THE WARS OF MARLBOROUGH
(1702–1709)

THE WARS OF
MARLBOROUGH

1702–1709

BY

FRANK TAYLOR
SOMETIME SCHOLAR OF LINCOLN COLLEGE, OXFORD

EDITED BY

G. WINIFRED TAYLOR
M.A. OXON.

VOL. II.

OXFORD
BASIL BLACKWELL
1921

CONTENTS OF VOL. II.

APPENDICES

LIST OF MAPS TO VOL. II.

ERRATA

VOL I

Page 340, line 15, *for* " Ivrea," *read* " Verrua."

VOL II.

Page 22, Note 2, *for* " 17 7," *read* " 1707 "
Page 24, line 20, *for* " contained," *read* " countered."
Page 64, lines 9, 14 and 19, *for* " De Guay Trouin," *read* " Du Guay Trouin '
Page 89, Ref 1, *for* " page 139," *read* " page 1392 "
Page 117, line 23, *for* " Zuerbeek," *read* " Zuenbeek "
Page 118, line 26, *for* " Zuerbeek," *read* " Zuenbeek "
Page 165, Note 4, *for* " and," *read* " an."
Page 171, line 23, *for* " M. de Sautai," *read* " M Sautai "
Page 254, line 24, *for* " M. de Sautai," *read* " M. Sautai "
Page 269, line 8, *for* " Bavaria," *read* " Hanover "
Page 348, line 31, *for* " Cambrai," *read* " Cambrin "
Page 349, line 29, *for* " Montroeul," *read* " Montreuil "
Page 352, line 20, *for* " Pont-à-Trenin," *read* " Pont-à-Tressin "
Page 362, line 22, " though exposed," *delete* " though "
Page 366, line 8, *for* " discovered," *read* ' discerned."
Page 405, line 39, *for* " Saltburn," *read* " Saltoun."
Page 458, line 34, *for* " proclaimed," *read* " proclaim "

THE WARS OF MARLBOROUGH
(1707–1709)

XVII.—ALMANZA, STOLLHOFEN, AND TOULON

On the morning of the day after his arrival at the Hague, as Marlborough sat in conference with Count Goes, the Pensionary, Heinsius, was announced. He brought unwelcome news According to reports from French sources, the allied army in Spain had been virtually annihilated

The truth was not so bad as the French pretended; but it was bad enough. In pursuance of the plans adopted at Valencia in January, Galway and Das Minas assembled their forces in April and prepared to invade Aragon. To protect their march and to ensure the safety of their base, they entered Mercia on the 10th, and destroyed the enemies' magazines. Berwick retired before them from Villena to Chinchilla, a distance of nearly sixty miles. Berwick was awaiting powerful reinforcements drawn from those garrisons in Lombardy which the convention with the Emperor had enabled Louis to divert to Germany and Spain He was expecting also the Duke of Orléans, who was eager to retrieve the disaster of Turin A part of his reinforcements joined him at Chinchilla; but the Duke of Orléans turned aside to visit the Court of Madrid. On the 18th Berwick advanced, and came on the 23rd to Almanza. Galway and Das Minas, who could get no reliable information from the hostile peasantry, imagined that, because the Duke had not yet joined, the expected contingent also was still upon the road They therefore determined to attack at once. Berwick made ready to receive them in an excellent position, south of the town of Almanza. At noon on the 25th the allies, after a march of eight miles, halted in presence of the enemy The odds were tremendously against them. Berwick's army numbered at the very least

25,400 men, of whom 11,900 were French and the rest
Spaniards. The allies did not exceed 15,500, of whom more
than half were Portuguese, less than one-third English,
and the remainder Dutch, Germans, and Huguenots. Both
sides drew up their forces in the orthodox fashion, the
infantry in the centre, and the cavalry on the wings; but
the weakness of the allied cavalry necessitated the interposition of some battalions of foot. At 3 o'clock the attack
was delivered On the left, Galway with his English
squadrons, supported by the 6th and 33rd regiments of
English Foot, more than held his own against very
superior numbers of Spanish horse. In the centre the
British infantry, aided by the Germans, Dutch, and Huguenots, carried all before them; indeed, the Guards and the
2nd Foot actually pursued the enemy to the very walls of
Almanza. But on the right, almost the whole of the
Portuguese cavalry bolted from the field Most of the
Portuguese infantry of the centre followed their example,
and the Portuguese gunners abandoned their guns. The
rest of the allied army stood up heroically against overwhelming numbers. But the situation was absurd. A
mixed force of English, Dutch, Germans, and Huguenots,
numbering fewer than 8,000, was fighting in an open plain
against more than three times their own number of French
and Spaniards. Galway, blinded by two sabre-cuts above
the right eye, retired temporarily from the field; but he
returned in time to organise the retreat. Covered by
gallant charges of English and Huguenot horse, he managed
to bring off 3,500 men and the English train of six guns.
Another body, 2,000 strong, cut their way out and escaped
to the hills, but were nevertheless compelled to surrender
on the following day. Berwick fixes the allied losses at
15,000, which is ridiculous The killed and wounded
numbered 4,000, the prisoners 3,000, and the Portuguese
train of twenty guns was captured Berwick's own losses
were heavy. Parnell[1] estimates them at 6,000. Armies
do not blazon their defeats, otherwise the name of Almanza,
like the name of Fontenoy, would be no disgrace to British
colours.

[1] Parnell, *The War of the Succession in Spain*, p 222

‹ If Marlborough's design upon Toulon was desirable before the disaster of Almanza, it was doubly desirable now. Nothing more likely to relieve the pressure on the remnant of the allied forces in the Peninsula could well be imagined. The Duke did not neglect to make this point A deputation from the States-General, which visited him after Heinsius had gone, arrived at the conclusion that nothing could save Spain but "a prompt and vigorous invasion of France with two different armies, by Provence and Dauphiné,"[1] and that all idea of an expedition to Naples must be abandoned. The Dutch minister at Vienna was instructed to make representations to that effect. And Marlborough wrote privately to Wratislaw[2] to advise him of the views of the States, and to warn him that, unless the Emperor bestirred himself, the peace party in Holland would gain the upper hand

The Duke left the Hague on the 11th and reached Brussels on the 13th. Here he discussed the military situation with Overkirk and the field-deputies, and directed the army to concentrate at Anderlecht on the outskirts of the city. The French were loudly boasting that they intended to quit their lines and to offer battle Though Marlborough was credibly informed that they had collected a numerous army, he did not anticipate that they would risk it in the open. He could not believe in the possibility of such a piece of good fortune, which was what at this moment he most ardently desired A second Ramillies would have more than compensated the coalition for Almanza. "Nothing," he wrote to the Margrave of Bayreuth, "nothing shall be neglected here to repair the unfortunate commencement of the campaign in Spain "[3] To Sunderland he said· "They talk very big since their success in Spain, but I hardly believe they will venture a battle, though nothing could be more desirable at this juncture."[4] And to Harley "Since their success in Spain they talk very big, and pretend to give us battle, for my part I think nothing could be more for the advantage of

[1] Murray, vol iii , p 360. Marlborough to Wratislaw, May 10, 1707.
[2] Ibid
[3] Ibid , p 365 Marlborough to the Margrave of Bayreuth, May 14, 1707.
[4] Ibid , p. 368: Marlborough to Sunderland, May 16, 1707

the allies."[1]   And to the Earl of Manchester: "They talk
no less than of giving us battle, which in my opinion is
what we ought most to desire."[2]   He wrote in similar
terms to Lord Raby, to the Prince of Hesse, to Noyelles,
and to Eugène.   It is important to note these declarations,
because the field-deputy, Goslinga, alleges in his memoirs
that Marlborough had no intention of fighting, if by any
means he could avoid it.   Goslinga maintains that, in
compelling the Duke to refuse the patent, the Dutch
government acted very imprudently, and that the Duke
decided to punish them for their ingratitude and to recoup
himself for his own loss by prolonging the war to the utmost
of his power.   If Goslinga was right, the Duke showed
himself remarkably and gratuitously careless of his own
reputation, when he went out of his way to excite in so
many different quarters the hope of victory.   That of all
men, a Dutchman and a field-deputy should advance this
of all accusations against the general who, but for Dutchmen and field-deputies, would long since have dictated terms
to Louis, argues a deficiency of humour.   It argues also
a deficiency of sense, seeing that Goslinga was, as he proudly
observes, one of the four or five persons in all Holland to
whom Marlborough had confided the secret of his design
on Toulon, than which nothing better calculated to end
the war had hitherto been devised.[3]

The reports which reached Marlborough did not exag-
gerate the magnitude of the French army.   In fact they
underrated it   Never was there a better illustration of the
use that could be made of the breathing-space allowed to
a half-beaten antagonist by the sacred custom of winter-
quarters.   Since the autumn large numbers of recruits had
been raised and drilled; and the treaty made with the
Emperor in the spring, by releasing thousands of trained
soldiers for service in other theatres of the war, had obviated
the necessity of drawing detachments from Flanders.
Thanks, moreover, to the inactivity of the Germans on the
Rhine, it was unnecessary to divert troops in that direction.
The result was that Vendôme and the Elector were enabled

[1] Murray, vol. iii., p 369 Marlborough to Harley, May 16, 1707.
[2] Ibid , p 371 · Marlborough to Earl of Manchester, May 19, 1707.
[3] Mémoires de Sicco van Goslinga, p 29

to concentrate in the vicinity of Mons an army of 124 battalions and 195 squadrons, or a total force which was one-third as big again as that which confronted Marlborough at Ramillies less than a year before   Certainly it contained a large proportion of young soldiers, but its spirit, particularly after the news of Almanza, gave every satisfaction to Vendôme.   At present it lay behind the lines which had been constructed to protect the counties of Artois and Cambrésis against hostile parties.   These lines had not entirely served their purpose.   On one occasion a daring band had even penetrated to the other side of Paris, and, mistaking the King's First Equerry for a Prince of the Blood, had kidnapped him on the Versailles road, and carried him as far as Ham before a rescue was effected   Vendôme, though he declined to accept a suggestion of Louis that he should capture Huy before Marlborough's forces were assembled, did not intend to make the campaign behind earthworks.   Believing that his army was equal in *moral* and very superior in numbers to that of the enemy, he purposed to take his chance in the open field.

Marlborough quitted Brussels on the 21st, and found 97 battalions and 164 squadrons assembled at Anderlecht. He advanced the same day by Hal to Lembecq   His information still led him to believe that the numbers of the enemy were inferior, or at most equal, to his own.   Their intentions he could not fathom.   He was still incredulous of their alleged anxiety to fight, but on the 23rd he wrote to Salm to complain that the slackness of the Germans had permitted the concentration of very large forces in Flanders,[1] and to Sinzendorf to say that he might in consequence be prevented from accomplishing anything material.[2]   On the 25th he wrote to the Duchess· "I am afraid they think they are strong enough to hinder us from doing anything."[3]   Having learned at midnight that the enemy would move at dawn, he advanced to Soignies on the 26th, in the hope of meeting them   The French, who were at Estinnes, marched out of their lines in six columns, towards Gosselies.   "Their camp is very strong," wrote

[1] Murray, vol iii , p 377 Marlborough to the Prince of Salm, May 23, 1707
[2] *Ibid* , p 378. Marlborough to Sinzendorf, May 23, 1707
[3] Coxe, vol ii., p 66 The Duke to the Duchess, May 25, 1707.

Marlborough to Godolphin, " and I believe they will not stay in any place where they may with reason be attacked."[1]

Nevertheless, the boldness of Vendôme's movement surprised the Duke. The march of the allies directly threatened Mons, and Vendôme apparently was leaving Mons to its fate But the Frenchman knew very well what he was about. If Marlborough menaced Mons, Vendôme would menace Brussels and Louvain. It was a bad exchange for Marlborough For Brussels and Louvain were comparatively open towns which could be carried with no great difficulty, while Mons was a place that could only be attacked in form, and could only be taken after a lengthy siege. Huy and Liège, too, lay open to Vendôme; and Huy and Liège would not detain him very long Moreover, it was more than doubtful whether the allied army could in any circumstances invest Mons, when an army that was approximately its equal in numbers was roaming at large upon its communications And it was certain that the loss of such places as Brussels, Louvain, and Liège could not for one moment be contemplated. The moral effect would be too disastrous Dutch misrule had already excited no little discontent among all classes in the Spanish Netherlands; and already the news of Almanza had been greeted in the capital and elsewhere with secret, and even open, rejoicing. The problem was a complex one. In only one way could it have been solved at once, and solved effectually Vendôme's army should have been fought and destroyed.

At dawn on the 27th, in a thick fog, Marlborough and the field-deputies, escorted by twelve squadrons, rode out towards Grand Rœulx to reconnoitre. Having failed to discover the enemy's camp, they dispatched a scout of Lord Albemarle's towards Piéton, and returned at once to Soignies Goslinga in his memoirs describes in detail the events of the day. By his account the field-deputies immediately held a private conclave They came to the conclusion that Brabant could be protected only in two ways, by a march to Brussels, or a march over the Senne to Nivelles The former expedient they regarded as " humiliating," and the latter as " subject to great risks "[2]

[1] Coxe, vol ii , p 69   [2] Mémoires de Goslinga p. 31.

In the former instance their reasoning appears to have been defective, because both movements could be represented as retrograde by anybody who was desirous of taking that view of them In the latter, their reasoning was sound, from their own standpoint By " great risks " they meant, of course, that a collision might ensue In other words, they were afraid to try the one sure remedy, a battle. They then consulted Overkirk and the Dutch generals. According to Goslinga, the meeting after mature consideration unanimously decided that it would be shameful to go to Brussels, and that the passage of the Senne should be essayed Some of the generals recalled the fact that William had once crossed the river at Arquennes, where, the country being difficult, Vendôme's numerous cavalry would be useless against the splendid infantry of the allies After dinner the company went to Marlborough's quarters. The Duke told them that Albemarle's scout had now returned with the report that the French were at Trazegnies and Cheval Blanc, that they had been very alert throughout the night, and that their cavalry had not even unsaddled. A discussion followed. Goslinga alleges that all agreed that it would be humiliating to retreat to Brussels, that Marlborough thereupon proposed to remain at Soignies and to send a detachment to level the enemy's lines in the neighbourhood of Mons (presumably with the object of compelling Vendôme to return), and that everybody, even Cadogan, condemned this suggestion as useless, impracticable, and very dangerous. Then Overkirk told the Duke what had passed at the previous council of the Dutch. After some debate, Marlborough and Cadogan consented to attempt the passage of the Senne at Arquennes It was unanimously resolved to march at 2 the next morning, and preparations were made accordingly. Goslinga went to bed in his clothes. At 2 he rose, and was astonished to find that the army was not moving An hour or so later Cadogan came to say that he and the Dutch Quartermaster had reconnoitred the passage of Ronquières, which was reported easier than that of Arquennes, that they had found it impossible, and that Marlborough had now resolved to go by way of Brussels and Louvain to the Dyle, where they must await a more favourable opportunity. The deputies mounted, and overtook Marlborough and Over-kirk on the road to Hal Marlborough had confided his opinion to Overkirk in the night, and to none other, and Overkirk, as usual, had adopted it. Goslinga told the Duke that he was augmenting Vendôme's reputation at the expense of his own, and restoring the *moral* of the French soldiery. Marlborough said but little. The deputies could do nothing. Their own Field-Marshal was against them. But Goslinga was certain from that moment that Marlborough intended to prolong the war out of pique for the loss of the patent.[1]

This curious narrative presents the leading characters in a new light. For the first time, after five campaigns, it is Marlborough who is running away, and the Dutch, both civilians and soldiers, who are thirsting for battle, or if not for battle, at any rate for a peep at the enemy. No wonder Marlborough had little to say to Goslinga

Unfortunately for Goslinga, his story is not supported. Even Cranstoun, who was never afraid to criticise the Duke, knows nothing about it. And it is flatly contradicted by Marlborough himself. Writing to Godolphin on the following day he said, " Instead of coming to this camp, I would have marched yesterday to Nivelles, but the deputies would not consent to it, telling me very plainly that they feared the consequence of that march might be a battle."[2] The two versions are irreconcilable. The issue is therefore between the compiler of memoirs, endeavouring to establish a thesis of his own, and the commander-in-chief, reporting at the time to the British Prime Minister upon a matter of fact which was well within the knowledge of several other persons.

The account published in the *Gazette*[3] referred merely to the risk of besieging Mons, while the open cities of Brabant were exposed to attack. The accounts given by Boyer and Lediard are vague and impersonal. " Upon intelligence that they were encamp'd in the plain of Flerus, a council of war was held in which it was resolved to march to

---

[1] *Mémoires de Goslinga*, p 34   [2] Coxe, vol ii , p 70
[3] *The London Gazette*, May 22-26, 1707.

Nivelle to attack them, and accordingly a detachment was sent to view the pass of Ronquièies, through which they were to pass "[1] This version, so far as it goes, is against Goslinga, because it declares that the final decision was made at a second council, and not on the responsibility of Marlborough and Overkirk. But it says nothing about the deputies' objection to a battle. The reason is obvious! Though Marlborough did not suffer fools gladly, in the public interest he did his utmost to shield them. "I take care," he writes to Godolphin, "not to let the army know that the Dutch are not willing to venture, since that must have an ill effect."[2]

But after all, it did not greatly matter whether the field-deputies were willing to go to Nivelles or not. The really important question was, what they were prepared to do when they got there, or before they got there, assuming that resistance were encountered on the way Marlborough was satisfied that they would not consent to a battle. And if they would not consent to a battle, there was no advantage in courting one. Indeed, there were grave disadvantages. The Duke had no desire to repeat upon the Senne the fiasco which had happened on the Dyle in 1705. And he had no desire to lead his troops into the presence of the enemy, as he led them at the Yssche and again and again in the campaigns of 1702 and 1703, only to give the order to retreat when the order to engage was eagerly expected. Such experiences conduced neither to good discipline nor to good *moral*. He knew, of course (none better), the value of *moral*. He had nothing to learn from Goslinga on that score. But his judgment told him that if it was humiliating to march to Brussels, it would prove to be a thousand times more humiliating to march to Nivelles.

It was not the question of the patent, but the question of the barrier which was at the root of the trouble At Ramillies the French had lost the barrier; but the Dutch had not yet gained it. Consequently the Dutch were now intensely interested in carrying on their diplomatic wrangle with London and Vienna, but they were not interested at all in continuing the war with vigour. Every guilder that they

---

[1] Boyer, vol vi., p 57   [2] Coxe, vol. ii , p. 70. Marlborough to Godolphin.

spent and every soldier that they lost they now regarded as a dead loss. Even the disaster of Almanza appeared to them as a blessing in disguise, because it might incline both England and Austria to thoughts of peace. "The States," wrote Marlborough on the 15th, "received the news of this fatal stroke with less concern than I expected."[1] To maintain the ground that had been won in Belgium until such time as the barrier was secured to them, was now their sole remaining interest in the struggle. Marlborough knew it, and he knew how strong must be the temptation to the Dutch government to impose restrictions on his action in the field.[2] "It is very likely," he continued, "their deputies may have orders to act here with more caution than the urgency of affairs requires." This danger was certain to be intensified by the startling revelation that the French army was so large and so full of confidence in itself and its commander His letter of the 29th to Godolphin, already quoted, supplies the key to his actions. "Unless," he said, "I can convince the Pensioner that I am not for hazarding, but when we have an advantage, they will give such orders to their deputies, that I shall not have it in my power of doing good, if an advantage should offer itself."[3] That was why he adopted a course not open to the least reproach of rashness. And that was why he wrote encouragingly to Heinsius to inform him that though the enemy had more battalions, they were very weak ones, and that the allied squadrons were "much better, and as many, if not more in number." "Upon the whole," he told the Pensionary, "I believe our army is stronger than theirs" Nevertheless, "I shall not be for venturing," he said, "unless we have the advantage on our side."[4] He had all the summer before him. If only the Dutch government could be convinced that he was to be trusted and that it was unnecessary to give special instructions to the field-deputies, excellent opportunities might yet arise. "Though it is a very unpleasant thing," he said to Godolphin, "not to have full power at the head of an army, yet I do please myself I shall do some consider-

[1] Coxe, vol ii , p 67. Marlborough to Godolphin, May 15, 1707.
[2] Ibid   [3] Ibid , p 70. Marlborough to Godolphin.
[4] Ibid , p. 70 Marlborough to the Pensionary.

able service this campaign, for I do believe we shall find the Elector and M. Vendôme grow insolent, by which they will either attack or give me occasion for attacking them."[1]

The " considerable service " which he had in mind may be gathered from the following passage, " I am also apprehensive that M Vendôme knows, from the French partisans in Holland, that the States are against venturing a battle, which encourages him to act as he does; for he can't but know that our army is better than his, and that if we should beat him, his master must submit to such terms as the allies should think reasonable."[2] In short, he hoped, if only Goslinga's employers would allow him, to finish the war at one stroke.

Why, then, it may be asked, should Goslinga invent a legend diametrically opposed to the truth ? It is quite conceivable that Goslinga honestly believed in his own theory His motives can be conjectured with some certainty He and his colleagues had been chosen at a time when disgust at the conduct of Schlangenberg and his like was universal. The new appointments were followed by the astonishing campaign of Ramillies. Goslinga, who did not suffer from excessive modesty, felt himself to be a partner in the military achievements of 1706. If the events of subsequent campaigns fell short of that high standard, he was anxious to dissociate himself from them And he probably had a higher motive than the merely personal one. He had been long enough with the army to know what the army thought of the treatment accorded to Marlborough in the past by the Dutch government, generals, and field-deputies. He knew what he thought of himself. He was not a soldier, but for that very reason he could see the imbecility of much that passed for military science among the orthodox soldiers of the age He was also a man of spirit and courage, and in his secret heart he was ashamed of the past dealings of his countrymen with the English general He probably found it extremely consoling to his patriotism to persuade himself that from the spring of 1707 onwards the responsibility for every failure rested entirely upon Marlborough himself.

[1] *Ibid*, p. 70 Marlborough to Godolphin.   [2] *Ibid.*

Having formed his plan, Marlborough executed it with celerity, because he knew that the French, moving on the chord while he was moving on the arc, might attempt to outpace him   On the 28th he marched to Hal; on the 29th he passed the Brussels canal at Dieghem, and encamped at Beaulieu, where he rested his men on the 30th. On the 31st he came to Bethlehem, bridged the Dyle, and crossing it on June 1, took post at Meldert   It gratified the French to picture this rapid manœuvre as a precipitate retreat.   Neither they nor Goslinga appear to have remarked that, in its latter stages, it was an advance.

Vendôme and the Elector proceeded now to Gembloux, where they encamped in a position reported to be impregnable.   They did not intend to besiege Huy, and on the 6th they reconnoitred the approaches to Meldert.   Vendôme reported to Versailles that an attack upon the enemy would be perfectly feasible   He declared that the disparity between the two armies had been greatly increased by the dispatch of 6,000 of the allies to their various garrisons. Relying on the numbers and the spirit of his men, he was honestly eager for a battle   But Louis was satisfied with what had been done.   The war had been removed from Flanders to the enemy's country, a real triumph, as triumphs were reckoned under the rules of the oldest game.   Though he left the general a free hand, he recommended caution, and advised delay until Marlborough should be compelled to send detachments to the other theatres of the war. Such a contingency was not improbable.   For the misfortunes of the coalition were not confined to Spain alone.

Two days before he arrived at Meldert, Marlborough received intelligence of a deplorable nature from the Upper Rhine.   Quitting a Strasbourg ballroom in the early hours of May 21, Villars, by a bold and skilful combination, had easily surprised and captured the renowned lines of Stollhofen, with all their stores, artillery, and magazines.   He had immediately advanced to Rastatt.   The army of the Margrave of Bayreuth had retired in disorder to Pforzheim, and the French marshal, adopting a tone of extreme arrogance and menace, was levying contributions in Franconia and Swabia within a radius of forty leagues.   This calamity, which was nearer to their own doors than Almanza, finally determined the policy of the Dutch government. They sent explicit instructions to the field-deputies at Meldert " to avoid every occasion where there could be risk of coming to an action," until such time as the enemy should be seriously weakened by detachments. Goslinga endeavoured, though without success, to get these instructions amended, not because he thought them bad in themselves, but because, as he argues, they could be used by Marlborough, to cover his own self-interested design of prolonging the war.

For ten weeks the two armies lay idle at Meldert and Gembloux within a few hours' march of one another   Both generals desired a battle.   But Vendôme, though nominally free, was in reality bound by the cautious spirit of the communications which he received from Versailles.   Marlborough was tied hand and foot by the instructions given to the deputies   " Our friends in Holland," he wrote to Harley on June 27, " are desirous of good success, but will not consent to the venturing a battle for it "[1]   The absurdity of the situation was enhanced by the fact that the soldiers upon both sides were as eager to fight as their commanders. The French were naturally uplifted by the triumphs of their comrades under Berwick and Villars.   The allies, despite the dismal prognostications of Goslinga on the march from Soignies to Hal, retained their unshaken confidence in themselves and their leader. " In the army," said Marlborough, " I must do them right, that there is all the desire imaginable to venture their lives for the public good, but all other sorts of people on this side of the water are so very wise, that I am afraid at last they will bring us to a bad peace   For myself, I am old, and shall not live to see the misfortunes that must happen to Christendom, if the French be suffered to get the better of this war "[2]

These ten weeks were not a holiday for Marlborough. He devoted them to a careful study of the military and political situation of the Grand Alliance, and to ceaseless

[1] Portland MSS., p 420 · Marlborough to Harley, June 27, 1707 (Hist. MSS Comm , 15th Report, Appendix, part iv) · Bath MSS., vol. i,. p. 173: Marlborough to Harley, June 5/16, 1707 (Hist MSS. Comm).
[2] Coxe, vol ii , p 72   The Duke to the Duchess, June 13, 1707.

endeavours to retrieve what had been lost in other theatres of the war. The camp at Meldert became at once the brain and the heart of the coalition Even Goslinga himself, if he could have perused that bulky portion of the Duke's correspondence which bears the address of Meldert, must have revised his ignoble hypothesis of the Englishman's motives, unless he was prepared to contend that Marlborough was an actor who carried his acting to useless and even stultifying extremes All that one man could do, under the difficult conditions of time and space, Marlborough now did, not only to check the progress of the French arms, but to shatter them utterly and that within the compass of this most unpromising campaign.

The problem which caused him the gravest anxiety of all was the Spanish one. After Almanza Galway had retired towards the coast Byng, who to illustrate the English seaman's habit of arriving at the right moment, had anchored at Alicante on the 20th with reinforcements, provisions, and money, embarked the sick, the wounded, and the stores upon his ships, and transported them to Tortosa. Galway conducted his army to the same place by land, and undeterred by his years, his wounds, and his misfortunes, prepared for an obstinate defence of Catalonia Aragon and Valencia were lost to Charles, but the heroic resistance offered by the garrison of Xativa, which surrendered only after a siege of thirty-nine days, as well as by the garrison of Denia, which, reinforced by English sailors, never surrendered at all, greatly delayed the operations of Berwick and Orléans, who were presently constrained by the July heats to go into summer-quarters. The respite, however, was only temporary It was necessary to provide for the future. " God knows," wrote Marlborough to the Duchess on June 6, "what is to be done for the recovery of the great disorders that are now in Spain "[1] To endeavour to exercise any useful control over military operations as to which he was often without any reliable information for months at a time, would become a hopeless task. He felt that his own position was in fact an impossible one. Both on military and political grounds, he had always recommended the occupation of Madrid. But

[1] Coxe, vol ii., p. 62. The Duke to the Duchess, June 6, 1707.

he never imagined that those who accepted his advice would be so mad as to divide their forces before they proceeded to execute it. He had supported the appointment of Peterborough; and Noyelles was one of his own men. But he could hardly have foreseen that the professional talents of both those officers would be more than neutralised by their talents for intrigue. His friend, Galway, was now accused on all hands of incapacity and even treason. Both Charles and Noyelles denounced him. The government of Vienna denounced him. Rochester's Tories assailed him as a foreigner. The Jacobites drank to the health of " the brave Englishman," Berwick, who had beaten the French--man. Peterborough, who at this time was roving from one European court to another on a self-imposed mission of meddlesome diplomacy, impressed upon everybody that if only his own advice had been accepted, the defeat of Almanza could never have occurred. The general clamour astonished Marlborough, but it did not shake his confidence in his valiant friend. He realised, however, that, in Galway's case, as in Peterborough's, individual merit or demerit was no longer in question. " It is impracticable," he wrote to Godolphin on June 23, " for Lord Galway to continue in that service "[1] And on the 27th he wrote to Sunderland, " Nobody can have a better opinion than I have of Lord Galway, but when I consider the court and King of Spain, I think it would be the most barbarous thing in the world to impose upon Galway to stay, for I am very confident he would rather beg his bread—I am sure I would "[2] Godolphin agreed with the Duke; but he was confronted by the opposition of the Whigs. " They are very uneasy," he wrote, " to think of recalling Lord Galway, though sensible he must be useless "[3] They considered, and not without reason, that Noyelles was " the principal occasion and contriver of Lord Galway's misfortunes,"[4] and that unless both officers were removed at the same time, it would appear as if England were admitting that she and her general were entirely to blame for the defeat of Almanza. In these circumstances both Marlborough and Godolphin decided that there was only one solution. The Emperor

---

[1] *Ibid*, p 89   [2] *Ibid*, p 102
[3] *Ibid*, p 88 Godolphin to Marlborough, June 13/24, 1707.   [4] *Ibid*.

must dispatch a commander of high standing to Barcelona to supersede all others. Galway could not complain of this decision, as he himself had long since recommended the appointment of Eugène. Stanhope, writing to Godolphin on July 8, had said, " I shall look upon his name as equivalent to an army "[1] They also decided that henceforward the war in Spain must be managed on a different basis. The allied army must be mainly composed of Imperialist forces, transported from Italy by the fleets of the maritime powers   " The war in Catalonia," wrote Marlborough to Godolphin on July 4, "must be carried on by troops from Italy, and not by the Queen's subjects, by which you may save money and the service be better done."[2] And on August 1 he wrote again, " I am glad that you are of opinion that the war in Spain ought to be carried on by subsidies, which may get foreign troops, for Her Majesty's subjects can never come in time, nor indeed be kept in good order in that country, for want of recruits."[3] As to the Portuguese, it was agreed to return them all to Portugal, where, if anywhere, they might conceivably do their duty. These decisions, while they relieved the Duke of intolerable responsibilities, made for greater efficiency in the field They were also dictated by considerations of high policy. The war was now exhibiting a dangerous tendency to develop from a civil war into a national one, in which Charles was identified in the popular mind with the alien. At Almanza, for example, the allied army consisted entirely of foreigners. If the French claimant was assisted by Frenchmen, the German claimant might be assisted by Germans. But it was very undesirable that he should appear to rely upon Englishmen and Dutchmen whom the Spaniards regarded as heretics, and upon Portuguese whom they regarded as hereditary foes.

The situation in Germany excited in the breast of Marlborough more anger than alarm. The successes of Villars had been rendered possible partly by the failure of the German princes to supply their proper contingents, partly by mismanagement of the available forces, which in Marl-

---

[1] Mahon, *History of the War of the Succession in Spain*, p 243 Stanhope to Godolphin, July 8, 1707.
[2] Coxe, vol ii , p 104   [3] *Ibid* , p. 118.

borough's judgment were fully adequate in numbers to
cope with the French, but principally by the criminal neglect
of the Austrian government to associate a competent
commander with the Margrave of Bayreuth   Because
Marlborough had opposed the transference of Eugène from
Italy to the Rhine, Vienna had ignored his suggestion that
Starhemberg be sent, and had sent nobody.   Otherwise,
as he told Eugène, " this misfortune would never have
occurred "[1]   The " misfortune " differed from the Spanish
one.   The Germans were not defeated; they were only
disgraced   Their consternation was ludicrous.   Express
after express, soliciting the Duke's assistance, arrived at
Meldert.   On June 7 he informed the Margrave that, confronted as he was by a superior enemy, he could make no
detachments for the Rhine   " If all the troops that you
have within reach," he added, " were assembled in a single
body, the army of the Empire would equal and perhaps
exceed that of the enemy "   He criticised the folly of shut-
ting up large numbers in fortified places at such a moment,
and suggested that "a good diversion" could be made with
" the numerous garrisons of Philippsburg and Landau "
" Your Highness," he said, " would do well to consider
that, if the advantage were on our side, and we had made
an irruption into their country, they would not leave 6,000
men at Strassburg with their arms crossed, as we are doing
at Philippsburg."[2]   He did not hesitate to declare that
Villars' army, which contained many raw soldiers, would
offer no resistance, if only the Germans could muster up
a little firmness.   He wrote in similar terms of severity to
the Margrave's officers.   At the same time, he urged the
Emperor to order up some Danish and other troops from
Bavaria, and he requested the Elector Palatine to send
two regiments of horse and three battalions of foot to the
threatened point.   His indignation against the Austrian
government he made no attempt to conceal   " If the
least attention," he wrote to Sinzendorf, " had been paid
to the pressing and oft-repeated representations which have
been made to you in favour of sending a general of authority,

[1] Murray, vol iii , p 391· Marlborough to the Prince of Savoy, June 6,
1707
[2] *Ibid* , p 396 Marlborough to the Margrave of Bayreuth, June 7, 1707.

capable of commanding the troops, our affairs would not be in their present exasperating condition, on the contrary, if M. de Staremberg had been sent in time, the enemy would never have ventured to attempt anything, and we should perhaps have had the advantage on our side."[1] " For God's sake," he exclaimed to Wratislaw, " lose no time in removing the Margrave "[2] In a letter to the King of Spain he spoke of " the unheard-of negligence and misconduct "[3] in Germany, where he had been led to expect a diversion in his own favour, and where for four months he had been exhorting the Emperor and the Princes to be early in the field. The Austrian ministers were slow to answer. Their replies, when they did arrive, were couched in terms of some asperity But Marlborough coldly declined to discuss the matter further Meanwhile the situation in Germany went from bad to worse. On May 30 Villars advanced to Pforzheim, and the Margrave retired precipitately, leaving a quantity of powder and bombs behind him. From Pforzheim the French pushed on to Stuttgart, and from Stuttgart to Schorndorf, which they captured on June 15. The Germans awaited them at Gmund, but only to withdraw at their approach. They still sent continual expresses to Marlborough for assistance. " Our people," he wrote to Eugène, " fly like a sheep before the wolf—their terror has already multiplied the enemy's numbers by two."[4] Villars could never overtake them, but far and wide he imposed his merciless exactions on the cities of Germany. He even had the effrontery to declare that arrears had accumulated since his campaign of 1703 and must now be paid. One of his parties crossed the Danube, and levied toll as far south as Memmingen. Refusal to pay was answered by the burning of villages. He was suspected of a design to restore the Elector; and on June 30 Vendôme dispatched 1,200 Bavarians to his assistance. He sent his hussars to the field of Blenheim to destroy a pyramid which was falsely alleged to have been erected

[1] Murray, vol iii , p 392 Marlborough to Sinzendorf, June 6, 1707.
[2] Ibid , p. 390. Marlborough to Wratislaw, June 6, 1707
[3] Ibid , p 404 Marlborough to the King of Spain, June 11, 1707
[4] Ibid , p. 405: Marlborough to the Prince of Savoy, June 11, 1707.

there in honour of Marlborough's victory. He recovered
many of the prisoners that had been taken in that battle.
The magistrates of Ulm were so terrified by his menaces
that they implored the assistance of the Englishman who
had saved Germany in 1704. Marlborough replied that if
the Germans would only concentrate their troops, they
could soon expel the enemy.[1] He agreed with Godolphin,
who said: " Whatever uneasiness happens to the court of
Vienna, they deserve it richly, who would not, in all this
time, send a general to the Rhine, though they have been
pressed to do it, to my knowledge, ever since last Christmas ''[2]
But though he had little pity for the Germans, he was
careful of the cause. The Elector Palatine proposed that
the Margrave should be removed and the Elector of Hanover
appointed in his stead. Marlborough welcomed the suggestion. The Elector of Hanover was a competent general;
his authority in Germany was such as to compel obedience, and the opportunity of shedding lustre upon the
family which was destined to succeed to the English throne
was not to be despised   But the Duke was not very hopeful
that the project would succeed, for no prince who valued
his own reputation would be eager to expose it to such
hazards. Nevertheless, at the Elector Palatine's request,
he strongly supported the proposal both at Hanover,
London, and Vienna. The Elector of Hanover demurred
at first, but eventually accepted   The Elector Palatine
had also suggested that the Saxon troops, which had been
hired by the maritime powers, should be sent to the Rhine
instead of to Brabant   Marlborough pointed out that
England and Holland did not subsidise soldiers for the
protection of Germany, and that Holland at any rate
would probably object to be deprived of the Saxon contingent at the present juncture   Yet he succeeded in
persuading the Dutch to consent to the proposal, on condition that the Elector of Mainz pledged himself to have
boats in readiness to transport the Saxons from Philippsburg to Cologne in case they should be urgently required
in Brabant. And without waiting for instructions from

[1] Murray, vol iii., p. 423· Marlborough to the Burgomasters and
Magistrates of Ulm, June 18, 1707.
[2] Coxe, vol ii , p 87

London, he took upon himself to give the Queen's consent
On June 23, in conjunction with the field-deputies, he sent
an express to the Saxon contingent, directing it to march
to Philippsburg This movement exercised a determining
effect upon the campaign On July 5 Villars learned that
the Margrave of Bayreuth, who had now been joined by
General Heister from Vienna, had doubled back towards
Heilbronn, that he had already obtained a good start, and
that not only the Saxons but Hanoverians, Prussians, and
all the available soldiers in Germany were concentrating
on Philippsburg. Fearful for his communications, and for
the safety of Alsace and Lorraine, the Marshal returned
with all speed to the Rhine He seized Heidelberg, and
levied his contributions from the Neckar to the Main.
But he was presently obliged to fall back before the very
superior forces of the Margrave For weeks the two armies
confronted one another in strong positions in the vicinity
of Durlach The Elector of Hanover took over the command in September But Villars still maintained his
footing, indeed he would have wintered in Germany had
his government allowed. At the end of October he repassed
the Rhine. He had rendered an extraordinary service to
France. The enormous sums which he had extorted from
the Germans he had divided into three parts. With the
first he both paid and supported his army, which cost the
French government nothing for the entire campaign With
the second he redeemed a mass of paper money which had
been issued to the officers in the preceding campaign.
And with the third, he proposed, in his own picturesque
phraseology, " to fatten his calf."[1] This last idea was
graciously approved by Louis, who was pleased to say
that he would have made the same provision if the Marshal
had forgotten it. " The Maréchal de Villars is making his
fortune," grumbled a French courtier. " Yes," retorted
Louis, " but he is making mine too."[2]

This German scandal, which Marlborough had laboured
so actively to terminate, could partly be explained, though
it could not be justified, by the continued presence of the
Swedes in Saxony. The Emperor and the princes had been

[1] *Vie de Villars*, t. 1., p. 438.   [2] *Ibid.*

so concerned about Charles XII that they had forgotten
Villars   The Marshal was by no means blind to the
strategical possibilities of the situation as it existed in
June. From the heart of Germany he dispatched a letter
to Alt-Ranstadt, suggesting that the Swedish army should
unite with his at Nürnberg   Had Charles accepted, the
results can only be conjectured   Charles was what is
termed in the language of the prize ring, 'a hurricane
fighter.' He would have stood no chance against soldiers
like Marlborough and Eugène, who combined a daring
equal to his own with a science to which he was a stranger.
But in conjunction with Villars, and assisted by the
Hungarian rebels, he would not easily have been put down.
Villars, however, got nothing for his pains but a portrait
and some compliments   His very success, no less than
Berwick's, was turned by the Swedish ministers against
the unhappy Besenval, who was reminded how from the
very first they had insisted upon the ability of France to
hold her own.   Charles XII, as Marlborough had correctly
judged, would never combine with Louis XIV to attack
the Grand Alliance.   But the presence of the Swedish army
in Saxony continued to create anxiety.   The quarrel with
Austria was still unsettled.   Indeed, it was aggravated by
the fact that the 1,200 Muscovites had actually escaped
from Germany with the connivance, as Charles had reason
to believe, of the Austrian government.   Relying upon the
influence of the maritime powers to prevent a rupture, the
Emperor adopted an impolitic line.   To show that he was
not afraid, he accorded a friendly reception to the Russian
ambassador, who proposed on behalf of the Czar that the
election of Stanislaus should be voided, and that Eugène
should be elevated to the Polish throne   To prove that he
was not at the end of his resources, he permitted Sinzendorf,
at Leipzig, to propagate a rumour that Austria was about
to make peace with France that she might be free to turn
her arms against the northern intruder.   But Charles'
nerves were not affected by these diplomatic manœuvres,
which merely exasperated him.   Although he was informed
on June 13 that Count Zobor's trial was about to begin
at Vienna, he declined altogether to believe in the Emperor's

sincerity, and he refused any longer to admit Sinzendorf
to his presence. Marlborough, who was in constant communication with Robinson and with the Austrian government, watched the course of events with some misgiving
He consistently advised the Austrians to temporise and to
" manage "[1] their dangerous antagonist   " I very much
fear," he told Godolphin, " that Count Wratislaw and the
other ministers may persuade the Emperor to such a
behaviour as may force the King of Sweden into war,
which I think would be destruction to themselves, as well
as to their friends   I have said all that is possible."[2]
" If it should come to a declaration of war," he wrote
to Wratislaw on June 6, " I will tell you frankly that I
consider that it will be the ruin of all the allies "[3]   On the
same date he wrote to Piper in language intended for the
eye of Charles, and well calculated to flatter that monarch's
vanity.   Having briefly referred to the disasters of Almanza
and Stollhofen, he declared that, serious as they were, they
troubled him less than the quarrel between Charles and
the Emperor   " Nevertheless," he added, " I want to
flatter myself that the King's moderation will prevail on
this occasion, for if he displayed his resentment at the
present juncture, it would be very fatal to the High Allies,
and indeed to all Christendom "[4]   This epistle, a copy of
which was forwarded to Hanover, was approved by the
Elector, who was also endeavouring to induce the Court
of Vienna " to make some advances to his Swedish
Majesty "[5]   It was also approved by Godolphin   But
neither Godolphin nor Marlborough was particularly san-
guine of the result. On June 16 the Duke transmitted
to Robinson a letter from Anne herself to Charles, in which
she expressed her regret at the dilatory course of the negotiations.   " I should have reason," she said, " to apprehend
some fatal consequences, if I were not strongly persuaded
that the zeal which you have always shown for the two

[1] Murray, vol iii , p 377 Marlborough to the Prince of Salm, May 23,
1707; p 390. Marlborough to Wratislaw, June 6, 1707
[2] Coxe, vol ii , p 85 Marlborough to Godolphin, June 9, 17 7
[3] Murray, vol. iii , p 390· Marlborough to Wratislaw, June 6, 1707
[4] Ibid., p. 393 Marlborough to Piper, June 6, 1707
[5] Lediard, vol. ii., p 194.

causes of religion and liberty, will never suffer you to
undertake anything in opposition to the allies " And she
concluded by offering " her offices with the Emperor . . .
with an entire confidence that Your Majesty will suffer
these differences to be adjusted by my care."[1]   But Charles
remained obdurate   The appeals of Anne and of Marlborough encouraged him in the belief that all the world
was frightened of him.   " If the Emperor does not give me
satisfaction," he exclaimed, after reading the Queen of
England's letter, " I will go myself and take it in his
dominions."   On June 25 his reply was handed to Robinson.   Its tone was "vague and menacing "[2] It gave, in
Marlborough's judgment, " but little satisfaction either as
to the purport or the style," and he described it to Godolphin
as " very discouraging."[3]   Piper wrote to the Duke in
" smoother " terms   But Robinson's reports excited
" melancholy apprehensions "   Robinson's fears were
shared by all the diplomatists at Alt-Ranstädt, with the
sole exception of Besenval   That cool observer, who
rightly considered that the inability of Charles to injure
the Emperor without at the same time injuring the maritime
powers, was the governing factor in the whole problem,
neither now nor at any other time believed in the possibility
of a war.

To elicit from Charles a clear definition of the satisfaction
which he demanded, was no easy task.   His policy at this
moment appears to have been guided by no particular
principle, but solely by personal vanity and pique.   But
at the end of June he slightly relaxed his attitude of sombre
mystery   Piper announced that if once the affairs of
Breslau and Count Zobor were settled, the King would
consent to discuss the business of the Muscovites.   The
Emperor, who had requested that, as the person of Sinzendorf
was no longer agreeable to Charles, Wratislaw might be
received at Alt-Ranstädt, was informed that if Wratislaw
were accompanied by Zobor and by the responsible officer
for Breslau, and were furnished with ample powers to treat,
the negotiations could proceed.   Marlborough was pleased.

[1] *Ibid* , p 199.
[2] Gabriel Syveton, *Louis XIV et Charles XII*, pp. 171, 172.
[3] Coxe, vol. ii , p. 109: Marlborough to Godolphin, July 18, 1707

" If they had done this sooner," he wrote on July 4 to Godolphin, " it would have been better, but I am glad he goes."[1] The situation seemed more hopeful, but it was speedily obscured. Wratislaw reached Leipzig on July 21, but before his arrival, four regiments of Swedish cavalry took quarters in Silesia, an event which appeared to Marlborough to afford " but a melancholy prospect "[2] Although the Swedish ministers pretended that their regiments had been forced over the frontier by the movements of Russian troops, the affront was very gross. Nevertheless Robinson, Kranenberg, and Sinzendorf decided to ignore it. Wratislaw remained at Leipzig, and negotiated with Charles' ministers through Robinson and Kranenberg. The mediation of the maritime powers was therefore tacitly accepted Charles declared that the only satisfaction which he would accept was a satisfaction of honour. Wratislaw desired an explication of the term He was told that, if the Emperor would restore religious liberty to the Silesian Protestants, everything could be settled. This proposition was a novel one. It expressly contained the definite promise which the King had given to Marlborough Wratislaw refused to assent to it, and wrote to Vienna for instructions. And on August 5 Piper dispensed with the services of Robinson and Kranenberg, informing them that his master now required him to treat with the Austrian direct " From what Count Wratislaw writes to me," said Marlborough to Harley on August 8, " he seems about to despair,"[3] and again on the 15th, " I see no likelihood of their coming to any accommodation."[4]

Godolphin's patience had already given out, and even Marlborough's was nearly exhausted. " If it be possible," wrote the Duke to his colleague on August 1, " the King of Sweden should use the Emperor hardly after the advances the latter has made, *I agree entirely with you that we must take such vigorous measures as may put a stop to his proceedings ;* but it must be not sooner than the end of this

[1] Coxe, vol 11., p 105
[2] Lediard, vol 11 , p 207.
[3] Murray, vol 111 , p 508 Marlborough to Harley, August 8, 1707
[4] *Ibid.,* p 513 · Marlborough to Harley, August 15, 1707

campaign "[1] At that date, however, he still refused to
believe that the necessity for such measures would arise.
But a fortnight later, on August 15, he wrote to Wratislaw
in cipher, " I am entirely of your opinion that we have
nothing else to do but temporise, *pending such time as
we may be able to take juster measures.*"[2] On the 16th he
wrote to Robinson emphasising the gravity of the risks
which Charles was running   There is no doubt that at
this time he was seriously considering the resources available for the destruction of the Swedish army[3]   He even
contemplated the possibility of an alliance between Russia
and the maritime powers.   One almost regrets that he
was denied the opportunity of chastising a monarch, whose
military reputation was absurdly inflated, and who profited
by the preoccupation of his neighbours to gratify his own
inordinate conceit   But the Austrian government gave
way suddenly   On August 18 Wratislaw, having received
instructions from Vienna, visited Piper. The Austrian
proposals were inadequate   Piper adopted a threatening
tone. Wratislaw sent for fresh instructions, and took to
his bed with the gout   On August 22 the Swedish army
began its march towards Silesia.   On the 24th Piper
appeared in the sick-room with a kind of ultimatum
Wratislaw still held out   But on the 28th his instructions
arrived   The Emperor conceded everything   On September 1 the treaty was signed, and duly guaranteed by
the maritime powers   And Charles departed for Russia,
where his peculiar talents eventually received their adequate
reward.

In the course of these long and irritating negotiations
the maritime powers got wind of a project for a secret
treaty between Sweden, Prussia, and Hanover.   It was
natural enough that the Protestant princes of Germany
should ally themselves closely with the upholder of the
nation of Gustavus, albeit his zeal for religion, according
to Burnet, was " not much enlightened "[4] But it was

---

[1] Coxe, vol ii , p. 117 Marlborough to Godolphin, August 1, 1707.
[2] Murray, vol iii , p 517 Marlborough to Wratislaw, August 15,
1707.
[3] *Ibid* , p 533 Marlborough to Sinzendorf, August 25, 1707.
[4] Burnet, vol iv , p 155.

very desirable to avoid the accentuation of theological
difference in a body like the Grand Alliance, which represented more religions than one. Accordingly, in July,
Marlborough approached the Prussian minister, Wartenberg, on the subject, and received from him the most satisfactory assurances.[1] Marlborough was at all times particularly anxious to conciliate and gratify the Court of
Berlin, for Frederick was sensitive, and his soldiers were
second to none in the armies of the coalition   In June he
reviewed the forces at Meldert, and he took the opportunity
of writing, both to the King and to the Prince Royal, to
congratulate them on the efficiency and the fine appearance
of the Brandenburgers, both horse and foot. In the same
month there occurred an event which made much stir in
Europe at the time, and which afforded an excellent opportunity of cementing the ties which united Prussia to the
Grand Alliance. The succession to the Principality of
Neufchâtel fell vacant   It was claimed by no fewer than
thirteen competitors, one of whom was the Prince de Conti
and one the King of Prussia   The King's pretensions,
according to Villars, who was not, however, the highest
authority on points of law, were purely " imaginary "[2]
But the decision did not depend on points of law.   It
depended on the relative strength of France and the Grand
Alliance   Louis, from the outset, adopted a menacing tone
towards the burghers of Neufchâtel, which roused at once
the spirit of Swiss independence   Protestants for the most
part, they were naturally inclined towards a Protestant
candidate, who, moreover, did not neglect to stimulate their
spiritual zeal by material means. But France was a close
neighbour, and a powerful one. Marlborough, who did not
desire that the Prussian troops in Italy should be diverted
to Switzerland, induced the English and Dutch governments
to promise the people of Neufchâtel both men and money.
He also instructed the English minister in Switzerland to
support and assist the Prussian representative, Metternich,
by every means in his power   " I pray you to assure His
Majesty," wrote the Duke to Wartenberg, " that nothing

[1] Murray, vol. iii , p 476: Wartenberg to Marlborough, July 25, 1707
[2] Vie de Villars, t. i , p. 419.

will be wanting on our side, and I am persuaded that the
minister of the States will also do his duty."[1] The King
was charmed with the activity which Marlborough showed
on behalf of what the Duke termed " his just pretensions."
The proceedings before the tribunal at Neufchâtel dragged
on for months   Frederick's cause was assisted by a letter
which the King of Sweden wrote in August to the canton
of Berne, kindly recommending him on religious grounds.
Conti and the other French candidates lost their tempers
from the beginning.   In open court, one of their representatives was promised the bastinado by an agent of the
King of Prussia, who was severely dealt with by the judges.
The French ambassador blustered   The English and Dutch
ministers, executing Marlborough's instructions to the
letter, derided his threats, and exhorted the burghers to
stand firm   In November, backed by the canton of Berne
and the other Protestant cantons, Neufchâtel gave its
allegiance to Frederick.   Thereupon Louis made military
preparations in Burgundy.   The cantons made counter-
preparations   But nothing happened   Villars reported to
Versailles that, though he would have been delighted at
an earlier stage to undertake the congenial task of bullying
a handful of Switzers into acknowledging the claims of
anybody, even himself, the moment was distinctly in-
opportune for an attack upon the whole Helvetian
body

At this time also Marlborough was apprised by the
Elector of Hanover's minister, Robethon, one of the Duke's
most trusted correspondents, that the Tory proposal to
invite the Electress Sophia to England had again been
revived, and that a secret intrigue to estrange the two
Courts was being busily conducted.   Marlborough informed
Godolphin, and effectual action was taken to frustrate the
scheme

During his stay at Meldert, Marlborough rendered the
Grand Alliance yet another service, which specially merited
the attention of Goslinga.   The control which Goslinga's
countrymen exercised in that age over the financial system
of the civilised world, made it impossible for France to

---

[1] Murray, vol iii., p 476 Marlborough to Wartenberg, July 18, 1707

obtain money in the various theatres of the war without
the co-operation of Dutch markets and bankers It had
long been a grievance in England that this co-operation
should not have been withdrawn. The government of
the Hague pleaded in justification that so lucrative a
business increased the taxable capacity of their subjects
But in June of this year Marlborough persuaded them to
prohibit the export of loans and " the commerce and currency of French bills within the United Provinces."[1] On
the 17th he instructed Stepney, with whom he was in
constant communication, to procure the adoption of a
similar measure in the Spanish Netherlands. " I need not
set forth to you," he said, " the advantages which the
public will receive from our stopping the source from
whence the enemy has been so long supplied in the remotest
parts with the only means of carrying on the war."[2] On
the 20th he informed Buys that Stepney anticipated no
difficulties at Brussels. " I hope," he added, " it will
prove the most efficacious means of cutting, for the enemy,
the nerves of the present war."[3] Goslinga has rightly
omitted to mention this incident in his memoirs, it does not
assist his argument.

In the midst of his multifarious and exacting labours at
Meldert, Marlborough was continually harassed by pessimistic accounts of the political situation at home. The
trouble there was with the Queen. The bishoprics of
Exeter and Chester being vacant, Anne, without consulting
Godolphin, promised to confer them on Blackhall and
Dawes, who by Burnet's admission were " in themselves
men of value and worth,"[4] but who were also Tories and
High Churchmen Taught by the humiliations which she
had suffered in the case of Sunderland, Anne deliberately
committed herself to these appointments, because she
desired to anticipate the advice of a minister who was
willing to be blackmailed The Junta sprang instantly to
arms It was contrary to first principles that the good
things in Church or State should fall to any but good Whigs
And it was quite intolerable that the small but permanent

[1] Murray, vol iii , p. 418: Marlborough to Stepney, June 17, 1707.
[2] Ibid   [3] Ibid , p 427· Marlborough to Buys, June 20, 1707.
[4] Burnet, vol iv , p 171.

Whig majority in the House of Lords should be imperilled Godolphin was required to explain the discrepancy between the Sovereign's practice and the minister's professions He knew that where the Church was concerned the Queen was peculiarly sensitive, but he was compelled to protest against an action which placed him in a false and embarrassing position   Anne remained deaf to his remonstrances. Both Godolphin and the Duchess appealed to Marlborough. " I am very sorry for it," wrote the Duke to Sarah on June 23, " but you know I have very little to say on those matters,"[1] in proof of which he referred to the case of the Whig, Potter, whom he himself had strongly, but hitherto unsuccessfully, recommended for the Regius Professorship of Divinity at Oxford. Godolphin admitted that the Queen had gone too far in the matter to withdraw, even if she wished. But he warned the Duke that the Junta were preparing to take vengeance. The blow was to fall upon Marlborough, who, because he considered Halifax unsuited for a diplomatic career, and had dared to say so, had already incurred their high displeasure. " One of the measures," wrote Godolphin on July 8, " which I fear is laid down by the Whigs, is to disturb your brother George, as soon as ever they have an opportunity."[2] The opportunity could easily be found. For many months the losses incurred at sea had been abnormal, and a popular clamour had arisen against the management of the navy. Churchill, as the Lord High Admiral's principal adviser, was therefore selected by the Junta for a grand attack in form, when Parliament assembled. " I see," wrote Marlborough to the Duchess on July 21, " that I am to be mortified by the prosecution of my brother George. I have deserved better from the Whigs, but since they are grown so indifferent as not to care what mortifications the Court may receive this winter, I shall not expect favour. My greatest concern is for the Queen, and for the Lord Treasurer England will take care of itself, and not be ruined because a few men are not pleased   They will see their error when it is too late "[3] He expressed a wish that his brother would

---

[1] Coxe, vol 11 , p 101· The Duke to the Duchess, June 23, 1707.
[2] Ibid , p 108   Godolphin to Marlborough, June 27/July 8, 1707.
[3] Ibid , The Duke to the Duchess, July 21, 1707.

resign; but he warned his wife that he would not tolerate attacks on Churchill by those " that I have a concern for." He suggested that she should speak " two words to Lord Sunderland " on the subject   " I expect," he said, " no more than what I would do if he had a brother attacked."[1] The firmness which the Queen exhibited at this time appears to have astonished Godolphin   He formed the opinion that she was receiving both encouragement and advice from some undisclosed quarter. The Duchess of Marlborough had long been convinced of what she terms the " secret practices " of Harley, and during the crisis which occurred over Sunderland's appointment, she had denounced both him and St. John to the Lord Treasurer   At the time both Godolphin and Marlborough had accepted the denials of their colleague. Before he departed for the continent, Marlborough had received a letter from Harley in which the following passage occurs. " I serve you by inclination and principle, and a very little time will make that manifest, as well as that I have no views or aims of my own."[2] But Godolphin's suspicions were now once more aroused. He communicated them to Marlborough, who replied on June 27: " You know my opinion was, and is yet, that you ought to take with you Mr. Secretary Harley, and to let the Queen see with all the freedom and plainness imaginable her true interest."[3]   Godolphin answered on July 5 that " Mr Harley does so hate and fear Lord Somers, Lord Sunderland, and Lord Wharton that he omits no occasion of filling the Queen's head with their projects and designs,"[4] but he added that no practical result would flow from the adoption of Marlborough's advice. The Duke replied on July 11 that the only alternative was to find " some way of speaking plainly to him."[5] In the very same letter he urged the Lord Treasurer to increase the emoluments of the Secretary at War, St. John, who was Harley's associate and friend. On the same date he informed the Duchess that Godolphin should " tell the Queen very plainly which way he thinks her business may be carried on; and if that be not agreeable, that she would

[1] Coxe, vol. ii., p 110. The Duke to the Duchess, July 11/22, 1707.
[2] *Conduct of the Duchess of Marlborough,* p 169
[3] Coxe, vol ii., p. 103   [4] *Ibid.,* p. 106.   [5] *Ibid.*

lose no time in knowing of Mr. Harley what his scheme is,
and follow that."[1]   A week later he told Godolphin that
he was "very desponding" "I am afraid." he said,
"there is too much conversation between the Queen and
Mr. Harley. You on the place can best judge what may
be proper to be done in it, but nevertheless one or both
should be spoke to." And he expressed the wish that
"some practicable scheme could be made by which Her
Majesty might be well served, and we both out of the
ministry."[2]

It is difficult not to sympathise with each and all of the
parties involved in this unfortunate affair The Queen
was honestly desirous of retaining the services of Godolphin,
but she objected strongly to his new system of pandering
to the Junta. Godolphin was honestly desirous of serving
her faithfully, but he, and he alone, was responsible for
the supplies which were essential to the conduct of the war,
and he could not guarantee that they would be passed by
the Commons, unless he conciliated the solid phalanx of
160 Whigs. Harley was honestly desirous of doing his
duty both to his Sovereign and his chief; but he shared
the Queen's detestation of the Whig oligarchy, and he
believed that it was unnecessary to submit to their blackmail It was natural that the Queen should turn for
consolation to the minister whose sentiments were identical
with her own; it was natural that the premier should resent
the intrusion of a colleague between himself and his
Sovereign; and it was natural that Harley should desire
to maintain the political system under which he had joined
the government. It must not, however, be supposed that
the Queen was taking action at this time on the advice of
a subordinate minister. Blackhall and Dawes had not
been nominated upon Harley's recommendation. "He
knew nothing of it, till it was the talk of the town,"[3] wrote
Anne to Marlborough, who had told her in August that
she must choose between Harley and Godolphin. Nevertheless, her intercourse with the Secretary of State was a
grave embarrassment to the Lord Treasurer. For Harley
was advising her it was a mistake to assume that her govern-

---

[1] *Ibid*, p. 107.   [2] *Ibid*, p 109.   [3] *Ibid.*, p. 158.

ment could not be carried on except by gracious permission
of the Junta   Reassured on this essential point, she was
only too likely to continue to pursue her independent
course   She had great opportunities.   The bishopric of
Norwich fell vacant in June   " There are now three
bishoprics vacant," wrote Godolphin to Marlborough on
July 19, " and I have so little hopes of their being well
filled, that I am resolved to use all my endeavours to keep
them vacant, till I can have Mr Freeman's assistance in
these spiritual affairs, which seem to grow worse and worse."[1]
On the principle that an open enemy is better than a blackmailing friend, it was Harley's plan to drive the Junta
into opposition. Thus, and only thus, would Godolphin
be saved from himself.

Marlborough's own position was a painful one. He had
always endeavoured to maintain a detached attitude towards
domestic politics. The views of the Queen and of Harley
upon party government had always been his views. On
the question of their practicability in the existing circumstances he did not set up for an authority, though he regretted
that Godolphin should disagree with Harley, who was
admittedly the foremost Parliamentary tactician of the
time   But if he was compelled to choose between the
Lord Treasurer and the Secretary of State, the Lord Treasurer
could rely upon his absolute loyalty.

Neither Godolphin nor Marlborough obtained any assistance from the Duchess. On the contrary, Mrs Freeman's
own situation was itself in danger. The misunderstanding
with the Queen, which was largely the result of Sarah's
intemperate zeal for Whiggery, was complicated by trouble
in the royal household. When Mrs. Morley was no more
than the Princess of Denmark, private friendship remained
unaffected by political and religious differences. But when
Mrs Morley became responsible for the supreme governance
of Church and State, the case was altered   That licence of
speech which Anne had formerly appreciated and enjoyed,
grew altogether intolerable when it was used to deliver
the decrees of the Junta to a Queen of England, who was
also " defender of the faith." From a state of chronic

[1] Coxe, vol ii., p. 108

friction Mrs. Freeman and Mrs Morley had approached violent rupture at the time when Sunderland was forced upon his unwilling Sovereign. It was then that Anne, unspeakably mortified, sought consolation outside the circle of her lifelong friends. But the comfort which Harley gave her was of the intellectual kind. She had need of something more. She had need of sympathetic contact with one of her own sex. She found what she wanted in the person of one of her bedchamber women, Abigail Hill. Abigail was the daughter of a wealthy merchant, who had ruined himself by speculation   Her mother was one of the twenty-two children of Sir John Jennings, grandfather of the Duchess of Marlborough   Sarah had befriended the family in the past. With Godolphin's help she had procured the elder boy a place in the Customs. " His brother, whom," to quote the Duchess's own words, " the bottle-men afterwards called ' honest Jack Hill,' " she had sent to school at St Albans, and had eventually induced her husband to take as an aide-de-camp, " though my Lord always said that Jack Hill was good for nothing "   Of the two sisters, the younger, having obtained by Sarah's influence the post of laundress to the Duke of Gloucester's family, had received an annuity after the Duke's death. For the elder, Abigail, Sarah had secured a place among the bedchamber women, where she conducted herself entirely to the satisfaction of both the Duchess and the Queen. It was to this poor relation, whose modest and unassuming demeanour excited no suspicion in the breast of the imperious favourite, that Anne had turned. Abigail was the very antithesis of her cousin   Respectful and submissive in manner, and in principles a High Tory, she was precisely the person to whom a woman, so lonely and so afflicted as the Queen now was, would be tempted to unbosom herself   Sarah's account of her is well known. It is distorted by personal resentment and the malice of the partisan. It ascribes to Abigail " a peculiar moroseness of temper," a " want of breeding," and an " incurable baseness," and of course " ingratitude "   Abigail was neither beautiful nor brilliant; but she was a clever woman, and a very brave one. She was at least as well educated as

II.   3

Sarah, and she had what Sarah never had, and never could acquire, both tact and judgment. It was not she who robbed her benefactress of the royal favour. Sarah fell by her own hand. And the rise of Abigail was the consequence and not the cause of her cousin's decline.

In the early months of the year 1707 the Duchess was warned by her friends of the Queen's intimacy with the bedchamber woman. But she attached no credence to the tale. She was then informed that Abigail had been privately married to Mr. Masham, groom of the bedchamber to the Prince of Denmark. Mr Masham, though a man of good family, owed his position, like Abigail, to Sarah's influence Sarah enquired of her cousin if this story were true. Abigail admitted that it was, and apologised for the secrecy which she had thought fit to observe. Sarah congratulated her warmly on the event, and showed a particular interest in the domestic arrangements of the couple. But on offering to break the news for her to their mistress, she was surprised to learn that Anne had already heard of it. " I went presently to the Queen," says Sarah, " and asked her why she had not been so kind as to tell me of my cousin's marriage " " All the answer I could obtain from Her Majesty was this, ' I have a hundred times bid Masham tell it you and she would not.' " The Duchess regarded the incident as mysterious. She made enquiries, and speedily discovered that Anne herself had been present at the wedding and had " called for a round sum out of the privy purse," that " Mrs Masham came often to the Queen when the Prince was asleep, and was generally two hours every day in private with her," and that Harley enjoyed " correspondence and interest at court by means of this woman "[1] In short, the Queen had transferred her favour, or at any rate a part of it, from Mrs. Freeman to Mrs Freeman's cousin, and what was worse, this cousin was in close touch with Harley. That Harley and Mrs. Masham should be on friendly terms, was not surprising, for, as it happened, Harley was a relative both of Abigail and her husband Presumably it was the knowledge of that fact which induced Abigail to conceal

[1] See *Memoirs of the Life and Conduct of Sarah, Duchess of Marlborough,* p 161.

her marriage from the Duchess, of whose hatred of Harley she was doubtless well aware. It may be assumed that Harley was at pains to fashion the Toryism of Abigail in the special mould which he himself recommended   But Sarah goes too far when she insinuates that he owed his influence at court to Abigail.   Harley was not an obscure adventurer, who could only obtain access to the Queen by a backstairs intrigue.   He was one of the most famous men in England; he had twice been offered a Secretaryship of State by William; he had thrice been chosen Speaker of the House of Commons; he was classed in the popular mind with Marlborough and Godolphin, and bracketed with them by Whig satirists as a " Triumvir ", and he was the holder of an illustrious office, which gave him of necessity free access to the presence of his Sovereign.   At the same time, his intimacy with the rising favourite could not fail to strengthen the grip which his opinions had acquired over the mind of Anne.   Sarah was alarmed, not indeed for herself, but for the Junta   She was indignant at this unexpected peril which threatened to confound the hopeful schemes of her blackmailing friends.   With her usual vehemence she attacked the Queen, and accused her of permitting Abigail to feed " Mrs Morley in her passion "[1] against Whiggery in Church and State   Anne's reply was affectionate in form but ironical in fact   Abigail, she said, was " never meddling with anything," though she believed that " in former times " others in the same station had been " tattling and very impertinent."[2]   The wrath of Sarah burst all bounds.   Godolphin found it necessary to speak to the Queen upon the subject   Thereupon Mrs Masham made some advances to the Duchess.   But a reconciliation between the cousins was impracticable

Marlborough was duly apprised of this affair at all its stages   He was at first disposed to minimise it   " The wisest thing," he wrote to Sarah on June 3, " is to have to do with as few people as possible   If you are sure that Mrs. Masham speaks of business to the Queen, I should think you might with some caution tell her of it, which would do good. For she certainly must be grateful and

---

[1] Coxe, vol II., p 99   [2] Ibid , p. 99.

will mind what you say."[1] But the endless complaints
which he received from the Lord Treasurer and the Duchess
convinced him that Mrs. Masham and Harley had combined
their forces "My apprehensions are," he wrote to Sarah
on July 21, "that somebody or other, I know not who,
has got so much credit with the Queen that they will be
able to persuade her to do more hurt to herself than we
can do good."[2]

In the midst of these manifold anxieties Marlborough
had one consolation and only one If the Dutch constitution had required him to submit his private correspondence
to the field-deputies, Goslinga would have been astonished
to see how continually the Duke recurred to his longing
for a speedy release from the public service. "If it were
not for the happiness I propose to myself, of living some
part of the remainder of my life quietly with you," he
wrote to his wife on June 26, "I could not bear with patience
the trouble I struggle with at this time" Referring to
the orchards at Woodstock, he requested her "to taste
the fruit of every tree, so that what is not good might be
changed" He was also concerned about the plans of the
ice-house. "The hot weather makes me think of these
things,"[3] he said. But in truth he was always thinking
of them He told Sunderland on June 27 that he was
"quite weary of serving"[4] He told Godolphin on July 18
that neither of them could have any peace "till we are
at Woodstock",[5] and again on the 27th he declared, "I
am so weary of all this matter that nothing can make me
happy but being in quiet at Woodstock"[6] He had already
asked the Lord Treasurer to inform Her Majesty that his
"heart and firm resolution" was "with her leave that
as soon as the war is at an end I might be master of myself,
by which I might have both time and quietness to reconcile
myself to God."[7]

These utterances, addressed to persons with whom it
was impossible, as well as unnecessary, for Marlborough

[1] *Memoirs of the Life and Conduct of Sarah, Duchess of Marlborough:*
Letter of the Duke of Marlborough to the Duchess of Marlborough,
June 3, 1707
[2] Coxe, vol ii., p. 110   [3] *Ibid*, p 102.   [4] *Ibid*, p 102
[5] *Ibid.*, p. 109   [6] *Ibid.*, p. 114.   [7] *Ibid*, p 103.

to play the hypocrite, are proof positive of the sincerity
of his public conduct.   But they do not stand alone.   Even
after the disasters of Almanza and Stollhofen the Duke
still hoped that the war could be terminated in the existing
campaign   He pinned his faith to the success of the design
against Toulon, a design which, if executed as he had
originally planned it, might have already brought France
to her knees, but which even now was capable of producing
a decisive result   He constantly referred to it in his letters
and dispatches as "the only way," "the unique remedy."
" All our hope is built upon it," he wrote to Salm on May 23,
" especially since the misfortune which has happened in
Spain "[1]   " England and Holland," he wrote to Wratislaw
on June 6, "found all their hope on the projects concerted in Italy."[2]   The same note was clearly sounded
in his communications to the King of Spain, to the Duke
of Savoy, to Chetwynd, the ambassador at Turin, and to
Prince Eugène.   He was convinced that, if this design
should miscarry, it would be more difficult than ever to
restrain the peace party in Holland, and no pleasant task
to face the English Parliament that winter.   Unfortunately
the Austrian government had assented to the scheme only
under compulsion from the maritime powers.   The suspicions, aroused at Vienna by the attitude of the Dutch
towards the Spanish Netherlands, had not been calmed
The Emperor's ministers believed that, if Toulon were
taken or destroyed, England would be as ready as Holland
to negotiate for peace, and that the Duke of Savoy, having
secured at the same time some footing in Provence, would
follow suit.   " We risk our army," wrote Wratislaw to
Marlborough on July 13, "in the sole view of pleasing
England "[3]   Godolphin was indignant   " Had they ever
had Italy or an army," he exclaimed, "but for the extraordinary efforts and expenses of England ?"[4]   But the
Emperor's ministers utterly refused to see that the capture
of Toulon was an object deserving of the utmost endeavours
of the entire coalition.   " A jealous humour," wrote Marlborough to Manchester on May 19, " prevails so much at

---

[1] Murray, vol iii , p 377· Marlborough to Salm, May 23, 1707.
[2] *Ibid* , p 390 Marlborough to Wratislaw, June 6 1707
[3] Coxe, vol ii., p 112   [4] *Ibid* , p. 119

the Court that they will not seriously weigh and consider their own interest "[1] They obstinately adhered to their expedition against Naples, and insisted upon detaching 12,000 men under General Daun for the invasion of that kingdom Marlborough left nothing undone to dissuade them from this blunder. At the Duke of Savoy's request, Chetwynd went from Turin to Milan to protest against it to Eugène But the palpable anxiety of England and Savoy only increased the suspicions of the Austrian statesmen, and confirmed them in their resolution to seize what they could, and while they could, for the House of Hapsburg. They declared that they had friends in Naples who expected them, and whom they could not desert, and that the forces in Italy were sufficiently numerous to execute both projects simultaneously. Daun marched on May 18. He encountered no serious opposition, and entered Naples on July 7. Eugène had promised Marlborough that he would " do his best " · but the army destined for the attack on Toulon was not ready until the end of June. The Austrian preparations were extremely backward, and at least 8,000 of their recruits never arrived at all. Hearing from Chetwynd that there was danger of a deficiency of ammunition, Marlborough authorised Shovel, who reached those waters early in June, to purchase powder and ball at Genoa and Leghorn, and to supply the army with all that the fleet could safely spare The King of Spain was pressing for reinforcements from Italy; but Marlborough told Eugène that the departure of Daun's 12,000 had sufficiently jeopardised the prospects of the design on Toulon, and that the maritime powers would never consent to another detachment on any pretext whatsoever.[2] The Duke considered that, after the attack on Toulon had either succeeded or failed, a part of Daun's army should be conveyed under the protection of the fleet from Naples to Barcelona These views eventually prevailed By the end of June Eugène and Savoy were ready to advance. Having made a feint towards Susa, as if they intended to attack Dauphiné, they started for Toulon on the 30th,

---

[1] Murray, vol iii , p 371. Marlborough to Manchester, May 19, 1707.
[2] *Ibid* , p 405 Marlborough to the Prince of Savoy, June 11, 1707

and reached Tenda on July 5. Shovel and the fleet kept
pace with their march Behind the Var a French force
threw up a line of earthworks, and prepared to dispute
the passage. But on July 11 Sir John Norris with four
British men-of-war and a Dutchman entered the mouth of
the river, cannonaded the trenches, and landed 600 seamen
and marines, who turned the flank of the French and compelled them to retire. Tessé, who commanded the French
armies on the Italian frontier, wasted no time in further
attempts of this description Satisfied that Toulon was
the allies' goal, he concentrated his forces there, and began
the construction of a fortified camp on the heights adjacent
to the city. On July 26 the allies arrived before the place,
both by land and sea. That very day dispatches from
Eugène and Shovel, recounting the passage of the Var,
reached Meldert Marlborough was delighted But
Eugène's dispatch, after referring to the fact that Tessé
was sure to be reinforced from other theatres of the war,
concluded with these words: " Whatever is possible, will
be done; but the enterprise is one of the most perilous."
Marlborough told Godolphin that these words " should
not be seen but by few." " You must not," he said, " be
too much alarmed at his expression; for it is his way to think
everything difficult till he comes to put it into execution,
but then he acts with so much vigour that he makes amends
for all his despondency."[1] At the same time, the Duke
suggested to Eugène, that now that Naples had fallen,
some of Daun's men might be shipped across to the Riviera.
He was very hopeful of success. " If the siege of Toulon
goes prosperously," he said, " I shall be cured of all diseases
but old age."[2] Neither Godolphin nor Wratislaw had ever
shared his optimism. But Marlborough had a boundless
faith in the genius of Eugène and the prowess of the British
navy. Already he foresaw in imagination the allied army
wintering on the Riviera, and the allied squadrons permanently based upon the port and dockyard of Toulon.[3]

The latest news from Provence was conveyed into the
Spanish Netherlands from French sources. It encouraged

[1] Coxe, vol ii , p 114   [2] Ibid , p 121
[3] Murray vol iii , p 467: Marlborough to Sinzendorf, July 11, 1707,
p. 491 Marlborough to Shovel, July 30, 1707.

Marlborough to anticipate an early change in the situation
in Brabant   When Vendôme had detached 1,200 Bavarians
for Germany at the end of June, the Duke had suggested
to the field-deputies that a march to Genappe would
threaten the French communications and would relieve
the country round Meldert of the burden of subsisting the
allied forces.   But he could not persuade them to consent
though he tried for six weeks.   They " will not own to
me," he wrote to Sunderland on July 7, " that they have
any other orders or directions but that of being cautious
not to venture anything till they hear what is done in
Provence."[1]   One of them, at any rate, was by his own
admission ashamed to confess the truth.   But the Duke
was not deceived.   " I have reason to believe," he said,
" that they have more positive orders from the States;
and let the success be good or bad in Provence, I believe
they will continue of the mind they are now in; since it is
the daily discourse in this army, as well as in Holland,
why should they venture, since they have already in their
hands what will be a sufficient security to them ?"[2]
Vendôme on the other hand had recurred to the project
of besieging Huy.   But Louis would not hear of it   He
was very well satisfied with things as they were.   On
August 1, however, Vendôme received positive orders from
Versailles to send thirteen battalions of foot and six
squadrons of dragoons to the assistance of Tessé.   They
started on the 5th.   Marlborough learned of their departure
on the 6th.   Goslinga asserts that the Duke now proposed
to the field-deputies to attack the French position at
Gembloux, and that the field-deputies, considering that
the numerical advantage which had been transferred to
the allies was of the very slightest, opposed the idea as
too hazardous   They consented, however, to a march to
Genappe.   " I can say without vanity," says Goslinga,
" that I animated the Duke to it as much as I could."[3]
Marlborough's version of the incident is altogether different.
He informed Godolphin on August 8 that he had pressed
the field-deputies to obtain fuller powers, and that they

---

[1] Coxe, vol ii , p 106   [2] Ibid.
[3] Mémoires de Goslinga, p 36

had that day handed him a copy of a modified resolution from the States   " You will see," he said, " by the reasoning of this resolution, the humour they are in."[1]   But he expressed the hope that the departure of the detachment for Toulon would " encourage the deputies so as that I may make the march I have been proposing to them for these last six weeks."   It would therefore appear that when Goslinga spoke without vanity, he spoke also without any sense of humour   However that may have been, Marlborough, Overkirk, and the field-deputies decided to quit Meldert, and by stealing a march upon Vendôme, to cut him off from Mons.   If he moved, a favourable opportunity for battle might present itself, if he continued at Gembloux, he could be attacked from the side of Genappe with less disadvantage than from that of Meldert

Preparations were made with secrecy and thoroughness   On the morning of the 10th the heavy baggage set off for Brussels, and the artillery moved towards the Dyle, where bridges had been prepared at Weert St. Georges.   At 3 in the afternoon Wurttemberg was ordered to advance with fourteen squadrons on the road to Piétrebais to alarm the French. He was to keep watch upon their movements throughout the night, and afterwards to follow the route of the allied army and form the rear-guard.   At 4 the tents were struck. Marching continually Marlborough passed the Dyle and the Lasne, and reached the neighbourhood of Wavre at daybreak   After a brief halt, he pressed forward to Genappe, where the heads of his columns arrived at 3 on the afternoon of the 11th, after a journey of twenty-four hours' duration. On the road, Goslinga overheard some of the Dutch generals complaining that the movement was a dangerous one   They had not been consulted

Meantime Württemberg had executed his orders well   He was seen within half a league of the French camp; and Vendôme and the Elector rode out to Walhain to reconnoitre.   Fully expecting to be attacked, they ordered the approaches to their position to be obstructed with timber, and made every preparation for a stout resistance.   It was not until midnight that they obtained reliable information

[1] Coxe, vol. ii., p. 126.

of Marlborough's march Then they lost no time They sent off their artillery and baggage to Charleroi, and in the small hours of the morning they took the road to Gosselies in seven columns. At 6 in the evening, when the last of Marlborough's men were trailing into camp at Genappe, the last of the French arrived in a strong position between Vanderbeek and Seneffe They had won the race by a very little, but they had won it. If they would not fight, it was practically impossible now to compel them " I hope," wrote Marlborough to Godolphin that evening, " this will convince our friends in Holland, as it has done our deputies, that if they had consented to my making this march six weeks ago, as I pressed to do, the French would then have made, as they now have, a shameful march, by which both armies see very plainly that they will not venture to fight."[1]

Goslinga alleges that Marlborough and the deputies decided overnight to make an early start on the morning of the 12th, but that nevertheless the Duke dined in camp, and did not resume his march till noon.[2] As it was obvious that at whatever hour the allies started the French did not intend to be caught, Marlborough and Overkirk may well have deemed it expedient to rest their tired troops. Soon after middle day they moved, and passing through Nivelles, came that evening by 6 o'clock to Arquennes, where they camped within less than a league of the enemy's position. The outposts of the two armies were almost within speaking distance.

Vendôme appeared to be in danger. But in reality he was safe enough He resembled a judicious runner, who deliberately permits his opponent almost to draw level. The allies had marched for twenty-four hours, rested twenty, and marched again for six. The French had marched for eighteen hours, and rested for twenty-four They were therefore comparatively fresh. Moreover, their army was the more mobile of the two, for it contained a larger proportion of mounted men and it had no artillery. At 7 o'clock it quietly prepared for the road. At 9, under cover of the darkness, it stole noiselessly away.

[1] Coxe, vol ii , p. 128.   [2] *Mémoires de Goslinga*, p. 37

Marlborough expected nothing else. He knew that the French would withdraw in the night, or at daybreak at the latest. But he knew also that at whatever hour the march was made, it would be covered by a strong rear-guard. If he could engage this rear-guard closely, he could either annihilate it, or compel Vendôme to return to its rescue and commit his main body to a battle   To accomplish this purpose he threw forward a detachment of forty squadrons and 5,000 grenadiers. He selected as their leader Count Tilly, the general commanding the cavalry of the Dutch army. Word was sent to Tilly that his men and his orders were awaiting him   He arrived at 11 and found the detachment under arms   " It rained heavily," says Cranstoun, " was pitch dark, and no house near "[1] Tilly's orders were in writing, but he could not read them for want of a light, which was not procured till midnight. The country was difficult; and another hour was lost in searching for guides. When he had obtained them, Tilly was afraid to venture forward in the rain and darkness   But a little before dawn, Ross extorted a reluctant permission to advance with two English squadrons. He speedily ascertained that the French were gone, and that their retreat was covered by a powerful body of horse and foot   It consisted in fact of two brigades of cavalry, two regiments of dragoons, 100 of the Garde du Corps, and twenty companies of grenadiers, the whole under the command of Albergotti   Ross sent back word to Tilly that the enemy were retiring, and that he with his two squadrons was dogging their rear-guard.   Tilly dispatched a messenger to Marlborough, and marched immediately on the heels of Ross. Marlborough ordered Lottum to support Tilly with twenty battalions and thirty squadrons   He himself followed with another detachment. The rest of the army stood to their arms. The morning was foggy, and the rain continued to descend. But it was the anniversary of Blenheim, and every soldier in the Duke's army was eager to do honour to the day. Tilly's grenadiers went forward at the double. They ran, says Cranstoun, " like horses for two leagues "[2]

[1] Portland MSS , p. 443 Lieut.-Colonel Cranstoun to Robert Cunningham, September 10, 1707 (Hist MSS Comm , 15th Report, Appendix, part iv.).   [2] Ibid

But they could not get up in time to retain Albergotti, who had secured too good a start. The country was intersected with hollow roads, and the French, retiring from hedge to hedge, easily kept Tilly's cavalry at bay. At 5 o'clock Vendôme learned that his rear-guard was attacked. Riding back with the Elector, he found Albergotti at Abbaye de l'Olive, retiring in perfect order, while the English troopers followed at a respectful distance. Seeing that his task was hopeless, Tilly drew off and returned to camp. His casualties reached a dozen   Lottum's detachment, and Marlborough's, returned likewise   Vendôme halted his army on the heights of Haine St. Pierre and Haine St. Paul, till Albergotti rejoined. He pretended to be offering battle, though he considered himself lucky to have saved his rear-guard. At 2 in the afternoon he resumed his flight.

In the opinion of Cranstoun " a fair opportunity " was lost that day, through want of judgment and of tact on Marlborough's part.[1]   Cranstoun declares that Tilly, though " a notable officer," was too old, too slow, and altogether too cautious for an enterprise of this nature, and that the treatment which he received from Marlborough disgusted him from the outset. Tilly, he says, as a man of family, and a soldier of high rank, " perhaps had a right to expect in good manners "[2] that he would have been summoned to the Duke's presence and personally instructed by word of mouth. Had that been done, he might have reconnoitred the ground, and possibly pushed forward his grenadiers before the daylight failed. These criticisms are recorded nowhere else   Even Goslinga does not refer to them   But they are put forward in good faith, and they are deserving of all respect.   " In war," wrote Clausewitz, " through the influence of an infinity of petty circumstances, which cannot possibly be described on paper, things disappoint us, and we fall short of the matter." As Cranstoun tells it, this story of driving rain, and impenetrable darkness, and unknown country, and orders illegible for want of light, and missing guides, and hollow roads, and private resentment, and an old man chosen for a young man's work, is

---

[1] Portland MSS., p. 442.   [2] Ibid, p 443

an admirable example of what Clausewitz meant by his phrase " friction in war."[1]

It was impossible to determine, from the direction of Vendôme's retreat, whether he intended to enter the French lines forthwith, or whether he would retire instead towards Tournai   But it was a certainty that in no case would he fight a battle.   Marlborough determined therefore to allow his soldiers some repose.   Later in the day his scouts and spies informed him that the French had headed for the west, and had halted for the night at St. Denis and Casteau. At 6 o'clock on the morning of the 14th the allied army set off for Soignies.   Nobody who witnessed their march ever forgot it.   It was made in the teeth of a rain-storm of unprecedented violence, over roads that had virtually ceased to exist, though a thousand pioneers had been at work upon them since the night of the 12th.   The majority both of the men and the horses left their shoes behind them in the tenacious mud of Belgium   The distance was barely a dozen miles, but the heads of the columns did not reach their destination till 5 in the evening, and it was noon on the 15th before the whole army marched in.   The guns and the baggage did not get through until the 17th [2]   The French, who had remained under arms throughout the night of the 13th, moved when the allies moved, and arrived at Cambron and Chièvres when the allies arrived at Soignies.

Both Goslinga and Cranstoun have plenty to say about the march to Soignies.   They both agree that it should have been made upon the 13th   In that event, according to Goslinga, the allies would have annihilated the French. He does not explain how one army can annihilate another, which travels lighter, is less fatigued, and is determined never to be overtaken   However, he lodged a complaint at the Hague,[3] and he seems to have considered that the

---

[1] Clausewitz, *On War*, book 1 , ch vii   " Friction in War," p 78.

[2] Every student of the Waterloo campaign will appreciate this story. On June 17, during the retreat from Quatre Bras, which was made in a remarkable storm of rain and thunder, some of the Life Guards' chargers at Genappe sank to their knees in the yielding soil   On June 18 Napoleon's artillery was unable to manœuvre before 11 30 by reason of the state of the ground   And on the same day, and from the same cause, the Prussians were greatly delayed in their march from Wavre to Planchenoit, and almost despaired of arriving at all

[3] Goslinga, p 42.

proof of his theory that Marlborough intended to prolong the war was now complete. Cranstoun's standpoint was different. "It is, I believe, most certain," he wrote, "that no general in the world ever desired more sincerely and anxiously to fight, and to push the war in earnest than my Lord Duke does, yet, by not taking all the right measures at that critical time that might have been taken, the enemy escaped out of our hands."[1] Cranstoun recognises apparently that the chances of a battle were small; but he argues that if the allies had moved on the 13th, Vendôme must have entered his lines at Mons, and Marlborough would have been free to invest Tournai, Lille, or Ypres. This point is spoiled by Cranstoun's own declaration in the very same letter that without a superiority of 25,000 or 30,000 men, no siege could be undertaken in that country [2] Marlborough at any rate did not propose to invest Tournai, Lille, or Ypres. If he could not fight, he was satisfied to keep Vendôme running But it was unnecessary to ruin his own army in the process. Neither Goslinga nor Cranstoun would appear to pay sufficient regard to the extraordinary efforts which had already been required of the soldiers. Cranstoun allows that Tilly's men could not, after their exertions and exposure, have moved again without some hours' rest. But Tilly's men numbered at least 10,000. He says nothing of Lottum's detachment, which was called out in the rain soon after daybreak They numbered at least 14,000 or 15,000. And he says nothing of the remainder of the army, which was roused from slumber at the same time, though one and all, and notably Wurttemberg's twelve squadrons, they must have sorely needed a more prolonged repose.

The condition of the French was pitiable In their precipitate march from Gembloux they had suffered extreme privations. For four nights they had not dared to pitch their tents They were two days at Cambron before their bread-waggons arrived. According to Marlborough 2,000 of them deserted, and according to Goslinga over 4,000.

---

[1] Portland MSS , p 442· Cranstoun to Robert Cunningham, September, 1707 (Hist MSS Comm , 15th Report, Appendix, part iv).
[2] *Ibid* , p 442

Cranstoun says that with one march more "almost all their infantry" would have disappeared [1]

This was an extraordinary summer in Belgium. At Meldert in June a torrent of rain had washed away whole tents and piles of arms; yet before the end of that month Marlborough complained that the heat had been more insufferable than in a Spanish August   It was then that he bethought him of the ice-house at Woodstock.[2]   But from Meldert on August 4 he wrote, "we have had so much rain that I can hardly stir out of my quarter, the dirt being up to the horses' bellies"[3]   The evil weather which had again set in on the night of the 12th, and which had so incommoded the march on the 14th, continued without any improvement until the 24th   "It is not to be expressed, the rains we have had," wrote Marlborough to Godolphin on the 18th, "so that if the common cause depended on our marching, neither the enemy nor we could stir out of our camps."[4]   He consoled himself with the reflection that the French were the greater sufferers, as "we have the grand chaussée to bring our bread and provision from Brussels."[5]   This inactivity is censured by Goslinga, who suggests that the weather was only a pretext for delay.[6]

At Soignies the army had a notable guest in the person of Peterborough, who had arrived on the 12th, having completed his circular tour of the courts of Europe. The British government had watched his proceedings at Turin, Vienna, Alt-Ranstädt and Hanover with some uneasiness. At Turin the Duke of Savoy had declined to listen to his projects, and had advised him to return home and clear his character.   At Milan, Eugène formed the opinion that he thought like a general, though he did not always "express himself with propriety."[7]   At Vienna he made a good impression by abusing Galway and Stanhope; and Wratislaw had advised Marlborough that it would be "dangerous to offend him, as he is an Englishman, and has been supplanted by a Frenchman, who has been the cause of this irreparable

[1] *Ibid*, p 444.   [2] Coxe, vol ii , p 102
[3] *Ibid*, p 121   [4] *Ibid.*, p 132
[5] Murray, vol iii , p 524 Marlborough to Portland, August 18, 1707.
[6] Goslinga, p. 40.   [7] Coxe, vol ii., p 79

loss "[1]   At Alt-Ranstadt he had endeavoured to persuade
Charles to intervene between France and the Grand Alliance, but the King had heard him with amused contempt,
and the ministers had treated him " as a madman."[2]   At
Hanover he " warmly declaimed against Lord Galway,"
showed himself " extravagantly Swedish and an enemy of
the Emperor,"[3] and won the favour of Sophia by approving
the proposal that she should visit England.   But the
Elector did not fail to let him understand that his presence
was unwelcome.   His mischievous conduct embarrassed
the English ministry, and particularly Marlborough, whom
he affected to regard as his friend and champion, and to
whom he wrote continually.   The Duke desired that he
should be summoned home   Godolphin thought that " he
would do less hurt abroad."[4]   " A little good advice from
you," he wrote to Marlborough on August 15, " will have
more weight than from anybody to hinder him from hurting
himself and being very troublesome to others."[5]   Harley
considered that he should be called to account.   " If,"
wrote the Secretary of State to the Lord Treasurer, " it
appears he has acted contrary to his instructions, ought he
not to be committed ? . . .   It is better to find him work
to clear himself, than leave him leisure to do mischief "[6]

On August 15 Marlborough wrote from Soignies to the
Duchess " I have at this time my winter clothes and a
fire in my chamber, but what is worse, the ill weather hinders
me from going abroad, so that Lord Peterborough has the
opportunity of very long conversations; what is said one
day the next destroys, so that I have desired him to put
his thoughts in writing "[7]   Peterborough complained that
he had lost a fortune in the service, and that he had been
" injured in everything that has been reported to his disadvantage."[8]   He exhibited " obliging letters "[9] from the
King of Spain, declared that he could convince Godolphin
and Sunderland that he had been greatly slandered, and
announced his intention of serving the Queen if she would
let him, and if not, of soliciting her permission to serve

[1] Coxe, vol ii , p 79   [2] *Ibid* , p 80   Letter from Besenval
[3] *Ibid* , p 124   [4] *Ibid* , p 109
[5] *Ibid* , p 126   [6] *Ibid* , p 137   [7] *Ibid* , pp 131, 132.
[8] *Ibid* , p 132   [9] *Ibid*

elsewhere. Marlborough was speedily weary of him.
'Lord Peterborough,'' he wrote to Godolphin on the 18th,
'has said all that is possible to me, but says nothing of
leaving the army."[1] Nevertheless he departed on the
20th   Marlborough advised him "for his own sake . . .
to clear up the objections against him"[2]   But the Duke
warned Godolphin that he would "not be governed," and
that it was desirable, if possible, "to make him easy."[3]
At the same time he sent a caution to the Duchess.   "If,"
he said, "Lord Peterborough should . . . at any time
write to you, pray be careful what answer you make, for
sooner or later it will be in print"[4]

It is not unworthy of remark that Peterborough was an
eye-witness of those events which Goslinga and Cranstoun
have criticised, but there is no evidence that he shared
their views.   Had he seen anything to censure, he was not
the man to keep it to himself.

During his depressing sojourn at Soignies Marlborough
was cheered by the reflection that the capture of Toulon
would fully compensate the Grand Alliance for its failures
elsewhere   "That," he wrote to Spaar on the 24th, "must
give a jog to all the rest."[5]   The silence of the French
encouraged him to hope that the reports from Provence
were little to their liking.   But he knew that their detachments, drawn from other theatres of the war, must turn
the balance in favour of Tessé; and he therefore wrote to
Salm and to Eugène, urging the adoption of his proposal
that 6,000 men should be shipped from Naples to the Riviera.
On the 25th he received letters from Chetwynd and from
the army in Provence.   They informed him, as he told
Godolphin, "that there is not that friendship and reliance
between the Duke of Savoy and Prince Eugène as should
be wished, for making so great a design succeed."[6]   He
learned with regret that on the arrival of the allied army
before Toulon, the Duke had proposed to storm the fortified
camp which Tessé had constructed, and that Eugène had
refused his consent to the operation.   At the same time
he was unable to believe that they would have continued

[1] Coxe, p 132   [2] Ibid   [3] Ibid.   [4] Ibid, p 133.
[5] Murray, vol iii, p 528 Marlborough to Spaar, August 24, 1707.
[6] Coxe, vol ii, p 134.

so long before the place, if the chances of success were other than favourable. But ominous rumours now began to arrive from the French frontier. Marlborough at first discredited them By the end of the month he could discredit them no longer. They were in fact too true. The allied army, which numbered only 35,000 men, was insufficient for the investment of Toulon To carry both the fortified camp and the town by a swift assault, was its only chance. When that idea was abandoned, the prospect became hopeless. But guns and gunners were landed from the fleet. There was furious fighting round the posts upon the hills On July 30 the Imperialists stormed the height of St Catherine. On August 15 the French recovered it, after a desperate struggle in which the gallant Prince of Saxe-Gotha was killed. Eugène reported to the Emperor that the enterprise was an impossible one, and that he only persisted in it because the naval officers, " who do not understand land operations, still consider it practicable." Day by day supplies diminished, and the numbers of the enemy increased. Even the communications with Italy were threatened There was no alternative but to retreat. Shovel embarked the sick, wounded, and artillery. At noon on the 21st the fleet stood in, engaged the forts, and bombarded the town and harbour till 5 on the morning of the 22nd, ruining buildings, destroying battleships, and setting fire to the magazine of cordage. That night the army retired in five columns Their march was ably conducted, and was unimpeded, save for some skirmishes with the peasantry who had been infuriated by the excesses of the soldiery. They passed the Var on the 31st. On September 16 they encamped near Pignerole. They finished their campaign by the capture of Susa.

Explanations and recriminations followed But the principal causes of this deplorable miscarriage are apparent. In the first place the Austrian government never had its heart in the enterprise, and it successfully communicated its own apathy to Eugène. Secondly, the suspicion and jealousy which existed between the Courts of Vienna and Turin reproduced themselves in the personal relations between Eugène and the Duke of Savoy. And thirdly, the

dispatch of 12,000 of the Emperor's men to Naples and
the absence of 8,000 of his recruits, rendered failure
inevitable, if time were allowed for the army of Tessé to be
reinforced.

Marlborough endured this crowning disappointment with
firmness   It was rendered the more bitter by the impudent
assertion of Wratislaw that "the retreat from Toulon
justifies the court of Vienna, and proves it to have been more
correct in its predictions than that of England."[1]   The
Duke said but little.   He endeavoured to console himself
with the reflection that the invasion of Provence had at
any rate created an extreme consternation in France, had
paralysed the armies of Louis in Spain, Germany, and
Flanders, had inflicted immense losses upon the peasantry
and upon the town of Toulon, and had caused the destruction of some twenty men-of-war, which had been sunk by
Shovel or by the French themselves.

But England's luck was surely out.   Off Scilly on a dark
autumnal night, Shovel, "the greatest seaman of the age,"[2]
by an error of judgment, struck upon the rocks and was
lost with four ships of the line   He entered the service
as a cabin-boy; he died a rear-admiral of England, and
commander of the confederate fleets

The roads having now recovered from the deluge, Marlborough prepared to advance.   On August 31 he marched
straight upon Ath   Vendôme fled, and never halted till
he was safe under the cannon of Tournai.   So excessive
was the hurry of the French that they left "a good deal
of provision and baggage behind them," which became the
loot of the allied soldiery   Goslinga says that the field-
deputies now suggested the siege of Mons, and that Marlborough raised objections which were quite invalid.[3]   On
the 3rd the Duke continued his advance towards Audenarde,
and on the 4th passed the Schelde below that town.   Moving
along the left bank of the river he reached Helchin on the
7th.   Vendôme, whose position was now threatened, did
not tarry.   He fled to Pont-à-Tressin, where he took refuge
behind the lines of the Marque, under cover of the guns of
Lille

[1] Coxe, vol 11 , p 150   [2] Burnet, vol iv., p 168.
[3] Mémoires de Goslinga, p. 40

At Helchin the army lived well. Both sides were now subsisting on French territory. On September 15 Marlborough made a last attempt to provoke a battle Learning that the enemy designed to forage that day in the direction of Templeuve, he marched at dawn with 20,000 foot, 5,000 horse, and 12 guns "in order to attack the escort that should cover them."[1] But the enemy declined to stir. Thereupon the Duke himself foraged "the villages between Lille and Tournai, within a little league of their army." The injury and insult were patiently endured "They will venture nothing this year,"[2] wrote Marlborough to Godolphin. All their efforts were in fact directed to fortifying the impregnable position which they had assumed.

The campaign terminated on October 10. As an exhibition of the orthodox war of the period, it was a masterpiece Both armies had done nothing at all for about seventeen weeks. Both had executed some long and fatiguing marches. Both had lost heavily from sickness and exposure, and hardly at all from shot or steel. And both had succeeded for a time in drawing supplies from the enemy's country. In this dreary contest Vendôme was regarded, on the whole, as the victor. But his victory was gained, not over the Duke of Marlborough, but over their High Mightinesses, the States-General of the United Provinces, and over those field-deputies, who in the words of Eugène, "ignorant of our profession, follow the opinion of their generals, who know nothing but defensive warfare."

It seems to have been universally accepted by historians that the summer of 1707 constitutes a blot upon the career of Marlborough. Never was there a worse mistake. It is true that he won no battle in the Spanish Netherlands— how should he, when neither he nor his antagonist was allowed to fight ? But his battles were won in other fields. The Grand Alliance, cowering in the shadow of the northern peril, riven by internal dissensions, and stricken by three successive defeats, seemed visibly to collapse But always in the background, and oftentimes unseen of the eyes of the multitude, stood the Captain-General of England,

[1] Murray, vol iii , p 560· Marlborough to Harley, September 15, 1707
[2] Coxe, vol ii , p. 149

exhorting one, counselling another, inspiring all, encouraging here, reprimanding there, supervising everywhere, contriving, uniting, foreseeing, organising, reorganising— a giant figure, supporting with labours that transcended the credible the tottering fabric of the coalition. How Marlborough would have borne himself at the head of a beaten army, posterity knows not, for he never commanded one. But the patience, the firmness, and the tenacity which he displayed through the long crisis of the summer of 1707 enable us to conjecture His own judgment on this matter is perhaps the best. It was delivered from Meldert to his wife, in language intensely English " I have done my duty, and God's will be done."[1]

[1] Coxe, vol. ii., p. 110. Marlborough to the Duchess, July 11/22, 1707.

XVIII.—HARLEY

IN September, while Marlborough was at Helchin, Godolphin at length adopted his advice, and spoke "plainly" to Harley He took the line that, if ministers at home were working in opposite directions, success abroad could never be achieved [1] But the interview produced no practical result. The Secretary of State indignantly repelled the imputations made against him, and emphatically asserted his fidelity to his colleagues He maintained that, now as always, he dreaded and detested the machinations of political extremists, but that now, as always, he would take his orders from none save Godolphin and Marlborough. He also objected that the charge was a general one, and demanded to know particulars. Godolphin could adduce nothing save the promises given to Blackhall and Dawes. Harley declared that he was the victim of misrepresentation, and he of course repeated the denial which the Queen herself had given in regard to the bishoprics. " I never knew those two persons," he said, " I never spoke of them, nor ever thought of them, or directly or indirectly ever recommended them." [2] In a similar strain he wrote to Marlborough, protesting that he had acted " with the nicest honour and by the strictest rules of friendship," [3] that he had on no occasion meddled in affairs of patronage or any other affairs, and that, if he had thought proper to interest himself on behalf of Blackhall and Dawes, he would never have condescended to lie about it afterwards All this was true enough The Queen knew how to fill the episcopal bench without the assistance of Defoe's employer. But Godolphin was continually assuring her that, unless she paid blackmail to the Junta, her government could not be

[1] MSS of the Marquis of Bath Lord Godolphin to R Harley, September 18 1707 (Hist MSS Comm , vol 1 , p 183)
[2] Coxe, vol 11 , p 171 Harley to Marlborough, September 16/27, 1707.
[3] *Ibid* , p 170

carried on. She had therefore appealed to Harley, who was generally recognised as the foremost authority in England on tactics in the House of Commons; and Harley had expressed the opinion that a way could still be found. Marlborough did not pretend to understand the scheme. " What it is, God knows,"[1] he said. But whatever it was, it was sufficient to encourage the Queen to resist payment to her tormentors

In appearance, however, the " Triumvirate " still continued to work as harmoniously as ever. " I never had, nor ever can have, a thought of your being out of the Queen's service while I am in it,"[2] wrote Godolphin to Harley on September 18. A week later, he declared that he had " not the least doubt "[3] of the honesty of his friend's intentions. And Marlborough, writing from the Hague on October 7, used language equally conciliatory " I beg you will do me the justice to believe," he said, " I am sincerely yours, and that I am sorry from my heart that you have any reason given you to be uneasy."[4] But the Secretary of State had every reason to be uneasy He had great and implacable enemies; and in his letter of thanks, he reminded the Duke that twelve months before he had prophesied that they would contrive to ruin him in the very manner which they had now adopted.

Anne believed that she could convince Marlborough, though she could not convince Godolphin, of the reasonableness of her conduct Godolphin thought that, where Mr Montgomery had failed, Mr Freeman might yet succeed. The Duke proposed at first to try the effect of a flying visit to England in September. But the idea was abandoned, as likely to excite unfavourable comment. By this time he was more than disgusted with domestic politics. " What I hear from England," he wrote to the Duchess on September 19, " sometimes vexes me so that I am not the same man "[5] He recognised that, as long as the war lasted, he must remain at the head of the army " Continue in

[1] *Ibid* , p 163. Marlborough to Godolphin, September 29, 1707
[2] MSS of the Marquis of Bath Lord Godolphin to R Harley, September 18 1707 (Hist. MSS Comm , vol 1 , p 183)
[3] *Ibid* , Lord Godolphin to R Harley, September 25, 1707. p 184
[4] *Ibid* , Marlborough to R Harley, October 7, 1707 p 184
[5] Coxe, vol ii , p 161 Marlborough to the Duchess, September 19, 1707.

the galley,"[1] as he called it   But as responsibility without power is intolerable, he thought that Godolphin should resign. " If you, the Lord Treasurer, and I were out of business," he told his wife, " I should be more capable of doing my duty here "[2]

It was indeed desirable that Marlborough should be free to devote his utmost energies to affairs upon the continent The Grand Alliance could never survive another campaign like that of 1707. "Nothing," wrote the Duke to Godolphin on September 29, " shall dishearten me from endeavouring to do all the good I can here abroad."[3]   Two vital questions called for prompt and adequate settlement It was necessary to augment the armies in the field, and it was equally necessary to select an efficient commander for every theatre of war   Though the French were boasting of the immense levies which they proposed to raise in the ensuing winter, no member of the coalition was likely to respond to an appeal for fresh sacrifices. And though the situation in Spain urgently demanded the presence of an Imperialist general, endowed with personal authority as well as with military genius, it was doubtful whether the Prince of Savoy, who in Marlborough's judgment was pre-eminently fitted for the service, would be allowed by the Emperor to carry his talents so far afield. The Duke wrote fully on these topics to Godolphin, Heinsius, Wratislaw, and Eugène. He realised that, while Great Britain was financially the strongest of the allies, the British Parliament would not be easily induced to vote more money for a war which had just been so woefully mismanaged in every part of it   At the same time, Eugène was enormously popular with all classes of the English people; their confidence in his prowess, especially since the Italian campaign of 1706, was unbounded; and if it became known that the Emperor intended to send him into Spain, they would never allow him to fail for lack of means. To ascertain the private views of the Prince, as well as those of the Duke of Savoy, Marlborough had already dispatched the Brigadier Palmes to Turin, and despite the pressing appeals of Godolphin

[1] Coxe, vol ii , p 156 Marlborough to Lord Sunderland, September 19 1707   [2] Ibid , p 161.
   [3] Ibid p 163 · Marlborough to Godolphin, September 29, 1707

that he himself should return immediately to England, he
now arranged to meet both Wratislaw and the Elector of
Hanover at Mainz or Frankfurt in the latter part of October.
On the 4th, he quitted Helchin for the Hague, where he
arrived on the morning of the 6th. He stayed for a day
and a half, interviewed the Pensionary and Slingelandt,
had two conferences with the deputies of the States, and
was back at Helchin on the 10th, his journey being somewhat delayed by the weather and the roads. The result
of the visit was not encouraging The deputies were
" very desirous " that he should go to Mainz, and that he
should press the Emperor and the Germans to hire 6,000
Saxon cavalry. But " I see very plainly," he reported to
Godolphin, " that the Dutch will not only not augment
their troops, but will act the next year as they have done
this last, which is so disheartening, that I do wish with all
my heart it were possible for me to be excused from being
at the head of their troops."[1]

On the 11th, Marlborough broke up from Helchin, and
moved towards Audenarde. The heavy rains had again
set in, and the Duke had " the spleen to see the poor soldiers
march in dirt up to their knees "[2] On the 14th, the army
arrived at Afflighem near Alost, and there encamped. On
the 15th, the Duke departed for Frankfurt. Anxiety and
fatigue had left their mark upon him. " If I studied my
own health," he said, " I should hardly undertake such a
journey at this time of the year."[3] He chose the circuitous
road by Liende, Grave, and Wesel, because he was advised
that the French had parties out upon the direct route.
He reached Düsseldorf on the 18th. On the 19th, he was
magnificently entertained by the Elector Palatine at Brück.
On the 21st, he came to Frankfurt, where he found the
Electors of Hanover and Mainz

Parliament was to assemble within a fortnight The
Duke, who was pursued by reiterated messages of recall,
had intended to make the briefest possible stay at Frankfurt.
But he was compelled to wait for Wratislaw, who did not

[1] *Ibid*, p 165 Marlborough to Godolphin, October 7, 1707
[2] *Ibid*, p 167· Marlborough to the Duchess, October 10, 1707.
[3] Murray, vol iii, p 619 Marlborough to Peterborough, October 13,
1707

arrive until the 27th. He was very unfavourably impressed
by the condition of affairs in Germany. " Their Electoral
Highnesses," he wrote to the King of Prussia, " display
much zeal—but Your Majesty knows that what is necessary
is a general and unanimous concurrence of the whole
Empire "[1] The King of Prussia had himself refused to
augment his own forces, though Marlborough had suggested
that the departure of the Swedes might enable him to
spare more men. The two Electors undertook to support
a proposal that " the Emperor and the Empire may entertain the 6,000 Saxon horse ", but the Duke was afraid that
trouble would arise over the question of payment. " I
have promised," he informed Godolphin on the 27th, " to
press Count Wratislaw that the court of Vienna may do
their part, which, it is said, ought to be one half of the
expense." He also reported that the Elector of Hanover
refused to continue in the command upon the Rhine, " if
the Empire do not put their army in a better condition."
In the same letter, he suggested that, if he could not prevail
"to have Prince Eugène sent to Catalonia,   . the next best
thing for the service will be that he commands in chief in
the Empire, and that the Elector of Hanover takes upon
him the command I have in Flanders; for if things go as
I think they will, both in England and Holland, nothing
shall prevail with me to lose that reputation I have hazarded
for this war."[2]

When Wratislaw at length arrived, it appeared that he
was armed with very inadequate powers. Everything
having been discussed and nothing decided, Marlborough
departed on the 29th. Wratislaw went with him. They
reached the Hague on November 3. Marlborough had
hoped that, with the assistance of the Austrian minister,
he might rouse the Dutch government from their dangerous
apathy. But he was disappointed. The reports of Louis'
preparations and the rumours that all was not well with
the ministry of Godolphin, had strengthened the hands of
the party clamorous for peace. Moreover, from his conversations with Wratislaw, Marlborough learned that the

[1] Murray, vol iii , p 631 Marlborough to the King of Prussia, October
28 1707
[2] Coxe, vol ii , p 160. Marlborough to Godolphin, October 27, 1707

Court of Vienna were desirous of keeping Eugène in Germany Heinsius promised to impress upon the Austrian minister the importance of sending the Prince to Catalonia. It was definitely settled that reinforcements should be dispatched to Charles from Italy, and that 4,200 men should be shipped at an early date. It was also understood that the Emperor would arrange for the Duke of Savoy to command an army at least 40,000 strong. But everything else was left undetermined The Dutch contended that they were completely crippled by lack of funds The Duke, however, still hoped that, if the British Parliament could be persuaded to set them a good example, they might change their tone. " I long to have one hour in which I may speak freely to you,"[1] he wrote to Harley on November 8.

Contrary winds detained him in Holland until the 16th On the 18th, he reached London. Cadogan, who had been chosen to succeed Stepney, remained behind at Brussels.

Parliament, the first Parliament of Great Britain, had already assembled The speech from the throne referred " with entire satisfaction " to the union of the two countries, passed lightly over the misfortunes of the recent summer, and emphasised the importance of prosecuting " this just and necessary war "[2] with undiminished vigour The Commons, in reply, informed the Queen of their determination " to exert the united strength of this island in such a manner as shall make it a terror to your enemies."[3] Before the end of December they proved their sincerity by voting a sum of nearly £6,000,000 for the various services by sea and land.

The Junta did not intervene to discourage the zeal of the Lower House. Enemies of France, so inveterate and so implacable, could not in decency obstruct supply. But they could criticise the use which ministers made of it. They were firmly resolved to inflict upon the government some humiliating proofs of their displeasure Before the opening of Parliament, Godolphin, who had yet to learn that the successful blackmailer never relents, endeavoured

[1] MSS of the Marquis of Bath Duke of Marlborough to R Harley, November 8, 1707 (Hist. MSS Comm , vol 1 , p 187)
[2] Boyer, vol. vi , p 246   [3] *Ibid* , p. 250

to appease the wrath of the tormentors. At a private
gathering of the most prominent Whig members of the House
of Commons, the Dukes of Devonshire and Somerset
announced that, although the Queen could not go back
upon her promise to Blackhall and Dawes, "yet, for the
future, she was resolved to give them full content."[1] The
Junta accepted the pledge for what it might be worth.
They had little confidence in Godolphin, they had less in
Marlborough and the Queen. An attack upon the management of the navy would convince both the Sovereign and
the general of the necessity of submission, for the Sovereign's
consort was Lord High Admiral, and his chief adviser was
the general's brother. It would, moreover, be popular
with the merchants and the manufacturers, who were for
the most part adherents to the Whigs. But there was
another, and perhaps stronger, reason why the Junta should
show their teeth. Godolphin's remonstrance had not been
wasted upon Harley. The Secretary of State was now
upon his guard. He did not intend to desert his mistress
without a struggle In conjunction with St. John and
Harcourt, he privately approached the Tory leaders in
the Commons, "to engage them in the Queen's interest,
assuring them that her heart was with them, that she was
weary of the tyranny of the Whigs, and longed to be delivered from it."[2] The Tories received his advances without
enthusiasm The Junta, getting wind of the intrigue,
grew more and more suspicious. They knew that the Queen
detested them; they conjectured that she possessed the
secret sympathy of Marlborough; and they were afraid
that even Godolphin was human and did not enjoy being
blackmailed They therefore hardened their hearts. And
they were right Harley was a dangerous foe. His influence over Anne became stronger every day. For years
she had written him letters, signed, "Your very affectionate
friend." She summoned him now to clandestine and
nocturnal interviews, which were arranged by Mrs Masham.
Furthermore, the breach between Abigail and Sarah was at
last complete. A few days after the conversation, in which
Godolphin spoke "plainly" to Harley, the ladies met in

[1] Burnet, vol. iv , p 171.   [2] Ibid.

the Queen's drawing-room. "As for her looks," wrote Abigail to Harley, "indeed, they are not to be described by any mortal but her own self."[1] Subsequent correspondence[2] and a very unpleasant interview merely aggravated the quarrel. And when Sarah complained to the Queen, it appeared that Mrs. Morley's sympathies were not with Mrs Freeman.

The Junta opened their attack on November 23, when the Queen's speech was to be discussed in the House of Lords, and the customary address of thanks to be moved. Marlborough was present. Wharton delivered a prepared oration, in which he particularly lamented "the great decay of trade and scarcity of money."[3] Somers followed, and threw the blame upon "the ill-condition and late mismanagements of the navy."[4] When the Earl of Stamford brought forward the address of thanks, Buckingham and Rochester objected, and demanded that the state of the nation should first be considered. This combination of the Junta and "the Tackers" was irresistible. It was therefore agreed that the state of the nation should be considered on the 30th. On that date, Marlborough was again in his place, and the Queen herself was a spectator Wharton presented a petition from the Sheriffs and 200 merchants of the City of London, complaining of the deficiency of convoys and cruisers. He began the debate with a speech, "laying open the miserable condition of the nation and the great decay of trade."[5] He was supported, as before, by both Whigs and Tories; but it was observed that, while the Junta directed their blows against the Admiralty alone, the Tory orators arraigned the ministry as a whole. Those who expected that on such an occasion Lord Haversham would distinguish himself were not disappointed Ironically apologising to their lordships for the use of the word "England" instead of "Britain," (" I have not yet forgot that beloved name," he said,) he declared the condition of

[1] Portland MSS · Abigail Masham to R Harley, September 29, 1707 (Hist MSS Comm , 15th Report, Appendix, part iv , p 454)
[2] Mrs Masham's letter dated September 24, and published in *The Conduct*, etc , is alleged by the Duchess to have been inspired, if not dictated, by Harley But Mrs Masham's letter to Harley, dated the 29th, and published in the Portland MSS , shows that he was not consulted
[3] Boyer, vol. vi , p. 252   [4] *Ibid.*   [5] *Ibid* , p 253.

the country to be " very low and desperate " " Your
trade," he argued, " is the mother and nurse of your seamen, your seamen are the life of your fleet, and your fleet
is the security and protection of your trade." It was
incredible, he protested, that interests so vital " should be
postponed to any foreign consideration whatsoever." He
then dilated upon the losses at sea " Your merchants
are beggared," he exclaimed, " your commerce is broke,
your trade is gone, your staple and manufacture ruined."
He alleged that in the past the sufferers had kept silence,
but that " the temper of the nation " had been changed
" in the space of one year's time," and that " now it is
hard to stop their mouths or keep them within any bounds "
Touching upon the question of responsibility, " I think it
very indifferent," he remarked, " which way you proceed . . .
but I must take leave to say that, begin where you will,
it you do not end with the ministry, we shall be in a worse
condition . . . than we were before." " As to the Admiralty,"
he said, " if the Prince's council have committed any fault,
it is very fit they should have what they deserve." But
he strongly deprecated the removal of the Prince himself,
because the Prince " owes not his commission to the favour
of any great minister whatsoever." In conclusion, he
insisted that the government, and the government alone,
must be held responsible, because the Queen was a Sovereign
of such " consummate wisdom as not to do anything without the advice of her ministry."[1]

Haversham's eloquence inflamed the House   Neither the
tone nor the direction of the debate was entirely agreeable
to the Junta, who presently deemed it advisable to call
a halt.   It was therefore proposed by Halifax that a committee be appointed to receive suggestions for the encouragement of trade and privateering to the West Indies.
Godolphin eagerly seconded the motion, which was carried.
It was also resolved to hear the evidence of the petitioners
in a fortnight's time.

Marlborough took no part in this discussion   He regarded
his brother, George, as " a very indiscreet Tory "; but he

[1] Boyer, vol vi , p. 253. see Lord Haversham's speech, November 19,
1707.

knew that, so far as the Junta was concerned, the attack
upon the Admiralty was a dishonest manœuvre, intended
as a personal affront to himself and to the Queen When
the House rose, he went up to Wharton, and expressed his
resentment in unmistakable fashion. As for the Queen,
she " seemed," says Burnet, " to be highly offended "[1]

Similar proceedings occurred in the Commons. Merchants, admitted to the House to substantiate their allegations, boldly charged the Admiralty with " fraud, malice,
and ignorance."[2] But here Churchill defended himself and
his colleagues with vigour and ability, he argued that the
petitioners had proved their losses, but had proved nothing
else, and he succeeded in inducing the House to suspend
its judgment until the official defence, which was in course
of preparation, should be in the hands of members.

This agitation, unscrupulously manipulated though it
was by the Junta, arose out of facts which admitted of no
denial Writing in December to the Pensionary, Marlborough laid emphasis on " the great scarcity of money
in the country and the decay of trade in our sea-ports."[3]
But Wharton, when he enlarged on these topics in the House
of Lords, must have been well aware that such consequences
flowed naturally from a war, which had already endured
for nearly six years, which was largely financed by England,
which injuriously affected or entirely closed the best markets
of the continent, and which opened every ocean in the
world to the commerce-destroyers of the enemy. It was
true that in 1706 and 1707 the losses at sea, both in their
number and their magnitude, exceeded all precedent But
the reasons were obvious After the hard-fought battle of
Malaga in 1704, the French had entirely altered their
maritime strategy Although their navy was neither
destroyed nor incapacitated, they never again attempted
to encounter the fleets of England and Holland upon equal
terms But they infested every sea with swift-sailing
squadrons and with single ships, besides privateers innumerable. These lay in wait upon the trade-routes,

[1] Burnet, vol iv , p 176   [2] Boyer, vol vi , p 263.
[3] Murray, vol iii , p 650 Marlborough to the Pensioner, December 5,
1707.

pounced upon defenceless merchantmen, fought victoriously
with convoys, cruised audaciously off English harbours,
kidnapped English peasants in their beds,[1] and generally
eluded all capture and pursuit   Whether this strategy was
right or wrong, it certainly achieved results. It owed its
success in great part to the character of the men to whom
it was entrusted. The French, at this moment, possessed,
says Clowes, " more brilliant cruiser-captains than at any
other period in their history, De Guay Trouin, the Chevalier
de St. Pol, Cöetlogon, Forbin, d'Iberville, and Cassard—
and seldom has any country disposed at one time of a more
gallant band of adventurous seamen."[2] In 1706 Forbin
fitted out a squadron at Dunkirk, and cruising sometimes
alone, and sometimes with De Guay Trouin, captured part
of an English convoy off Ostend and played havoc with the
Dutch merchantmen. In May, 1707, he captured the
convoy, Grafton, and twenty merchantmen in the Channel.
In July, he captured fifteen merchantmen bound for Russia.
In October, in company with De Guay Trouin, he engaged
a convoy of five men-of-war off the Lizard   Many of the
merchantmen, which were bound for Lisbon, escaped; but
one of the convoy was burned, and three captured. These
were some of the more notable among a multitude of exploits,
which had reduced the traders and manufacturers of England
to despair.

Possessed as they were of excellent naval bases upon
both sides of the Straits of Dover and the Straits of Gibraltar,
as well as in the New World, the French enjoyed peculiar
advantages for warfare of this kind. The maritime powers,
on the other hand, had no longer access to the ports of
Spain in Europe and America, which had been open to them
in the preceding war   Yet the French could hardly have
succeeded as they did, if the British Admiralty, after the
battle of Malaga, had changed its strategy in imitation of
the enemy. Beset upon all sides by the clamours of the
merchants and the unemployed, and by what Haversham
called " the tears of the fatherless and cries of the widows,"
they must have been sorely tempted to dissolve their great

[1] Portland MSS . Richard Duke to Harley, September, 1704 (15th Report,
Appendix, part iv , pp 122, 123)   The case of Ura Arnop, of Crookhaven,
in the Kingdom of Ireland   [2] Clowes, *Royal Navy*, vol ii , p 507

fleets into handy squadrons and swarms of cruisers, which would have speedily hunted down the more obnoxious of the enemy's commerce-destroyers. Yet they did nothing of the kind. They adhered to the strategy of "supporting," in the words of their own defence, "a superiority at sea upon the coasts of Portugal, Spain, and Italy "[1] That was the strategy of the Cabinet, or, in other words, of Marlborough It aimed at the total destruction of half the naval resources of France by the capture of Toulon. And it aimed at an early decision of the whole contest by the assistance and encouragement which it gave to the military operations on Spanish and Italian soil. Already it had borne good fruit in the acquisition of Barcelona, Gibraltar, and the island of Majorca. It had succoured the allies on the morrow of Almanza; it had inflicted enormous damage on the fleet and arsenal of Toulon; and it had transformed the Mediterranean into a highway for the transit of the Imperialist forces from Italy to Spain. More than anything else, it had contributed to detach both Portugal and Savoy from the French connection, and to keep them faithful to the Grand Alliance. It maintained the credit of the coalised powers in the money-markets of Italy Its moral effect upon Catalans, Camisards, and all other friends and soldiers of the coalition in Southern Europe was incalculable. That he should have foreseen the value of such strategy, and that he should have steadily pursued it in face of the heavy sacrifices, which it entailed elsewhere, and of the public outcry, which those sacrifices of necessity produced, is perhaps the strongest of Marlborough's many titles to the admiration of posterity It is certainly the least known. Haversham, who talked so often and so much that he could not fail to hit the mark at times, if only by accident, did the Duke no more than justice when he insisted that the entire responsibility for the use made of the naval forces of the Crown must rest upon the Cabinet. It did rest upon the Cabinet Neither George Churchill nor George of Denmark could lay claim to so much honour But the Cabinet, in this connection, meant Marlborough, and Marlborough alone.

[1] Boyer, vol vi., Appendix, p. 119

The attack upon the Admiralty was " feebly managed "[1] in the House of Commons, where everybody knew that it was resented by the Queen, and where the Tories suspected that it was engineered in the interest of Orford, whom the Junta would have thrust into the place of Churchill. It ended, at any rate, in nothing worse than a motion for the employment of more cruisers. But the Lords appointed a committee, who examined the evidence of the merchants, compared it with the official defence, and reported in terms adverse to the Admiralty. The Admiralty had in fact admitted nothing On the contrary, they had accused the merchants of negligence and stupidity, and had outraged one of the most sacred principles of Whiggery by reflecting upon the naval administration of William's reign. The Lords addressed the Queen upon the whole matter in a style that was intended to be extremely offensive to Marlborough's brother. " Some persons," they said, " employed by the Lord High Admiral, had made the worst use imaginable of the trust he honours them with."[2] Anne's reply was curt and enigmatic. It merely informed the House that she had always understood the importance of the navy and of trade, and that they could rely on her to encourage both.

Upon the evidence, and at this distance of time, he would be a daring and expert judge who could determine to what extent, if any, the criticisms levelled at the Admiralty were justified Godolphin apparently believed that they were not without foundation. " The Admiralty," he said, in a private letter to Harley, in July, 1706, " are not so lively and vigilant as they ought to be, I see it every day upon twenty occasions."[3] But the Admiralty were in contact with a problem, which had taxed the ingenuity of more brilliant seamen than any who existed in that age, the problem of apportioning cruisers between the battle-fleet which ensures control of communications, and the communications themselves where that control is exercised. But in any event, the following observations by Mr. Julian Corbett deserve to be remembered. " No degree of naval superi-

[1] Burnet, vol iv , p 172   [2] Boyer, vol vi , Appendix, p 141
[3] MSS of the Marquis of Bath Lord Godolphin to Harley, July 20, 1706 (Hist. MSS Comm., vol. i., p 83),

ority," he says, " can ensure our communications against
sporadic attack from detached cruisers, or even raiding
squadrons, if they be boldly led and are prepared to risk
destruction . . . By no conceivable means is it possible
to give trade absolute protection. . . . We cannot make
war without losing ships. . . . In 1870 the second naval
power in the world was at war with an enemy that could
not be considered a naval power at all, and yet she lost
ships by capture. Never in the days of our most complete
domination upon the seas was our trade invulnerable, and
it never can be "[1]

The combination between the Junta and " the Tackers "
was essentially an immoral one   No real community of
aim existed. The object of the Junta was to squeeze
places for themselves and their friends out of a Prime
Minister, whose general policy they cordially approved.
The object of " the Tackers " was to overthrow the government. When Parliament turned its attention from naval
to military affairs, the essential discord between these strange
bedfellows appeared at once. To that misguided strategist,
Rochester, the Spanish muddle was a perfect godsend.
Although, after Almanza, the summer heats and the stubborn
energy of Galway had saved Catalonia for Charles, operations had been resumed in the autumn, and both Lerida
and Ciudad Rodrigo had fallen to the Bourbon arms. The
British public were intensely disgusted. They were also
suspicious. Peterborough, whom they regarded as a hero,
was supposed to have prophesied the disaster of Almanza;
yet Peterborough was now in disgrace. The government
required him to explain why he had failed to carry his
army to Madrid in 1706, why he had not advanced to
Charles the moneys placed at his disposal, and why he had
withdrawn to Genoa and raised a loan upon unfavourable
terms without any authority from London   The Earl
pretended that he was very ill-used. His physician,
Freind, published an overdone panegyric on his exploits.
His admirers declared that the ministry persecuted him
because they were afraid of him. And now Rochester took
up his case. Though Peterborough's Whiggery had always

---

[1] Julian Corbett, *Some Principles of Maritime Strategy*, pp 102 and 284.

been notoriously violent, the leader of the extreme Tories became his champion in Parliament. It was a clever move, for it suggested that Rochester was animated by higher motives than those of party. And so, in a sense, he was. He sincerely believed that Marlborough's strategy had been wrong from the beginning, and he wanted a peg on which to hang that text. On December 30, the House of Lords being in committee, and the Queen and the Duke being both present, he recited the services which Peterborough had rendered, and expressed surprise that they had not been recognised by a vote of thanks. He was followed by Halifax. The Junta were willing enough to worry Godolphin; but they suspected a trap. Halifax, therefore, while he extolled the achievements of Peterborough, contended that the vote of thanks should be postponed, " till the whole tenor of his conduct had been examined."[1] In the course of the discussion, Haversham observed that it was " no wonder our affairs in Spain went so ill, since the management of them had been entrusted to a foreigner."[2] Several of the speakers insisted that the war must be prosecuted till the whole of the Spanish monarchy was recovered for Charles. Peterborough himself declared that " they ought to give the Queen nineteen shillings in the pound rather than make peace upon any other terms," and added that, " if it were thought necessary, he was ready to return to Spain and serve even under the Earl of Galway."[3] The debate turned naturally to the practical question of the measures to be adopted It was the moment for which Rochester was waiting.

" The principal business," he declared, was neglected in favour of " accessories." To explain his meaning, he cited an alleged dictum of the old Duke of Schomberg, whom he now thought proper to describe as " a great general," which was hardly the orthodox, Tory view of William's foreign mercenaries. This " great general," he told the House, had laid it down that to attack France in the Netherlands was " like taking a bull by the horns." He therefore proposed that, in the next campaign, the army of Flanders should remain on the defensive, and should

---

[1] Boyer, vol. vi , p. 296.   [2] *Ibid.*, p. 297.   [3] *Ibid.*

detach 15,000 or 20,000 men to Catalonia. He was seconded
by Nottingham, who complained that Spain was " in a
manner abandoned "[1]

Thus plausibly presented, the argument wore so dangerous
an aspect that Marlborough was constrained to intervene.
" With some warmth," he told the Peers plainly that the
forces in Flanders, instead of being diminished, required to
be increased. He gave two reasons. The first was that
the conquest of the great towns of Brabant had injuriously
affected the relative strength of the armies in the field,
because the French could garrison most of their fortresses
" with one battalion in each," while places like Brussels,
Louvain, and Ghent, the defences of which were obsolete,
" required twenty times that number of men for their
preservation " The second was that, if Rochester's suggestion were adopted, and the French obtained, as they
not improbably might, some " considerable advantage " in
Flanders, " the discontented party in Holland, who were
not a few, and bore with impatience the necessary charges
of the war, would not fail crying aloud for peace."[2]

As these arguments admitted of no effective rejoinder,
Rochester fell back upon personalities. He wondered, he
said, that " that noble peer, who had been ever conspicuous
for his calmness and moderation, should now be out of his
temper "[3] Marlborough's serenity is still proverbial, but
fully to appreciate the spectators' enjoyment of this passage
of arms, it should be remembered that Rochester was a
particularly passionate man, and that, however good his
case, and however ably he might be arguing it, he could
usually be driven into furious incoherence by the scientific
goading of the Whig tacticians.[4] His taunt, however, had
a deeper significance. It was intended to suggest that the
interests of sound strategy had been subordinated to the
private interests of the general. He went on to observe that
" there being an absolute necessity to succour Spain, His
Grace would oblige their lordships if he would let them
know where they might get troops to send thither," particularly as Lord Peterborough had just informed the

[1] Ibid   [2] Ibid   [3] Ibid
[4] Memoirs of John Mucky· *Characters of the Court of Great Britain:*
Lawrence. Earl of Rochester, p 30.

House, on the authority of Prince Eugène, that "the German soldiers had rather be decimated than sent into Spain "[1]

Marlborough had entirely recovered his self-control. He might have explained that the opinion attributed to Schomberg had always been his own, and that nobody had laboured more indefatigably than he to persuade the Grand Alliance that the true line of invasion was not through Belgium But he chose to ignore the attack upon himself. Remarking merely that "the thing was of too great importance to be spoken of without concernment," he told the House that, although the public interest forbade the disclosure of "secret projects," he was free to state that arrangements had been made with the Emperor for the maintenance of an army of 40,000 men in Savoy, and for the rapid transport of reinforcements from Italy to Catalonia. He expressed the hope that Eugène would be sent to Barcelona, "in which case the Germans would gladly follow him thither." He admitted that "the usual slowness of the court of Vienna," which had ruined the expedition to Toulon, did not inspire confidence, but he pledged his word that "for the future his Imperial Majesty would punctually perform his promises "[2] This reply gave general satisfaction, and Rochester's proposal collapsed.

But the debate did not terminate here. Those expert fishers in troubled waters, the Junta, put up Lord Somers to move that no peace could be "safe or honourable, . . if Spain and the Spanish West Indies be suffered to continue in the power of the House of Bourbon."[3] Nobody objected. Then Wharton proposed that, in view of the information contained in Marlborough's speech, the Queen be presented with an address of thanks for the care which she had taken for the conduct of the war in Spain. And finally, Halifax suggested that she be desired "to make the most pressing instances to the Emperor,"[4] to dispatch a prompt and powerful reinforcement to Catalonia under the command of Eugène, to fulfil his promise in regard to Savoy, and to use his best endeavours to strengthen the army on the Rhine. All three resolutions were adopted, and a

[1] Boyer, vol. vi , p. 208.   [2] Ibid   [3] Ibid , p 299.   [4] Ibid., p. 300.

committee was appointed to draw up the address. It was a
committee of Whigs, but the Junta were graciously pleased
to permit the Captain-General and the Lord Treasurer to
serve on it. As a congenial colleague for ministers, who
were supposed to be persecuting him, Peterborough was
added to the company. And to crown the joke, Rochester
was included.

Coxe drew attention to the remarkable fact that when
these important resolutions were moved and carried by
irresponsible politicians, the head of the government was
absent from the House   But there is no reason to suppose
that, if he had been present, a different course would have
been taken. It is true that, if a foreign observer, ignorant
of English affairs, had witnessed the debate, he might easily
have inferred that the rulers of England were the Whig
Junta. And so in fact they were. They were now exhibiting their authority for the express purpose of humiliating Godolphin, who was not bound to assist at the spectacle.
Both he and Marlborough readily concurred in the address.
When the terms of it came to be considered, Somers proposed to alter the words, " Spain and the West Indies " to
" Spain, the West Indies, or any part of the Spanish
monarchy."[1] This modification, which afterwards became
famous, seems at the time to have attracted less attention
than it deserved. It meant that no treaty of partition
must ever be considered   It meant that no compensation,
however small or insignificant, must ever be conceded to
Philip. It meant, in short, that even if " the exorbitant
power of France " were reduced to the proper level, or
below the proper level, the war must still go on so long as
a single acre of the Spanish Empire denied the sovereignty
of Charles. Yet nobody objected   The House of Lords
adopted the address, the House of Commons agreed with
the House of Lords; and the Queen in her reply declared
herself to be fully of the opinion " that no peace can be
honourable or safe for us or for our allies till the entire
monarchy of Spain be restored to the House of Austria."[2]

" This new language of ' no peace without Spain ' "[3] was

---

[1] *Ibid*, p. 302   [2] *Ibid*, p 303.
[3] Swift, *Conduct of the Allies*, pp 67 and 69

afterwards denounced by Swift as "contrary to common prudence and justice," and as "unfair," "dishonourable," and "imperious" Certainly the terms of the Grand Alliance did not commit the signatories to any such condition. The ruling motive of Somers and the Junta was then, as ever, implacable hatred of the Catholic and autocratic monarchy of France. But the motive of Marlborough and Godolphin was entirely different. They did not conceive themselves to be engaged in a vendetta or a crusade. They were fighting for the restoration of the balance of power, and any terms of peace which would secure that end they were prepared to accept. They had no desire to fetter their own freedom of action beforehand In subscribing, therefore, to the resolution of Somers, they acted, in appearance, at any rate, without due regard to sincerity or logic. But they were not, at this moment, thinking about terms of peace at all They were thinking rather of the efficient conduct of the war. This resolution would have a good effect upon the allies. It would convince the Dutch that England would never permit them to retire from the contest merely because a potential barrier had been acquired for Holland. It would convince the Emperor of his mistake in supposing that England, if only she could compass the capture of Toulon, would be satisfied to withdraw from the Grand Alliance. Coxe regarded it as an open question whether the original motion of Somers was made with the approval of Marlborough and Godolphin. He seems to have overlooked a letter, written on August 5 by Godolphin to Marlborough, in which the following passage occurs "If the Emperor has any doubt whether England would make use of the success we hope for at Toulon not to continue the war, his Imperial Majesty has but to make it his request to all the allies *not to make peace till the monarchy of Spain be restored to the House of Austria,* and he will soon see if England will not be ready to join with him in procuring such a declaration from them. And perhaps this would not give a very improper rise for what will be necessary to be said to the States." Coxe seems also to have overlooked the fact that "no peace without Spain" was one of the preliminaries agreed upon by Marl-

borough and the Dutch deputies in the critical autumn of
1706, when Louis was endeavouring to bribe Holland with
the offer of the Spanish Netherlands. The idea of stimulating and reassuring the allies by a formal asseveration of
this principle was therefore in the minds of Marlborough
and Godolphin many months before Somers moved his
resolution. Swift alleges that " when the vote passed in
the House of Lords against any peace without Spain being
restored to the Austrian family, the Earl of Wharton told
the House that it was indeed impossible and impracticable
to recover Spain; but, however, there were certain reasons
why such a vote should be made at that time."[1] If Swift's
testimony is true, it supports the view that Godolphin and
Marlborough did not endorse the resolution so much for
its own sake as for the sake of the beneficial results it might
produce at Vienna and the Hague.

These proceedings quite overshadowed the private
grievances of Peterborough. Parliament was not really
interested in Peterborough, except in so far as his complaints affected the credit and position of the ministry.
Nevertheless, the Lords spent several days in listening to
his arguments and to the voluminous, documentary evidence with which he bored them. In the end, although the
view prevailed that he had exonerated himself, no vote
of thanks was granted him.

The notion that the ministry were afraid of Peterborough
was true only in the very restricted sense that they knew
him to be capable of making himself a perennial nuisance,
and that they knew " the Tackers " and the Junta to be
capable of exploiting him to any extent. But in the sense
that he could, if he chose, convict them of responsibility,
other than technical, for the disaster of Almanza, they were
not afraid of him at all. The political importance of
occupying Madrid, and the great success which had attended
the Spanish campaign in 1706, justified Galway and Stanhope in insisting, in January, 1707, that the army should
again take the offensive. This opinion was backed by
Marlborough and the Cabinet. In opposing it, Peterborough had been animated, in part at any rate, by a

---

[1] Swift, *Conduct of the Allies*, p 63.

motive which was altogether inadmissible, he had wanted
to transfer troops from Spain to Savoy, that he might
conduct an expedition of his own against Toulon. In
supporting it, Marlborough and the Cabinet had of course
assumed that the army would not be divided, and that it
would not be committed to an action against odds so heavy
as those which it encountered at Almanza. It was not
their fault if these assumptions were incorrect. Telegraphy
not being then invented it was impossible to control operations in Valencia from London or Leipzig. When Marlborough learned of the departure of Charles and Noyelles
for Barcelona he expressed his misgivings to Wratislaw.[1]

Yet he did not boast, as Peterborough boasted, that he
had prophesied the defeat of Almanza. Even as it was,
that battle was so evenly contested that, if the forces in
Catalonia, or only a part of them, had been present, as
they ought to have been present, the strategy of England
would have been fully vindicated. If, on the other hand,
the strategy of Peterborough had been adopted, those who
now threw out suggestions of incompetence, would have
been the first to insinuate that ministers were prolonging
the war for their own private ends.

The Junta considered that enough, and perhaps more
than enough, had now been done. Godolphin and Marlborough were evidently impressed. On January 18, when
the appointments of Blackhall and Dawes were publicly
announced, the bishopric of Norwich was conferred upon the
Whig, Trimmel, who had been Sunderland's tutor, and the
Regius Professorship of Divinity at Oxford upon the Whig,
Potter, who had long been recommended by Marlborough

Yet the Junta were far from happy. There was a lion
in the path. Ever since the meeting of Parliament, Harley
had been endeavouring to convince Godolphin by argument,
and incidentally, to coerce him by intrigues, which were
calculated to damage the ministerial majorities. But
Godolphin only grew restive under this treatment. Thus,
for example, on December 5, he complained to Harley that
at a by-election " all the Court Tories were for a ' Tacker,' "
and denounced the " very weak and foolish behaviour of

---

[1] Murray, vol. iii., p 240   Marlborough to Wratislaw, May 1 1707.

those who are in office, to say no more."[1] Harley sent him a note, requesting an interview in the presence of Marlborough. The Prime Minister consented; but the tone of his reply shows that relations were beginning to be strained.[2]

To procure the removal of a Secretary of State, who was also the personal friend of the Queen and of the Queen's new favourite, would be difficult in the extreme. Marlborough, at any rate, hated the business of bullying his Sovereign. And both Marlborough and Godolphin knew that, if Harley went, St. John and Harcourt would go with him It was true that Harley's talents had ceased to be indispensable, now that Harley's system of managing the Commons had been virtually abandoned. But Harcourt was an able Attorney-General, whose services the government did not desire to lose, and St. John was recognised as a man of exceptional promise. For St. John, moreover, the Duke had a particular affection. The expulsion of Harley and his associates from the ministry would involve a painful severance of ties both political and private. It would involve also the complete subjection of Marlborough and Godolphin, and ultimately of the Crown itself, to the Whig Junta.

Why, it may be asked, did Harley not resign ? The answer given by the Whigs was the answer to be expected from a party which was led by office-hunters. Harley, they said, was scheming to supplant Godolphin. But was he ? Harley was certainly advising the Queen that Godolphin's system, which she so detested, was not the sole alternative. But because he believed that by courage and address Godolphin and Marlborough could carry on without paying perpetual blackmail to the Junta, it does not follow that he also believed that he himself could form an administration in existing circumstances Still less does it follow that he desired to try the experiment But as long as he saw any prospect of converting his political chief, he had a reasonable ground for continuing in the ministry. And he was also under the influence of another

[1] Portland MSS. Godolphin to R Harley, December 5, 1707 (Hist. MSS. Comm , 15th Report, Appendix part iv , p 464)
[2] Somerville, *History of the Reign of Queen Anne*, Appendix, No xix.; Godolphin to Harley, December 5, 1707; Hardwicke Papers.

and a stronger motive. The lonely Queen clung to him as to her only friend. His natural kindliness of heart forbade him to desert her. In modern times a minister, situated as Harley then was, would almost certainly resign. But the analogy with modern times does not hold good, because in Harley's day the Sovereign still enjoyed real power, while the authority of the Prime Minister over his colleagues was less absolute than it afterwards became. For the rest, the temptation to escape must have been very strong. For Harley was an easy-going, indolent man, and not a particularly ambitious one.

Accident, or what is generally regarded as accident, provided the Junta with a powerful weapon when they most needed it. The recent abnormal successes of the French commerce-destroyers had given birth to the theory that some specially well-informed traitor was selling secrets to the French government. Godolphin himself was unable to explain the loss of the Russian fleet upon any other hypothesis.[1] The private correspondence between the French prisoners in England and their friends in France underwent an official scrutiny in Harley's department. Towards the end of 1707 it began to be suspected that somebody there was taking advantage of this regulation to insert intelligence which was subsequently transmitted by the receiver to the government at Versailles. On Harley's instructions the mail-bags were detained and their contents examined. Enclosed in communications from Tallard to his steward, and intended to be forwarded to Chamillart, were notes of the proceedings in the British Parliament and a copy of the letter which the Queen had sent to the Emperor in reference to the appointment of Eugène to the command in Catalonia. The handwriting was recognised as that of William Greg, a junior clerk in the department

Greg, " a man of parts, born in Montrose, and brought up in the University of Aberdeen," had been attached for nearly six years to the embassy at Copenhagen. He owed his appointment there to a relative, who was British representative at the Danish court in King William's time.

---

[1] MSS of the Marquis of Bath · Godolphin to R Harley, August 7, 1707 (Hist MSS Comm vol 1 , p 177)

After the death of this relative, he was retained by the new envoy till the end of 1704, when the irregularity of his private life led to his dismissal. Returning to England, he applied to Harley for a post [1] Harley, being satisfied that he was a person of some ability and experience of affairs, used him in the summer of 1705 as a secret agent in his own country of Scotland. Recalled to London in October, Greg petitioned to be sent abroad His reason was that, owing to his vicious mode of life, he had incurred debts which the slender salary attached to departmental appointments would not enable him to liquidate. Harley treated him with considerable generosity, and promised to remember his application for foreign employment. Meanwhile, a place was found for him in the office at Whitehall. As time went on, and his creditors grew pressing, Greg became desperate. On April 15, 1707, he was imploring Harley to advance him £10, lest he should " be affronted "[2] before he reached the office on the next morning. In October he was being dunned for another account of £14, on which occasion Harley advanced him half that sum. In the same month he encountered a tremendous temptation. " He had been long acquainted with one Crookshanks," whose father-in-law was a merchant named Brown. Crookshanks offered him two hundred guineas, which Brown was to pay, " if he would procure a French pass "[3] for a vessel, the *Mary of London*, trading to the West Indies Greg had great opportunities. Ever since he entered the office, the duty of perusing the correspondence of the French prisoners had been largely delegated to him, because he possessed a good knowledge of the language. He told his colleagues that he found the business " very entertaining "[4] He also

---

[1] " Up to comparatively recent times, there were fewer departments in the Civil Service than now, they were smaller, and they were self-contained. The Secretary of State, or other Minister at the head of an office, was the final authority to which his subordinates ever thought of looking, he was hardly at all checked by rules of service in making appointments and promotions, and he had not much need to regard either a controlling Treasury or a recording Auditor-General" (2nd Report of the Royal Commission, appointed to enquire into the Civil Establishments of the different offices of State at home and abroad, p xii, 1888)

[2] Portland MSS · W Greg to R Harley, April 15, 1707 (Hist MSS. Comm., 15th Report, Appendix, part iv , p 401)

[3] *Journals of the House of Lords*, vol xviii , March 18, 1708

[4] Portland MSS.: Memorandum on French Prisoners' Letters, 1707-8, January 18, p 475

had access to state papers of supreme importance. He now conceived, and began to execute, the idea of enclosing in letters from Tallard information of interest to the French government, in the hope of obtaining in return the pass which was to rid him of his financial embarrassments. But on January 11, Harley confronted him with the intercepted documents, and extorted a full confession on the spot. Greg was arrested, examined in the presence of Marlborough, Godolphin, Harley, Sunderland, and other ministers, and committed to Newgate. Valentine and Barra, two spies whom Harley had employed to collect intelligence in the northern seaports of France, were also arrested at this time. " Having a white kerchief at his eyes, in a weeping posture," he pleaded guilty, and received the customary sentence. He was a pitiable wretch. Such information as he had betrayed to the enemy was of very trifling value, and he had never received one penny of money, either French or English, in payment for his crime.

This dismal affair created no little stir. The Junta regarded it as happily adapted to their immediate needs. Though Greg, in his examination and confession, incriminated nobody but himself, and though Valentine and Barra steadily denied that they had been playing a double game, the Whigs gave out that the Secretary of State was in correspondence with Versailles, and that creatures such as these were the agents of his treachery. The lords of the Junta must have been well aware that the suggestion was ridiculous. " Some of them, I should think," said the mordant Swift, " knew better what belonged to such a correspondence, and how it ought to be managed "[1] But the nation at large, exasperated by its expensive failure at Toulon, and hard hit by its extraordinary losses at sea, was only too ready to absorb the idea that somebody in high place had been betraying its secrets to the enemy. It is alleged by Swift, and also by Harley's brother, Edward, that a person, employed by the Junta, gave Greg a warning to escape before he was arrested. Of course, in the absence of the real criminal, no limits could have been set to the

---

[1] Swift, *Some Remarks upon a Pamphlet entitled "A Letter to the Seven Lords of the Committee appointed to examine Gregg."*

possibilities of malicious insinuation against his master.
Even as it was, Greg's plea of guilty was represented as a
highly suspicious circumstance. For it did away with the
necessity of summoning witnesses, from whom evidence,
tending to inculpate Harley, might presumably have been
extracted at the trial. The Junta knew that Marlborough
and Godolphin, however much they might despise the
slander on their colleague and the men who circulated it,
could not afford to disregard it Harley was already a
nuisance to the Cabinet, if a sufficient number of fools
could be persuaded to believe that he was Greg's accomplice,
he would become a menace to its existence. The general
election was approaching. The ministry, which harboured
such a man, would get short shrift from the constituencies.
Rendered desperate by their realisation of that fact, Marlborough and Godolphin would be forced to engage in that
supreme contest with the Queen from which they shrank.

Harley saw his peril. He saw that he was destined for
the sacrifice. But he did not intend to go down without
a struggle. He had now an additional motive for continuing in office. Resignation now would be imputed to the
terror of conscious guilt He therefore resolved to stand
his ground Unfortunately, he could not strike at his
enemies except through those who had been his friends.
He could not reach the Junta except through the bodies of
the ministers on whom the Junta fattened. A blow at
Godolphin and Marlborough would lay him open to the
charge of disloyalty. But a blow at Godolphin and Marlborough was the only resource left him. And doubtless
he regarded himself as morally absolved from allegiance
to colleagues, who chose the counsel and support of his
mortal enemies in preference to his own. To this tragical
ending had the famous " Triumvirate " come

It is possible that Harley made his first move on
January 31, when the government endeavoured to procure
the assent of the Commons to a measure for raising 16,000
recruits by a compulsory levy upon parishes and counties.
The proposal was lost by eight votes, much to Marlborough's
vexation. It could hardly have been popular in the constituencies at the approaching general election; but the

closeness of the division suggests that Harley might have
saved it, had he wished.

The game of misleading the ignorant and the uninformed
is a game at which two can play. In challenging Harley
to a contest of that character, the Junta displayed more
malice than discretion. For Harley knew more about
public opinion and the forces which controlled it than any
man in the kingdom. And he was resolved to use his
knowledge. The House of Commons had called for an
account of the number of the British forces in Spain at
the time of Almanza. On February 9, St. John laid upon
the table a paper giving the total as 8,660. No proceeding
could appear more correct   The House had demanded
some military statistics, and the Secretary for War had
provided them. But no proceeding could in fact have
been more deadly. Parliament had granted supplies for
a total force of 29,395. At once the House was in a flame.
Here was a deficiency of more than 20,000 men, or of the
money voted in respect of them. The answer was that
the larger figure included, and the smaller figure excluded,
both officers and their servants, that over 4,000 of the men
who sailed with Rivers had perished on the voyage, that
an allowance of nearly 1,800 must be made for prisoners,
and that the time between the date when the money was
voted and the date when Almanza was fought was insufficient to enable complete effect to be given to the intentions of Parliament   But this answer was not in print.
Common prudence dictated that, in publishing such
statistics, the government should have appended an explanatory note.   Yet without consulting or forewarning
Godolphin, St. John flung the naked figures to the
House.

In the heated debate which ensued, St. John and Harley,
as in duty bound, defended the ministry.   But the mischief
was done. Both Whigs and Tories were in arms. A
damaging lie had been started, and in the country at any
rate it could never be overtaken. It never was. Subsequent explanations came too late. The suggestion that,
through negligence or fraud, or both, two-thirds of the
British army in Spain were missing at the moment of trial,

was never killed. It was precisely a thrust which none but an old Parliamentary hand could have invented.[1]

Godolphin determined at once that either he or Harley must go. No government which desired to exist could tolerate such tactics. That same evening he intimated that relations were at an end The Attorney-General carried his message.

Harley appealed to Marlborough, who saw him personally, and told him the truth He wrote to Godolphin, whose brief reply concluded as follows. " I cannot help seeing nor believing my senses. I am very far from having deserved it of you. God forgive you."[2] Nevertheless, the Secretary of State did not resign. Marlborough and Godolphin laid the facts before the Queen, and requested his dismissal. But Anne refused to credit their allegations. Then they played their last card They informed her in writing that they could no longer serve in the same Cabinet with one whose proceedings were described by Marlborough as " false and treacherous." The Duke, who knew that the stability of the Grand Alliance depended largely on the prestige of the British government, warned the Queen that this event would be " attended with the sorrow and amazement of all Europe." He expressed his deep devotion to her interests; but, " I beseech Your Majesty," he wrote, " to look upon me, from this moment, as forced out of your service."[3]

A Cabinet council was summoned for Sunday, February 19. The two ministers waited on the Queen beforehand, and again tendered their resignations In Godolphin's case, " she seemed," says Burnet, " not much concerned, . . but she was much touched with the Duke of Marlborough's offering to quit, and studied with some soft expressions, to divert him from that resolution, but he was firm "[4] She also was firm, and they left her presence together. The Cabinet met. Harley introduced some business relative to the quota of Imperialist troops But the Duke of Somerset observed with some warmth that he did not see how they could deliberate on such a question in the absence of the

---

[1] From the nature of the case this view of Harley's conduct rests upon the inferences of contemporary observers (see Leadam and Von Noorden).
[2] Somerville, Appendix XXI : Godolphin to Harley, Hardwicke Papers.
[3] Coxe, vol. ii , p 191   [4] Burnet, vol iv , p 180

Lord Treasurer and the Captain-General   Both he and
Pembroke proposed to leave the meeting.   Everybody else
looked "cold and sullen"[1]   Harley was embarrassed; the
Queen remained silent, and the council terminated abruptly.

The Whigs were perfectly aware that the conflict between
Harley and his colleagues was in reality a conflict between
Harley and the Junta.   Believing that as long as Marlborough refused to serve, no new ministry could be constituted, they had already informed the Duke of their
sympathy and support.   The Duke, for his part, had acted
with perfect loyalty to Godolphin; but Harley still stood
fast.   It was necessary therefore that the Junta themselves
should take a hand in the game.   On Monday, the 20th,
they induced the Upper House to appoint a committee of
seven to examine Greg.   As Greg had been three times
examined by the Cabinet before he was sent for trial, this
proceeding appeared to be superfluous.   But the object of it
was very well understood.   The seven peers were selected
by ballot.   They were all Whigs, and three of them were
members of the Junta.   Their names were Devonshire,
Somerset, Bolton, Wharton, Townshend, Somers, and Halifax.

The issue, however, had already been determined.   On
that same Monday the Queen sent for Marlborough, and
"after some expostulations," told him that Harley "should
immediately leave his post."[2]   Impressed by the events
of Sunday, she had finally yielded to the arguments of the
Prince of Denmark, who had been persuaded by Admiral
Churchill to intervene at this critical juncture.   Apparently
it was in opposition to Harley's own wishes that she had
held out so long.   For none knew better than he that,
if Marlborough refused to serve, a new administration could
not be formed in face of the hostility of the Prince and his
friends as well as of the growing alarm of Parliament and
of the moneyed class.

On the 22nd Harley resigned.   "Between ourselves,"
wrote Marlborough to Wratislaw, "he has well deserved
what has just happened to him."[3]   St. John, Harcourt,
and Mansel, Comptroller of the Queen's Household, resigned

---

[1] Burnet, vol iv, p 180   [2] Ibid
[3] Murr. y, vol iii, p 676 Marlborough to Wratislaw, February 10, 1708.

also Boyle, the Chancellor of the Exchequer, became Secretary of State, his place being taken by Smith, the Speaker of the House of Commons. St. John was succeeded by Walpole, and Mansel by Lord Cholmondeley. The new ministers were all Whigs. But when the name of Halifax's brother, Montagu, was proposed for the attorney-generalship, Anne, who was burning with rage and resentment, refused to accept it. This important post was therefore left unfilled.

It was thus that Harley fell. The Whig version, which is also the Duchess of Marlborough's, depicts both him and Mrs. Masham as a couple of treacherous self-seekers, biting the hands that had fed them Perhaps it was natural that Sarah should so regard her poor relation. It was certainly natural that the Junta should ascribe to Harley that thirst for office which, in their own case, amounted to a disease. But there are more ways than one of telling the same story. Harley's real offence was rank, and unpardonable. He had dared to adhere to a system of government which Godolphin and Marlborough had originally approved, and which Anne herself preferred. He had dared to advise a Queen of England that she was not bound to abdicate, in all save name, in favour of a self-appointed oligarchy of five. And he had dared to tell her that a minority ought not to be allowed to dictate to the House of Commons. For crimes like these it was difficult to devise an adequate punishment; but the Lords' Committee, appointed to examine Greg, were resolved to try their hand.

On the constitutional issue, which underlay the contest between Harley and the Junta, it is frequently assumed that the Junta were right, and that the opinion and the practice of posterity have shown that they were right. This judgment is a somewhat superficial one. It has certainly come to be recognised that a Cabinet, composed of men of both parties, is neither an ideal nor a practical instrument, except upon abnormal occasions. But the greatest war in which England had ever been engaged was at any rate an abnormal occasion. And Harley's system, by excluding fanatical partisans, both Whig and Tory, aimed at a combination of the moderate men of both

sides. Politicians of this description have frequently more
in common with one another than with the extremists of
their respective factions.   When they unite to rule, government by party is virtually suspended.   It cannot be said
that, after two centuries of political experience, modern
opinion is reconciled to government by party.   It has long
been conceded that partisans in power must as far as possible
forget that they are partisans   In other words, the system
of the Junta is accepted and tolerated only on the understanding that it is worked in a spirit to which the Junta
themselves were strangers.   And that, after all, was Harley's
goal, though reached by a different road

The Lords' Committee went to Newgate on February 12
to examine Greg.   They told him, at the outset, that " if
he, by a true, ingenuous, and full confession, would deserve
it, he might have ground to hope the House of Lords might
intercede in his behalf for mercy from Her Majesty."   They
told him also that " being a man of understanding, he was
not to expect to be asked questions," but was himself to
tell them " when and by what instigation he was drawn
in to correspond with the Queen's enemies "[1]   It was a
promising opening; but it hardly fulfilled expectations.
Greg described his official career and the origin and nature
of his crime with a richness of detail which might be invaluable to a historian of the Civil Service, but which was
very unsatisfying to the noble seven   They interrupted
him once, by their own admission, to tell him that the
House would expect him to be " very clear and particular
in declaring by what advice or encouragement he first
began such a correspondence.   He said, ' By none at all.
He was tempted to it by the Devil and the hopes of getting
money.' "   He told them that official documents, not
excepting those of the highest importance, were very
negligently kept in the department, but no amount of
suggestion or exhortation could induce him to say what
he was required to say   According to Hoskins, the Duke
of Somerset's steward, whom they employed to assist them
in their dirty work, " the Lords asked Greg a great many

---

[1] For the examination of Greg by the Lords' Committee, see *Journals of the House of Lords*, vol xviii , March 18, 1708.

very hard questions about Mr. Secretary Harley, insomuch
that, had Greg been a thorough-paced rogue (as he said),
he might have saved his life by giving pertinent answers
to them."[1] The Committee then turned their attention to
Valentine and Barra. They raked up a quantity of evidence
from the seaport towns, but they merely succeeded in
establishing a possibility that Valentine, like other spies
before and since, had "played Jack on both sides "[2] It
would appear that Valentine, like Greg, was what the Committee called " a man of understanding," for he remarked
that " he knew very well for what he was confined, but
that he would sooner be torn in pieces by horses than do
so vile a thing " The impotent conclusion was that Valentine
and Barra were " unfit to be trusted or employed."[3] Six
weeks were spent in these unfruitful investigations. Greg,
in the meantime, was not left undisturbed. Mysterious
visits and " strange promises were often made him by men
of note."[4] Hoskins was sent to him from the Committee
with a definite offer of intercession with the Queen; but
Hoskins came empty away. Except for some trivial
details of his crime, which the prisoner displayed a meti-
culous anxiety to reveal, he had nothing to say to his
tempters. In his conversations with the Ordinary of
Newgate, over and over again "with the greatest and
solemnest asseveration and protestation imaginable (he
being all the while upon his knees and calling the great
God to witness),"[5] he proclaimed the innocence of Harley.
The Ordinary, no inexperienced judge of such matters,
believed the word of the condemned man, who behaved
throughout like a sincere penitent. Yet one of the distinguished visitors had offered Greg his life and a pension
of £200 a year. No wonder the good priest was uneasy.

On March 18 the House of Lords presented the report
of their Committee to the Queen, and requested her to

[1] Portland MSS : W. Greg's Examination, March 31, 1708 (Hist. MSS.
Comm , 15th Report, Appendix, part iv , p 484)
[2] Ibid , p 479 " K O " so endorsed to E Harley, March 4, 1708.
[3] Journals of the House of Lords, vol xviii , March 18, 1708
[4] Swift, Some Remarks upon a Pamphlet entitled "A Letter to the Seven
Lords of the Committee appointed to examine Gregg."
[5] State Trials, T B Howell, vol. xiv The Ordinary of Newgate's letter
to Francis Hoffman

make "an example."[1] In this report, according to Hoskins,[2] the account of Greg's examination was deliberately garbled, and certain of his replies were modified or suppressed without his knowledge. The Committee had now discovered that as long ago as 1697 one, W. Greg, had been tried for coining Two witnesses had identified the prisoner, after eleven years, as the same man. Greg "very positively"[3] denied it. But it was necessary now to discredit one whose word, if only it had been given against Harley, would have been greedily accepted. The irritation of the Whig peers was natural enough. The party which had patronised Titus Oates was at a loss to comprehend the inconvenient squeamishness of Greg They reasoned on the common, but childish, assumption that a man, who has ignored the claims of honour, religion, and gratitude upon certain occasions, will ignore them upon all. They attributed the firmness of the prisoner to his expectation of the royal clemency. The Committee, in their report, drew attention to the fact that "they did not observe Greg to be under any disorder or terror from the apprehension or sense of his danger."[4] Why should he have been ? Courage, or the appearance of it, has often been exhibited under similar circumstances. It was true that the Queen, in accordance with her laudable custom, had bestowed some charity upon the prisoner. But the Lords must have been aware, and Greg, as "a man of understanding," must have been aware also, that this was a very flimsy foundation upon which to build. For if Anne had exercised her prerogative on Greg's behalf, she would have done a cruel disservice to Harley

Even now justice was not permitted to take its course. It was apparently assumed that the address to the Queen would convince Greg of the hopelessness of his position. He was therefore allowed a week for meditation, and was then again examined at Lord Sunderland's house, but without result. Finally, he received a respite of yet another month. The Queen was indignant at so gross a scandal. "The usage he had," she declared, "was hanging him over

[1] Boyer, vol vi , p 363
[2] Portland MSS · Memorandum, March 31, 1708 (Hist MSS Comm., 15th Report, Appendix, part iv , p. 484)
[3] Journals of the House of Lords, vol xviii , March 18, 1708   [4] Ibid.

and over."[1] But the prisoner continued inflexible to the end. He seemed to be truly sorry for his crime, which was caused, as he told the Ordinary, by his poverty His poverty he ascribed to his vicious habits, confessing that he " had formerly indulged himself in lewdness and filthy pleasures." This last circumstance might reasonably have been expected to recommend him to some, at any rate, of the Lords' Committee.[2] And as Swift remarked, " the party was bound in honour to procure Greg a pardon, which was openly promised him, upon condition of making an ingenuous confession. . . . A confession may be never the less ingenuous for not answering the hopes or designs of those who take it."[3] When the Junta got to work on Greg, he was, as the same writer remarks, " a poor, profligate fellow ",[4] when they had finished with him, he was a hero, and a veritable martyr for the truth.

From the date of the sentence to the date of its execution nearly a hundred days elapsed Most men in Harley's situation would have suffered acutely throughout that period. His honour, and possibly his life, depended on the firmness of one whose ability to resist temptation might well be doubted. But Harley showed himself " totally unmoved," and never once exhibited " the least discomposure." His friends, however, were consumed with anxiety. Atterbury said to Edward Harley, " Your brother's head is upon the block, and yet he seems to have no concern about it; you should persuade him to do something that may prevent the impending danger."[5] But Harley's only comment was, " I know nothing that I can do, but entirely to be resigned to, and confide in, the providence of God "[6] His faith was rewarded. " God," he exclaimed, " has miraculously touched the conscience of that unhappy man "[7]

[1] Portland MSS · W Thomas to E Harley, March 30, 1708 (Hist MSS. Comm , 15th Report, Appendix, part iv , p 483)
[2] The following notes are taken from the *Characters* of John Macky, who was no Tory Wharton, " Much of a Libertine ", Devonshire " Loves the Ladies ", Somers, " Something of a Libertine "
[3] Swift, *Some Remarks upon a Pamphlet entitled " A Letter to the Seven Lords of the Committee appointed to examine Gregg "* [4] *Ibid*
[5] Portland MSS , vol v , p 648, Appendix (Hist MSS Comm) [6] *Ibid*
[7] *Ibid* Edward Harley to his aunt, Abigail Harley, December 3, 1708 (Hist. MSS Comm , 15th Report, Appendix, part iv , p 511)

The Queen wavered at the last, and hesitated to send Greg to his death. In spite of the fact that, if she had spared him, the Whigs would have accused her of purchasing his silence, it was possible to suggest that Greg was a hypocrite, that his confession, his repentance, and his refusal to incriminate his old employer, were artfully designed to procure him a pardon from a Sovereign who always detested the signing of death warrants, who was always favourably impressed by Christian behaviour, and who notoriously resented the Junta's conspiracy to ruin her friend It was possible to suggest it, and the Whigs did suggest it. Only in one way could Greg reply to them; but that way was effectual. There came an hour when he learned that his prolonged respite was really finished. There came an hour when he was dragged upon a hurdle from Newgate to Tyburn, when he stood beneath the gallows and beheld the horrid apparatus of a traitor's doom. Even then he could still have saved his life by a lie, but that lie remained unspoken He did not flinch. His presence of mind did not desert him. His behaviour was described by those who witnessed it as " extraordinary devout."[1] At that solemn moment, one of the sheriffs, Sir Charles Piers, to his eternal shame, tempted the dying man for the last time. He interrupted the final offices of the Church with unseasonable questions. He whispered a communication to the executioner, who conveyed it to Greg as he stood upon the cart with the rope around his neck. " What would they have me say?" exclaimed Greg. " I have told all I knew " And then, with " a very strong voice," audible above the tumult of the great multitude, he cried aloud. " Mr Harley is perfectly innocent as to any knowledge of the correspondence I was engaged in, neither he nor anybody had any hand in it, and I call God to witness that I die with a conscience clear from having concealed anything I knew relating to the Queen and the government "[2] He was somewhat nobler then than the noble seven of the Lords' Committee. He had sinned He had betrayed his trust. He had brought disgrace and

[1] Portland MSS . W Thomas to E Harley, April 29, 1708 (Hist. MSS. Comm 15th Report, Appendix, part iv , p 488).   [2] *Ibid.*

peril upon one who had been too kind to him. But for a hundred days he had wrestled against all the powers of darkness, and had prevailed. For a hundred days of his misspent life he had borne himself like a gentleman; and like a gentleman he died.

He left behind him a written declaration, in which he repeated that he was guiltless of all responsibility for " the miscarriage before Toulon " or " the losses by sea," utterly repudiated the suggestion that he had formerly been charged with coining, and entirely exonerated Harley, " as I shall answer it before the judgment-seat of Christ."[1] The Whigs were stupid enough to pretend that this document was composed for him by a clergyman. It was, in fact, so devoid of literary merit that Greg himself, conscious perhaps that it did no particular credit to his University of Aberdeen, described it as a " poor paper."[2] Nevertheless, this " poor paper " so terrified the Junta that they contrived to delay its publication for eight days. But the existence of the document was already known, for Greg had alluded to it at Tyburn. To postpone its appearance was therefore a foolish and unprofitable proceeding, which made the worst impression.

The treason of Greg has always been regarded as a stroke of good fortune for the Whigs, who gained enormously by it. But the admitted facts, as they affect the leaders of that party, are of so infamous a character, that the question arises how far the affair was an accident at all When the Whig Lords enquired of the condemned man what persons were behind him, it is at least within the bounds of possibility that they themselves could have supplied an answer which would have astonished even him. The known circumstances of the case are by no means inconsistent with the hypothesis that Greg was originally incited to his crime by secret agents of the Junta It is to be observed that, despite his great and obvious temptations, he did not set up as a traitor spontaneously, or in the hope of obtaining French money from Chamillart. It was " one, Crookshanks," who offered him 200 guineas, if he would procure

[1] *State Trials*, T B. Howell, vol xiv , p. 139 a copy of William Gregg's paper   [2] *Ibid.*

a French pass for the merchant, Brown   Crookshanks must have approached him some time before October 24 (O S.), the date on which Greg began operations. The weeks preceding October 24 (O.S.) were precisely the weeks when the Junta realised that the " plain " talk between Harley and Godolphin had not resulted in the resignation or removal of the obnoxious minister. Both the time and the manner of the commencement of Greg's correspondence with France are therefore consistent with the theory that an *agent provocateur* was employed. Such a theory is assuredly not damaged by the assertion both of Edward Harley and of Swift that, immediately before his arrest, Greg received a warning of his peril from a Whig source. If the whole affair was engineered by Harley's enemies, it may well have been their original plan that, as soon as ever the fact of a treasonable correspondence, emanating from Harley's department, had been clearly established, Greg should vanish For he would leave behind him an atmosphere of vague suspicion, calculated to inflict more injury on Harley's reputation than a public trial, at which nothing could be proved against the minister, and something might possibly emerge to expose the machinations of his enemies. If more were known of Crookshanks, or if it could be ascertained what persons first drew Harley's attention to the probability that the correspondence of the French prisoners was being utilised by a traitor in his own department, a decisive judgment could perhaps be formed. Greg himself declared before the Lords' Committee that, after he had embarked on his correspondence with France, he was guilty of what he called the " downright madness " of exhibiting extracts from it to both Crookshanks and Brown, and also to a certain Bollinger, who was another merchant, and a friend of Brown. There were too many merchants in the case. Merchants, as a class, were generally Whigs; as a class, also, they were exasperated against the Tory element in the Cabinet, which they identified with Churchill's domination at the Admiralty. As the matter stands, the Whig peers, or some of them, are at least suspect of an act of baseness, of which their conduct after Greg's arrest demonstrates only too plainly that they were entirely capable.

This story has been told in full, because it shows how intense were political passions at that time, and how intense they were likely to become. It shows also what manner of men were they into whose power Godolphin and Marlborough had now delivered themselves "O most implacable hell-hounds!"[1] exclaimed Edward Harley And finally, it shows how low was the standard of public conduct which prevailed under the later Stuarts. The members of the Lords' Committee, which endeavoured to suborn Greg, were some of the most influential and prominent persons then alive. Though most of them are now forgotten, one of them, Somers, is honoured to this day. Those who still cherish the legend that the career of Marlborough was disfigured by peculiar and exceptional brands of infamy, must be singularly ignorant of the code of morals accepted by the men who were his equals and contemporaries.

Godolphin was a great and a justly famous statesman. He made the Union with Scotland, and he successfully financed a war more gigantic than any in which England had previously participated But he suffered from an excess of caution. He loved to play for safety, and to choose the line of least resistance. To purchase in the open market the votes which the Junta put up for sale was less dangerous and less difficult than to follow the advice of Harley. But the costs were accumulating at an extravagant rate By the beginning of 1705 he had alienated the mass of the parochial clergy, the strongest body of organised thought in the country. By the beginning of 1707, he had alienated the Queen, who, in addition to the personal power which she enjoyed under the constitution, enjoyed also as large a measure of personal popularity as has ever fallen to the lot of an English Sovereign By the beginning of 1708 he had alienated Harley, a politician who knew more about parties in Parliament and about opinion outside Parliament than any other politician of that day, a statesman, who, unlike the Rochesters and the Nottinghams, would be fully capable of forming a ministry and formulating a policy that would appeal to both the

---

[1] Portland MSS Edward Harley to his aunt, Abigail Harley, December 3, 1708 (Hist. MSS Comm , 15th Report, Appendix, part iv., p 511).

country and the Queen. In exchange, he had secured the
assistance of five domineering oligarchs, who controlled
150 votes in the House of Commons, and who did not
shrink from subornation itself, if subornation was conducive
to the ends of Whiggery. With the merchants aggrieved
by their losses, and the country gentlemen impatient of their
taxes, what expectation of life had a ministry, that relied
upon such friends to protect it against such foes ? It is
not surprising that Marlborough should have been in haste
to finish the war.

XIX.—DUNKIRK, GHENT, AND BRUGES

THE resolutions of Parliament and the representations of the Queen in favour of the dispatch of Prince Eugène to Catalonia were supported by emphatic letters from Marlborough to Wratislaw, Sinzendorf, and Salm. He insisted that public opinion in England was unanimous upon the point; and he warned the Austrian ministers that a refusal would produce a very bad impression. Nevertheless, the Emperor declined to grant this most reasonable request, which was framed in the obvious interest of his own family as well as of the coalition as a whole. Starhemberg was selected to command in Spain, and in signifying this decision to Marlborough, Wratislaw took exception to the address of the British Parliament upon the subject. Angry and disappointed, Marlborough replied on February 5 that the ministry, as Wratislaw from his knowledge of the British constitution must be well aware, was not responsible for the address, and that, if English opinion was to be tranquillised, Starhemberg must start at once. "As to his merit, his experience, and his capacity for commanding an army," wrote the Duke, "everybody is agreed, but these are not the only motives which have operated here. It has been considered that the authority of the Prince of Savoy was absolutely necessary to direct affairs at the court of His Christian Majesty as well as at the head of the army."[1] Writing again on the 17th, he said "Let us speak no more of this business; it is now only a question of having M Starhemberg at the head of the army as soon as possible—and I flatter myself that he is even now upon his way."[2] To Sinzendorf he wrote on the same date: "If he has not already started, I conjure you to hasten his journey as much as possible."[3] Beyond all challenge

[1] Murray, vol III, p 673 · Marlborough to Wratislaw, February 5, 1708.
[2] Ibid, p 677 Marlborough to Wratislaw, February 17, 1708.
[3] Ibid, p 678 Marlborough to Sinzendorf, February 17, 1708.

England was right in this dispute. But it was not the first occasion on which the government of Vienna had deliberately obstructed the common cause. And even after Marlborough's insistence upon urgency, Starhemberg did not arrive till the end of April Luckily for him and for the Grand Alliance, he found Count Noyelles dead.

It was arranged in February that Marlborough and Eugène should meet at the Hague in the last week of March, to concert the operations of the forthcoming campaign. But the date was postponed until April 11, by reason of an event, which excited the interest of Europe in the highest degree.

At the time of Harley's downfall, the maritime powers were perturbed by an incessant rumour of naval and military preparations at Dunkirk The Hague was nervous on account of Zealand; but London suspected, and with better cause, that Scotland was the threatened point. The great majority of the people of that country, without distinction of class or party, detested the Act of Union; their first experience of its operation, which was attended by a variety of grievances, only augmented the prevailing bitterness. In the autumn of 1707 Harley had been instructed by his secret service that the northern kingdom was in a highly explosive condition. He had been definitely warned of the existence of a project for a French descent, which was to be the signal for a national insurrection. Louis was to land 10,000 regular troops, who were to be joined immediately by Highlanders and Lowlanders, by Whigs, Cameronians, and Jacobites, to the number of 30,000. It was only natural, therefore, that the British government should associate the mysterious activity at Dunkirk with this design At a moment so critical, the unwisdom of removing Marlborough from the control of British strategy must have been fully realised at the Admiralty, and probably the Prince of Denmark made use of this argument in the final tussle with the Queen

Louis, in fact, had yielded to the representations of the exiled court of St Germain, which was in a position to produce authentic evidence of Scottish disaffection. His personal pride, which had been sorely hurt by the recent attack on Toulon, welcomed the idea of retaliation in kind, while his knowledge of strategy told him that a diversion, intended to produce a civil war upon a grand scale in the British Isles, was worth some sacrifice. It was decided that the brilliant Forbin should command the expedition, and that the Pretender should accompany it. A fleet of eight sail of the line and twenty-four frigates was collected at Dunkirk. Transports to the number of sixty-six were provided for the troops. Twelve battalions received orders for this service. Irish and Scottish officers were specially selected Arms, clothing, and money were furnished for the use of the insurgents, and plate, liveries, and uniforms for the Pretender's Court. The Pope bestowed his blessing and 100,000 crowns upon an enterprise, the " principal end " of which was described by the Pretender's mother as " the conversion of three kingdoms." And James put out a proclamation from St. Germain, characterising Anne as " the usurper," and promising an amnesty for all who did not oppose him.

Ever since the battle of Malaga, France had virtually retired from the contest . for the command of the sea. England was safe from invasion, but it was not in the power of her navy to guarantee her absolutely against ar aid. Given the skill and daring of such a sailor as Forbin in combination with the accidents which in maritime warfare invariably occur, a raid was always possible On February 17 Leake sailed for Portugal with a convoy of seventeen men-of-war. The French were hopeful that the resources remaining to the British Admiralty might prove insufficient to maintain an effectual blockade of Dunkirk. But the British Admiralty knew their business better than some of their Parliamentary critics had imagined By the first week in March, they had assembled in the Downs a fleet of twenty-three men-of-war and a fire-ship, besides three Dutchmen, all under the command of Sir George Byng. On the 9th Byng appeared before Dunkirk and Gravelines. From that time onward it was obvious that Forbin's chance was a very slender one.

Such as it was, however, Marlborough had already insured against it. The Scottish garrisons were few in number, and according to Harley's spies, by no means to be trusted. But Marlborough did not rely upon the Scottish garrisons. On February 17 he desired Cadogan to proceed to Flanders, to spare no pains to ascertain the designs of the French, and to keep the Cabinet informed of them, if necessary " by frequent expresses both by Ostend and the Brill." Having satisfied himself of the intentions and the strength of the enemy, Cadogan was to see that " a proportionable number of Her Majesty's foot-forces " were " kept in readiness to embark immediately." If Forbin should escape the vigilance of Byng, Cadogan, without waiting for orders from England, was to put his men aboard " with all possible speed," and convey them himself to " the first convenient port "[1] He was to concert the necessary arrangements with Lumley, who commanded the British army in Marlborough's absence, and also with Overkirk. And he was to apply to the Dutch government to assist the operation with such men-of-war as they might have available. On the same date, the Duke instructed Lumley to select battalions " most proper for this service,"[2] and to obtain and forward such intelligence as he could collect. He also requested Overkirk to fill the vacancies in the garrisons with Dutch troops. To all three officers he recommended the strictest secrecy.

On the arrival of these dispatches, Cadogan approached the Dutch government, and directed that transports should be prepared at Ostend. Having taken counsel with Overkirk at Brussels, he set off for Ghent, where he conferred with Lumley. Ten battalions having been chosen for the work, Lumley and he proceeded to Ostend, to supervise the arrangements at that port.

Marlborough, in the meantime, was diligently mobilising the forces in London and the southern counties. These consisted of seven regiments of infantry, besides a contingent of Household Troops, both horse and foot, and a detachment of dragoons. With the recruits that were actually being raised for the regiments which had suffered so heavily at Almanza, he hoped to form two or three additional battalions. He also gave orders for a regiment

[1] Murray, vol III , p. 680 Marlborough to Cadogan, February 17, 1708.
[2] Ibid , p 680. Marlborough to Lumley, February 17, 1708

of horse and two of dragoons to be got ready in the north of Ireland.   But as long as he was ignorant of the precise point selected for the descent, he very properly made no movements.   As against the French alone, or as against the known partisans of the House of Stuart, his preparations at home and in Flanders were crushing.   As against the two together, they were ample.   But as against an insurrection on a national scale, something more was required.

On March 15, the government put up Boyle to inform the Commons of the situation at Dunkirk   On the following day, both Houses returned thanks to the Queen for the measures taken, and prayed her " to order that the laws against papists and non-jurors be put into execution,"[1] and that all suspected persons be seized with their horses and arms   The Queen gave effect to these proposals by a proclamation, in which she described her brother and his friends as " traitors and rebels."   On the 22nd, Parliament suspended the Habeas Corpus Act.   The government, which had been supplied by informers with lists of the Pretender's secret adherents, was now in a position to strike.

" Since we have got a greater strength of shipping together than in all likelihood they can put to sea," wrote Marlborough to Robinson on the 2nd, " I think we have nothing to apprehend, whatever their design may be."[2] This opinion was justified.   The startling apparition of Byng's formidable fleet had disheartened the French. Forbin stopped the work of embarkation, which had already begun.   The Pretender, who reached Dunkirk on the 9th, protested loudly and appealed to Versailles   Then he fell ill of the measles.   Forbin represented that, although he might slip through the blockade, and might even land the troops in Scotland, he could not be answerable for the safety of the King's ships   But if a raid was seriously intended, the safety of the King's ships was not the first consideration   Forbin was ordered to make the attempt.   Fortune favoured him   On the 13th great gales drove Byng from his station to the Downs.   On the 17th, the wind changed.   The Pretender

[1] Boyer, vol vi, p 335
[2] Murray, vol iii, p 686 Marlborough to Robinson, March 2, 1700.

recovered from his measles, the soldiers hastened on board, and hidden by a dense fog, Forbin put to sea. That night the wind changed again, and compelled him to cast anchor at Nieuport, where he remained until the evening of the 19th, when he steered for Scotland   Byng, in the meantime, had returned from the Downs on the 17th. His fleet had now been reinforced " to the number of above forty men-of-war of the line of battle besides frigates and fire-ships."[1] At 1 o'clock on the morning of the 20th, as he cruised between Calais and Dunkirk, an Ostend boat, dispatched by Cadogan, informed him that the French had sailed from Nieuport the preceding evening   They had twelve hours' start. There was no time to lose.   Byng immediately detached a squadron to protect the crossing of Cadogan's men to England, and to watch the warships remaining at Dunkirk.   He himself with the remainder of the fleet set off in hot pursuit   Rightly concluding that the Pretender's goal was Edinburgh, he steered for the Firth of Forth.

The Queen informed Parliament on the 22nd that the French were out, that Byng could be trusted to " give a good account of them,"[2] and that the ten battalions had embarked at Ostend   Two days later, the Commons presented an address, wherein they pledged themselves to make good all such expenditure as the Queen thought proper to incur, and entreated her not to be diverted from vigorously supporting her " allies in all parts, whatever attempts are made at home "   At the same time, while they expressed their contempt for " the small number of ships and troops " employed in the design on Scotland, they drew the obvious inference that the enemy was relying upon domestic traitors.   And finally they besought her " to discountenance " the persons who had endeavoured " to create divisions and animosities . . . or by any artful methods lessen the just esteem Your Majesty has for those who have so eminently and in so distinguishing a manner commanded your armies and managed your treasure "[3]— a palpable hit at Harley and his friends.   The address of the Lords was similar in its substance, but more violent in its

[1] Boyer, vol. vi , p 338.   [2] Ibid , p. 341.   [3] Ibid., pp. 342, 343.

tone " We hope," said this document, which was really
a manifesto from the Junta to the Sovereign, " we hope
Your Majesty will always have a just detestation of those
persons, who at a time when this hellish attempt was afoot,
and so near breaking out, were using their endeavours to
misrepresent the actions of your best subjects, and create
jealousies in Your Majesty of those who had always served
you most eminently and faithfully · and we beseech Your
Majesty not to give so just a cause of uneasiness to your
people, as to suffer any such hereafter to have access to
your royal person."

From the 22nd to the 27th the government remained
without news. On the 24th the forces which Marlborough
had mobilised began their march towards Scotland
Recruiting proceeded apace, and the Duke commenced to
arrange for the embarkation of seven squadrons of cavalry
in Flanders The Queen's proclamation was vigorously
enforced Many suspected persons were arrested, notably
the Dukes of Hamilton, Athol, and Gordon. Public opinion
continued tranquil on the whole. But on the 23rd, on a
rumour that the French had landed and that the Scots
had risen, the funds dropped fifteen points, and a run upon
the Bank began The panic was partly spontaneous, and
partly organised by goldsmiths, who were envious of the
Bank's success, and by Jacobites, who hoped to ruin the
credit both of England and the Grand Alliance. But the
directors called upon the shareholders for 20 per cent. of
the capital; Godolphin paid in all the money at the Treasury;
the Queen herself, as well as the Dukes of Marlborough,
Somerset, and Newcastle, and other peers, made large
advances; and the Whig merchants, together with the
Jewish, Dutch, and Huguenot houses, rushed in a body to
the rescue. The only result of a disreputable manœuvre
was the passage of a unanimous resolution through the
Commons to the effect that, " Whoever designedly endeavours to destroy or lessen the public credit, especially
at a time when the Kingdom is threatened with an invasion,
is guilty of an high crime and misdemeanour, and is an
enemy to her Majesty and the Kingdom."[1]

[1] *Ibid*, p 354.

On the 27th came dispatches, written by Byng off the Firth of Forth. He was in touch with the enemy, who had not as yet succeeded in landing a single man. " They stand from us," he wrote, " and we after them with all the sail we can "[1]

The luck had turned. With more than twelve hours' start, and with cleaner ships than Byng's, Forbin had a reasonable chance of making the Firth of Forth in time to disembark the troops and put to sea again before Byng could intercept him. But owing to the strength of the gale or to an error in navigation, he overshot his mark, and was first sighted off Montrose. Working back towards the Firth, he reached the entrance on the evening of the 23rd, and anchored off Pittenween and Creil on the northern side. He made some signals, which ought to have been answered by Jacobites on shore, but which met with no response. The loss of time had been fatal to his plans. That same night Byng dropped anchor on the southern side of the Firth When daylight broke on the 24th, Forbin perceived that he was almost trapped He ran for the open, and by skilful seamanship he outmanœuvred Byng, who was hampered by a land breeze. Byng gave chase. The enemy steered north-east, but their slowest ships were overhauled by the fastest of the English, and a running fight ensued until nightfall. The *Salisbury*, of fifty-two guns, which had been captured by the French in 1703, was boarded by the *Leopard*, and easily re-taken She carried, besides her regular crew, a considerable contingent of soldiers, a number of Jacobites, including the aged Lord Griffen, and a quantity of money, arms, and ammunition. Off Buchan Ness Byng abandoned the pursuit, and sailed for Leith. On the 25th, although the primary aim of the expedition, the capture of Edinburgh, was now impossible, the enemy continued their course with the object of effecting a descent at Inverness. But that night " there arose a strong contrary wind," which " continued the next day with violence."[2] Forbin refused to hazard his ships in unknown waters for the sake of what he now regarded as a hopeless and unprofitable adventure. To the intense

---

[1] Boyer, vol vi , p 351   [2] *Ibid* , p. 347.

disgust of James, it was decided to return to Dunkirk.
They did not regain that port until April 9 One ship
foundered at sea; and it was estimated that from sickness,
confinement, insufficiency of water, and other causes they
lost no fewer than 4,000 men during their three weeks'
voyage They arrived "in so miserable a condition,"
according to the account of a Jacobite officer, "that the
soldiers when they crept ashore looked more like rats than
men." The Pretender, according to the same authority,
was received "by abundance of ladies in their coaches,
with looks that put me in mind of an English funeral.
When he went off, the noise was all over, 'Long live the
King'; but at our return, shrugging of shoulders and
shaking of heads gave a dismal welcome."[1]

Meantime, the English troops had continued their march
towards Scotland. The detachment from Ostend had
arrived off Tynemouth on March 31. But as day after
day went by, and nothing more was heard of the French,
the government and the nation realised that the attempt
had failed.

This expensive fiasco gave rise to some recriminations
between the Jacobites and the French. Doubts were
thrown upon the sincerity of Louis, who was represented
as eager to provoke a civil war in the British Isles, but
very reluctant to risk his own soldiers and ships It is
probable that a landing could have been effected in the
Firth of Forth, had Forbin been willing to sacrifice his
squadron; and it is possible that his instructions forbade
him to pay so heavy a price. Assuming that something
was left to his discretion, it should be observed that, when
he lay off the coast of Fifeshire, he formed the opinion that
the reports of Scottish disaffection had been grossly exaggerated In a sense, they had. It was one thing to follow
a Stuart prince against the presumptuous English; but it
was another to march under banners that had been blessed
by the Pope in a crusade for "the conversion of three
kingdoms" At the same time, if James had once set foot
on Scottish soil, and certainly if he had carried the Castle
of Edinburgh by assault, he would have found himself at

[1] *Ibid*, p. 350.

the head of an army.   But whether that army could have stood before the veterans of Marlborough, may well be doubted.   Upon the whole, and particularly in view of the fact that, except for the best of good luck, the expedition could never have sighted Scotland at all, it deserved to be regarded from the very outset as a desperate venture; and its issue must be judged accordingly.

The political results of this affair were very unfavourable to France.   The energy and efficiency, displayed by the British government, inspired and encouraged the members of the Grand Alliance.   In England, the Admiralty was rehabilitated; Marlborough's activity and foresight were everywhere applauded; and the ministry of Godolphin recovered the popularity which it had recently lost.   The Queen was overwhelmed with congratulatory addresses from all parts of the kingdom   " All which is dear to you," she said in her speech from the throne on April 12, " is perfectly safe under my government; and must be irrecoverably lost, if ever the designs of a Popish Pretender, bred up in the principles of the most arbitrary government, should take place."[1]   The Junta in particular profited by the widespread indignation which the expedition had aroused   Representing in accordance with their custom that everybody who was not a Whig was certainly a Jacobite or a tool of France, they prepared the way for a general election which should complete the overthrow of Harley and his friends.   One mistake, which it was open to the government to make, was carefully avoided.   The Jacobite prisoners were treated with extreme clemency.   Many were acquitted, or discharged.   Griffen indeed was condemned to death, but he was respited from month to month until, in 1710, he expired of old age.   Marlborough and Godolphin, who personally detested the shedding of blood, were wisely desirous of conciliating Scottish opinion.   Moreover, in common with the majority of Englishmen, they felt in their hearts a sympathy with the Pretender, which they could not openly express.   Nothing but his religion stood between him and the succession.   But the Pretender took his religion more seriously than Henry of Navarre, a

[1] Boyer, vol vi , p 360.

mistake to be avoided by all such as seek after temporal crowns.

Marlborough quitted London on April 9, and reached the Hague on the evening of the 10th. Eugène was awaiting him. The meeting of the two illustrious commanders, and the fact that Eugène had never before been seen in Holland, excited the interest and curiosity of the populace to the highest pitch. In the conferences which ensued, the Duke represented the importance of satisfying the claims of Savoy to a portion of the Mantuan territory, and the unreasonableness of the Emperor's demands upon England for levy-money in respect of troops, raised to replace those that were sent to Catalonia. But the principal business to be determined was the plan of the forthcoming campaign in Germany and the Netherlands. Eugène was at first desirous of borrowing 30,000 men from Marlborough's army, and attempting to invade France by the valley of the Moselle. The Duke opposed the design, because, having tried it himself in 1705, he knew that it would fail again, as it had failed then, through the apathy of the Germans, the inefficiency of the Austrians, and the nervousness of the Dutch. He was also afraid that, if the forces in Flanders were materially weakened, the French might be tempted to essay a fresh descent on Scotland, although, as the Dutch truly said, " the best way of hindering it would be to keep a good squadron constantly before Dunkirk "[1] He believed that the enemy intended to concentrate their greatest strength in Flanders, and it was in Flanders that he hoped to crush them. If the allied army there could be augmented, and above all, if Eugène himself could join it, the war might be ended by a second Blenheim. The Duke succeeded in convincing Eugène of the soundness of his judgment. But the execution of the idea was difficult. As in the case of the campaign of Blenheim, friends must be deceived as well as foes Then it was the Margrave of Baden and the Dutch, whom it was necessary to hoodwink; now it was the Elector of Hanover The Elector, who was intensely jealous of Eugène, would certainly view with resentment any distribution of forces which diminished

[1] Coxe, vol. ii., p 205. Marlborough to Secretary Boyle.

either the numbers or importance of his own command upon the Rhine. It was eventually agreed that three separate armies should take the field, one in Flanders under Marlborough, one on the Rhine under the Elector, and a third, which was to be formed out of detachments from the other two, on the Moselle under Eugène. This last was to number 40,000 men. The Elector was to be left with 45,000, and Marlborough with approximately 80,000. All three generals were to act offensively, and to be at liberty to march to one another's assistance, if circumstances required. This project, which was intended to be communicated to the Allied Courts, and which now received the approval of the government at the Hague, was not the real project. By a secret understanding between Marlborough and Eugène, it was definitely arranged that, as soon as ever the army of the Moselle was assembled, Eugène should carry it to the Netherlands, and in conjunction with the Duke, deliver a decisive blow. To this innocent, but necessary conspiracy, Heinsius and Godolphin were admitted. And doubtless it was largely due to Heinsius that the field-deputies' instructions were not so drawn as to defeat the purpose which the two commanders had in view.

As it was anticipated that the Elector Palatine, the Elector of Saxony, and the Landgrave of Hesse would refuse their co-operation, unless the Emperor agreed to satisfy certain claims which they were advancing, Eugène undertook to negotiate with those princes on his road to Vienna. He also proposed to call at Hanover, and knowing himself to be personally unacceptable at that Court, he earnestly requested Marlborough to rejoin him there. Marlborough refused Before quitting England, he had given a promise to return, which, since his arrival at the Hague, he had been earnestly pressed to redeem. The Junta, elated by the access of strength which they derived from the Pretender's failure, had again applied the screw. They had called upon Godolphin to bestow the office of President of the Council, which was one of the offices held by the Earl of Pembroke, upon that great exponent and embodiment of all that Whiggery understood by the Revolution, Lord Somers. The Queen declined to listen to the suggestion, the Junta insisted; and Godolphin and the Duchess summoned Marlborough to the rescue. It seems to have been fully recognised by this time that Marlborough was the only member of the administration who possessed any real influence over the Sovereign. He was willing now to return, but the strong solicitations of Eugène, coupled with the attitude of the States-General, who, fearing lest he should be detained in England by contrary winds, addressed a remonstrance to Anne upon the subject, convinced him that he must abandon the idea, and proceed instead to Hanover

Eugène departed on the 20th for Düsseldorf On the 22nd Marlborough set off for Hanover. He travelled with Count Rechteren, envoy extraordinary from the States, and on the last stage of the journey he fell in with Eugène. It speedily appeared that the prince had correctly estimated the nature of the task The Elector plainly showed that he regarded Eugène as an interloper, and that he would not co-operate in any scheme which was intended to reduce the army of the Rhine to the defensive. The project, adopted at the Hague, did not of necessity have that effect; nor did it show, upon the face of it, that the army of the Moselle was more likely to combine with that of Marlborough than with that of the Elector The Elector was eventually persuaded to adopt the idea, but only on condition that his forces were augmented by 2,000 cavalry, originally intended for Eugène, and a detachment of 5,000 men from Flanders. " After a very great deal of uneasiness," wrote Marlborough to Godolphin, " the Elector has consented to the project for three armies . . as for the joining the two armies, we thought it best not to acquaint the Elector with it, so that I expect when that is put in execution, he will be very angry; but since the good of the campaign depends upon it, I know no remedy but patience."[1]

Quitting Hanover on the 30th, Marlborough reached the Hague on May 3 Here he found several letters from Godolphin and the Duchess, who seemed to be deeply hurt by his failure to return to England Godolphin described it as " a great mortification,"[2] and complained that it

[1] Coxe, vol ii, p 215 Marlborough to Godolphin, May 3, 1708
[2] Ibid , p 213: Godolphin to Marlborough, April 11/22, 1708.

would be misrepresented by the Tories. They both insinuated that he was not very eager to assist them in the
business of coercing the Queen at the dictation of the
Junta. The Duke, who had been absolutely bound to
go to Hanover, but who probably in his heart had been
only too glad to escape the visit to England, was extremely
vexed. He told Godolphin that the Dutch believed the
Cabinet to be out of favour with the Queen, that the city
of Amsterdam, which had always been zealous for the war,
was pressing him to come to terms with France, and that
he should despair, " were it not for the hopes that God
will give me, this campaign, an opportunity of serving the
Queen and common cause."[1] " I own to you," he added,
" that I expect no good nature from my dear countrymen,
but I beg that justice and friendship of you to believe, that
I could no ways avoid my journey to Hanover, without
hazarding the project we have made for this campaign."
He told his wife that he could endure all things so long as
he was possessed of her " love and esteem."[2] And he
confessed to Sunderland that, after the campaign was
finished, he would be glad to see his " place well filled, so
that for the remaining part of my life I might have a little
quiet, and be sometimes with my children "[3] The patent
sincerity of these aspirations is in glaring antagonism to
Goslinga's theory that the Duke was deliberately protract-
ing the war. Marlborough indeed was in most evil case.
Never had his detestation of party politics been keener
than it was at this moment, when party politics meant
nothing but the continual humiliation of a Sovereign to
whom he was genuinely attached   Yet it was precisely at
this moment that the wife whom he adored, and the friend
to whom he was invincibly loyal, were relying more and
more upon him, of all men, to procure the Queen's submission to the edicts of the Whig oligarchs

Marlborough quitted the Hague on May 7, and passing
through Antwerp, reached Ghent on the 9th. On the road
he received letters from Godolphin and the Queen. The
Dukes of Devonshire and Newcastle had suggested to Anne

---

[1] Coxe, vol ii, pp 215, 216· Marlborough to Godolphin, May 3, 1708
[2] *Ibid* p 214 Marlborough to the Duchess, May 3, 1708
[3] *Ibid.*, p 216. Marlborough to Sunderland, May 4, 1708.

that, since she objected to deprive Lord Pembroke of a place for the benefit of Lord Somers, the simplest solution would be to admit Lord Somers to the Cabinet council without bestowing on him any office. Anne had replied that the proposal was unprecedented, and that in any case the Cabinet council was sufficiently large already She had then summoned Godolphin, who had recommended her to consent, and had assured her that Marlborough would have given the same advice. Thereupon the Queen appealed to Marlborough She told him that she regarded it as " utter destruction to me to bring Lord Somers into my service." " I hope," she said, " you will not join in soliciting me in this thing, though Lord Treasurer tells me you will; for it is what I can never consent to."[1] Her pathetic craving for the Duke's support rendered the task of upholding his colleague an extremely painful one. Marlborough discharged it with much ability He began his letter by a reference to the representations of the city of Amsterdam in favour of a peace, " which," he observed, " I think not for the honour or interest of your character." This movement of Dutch opinion he ascribed to the evil effect of the recent troubles in the Cabinet, and of " the continued intelligence they have of Your Majesty's being resolved to change hands and parties." He emphasised the folly of supposing that a general election, following so soon upon the Pretender's attempt, could result in a Tory majority. " If," he exclaimed, " what I have the honour to write to Your Majesty be the truth, for God's sake consider what may be the consequences of refusing the request of the Dukes of Newcastle and Devonshire; since it will be a demonstration not only to them, but to everybody, that Lord Treasurer and I have no credit with Your Majesty, but that you are guided by the insinuation of Mr. Harley." In conclusion he told her that the enemy had " orders to venture a battle," that " so far from avoiding it," he should " seek it," and that this letter might therefore be the last he should ever write to her, " which makes me beg with the same earnestness as if I were sure it were to be my last that Your Majesty will let no influence or persuasion hinder

[1] *Ibid.*, p. 220: The Queen to Marlborough, April 22/May 3, 1708.

you . to follow the advice of Lord Treasurer, who will
never have any thought but what is for your honour and
true interest."[1] This appeal, skilfully drawn as it was,
was not expected by the writer to succeed. Nor did it.
In regard to Lord Somers, as also in regard to Halifax's
brother, Montagu, the Queen continued, in Godolphin's
language, "inflexible."[2] Her reply to Marlborough was
affectionate in tone, but it entirely ignored the real issue.
She agreed with him that a peace was out of the question,
and she begged him to be careful of his life In excuse
for the brevity of her letter, she said: " I have been so tired
to-day with importunities that come from the Whigs that
I have not spirits left to open my afflicted heart so freely
and so fully as I intended."[3] At the same time, she assured
Godolphin that she discussed politics with nobody but
her husband. " From whence the Prince's notions come,"
said Godolphin, " is not hard to conjecture."[4] Admiral
Churchill was now the villain of the piece, and both the
Duchess and the Lord Treasurer denounced him to the
Duke, who was obliged to remonstrate by post with that
" very indiscreet Tory."

Having reviewed the British forces, and visited the
Duchess of Tyrconnel, whose beautiful face he found " a
good deal changed,"[5] Marlborough went to Brussels on the
11th The backwardness of the season and the consequent
lack of forage seemed likely to delay the opening of the
campaign But the French preparations were on an
imposing scale. Chamillart himself had inspected the
arrangements on the frontier The army, which was
assembling in the neighbourhood of Mons, was to number
between 90,000 and 100,000 men It included the Guards,
the Gendarmerie, and the Maison du Roi. Conspicuous
among a brilliant company of officers were the Duke of
Berry and the Pretender, who served incognito as the
Chevalier de St. George. The chief command was invested
in the Dauphin's son, the Duke of Burgundy, who was,

[1] Coxe, vol ii , p 221 · Marlborough to the Queen, May 9, 1708.
[2] *Ibid* , p 222 Godolphin to Marlborough, April 29/May 10, 1708
[3] *Ibid* , p 225 The Queen to Marlborough, May 17, 1708
[4] *Ibid* , p 223: Godolphin to Marlborough, May 17, 1708
[5] *Ibid* , p 224. Marlborough to the Duchess, May 14, 1708.

however, instructed to bow to the decisions of Vendôme, whenever Vendôme proved obstinate.   It was a bad combination, a mixture, as Saint-Simon observed, of " fire and water."[1] For Burgundy was a devout and clean-living prince, as modest as he was conscientious, Vendôme a sluggard, a glutton, a practitioner of nameless vices, and notoriously conceited and self-confident.   Vendôme enjoyed a certain popularity among the soldiery; but the general-officers entertained a profound mistrust of his leadership, and looked to Burgundy to curb the excesses of his incurable optimism.   The situation, which resulted, was really an impossible one, and it was not unknown to Marlborough, who never failed to study, and to profit by, the personal idiosyncrasies of the commanders opposed to him.   For the rest, the Elector of Bavaria was transferred to the Rhine, where he was associated with the Duke of Berwick, Villars, greatly to his own disgust, being removed to Dauphiné   Orléans and Noailles remained in Spain.

The magnitude of the French army and the presence of the princes, who were all eager for distinction, encouraged Marlborough to anticipate a battle, or operations that must soon result in one.   But from the very outset the plans of the French were lacking in decision.   At the time when the expedition to Scotland was in preparation, the Comte de Bergueick, a Flemish noble, whose knowledge of his countrymen was as great as the influence which he possessed over them, proposed to Louis a plan for recovering the Spanish Netherlands by the connivance of the principal inhabitants of the great towns   As Marlborough had long been aware, the people were extremely dissatisfied with the new administration   " The Dutch," says Burnet, though he was ever their partisan, " were severe masters, and the Flandrians could not bear it; though the French had laid heavier taxes on them, yet they used them better in all other respects."[2]   Bergueick's design was cordially approved at Versailles, but as it was in part dependent on the Pretender's success in Scotland, it had eventually dropped   A correspondence with the disaffected Flemings however, was still maintained   The departure of the

[1] Saint-Simon, vol. xi , p 106   [2] Burnet, vol iv , p 190.

Elector, who in his capacity as governor had acquired no little popularity, especially among the ladies, increased the prevailing discontent, because it was regarded as an indication that the French were minded to make over the country to the Dutch as the price of peace. Bergueick had therefore no difficulty in organising a conspiracy for the surprise of Antwerp. When Marlborough was at Ghent, a letter, opened in the post, revealed the plot. The correspondence was permitted to continue, and was regularly tapped until the allies were in full possession of the facts. This enterprise, the success of which must have affected the movements of the French army, had now to be abandoned Louis had originally desired to begin the campaign with the siege of Huy. He was anxious to remove the war from Flanders, both because that country had suffered severely in the late campaign, and because it was specially adapted to combats of infantry, an arm in which Marlborough was rightly considered by the French to have all the advantage of quality. But in a dispatch of May 20, the King announced that he had changed his mind. He was afraid that a move towards the Meuse might be answered by a move towards the Schelde. Vendôme was surprised. He still adhered to the idea of besieging Huy. But Burgundy, who regarded such an operation as beneath his dignity, favoured a direct march on Brussels. Vendôme agreed. Considering that they enjoyed a numerical superiority of at least 10,000 over Marlborough's forces, the decision was a correct one. Unfortunately for them, they did not abide by it. On May 26, they crossed the Haine and advanced to Soignies. Simultaneously, Marlborough, who had been collecting his army at Anderlecht, moved out to Hal. Thereupon the French stopped dead. Burgundy was anxious to press on through Braine and Tubize; but Vendôme contended that Marlborough's position was too strong to be attacked, and once more reverted to the idea of besieging Huy Heavy rains threatened to paralyse both armies. But the French continually gave out that they were "resolved to venture a battle."[1] On the 29th, "to show them we will not decline it,"[2] Marlborough again

[1] Murray, vol iv, p. 35 Marlborough to Boyle, May 28, 1708. [2] *Ibid.*

advanced, and encamped between Lembecq and Herffelingen.
But Vendôme and Burgundy could think of nothing more
original than the strategy of the preceding campaign.
This strategy consisted in a march towards the Dyle, and
the occupation of some point whence they could threaten
Brussels, Louvain, and the places on the Meuse. Fearful
lest Marlborough should attack them on the road, they
took precautions to deceive him. On the 31st, they sent
away their heavy baggage; and the Duke, too hastily concluding that they meant, after all, to fight, ordered his army
to be ready to move at an hour's notice. But on June 1,
he learned that the baggage was countermanded, and that
the French had been busy foraging, as though they intended
to remain at Soignies On the morning of the 2nd, however,
at 8 a m., he was apprised that they had decamped on
the preceding evening, and had taken the road to Nivelles.
Divining their intention, he instantly fell back to Anderlecht, and marching all night, "in a heavy, thick rain,"[1]
passed round Brussels on the north side, and came, on
the afternoon of the 3rd, with a wet and weary army, to
Terbank, on the outskirts of Louvain. The French encamped between Braine l'Alleud and Genappe They had
accomplished one of those "daring marches," which they
affected to regard with so much satisfaction. The net
result was the reproduction of the situation of 1707, when
Marlborough had lain at Meldert and Vendôme and the
Elector at Gembloux It was a poor achievement for an
army which enjoyed a numerical advantage of 12 per cent.,
and comprised in its ranks some of the most renowned
regiments in Europe.

Relying as ever on "the goodness of the troops," Marlborough was perfectly confident of his ability to hold his
own until Eugène arrived He had already written, on
May 30, a letter, which was intended to be exhibited by
the Prince to the Elector of Hanover, and which depicted
the combination, secretly pre-arranged at the Hague, as
an excellent idea, suggested naturally by existing circumstances. On June 1, he instructed Captain Armstrong,
one of the assistant quartermasters, who in 1705 had studied

---

[1] *Millner's Journal*, p 210, June 22, 1708.

the country between the Moselle and the Meuse, to proceed to Coblenz and assist Eugène with his experience and counsel.   But these steps had been somewhat premature It had been part of the project, as approved both at Hanover and the Hague, that the three armies should assemble simultaneously between May 20 and 25   But Marlborough's was the only one which was punctual in the field.   When the Duke arrived at Terbank on June 3, the army of the Moselle was but partly formed, artillery and horses were lacking, Eugène had only quitted Vienna the day before, and the Elector, who was reported to be " very much out of humour,"[1] had not yet got as far as Frankfurt. The Elector Palatine, who had refused to allow his contingent of 10,000 men to march to the Moselle until he could obtain the investiture of the Upper Palatinate from the Emperor, had at last given orders to the troops to start; but two days later, some new difficulty having arisen with Vienna, he had revoked those orders.   " You may by this see," wrote Marlborough to Godolphin on the 4th, " the great advantage the King of France has over the allies, since we depend upon the humours of several princes, and he has nothing but his own will and pleasure "[2]   Ten days later, he learned from Rechteren that the army of the Moselle could not be expected " till the beginning of July " He forwarded Rechteren's letter to Godolphin, that the Queen and the Cabinet might judge " how uncertain all measures taken with the Germans are."[3]   He himself, remembering his own bitter experience of 1705, could hardly have been surprised.   " The slowness of the Germans is such," he wrote to the Duchess, " that we must be always disappointed."[4]   And to Godolphin he observed, " Patience is a virtue absolutely necessary, when one is obliged to keep measures with such people."[5]   As for Vienna, he doubtless agreed with Hare, whose comment was· " That Court plays the fool eternally."[6]

Nevertheless, the Duke realised that his project was

[1] Coxe, vol ii , p 236 Marlborough to Godolphin, May 17, 1708
[2] Ibid , p 240 Marlborough to Godolphin, June 4, 1708.
[3] Ibid , p 242 Marlborough to Godolphin, June 14, 1708
[4] Ibid , p 241 Marlborough to the Duchess, June 11, 1708
[5] Ibid , p 242 Marlborough to Godolphin, June 14, 1708
[6] Hare MSS . Letter of June 11, 1708 (Hist MSS Comm , 14th Report Appendix, part ix , p 216)

already partly spoiled. He had hoped that a rapid concentration of the army of the Moselle would compel both Vendôme and the Elector of Bavaria to detach troops to that quarter, and that before the French could understand or counteract his strategy, a great blow might be struck in Flanders, and possibly another on the Rhine. But as the matter was managed, or rather mismanaged, the French paid little attention to the Moselle until June 5, when Berwick and Max Emanuel, leaving their main army to watch the Germans on the Rhine, carried to the Saar a reinforcement, which raised the number of French troops in that region to 35,000. It was already suspected at Versailles that the army assembling at Coblenz was destined, not for Lorraine, but for the Netherlands. But as the distance from Trèves to Genappe was much shorter than the distance from Coblenz to Louvain, Berwick, if he kept himself well informed, could probably hope to outmarch Eugène, or at least to reach the scene of action at the same time. Marlborough realised that a surprise on a grand scale was now impossible "For a beginning," he wrote on the 11th, to Eugène, "we can rely only on the cavalry, with which I request you to hasten in all diligence. . . . If the Palatines are not yet arrived, you will please not to wait for them. . . If you can gain only forty-eight hours, I will make my dispositions for the moment of your arrival; and with the blessing of Heaven, we may profit so well by the two days as to feel the good effects of it the rest of the campaign."[1]

Meanwhile, chronic irresolution had reduced the army of Burgundy and Vendôme to complete inactivity. Vendôme insisted still upon the siege of Huy, and at last induced the King to give his consent. But Burgundy delayed, and sent a protest to Versailles. Finally, the King decided that, in view of the strong probability of a junction between Marlborough and Eugène, the siege of Huy must not be undertaken. Vendôme was indignant, but to little purpose Marlborough perceived with satisfaction that it was not the Germans alone who were wasting all the month of June. He himself, however, was not altogether idle.

[1] Coxe, vol. ii , p. 243. Marlborough to Eugène, June 11, 1708.

He spent some days in a businesslike inspection of his forces He was more than satisfied with their condition. " It would gratify Your Highness to see them,"[1] he wrote to Eugène The British cavalry " appeared with a great deal of distinction," and the Prussians, both horse and foot, were universally admired. One and all, they were "eager to engage an enemy they despised."

Occupation less agreeable was provided for his leisure by the English mails Godolphin continued to lament the obstinacy of the Queen, whom he begged " to dismiss him and not let him bear the burden of other people's follies."[2] He continued also to criticise the attitude of Prince George and of Admiral Churchill. He warned the Duke that, " unless it may consist with Mr. Freeman's affairs to see England and settle measures both with me and the Queen before the meeting of Parliament,"[3] he could not face another session. The general election was now in progress. The results, which were regularly reported to Marlborough, were distinctly adverse both to Harley and " the Tackers." But the government were gravely embarrassed by the action of the Junta, who, having decided to give another turn to the screw, took the field as an absolutely independent party. To secure a majority of the Scottish peers, they even coalesced with the Jacobites. They exerted, or pretended to have exerted, their influence on behalf of the persons arrested in Scotland on suspicion of complicity with the attempted invasion, and Newcastle, Wharton, and Halifax stood bail for Hamilton. They endeavoured to discredit the Earl of Mar, who was managing the candidature of the government's supporters. Sunderland himself took an active and prominent part in this discreditable intrigue. By his letters to various Scottish noblemen, he succeeded in diverting votes, on the very eve of the election, from the friends of the ministry to which he belonged to the nominees of the Junta Writing to the Duke of Roxburgh, this remarkable Secretary of State declared that the new Parliament would be " the most Whig Parliament by an extraordinary majority, and consequently the best Parliament

---

[1] Coxe, vol ii , p 243 Marlborough to Eugène, June 11, 1708.
[2] Ibid p 229 Godolphin to Marlborough, June 24, 1708.   [3] Ibid

that ever we saw." "And the Court," he added, "will be
forced to give in to it "[1] Yet no member of the Junta had
been louder than Sunderland in denouncing Harley for
disloyalty to his chief and to his colleagues. But it was
necessary, at all costs, to maintain the permanent, but
slender, Whig majority in the House of Lords By these
methods and especially by the canvassing of Hamilton and
the Jacobite prisoners, the Junta established a powerful
interest among the Scottish peers Strong complaints of
these extraordinary proceedings, and especially of "the
influence from London," exercised by the Queen's "immediate servants," were forwarded from Edinburgh to Anne
by the Earl of Mar.[2] Anne was furious. She informed
Mar that she was very sensible of the "ill-treatment"
which she was receiving, and "which," she said, "I do
resent extremely."[3] She accused the Secretary of State of
prostituting his ministerial office and degrading the royal
authority for the ends of faction. She even threatened to
dismiss him from her service. Marlborough was eventually
compelled to intervene on behalf of his son-in-law. But
Marlborough and Godolphin shared to the full in the
indignation of the Queen. The Duke, as a Scottish peer,
transmitted his proxy to the Earl of Mar, to use as the
Earl thought best; the Presbyterians supported the government, and in the end the Junta were beaten by 10 to 6.
Mar reported that, in the circumstances, the result was
good, but that it ought to have been better. The political
situation was still further complicated by an attempt of
the Duke of Somerset to reconstitute Harley's system, but
on a basis of moderate Whiggery The Queen was pleased;
but the Junta accused Marlborough of encouraging Somerset
to create a division in the ranks of their party Marlborough disclaimed all interest in the design But the
wrigglings of his various victims have never yet been
known to melt the heart of the professional blackmailer.
The Junta continued on their turbulent course They

[1] MSS of the Earl of Mar and Kellie· Notes of the Earl of Sunderland's
letter to the Duke of Roxburgh, June, 1708 (Hist MSS Comm , p 448).
[2] *Ibid* · The Earl of Mar to the Queen, June 14, 1708 (Hist MSS. Comm.,
p 445).
[3] *Ibid* : Queen Anne to the Earl of Mar, June 24, 1708 (Hist. MSS.
Comm , p 453)

even threatened to revive the old Tory project of an invitation to some member of the House of Hanover to reside in England. Apparently there was no trick of the party game, however disreputable, to which they were not willing to descend.

At last, to his intense relief, Marlborough learned on the 23rd that the trouble with the Elector Palatine was settled, and that Eugène's army would be ready in a few days to take the road. The Duke's letter of May 30, intended for use as against the Elector of Hanover, was now obsolete. He therefore provided Eugène with a second edition, modified to meet the altered circumstances, and even more artfully worded than the first. Eugène, who was afraid that the Elector might endeavour to hinder his departure, did not propose to forward a copy of this document till the night before he marched. On the 25th, Marlborough himself, in writing to the Elector, to congratulate him on the recent arrival of the Electoral Prince at Louvain, respectfully stated the case in favour of the impending movement. On the 27th, he wrote once more to Eugène, promising to send Cadogan to meet him at Maestricht, and reminding him that everything depended " on the diligence of the cavalry in gaining some days "[1] on the cavalry of Berwick. On July 1, he learned that the march from the Moselle had begun on June 29. He therefore communicated an exact account of the situation to the States-General. " As soon as the cavalry shall approach," he said, " we shall move directly upon the enemy, and bring on a battle."[2] He had already written two letters to his wife. " You are so kind," he observed in one, " to be in pain what may happen when Prince Eugène comes. Put your trust in God, as I do, and be assured that I think I can't be unhappy as long as you are kind."[3] In the other, " I earnestly long," he exclaimed, " for doing something that may put an end to this war, so that I might have the happiness of being in quiet with you "[4]

The French, in the meantime, had not been wholly idle.

[1] Murray, vol iv., p 86 Marlborough to the Prince of Savoy, June 27, 1708.
[2] Ibid , p 94· Marlborough to the States-General, July 2, 1708.
[3] Coxe, vol. ii., p. 228 Marlborough to the Duchess, June 25, 1708
[4] Ibid , p. 229· Marlborough to the Duchess, July 1, 1708

Reluctant to let go of all the threads of the grand conspiracy which he had woven in the spring, and undeterred by the recent miscarriage at Antwerp, Bergueick had put forward a plan for the surprise of Brussels. The execution of it being deemed too difficult, he next proposed a scheme for the seizure of Ghent and Bruges, which was approved at Versailles. The secret was well kept. Marlborough obtained no inkling of it, but on July 2, he was aware that the enemy were contemplating an early move,[1] and he ordered his army to be ready to decamp at an hour's warning. On the 3rd, Vendôme sent out a detachment of 2,000 horse and 2,000 grenadiers in the direction of Enghien, as if to forage. But on the 4th they passed the Dendre at Ninove, and dashed forward upon Ghent. At the same time, another detachment under La Motte was moving from the lines of Comines upon Bruges. At 7 o'clock, on the evening of the 4th, Vendôme and Burgundy suddenly struck their tents, and marched in four columns on the way to Tubize. It rained heavily from 10 onwards, and the roads were bad, but they passed the Senne at Tubize soon after sunrise on the 5th and pressed on towards Ninove. Presently the rain ceased. At midday they were resting on the banks of the Zuerbeek, when an express galloped in with the news that Ghent had been taken that morning with the connivance of the citizens. They immediately resumed their march.

It was noon on the 4th before Marlborough learned of the departure of the detachment of horse and grenadiers; and it was after 10 at night when he first heard that the whole French army was moving towards the Senne. Ignorant of their intentions, but resolved to keep close touch, he waited only for confirmation of the news, and then decamped at 2 on the morning of the 5th. At the same hour he dispatched an express to Major-General Murray, who commanded a small body of troops in the neighbourhood of Ghent, with orders to throw a British regiment into Audenarde, which was weakly garrisoned. Despite the softness of the roads, his columns were skirting the north

[1] Hare MSS, July 2, 1708 (Hist MSS Comm., 14th Report, Appendix, part ix, p 217)

side of Brussels at midday, when he learned that the enemy's detachment had passed the Dendre at Alost, and had broken down the bridges in its rear. Goslinga, who was at Brussels at the time, and not with the army, declares that the Duke received the news from Alost at 10, but Marlborough's own dispatch to Boyle, written on the same day, fixes the hour as noon. Goslinga boasts that he himself knew instinctively that Ghent was betrayed. He contends that Marlborough ought to have known it too, and that the army ought to have marched straight for Alost, though he does not explain how any such movement could have saved Ghent. Marlborough's dispatch to Boyle gives no indication that the Duke suspected treachery; but if he suspected it, he must have known that nothing could be done. On the reasonable assumption that the detachment might be meditating a raid, he ordered Bothmar with 2,000 cavalry and dragoons to pass the Dendre at Dendermonde, " to observe them and to protect the Pays de Waes."[1] But instead of uncovering the capital and plunging out into the unknown, he very properly decided to keep as near as possible to the French army, which he always regarded as his true objective. He therefore continued his own march in the direction of Anderlecht. That afternoon his advanced parties were sighted in the neighbourhood of Goyck by the weary columns of Vendôme and Burgundy, as they trudged from the Zuerbeek on the road to Ninove. At 5.30, Marlborough, who had passed a sleepless night, was resting on a bed at Anderlecht, when a report of the enemy's proximity came in from Goyck He mounted his horse, and at 6.30 rode out to reconnoitre. According to Goslinga, who accompanied him, he proceeded a good half-league, remarked that it was then too late to accomplish anything, and returned to Anderlecht. Goslinga, who, by his own account, was anxious to prolong the ride, alleges that the Dutch general, Welderen, urged him and another field-deputy, Gueldermalsen, to summon the generals to a council, but that out of a mistaken consideration for the Duke, they refused. Such unusual delicacy on their part certainly deserved to be recorded.

[1] Murray, vol iv , p. 96. Marlborough to Boyle, July 5, 1708

It was true that a portion of the French army was taking dangerous risks Marlborough's right, which encamped at Lennick St. Quentin, lay within striking distance of their line of march. But it did not finish its sixteen hours' tramp till 6 that evening, and the left did not finally get into Anderlecht till 2 the next morning, and even then the artillery had not arrived If the march of the allies had finished two or three hours before it did, the French could hardly have escaped a disaster.[1] But as it was, darkness would have descended before anything material could be effected. Realising that Marlborough's judgment was correct, Goslinga falls back upon the assertion that the necessary hours of daylight had been thrown away by the Duke himself, who had conducted the whole movement in a casual and dilatory fashion He makes no reference to the rain, or the condition of the roads. As he did not accompany the troops, his evidence, apart from the malicious bias which always attaches to it where Marlborough's reputation is concerned, possesses no special value. The map shows that the allies travelled at least as fast as the French.

At 6 o'clock, when Burgundy and Vendôme perceived the right of Marlborough's army at Lennick St. Quentin, they had already taken precautions to secure the uninterrupted progress of their columns until nightfall at least. Albergotti was detached with four brigades of infantry to cover the exposed flank Advancing to within half a league of the mill of Goyck, he occupied a position barring the approaches to the line of march The officers, commanding on the allied right, misjudged the nature of this movement, and sent word to Anderlecht that the French army had halted. Marlborough, who had now returned from his ride, was discussing the general situation with Tilly, Dopf, and Goslinga. Goslinga was suggesting that the enemy's rear-guard might be attacked in the morning, and Dopf was arguing that the ground was unfavourable. Then came a second message from the right Bülow reported that, according to the statements of deserters, the whole French

---

[1] Hare MSS , July 8, 1708 (Hist. MSS Comm , 14th Report, Appendix, part ix., p. 217).

army was preparing to attack. Other and more alarming messages followed. Albergotti had made his dispositions with so much skill that he completely imposed upon the officers confronting him, and succeeded in convincing them that Vendôme and Burgundy intended to fling their entire force upon Marlborough's right flank Yet, at this very time, the French columns were traversing the Dendre at Ninove. The passage began at 8.

On this occasion Marlborough was not well served by his intelligence department. Cadogan, who had gone to Maestricht to meet Eugène, was sorely missed. Acting on the erroneous information received from the right, the Duke transferred thirty battalions and forty squadrons to that quarter, and ordered the remainder of the army to be under arms at dawn Although he was "mightily indisposed for want of rest,"[1] he left his bed at 1 a m in response to an urgent summons, and after prayers drove off in a chaise towards the point of danger. He found Bulow and the other generals at the mill of Lombeek. In that mysterious twilight which precedes the dawn, they could all see what they expected to see and some could even count the squadrons and battalions in the opposing line of battle But when the shadows melted from the landscape, not a Frenchman was visible. After some discussion, a detachment was thrown forward towards Ninove. At 6 it overtook the enemy's rear-guard, and captured 300 prisoners and a column of mules and baggage. But by 7 Vendôme and Burgundy had completed the passage of the Dendre, having made, in the words of Marlborough's chaplain, "one of the boldest marches in the world."[2]

So bold it was that its final stages were attended by a degree of precipitation, disorder, and desertion, not far removed from panic. Throughout the night, the whole of the artillery and baggage had remained on the south side of the river, the horses being too exhausted to proceed. Had Marlborough known the facts, and pressed forward with the bulk of his army before sunrise, he must have reaped a considerable advantage. It is probable that "this fair chance of retrieving all at once," as Hare calls it,

[1] Hare MSS , July 8, 1708.   [2] Ibid.

would not have been lost, if Cadogan had been there. For
Cadogan would have known " the difference between their
coming to us and marching by us "[1]

That day the French encamped at Lede between the
Dendre and the Schelde. In this position they covered
Ghent and threatened Brussels   Marlborough was greatly
troubled. He now learned that Ghent had opened its gates
to the enemy on the morning of the 5th. The treason
was flagrant, for at 8 a m., when the French were not yet
entirely in possession, Murray had been refused admission
by the citizens. A few hours later, Bruges had suffered
the same fate as Ghent. Marlborough, who had long been
aware of the secret hostility of the people to their present
rulers, knew not where next the blow might fall, or which
of the fruits of Ramillies might next be stolen from him.
" The States," he wrote to Godolphin, " have used this
country so ill that I no ways doubt but all the towns . . .
will play us the same trick as Ghent has done, whenever
they have it in their power "[2] Brussels was his chief
anxiety. To cover the capital, and to intimidate the
French partisans among its inhabitants, he moved the
army to Assche, where they encamped on the morning of
the 6th. Goslinga, of course, objected. He advised the
Duke to pass the Schelde, and ensure the safety of Audenarde
and Menin. But Marlborough was resolved to go to Assche,
and await Eugène. He must have needed all his wonderful
patience to endure the chatter of Goslinga. Official personages of Goslinga's class and nationality were directly
responsible for the dangerous and embarrassing disaffection
of the Spanish Netherlands.

From Assche Marlborough sent an express to the governor
of Antwerp, warning him to be on the alert, and promising to
assist him, if possible, with two companies of dragoons. He
sent another to the governor of Dendermonde, urging him to
endeavour to throw two or three hundred men into the castle
of Ghent, which still held out   The governor of Audenarde
acted with all the vigour and resolution which the emergency
required   Knowing that parties of French cavalry were

[1] *Ibid*
[2] Coxe vol ii , p. 252. Marlborough to Godolphin, July 9, 1708.

prowling in the neighbourhood, he summoned the magistrates, and having told them plainly that he had no doubt of his ability to hold the place against the enemy without, he warned them that, at the first symptom of treachery within, he would fire the town in several quarters This speech produced an admirable effect   On the 9th, Chanclos, the governor of Ath, entered Audenarde with reinforcements. Chanclos was acting under orders from Marlborough, who chose this course in preference to the suggestion of Goslinga that two battalions should be sent to the town from Anderlecht through a country, in which every second person was a spy, and in which the enemy's cavalry were roaming at large.

When Marlborough arrived at Assche, he found Cadogan and Eugène. The Prince's foot were still several marches from the Meuse; his horse were approaching that river; but he himself, with an escort of a hundred hussars, had dashed on to join the Duke. His coming was hailed with delight by the entire army. Goslinga says that both Cadogan and Eugène considered the movement to Assche a mistake, and asked him who was responsible for it, and that he laughingly replied to the Prince, " Lord, if thou hadst been here, my brother had not died."[1] This story is intended to show the author's wit, as well as his intimate relations with the great, it reveals him in fact as a blasphemer and a snob. It also marks the opening of a new line of attack on Marlborough. Henceforward the Duke is depicted not only as prolonging the war for selfish ends, but also as reaping laurels which belonged in reality to Eugène

The Prince reported to Vienna that he found the English staff considerably demoralised by recent events   He and Cadogan between them speedily restored confidence. Both Marlborough and Eugène agreed at once that the enemy must be brought to battle. It is said[2] that Marlborough would have preferred to effect a junction with the army of the Moselle in the first instance, but that he was dissuaded from this course by Eugène, who prophesied that, if the French were given time enough, they would show

[1] *Mémoires de Goslinga*, p 51
[2] *Mémoires du Prince Eugène (Campagne des Pays-Bas avec Marlborough)*, p 77.

a clean pair of heels. None knew better than Marlborough their predilection for this form of strategy. But he may naturally have desired to adhere to the original plan of campaign, more especially as Eugène's men had secured a lead over Berwick's Whatever may have passed in private between the two commanders, no hint of any divergency of views could have reached the ears of the Dutch generals or field - deputies. Otherwise Goslinga would not have failed to draw the usual moral. But he merely records that it was unanimously decided to march, as soon as ever the army was rested, and to pass the Dendre at Lessines before the French could occupy that post. By this movement, Audenarde, Menin, and possibly the castle of Ghent, were to be saved But the real object of Marlborough and Eugène was not the preservation of fortresses, but the destruction of the enemy. If they could once interpose between the French army and the frontiers of France, a battle would be almost certain. For Vendôme and Burgundy must either fight their way through, or abandon the rich cities and fertile provinces of the northeast to the mercies of the invader.

The capture of Ghent and Bruges created an undue elation at the court of Louis,[1] where many people imagined, as many people imagine in England at the present time, that successful war can be waged without bloodshed. Nor did the French generals themselves appreciate the true position. " Marlborough has been caught this time,"[2] wrote the exultant Burgundy, while Vendôme appears to have relapsed into his natural indolence. They did not realise that, as long as Marlborough remained unbeaten in the field, their conquests rested on no solid foundation Even less did they realise that now was pre-eminently the time to strike. The numerical superiority was still theirs; but in a few days it would be theirs no longer, for the army of the Moselle was approaching, and approaching more rapidly than their own reinforcements under Berwick. Their soldiers were in high spirits, which would be all the higher if the order were given to attack the enemy. It was a fair chance;

---

[1] Saint-Simon, vol xi , p 205.
[2] Vogüé, *Le duc de Bourgogne*, p 53: Lettre du 6 juillet.

and it was the last which offered in that campaign, and indeed, in the remainder of the war. Yet Vendôme and Burgundy did not so much as see it. They had their own plans; and the plan of Vendôme possessed nothing in common with the plan of Burgundy save feebleness. In the face of commanders, informed with the true spirit of war, the French generals were discussing which fortress to invest and which river to defend. Vendôme proposed to besiege Audenarde, while the covering army encamped at Lessines on the Dendre. Burgundy proposed to besiege Menin, while the covering army entrenched itself near Audenarde, and fortified all the passages of the Schelde. These hopeful schemes were both submitted to Versailles for judgment. When the answer arrived, it was already obsolete. Marlborough and Eugène had determined the issue in a manner very disconcerting to both appellants.

XX.—OUDENARDE[1]

IF Burgundy and Vendôme could have perceived that the only road to follow was the road to Assche, and could have summoned up courage to follow it without waiting to consult Versailles, Sunday, July 8, would have been an admirable day for the attempt. On Saturday afternoon Eugène had departed for Brussels on a visit to his mother, whom he had not seen for 25 years. Marlborough had arranged to be in the capital on Sunday. So accurately had they gauged the calibre of their antagonists that they were both content to be absent from the army together at the very moment when a decisive struggle ought to have been imminent. But when Sunday came, Marlborough was too unwell to transact business. He was suffering from fever, the result, as he himself said, of " the treachery of Ghent, continual marching, and some letters I have received from England."[2] One general being away, and the other incapacitated, the chances of the French were certainly fairer than they had any right to expect. " His Grace," wrote Hare, " has been confined to his bed all day by a hot fever-fit, but something he took in the afternoon carried it off, with a gentle sweat, and he was much mended."[3] His condition, however, still gave anxiety to the doctor, who urged his removal to Brussels. But the Duke refused to quit the camp. The army was to start at dawn on Monday He intended to accompany it. For he could not entrust to others the execution of strategy which, at a few hours' notice, might precipitate a battle.

That Sunday, four battalions were sent in to Brussels to reinforce the garrison, Cadogan set off with a detach-

[1] Following the plan adopted in the spelling of Blenheim and Blindheim, Oudenarde will be used for the battle and Audenarde for the place — G W. T.
[2] Coxe, vol. ii., p. 252. Marlborough to the Treasurer, July 9, 1708
[3] Hare MSS , July 8, 1708 (Hist MSS Comm , 14th Report, Appendix, part ix , p 218)

ment to prepare the ways in the direction of Enghien; and by an order of unexampled severity, the interposition of baggage on the line of route was sternly prohibited.

At 2 a.m., on the morning of Monday the 9th, the army decamped They moved in four columns, two of infantry in the centre, and one of cavalry on either flank Albemarle, with thirty squadrons and all the grenadiers, was directed to cover the rear, and to guard against the possibility of a dash by the French upon Brussels. The weather was beautiful The regulation as to baggage was strictly observed. There were no stragglers and no laggards. Every man stepped out with a will, for every man deemed it a point of honour to chastise the foe before the Imperialists arrived. The order and celerity of their march impressed all who witnessed it. Before 11 they had passed the village of Herffelingen, five leagues from Assche. Then the Duke, who " in all appearance was very well," called a halt, and commanded the tents to be set up [1]

Vendôme and Burgundy received the reports of Marlborough's departure from Assche with a somewhat languid interest. It undoubtedly surprised them, because they had imagined that he would be afraid to uncover Brussels. But they were too well satisfied with the progress of their own designs to feel any anxiety about his. La Motte had stormed the post of Plasschendaele on the Bruges canal. The castle of Ghent had surrendered on Sunday morning. A detachment of their horse was already investing Audenarde, for pending a response from Versailles, they were proceeding on the assumption that Vendôme's plan would be ultimately adopted. Marlborough's precise aim, which was not certainly disclosed by the march to Herffelingen, remained for them a matter of conjecture. They deemed it more than possible that he was meditating the investment of Namur or Charleroi, as though he would compensate himself for the loss of Flemish towns by the capture of Walloon ones. So incapable they were of understanding the art of war as it was understood by Marlborough and Eugène. Like Tallard, Marsin, and Max Emanuel on the eve of Blenheim, they lived in a world constructed of their own hypotheses

[1] Hare MSS., July 9, 1708

and bounded by the canons and the maxims beloved of all second-rate exponents of the art.

But inasmuch as Marlborough at Herffelingen was within a march of the position at Lessines which Vendôme designed to occupy during the siege of Audenarde, the French commanders struck their camp at 3 in the afternoon and moved towards Ninove. At Ninove they would be nearer than the enemy to Lessines. But they started late, and they did not hurry. Their spies having reported that the allied army had not only halted but had pitched its tents, Burgundy and Vendôme concluded that Marlborough proposed to spend the night at Herffelingen They reasoned exactly as the Duke intended them to reason.

At 4 in the afternoon Cadogan set off with eight battalions and eight squadrons on the road to Lessines. At sunset, the whole army decamped, and followed Cadogan. Eugène, who had now rejoined from Brussels, rode with them. In the darkness, Marlborough and his horse fell into a big ditch. At midnight, 800 of Cadogan's men crossed the Dendre, and occupied the town of Lessines. The rest of the detachment arrived at 4 a.m. on Tuesday, and posting themselves upon the left bank of the river, began to construct bridges. Marching steadily throughout the night, Marlborough's columns made a brief halt at Ghislenghien soon after daybreak, and reached the Dendre about 11 They had now completed another five leagues. Without delay they traversed the bridges, and set up their tents on the very ground which Vendôme and Burgundy had selected for themselves.

The vanguard of the French had arrived at Voorde, to the west of Ninove, about midnight. Here they must have learned before many hours had elapsed that Cadogan was in Lessines. They must have learned also that the allies had quitted Herffelingen. A council of war was held. It was evident now that Vendôme's plan was impracticable, and it was decided to fall back on Burgundy's. Orders of recall were dispatched to the squadrons investing Audenarde. The army turned to the right, and after a halt of two hours, took the road to Gavre, intending to pass the Schelde on Wednesday. Their leisurely procedure shows that the French generals had entirely failed to penetrate the design of their antagonists. In the course of the morning, they were informed by their spies, who had seen some tents hung up to dry during the halt at Ghislenghien,[1] that Marlborough had encamped there, and that he did not intend to join Cadogan until Wednesday. This report only confirmed them in their belief that the Duke's strategy was purely defensive, that the initiative remained with them, and that there was no occasion for haste. Later in the day, they must have learned that Marlborough was passing the Dendre. But inasmuch as the last of his weary columns did not get into Lessines before midnight, their sense of security remained undisturbed.

At 1 o'clock, on the morning of Wednesday the 11th, Cadogan and Rantzau quitted the camp at Lessines with sixteen battalions, eight squadrons of Hanoverian dragoons, and thirty-two guns. Their instructions were, to prepare the roads in the direction of Audenarde for the march of the allied columns, and to bridge the Schelde a little above the village of Eename, which is a mile below the town. When Cadogan reached the hills overlooking Eename, he could descry the French army six miles to the northward and still upon the same side of the river as himself. By 10 30 the whole of his detachment had arrived. The work of laying the pontoons began immediately Already the French were seen to be in motion to pass the Schelde by bridges which they had previously prepared By noon Cadogan's task was completed Rantzau crossed at once with the eight squadrons of Hanoverian dragoons, and Cadogan followed with twelve battalions of foot The other four battalions remained to guard the pontoons.

Moving due north, Cadogan and Rantzau advanced to the edge of a marshy stream, which flows into the Schelde over against Eename Here they halted, the infantry on the right and the dragoons on the left. In this position they covered the projected passage of the allied army. For beyond the stream, and opposite to the twelve battalions of foot, stood the village of Eyne, where the road from Ghent to Audenarde is joined by the road which runs parallel to the left bank of the Schelde; and by one or other

[1] *Leben und Denkwürdigkeiten Reichsgrafen von der Schulenburg*, p. 326.

of these two approaches the French, who were now traversing the river at Gavre, must defile to the attack.

Meantime, the allied army had decamped from Lessines
between 7 and 8, and was moving rapidly in four columns
upon Audenarde. They had five leagues to travel, and
the ways were none too good, but the bearing of the soldiers
exhibited no trace of the fatigues which they had already
undergone. Eager as they always were to follow the Duke
to battle, they were marching now as if every man hoped
to avenge a private quarrel. And every man, in fact,
regarded the betrayal of Ghent and Bruges as a personal
affront to himself. When horsemen from Cadogan rode
up with the good tidings that the French had not yet passed
the Schelde, but were still in the very act of passing it,
a thrill of stern delight ran down the dusty columns.
They needed neither command nor exhortation to urge
them to the front. Spontaneous enthusiasm drove them
forward at an ever quickening pace. Some baggage-
waggons, which in defiance of the Duke's express regulation,
appeared upon the line of march, were instantly overturned
and rifled of their contents. Nothing in the whole war
was quite like the demeanour of Marlborough's men on the
day of Oudenarde Convinced of their own superiority,
and supremely confident in their commander's skill, they
were seething with suppressed indignation against an
enemy, who ever since his defeat at Ramillies had been
acquiring a sort of spurious reputation by successful running
away, and who had recently achieved a conquest which
every man in the allied ranks roundly denounced as un-
soldierlike and unfair.

Cadogan, having posted his detachment, rode on to
reconnoitre. The vanguard of the French, consisting of
twenty squadrons and seven Swiss battalions under Biron,
had already crossed the Schelde. Totally unconscious of
the enemy's proximity, Biron's foragers were busy in the
fields about Heurne. Cadogan saw them, and ordered
Rantzau's dragoons to advance. Rantzau succeeded in
capturing some prisoners, but the fugitives warned Biron,
who, hastening to the scene with twelve squadrons, compelled Rantzau to retire to his original position. Biron

rode as far as Eyne, whence he plainly saw the twelve battalions beyond the stream, and the four which guarded the pontoons. He saw also a long column of Prussian cavalry descending from the hills above Eename, and already traversing the bridges at a rapid trot. Leaving one half of their horse to screen the right flank of the army's march, Marlborough and Eugène had dashed forward with the other half at the gallop. They had reached the hills soon after noon.

Biron was amazed Judging from what he saw that he was confronted by the whole of the allied forces, he instantly dispatched the news to Vendôme and Burgundy, while he himself retired with his twelve squadrons to Heurne.

It must have been 1 o'clock or thereabouts, and half the French army had crossed the Schelde, when Biron's first report arrived at headquarters. Two courses were now open to the French commanders. Parallel to the stream, behind which Cadogan's men were posted, and about three miles to the north of it, runs a longer and a larger stream, the Norken, which flows into the Schelde a little above Gavre Beyond the Norken stands the low plateau of Huysse, an admirable position, which the French could have occupied at their leisure, and which they might have defended with a reasonable prospect of success On the other hand, they had it in their power, by a swift offensive movement, to inflict a severe check, if not a grave disaster upon their daring foe ' Had they, without any delay, formed their line parallel to the Schelde, setting their left at Heurne, their centre at Eyne, and their right towards the outworks of Audenarde, they could have rolled Cadogan and Rantzau back into the river, and crushed the heads of the allied columns as fast as they arrived. A Berwick would have chosen the one course, a Villars the other Vendôme and Burgundy attempted both and accomplished neither.

Exactly how or why the French army came to be handled as it was handled will probably never be known. So many persons of importance were interested in misrepresenting the facts and in disclaiming responsibility for the result, that from the very outset the truth was obscured at its proper sources. It would appear, however, that Vendôme,

who habitually believed only what he desired to believe,
greeted the first report from Biron with incredulity. But
when a second and a third arrived he was compelled to act.
He ordered Biron to charge the enemy, and placing himself
at the head of the cavalry of the right wing, which included
the Household, he advanced to support the attack.
Burgundy followed with the rest of the army. Biron's
seven Swiss battalions occupied Heurne, whence four of
them subsequently pushed forward to Eyne His horse
were preparing to pass the stream, when Puységur, whose
topographical knowledge was highly esteemed, warned him
that the ground was impracticable. Then the Maréchal
de Matignon rode up, and forbade him to charge. Vendôme
was now approaching. Two hundred paces from Eyne he
was met by Puységur, who repeated the warning already
given to Biron, and recommended the occupation of a line
behind the Norken. Thereupon the offensive plan was
abandoned. The columns changed direction from left to
right, and moved towards the plateau of Huysse. Vendôme,
with the Household and the rest of the cavalry of the right
wing, accompanied them Only a dozen squadrons remained in the vicinity of Heurne. But the three battalions,
which had occupied that village, and the four, which had
occupied Eyne, were not withdrawn. Presumably they
were intended now to cover the flank of the army, as it
defiled towards the right If so, they were dangerously
exposed, and virtually unsupported.

Meanwhile, Marlborough and Eugène had not been idle.
They had passed one half of their cavalry over the bridges,
and ranged them on the northern side of Audenarde; and
they had posted a battery of six guns on the left of Rantzau's
dragoons. But without infantry they could do nothing.
They were, in fact, in peril of a sharp reverse. Horseman
after horseman dashed back along the road to Lessines
to urge the oncoming columns to the front But the allied
soldiery stood in no need of urging Like Nelson's men
at Trafalgar, they had but one idea, to close as swiftly as
possible with an elusive foe The very baggage-guards
deserted their charge, and joined in the impetuous rush
towards the Schelde.

Before 3 the infantry began to arrive. Cadogan, who had reported the presence of the Swiss at Eyne, and had been instructed to use his own discretion in regard to them, considered that his opportunity had come. He called up the brigade, which he had left behind to guard the pontoons, and with his other three he advanced to storm the village, while Rantzau and the eight squadrons passed the stream to the west, and threatened the line of the enemy's retreat. The leading brigade was Sabine's, which consisted of four British battalions. With bayonets fixed and firelocks shouldered, they moved proudly forward, as if to enter some citadel already fallen. Not a shot did they fire, and not until they came within pistol range of the enemy did they bring their bayonets to the charge. Their cold and haughty bearing, most eloquent of the temper of Marlborough's men that day, chilled the courage of the sturdy Swiss. The conflict was sharp, but very brief. Three battalions out of four laid down their arms. The fourth endeavoured to fall back along the highway to Heurne; but the Hanoverian dragoons, crossing the great road to Ghent, swept down upon the fugitives, killing, capturing, or dispersing all. The three battalions in Heurne, which had advanced to support their comrades, fled in panic towards the Norken. But Rantzau was not content with his easy triumph. Before him on a fair and open plain were twelve French squadrons. His own men, though inferior in numbers, were precisely in that mood which makes the mounted arm most formidable; and with them, conspicuous among a knot of high-born volunteers, rode their young Electoral Prince, the heir-presumptive to the British Crown. Without a moment's hesitation Rantzau flung them forward to the charge. The French cavalry, unnerved by the spectacle of the Switzers' fate, were already in full retreat towards the Norken and the sheltering enclosures on its southern banks, when the Hanoverians came up at the gallop, charged them instantly, and scattered them in shameful rout. Still pressing on towards the north, and driving the mob of terrified horsemen before him, Rantzau perceived the cavalry of the French rear-guard, defiling across his front. He was unsupported; but his men were well together, and their blood was up. Right into the flank of the astonished column broke the rabble of runaways, and close on their heels crashed the German troopers. In the confused combat which ensued, the Electoral Prince displayed the well-known valour of his race. His horse was brought down by a pistol-bullet in the neck, the Count Lusky was killed at his side. Several French regiments were entirely broken. The Hanoverians paid cheaply enough for their daring exploit. When Rantzau rallied them and drew them off towards Heurne, four French guns, which had been rushed up to the high ground near Mullem, opened fire, and fifteen or sixteen squadrons advanced at the gallop. Some confusion ensued, but it was only momentary. Presenting a firm front to the enemy, they eventually came off unpunished and unpursued. They brought with them as trophies of their victory a French colonel of cavalry, mortally wounded, and many other officers, besides ten standards, two pair of kettle-drums and some horses. No fewer than forty officers of the Swiss infantry, including Pfeiffer, a general of brigade, were already in Cadogan's hands.

It was 4 o'clock when the news of this brilliant success was passed backward to the Schelde. Along the ranks of the assembled troops, and all down the marching columns on the Lessines road, ran a thrill of savage exultation. But Marlborough knew well that the situation was still full of danger. Cadogan's cavalry had completely cleared the plain of the enemy's squadrons; and after capturing Eyne, his twelve battalions had advanced to Heurne. But Burgundy and Vendôme were now in position behind the Norken. If they threw their right wing forward, they could outflank Cadogan's detachment, and drive it into the Schelde. To resist such a manœuvre, very few of the allied infantry had as yet arrived. Fortunately, however, the nature of the ground was not very favourable to its execution.

The country between Audenarde and the Norken is flat. It is bounded on the south and east by the circuitous line of the Schelde, and on the west and north by a semi-circle of gentle upland. This semi-circle begins a little to the south of Eyne, and sweeping to the west by Bevere and the hill of Oycke, which is its highest summit, curves round behind the valley of the Norken till it gradually descends towards the Schelde over against Gavre. The northern side of it was already in possession of the French army, the southern was rapidly being occupied by the allied troops. From its western slopes two rivulets run eastward, parallel to the Norken and to one another. At a point called Groenewald, the northern rivulet turns at a right angle, and flowing due south for the distance of a mile, unites with the other at a point called Schaerken, where the two together form the stream behind which Cadogan had posted his detachment at noon. The line from Groenewald to Schaerken divided the battlefield of Oudenarde into two parts. On the east of it was the comparatively open plain of Heurne, where the Hanoverian dragoons had delivered their charges. On the west of it was country in which no cavalry could operate effectively. It was to a large extent enclosed, it was dotted with country houses and farm buildings; it was intercepted by lanes which were bordered by avenues of trees; and it was surrounded by streams, the banks of which were obstructed with coppice and underwood. Any forward movement of the French right wing must proceed across this difficult ground.

If the eastern bank of the rivulet from Groenewald to Schaerken were stoutly held, the manœuvre which Marlborough feared could be checked until sufficient infantry had arrived to enable the allies to take the offensive. But as yet, except for two Prussian battalions, which Cadogan had pushed up to Groenewald, and the six guns which the Duke had posted near Schaerken, this critical line lay altogether open to attack. The rest of Cadogan's detachment was watching the centre and left of the French army.

The choice before the French commanders was simple. Retreat, in the daylight, in any direction, was impracticable There were only two alternatives They might remain where they were, affecting to invite an onslaught which could hardly be delivered before the morrow, by which time they would have disappeared; or they might fall upon the fraction of the allied army, which they saw before them, and tumble it back into the Schelde. If they could have communicated with Versailles, they would have been instructed to pursue the former course, but tempted by the temerity of the enemy, and stung by the losses they had just incurred, they selected the latter.

At 4 o'clock, Burgundy directed Grimaldi to pass the Norken with sixteen squadrons of the right wing. It was the beginning of the movement dreaded by Marlborough. That movement was sound enough in conception, but because it eventually failed, Burgundy, who commanded it without consulting Vendôme, has of course been censured. As soon as Marlborough perceived Grimaldi's squadrons in motion, he ordered the rest of Cadogan's infantry to Groenewald, while he himself, with the Prussian cavalry, joined the Hanoverian dragoons on the plain of Heurne. Grimaldi led his squadrons across the Norken, traversed a small plateau, which was crowned by the windmill of Roijgem, and arrived at the brink of the northern rivulet. Here he halted, and having duly noted the intricate nature of the country and the dispositions which the enemy were making, he fell back to the windmill, and reported to Burgundy the result of his observations. Thereupon Burgundy directed six battalions of the King's regiment and the regiment of Poitou to drive the Prussians from Groenewald The Prussians, though outnumbered by three to one, met the assault with great firmness, and repulsed it   Vendôme hastened to the scene, and at once assumed control   He rallied the six battalions, reinforced them with another six of Picardy and Piedmont, and again advanced   At the same time, he ordered the remainder of the right wing, which contained the flower of the French infantry, to push steadily down towards the south, and wheeling to the left as fast as it arrived, to prolong the line from Groenewald to Schaerken.

But before Vendôme could engage the Prussians at Groenewald a second time, the rest of Cadogan's foot appeared, and posted themselves among the avenues, running northward from Groenewald to Herlegem.   In this situation they threatened the flank of the French columns descending towards Groenewald and Schaerken.

Thereupon, Vendôme attacked with fury from Herlegem to Groenewald, and under cover of this engagement, the whole of his right wing came into action as he had directed.

If this manœuvre had been accompanied by a simultaneous advance of the French left, the exposed portion of the allied army might have been crushed between the two converging attacks, or at any rate rolled back upon the Schelde. Vendôme dispatched the necessary orders to the left, but before they could be executed, Burgundy intervened. Burgundy had been advised that the ground to be traversed was impassable by reason of a swamp, which in fact had no existence. The French staff would appear to have been extremely ignorant of the country north of Audenarde. They were therefore at a disadvantage in comparison with Marlborough's officers, who at the close of the preceding campaign had been twice in the locality. By Burgundy's caution an excellent chance was lost. The French left, which, as it now disposed of ten cannon, had been converted into a force of all three arms, had only to cross the Norken as Marlborough had crossed the Nebel at Blenheim and the hollow road at Tirlemont. Doubtless, the allied cavalry would have rendered a good account of itself. But it would hardly have been in the power of cavalry alone to frustrate the operation.

It was 5, or later, before the offensive movement of the French right had fully developed. Marlborough watched it with intense anxiety. Horseman after horseman galloped back towards the river with urgent demands for infantry. From Herlegem to Groenewald, a stubborn contest was already raging; and from Herlegem to Schaerken, the French were pressing forward to the edge of the stream with loud shouts of " Vive le Roi ! " At this critical moment, Argyle came up with twenty battalions and took post upon Cadogan's left. He was instantly attacked with vigour all along the line. The French, continuing to arrive with great rapidity, soon outflanked Argyle at Schaerken. They deployed along the edge of the southern rivulet, crossed it, and occupied the farms and enclosures on the other bank, dislodging at the same time some Prussian regiments on Argyle's left. Here, however, they were checked by twenty battalions of Hanoverians and Prussians under Lottum. At 6 o'clock, Lottum advanced in turn, recovered the farms and enclosures, and forced the enemy back to their own side of the rivulet. Argyle's Prussians participated in this counter-stroke, and regained their positions at the point of the bayonet.

From 4 to 6 Marlborough had continued on the plain of Heurne, presiding over the combat between Herlegem and Groenewald, and anxiously watching the centre and left of the French army for the first sign of a forward movement. He now entrusted the command of the right to Eugène, who was always proud to have the leadership of English troops. He himself rode round towards his centre, where he found the twenty battalions of Lottum, which had just repulsed the enemy, and which were now securely established along the southern rivulet. Knowing that Eugène, who was already closely engaged with some of the finest infantry in the French army, might at any moment be attacked by the hostile centre and left, the Duke profited by the success of Lottum to transfer that general with his twenty battalions to the right wing. The interval, which was thus created, he filled at once by eighteen battalions of Dutch and Hanoverians, which had just arrived.

Eugène had now at his disposal no fewer than fifty-six battalions, or exactly half the infantry of the allied army And he needed them. The French had just expelled Cadogan's force from its position between Herlegem and Groenewald, and were driving it back across the plain towards the road to Ghent. With Lottum's help, the Prince checked their advance, broke their first line, and flung it back upon their second, which began to give way in turn, though here Vendôme, pike in hand, fought courageously at the head of his men Lottum, perceiving that, if the allies pushed on into the plain of Roijgem, they would be charged by the French horse, sent officer after officer to the rear for cavalry The Prussian general, Natzmer, with twenty squadrons responded to the call. The infantry opened to let them pass. Within musket-shot of the French, who made no motion to attack them, they calmly formed their line. Natzmer detected a wavering in the enemy's ranks, and instantly led his squadrons to the charge. Just as at Blenheim, the French fired from the saddle, and some of them even fired into the air, and then, just as at Blenheim, they bolted. Pressing forward in pursuit, the Prussians came upon fresh battalions of the enemy's foot, who saluted them with a deadly fire at close quarters. Natzmer's squadrons recoiled in some disorder, and swerving to the right, dashed upon the hedges skirting the plateau. The infantry, posted there, received them warmly The Prussian Gendarmes rode over two battalions and captured some colours, only to be surrounded at last by the Household Cavalry and partially destroyed. In the course of this terrible conflict, Natzmer was for a long time quite alone in the midst of the enemy He sustained a cut above the eye, besides three other wounds; and he narrowly escaped in the end by leaping his charger over a wide, wet ditch. His squadrons rallied on the infantry of Lottum and Cadogan. They had suffered much. More than half the Prussian Gendarmes were out of action. But Natzmer and his men fully deserved the eulogies which they obtained from Marlborough, who specially mentioned them in his dispatch to the King of Prussia. Like Von Bredow and his devoted horsemen at Rezonville, they had sacrificed themselves to render a vital service. Apart from the actual casualties which the French incurred, this charge unnerved their infantry at the most critical point on the field, and robbed them of all desire to advance a second time into the open, where the whole of the cavalry of the allied right was waiting to repeat the lesson.

Meantime, Marlborough with the Dutch and Hanoverian foot had passed the southern rivulet, and attacked the hedges and enclosures on the opposite side. He encountered the most obstinate resistance, and though he gradually pushed back the enemy as far as the hamlet of Diepenbeke, a few hundred yards to the north of Schaerken, he could make no further progress But the bulk of the infantry of the allied left had now arrived. Their cavalry, which had crossed the Schelde by the bridge of Audenarde, was already awaiting them. Marlborough sent instructions to Overkirk to throw the weight of this new force against the right flank of the French. Overkirk, who was sixty-seven and had been ailing all the winter, executed the order with alacrity and skill. The lower slopes of the hill of Oycke were partially covered by a belt of woodland. But between this obstacle and the source of the southern rivulet there was a gap. Overkirk directed General Week with a couple of Dutch brigades to penetrate here. Week moved briskly to the attack He was warmly received, but his two brigades, which comprised some of the choicest troops in the Dutch service, continued to gain ground, and joining hands with Marlborough's left, began to encircle the enemy.

It was 7 o'clock From end to end of the curving line the conflict raged What Louis had expressly forbidden had come to pass, a combat of infantry in enclosed country In such a combat, where single battalions, and often single companies, met in isolated duels, and where unusual responsibilities devolved upon junior officers, the superior training and confidence of Marlborough's veteran, and always victorious, troops was bound to tell. But Malleson is unjust to their opponents when he says that " in no pitched battle . . . have the French soldiers less distinguished themselves."[1] Competent eyewitnesses on both sides deposed that they had seldom seen so close an engagement, or firing so heavy and so well sustained. They " behaved very gallantly,"[2] said Kane. " They made a better defence than they used to do,"[3] said Hare. " It must be acknowledged," wrote Lediard, " that, in general, they fought better at this time than they had done upon any other occasion."[4]

No sooner was the movement of Week's brigades successfully launched, than Overkirk with the remainder of the left wing ascended the hill of Oycke. Arrived at the summit, he looked down upon the entire field of battle as upon a map. He saw at once that, if he wheeled to the right, and extended his left towards the Norken, the formation of the allied army would then resemble a horseshoe, and that if the tips of the horseshoe closed, the right wing

[1] Malleson, *Prince Eugène of Savoy*, p 164
[2] Kane, *Campaigns of King William and Queen Anne*, p 75
Hare MSS , July 12, 1708 (Hist MSS Comm , 14th Report, Appendix, part ix , p. 218) [4] Lediard, vol ii., p 269.

of the French would be entirely surrounded. He wheeled and extended accordingly, and reported the situation to the Duke. Marlborough replied that he was to spare no pains to complete the envelopment of the enemy. Thereupon, the youthful Prince of Orange-Nassau, with General Oxenstiern and four brigades of Dutch foot, supported by Tilly with twelve squadrons of Danes, rapidly descended the eastern slope of the hill, and advanced between the Norken and the belt of woodland towards the plateau of Roijgem. Surprised and alarmed by the manœuvre, the French hastily lined the hedges upon this side with grenadiers, who were sustained by the Household Cavalry. It was now 8 30. The Dutch attacked with vigour. Their flashing volleys, plainly visible in the gathering twilight to Marlborough in the centre and to Eugène upon the right, revealed to the dullest soldier in both armies the nature of the movement that was now in progress. In the French ranks ammunition was beginning to fail; and the men were refusing to follow their officers. But the allies, certain of victory, closed resolutely in, girdling the despondent foe with an ever-tightening semi-circle of musketry and steel.

Vendôme endeavoured to avert the imminent annihilation of his right wing by pushing up battalions from his centre. This manœuvre, which was exposed to a flanking fire from Cadogan's men, proved worse than useless. For as the French were everywhere giving way and receding towards the windmill of Roijgem, and the narrow pass whereby they could still communicate with their centre and left, the advance of fresh troops served only to increase the congestion and disorder at this critical point. Nevertheless, at 8 30, a desperate charge was delivered against the allied right. It collapsed before the murderous fire of the Hanoverian and Prussian infantry Vendôme displayed the most reckless, personal bravery; but neither by exhortation nor example could he restore the discipline or revive the courage of soldiers, who believed themselves to be entrapped. Night was descending fast, and a drizzling rain had begun to fall, when a council of war was held on the plateau of Huysse. Burgundy had begun to speak, but Vendôme, who was beside himself with fury, told the

heii-presumptive to hold his tongue. He then pioceeded
to contend that the battle was by no means lost, that half
the army had not even been engaged, and that they had
only to stand their ground behind the Noiken and renew
the combat on the ensuing day He was heard in silence
Puységur, Matignon, and other officers, arriving with alarming news from various quarters, Vendôme perceived that
he was virtually alone in his opinion. " Very well, gentlemen," he exclaimed, " I see clearly that you all wish it.
So we must retreat. And you, Monseigneur," he added,
turning to the Duke of Burgundy, " have long desired it."[1]
Again he was heard in silence. Then the order was given
to retire on Ghent. All who could, fled incontinently.
The whole of the left wing and a part of the centre marched
off without striking a blow. The men who had done
their duty were deserted and forgotten. Within the now
almost completed circle, which the allies had drawn about
the vainly struggling enemy, organised resistance was
virtually at an end. The demoralised foot were crowding
back upon the horse, who for want of space were unable
to act. Darkness augmented the panic and confusion.
Battalion was heaped upon battalion, and squadron upon
squadron. Cavalry and infantry were inextricably mixed,
and friends and foes no longer distinguishable Few orders
were given, and fewer still obeyed. And always the fire-
fringed line of the allies closed in remorselessly upon the
terrified mob

The Household Cavalry and the Gendarmerie were well-
nigh surrounded, but by a desperate effort they cut their
way out with heavy loss Their retreat was partially
covered by seven regiments of dragoons, the greater number
of whom were killed or taken. A little before 9, Cadogan's
right and Orange-Nassau's left approached so closely to
one another that their volleys crossed. Fearful of some
calamitous blunder, Marlborough and Eugène now issued
peremptory orders to cease firing Yet even so, the French,
entangled in a country of hedges and enclosures, and
enveloped by enemies, found it no easy matter to escape.
Some were protected by the darkness, but others were only

[1] Saint-Simon, t. xi , ch. cciii., p. 213.

perplexed by it. A considerable body, slipping through an interval between the allied centre and left, made off towards the frontiers of France. But many, less fortunate, were captured in similar attempts. Then, into this welter of distraction and despair strode the Huguenot officers in the allied service. Commanding their drummers to beat the French retreat, they cried in a loud voice, "A moi, Picardie!" "A moi, Roussillon!" "A moi, Piedmont!" All within earshot rallied to their call. By this device, which was Eugène's, a goodly harvest of prisoners was reaped.

Throughout the night the allied troops continued under arms. Marlborough and Eugène remained on horseback in "a very soaking rain."[1] Sunrise showed that the enemy had abandoned all his positions and disappeared The Duke immediately dispatched Lumley and Bülow with forty squadrons of the right wing to take up the pursuit along the road to Ghent They were supported by Meredith with a brigade of foot. They soon came up with the French rear-guard, which consisted of a large body of horse and twelve companies of grenadiers. The country being difficult for cavalry, and the road being lined with grenadiers, a sharp conflict ensued. Two of Bülow's squadrons suffered severely; Meredith was slightly hurt, and several officers of foot were killed and wounded. On the other hand, a couple of French companies and a lieutenant-general were taken Thereupon the chase was abandoned. The enemy passed the canal of Ghent, destroyed the bridges behind them, and began to throw up earthworks. Vendôme took to his bed, and remained there for thirty hours. Those fugitives who made for the French frontier were pursued by eight of Overkirk's squadrons as far as the Lys. Some were drowned in passing that river; and more than 300 officers and men surrendered.

Marlborough, in the meantime, was giving directions for the disposal of the wounded of both armies, who had suffered cruelly during the wet night. Not until 9 o'clock did Eugène and he ride into Audenarde. It was a memorable day for the inhabitants of that ancient town. Their

[1] *Millner's Journal*, June 30, 1708, p. 217.

beautiful hôtel-de-ville looked down upon a market-place, swarming with French prisoners, many of them in the brilliant uniforms of world-famous regiments " They have been coming by droves into this town, for many hours,"[1] wrote Hare.

It was a crippling blow to France. Her killed and wounded were at least 6,000. The prisoners, by Berwick's admission, amounted to 9,000, and probably exceeded that number Among them were Lieutenant-General Biron and 700 officers of various grades. " At least forty of our regiments," wrote one of the captives, " are reduced to a wretched condition, the greatest part of them being killed or taken, so that it will be long before they can be re-established."[2] The desertions also were very numerous. " It is most certain," wrote Marlborough, a fortnight after the battle, " that the success we had at Audenarde has lessened their army at least 20,000 men "[3] Among the trophies of the allies were " upwards of a hundred standards, colours, and kettle-drums, 4,500 horses, and ten pieces of cannon."[4] " Now by that time," wrote Sergeant Millner with grim satisfaction, " they had bought Ghent and Bruges somewhat dear."

The casualties of the allies were comparatively light. They numbered 3,000, or rather more, " which loss," says Lediard, " was abundantly repaired by deserters and prisoners, Germans, Switzers, and Spaniards, who listed themselves voluntarily."[5] In the British regiments the killed and wounded did not exceed 230 men. But it must be remembered that the British cavalry can scarcely be said to have been engaged at all.

As usual, the French made the most extravagant attempts to minimise their defeat. Marlborough wrote to Galway that they would " hardly own it in their prints to have been a battle."[6] Burgundy, writing ten days after the combat to Madame de Maintenon, fixed the total deficit

---

[1] Hare MSS , July 12, 1708 (Hist MSS Comm , 14th Report, Appendix, part ix , p 218).   [2] Lediard, vol ii , p 287
[3] Coxe, vol ii., p 273: Marlborough to Godolphin, July 26, 1708
[4] *Millner's Journal*, p 218. July 1, 1708
[5] Lediard, vol. ii , p 272.
[6] Murray, vol. iv., p. 137· Marlborough to the Earl of Galway, July 30, 1708

from all causes at 6,000. D'Artaignan reported that both sides had suffered equally.[1] He gave the figures at 3,000. He also denied that any guns or colours had been lost. Vendôme's creature, Albergotti, announced that, by retiring behind the canal, that general had "thrown the enemy out of action"[2] It was industriously suggested that an encounter, in which half the French army did not participate, must of necessity have been a very insignificant affair It was also contended that the safe arrival of almost all the artillery at Ghent was inconsistent with the notion of defeat. The fact that the artillery had apparently been forgotten during the action, and left without orders a long way in the rear, was conveniently suppressed But the truth could not be hidden for ever. Certain circumstances, which were public property, gave the lie to the theory that only a trifling collision had occurred. That theory did not explain why generals, who had just been discussing whether they should invest Audenarde before Menin or Menin before Audenarde, had now retired to Ghent without investing either. It did not explain the presence of more than 9,000 prisoners, including 700 officers, in Marlborough's camp. It did not explain why Vendôme and Burgundy with the bulk of their forces were at Ghent, while 10,000 fugitives had gradually assembled at Tournai, Courtrai, and Lille And it did not explain the furious recriminations between those two commanders and their partisans in the army and at Versailles. Louis learned the facts from the lips of Biron, who was permitted by Marlborough to visit Fontainebleau upon parole. " I see," wrote the King to Burgundy, " that the combat was very obstinate, and the loss more considerable than I had reason to suppose from the first letters and the relations which some private persons had received."[3]

Yet even the ingenuity of French fiction seems but a poor thing in comparison with the standard of imaginative art set up by Sicco van Goslinga. All the world knew

[1] It is to be regretted that in so valuable a work as Pelet's these absurdities should be repeated as historical facts· Pelet, t viii., p 388: Lettre de M. D'Artaignan, 11 juillet, 1708.

[2] Saint-Simon, t. xi , ch cciv , p 225.

[3] Pelet t viii , p 399 Lettre du Roi à Monseigneur le duc de Bourgogne, 16 juillet, 1708.

that a victory, gained under the conditions which prevailed
in the case of Oudenarde, could be gained only by exceptional energy and daring But energy and daring were
the very qualities which, by Goslinga's hypothesis, Marlborough was precluded from exhibiting. Therefore they
must have been exhibited by somebody else. Who that
somebody else was, Goslinga has explained in memoirs
which an engaging modesty forbade him to present to his
contemporaries. After premising that Marlborough not only
loitered at Lessines three hours longer than was necessary,
but even tolerated the presence of baggage on the line of
march in defiance of his own orders, the field-deputy observes
that, on receipt of information from Cadogan that the
enemy were crossing the Schelde, the Duke did not display
" all the ardour and *empressement* required."[1] Luckily,
however, the zeal of the soldiery more than compensated
for the slackness of the general At 4 o'clock, when the
situation began to be critical, Marlborough, instead of
choosing his ground, " appeared visibly embarrassed," and
" gave no positive order for the arrangement of the troops "[2]
Thereupon Goslinga and Rechteren requested Eugène to
assume the command Eugène demurred He admitted
that delay was dangerous, but he represented that he was
only a volunteer, and that he had no army. Goslinga and
Rechteren exhorted him in the name of his fatherland, of
his Emperor, and of glory in the abstract. Unable to
resist so much eloquence, the Prince accepted their offer,
and immediately made such dispositions on the right as
entirely frustrated the enemy's designs. He then dispatched
Goslinga and Gueldermalsen at full gallop to the left with
instructions to Overkirk to attack the French in flank.
Goslinga found Overkirk, Tilly, and other officers, executing
a singular movement of cavalry in the direction of Courtrai.
He delivered his orders; but Overkirk, who, because he
loved and trusted Marlborough, is always depicted by the
field-deputy as an amiable dotard, virtually told him to
mind his own business. Then Goslinga was taken up into
a high mountain, whence he beheld the inside of the French

[1] *Mémoires de Goslinga*, p. 54.
[2] *Ibid*, p 55.

position. On his descent, he repeated Eugène's orders to
Oxenstiern, whom he saw at the head of five or six battalions.
Oxenstiern answered that the country was difficult, and
that they must wait for the French to attack. Goslinga
retorted that the French would never attack, but Oxenstiern refused to budge. Then the doughty Dutchman
dismounted, went to the head of two Swiss battalions of
Sturler, paid them a pretty compliment, and himself led
them forward against the enemy's flank. This example
encouraged five other battalions to join the party After
these seven had deployed, Orange-Nassau appeared on their
right with eight more   The whole fifteen then resumed their
advance. They were charged by the Household Cavalry;
but Goslinga's Swiss repelled the charge with the bayonet.
The French infantry either ran away or surrendered.
Goslinga and Orange-Nassau sent to Overkirk for cavalry;
but Overkirk of course did not respond. After the battle,
Overkirk ordered all the colours and kettle-drums taken
by the left wing to be brought to him   Sturler's Swiss,
however, who had secured a couple of kettle-drums, brought
them to Goslinga instead. These simple heroes evidently
cherished the principle that the spoils belong to the victors,
and that the laurels should be borne by him who has reaped
them. But Goslinga magnanimously surrendered his perquisites to Overkirk, because the old man was exceeding
wroth. Perhaps, by that time, the official list of trophies
and their takers had already been compiled. Otherwise,
the profane might be tempted to enquire why Sturler's
battalions and their kettle-drums do not figure in it.
Goslinga pretends that he knows nothing of what was done
by the allied right and centre, after 5 o'clock   But what,
after all, does it matter ? The battle of Oudenarde can be
explained in a sentence. Eugène of Savoy, acting with
some reluctance on instructions received from Sicco van
Goslinga, amused the enemy, while the said Sicco delivered
the *coup de grâce*. This narrative, while it certainly illus-
trates the superiority of the Dutch school of historical
romance to the French, defies comment. One can only
reflect that

"Vixere fortes ante Agamemnona,"

1 to 6 p.m.

Wannegem

Huysse

Lede

Oyeke

Roygem
Mill

Mullem

GRIMALDO

Boser
Couter

Herlegem

Diepenbeke

Schaerken

MARLBOROUGH

Mooregem

Heurne

Bevere

Eyne

OUDENARDE
AUDENARDE

Abbey

Eename

which is as much as to say that there were mighty men of war before Bill Adams.

Marlborough dispatched Lord Stair to England with the tidings of victory. The exultation of the people was mingled with an intense curiosity as to the manner in which the youthful representatives of the Houses of Hanover and Stuart had borne themselves in action. The Whigs were particularly delighted with the prowess of the Electoral Prince. To point the moral, they circulated a slanderous report that the Pretender, who had done his duty with the Household Cavalry, had played the poltroon, and had witnessed the battle from the safe and convenient shelter of a windmill. The contrast was enforced in a popular ballad, *Jack Frenchman's Lamentations*, in which the following stanza occurred

> " Not so did behave
> Young Hannover brave
> In the Bloody Field I assure ye·
> When his War-Horse was shot
> He valu'd it not,
> But fought it on Foot like a Fury."[1]

The army, however, knew better. Biron told Saint-Simon[2] that, on the day after the battle, he was suddenly asked by Marlborough during dinner, and in the presence of a number of British officers, for news of the Prince of Wales, a title which the Duke apologised for using. Biron replied that there was no necessity to use it, as the Prince was always known in the French service as the Chevalier de St. George. He then expatiated at length on the Chevalier's admirable qualities When he had finished, Marlborough, who had listened attentively, confessed his gratification, and remarked that he could not do other than take great interest in that young prince. Biron noted the evident satisfaction on the Duke's face, and on the faces of most of the company.

Oudenarde, like Walcourt, is dismissed by Feuquières with one contemptuous sentence It interested him little, but it interests the modern student much, and for the same reason. No battle of that epoch conformed so badly

1 *Swift's Poems*, vol iii., p 6
2 Saint-Simon, t xi , ch. cciv , p. 219.

to the then accepted type of what a battle should be, or approached so closely to later developments of the combat. There was no leisurely deployment of the opposing hosts in parallel lines, with infantry in the centre and cavalry on the wings. The advance-guard, which had covered the passage of the Schelde by the allied army, forced on the action by successfully attacking the detachment which protected the march of the enemy's columns to the defensive position behind the Norken   The French were either tempted or provoked to throw forward the whole of their right wing against the left flank of the victors, who wheeled to meet the onset, and were sustained by the rest of the allied army as fast as it arrived. The assailants, though supported by their centre, were first held, then attacked in flank, and finally enveloped   Owing to the nature of the ground, the brunt of the engagement was borne by the infantry on both sides, and by the infantry the issue was determined. On both sides, the horse were drawn up in rear of the foot as much as upon its flanks. The work done by the cavalry of Rantzau and of Natzmer was brilliant and effective; but it was work which could have been equally well done in 1870.   The decisive blow at Oudenarde, unlike the decisive blow at Blenheim, Ramillies, and Malplaquet, was not delivered by the mounted arm.

But the glory and the lesson of Oudenarde lay not in the combat itself, they lay in the consummate skill with which Marlborough forced that combat on the enemy.   In many histories the true nature of the strategy which preceded the battle is misrepresented, or at best obscured. The reader is left with the impression that in a three days' race over a course, in which the allies had three times as far to go as the French, the allies won.   Nothing could be farther from the truth.   In such a race, had it ever occurred, it would have been physically impossible for the allies to win.   They could not have done it against any troops in Europe, and least of all against such renowned marchers as the French.   But it takes two to make a match; and for this particular event the French never entered.   From the afternoon of Monday the 9th, when they quitted Lede, until the afternoon of Wednesday the 11th, when they learned from Biron that the allies were crossing the Schelde, their movements were leisurely in the extreme. So far were they from engaging in a race, that they were perfectly unconscious that there was any necessity for hurry. From beginning to end, they were deceived by the strategy of Marlborough, a strategy essentially similar to that which carried him in 1704 from the Meuse to the Danube. In moving to Herffelingen, he led them to suppose that he desired to threaten Charleroi or Namur without exposing Brussels, in camping at Herffelingen, he induced them to believe that, whatever his ultimate intention might be, they had plenty of time to occupy Lessines; in seizing Lessines, he convinced them that his aim, after all, was the purely defensive one of hindering the siege of Audenarde. They thought that Lessines was the goal of a defensive movement, they did not dream that it was the penultimate stage of an offensive one. They never imagined that Marlborough had conceived the idea of dashing across the Schelde and intervening between them and France. Still less did they imagine that he would risk such an operation and even provoke a battle, when his troops were thoroughly fatigued, and by the nature of the case, could only arrive piecemeal. Misunderstanding everything, they foresaw nothing; and Marlborough succeeded, in the end, in effecting a grand strategical surprise, and even a tactical one.

" I must ever acknowledge the goodness of God in the success He was pleased to give us," wrote Marlborough to Godolphin, " . . . but you know when I left England I was positively resolved to endeavour by all means a battle, thinking nothing else would make the Queen's business go on well. This reason only made me venture the battle yesterday, otherwise I did give them too much advantage; but the good of the Queen and my country shall always be preferred by me before any personal concern, for I am very sensible if I had miscarried I should have been blamed "[1] And to Anne herself he wrote: " The circumstances in this last battle, I think, show the hand of God; for we were obliged not only to march five leagues that morning, but to pass a river before the enemy, and to

[1] Coxe, vol. ii , p 265· Marlborough to Godolphin, July 12, 1708.

engage them before the whole army was passed, which was a visible mark of the favour of Heaven to you and your arms "[1] These letters breathe the old spirit, the spirit of the eve of Blenheim, and of Jervis's immortal words, " A victory is very essential to England at this moment "[2] And certainly the Duke accepted no ordinary risks at Oudenarde. But he accepted them only after a calculation which showed him that they were less formidable than they appeared. The enemy had material advantages of first-rate importance; in numbers, in position, and in the comparative freshness of their troops, they enjoyed a palpable superiority. Marlborough had only one, a larger proportion of experienced and highly trained men in the ranks of his infantry. But all the moral advantages were indubitably his. Thanks to the perfect understanding which existed always between himself and Eugène, he knew that the whole of the allied army would be handled with equal method and determination, whereas he had every reason to believe that the notorious friction between the French commanders would give birth to irresolution and disorder in the field He knew too that this result would be surely and greatly intensified by the surprise which he had effected. And above all, he knew that what he was accustomed to call " the goodness of the men," a quality compounded of immense contempt for the enemy and immense confidence in themselves and their commander, was the most valuable asset that a general could possess. This quality the allied troops, and particularly the British, had never failed to exhibit since first he led them in the field; but on the day of Oudenarde it was reinforced by an intense and bitter indignation, unusual in professional armies, and springing entirely from the fact that every private soldier regarded the treacherous surrender of Ghent and Bruges as a personal insult to himself [3] " Most marvellous of all," says Fortescue, " was the spirit of the troops. They had started at 2 a.m. on Monday and had marched fifty miles, including the passage of two

[1] Coxe, vol 11 , p 280· Marlborough to the Queen, July 23, 1708
[2] *Life of John Jervis*, by Captain Anson, p 157
[3] *Millner's Journal*, p 218, July 1, 1708   "Now by that time they had bought Ghent and Bruges somewhat dear "

large rivers, before they came into action at 2 p m. on Wednesday afternoon."[1] The captive French officers complained that they had " had to deal with devils "[2] It was upon factors such as these, factors which are entirely neglected or ignored by writers like Feuquières, that Marlborough relied. A better illustration of the relative values of the spiritual and the material in war it would be difficult to find

Knowledge of these values is essential to a right understanding of the consequences, both immediate and remote, of the battle of Oudenarde. France was weaker by the loss of 20,000 men. " If we had been so happy as to have had two more hours of daylight," wrote Marlborough to the Duchess, " I believe we should have made an end of the war."[3] But those two hours had been denied him. And now that Berwick had arrived, France had still 100,000 soldiers in the Spanish Netherlands. Apparently, therefore, the destruction of the enemy's armed force by the allies had yet to be accomplished But " if we speak of the destruction of the enemy's armed force," says Clausewitz, " we must expressly point out that nothing obliges us to confine this idea to the mere physical force; on the contrary, the moral is necessarily implied as well, because both in fact are interwoven with each other, even in the most minute details, and therefore cannot be separated "[4] These words reveal the true nature of the blow which the French had sustained. They also supply the key to the remainder of the campaign. " That which is our greatest advantage," wrote Marlborough to Godolphin a fortnight after the battle, " is the terror that is in their army ",[5] and again, " that which I think our greatest advantage consists in the fear that is among their troops "[6]

[1] *Cromwell to Wellington*, edited by Spenser Wilkinson, p 79.
[2] *The History of Francis-Eugène* (1741), by an English officer, p 274
[3] Coxe, vol 11 , p 267 Marlborough to the Duchess, July 16, 1708   In a letter to Godolphin the Duke put it at "one hour ", Schulenburg puts it at two hours *Leben der Schulenburg*, p 331
[4] Clausewitz, vol 1 , book 1 , ch 11
[5] Coxe, vol 11 , p. 272 Marlborough to Godolphin, July 26, 1708.
[6] *Ibid*

XXI.—LILLE

ON the morrow of Oudenarde, that sound instinct for
offensive warfare which characterised both Marlborough
and Eugène, told them imperatively what they had next
to do. Before their weakened and demoralised foe could
at all recover from the stroke, they must deal him another.
But the difficulty was to come at him a second time   An
entrenched position, flanked by the cannon of Ghent and
Bruges, and moated by the canal connecting those places,
could not be forced by an army equipped with the field-
guns of that epoch. The only alternative was to entice
or to constrain Vendôme and Burgundy to return once
more into the open country.   To that end, the allied commanders resolved to move at once towards the French
frontier and bring home to the populations of Picardy and
Artois the realities of war.

On the afternoon of Thursday, July 12, they unfolded
their views in the presence of Overkirk, Dopf, Cadogan,
and the six field-deputies   Everybody approved, save
Goslinga and Gueldermalsen.   Goslinga contended that the
beaten army, with its back to the sea, was plainly in a
trap, and that the allies had nothing to do but to close the
door. He therefore suggested that the united forces of
Marlborough and Eugène should establish a blockade of
the French until such time as the pressure of hunger compelled a capitulation   He was seconded by Gueldermalsen,
whom he had previously converted to this heroic strategy.
It was one of those pretty conceits which laymen and
theorists invent at leisure, and which practical soldiers
reject on sight. In the first place, the trap itself was not
complete. Holding Nieuport and the fortified post of
Plasschendaele on the canal between Bruges and Ostend,
the enemy still retained his communications with his own
country. Secondly, the line to be guarded was of enormous

152

extent. Even with the united forces of Marlborough and Eugène, an effective blockade from Nieuport to Dendermonde could not be guaranteed. Thirdly, the allied army, strung out at perilous length, would be exposed to an attack in rear from Berwick's corps, reinforced from the garrisons of half a dozen fortresses at least   If such an attack formed part of a combined movement, previously concerted with Vendôme and Burgundy, the result might be altogether disastrous to the allies, who in point of numbers, at any rate, would certainly be overmatched. And fourthly, the process of starvation might easily prove to be a very tedious one   Even assuming that the blockade were continuously and entirely effective (itself a very generous assumption), the area of the Spanish Netherlands, available for the subsistence of the imprisoned army, was not inconsiderable; and it was fringed on the north by a strip of Dutch territory, the inhabitants of which would be made to learn far sooner than the French what famine meant. If the approach of winter found the blockade still unsuccessful, the net result of the campaign would not be in favour of the coalition. This was a contingency, which, in the existing temper of Goslinga's countrymen and employers, Marlborough was not prepared to face. Referring to Oudenarde, " I am assured," he wrote to Godolphin on July 26, " that, if this action had not happened, some proposal of peace was to have been made towards the end of August."[1]   In other words, the fidelity of the Dutch to the Grand Alliance was a plant that needed perpetual refreshment. Unless they were presented with tangible profits at frequent intervals, they would retire from partnership. But the Duke could hardly be expected to tell this not very flattering truth to the patriotic field-deputy. Goslinga was highly indignant when his beautiful plan was rejected. He consoled himself with the reflection that it was not rejected on its merits. Marlborough, of course, opposed it, because Marlborough opposed everything that was calculated to put a speedy termination to the war   Eugène agreed with Marlborough, because it was Austria's policy to curry favour with England. Overkirk was a venerable puppet, Dopf a mere parasite,

---

[1] Coxe, vol. ii., p. 273: Marlborough to Godolphin, July 26, 1708.

Cadogan a money-grubber, growing fat like his patron on the prolongation of the struggle   Even the faithful Gueldermalsen proved but a feeble support. For Gueldermalsen was jealous of the martial Sicco, who seemed in a fair way to add the laurels of the strategist to the laurels of the tactician.

Marlborough allowed his exhausted soldiers two days' rest at Audenarde. On the morning of the 13th Eugène departed for Brussels, where his army was now assembled. In that city the Comtesse de Soissons had her residence. Mother and son, who had not met for twenty-five years, exulted together over the humiliation of the King of France.

Marlborough had hoped that the enemy would abandon Ghent and Bruges without delay. But all the intelligence which he could procure, indicated that they were resolved to continue in the position which they were daily fortifying behind the canal. At midnight, therefore, on the 13th, he detached Lottum with thirty battalions, forty squadrons, and some field-guns, to seize the lines of Comines, which ran from Ypres to the Lys. It was necessary to hasten, because Berwick with twenty squadrons had already reached Mons. Marching by Courtrai and Menin, and meeting with no resistance, Lottum was in full possession of the lines by the afternoon of the 15th. He took five hundred prisoners and ten cannon   But he was only just in time. For La Motte with a detachment from the army of Burgundy and Vendôme had already reached Ypres. Marlborough, who had started a few hours after Lottum with the main body, arrived that same evening, and encamped at Wervicq. He immediately engaged 3,000 labourers to level the works.

Yet even now Burgundy and Vendôme refused to move. "At the same time," wrote Marlborough to Godolphin on the 16th, "they leave all France open to us, which is what I flatter myself the King of France and his council will never suffer, so that I hope by Thursday" (the 19th) "M. de Vendôme will receive orders from court not to continue in the camp where he is, from whence we are not able to force him but by famine."[1]   To increase the pressure on the French government, the Duke proceeded to levy

[1] Coxe, vol II., p. 267: Marlborough to Godolphin, July 16, 1708.

contributions in Artois. His parties penetrated in every
direction. Eight hundred of his horse rode to the very
gates of Arras, where, failing to obtain the sum for which
they stipulated, they fired the suburbs Lens, which was
threatened with similar execution, gave hostages for payment The inhabitants of Richebourg, who offered armed
resistance, saw their village laid in ashes. On the 19th,
Marlborough informed Godolphin that the affair at Arras
" and some other burnings " had created " a very great
consternation," and that the people of the country had
already " sent to the King for leave to treat for the contributions."[1] But although the Duke's parties made daily
excursions into French territory, Vendôme and Burgundy
continued to entrench themselves behind the canal, as
though they intended " to stay there for the rest of this
campaign."[2] Berwick appears to have protested to Marlborough against the treatment accorded to the civilian
population Marlborough replied that he was in no
way transgressing the recognised laws of war. Berwick
deserved this snub at the hands of his uncle. For his
own severities in Spain are a lasting blot upon his
reputation.

The military situation was now, in appearance at any
rate, extremely complicated No fewer than four armies
were in the field Marlborough at Wervicq was holding
the enemy's country to ransom, and at the same time
menacing the three fortresses of Ypres, Lille, and Tournai.
Berwick at Douai was distributing among the garrisons of
those places reinforcements largely drawn from the fugitives
of Oudenarde, while he endeavoured, with little or no
success, to protect the harassed population of Artois
against Marlborough's raids Burgundy and Vendôme
behind the canal of Ghent and Bruges were busily occupied
in erecting earthworks and mounting cannon. And Eugène
at Brussels was keeping open the communications between
Marlborough and the capital, and covering Brabant against
retaliatory attacks. To a certain extent, each side was
waiting for the other to make the first move. Marlborough
was hoping that Vendôme and Burgundy would be either

[1] *Ibid*, p. 268: Marlborough to Godolphin, July 19, 1708.   [2] *Ibid*

lured or forced into the open by his operations in Artois;
and Vendôme and Burgundy were persuading themselves
that, as long as they remained where they were, Marlborough
could effect nothing of importance during the remainder
of the campaign, which must eventually end in a sort of
stalemate.

It must not, however, be supposed that, during these
days of uncertainty, Marlborough was simply marking time.
In the council which he had held at Audenarde, it had
been decided that, if Vendôme and Burgundy declined to
stir, and no second opportunity of battle offered, the allies
should undertake the siege of Lille. Now, as long as the
French at Ghent controlled the waterways of the Lys and
Schelde, the business of transporting the siege-train would
be lengthy and difficult. Sixty pieces were at Sas van Gent
in Dutch Flanders; many others must be procured from
Antwerp and from Maestricht, and one and all must be conveyed to Brussels in the first instance, and thence escorted
overland to the scene of operations Marlborough was hoping
and endeavouring to avoid the necessity for this most
tedious and roundabout process; but in case he should be
obliged to adopt it in the end, he gave orders on the 15th to
dispatch the cannon at Sas van Gent by water to Brussels.
The news of the concentration of heavy artillery in the capital
did not alarm Vendôme. He regarded it as one more ruse
of his antagonist to tempt or frighten him into the evacuation of his fortified position behind the canal. For in
common with the great majority of French officers he
refused to believe that, in the existing situation, generals
so able as Marlborough and Eugène would venture to
entangle themselves in any important siege whatsoever,
seeing that the total number of the allied forces was inferior
to that of the French, and that everything necessary must
be carried from Brussels by a road which was exposed to
attack from Douai in the front, and more particularly
from Ghent and Bruges upon the flank. It is instructive
to note that, on this occasion, Feuquières for once upholds
his countrymen   " Although the siege of Lille was successful," he says, " I shall not blame the project of it any the
less on that account. . . . The project of the siege ought

to have appeared chimerical to every man in his right
senses "[1]

This judgment is an admirable illustration of the fundamental weakness of Feuquières' philosophy of war. It
was not by the slight numerical advantage which the
French enjoyed, nor by the material difficulty of transporting overland a siege-train which was estimated to
require no fewer than 16,000 draught horses, that this critic
was impressed. For he knew, as a practical soldier, that
skill and patience could surmount such obstacles. In
Feuquières' eyes, the dominating factor was the possession
by Burgundy and Vendôme of an entrenched position on
the flank of Marlborough's communications with his base.
Theoretically, the siege of Lille under such circumstances
was impracticable. But Marlborough and Eugène paid
no respect to theory, they did no homage to ideas, however
axiomatic, or to maxims, however solemn. They looked
solely to facts. They recognised that a resolute general,
operating with trustworthy troops on the flank of their
communications, would have been extremely inconvenient,
if not fatal to their plans. But a couple of squabbling
commanders at the head of a demoralised soldiery excited
a much less lively apprehension. As no convoy of importance would travel without a covering army, any attempt
by Burgundy and Vendôme would necessarily bring on
a battle But a battle was the one thing which Burgundy
and Vendôme abhorred, and which Marlborough and
Eugène most ardently desired. On this view of the matter,
the precise position in which the French army elected to
play the part of spectators, mattered not at all. As long
as they were afraid to face the allies in the field, they exercised no more effective control over the operations than
the placid canal behind which they were encamped. So
true it is that, in war, everything depends ultimately upon
the ability and the will to fight If these be lacking, all
the fine phrases in the text-books avail no more than mean-
ingless incantations, and the whole body of military science
can be discarded as an idle superstition

From the morrow of Oudenarde almost to the end of

[1] Feuquières, t. iv., p. 162

the campaign Berwick corresponded with Burgundy and
Vendôme, and Louis and Chamillart with all three. Between
them they produced an enormous mass of dispatches, the
perusal of which tends little to edification. The impression
conveyed is one of indecision, procrastination, misunderstanding, and gigantic muddle Louis and Chamillart had
lost their nerve, Burgundy was in very deep waters, and
he knew it; and Vendôme persisted in believing only what
he wished to believe. Berwick alone had any grip upon
realities Berwick never doubted from the first that the
allies intended to undertake an important siege And
Berwick foresaw that, if once they were established before
the place selected, they could not be dislodged, because,
as he frankly declared to Burgundy, "they will choose a
good position, they will entrench themselves, and our
infantry is not the best in the world for an attack upon
entrenchments "[1] He argued, therefore, that no such
situation should be permitted to arise. If the enemy's
convoys were ruthlessly destroyed, or if Burgundy and
Vendôme marched out to Audenarde, occupied a strong
camp, and severed the forces of Marlborough from the
forces of Eugène, a siege would, in Berwick's judgment,
have been impracticable. But Burgundy and Vendôme
declined to move On the 21st, the heavy baggage of
Marlborough's army set off from Brussels on the Enghien
road, the main body of the Imperialists doing duty as
escort. Both Berwick and Bergueick sent early intelligence
of this movement to Ghent. But Vendôme, affecting to
despise a convoy which contained no cannon, did nothing.
Marlborough had six battalions at Ath On the 23rd, he
dispatched 2,000 horse towards the Schelde On the 24th,
upon information that Berwick was proceeding towards
Tournai, he sent six squadrons more On the 25th, the
baggage arrived safely at Wervicq. Eugène's army encamped in the vicinity of Ath.

Marlborough regarded the project of besieging Lille with
no enthusiasm He had little liking for sieges at any time.
He believed with Clausewitz that " nothing so much weakens

[1] *Mémoires du Maréchal de Berwick* (1778), t. ii , p. 429: Letter of
August 12, 1708.

the force of the offensive," and that "therefoie there is
nothing so certain to rob it of its preponderance for a
season."[1] The siege of Lille could only be undertaken if
the allies weic prepared to accept what the military science
of the age considered as extraordinary risk. It seemed to
Marlborough that, if they were really prepared to accept
that class of risk, they might get better value for their
money He therefore suggested to Eugène that, ignoring
Tournai, Ypres, and even Lille itself, they should march
boldly into the heart of France. He named as an immediate
objective the town of Abbeville on the Somme, and he
proposed to combine his advance with a naval descent from
England on the adjacent coast. In the Isle of Wight a
force lay ready for the purpose under General Erle. So
strong and daring a move would almost certainly have
compelled Vendôme and Burgundy, as well as Berwick,
to return with every available man for the protection of
the capital itself. But if, on the other hand, they had
preferred to attempt a diversion in Brabant, nothing that
they could have done in that region could have been half
so dangerous to the coalition as the march of Marlborough
and Eugène through Picardy on Paris would have been to
France. Doubtless the problem of supply would have
proved extremely troublesome, but handled on uncon-
ventional lines, it need not have been insoluble, seeing that
the province of Artois was so rich that it was popularly
known as "the granary of the Low Countries."[2] In any
event, however, their habitual dread of the unorthodox in
war would have moved the Dutch government to oppose
such a project. The Duke did not allow them the opportunity. "By what I hear from Buys," he wrote to Godolphin on the 26th, "it is plain that they think enough is
done for peace, and I am afraid they will not willingly give
their consent for the marching their army into France,
which, certainly, if it succeeded, would put a happy end
to the war."[3] And a week later, he wrote. "I have spoke
of it to nobody but the Prince; for by several observations
I have of late made of the deputies of our army, I am

[1] Clausewitz, vol iii., book vii , ch xvii , p 41.
[2] A Journey through the Austrian Netherlands (1732), p 203, letter xii.
[3] Coxe, vol. ii., p 272. Marlborough to Godolphin, July 26, 1708.

afraid the States would not be for this expedition nor anything else where there is a venture."[1]

If Marlborough and Eugène had been both of one mind in the matter, civilian opposition might have been overborne. But for once Marlborough and Eugène disagreed. " He thinks it impracticable," wrote the Duke in his letter of the 26th, " till we have Lille for a *place d'armes* and magazine."[2] The Dutch were willing to besiege Lille, because every fortress captured increased their chances of obtaining a powerful barrier at that early peace on which their hearts were set. In these circumstances, Marlborough was compelled to relinquish a conception which could only have arisen in a mind of the Cromwellian or Napoleonic order. But in a letter of July 26, to Lord Halifax, he made this very significant comment· " Were our army all composed of English, the project would certainly be feasible, but we have a great many among us, who are more afraid of wanting provisions than of the enemy."[3]

If Goslinga, who pretended to a knowledge of so many secrets, knew anything at all about this episode, he very prudently excluded all mention of it from his memoirs. For it is sufficient by itself to demolish his whole theory of Marlborough's conduct. The design which the Duke unfolded to Eugène, and which even Eugène rejected as too hazardous, was open to criticism of various kinds. But to one objection it was not exposed. Nobody could say that it was calculated to prolong the war. Nobody could say that it tended to anything other than a decision, and a rapid decision, of the whole struggle in favour of one side or the other. Yet it was suggested by Marlborough, who, on Goslinga's hypothesis, had maliciously resolved to protract hostilities, and it was thwarted by Eugène, who, also on Goslinga's hypothesis, invariably acquiesced, from motives of Austrian statecraft, in the dilatory and half-hearted operations of the English commander The true situation, both military and political, as it existed at this moment, is revealed in a couple of sentences of the Duke's

[1] Coxe, vol ii , p 275· Marlborough to Godolphin, August 3, 1708.
[2] *Ibid* , p 272· Marlborough to Godolphin, July 26, 1708
[3] Murray, vol iv., p. 129: Marlborough to Halifax, July 26, 1708.

correspondence. On July 26, he wrote to the Duchess: " Prince Eugène and I consult daily, not only how to end this campaign, but also the war, with advantage."[1] And on August 3, he wrote to Godolphin in reference to the Dutch. " I am confident they think themselves sure of peace, the thoughts of which may ruin themselves and the allies, for I verily believe the intention of the King of France is to amuse them, in order to gain time."[2]

When Marlborough consented to the siege of Lille, he anticipated that he would be master of that place in September, and Abbeville at any rate might still be taken, and garrisoned by English troops throughout the winter. He therefore sent urgent orders to General Erle to utilise the month of August in alarming the coasts of Normandy and Brittany. " No attempt should be made on Abbeville," he wrote to Boyle on August 3, " nor the least jealousy given that way till towards the end of September."[3] But Erle had sailed from Spithead on August 7. On the 13th and 14th, he made a demonstration off Boulogne, and on the 15th, he actually effected a landing near Etaples. Here, however, he received his new instructions. He re-embarked at once, and eventually set sail for Cherbourg and La Hogue.

During the concentration of the siege-train at Brussels, Marlborough redoubled his efforts to compel Vendôme and Burgundy to quit their position " If we could get them out of their entrenchments, and from behind the canal of Ghent and Bruges," he wrote to Godolphin on the 23rd, " we should beat them with half their numbers, especially their foot. This is one of their reasons for their staying where they are."[4] But whether they could be brought a second time to battle or not, their mere continuance in their present situation was a great impediment to the siege of Lille Pressure was therefore applied by Marlborough in two directions To deprive them as far as possible of necessary supplies, he dispatched ten squadrons on the 21st towards Audenarde, and another body of 500 horse to Rousselaere, with orders to intercept such convoys as

[1] Coxe, vol ii., p. 274· The Duke to the Duchess, July 26, 1708.
[2] Ibid. pp 275, 276 Marlborough to Godolphin, August 3, 1708.
[3] Ibid. p 276 Marlborough to Boyle, August 3, 1708
[4] Ibid. p 272. Marlborough to Godolphin, July 23, 1708.

might be fitted out at Tournai and Ypres for the use of the army at Ghent. With a similar object, the governor of Ostend endeavoured to destroy communications between Bruges and Nieuport by laying the intervening country under water, while the inhabitants of the Spanish Netherlands and Dutch Flanders were forbidden by proclamation to carry foodstuffs to the markets of the towns occupied by Burgundy and Vendôme At the same time, to increase the popular dismay and clamour in France to the highest pitch, the Duke bore every day more heavily on the unfortunate provinces which lay within his reach On the 23rd, he occupied the town of Armentières with 1,600 men. His purpose was, as he described it to Boyle, " to encourage the parties we send daily into France to continue the alarm and consternation among them, and to cover our army from the insults of small parties from the enemies' garrisons "[1] On the 25th, he made his last and greatest effort. Tilly "was commanded out " with 50 squadrons of horse, 12 battalions of foot, 1,000 grenadiers, 6 field-guns, and all the hussars " The foot under the command of the Earl of Orkney," wrote Marlborough to Boyle, " are to take post at La Bassée, while the horse advance towards Arras, and send parties to make excursions as far as Picardy."[2] According to Hare, Tilly was to let loose " 1,000 horse with the hussars into Picardy, to play the devil for twice twenty-four hours."[3] A raid upon so large a scale was tantamount, in its moral effect, to an invasion. Marlborough anticipated that it would " soon oblige the enemy to quit the canal of Bruges to secure their own frontiers."[4] Hare, writing on the 26th, expressed the opinion that Burgundy and Vendôme would march into France by way of Nieuport, "leaving only a small body under Count La Motte to keep the canal and their stolen goods "[5]

Tilly occupied La Bassée on the 26th. The same day, his

[1] Murray, vol. iv., p 126· Marlborough to Boyle, July 23, 1708.
[2] *Ibid* , p. 131. Marlborough to Boyle, July 26, 1708.
[3] Hare MSS , July 26, 1708 (Hist MSS Comm , 14th Report, Appendix, part ix., p 219).
[4] Murray, vol. iv., p. 132: Marlborough to Major-General Murray, July 26, 1708
[5] Hare MSS., *ibid.*

horse, advancing towards Arras, encountered 800 of the enemy's cavalry, whom they defeated, and pursued to the walls of Lens. Finding that post to be garrisoned by 1,400 of Berwick's foot, they returned to La Bassée with more than 200 prisoners, including several officers. In the night, the French abandoned Lens, and Tilly took possession of the place with his cavalry on the 27th Marlborough, in the meantime, had ascertained that 34 squadrons were marching from Ghent by way of Nieuport to reinforce the army of Berwick. He therefore detached 20 squadrons and 15 battalions to the assistance of Tilly. The province of Artois having compounded for 500,000 crowns, or 1,500,000 livres, Tilly invited the inhabitants of Picardy to adopt a similar course He suggested for their guidance that arrears were due as from the year 1702, when the war had begun, and that the contribution should be calculated upon this basis Seeing that in the previous summer Villars had perpetrated the same bad joke in Germany,[1] the indignation of the French at the exorbitance of the demand need not be taken seriously. Tilly, at any rate, with 25,000 men at his back, was in a position to dictate his own arithmetic Appearing in force in the neighbourhood of Arras, he threw his hussars and 2,000 cavalry across the Scarpe. They almost surprised the town of Doullens, and spreading over the country far and wide, they burned and ravaged to the gates of Guise, St. Quentin, and Péronne For a whole week the scourge descended Not until August 3 did Tilly march back to Wervicq, laden with booty and hostages The universal panic which prevailed from the frontier to the walls of Paris, showed how deadly would have been the effect, if Marlborough's proposal to advance on Abbeville had been tried. "The alarm in France," wrote the Duke to Godolphin on July 30, "is very great, so that we should bring them to reasonable terms, if Holland would let us act as we ought to do "[2]

But the principal object of Tilly's incursion was not achieved. "We are assured," wrote Marlborough in the same letter, "that the Dukes of Burgundy and Vendôme

---

[1] Vogué, *Mémoires de Villars*, t ii , p 229
[2] Coxe, vol ii , p 274: Marlborough to Godolphin, July 30, 1704.

have obtained the King of France's consent to continue in their camp behind the canal of Bruges and Ghent "

Burgundy and Vendôme, moreover, were in a position to inflict reprisals of a sort. They had captured Fort Rouge on the Sas canal on the 19th, they had carried off all the corn in the Pays de Waes as far as Alost, and now, while Tilly was in Picardy and Artois, they detached Rosel with 10,000 men to penetrate the lines which covered Dutch Flanders. Fagel and Murray, who with a handful of troops commanded in those parts, were compelled to retire Rosel burned 100 houses in Cadzand, levelled a portion of the lines, and returned to camp with horses, cattle, hostages, and other spoils. Marlborough dispatched seven battalions from Wervicq, and three from Brussels, to the assistance of Murray and Fagel. He dreaded the consequences which this diversion might produce in Holland. " Those that are for peace," he wrote on August 2, " will endeavour to make all the noise they can "[1]

Though Tilly's work had failed to draw Vendôme and Burgundy into the open, it had, nevertheless, fulfilled three useful purposes which Marlborough had much at heart. By demonstrating the ease with which heavy contributions could be extracted from wealthy French provinces, it kindled the cupidity of the Dutch, and encouraged them to continue the war as a profitable concern. By augmenting the supply of draught-horses, it assisted to solve the problem of transporting the siege-train from Brussels to Lille. And by fixing the attention of Berwick, and compelling him to remain at Douai, it facilitated the safe conveyance to the capital of such teams and waggons as had already been collected Berwick's task was in fact an impossible one. With the forces at his disposal, he could not, at one and the same time, strengthen the garrisons of the threatened fortresses, check the irruptions of the allies into Artois and Picardy, and operate effectively against the communications between Wervicq and Brussels He, at any rate, believed firmly that Marlborough intended to undertake the siege of an important place; he believed also that, only by spoiling the preliminary arrangements

[1] Coxe, vol. ii., p. 275. Marlborough to Godolphin, August 2, 1708

could this design be frustrated.   But Louis, who, according
to Saint-Simon, was deeply distressed at the ruin of the
country so close to Paris, a thing "which he had never
heard mentioned since his minority,"[1] sent the Marshal
explicit and repeated orders to remain at Douai.   "In
preference to everything," wrote Chamillart on August 1,
" you are to be very attentive to the movements which
the enemy might make towards the Somme or the Authie
with a considerable corps.   That would be a sure means
of completing the ruin of Picardy, and of spreading terror
into Normandy, and up to the gates of Paris."[2]   Louis
had already warned Burgundy, on July 30, that, if the
allies passed the Somme or the Authie, the army must
immediately abandon Ghent, join forces with Berwick, and
compel the invaders to fight or retire.[3]   The Somme and
the Authie are the rivers that water the country adjacent
to Abbeville   With so true an eye had Marlborough
detected the vital spot.

All this time, the cannon from Antwerp, Sas van Gent, and
Maestricht had been converging upon Brussels, and Marlborough had been diligently accumulating the horses and
waggons, necessary to convey the siege-train to the front.
" On the rapidity with which it shall enter into action," he
wrote to Heinsius, " depends the future of Europe."[4]   But
16,000 horses were not easy to procure.   The districts dependent upon Ypres, Lille, and Tournai were summoned, "on
pain of military execution," to supply their quotas.   Berwick
retorted by ordering the inhabitants to send all their horses
to him at Douai.   " But I trust," wrote Hare, " our arguments will have most force with them,"[5] and Louis wrote
to Burgundy that it was impossible to require the people
of French Flanders to adopt a course which would result
in the burning of their homes.   Tilly had collected as
many horses as possible in Artois and Picardy.   But even

[1] Saint-Simon, t vi , ch xxv , p 317
[2] *Mémoires de Berwick*, t ii., p 448
[3] Pelet, t viii., p 57: Lettre du Roi à Monseigneur le duc de Bourgogne,
30 juillet, 1708
[4] Von Noorden, *Europäische Geschichte*, vol iii., p 273· Marlborough and
Heinsius, 30 July, 1708 (*Heinsius Archiv*)
[5] Hare MSS , July 26, 1708 (Hist MSS Comm , 14th Report, Appendix
part ix , p 219)

so, the numbers were quite insufficient. It became necessary to call on friends as well as foes. The district of Ath was directed to furnish 705 waggons with teams of four, and the town of Audenarde, fifty with teams of three. The army itself did not escape its toll of horse-flesh. " A certain number," wrote Hare, " is supplied by the army out of the equipage of the officers, so many per regiment, the general officers left to their honour and to do as their zeal prompts them."[1] Even the contractors and the field-deputies were expected to assist. By these devices the requisite total was at last obtained. As fast as the horses and waggons could be got together, they were forwarded to Brussels, where Cadogan had charge of the arrangements. But although this process continued from day to day for upwards of a week, it was never once impeded by Berwick, who was tied to Douai by the King's commands.

The siege-train was composed of 80 cannon with 20 horses apiece, 20 mortars with 16 horses apiece, and 3,000 ammunition-waggons with 4 horses apiece. It formed a column fifteen miles in length. It had seventy-five miles to travel from Brussels to Lille, and two rivers to cross, the Dendre and the Schelde. The route which it must take was exposed to attack from the army at Ghent upon the right flank, and from the army at Douai upon the left, as well as from the garrisons of Mons, Tournai, and Lille. In these circumstances, the overwhelming balance of contemporary opinion, both civil and military, was adverse to the probability of its safe arrival. Marlborough and Eugène were well aware of the chances which they were offering But they trusted to the moral paralysis of the enemy's forces and to the perfection of their own arrangements. Every detail of the operation had been carefully concerted. Cadogan and the Prince of Hesse-Cassel were to move the train from Brussels; Eugène was to meet and escort it; and Marlborough was to hold himself in readiness to act immediately as circumstances should dictate. Constant communications were to be maintained between the various commanders, and also with the governors of Aude-

[1] Hare MSS : July 26, 1708 (Hist. MSS. Comm., 14th Report, Appendix, part ix., p. 219).

narde and Ath. And the intelligence departments of both the allied armies were to leave nothing undone to procure the earliest information of the enemies' plans.

On August 3, Marlborough dispatched twenty-five squadrons and twenty-five battalions to reinforce the army of Eugène at Ath. On the morning of the 4th, Eugène himself quitted Wervicq for the same destination. He was accompanied by Dopf, who possessed an invaluable acquaintance with the topography of the Spanish Netherlands. In the course of the day Marlborough was apprised that a powerful detachment of the enemy had marched from Ghent upon the way to Ninove. He therefore ordered twelve squadrons more to proceed to Audenarde. On the evening of the 5th, Eugène learned from Cadogan that the convoy would quit Brussels on the 6th, and would take the road to Mons, which was by no means the direct route to Lille, but was the route least open to attack from the side of Ghent. On the 6th, the Prince moved to Soignies with 40,000 men. The convoy, jealously guarded by Hesse-Cassel, arrived safely at that town on the 7th. On the same day, Marlborough having heard that the French at Ghent had sent out a second detachment on the way to Ninove, ordered Wurttemberg with an additional thirty squadrons to Audenarde, and promised Eugène to send him as many more troops as he chose to demand.

The march of the convoy to Soignies puzzled the French. They had supposed that the siege of Ypres, Lille, or Tournai was intended; but now, as it seemed, the selected fortress must be Mons On this assumption, Berwick, who had advanced to Mortagne, threw seven battalions and three squadrons into the city, thereby weakening himself without endangering the convoy.

At this time Marlborough's information suggested that Burgundy and Vendôme had some idea of flinging themselves on Brussels. He therefore warned the garrison, and reinforced it. He did as much for Antwerp. And he held himself in readiness to fall upon the rear of any force which might attempt to carry the capital.

On the 8th, at dawn, the convoy struck off from Soignies on the road to Ath. It was closely guarded by a special escort; its right flank was covered by Hesse-Cassel with thirty-five squadrons, its left by the army of Eugène, marching in two columns, and its rear was protected by a body of Hessians, who threw out parties in the direction of Mons But nothing happened The convoy passed the Dendre at Ath on the 9th, and the Schelde at Pottes on the 10th On the 11th, Marlborough sent Wood with thirty squadrons to Petegem, while he ordered the Prince of Orange-Nassau with thirty-one battalions and thirty-four squadrons to observe the garrison of Lille. On the 12th, he marched himself, with the rest of the army, to Helchin On the same day, the convoy arrived safely at Menin. The Duke was immensely relieved. How great had been his anxiety may be judged from his message to Cadogan on the eve of the departure of the train from Brussels. " For God's sake, be sure you do not risk the cannon, for I had rather come with the whole army than receive an affront."[1]

This achievement astonished Europe " Posterity," wrote Feuquières,[2] " will have a difficulty in believing it." Saint-Simon, the steady champion of the Duke of Burgundy, admitted his inability to comprehend that prince's inaction. But the responsibility rests no more heavily upon the Duke of Burgundy and the other officers in the field than upon Louis and Chamillart, who could, if they had wished, have insisted that the convoy should be attacked. Louis and Chamillart, however, could think of nothing better than a suggestion that some of Bergueick's agents should burn the train before it quitted Brussels. The explanation is simple. Eugène had 50,000 men under his command. Whoever would destroy the convoy, must first fight a battle. Rightly or wrongly, the French were afraid to fight a battle. Marlborough and Eugène knew it; and posterity, knowing it also, has been less incredulous than Feuquières foretold

Eugène encamped on the 12th at Templeuve between Lille and Tournai. On the same day, Orange-Nassau marched down from Menin, crossed the Marque, and beat the enemy from a post which they held on an island in the Dyle The English grenadiers dashed into the water with

[1] Murray, vol iv , p 144 Marlborough to Cadogan, August 2, 1708.
[2] *Mémoires de Feuquières*, t. iv., p 162

fixed bayonets, and Sergeant Littler of Godfrey's regiment
swam the river and let down the drawbridge, for which
fine service he obtained a commission   Orange-Nassau
sent forward a detachment towards Lille.   It advanced
into the suburb of La Madeleine, whence it was expelled
by a sortie of the garrison.   On the 13th, Eugène passed
the Marque at Pont-à-Tressin, and in conjunction with
Orange Nassau invested the city.   "This," wrote Marlborough to Maffei on the same day, " may at last convince
the enemy that they lost the battle of Oudenarde."[1]

Thirty-three days had now elapsed since that victory was
gained.   According to Goslinga, these thirty-three days
had been wasted, and worse than wasted.   No sooner had
the field-deputy's plan for starving out the army of Burgundy
and Vendôme been rejected by Marlborough and Eugène,
than he had produced another   It was his contention that,
instead of seizing the lines of Comines and raiding Artois
and Picardy, the army should have immediately blockaded
Lille.   By his account of it, the place was at that time in
so miserable a condition that, with the assistance of the
artillery in Menin, it could have been carried by assault.   He
admits, however, that the engineer, Du Mey, whose courage
and skill were highly esteemed, refused to listen to his last
suggestions.   It was obvious, of course, that, if the army
had blockaded Lille, neither reinforcements nor supplies
could have entered the place.   But Berwick and all the
neighbouring garrisons would have been free to act against
the communications of the allies.   The necessary horses
would not have been obtained, or would not have reached
Brussels   And the siege itself, instead of being shortened,
would never have been formed   Goslinga's strategy was
sadly at fault.   His motives were sincerely Dutch   He
wanted Lille, and he wanted it quickly, because it was to
figure in that barrier, in return for which Holland was
ready to make peace at any moment   Marlborough, on
the other hand, though he wanted Lille and intended to
get it, wanted still more to crush the power of France.
And he had skilfully combined the essential preparations for
the siege with the infliction of such chastisement on French

[1] Murray, vol. iv , p. 165. Marlborough to Maffei, August 13, 1708.

provinces as was well calculated to teach both government
and people the inexpediency of continuing the struggle.
The difference between him and Goslinga can be explained
in a sentence. Goslinga desired a peace that would be
satisfactory to the Dutch, Marlborough a peace that would
be satisfactory to the coalition. As Goslinga failed to
appreciate the distinction, he charged the Duke with
prolonging the war for private gain.

The city of Lille was not unworthy of the immense exertions without which it could never be taken. There were
places like Dendermonde and Menin, which were fortresses
and nothing else; there were places like Ghent and Brussels,
which were populous and wealthy, but in the language of
the period, " of no defence." Lille belonged to neither
category. Its strength was in proportion to its riches
Vauban had bestowed upon its elaborate system of works
and inundations the utmost of his genius. He had given
it a citadel, which he regarded as " the finest and most
finished in the kingdom."[1] Napoleon said that " the true
boulevards of France " were Metz and Lille. He spoke
only as a soldier; but in the political and economic sense,
Lille, in the days of Louis XIV, " next to Paris, was reckoned
the chief place of His Most Christian Majesty's dominions."[2]
Its population was estimated at 60,000. The fertile country
dependent on it contained no fewer than 138 villages. Its
streets and edifices were nobly planned It was " the
staple of all the trade between the Netherlands and France."[3]
" This city," said an English traveller, " hath a face of
trade like London or Amsterdam, and makes a better
appearance than Antwerp; for in the coffee-houses round
the market-place, before and after Change a world of
business is transacted, and here is a good manufactory
for camblets and light stuffs, which they send to Spain and
the Spanish West Indies."[4] Moreover, the merchants of
Lille were " the principal owners of the Dunkirk privateers,
which, without their assistance, could not have been fitted
out in near so great numbers. As they were rich, they
generally supplied the wants of the French King's armies,

[1] Sautai, *Le Siège de Lille*, ch ii , p 19
[2] Lediard, vol ii , p 303   [3] *Ibid*
[4] *A Journey through the Austrian Netherlands*, p. 183, letter xi.

and the customs they paid him were a considerable part of his revenue "[1] Louis himself had a sentimental attachment to the place, which was "the first and fairest" of his conquests. In consenting, therefore, to sacrifice his own strategy in favour of the siege of Lille, Marlborough was not transgressing the fundamental principle of war, as he understood it. For obviously, if the allies succeeded in wrenching from the side of France all the wealth, power, and prestige which were accumulated in that city, a very terrible wound would have been inflicted on the vital resources of the enemy.

Vauban had estimated that a garrison of 16,000 men was necessary for the proper defence of his masterpiece; and according to Coxe, there were 15,000 soldiers in the place when the siege began Goslinga, whose official position afforded him special opportunities of ascertaining the truth, says that there were more than 16,000. During the time that Marlborough lay at Wervicq, the garrison had been reinforced under Berwick's supervision, by fugitives from Oudenarde, gunners from Dunkirk, the regiments of Touraine and Châteauneuf from Valenciennes, three of Berwick's own battalions, and a number of selected officers and other troops. But M de Sautai, whose history of the siege is a model of what such a work should be, fixes the total of all the fighting men in the town at 9,000. He complains that the allies, who were anxious to palliate their own losses, purposely exaggerated the numbers of the French to the magnitude of "a little army."[2] Though M. de Sautai's figures must be accepted in preference to all others, it must be stated, in justice to those whose motives he impugns, that so high a French authority as Feuquières declares that the garrison amounted to "about 15,000 men."[3]

To a city menaced with the agonies of a stern and protracted siege, the precise number of its soldiers is of less account than the character of him who commands them. The story now to be told is an example of the truth that only a great soul can inspire a great defence. When Marl-

[1] Lediard, ibid   [2] Sautai, Le Siège de Lille, ch. v , p 60.
[3] Mémoires de Feuquières, t. iv , p 342

borough encamped at Wervicq, Louis François Boufflers, governor of Flanders and of Lille, divined instinctively which of the frontier fortresses the allied generals would eventually invest. Although he was now in his sixty-fifth year, and already at the summit of his profession, he privately solicited the King's leave to proceed at once to the centre of his government. Louis refused; but the Marshal, who had made every preparation for immediate departure, persisted in his request. On July 26 his prayer was granted He quitted Paris the same day. He interviewed Berwick at Douai on the 27th. On the 28th he entered Lille, accompanied by only two servants He was received with rapture. For Boufflers was the very finest type of soldier produced under the old monarchy of France. He came of a race which had shed its blood at Agincourt and Pavia He had first distinguished himself in 1667 at the siege of the very town which he came now to defend. He had stood beside John Churchill in the bloodstained wood at Enzheim He was prominent in that desperate rearguard action which saved Turenne's army when Turenne himself was no more He fought under Luxembourg at Fleurus; and at Steinkirk he proved himself, in Marlborough's words, "a brave and intelligent captain." He held Namur against William for more than sixty days. He won the hard-fought battle of Eeckeren. A Duke and a Marshal of France, he was modest with the modesty of a simple gentleman. A successful courtier, he was adorned by virtues which rarely thrive in the corrupting atmosphere of courts He was a man of stainless honour, of large generosity, of the most unselfish patriotism. In his active care for the persecuted and the distressed, no less than in his romantic devotion to the person of his sovereign, he illustrated the noblest ideals of his class and of his time.

" He was a verray parfit, gentil knyght "

He knew that ready money would be urgently needed at Lille, and before he left Paris, he borrowed 100,000 crowns, which he devoted entirely to the King's service. He demanded, and obtained, the assistance of two admirable officers, Surville and La Frézelière, who happened to be out of favour at Versailles. Surville had suffered imprison-

ment in the Bastille, and La Frézelière was actually there
at the moment. They were nothing to him, and he was
free to choose whom he would; but he snatched at the
opportunity of restoring their fortunes, though neither they,
nor any of their friends, had the slightest knowledge of his
intention He had accomplished these good deeds, and
made his unostentatious entry into Lille, almost before the
Court was aware of his departure. In the school of Bayard
they did not teach the democratic art of self-advertisement.

Boufflers was not endowed with an intellect of the first
order. But he had studied his profession under Turenne,
Créqui, and Luxembourg; he had been educated by long
and manifold experience; and he was capable of immense
application and untiring attention to detail. In Lille he
surrounded himself with an able and devoted body of
advisers and lieutenants Lee, a valiant Jacobite, six
times wounded at the battle of Höchstadt, and greatly
distinguished at the Schellenberg, had assumed the command by Berwick's orders, and had already opened the
sluices, filled the moats, formed the inundations, and
borrowed largely from the arsenals of Tournai. And
besides La Frézelière, who had inherited from his father
the talents of a successful officer of artillery, besides Surville, a veteran of Steinkirk, Fleurus, and Speyer, Boufflers
was assisted by a notable band of engineers, headed by
Puy-Vauban, who knew the secrets of his cousin, the dead
Marshal, and exhibited not a little of that famous man's
capacity. With the help of these, and of many others as
good as they, and with the cordial co-operation of the
magistracy, Boufflers completed his preparations. He
victualled the place with abundance of wine, beer, and meat
both fresh and salted. He collected cattle, sheep, and
pigs from the surrounding country. He cleared the hospitals
of their occupants, whom he removed to Douai. He levelled
all the trees and hedges in the vicinity of the outworks.
He organised the citizens as firemen and stretcher-bearers,
and employed 800 of them in the construction of palisades.
He erected batteries, mounted cannon, and established a
code of signals to be used with Berwick. And above all,
he breathed into the rank and file of the garrison, many

of whom were neither choice nor seasoned troops, something of his own great spirit of cheerful endurance of privation and calm contempt of suffering and death ,

The Elector of Cologne, who resided at Lille, refused to credit the possibility of a siege, and Boufflers experienced considerable difficulty in inducing him to quit the town The Elector's doubts were shared by Vendôme and many others. On August 9, however, when the artillery of the allies took the road to Ath, it was obvious that either Lille or Tournai had been chosen. On the 12th, when Orange-Nassau's detachment came down from Menin, the truth was known   Thereupon Boufflers burned all farms and houses adjacent to the works. The next move lay with the allies.

Eugène was to conduct the siege, and Marlborough to cover it. Eugène's army, which had been reinforced by a detachment from Marlborough's, consisted now of 53 battalions and 90 squadrons, or 40,000 men in all. The infantry were commanded by the Prince of Orange-Nassau, the cavalry by the Hereditary Prince of Hesse. Marlborough could still dispose of 69 battalions and 140 squadrons, a total of 55,000 men. The whole of the British cavalry, and all the British infantry save five battalions were attached to the covering army. A combat was still a possibility, and for a combat the Duke trusted, as always, to his own countrymen   " Observe," said a news-letter of September 6, " that there are but very few English or Scotch at the siege of Lille; Duke Marlborough has them in a manner all with him, relying and depending mostly on them as the best troops."[1]

Eugène employed 10,000 pioneers on the lines of circumvallation, the circumference of which was six and a half leagues. During the progress of the work, the French fired with effect on the besiegers' quarters. One of their round shot, passing within six inches of the Prince of Orange-Nassau, took off the head of his principal valet. Several ladies of quality, having requested permission to leave the city, Eugène on the 19th, sent an escort to the barriers to bring them away. Some engineers, disguised

[1] Portland MSS · Newsletter, September 6, 1708 (Hist MSS Comm., 15th Report, Appendix, part iv., p 503)

as private soldiers, obtained on this occasion a good view of the fortifications. By the 20th, the entire siege-train had arrived It consisted of 120 guns, 40 mortars, 20 howitzers, and 400 waggons of ammunition On the 21st, after visiting Marlborough at Helchin, the Elector of Saxony and the Landgrave of Hesse arrived in the camp of the besiegers.

It was resolved to attack the city on its northern side, between the horn-works of Saint-André and La Madeleine. The defences here were exceptionally strong; but the decision of Eugène and his advisers was based upon solid ground. In the first place, the high road from Menin, which entered Lille by the suburb of La Madeleine, afforded excellent facilities for transport, and in the event of failure ensured a good line of retreat for the artillery. Secondly, by manipulating the waters of the Dyle, which flowed between the two horn-works, the contents of the moats might be drained away. And thirdly, the rising ground of La Madeleine was the one position which could be considered to dominate the city. The French were not in the least surprised at Eugène's selection Vauban himself had foreseen that, if ever the place were attacked, it would be attacked here, and in a memoir compiled by his own hand, he had enumerated his reasons for this belief. The particular attention, which he bestowed upon the fortifications on this side, was a practical evidence of the sincerity of his opinion.

The trenches were opened on the night of the 22nd. The loss incurred was trifling Two separate attacks had been planned, one on the right under the engineer, Des Roques, the other on the left under the engineer, Du Mey. On the night of the 24th, a fortified chapel, which impeded the advance on the left, was stormed by 300 grenadiers, and seventy prisoners were taken. But on the evening of the 26th, the French made a brilliant sortie, recovered the chapel, and before retiring, destroyed the works of the allies. Meantime Eugène had been preparing his batteries. On the 27th, he opened fire with nearly 100 cannon, mortars, and howitzers. It was estimated that, on that day alone, 7,000 projectiles were discharged against the place. Before sunset great breaches appeared in two bastions. At dawn

on the 28th, the bombardment was resumed   The French
gunners replied vigorously.   They themselves suffered little;
but the town was badly damaged, and the ruin of the bastions
was described by Boufflers as incredible   Under cover of
the bombardment, the besiegers continued to approach.
In front of the French left was a fortified mill, which the
English attacked and carried on the night of the 28th.
But the fire from the ramparts compelled them to abandon
the post as soon as they had won it.   The French re-
occupied it; but instead of holding it against a fresh assault,
which was to have been delivered on the following night,
they burned it, and retired into the town.   The allies were
now so close to the defences that they found it necessary
to sap.   They were constantly augmenting their batteries,
and by the 30th, they had mounted nearly 150 pieces of
various types   Their fire was terrific, but the French
responded stoutly, and on the 31st, succeeded in blowing
up the magazine attached to the biggest battery.   And
every night they sallied out, and endeavoured to destroy
the saps, which were drawing perilously near to the outworks of the place.

From the 12th to the 23rd Marlborough remained with
the covering army at Helchin.   Burgundy and Vendôme
were still between Ghent and Bruges, and Berwick was
at Mortagne with as many men as he could draw together.
If the French generals effected a junction, they would enjoy
an advantage of numbers over Marlborough and Eugène
together, and a very great one over Marlborough alone.
But the Duke was much more afraid of the political machinations of the enemy than of their armed forces in the field.
" The next thing we have to apprehend," he wrote at this
period to Godolphin, " is the intelligence they may have
in our great towns, and particularly that of Brussels; for
it is most certain the people are against us."[1]   To Heinsius
he complained that for some time the Council of State
had " attributed to itself a species of independence, which
causes inconceivable confusion and disorder in affairs, particularly in all that relates to the payment of the troops."[2]

[1] Coxe, vol ii , p 302 Marlborough to Godolphin, August 9, 1708.
[2] Murray, vol iv , p 195: Marlborough to the Pensioner, August 28,
1708.

The unpopulaiity of the Dutch in the Spanish Netherlands had now become a serious impediment to the stiategy of the allies. For the preservation of the capital from the fate of Ghent and Bruges, Marlborough was compelled to sacrifice no fewer than eight battalions and six squadrons, which were badly needed at the front. He ordered Fagel's detachment to hold itself in readiness to reinforce the garrison of Antwerp with four battalions, and he issued some very stringent regulations in favour of the detection of any spies and traitors who might be lurking in that city. He was convinced that the French would endeavour to relieve Lille; but he anticipated that the attempt would take the form of a powerful diversion, and not of a direct attack "There is reason to believe," he wrote to the field-deputies on the 16th, "that the enemy are desirous of uniting all their forces to operate in Brabant, in which case we must not think twice about marching straight upon them (*on ne pourra balancer d'aller droit à cux*)"[1] For such a contingency he had already concerted his own arrangements with Eugène, whom he now advised of the possible imminence of battle. "If the enemy enter Brabant," he wrote, "as I believe they will, we must fling ourselves upon them (*il faut aller tête baissée à eux*)."[2] He had very little doubt of the result. "If God continues on our side," he wrote to Godolphin on the 20th, "we have nothing to fear, our troops being good, though not so numerous as theirs I dare say before half the troops have fought, the success will declare, I hope in God, on our side, and then I may have what I earnestly wish for, quiet."[3] Nevertheless, the expected diversion did not occur Berwick, who was fully persuaded that it would be madness to throw the French infantry against any sort of prepared position, held by the soldiers of Marlborough and Eugène, did indeed propose that he himself should march on Brussels, Malines, and Louvain, while Burgundy and Vendôme took station in the neighbourhood of Audenarde. But Burgundy rejected the project.

[1] *Ibid.*, p. 172. Marlborough to the Deputies of the States, August 16, 1708.
[2] *Ibid*, p 173· Marlborough to the Prince of Savoy, August 16, 1708.
[3] Coxe, vol. ii., p 303. Marlborough to Godolphin, August 20, 1708.

On the 23rd, Marlborough crossed the Schelde, and advanced to Amougies, a movement calculated to diminish the chances of a successful diversion, and even to impede the junction of the French armies " I begin to think," he wrote to the field-deputies on the 24th, " that they no longer intend to act in Brabant."[1]   " I will tell you candidly," wrote Berwick to Chamillart on the 25th, " that I am still uneasy because of the movement of M. de Marlborough, for he wants to fight, and that, if it be possible, before I join."[2]

There was, in fact, no question of any diversion. Louis' orders were that his generals should unite their forces, and march to the relief of Lille. Vendôme, as late as the 20th, had refused to believe that the place could be besieged at all. But on the 25th, when he learned that the trenches had been opened, he prepared to move. " He must not lose much time," wrote Marlborough to Godolphin on the 27th, the date on which the batteries began to play, " since our engineers promise that we shall have the town in ten days "[3]

Leaving La Motte with 20,000 men to hold the lines between Ghent and Bruges, Burgundy and Vendôme marched on the 27th. They passed the Dendre near Ninove, and on the 30th, in the neighbourhood of Lessines, they joined hands with Berwick, who had started from Mons on the 28th. Their combined forces amounted to 140 battalions and 250 squadrons, or 110,000 men in all. According to Saint-Simon, an army at once so numerous, so brilliant, and so well equipped had not been seen within living memory. The same authority alleges that they were penetrated with the fighting spirit. Marlborough, on the other hand, had formed a somewhat qualified opinion of their military value " Their foot," he described to Godolphin on the 27th, as being " in a bad condition,"[4]

---

[1] Murray, vol iv , p 185 Marlborough to the Deputies of the States, August 24, 1708.

[2] *Mémoires de Berwick*, t ii., p. 450.

[3] Coxe, vol ii , p 305 Marlborough to Godolphin, August 27, 1708. According to another forecast, Lille was to fall on September 15 (see Sautai) And an English news-writer gave the date as September 3 " at furthest " (see Portland MSS. Pauncefort to Robert Harley, August 31, 1708 [Hist. MSS. Comm , 15th Report, Appendix, part iv , p. 502]).

[4] *Ibid*

a judgment which virtually coincided with that of Berwick. Even assuming that the French army was all that Saint-Simon pictured it, it was gravely handicapped by weak and divided leadership. Since the day of Oudenarde, Burgundy had been invested with supreme powers; but he was very unwilling to exercise them as against Vendôme. Vendôme, by reason of his semi-royal descent, enjoyed precedence over all the Marshals of France. Berwick, the son of a King of England, had appealed to Louis for exemption from the operation of this rule; but Louis had refused. When, therefore, the forces joined, Berwick, having submitted once to the formality of receiving orders from Vendôme, resigned his own command, and attached himself to the staff of the Duke of Burgundy. Except when he was in the company of that prince, he studiously avoided Vendôme. In these circumstances the French army gained less than nothing from the presence of the victor of Almanza. "Upon the whole," said Marlborough, "I cannot think they will venture a battle, though it is said they have positive orders to succour the place."[1]

Heading straight for Lille, the relieving army reached Tournai on September 1. On the 2nd, they passed the Schelde in eight columns. Vendôme had written to Louis on the 22nd "The more I think of it, the more I marvel at the temerity of the enemy."[2] From Tournai he now wrote to Chamillart: "I promise you that we shall attack them, or else the thing will be altogether impossible."[3]

To Marlborough at Amougies every move in the enemy's game was reported as soon as it was taken, and even before. On August 28, when the French armies were both in motion, but had not yet joined hands, he sent Athlone with 1,500 horse to observe them, while he himself made ready to march at a moment's notice. Near Leuze, Athlone attacked 100 of Berwick's cavalry and captured thirty of them. On the evening of the 29th, Marlborough detached Ross with 2,500 horse, towards Ath. Ross was to cover the march of

[1] *Ibid* : Marlborough to Godolphin, August 27, 1708.
[2] Sautai, ch viii, p 99, D G 2082 Vendôme au Roi, 22 août, 1708
[3] *Ibid*, p 101: D G 2083, Vendôme à Chamillart.

a valuable convoy of 700 waggons, and, at the same time, to push forward parties as far as Lessines. On the morning of the 30th, the convoy reached Amougies in safety The Duke, being satisfied now that the enemy intended at any rate to approach Lille, returned that same afternoon over the Schelde to his own camp at Helchin Thence he sent orders to Fagel to rejoin at once with four Dutch battalions from Flanders and some Saxon, Hessian, and English troops from Brussels. On the 31st, he moved south to Templeuve. And on September 1, the day that the French arrived at Tournai, he passed the Marque at Pont-à-Tressin, and encamped behind it with his centre at Péronne In this position he barred the enemy's advance from the east. If they made a circuit round the sources of the Marque, and then marched up from the south between that river and the Dyle, a simple movement by the right would place him once more between them and Lille.

"When I came to this camp on Saturday," wrote the Duke to Godolphin from Péronne, " I immediately went to the siege, where I had the dissatisfaction of finding every-thing backwarder than was represented to me by letter."[1] On the 2nd, Eugène returned his colleague's visit Accom-panied by Overkirk and other officers, the two commanders examined the country to the south of Lille. " We rode out to view the ground," said Marlborough in his report to Boyle, " and mark the place for the field of battle, in case the enemy should, as they still give out, attempt to succour the town "[2] To Godolphin he wrote " We have marked the camp where we are resolved to receive the enemy, if they make good their boasting. The ground is so very much for our advantage, that with the blessing of God we shall certainly beat them; so that it were to be wished they would venture, but I really think they will not."[3] These words were written on the 3rd, when the Duke had already interrogated a spy, who was endeavouring to enter Lille, and who " confessed that he was to assure the Marshal de Boufflers, from the Duke of Burgundy, that he would attempt

---

[1] Coxe, vol 11 , p. 306: Marlborough to Godolphin, September 3, 1708.
[2] Murray, vol iv., p 203 Marlborough to Boyle, September 3, 1708.
[3] Coxe, vol. 11., p 307 Marlborough to Godolphin, September 3, 1708.

the relief."[1]   Marlborough attached no credit to the story.
Never once, throughout the campaign of 1708, did he
modify the very low estimate which he had formed of the
military value of the French army in the field

His judgment was vindicated by the event.   But equally
well justified were the grave misgivings which he was
beginning to entertain as to the progress of the siege.   "Our
engineers," he wrote to Maffei on the 3rd, "lead us to
expect that we shall take the town in four or five days."[2]
But on the same date he confided to Godolphin that he was
"afraid the town and citadel will cost double the time
which was first thought."[3]   In Lille itself the French were
in high spirits   It was true that Boufflers regarded the
situation with some uneasiness, and suggested a sortie on
a grand scale with 2,600 men.   But the majority of his
officers considered it unnecessary to jeopardise so large a
portion of the garrison.   They could see from the ramparts
the columns of the covering army in motion in the east,
and they believed that the hour of deliverance was at hand.

At Tournai the French generals had disagreed as to the
next move.   Berwick desired to march straight towards
Lille, to encamp between Cysoing and Willems over against
Marlborough's centre and left, and to endeavour to pass the
Marque by surprise.   Vendôme, on the other hand, pinned
his faith to the heavy artillery, which had been ordered up
from Douai under Saint-Hilaire.   He favoured a march by
Cysoing to Pont-à-Marcq, where the army would strike the
Douai road   Burgundy adopted this opinion in preference
to Berwick's.   On the 3rd, they started, but in the neighbourhood of Cysoing, Burgundy and Berwick were warned
by the peasantry that the country between that place and
Pont-à-Marcq, which Vendôme had depicted as an open
plain, was covered with woods and marshes   Considering
that, if the army were once entangled in such a locality,
Marlborough might dash across the Marque and destroy
its rear-guard, Burgundy proposed to adopt the circuitous
road by Orchies.   Vendôme was furious, and roundly
abused Berwick; but Berwick kept his temper, and said

[1] Ibid . Marlborough to Godolphin, September 3, 1708
[2] Murray vol iv , p 204 Marlborough to Maffei September 3, 1708.
[3] Coxe, vol ii , p 307, ibid.

nothing. The peasants were summoned, and questioned
by Vendôme, who eventually gave way. The army marched
to Orchies, where it encamped that night. The partisans
of Vendôme gave out that he had been eager to attack
the allies, and that Berwick had prevented him   It was
no wonder that Marlborough regarded such antagonists
with an almost contemptuous equanimity

On the 4th, the French army turned westward to Mons-
en-Pevèle. Here they were joined by Saint-Hilaire with
100 cannon. They encamped that evening across the
high road from Douai to Lille, extending their left to the
wood of Phalempin, and occupying the village of Pont-à-
Marcq and a couple of châteaux on their front. But at 10
in the morning, when they started from Orchies, Marlborough
began the necessary movement by his right, and long before
they had completed their day's march he had assumed the
position which Eugène and he had already selected. Eugène
arrived in the early hours of the 5th with twenty-six battalions and seventy-two squadrons from the besieging army
The Elector of Saxony and the Landgrave of Hesse accompanied him as volunteers.

The allied position extended from Noyelles-les-Seclin on
the west to Fretin on the east. It was traversed by the
highways from Lille to Lens and Douai, much as the ridge
of Mont St. Jean by the highways from Brussels to Nivelles
and Charleroi. The right flank rested on the marshes of
the Dyle, the left on the water-meadows of the Marque.
The right was protected against cavalry by hollow roads,
the left lay in front of Fretin village with a gentle slope
before it. The centre stretched across a broad and level
plain, and except for a small, natural bastion, provided
by the hamlet of Ennetières on the Douai road, this portion
of the allied line was entirely open to attack. Such a situation would seem to have conferred no extraordinary, and
certainly no overwhelming, advantage upon those who
occupied it   Marlborough, however, did not attempt to
fortify it. Incredulous as he was of the sincerity of the
declared intention of the French, he was resolved to allow
them every opportunity to make it good. Having garrisoned
Ennetières with the brigade of Nassau-Woudenberg, and

posted twenty battalions, supported by twenty squadrons, upon each of his wings, he drew up his centre in three long lines   Contrary to custom, the first two were composed of cavalry, and the third of infantry, " which disposition," says Lediard, " was judged the most proper, as they were in a plain "[1]   Most proper it was from the standpoint of the French, whose strength lay chiefly in the mounted arm.   If, as they alleged, they were genuinely anxious to come to close quarters, they could hardly have expected a fairer opportunity.   They themselves, in Marlborough's situation, would have taken no such risks   They would have been busy at work with pick and shovel, if indeed they would not have prepared themselves an entrenched position several days before.   It is therefore not a little surprising that, although the singularity of the Duke's order of battle must have excited universal comment, the French historians do not refer to it.   Even by such high authorities as Pelet and Sautai it is altogether ignored.

When the sun rose on the morning of the 5th, which was the birthday of the King of France, the allied army made ready to receive the enemy.   The expectation of combat appears to have been very general among all ranks; but Marlborough's incredulity remained unshaken.   Hour after hour went by, and still the many glasses, turned towards the south, could detect no movement of advancing columns.   The French commanders did indeed ride forward to reconnoitre.   Vendôme was in favour of an immediate attack; but Berwick objected, and pointed out that the troops might be charged before they could complete their deployment.   Vendôme adhered to his opinion.   Eventually, however, it was agreed that the army could not, with safety, debouch into the plain until the approaches had been opened out   A numerous body of workmen was employed upon this task, which was finished only on the evening of the 7th.

Until 10 o'clock, Marlborough and Eugène waited patiently for the promised battle.   But when they perceived that an enemy, who possessed a numerical advantage of at least 20,000 men, was unwilling to engage them in

[1] Lediard, vol ii, p. 317.

what was virtually an open plain, they rightly decided
that, in the backward condition of the siege of Lille, where
every day's delay aggravated the problem of supply and
increased the risk of ultimate failure, their time was too
precious to be squandered in unprofitable parades. Thereupon Eugène's infantry marched back to camp. Marlborough set up his tents, and as he was now outnumbered
by nearly two to one, he began that same evening to entrench. Eugène had insisted upon this precaution. It
was very characteristic of the Duke's conception of the
art of war that he should have at first objected to employ
the spade, alleging that " since he commanded, he had never
accustomed his army to entrench itself in presence of the
enemy "[1] But he yielded at length to the representations
of his colleague, which were endorsed by the general-officers
and the field-deputies. The works were commenced at
Ennetières, and in front of the exposed centre. They consisted of a ditch, twelve feet broad and six deep, and a
parapet, four feet high. They were not completed until the
8th. As soon as Eugène's detachment had returned to the
siege, Marlborough changed his order of battle. He now
occupied the position from end to end with a double line
of foot. The Hessians and the Imperialists were on the
right; the Hanoverians, the Palatines, the Prussians, and
the Dutch were in the centre, the Danes and the English
were on the left. Two lines of horse supported each wing,
and the artillery was distributed at the most commanding
points. This was the arrangement which the Duke, according to the French historians, adopted from the outset.
They would seem to have deliberately suppressed the fact
that on the 5th, a challenge to combat in the open field
and upon approximately even terms, was deliberately
proffered by Marlborough and Eugène, and deliberately
declined by the generals of the larger army.

The French might even have attacked on the afternoon
of the 4th, when they arrived at Mons-en-Pevèle. Berwick
declares that, owing to the lateness of the hour at which
some of their troops marched in, this idea was impracticable.
But seeing that Marlborough had not at that time been

---

[1] Lamberty, vol v , p. 21.

joined by Eugène's detachment, Berwick's reasoning
appears to be defective. Marlborough's own opinion of
the whole matter may be read in a letter of the 7th, to the
Prince of Denmark, in which he said. " We drew up the army
twice before them, and gave them fair opportunity of
coming to us, which having declined, they may now find
it more difficult, since we have thrown up a line at the
head of our camp before the *ouvertures* that lead into
the plain, that we may not be subject to sudden alarms,
and draw part of the troops from the siege to no purpose."[1]

On the 6th, the French commanders dispatched their
reports to Versailles. " It is a pitiable thing," wrote
Vendôme to Chamillart, " to see how the goodness of this
army is neutralised by the counsels of M. de Berwick, and
certain general-officers, who destroy in one moment, in
the opinion of Monseigneur, the Duc de Bourgogne, everything with which I can inspire him "[2] This situation, he
explained, had existed from the beginning, and had now
become so intolerable that he must request the minister
to procure him permission to resign, as soon as the business
of Lille was settled Vendôme wrote also to Louis, maintaining that Ennetières could be annihilated by the heavy
artillery, and that the right of the allied position could
be easily carried. " Nevertheless," he complained, " the
majority of the general-officers have implanted doubts in
the mind of Monseigneur, the Duc de Bourgogne." With
the soldiers nothing was wrong, with the general-officers,
everything. " What I see," he exclaimed, " makes my
heart bleed."[3]

Berwick informed Chamillart that the enemy's flanks
were well supported, and that only a frontal attack was
possible. He expressed the opinion that, even if the French
troops had been as good as once they were, the thing would
have been impracticable. " It is sad," he said, " to see
the capture of Lille, but it is sadder still to see the destruction of the only army that is left us, or which can stop the
enemy after Lille is lost "[4] He protested that, if there

---

[1] Murray, vol iv., p 208. Marlborough to the Prince of Denmark,
September 7, 1708.
[2] Pelet, t viii , p 90 · Lettre de Vendôme à Chamillart, 6 septembre, 1708.
[3] *Ibid* , p 89 Lettre de Vendôme au Roi, 6 septembre, 1708
[4] *Ibid* , p 91 · Lettre de Berwick à Chamillart, 6 septembre, 1708.

were any chance of success, he would be willing to venture, but that he saw none.

Burgundy wrote to Louis and to Madame de Maintenon. He frankly admitted his own inability to decide, as between Berwick and Vendôme. He was impressed by the number of brave and intelligent officers who agreed with Berwick; but while he was convinced that Vendôme was constitutionally too rash, he did not deny that the others might be too timid. He recognised that the spirit of the army was good, but he recognised also that France possessed no other Vendôme, he said, " finds easy what the rest of the generals find impossible."[1]   He therefore cast upon the King the responsibility of determining whether they should run the risk of a disaster, or whether they should fall back upon the less heroic course of harassing the enemy's convoys.

Saint-Simon has drawn a vivid picture of the intense anxiety which prevailed at this time in the Court and kingdom of France, where tidings of a decisive collision were hourly expected. Everybody at Versailles had intimate friends and near relations at the front. It was known that Berwick had successfully effected a junction with Vendôme and Burgundy, it was known that the King had given orders that Lille should be relieved at any cost. The atmosphere of the palace grew heavy with intolerable suspense. The card-tables were deserted for the churches, fasting was preferred to supper-parties, and for once prayer became more fashionable than malicious gossip   The Duchess of Burgundy passed whole nights in chapel   A column of lackeys, deputed to announce to their employers the arrival of each fresh courier from the seat of war, blockaded the apartments of Chamillart. The clatter of every passing horse set all the courtiers running. Paris, which had longer to wait for its news, was even more agitated. In the provinces, where, in accordance with the King's commands, the bishops were offering public intercessions for the army, the general alarm was at its height.

The letters of Burgundy, Berwick, and Vendôme reached Versailles on the morning of the 7th. They shocked and disgusted Louis. He had hoped for victory, he had steeled

[1] Pelet, t. viii., p. 93: Lettre de Bourgogne au Roi, 6 septembre, 1708.

himself against defeat; but for vacillation and discord at so supreme a crisis he was not prepared. He saw that France was threatened with a blow to her prestige more dangerous perhaps than a lost battle. Three hours later, the courier who had brought these ominous dispatches was again in the saddle with the King's reply. It expressed the amazement of Louis that his orders had not been executed, and it reiterated them in peremptory tones. That same night, Chamillart himself quitted Versailles for Mons-en-Pevèle, where he arrived on the evening of the 8th.

The situation there had undergone a slight change. By the morning of the 7th, the entrenchments of the allies were so far advanced that Marlborough felt justified in sending back the Imperialist cavalry to Eugène. So confident was he of the ability of his own troops to defend their position against double their numbers that he actually detached 2,000 of his infantry for service with the besieging army. It was the day chosen by the Prince for an attack upon the counterscarp of Lille. From 3 in the afternoon until 7, the batteries maintained a continuous fire from 150 pieces. At 7.30 two columns of assault dashed out of the trenches, one against the horn-work of Saint-André, the other against the horn-work of La Madeleine. They were accompanied by carpenters, who were to cut away the palisades, and by labourers, who were to make good the positions won The French, however, were well prepared. They sprang no fewer than fourteen mines, and they met the assailants right manfully hand to hand. Their forty-five cannon discharged as many as fifty rounds apiece, a very high average in that epoch The allies suffered cruelly; and most of their workmen ran away in the darkness. Eugène had hoped to capture the entire length of the counterscarp from Saint-André to La Madeleine; but after a desperate encounter of three hours' duration, he succeeded only in obtaining a lodgment on the salient angles of the two horn-works His casualties amounted to 2,667. Three of his engineers were killed, and eleven wounded. Of a detachment of 172 Prussian grenadiers only forty emerged unscathed The losses of the defenders were returned at the low figure of 300. Marlborough's pessimistic views of the progress of the siege were now seen to be amply justified. The engineer, Des Roques, writing on the 10th, was fain to admit that the town might " yet hold out eight or ten days."[1] Marlborough reported to Boyle on the same date in guarded terms. " I went this morning to see Prince Eugène," he said, " and left everybody in good heart, but I must own it is not so forward as were to be wished "[2]

The engineers resorted now to the sap. To hinder their operations, the garrison sallied out on the 9th, 11th, and 12th. The consumption of powder and ball by the besieging army was very heavy. Pending the arrival of a convoy of munitions, which quitted Brussels on the 8th, the fire of their batteries slackened considerably To intercept this convoy, thirty squadrons rode off from Mons-en-Pevèle on the 8th; but Marlborough replied at once by detaching an equal force under Albemarle to Grammont. On the same day, while the Duke was dining in his quarters at Fretin, the enemy's foragers, supported by a powerful guard, approached to within a quarter of a league of the allied lines. General Wood requested permission to drive them off. He undertook to do it with a couple of English battalions. Marlborough gave him the regiments of Howe and Temple Argyle, Stair, and Webb accompanied him as volunteers The French retired before them as far as the château of Ennevelin, a good post, encompassed by two ditches. According to Hare, it was " a place which ten men might have kept against 1,000."[3] With charac- teristic temerity, the English, who had neither cannon nor supports, hurled themselves against it, but on the appear- ance of six fresh brigades and all the grenadiers of the enemy they were compelled to abandon the attempt. They retreated in good order, and several times beat off their pursuers. Their losses amounted to 200 privates and six or seven officers, killed and wounded.[4] The Duke was extremely vexed at this folly [5] " But," says one of his historians, " it was impossible to express how much this

[1] Boyer, vol vii , p 99 Letter of M des Roques, September 10, 1708.
[2] Murray, vol iv , p 217 Marlborough to Boyle, September 10, 1708.
[3] Hare MSS , September 10, 1708 (Hist MSS Comm , 14th Report, Appendix, part ix., p 222)
[4] Boyer, vol vii , p 101   Hare gives the figures as 150.
[5] Hare MSS , ibid

vigorous action encouraged the whole army; it being very remarkable that two battalions alone could repulse such a body of men."[1]

Chamillart, on his arrival at Mons-en-Pevèle, effected a sort of reconciliation between Berwick and Vendôme. A council of war was held on the night of the 8th. On the 9th, the minister and the princes reconnoitred the allied position from end to end, and were fired upon by Marlborough's cannon Vendôme adhered to his opinion that an attack was feasible; but Chamillart was converted to the views of Berwick. To try the effect of that artillery, in which Vendôme confided, and to obey, in appearance at any rate, the King's injunctions, the army marched on the morning of the 11th, crossed the Marque, and encamped with their right at Ennevelin, their centre at Avelin, and their left towards Séclin. Marlborough, who was aware of Chamillart's arrival, recognised as a possibility that his antagonists might be galvanised from Versailles into serious action. "We did begin to believe,"[2] he admitted to Godolphin The trenches were manned; the brigades of Evans and Wertmuler were thrown into Ennetières, and messengers were dispatched to Albemarle and Eugène. The French proceeded to set up a battery of heavy cannon over against Ennetières At 10.30 they opened fire. They were vigorously answered by Marlborough's guns. Their left advanced, and occupied Séclin, which was partially burned and then abandoned by the allies Here they erected more batteries, to play upon the right of the Duke's position. The firing continued without cessation until daylight failed. Eugène had now marched in with a detachment from the besieging army. Throughout the night, the allies remained upon the alert. At 7, on the morning of the 12th, the cannonade was resumed It lasted, wrote Marlborough to Boyle, "almost the whole day without making any impression, their balls having done very little mischief"[3] At noon Albemarle rode in. He had already conducted the convoy in safety to Menin. When night

[1] *The History of John, Duke of Marlborough*, by the Author of *The History of Prince Eugène* (1742), p 227
[2] Coxe, vol ii , p 310 Marlborough to Godolphin, September 13, 1708.
[3] Murray, vol iv , p. 222 Marlborough to Boyle, September 13, 1708.

descended, Marlborough ordered the works about Ennetières to be repaired   Vendôme, who had expected to destroy the place or at least to render it untenable, perceived with amazement the resisting power of earth   He was now in a party of one.   He recognised that it would be worse than wasteful to renew the cannonade on the 13th, for Marlborough's men were amusing themselves in collecting the French balls and forwarding them to the besieging army, which had need of ammunition for the pieces of large calibre.   Under cover of darkness, therefore, the French drew off their cannon.   Daylight revealed to the allies the completeness of the fiasco.   Thereupon Eugène and his detachment returned to Lille.

The farce was quite played out.   Vendôme himself reported to Versailles that it was impossible to execute the King's orders; but he laid the responsibility upon "certain general-officers," whom he accused of fostering such "an evil spirit throughout the army" that the soldiers could no longer be trusted to follow.   "When I see what I have seen during the last six days," he exclaimed, "I shed tears of blood."[1]

It was decided on the 14th to repass the Schelde, and to endeavour, by indirect means, to raise the siege. Boufflers and his men, hearing the rumble of the cannon on the 11th and 12th, had exulted in the expectation of immediate relief.   By the instrumentality of a gallant officer, who twice swam seven moats and watercourses with a letter in his mouth, the Marshal exchanged ideas with Chamillart.   He impressed upon the minister the necessity of a prompt attack   He argued that a retreat, by reason of its moral effect, would be tantamount to a disaster   But on the 13th, the welcome thunder in the south was heard no more   That same day, the expected convoy arrived in the camp of the besiegers, and Eugène's batteries roared as loudly as ever   Boufflers repaired the breaches as best he could.   La Frezchère constructed gun-boats which operated on the moats; and the garrison, abandoned to its own resources, cheerfully resolved to continue a resistance,

---

[1] Sautai, *Le Siège de Lille*, p 139. Vendôme au Roi, 13 septembre, 1708, D G 2083.

which had already astonished the allies by its tenacity and skill.

At break of day on the 15th, Vendôme and Burgundy decamped from Mons-en-Pevèle, and marched due east to Orchies. According to Saint-Simon considerable anxiety prevailed lest Marlborough should honour them with his company ("faire à l'armée du Roi la civilité de la reconduire ").[1] Berwick asserts that Marlborough and Eugène were desirous of taking the offensive, and that the French were only saved from a catastrophe by the refusal of the field-deputies to sanction what they regarded as an unnecessary hazard. But Goslinga tells a very different story. By his account, some Dutch generals were thirsting for battle, but Marlborough and Eugène refused to move, because (presumably) they were afraid of finishing the war too soon. One can only say that Goslinga was more likely to know the truth, but that Berwick was more likely to speak it The issue, however, is finally settled, and not in favour of Goslinga, by a letter, written three weeks later by Petkum, the ambassador of Schleswig-Holstein at the Hague, to Torcy, the French minister for foreign affairs. In this letter Petkum observes " The States now blame the deputies for preventing the generals from attacking the French army before Lille."[2] On this occasion, at any rate, the malignant mendacity of Goslinga is signally established.

Thus tamely ended the much advertised attempt to raise the siege of Lille. " Shameful for the nation," says Sautai, " the retreat which was to follow on the waste of time at Mons-en-Pevèle was equivalent to a defeat, as prejudicial to the *moral* of the troops as the check at Oudenarde."[3]

[1] Saint-Simon, t vi., ch. xxvii , p 347
[2] Round MSS Petkum to Torcy, October 4, 1708 (Hist MSS Comm , 14th Report, Appendix, part ix., p. 331).
[3] Sautai, ch. xi , p 144

XXII —LILLE, WYNENDAEL, AND BRUSSELS

MARLBOROUGH remained motionless in his position until the afternoon of the 16th, when upon information that the enemy had continued their march as far as Tournai, he swung round to the east, and encamped behind the Marque from Péronne to Forest On the 17th the French passed the Schelde at Tournai, giving out that they would capture Audenarde before the allies could capture Lille. But Marlborough, writing to Godolphin on the same day, expressed the opinion that they would encamp "between us and Audenarde, in order to hinder our convoys from Brussels, as also the provisions which come from that side of the army."[1] He judged correctly. The French encamped by detachments along the right bank of the Schelde, from the vicinity of Tournai to the vicinity of Ghent They guarded every crossing; they erected batteries at various points; and they rapidly threw up entrenchments of a very formidable description. "These lines," says Lediard, "were about seventy miles long, and in some places, near Audenarde, they had more the appearance of the ramparts of a fortress "[2] This new strategy resulted in a practical blockade of Audenarde, and a complete severance of the communications between the allied army and both Brussels and Holland.

But Vendôme and Burgundy had a second string to their bow. Bergueick was at work once more. A conspiracy to betray the town of Ath was detected in time, but the enemy's designs on Brussels gave Marlborough some anxiety. Pascal, who commanded there, was an energetic and alert officer He had warned the Duke, while the army lay at Fretin, that La Motte, with most of the troops from Ghent and Bruges, was moving out towards Ninove. Marlborough

---

[1] Coxe, vol ii , p 311 : Marlborough to Godolphin, September 17, 1708.
[2] Lediard, vol. ii., p. 329.

had directed that a regiment from the garrison of Antwerp, and four battalions, which were stationed under Murray at Hulst, should proceed forthwith to Brussels, while Eugène had sent orders to six squadrons of Imperialist dragoons and hussars, which were on their way to the front, to remain for the present in the capital. " You can assure the citizens," wrote the Duke to Pascal on the 17th, " that in the event of the enemy's army approaching them, I shall leave nothing undone to secure their safety, being resolved to come with the army to guarantee them against any assault."[1] This promise alone must have gone a long way to restore confidence, for if the French were afraid to fight a battle for the preservation of Lille, they would never venture one for the capture of Brussels.

On the 18th, the Duke advanced three leagues towards the enemy, and encamped at Templeuve. He found that the French had bridged the Schelde between Warcoing and Pecq, and fortified those villages, with the object of disturbing his communications between Audenarde and Courtrai. But on the 19th, he sent Dedem with all the grenadiers and thirty-six guns to dislodge them from those posts They immediately retired behind the river, and took their bridges with them. On the 20th, Marlborough fell back a little towards Lille, and encamped at Lannoy, " the better to observe the enemy and to cover the siege at the same time."[2]

Eugène, in the meanwhile, had made little, if any, progress since the great assault on the 7th. Continually inspired by the example of the chivalrous leader whom they adored, the weary and dwindling garrison displayed such vigilance and activity as amazed and baffled the besiegers. Marlborough visited the lines on the 17th, and dined with Eugène and the field-deputies. The situation of affairs impressed him unfavourably " The siege," he wrote to his wife, " goes on so very slowly, that I am in perpetual fears that it may continue so long, and consequently consume so much stores, that we may at last not have wherewithal to finish, which would be very cruel. These are

---

[1] Murray, vol. iv., p 227: Marlborough to Pascal, September 17, 1708.
[2] Ibid , p 230 Marlborough to Boyle, September 20, 1708.

my fears, but I desire you will let nobody know them "[1]
To Godolphin he wrote: " For these last five or six days the
siege has advanced very little, which makes everybody
uneasy." He added that he had found " everything in
a bad way, which gives me the spleen."[2] His official
report to Boyle was equally ominous. " I can give you
no very good account of its forwardness," he wrote " It
advances still slowly, and that is all that can be said."[3]
The enormous expenditure of ammunition and stores, which
Marlborough afterwards suspected to have been partially
due to embezzlement,[4] aroused the alarm of the field-
deputies, while the recollection of the arrogant prophecies
of the engineers excited the indignation of the soldiery,
who considered that culpable blunders had been committed. " It is commonly said now," wrote Hare, " that
our engineers have attacked the town in the strongest
part."[5] This particular criticism was not altogether just.
They had attacked the town in the part which Vauban
himself considered the most vulnerable, and which he had
specially fortified for that very reason. " Their outworks,"
wrote an officer on the 20th, " are so large and numerous
that, wherever we make our approaches, we are always
flanked and our men very often killed both with small and
cannon shot in the very bottom of the trench. . . . It's
generally believed our engineers have been very much
mistaken."[6] Mistaken they certainly had been, but not
precisely in the way that Hare suggests. Their error was
one of method rather than locality. It was in attempting
to ruin the bastions before destroying the outworks that
they had caused the terrible losses incurred in the assault
of the 7th. Both Marlborough and Eugène were very
dissatisfied with them. Eugène complained to the Emperor
that they knew next to nothing of their business, and
Marlborough wrote to Godolphin in the following terms:

---

[1] Coxe, vol ii , p 310 Marlborough to the Duchess, September 17, 1708.
[2] Ibid., p 311· Marlborough to Godolphin, September 17, 1708
[3] Murray, vol. iv., p 227. Marlborough to Boyle, September 17, 1708.
[4] Coxe, vol ii , p 336: Marlborough to Godolphin, November 29, 1708
[5] Hare MSS Letter, September 10, 1708 (Hist MSS Comm , 14th
Report, Appendix, part ix., p. 221).
[6] MSS of Earl of Mar and Kellie· Lieutenant William Nodding to the
Earl of Mar, September 20, 1708 (Hist MSS Comm., 1904, p 464).

" It is impossible for me to express the uneasiness I suffer for the ill-conduct of our engineers at the siege, where I think everything goes very wrong. It would be a cruel thing if, after we have obliged the enemy to quit all thoughts of relieving the place by force, which they have done, by repassing the Schelde, we should fail of taking it by the ignorance of our engineers, and the want of stores, for we have already fired very near as much as was demanded for the taking of the town and citadel, and as yet we are not entire masters of the counterscarp, so that to you I may own my despair of ending this campaign as in reason we might have expected."[1] It was already evident to Marlborough, that even if the siege were eventually successful, his project for the invasion of France must be abandoned, so far as the campaign of 1708 was concerned.

On the 21st, between 6 and 7 in the evening, Eugène delivered a second assault. The resistance of the garrison was as determined as ever. The Prince himself was wounded " with a small shot in the forehead,"[2] and compelled to withdraw As the result of a furious and protracted struggle, which lasted until 10 o'clock, and at one point until midnight, the besiegers obtained some additional lodgments on the counterscarp. Their casualties amounted to 2,000, while those of the French did not exceed 400.

On the 22nd, Marlborough rode over from Lannoy to visit his colleague. The Prince was about to mount his horse, when the Duke and King Augustus arrived, and persuaded him to continue under treatment for a few days. Fortunately the wound was only a slight one. But the knowledge that Eugène was out of action, depressed the spirits of the soldiers, and so alarmed the States-General that they instructed the field-deputies to urge him to be more sparing of his person in the future.

Marlborough now assumed command of both armies. He decided to deliver a third assault the same evening, and ordered up 400 British and Prussian grenadiers from Lannoy to take part in it. They came so late that he was compelled

[1] Coxe, vol ii , p 312 Marlborough to Godolphin, September 20, 1708.
[2] Murray, vol iv , p 237 Marlborough to the Earl of Sunderland, September 24, 1708.

to postpone the event until the 23rd To escape the notice
of the garrison, they entered the trenches in small groups.
The attack was made at 7 o'clock, in two columns, and
on a less extended front than on the previous occasion.
It was not announced by signal, as the Duke hoped to
surprise the defenders. But when the allies dashed forward
in the teeth of a blinding rainstorm, they found the enemy
well prepared. Nevertheless, they met with a considerable measure of success, and at 9 o'clock, when the fighting
terminated, they had materially added to their lodgments
on the counterscarp. But Marlborough was far from
happy. "We made a third attack last night," he wrote
to Godolphin on the 24th, "and are not yet masters of the
whole counterscarp; but that which is yet worse, those
who have charge of the stores have declared to the deputies
that the opiniatrety of the siege is such, that they have
not stores sufficient for the taking of the town. . . . My
next will acquaint you of what is resolved, but I fear you
must expect nothing good. . . . I am so vexed at the
misbehaviour of our engineers, that I have no patience, and
beg your excuse that I say no more till the next post "
In the same letter, he observed: " I have been obliged to
be every day at the siege, which with the vexation of its
going so ill, I am almost dead."[1]

It is evident that the Duke was exceedingly discouraged
by the evil turn of affairs. Nobody deplored it more than
he, and nobody was less responsible for it. Yet at this
very time he was advised that there were some who suspected him of deliberately prolonging the war in his own
interest There was more than one Goslinga at work both
in England and the Low Countries. The Duke told Bothmar
that the people who propagated this slander did him " great
wrong." " You who know me better," he said, " know
the contrary, and you have very rightly judged that if I
could finish it in one day, I should not take two."[2]

Marlborough's misgivings were shared by many of the
generals. The prevailing anxiety was legitimate enough.
The season was very far advanced, and at any moment,

---

[1] Coxe, vol. ii , p 314. Marlborough to Godolphin, September 24, 1708.
[2] Murray, vol. iv., p 238. Marlborough to Bothmar, September 24, 1708.

the autumnal rains, which in that country are frequently severe, might flood the trenches and destroy the roads. Thanks to the vigorous measures which the Duke adopted for the protection of the countryfolk against marauders from both sides, the subsistence of the allied forces was assured. But without ammunition the siege must come to an impotent conclusion. It was no longer possible to replenish the dwindling stock by means of overland convoys from Brussels. Communications with Brussels, and indeed with almost all the country in rear of the allied forces, were so badly cut that even ordinary dispatches had little prospect of passing, and fifty troopers were necessary to convey a letter from Marlborough to the governor of Audenarde and to deliver the governor's reply. But the Duke was not yet at the end of his resources. The expedition under General Erle, having failed to accomplish anything material upon the coasts of France, had been subsequently destined for Portugal. But on September 7, when Vendôme and Burgundy were at Mons-en-Pevèle, and La Motte was threatening Brussels, the field-deputies sent the Duke a petition, wherein they prayed him to move the Queen to divert the expedition to Ostend, whence it might attempt the recovery of Bruges and Ghent. Marlborough endorsed the document with his own approval and forwarded it to England. The idea was adopted by the English government. On September 21, Byng brought the transports to Ostend. It was impossible now to execute the original suggestion of the field-deputies, for La Motte, who, in consequence of the precautions taken, had already abandoned the design on Brussels, returned immediately to Bruges. But Marlborough judged correctly that here was a case in which the command of the sea might enable him to frustrate the enemy's strategy on land. He decided to restore communications with Antwerp, Brussels, and Holland by the new way of Ostend.

This plan had much to recommend it. The line from Lille to Ostend was shorter by one-third than the line from Lille to Brussels; and it was not intersected by any great river, which could be utilised as Vendôme and Burgundy had already utilised the Schelde. If those commanders

vacated their present position and endeavoured to destroy
the fresh connection, they would not only reopen the road
to Brussels, but they would also incur the risk of a pitched
battle upon level terms. Marlborough knew well, therefore, that he had little or nothing to fear from them La
Motte, however, with his small army at Bruges, might be
troublesome and even dangerous, by reason of his close
proximity to the flank of the new communications. He held
the post of Plasschendaele at the junction of the canals from
Bruges and Nieupoit to Ostend, and already, in concert
with the garrison at Nieuport, he had opened the dykes
and flooded the country to the south of Ostend. But at
this kind of warfare he had met his match in Erle, a methodical and laborious officer, who could organise a depôt much
more successfully than he could conduct a raid. On the
21st, Captain Armstrong brought him verbal instructions
from Marlborough, and on the 22nd, he was visited by
Cadogan With the fourteen battalions under his own
command, and with the help of the Dutch garrison of
Ostend, he partially drained the inundation, bridged the
canal at Leffinghe[1] on his right front, occupied that village
as well as the village of Oudenburg on his left front, and
rapidly landed the munitions and stores, with which he
was abundantly provided. On the arrival of 600 waggons,
which Marlborough sent him under a strong guard from
Lannoy, he prepared a convoy, well stocked with necessaries
for the army of Eugène. Meantime, to observe the movements of La Motte, the Duke, on the 23rd, ordered Landsberg
with six battalions and 800 horse to advance from Courtrai
on the road to Bruges, while on the 24th, he posted six
battalions and ten squadrons in the vicinity of Menin.
These dispositions had one immediate result They riveted
the attention of the French generals upon Ostend, and
terminated all anxiety for the safety of Brussels.
   On the 25th, a momentous council of war was held in
the camp of the besiegers. Marlborough, Eugène, Overkirk, Cadogan, Dopf, and five field-deputies were present.
They met to determine whether they should now abandon

---

[1] This village was already famous in history as the scene of the combat
which preceded the battle of Nieuport in 1600

an enterprise, which had already involved a totally unforeseen expenditure of blood and treasure, or whether they
should still persevere under obvious risks of a disaster.
Eugène declared in uncompromising language for the continuance of the siege   But conscious that he himself was
responsible not only for the operation but also for the
original decision to undertake it, he insisted that his opinion
was founded upon public considerations, and he disclaimed
all concern for his private honour.   He was supported by
three field-deputies, Rechteren, Van Collen, and Hardenbrok.
Strange as it may seem, by his own confession the fire-
eating Goslinga, the man who had won the battle of Oudenarde by himself, was now an advocate of retreat.   He
had been in a state of panic for a week.   Gueldermalsen, as
usual, shared his sentiments.   On the 19th, these two had
submitted to their colleagues a reasoned argument for
abandoning the siege, but they had made no converts
among men whose confidence in Eugène was boundless.
Goslinga of course ascribed their opposition to jealousy of
his own laurels.   On the 20th, he had reported to Heinsius
in most dismal style.   " When I consider," he wrote, " all
the drawbacks, the late season, the danger run by Brussels,
Antwerp, and consequently by our country, the necessity
of securing Ghent, and above all, of passing the Schelde,
I begin to despair of the success of our enterprise."[1]   He
had prophesied the failure of the forthcoming assault, and
had complained that Marlborough had allotted to Eugène
too small an army for so great a siege   On the 23rd, he
had written again in agonised terms.   " Our incomparable
chief is wounded," he exclaimed.   It would be better, he
argued, to save both the army and Brabant than to persist
in an enterprise which he regarded as desperate.   He
admitted that a retreat would be " a heavy blow for the
Republic," and would efface the glory of Oudenarde, but
he could see no feasible alternative   He added that Eugène
was now proposing to supply the army from Ostend; " but
for all that," he concluded, " I fear more than I hope "
On the same day, in conjunction with Gueldermalsen, he
had drawn up a memorandum in support of his views.

[1] *Heinsius Archives.*

Fortunately for the Grand Alliance this document did not impress his colleagues A reply to it was immediately drafted, and signed by four field-deputies. Three of these four were now present at the council, where they took their stand by Eugène Goslinga urged that a guard should be left over the camp before Lille, and that the rest of the army should march forthwith upon the Schelde and force a passage to Brussels. Gueldermalsen advocated the raising of the siege, and according to Goslinga, Marlborough, Overkirk, Cadogan, and Dopf " seemed to lean "[1] as strongly as Gueldermalsen in the same direction. During an adjournment for dinner, excellent reports arrived from Ostend. Thereupon, it was unanimously agreed that, until they had seen the fate of the convoy, which Erle was preparing, no new decision should be taken.

Goslinga plumes himself upon his candour in confessing in his Memoirs that he opposed the continuance of the siege. Apparently he considers that the course which he pursued on this occasion was in some way discreditable to himself. But only a very conceited amateur would consider it discreditable. The case for a retreat rested upon arguments of a respectable and even powerful order. In sincerely placing them before the council, Goslinga did nothing of which he had any need to be ashamed. The same can hardly be said of his assertion that Marlborough publicly opposed Eugène. It is highly improbable that Marlborough would, in any circumstances, have publicly opposed Eugène upon an issue of the highest consequence; it is simply incredible that the man, who had been working and planning for a week to establish a new line of communications, should have suddenly advocated a proposal, the adoption of which would have rendered his thought and labour a mere waste of time.

For the moment, the situation had been saved by the admirable firmness of Eugène A general, less highly endowed with that moral courage which infinitely transcends the physical bravery of the battlefield, might have lost his confidence in himself, and with it, the confidence of others. The Prince of Savoy retained both. Had he

[1] *Mémoires de Goslinga*, p. 95

manifested the slightest weakness, the field-deputies would have adopted the opinion of Goslinga, and the campaign of 1708 would have terminated with a costly and humiliating check to the arms of the Grand Alliance.

But even Eugène could not take Lille without powder and ball If Marlborough could supply him at once, and could keep him supplied, with ammunition from Ostend, the place must eventually be captured, provided always that the advent of torrential rains did not convert the lines and trenches of the besiegers into uninhabitable swamps. To a very serious, if less vital, degree, the chances of the defence were affected by the same imperative consideration. The consumption of powder by the garrison had been enormous; and Boufflers was advised that his magazines were dangerously depleted. Chamillart suggested that a fresh supply might be introduced into the place by a detachment of 2,000 men. The idea was coldly received. Boufflers himself was doubtful of its feasibility. Such an operation, it was thought, would require to be supported by a small army. But all imagination and daring were not yet extinct among the nobility of France. They flourished, at any rate, in the youngest and only surviving son of that victor of Fleurus, Steinkirk, and Neerwinden, whom, by reason of his bounteous prodigality in captured colours, the people had christened " the upholsterer of Notre Dame." Christian Louis de Montmorency-Luxembourg was a warrior well proven in famous fights. It was said that at Oudenarde he had rallied his men no fewer than fifteen times. Every soldier of France loved him for his valour and the great tradition of the name he bore. He was now to show himself well worthy of his reputation and his race. What Chamillart had suggested, the Chevalier de Luxembourg volunteered to execute

At Douai, with the assistance of Saint-Hilaire, the commander of the French artillery, he matured his plan. He conceived that, under cover of darkness and under the leadership of officers who spoke the languages current in the allied camps, a column of some 2,000 horse might cross the lines of the besiegers and enter the city without striking a blow. Acting on the advice of an excellent guide, who knew how thinly the enormous circuit was in many places guarded, he proposed to follow the main road from Douai to Lille as far as Ennetières, to wheel to the left at that village, to pass the barrier under the pretence that he was carrying ammunition from the army of Marlborough to the army of Eugène, and once inside, to dash for the nearest gate, the Porte des Malades. For the execution of this audacious project, he selected forty dragoons from the garrison of Tournai, who were well acquainted with the country, and 300 British and Germans in the service of France, who could easily masquerade in the darkness as soldiers of Marlborough. But the bulk of the detachment consisted of French cavalry and French dragoons. Every man exchanged his carbine for the firelock of the infantry. Every man fastened in his hat a green badge, the emblem of Marlborough's army. And every man carried on his horse's crupper a sack of gunpowder between fifty and sixty pounds in weight.

On the 28th, the day selected for the attempt, the gates of Douai remained strictly closed, that neither spies nor traitors might report the preparations to Eugène. At 3 in the afternoon, Luxembourg's long column trotted out along the northern road. Neither drum nor trumpet accompanied their march. At the bridge of Raches they were joined by the British and Germans and the dragoons from Tournai. Luxembourg briefly addressed the men. " Come, friends," he said, " it is necessary to get into Lille, and it is not necessary to get out again. We must sacrifice ourselves for the glory of the fatherland "[1] At 7 in the evening he resumed his march in absolute silence. He had timed himself to reach the besiegers' lines an hour after midnight. The dragoons from Tournai led the way. One hundred and fifty grenadiers on horseback brought up the rear. These, if the enterprise should miscarry, were to dismount at Ennetières and cover the retreat of the cavalry. It was speedily and terribly realised that, when Luxembourg spoke of sacrifice, he was not gasconading. As the column rode out of Raches, a charger of Saint-Aignan's

[1] Sautai, *Siège de Lille*, ch xvi , p. 190 (D'après le récit du chevalier de Bellevue).

regiment stumbled and fell. The road was paved; and the
sparks from the multitude of hoofs set fire to the powder
which the unfortunate animal carried, and which had
escaped from the sack. An explosion followed, and another,
and another. Twenty-five men were blown to pieces in
as many seconds If the risks were such at this stage of
the adventure, it needed no very powerful imagination to
estimate what their magnitude would be in presence of the
enemy. But Luxembourg was nothing daunted. He
simply directed the column to abandon the fatal pavement
and to ride only on the grassy side-tracks.

It was a fine and cloudless night. Northward they went,
past Mons-en-Pevèle, and through Pont-à-Marcq, across the
forsaken encampment of Burgundy and Vendôme, and out
into the vast and moonlit plain beyond. A black mass
barred the road. It was the sleeping village of Ennetières,
that much tormented outwork of Marlborough's unconquerable lines They passed unchallenged, and emerging
from the shadows, wheeled from the great high road, and
struck away towards the left across the open fields The
crucial moment was at hand. Suddenly a dragoon dashed
out of the column, and galloped madly off into the night.
It was nothing strange that among all those 2,000 riders
there should have been one whose nerve was unequal to
the test. It was very glorious for France that there should
have been only one. But Luxembourg, who dared not fire
upon the runaway, and who knew not whether the man
was a traitor or a coward, decided that there was no time
to lose Setting spurs to his horse, he took the column
at a gallop across the moonlit plain. The night was so
fine that he could not easily mistake the path. Soon they
were in sight of the besiegers' lines. As the head of the
column rode up to the barrier, they saw that it was open.
A few paces off, the guard were warming themselves beside
a fire. Short and sharp came the German challenge, " Who
goes there ?" " Holland !" was the answer, given with
easy confidence by the Silesian baron, Sandreski, " Holland ! Regiments of the army of Marlborough bringing
munitions to the besiegers."[1] And they began to pass.

[1] Sautai, p. 191.

Sandreski engaged the officer of the guard in idle converse. In explanation of the precipitate manner of their arrival, he told how they had been seen and chased by a party of French. And while he talked, they passed   Being thoroughly posted in the gossip of the allied camp, he sustained his part with a sublime assumption of calm, though he must almost have heard the pulsations of his own heart. And still they passed, troop after troop, and squadron after squadron, and no man said them nay Already the Chevalier de Luxembourg was through, and the British, and the Germans, and the dragoons of Tournai, and the dragoons of La Reine, and the regiment of Bourgogne, and the regiment of Saint-Aignan, and La Bertoche, and Macteville, and Fontaine. But not every man of them was endowed with the wonderful coolness of the Silesian. The strain upon the nerves of the later squadrons was well-nigh intolerable. "Close up ! Close up !"[1] roared a captain of Fontaine's, as the last of his men swung through the barrier. He spoke in French, and the onlookers started at the sound of his accent. Already the length of the column, and the ever-increasing velocity of its march, had excited some remark. Curiosity turned now to swift suspicion. A subaltern officer stepped forward, and challenged the regiment of Forsat which had begun to pass Again and again he challenged them, but no man answered. And still they passed, and still the smiling Silesian sat his horse beside the barrier and talked his German small-talk. Suddenly the guard rushed to arms, flung themselves into an adjacent redoubt, and opened fire upon this mysterious cavalry. The soldiers of the nearest regiments poured out from their tents, and hastily fell in in "their shirts and cartridge-boxes."[2] But Forsat still rode on. Then the worst happened. Hand-grenades were hurled into the ranks of the French with fatal accuracy. Two deafening explosions followed; and each explosion tore out the lives of thirty men. With a touch of the spur, Sandreski, who was mounted on a thorough-bred, bounded off unscathed to rejoin Luxembourg. But the regiment of Tourot, coming up now to the barrier, found the roadway blocked

[1] Saut a, p 191.   [2] *Millner's Journal*, p 236, September 17, 1708

with a mangled heap of men and hoises. Their terrified chargers refused to move The officers of Tourot and of the grenadiers dashed forward to the front. They saw at a glance what had befallen; they saw the guaids advancing to close the gates, the pickets running to arms, and all the camp alarmed, and they very properly gave the order to retiie upon Ennetières. There was no panic The movement was conducted with rapidity, but in good order. Some Hessian hussars gave chase, and captured thirty-one prisoners, but at Ennetières the grenadiers dismounted, and checked the pursuit.

The Chevalier de Luxembourg, in the meantime, drew rein before the Porte des Malades with no fewer than 1,500 men But the headlong gallop fiom Ennetières had upset his calculation, and he had arrived in advance of the appointed time. The garrison, suspecting a ruse, refused to open the gate. Some delay ensued. Luxembourg's peril was imminent, for the Prince of Hesse-Cassel had got the Palatine dragoons of Wittgenstein to horse, and was rapidly approaching. At length, in response to loud and repeated cries of " Vive Bourgogne !" the gate was opened, and amid the acclamations of an admiring throng, the gallant 1,500 rode into the town. They brought with them 50,000 pounds' weight of powder and 1,200 firelocks It was a night not soon to be forgotten by the citizens of Lille. The tumult of cheering was plainly audible in the camp of the besiegers. The whole population went delirious with joy, and many, in the ecstasy of the moment, did not hesitate to declare that the raising of the siege was close at hand.

" The action which M. le Chevalier de Luxembourg has just performed," wrote Boufflers to Versailles, " is so replete with courage and daring, and of such great distinction, that I think that it merits that the King should be graciously pleased to make him a lieutenant-general of his armies without waiting for the end of the siege."[1] The Marshal could ask no less Luxembourg had brought him both powder and men. Luxembourg had uplifted the hearts of the exhausted garrison and revived the hopes of the despon-

[1] Sautai, ch xvi., p. 192: Boufflers au duc de Bourgogne, D G 2083.

dent citizens. And Luxembourg had performed an exploit which the great majority of soldiers had deemed to be impossible. One may search very far in the history of war for a more splendid feat of arms.

The allies were so profoundly mortified at their unexpected reverse that they foolishly attempted to belittle it. The Prince of Hesse-Cassel, in his report upon the night's proceedings, dwelt upon " the dreadful spectacle " of "the way strewed with dead carcasses, horses, heads, arms, and legs, half-burned,"[1] and pretended to believe that no more than 300 men had actually entered the place. If Goslinga can be credited, the vexation of the besiegers is easy to understand. For the Dutchman alleges that Eugène had been warned in time by a gentleman of Douai, and that a party, commanded by a famous scout-master, was abroad that very evening for the express purpose of discovering the enemy's column. And then, with an affectation of reluctance, he regretfully confesses that even the great Eugène (" our incomparable chief ") was prone to neglect the minor details of his profession. Coming from Goslinga, the criticism is suspect. At all other times, it is his cue to represent Eugène as impeccable and infallible. But for this occasion only, the childish game of disparaging Marlborough by unduly exalting his colleague is suspended, in order that the soldier who had just refused to abandon the siege of Lille, in deference to the opinion of a conceited civilian, may be suitably chastised.

The exultation of the beleaguered city was short-lived. The devoted ride of Luxembourg was not all that happened on Friday, September 28. Even before that ride was well begun, something far bigger, something much more decisive, had befallen elsewhere

The resolution, unanimously adopted at the council of war on the 25th, was the logical outcome of unquestionable facts. If communications with Ostend could not be opened, the siege must be raised. Everything depended on the fate of the convoy which Erle was now preparing. To this truth the French commanders were as fully alive as Marlborough and Eugène. They therefore dispatched con-

[1] Lediard, vol. ii., p. 336.

siderable reinforcements to La Motte at Bruges. La Motte, who had served for many years in those parts and knew the country thoroughly, was assisted in the preparation of his plans by Berwick and Bergueick, who specially visited him at this time. His orders were to destroy the convoy at all hazards. But the concentration of a small army at Bruges did not escape the vigilance of Marlborough. Reckoning that the two detachments, which he had dispatched on the 23rd and 24th to observe La Motte, were no longer sufficient for their purpose, the Duke, on the 26th, instructed Major-General Webb to march with twelve battalions to their support. Webb was followed by Cadogan with twelve battalions more, and twenty squadrons On the 27th, Cadogan encamped at Rousselaere, and Webb at Thourout. On the 28th, Marlborough transferred his own camp from Lannoy to Roncq, which is a little south of Menin The convoy was already in motion. It had started on the evening of the 26th; and on the morning of the 27th, it crossed the canal at Leffinghe and took the road to Slype. Thereupon La Motte detached 1,000 foot and 300 horse to seize the post of Oudenburg. They met with a sharp repulse, and retired with a loss of 200 men. The same evening, Webb ordered a couple of battalions and 600 grenadiers under Landsberg to proceed to the assistance of the garrison, to cover the march of the convoy as far as Couckelaere, and then to rejoin him at Thourout.

The situation, on the morning of the 28th, was extremely interesting. The convoy was hastening south from Slype to Couckelaere. Landsberg was marching on the same point. Webb, with twenty-two battalions, was waiting at Thourout. Cadogan, with the cavalry, was at Hooglede. And La Motte had moved down with his entire force to Zedelghem. He had no fewer than 22,000 men under his command; but he was nervous and embarrassed. He had received a report that Marlborough in person had started for the north. If, therefore, he advanced too far, he might find himself in contact with overwhelming numbers. On the other hand, his instructions were explicit and peremptory. He was to destroy the convoy at all costs. And the convoy, as he was now informed, was approaching Couckelaere.

He decided to dash forward at once and intercept it at Wynendael.

In this, the supreme crisis of the whole campaign, Marlborough's officers made no mistakes. During the night, Cadogan had dispatched 150 horse under Lottum on the road to Oudenburg, to meet and reinforce Landsberg's detachment. Lottum had passed Cortemarck, and was already nearing Ichteghem, when he suddenly fell in with a party of the enemy's horse. Chasing them northward, he presently emerged into an open plain, where he descried a numerous body of French cavalry mounting in haste at his approach. He estimated their strength at sixteen squadrons. He immediately went about, and rode at full speed for Thourout. Arriving there at noon, he made his report to Webb.

Webb concluded rightly that La Motte was at hand. His own decision was instantly taken. Ordering Lottum to precede him, he marched out of Thourout with his twenty-two battalions on the road to Ichteghem. At the hamlet of Wynendael he found what he wanted, a position in which with his numerically inferior force he might hope to hold the enemy in check until the convoy had passed. The right flank was protected by a considerable wood, attached to the château of Wynendael, and the left, though to an inferior degree, by a low coppice. Lottum and his men advanced through the intervening space, and Webb in person rode with them to reconnoitre. It was now 2 o'clock. The enemy was plainly visible in the open country beyond. To impose upon them as long as possible, Webb boldly deployed his handful of troopers, while he occupied the coppice on the left with his grenadiers, who had led the march of the column. As fast as the remainder of the infantry arrived, he drew them up at the entrance of the interval between the coppice and the wood.

It seems to have been generally assumed by contemporary historians, other than French ones, that Webb was confronted by the whole of La Motte's army of 22,000 men. La Motte, however, had made his precipitate rush on Wynendael in two columns, one of which outpaced the other by several hours. This first column, according to

La Motte's own narrative, contained 18 battalions of infantry, 13 squadrons of cavalry, and 13 squadrons of dragoons. It was also equipped with 19 guns, 9 of them being of triple bore. It numbered probably between 11,000 and 12,000 men. Webb's force, with the exception of Lottum's 150 sabres, which in actual combat would be almost negligible, consisted solely of infantry. It had no artillery. In Landsberg's absence, its numbers apparently did not exceed 6,000

Six of the allied battalions had already arrived, and had formed their line across the gap between the coppice and the wood, when La Motte's gunners opened fire. It was impossible to respond in kind. But Lottum's troopers, with magnificent courage and discipline, steadily sat their horses in the very teeth of the cannonade. Behind this living screen Webb completed his deployment as rapidly as possible. He drew up his men in two lines, resting his right on the wood and château of Wynendael. His left, which was more exposed, and more easy to be turned, he extended behind the coppice and beyond it. He concealed a battalion in the wood, and three more in the coppice, with parties of grenadiers forty paces in advance, crouching in the undergrowth These troops he instructed to remain hidden, until such time as they could fire directly into the enemy's flanks.

As soon as he had completed his dispositions, he directed the survivors of Lottum's gallant cavalry to fall back. The welcome order was executed in perfect form He posted them now 300 paces to his left rear, which he regarded as his most vulnerable point. Meantime, the French came on but slowly. La Motte was waiting for his second column, the arrival of which would have increased the numerical odds in his favour to more than three to one. It was this delay which enabled Webb to elaborate his preparations at his leisure. But for three hours the French artillery was playing, without any risk to itself, on the ranks of the allies. Webb ordered his men to lie down.[1] In this position they were, for the most part, invisible to the French gunners, by reason of the fact that the land between the coppice

[1] Burnet, vol v., p. 391.

and the wood dips gently[1] from the plain, where La Motte's army was stationed, to the line which Webb had occupied. Consequently, the actual losses of the allies during this prolonged and nerve-racking cannonade were inconsiderable.

At 5 o'clock, La Motte could tarry no longer, for the convoy was passing beyond his reach, and darkness was rapidly approaching. Trusting that the allies had been severely shaken by the fire of his artillery, and relying on the weight of numbers to crush their centre, he advanced into the gap. His infantry was deployed in four lines, eight battalions of Spaniards being posted on the right, a position of honour which had been conceded to them only after a warm dispute. The cavalry and dragoons, in two lines, acted as supports. As they moved forward to the attack, they threw out the Royal Marine regiment on their right and three companies of grenadiers on their left, with the evident intention of clearing their flanks. This manœuvre did not escape the vigilance of Webb. He immediately reinforced the troops in the wood and the coppice with a battalion apiece. Scarcely had this final order been executed, when Landsberg, who had been escorting the convoy throughout the day, arrived with his detachment. Like a prudent officer, he had marched to the sound of the cannon. His two battalions and 600 grenadiers were utilised by Webb for the formation of a third line.

The troops, concealed in the coppice and the wood, obeyed their instructions to the letter. When the flanks of the enemy's infantry were fully exposed, but not before, they opened fire. Thereupon, the three companies of grenadiers which La Motte had detached towards the wood, instantly recoiled upon the main body, and the entire left wing shrank inwards on the centre. The same tendency, though not to the same degree, was exhibited on the right. Disorder and congestion ensued, and the whole of the advancing line staggered and paused. Encouraged by their officers, however, they recovered, and again went forward. Meantime, the Royal Marine regiment had penetrated the coppice, and had engaged the Prussians, who were posted

---

[1] The writer ascertained this fact upon the spot.

there, in deadly combat. Partially relieved by this diversion, the French right pushed in upon the allied centre. But the left could make no headway. La Motte had enjoined upon his men the use of the bayonet, but on the left, at any rate, the French soldiers insisted on burning powder at an ineffective range. The attack of the right created some disorder in a couple of allied battalions, and at this moment La Motte threw forward his dragoons to the assistance of his left. But the Swiss regiment of Albemarle moved out to meet the dragoons, and completely repulsed them with severe loss, while Webb brought up three fresh battalions to the relief of those which had been shaken. The French and Spanish infantry recoiled upon their mounted supports, recovered themselves a little, returned to the attack, and unable to endure the steady volleys which rolled them in upon their centre, again recoiled. The allies stood very firm. Indeed, they were eager to advance; but Webb forbade it, lest the advantage of the flanking fire from the coppice and the wood should be thrown away. Slowly, but in great confusion, the French and Spaniards fell back. Neither the exhortations nor the threats of their officers could induce them to do more than discharge their pieces from a distance. But in shooting, as in all else, they were hopelessly outclassed. The allied infantry, in the words of an old writer, "went out by platoons, and made a continual fire upon the enemy, in as good order as if they had been exercising."[1]

Before 7, the army of La Motte was in full retreat. In their haste to escape, they left their cannon in a wood, and only returned to fetch it on the ensuing day. The retirement was covered by their numerous cavalry. Towards the end of the action, Cadogan, who had hastened like Landsberg to the sound of the cannon, rode up with a couple of squadrons and courageously offered to charge the enemy's rear-guard. But Webb was unwilling to hazard a repulse. He had every reason to be satisfied with what had already been done. He had lost 138 killed and 800 wounded. But he had beaten an army that was almost

---

[1] *A Journey through the Austrian Netherlands*, p 188, letter xi (see also Webb's account, given in Boyer, vol. vii, p. 123)

twice as large as his own,[1] inflicting on it casualties that were at least three times as numerous as those which he himself had incurred; and he had saved the convoy.

" All the world wondered." Even the Dutch government were convinced at last. " Their confidence," wrote Petkum, " is now so great, that they have ordered their deputies to forbid no battles when the generals are agreed on them."[2] " So unequal an action," says Burnet, " and so shameful a flight, with so great loss, was looked on as the most extraordinary thing that had happened during the whole war."[3] And indeed a parallel case could not be easily discovered in any war   The numerical disproportion between the armies was very considerable; but the historians, some of whom have exaggerated the figures, dwell too much upon that aspect of the matter.   The vital distinction between the contending forces lay rather in their composition than in their numbers.   Properly speaking, Webb's command was not an army at all   It was simply a detachment of infantry, for Lottum's troopers were so few that they must be disregarded.   La Motte, on the other hand, disposed of a combined force of all three arms.   His horse included a proportion of mounted infantry; and half his artillery was of the newest pattern.   Against such a force, Clausewitz observes that " it is hardly conceivable " that an army consisting of infantry and cavalry only " could keep the field at all."[4]   Yet at Wynendael such a force sustained a shattering and decisive defeat at the hands of infantry alone.

Feuquières wrote with even more than his accustomed pungency of the incapacity of La Motte, who " not only failed to destroy the convoy with a body of troops infinitely superior to the escort, but found a way to get his own men beaten by that feeble escort."   " Truly a rare occurrence ! " he exclaims   " For cases have been fairly common, where convoys, which have taken great risks, have got through in safety, thanks to the diligence and secrecy of their

---

[1] Petkum says that the odds were 4 to 3 (see Round MSS).   But they would seem to have been more nearly 2 to 1
[2] Round MSS · Petkum to Torcy, October 4, 1708 (Hist. MSS. Comm., 14th Report, Appendix, part ix , p. 331).
[3] Burnet, vol v , p. 392
[4] Clausewitz, *On War*, vol ii , book v , ch. iv., p 10.

march. But hitherto there has never been a case where, when a convoy was attacked by forces infinitely stronger than its escort, not only did the convoy itself get through intact, but its feeble escort beat the superior assailant. The creation of so singular a precedent was reserved for M. de la Motte."[1]

It is doubtless true that La Motte, though an old and experienced officer, was not a brilliant one, and that he was confronted by an opponent in whom courage, resolution, and professional skill were united in no ordinary degree. He was told, of course (what beaten general is not told ?), that if only he had made a turning movement, all would have been well. But his fundamental error seems rather to have been that he ever permitted the convoy to proceed so far on its journey to the south. Whatever were his blunders (and the usual catalogue is to be found in Feuquières), his soldiers were certainly not the men to save him from the consequences of his own incompetence. " The infantry did very ill,"[2] wrote a French officer to Chamillart. Vendôme described them as " vagabonds," and as guilty of " the most frightful panic ever seen."[3] The bulk of them were incapable of obeying La Motte's order to use the bayonet. When their conduct is contrasted with that of the allied troops, the essential cause of a victory, which was regarded at the time as almost a miracle, becomes at once apparent. Webb's soldiers were mostly Prussians, Hanoverians, and Dutch. It is doubtful if there were more than two or three British battalions present But British and foreign, they were all of them Marlborough's men; and never was that overwhelming superiority of *moral*, to which Marlborough's men, without distinction of race, had now attained, more splendidly illustrated than on the field of Wynendael. And besides superiority of *moral*, they had something else not wholly unconnected with it, a signal superiority of fire discipline. Fire discipline was a matter on which the Duke had bestowed an immensity of time and pains. At Wynendael he was

---

[1] *Mémoires de Feuquières*, t iii , p 72
[2] Sautai, ch xvi , p 197 M de Bernières à Chamillart, 4 octobre, 1708, D G 2085
[3] *Ibid* Vendôme au duc de Bourgogne, D G. 2083.

abundantly rewarded by such an exhibition of coolness and precision as astonished all beholders.

Webb remained on the field of battle until two hours after midnight, when he collected his own wounded and many of the French as well, and returned to Thourout, while the convoy was proceeding in all security on the road to Rousselaere and Menin. From this time onward, the continuance of the siege was virtually assured, and that for two good reasons. In the first place the immediate requirements of the army of Eugène could now be met; in the second, it had been demonstrated that the new communications were a working substitute for the old ones. The test, accepted by the council of war on the 25th, had now been applied. Had the result been different, "the consequence," wrote Marlborough to Godolphin, "must have been the raising of the siege the next day."[1]

The *London Gazette*, in its first account of the battle of Wynendael, ascribed the honour to Cadogan. Cadogan, who was responsible for the general arrangements made for the safety of the convoy, deserved all credit for his skill. But Wynendael was Webb's victory, and Webb's alone. The gallant soldier was naturally indignant. He applied at once for permission to return to England, that he might lay the true facts before the Queen herself. Marlborough consented, and at the same time requested Godolphin to present Webb to Her Majesty, and repeatedly and warmly urged that he should be made a lieutenant-general at the earliest possible date. The Queen received him " very kindly and with a great deal of distinction"; and his own narrative of the battle was subsequently printed in full in the *Gazette* Webb got his promotion in the following January; and the King of Prussia, whose troops had played a conspicuous part in the battle, conferred on him the Order of Generosity But the Duke's enemies did not hesitate to turn the affair to their own vile uses. As Webb was a Tory, and Cadogan was Marlborough's favourite, they affected to consider that the case against the Duke was complete. The Duke, in reality, was altogether blameless. On the day after the battle, he had written

---

[1] Coxe, vol ii, p 321. Marlborough to Godolphin, October 1, 1708.

to Webb in these terms· " Mr. Cadogan is just now arrived, and has acquainted me with the success of the action you had yesterday . . . which must be attributed chiefly to your good conduct and resolution. You may assure yourself I shall do you justice at home, and be glad on all occasions to own the service you have done in securing the convoy upon which the success of our siege so much depends."[1] And on the same day he forwarded to the Secretary of State an official report in which no name save Webb's was so much as mentioned. Whoever, therefore, may have been responsible for the misleading notice in the *London Gazette*, Marlborough most certainly was not. It was not the first occasion on which serious ground for complaint had been given by that journal. Marlborough himself, and notably in the campaign of 1705, had been one of the sufferers from its antics. In the present instance the error may have been due to the malignant partisanship of the Whig editor, Steele. Or it may have originated from a mistake in a report sent by the Prince of Hesse to the Hague, and thence forwarded to London. But any weapon, however unclean, was good enough for the exasperated Tories to use against the Duke. And more than a century later, the Whig, Thackeray, made his Esmond such a hater of Marlborough as to believe and repeat these slanders.[2]

The catastrophe of Wynendael intensified the demoralisation of the enemy's forces, and gave rise to embittered recriminations between the French, who had done least, and the Spaniards, who had suffered most. It would have ruined La Motte but for the protection of powerful friends. It so infuriated Vendôme that he proceeded in person with a considerable body of troops to take command of the operations in the vicinity of Bruges. On October 5, he encamped at Oudenburg with 30,000 men. He ordered the sluices to be opened, and flooded the country far and wide. He reinforced the garrison of Nieuport, threatened the post at Leffinghe, and demonstrated against Ostend itself. But Erle was everywhere on the alert. The French were

---

[1] Murray, vol. iv., p. 242: Marlborough to Major-General Webb, September 29, 1708.

[2] *The History of Henry Esmond*, bk. ii., ch. xv, and the explanatory footnote

entrenching themselves at Oudenburg, when Marlborough moved. Hoping to catch them with their backs to the inundation, in which position, in the event of a defeat, it would have been impossible, says Berwick, "that a single man should escape,"[1] the Duke quitted Roncq on the 7th, with 60 battalions and 130 squadrons. He left behind him 20 squadrons and 20 battalions with instructions to join Eugène, if the Prince should need them   Passing through Rousselaere he came on the morning of the 8th to Wynendael, where he learned that the French, not daring to face him in the field, had fled precipitately to Bruges. According to Berwick, the general-officers, after fruitless endeavours to persuade Vendôme "to move out of the hole in which he had put himself,"[2] cut the dykes and rendered the camp untenable   There being no prospect of an action, the Duke marched back, on the 9th, to Rousselaere, whence he dispatched Lottum with half the infantry to Moorslede, to be nearer to the siege.   But learning that Vendôme was still at Bruges, and was continually drawing fresh troops in that direction, he recalled Lottum on the 10th   It is evident that his situation was a somewhat uneasy one. If he moved too far to the south, he uncovered the communications with Ostend, if he moved too far to the north, he uncovered the army of Eugène.   On the one hand, it was necessary to keep an unceasing watch upon Vendôme, but on the other, the precedent which Luxembourg had set might be imitated at any moment Indeed, at this very time, the French were seriously considering a definite proposal to dash through the besieger's lines with 6,000 men from Tournai.   Moreover, Burgundy and Berwick[3] were resolved to attack Eugène, if Marlborough proceeded farther north than Rousselaere.   In fixing his camp at that town, the Duke selected the most convenient point for the discharge of his twofold duty.

The besiegers, in the meanwhile, greatly encouraged both by the arrival of the convoy from Ostend and by the complete recovery of Eugène from his recent wound, were making indisputable progress.   Their replenished batteries

---

[1] *Memoirs of the Duke of Berwick*, vol ii , p 38   [2] *Ibid*

[3] *Ibid* , p 431 : Berwick to Chamillart, October 10, 1708

maintained a vigorous fire, and the insidious work of sapping went on apace On October 3, an assault was delivered on a ravelin. Marlborough was present; and 300 grenadiers from his army took part in the affair. The Duke himself is said to have suggested both the time and manner of attack Previous attempts had been made during the hours of darkness, in pursuance of the advice of the engineers, and "against the opinion of most of the general officers."[1] But on this occasion, the hour selected was noon No signal was given. The French, who were asleep at the moment, were completely surprised. The ravelin was easily taken, and despite a murderous cannonade from the ramparts, successfully held In the course of the action, a bomb from the besiegers' batteries blew up a French magazine, containing 1,600 grenades besides a quantity of powder. "There remains now," wrote Marlborough to Sunderland, "little more to be done than filling up the fossé "[2] Boufflers was in despair He recognised that the loss of the ravelin was fatal. At first, he proposed to recover it by a sortie on a grand scale; but he was dissuaded by Lee from so hazardous a venture. In this hour of bitterness his chivalry did not desert him. When it was suggested that he should punish the officer whose carelessness was responsible for so grave a disaster, he absolutely refused to allow that a man of proved competence and courage should suffer for a solitary act of negligence. Small wonder that he was loved and served with infinite devotion.

On October 5, the garrison, undismayed by the increasing peril of their situation, frustrated an attempt of the besiegers to extend their lodgment on the counterscarp. It was the forty-fifth day of open trenches. " I think that the thing is without example,"[3] wrote Boufflers to Louis. From this time onward both he and his men subsisted upon horseflesh. Such cows as they still possessed were reserved for the service of the hospitals. By the middle of the month they were slaughtering a hundred horses a day. The supply of powder was dangerously low. There was a growing insufficiency of guns, bombs, and grenades. Boufflers

[1] Murray, vol. iv., p 252 Marlborough to Sunderland, October 4, 1708.
[2] Ibid
[3] Sautai, p 211, ch. xviii : Boufflers au Roi, 6 octobre, 1708, D.G 2083.

himself had never undressed since the first day of the siege. He slept but little He converted his own house into a hospital. And the nobles of France lived up to this ideal. The regiment of Angennes had no captains for its grenadiers. The regiment of Touraine would soon have no captains at all. And almost every general and colonel had been wounded.

Eugène's army was likewise in evil case. Provisions were by no means abundant The soldiers were shoeless and ill-paid The Germans, in particular, were discontented, and eager to return to their own country. The total casualties of the siege were estimated on October 18 at 10,000. No fewer than sixty engineers had been killed or wounded Neither the staff of surgeons nor the supply of drugs was adequate for the treatment of the suffering multitude which crowded the hospitals of Menin and of Courtrai.

It was fortunate indeed for the allies that the weather continued to be dry and mild. Only two slight showers had fallen since the commencement of the siege. If the autumn rains, so long overdue, had even now set in with some severity, Eugène would probably have been compelled to abandon the enterprise even at the eleventh hour, or lose his army. But the stars in their courses were fighting for the coalition. Louis beheld, with bitter incredulity, the second city in his kingdom fast slipping from his grasp. "It is a strange thing," wrote Chamillart to Berwick on October 3, "that being masters of the places and the country, and having an army at least equal to the enemy's, you suffer all their convoys to pass, and let them take Lille without the Duke of Burgundy's forming any obstacle against it. The uncharitable public attribute this to the little union that subsists between the Duke of Vendôme and yourself. I wish you had already found an opportunity to show that they are mistaken."[1] And again, on the 8th, he wrote: "Absorbed as I am, and as I ought to be, with grief, at seeing Lille fall into the hands of the enemy, who do just what they please in the face of an army of a hundred thousand men, I think the Duke of Burgundy

---

[1] *Berwick's Memoirs*, vol ii , p 421 · Chamillart to Berwick, October 3, 1708.

might make a better use of his army than in guarding the Schelde."[1] The minister did but give utterance to the painful emotions of the orthodox school of warfare, confronted now with the nemesis of its own system. His insinuations produced no result. Burgundy and Berwick did not dare to fling such infantry as that which had disgraced itself at Wynendael against the confident veterans whom Marlborough had trained to the temper and the habit of victory in the field. One chance of saving Lille, and one alone, remained If only Vendôme could immediately destroy the communications with Ostend, the siege must even now collapse.

Vendôme was by no means idle. The besiegers had need of a second convoy; and although 900 waggons, mounted on wheels of exceptional height, had succeeded in reaching Ostend, it was doubtful whether they could return. The inundation extended as far south as the village of St. Pierre Cappelle, and it was rising daily. Only the village of Leffinghe, which was strongly held by the allies, stood up like the ark in the midst of the waters. Erle provided boats for the conveyance of the stores as far as St. Pierre Cappelle, where Marlborough's carriages were waiting to receive them. But Vendôme brought galleys from Dunkirk, and sloops from Nieuport and Bruges, and erecting a battery on a small island, formed out of the débris of a broken dyke, he cannonaded Leffinghe itself as well as the boats from Ostend. On the 12th, Marlborough dispatched eight battalions and nine squadrons to Couckelaere, and five battalions to Cortemarck. On the 13th, he ordered pioneers, carpenters, and pontoons to proceed to St Pierre Cappelle, where Cadogan was supervising the operations. On the 14th, 500 barrels of powder came through Rousselaere. Anticipating that Vendôme might be tempted, out of sheer despair, to risk all upon a battle, Marlborough dispatched a reinforcement of twelve battalions and twenty squadrons, on the 15th, to Cortemarck, and directed his army to be ready to march at an hour's notice. But Cadogan continued to transmit in safety ammunition, money, and provisions for the army of Eugène until the 18th, when he

[1] *Ibid*, p 429 Ch. nullart to Berwick, October 8, 1708

reported that the business was no longer feasible. " The enemy having cut the dykes in other places," wrote Marlborough to Sunderland on the 19th, " the spring-tides threw in so much water that their galleys and boats rowed over the very places where we had posted our men, whereby they have destroyed a great tract of land for many years,"[1] (an interesting achievement on the part of those who affected to be shocked at the devastation of Bavaria in 1704). Nevertheless, nearly 1,700 barrels of powder had now come through, to feed the powerful batteries which Eugène was mounting on the counterscarp, and " a vast quantity of brandy, salt, cheese, hams, etc." to feed the gunners who manned them. The fall of Lille, either by capitulation or by storm, was virtually assured.

The happiness of witnessing so proud a triumph for a cause which none had served more devotedly than he, was denied to Overkirk. His health, which had begun to fail in the preceding winter, had broken down completely under the anxieties and fatigues of this trying campaign. On the 18th, while Marlborough and Eugène were conferring with the field-deputies at Menin, he expired in his quarters at Rousselaere, in the sixty-seventh year of his age, and in the Duke's own words to Sunderland, " very much lamented as well in the army as by all who knew him."[2] He was a wise and noble captain, who had fought in many famous fields. It was exactly thirty years since he had saved the life of William at the battle of St. Denis, in days when the fortune of the Dutch Republic was low indeed. The wheel had come full circle now, and Overkirk had lived to lead the once despised horsemen of Holland in the winning charge at Ramillies, and to launch the culminating movement on the day of Oudenarde. Marlborough recommended that, as " an act of goodness and generosity," the Queen should bestow a pension upon Overkirk's son, Nassau-Woudenberg, who had distinguished himself at Wynendael. " He is," said the Duke, " as virtuous and as brave a man as lives. His father has been able, I fear, to leave him nothing."[3] Marlborough, indeed, had every

---

[1] Murray, vol iv., p 269: Marlborough to Sunderland, October 19, 1708.
[2] *Ibid.*
[3] Coxe, vol. ii , p. 324. Marlborough to Godolphin, October 19, 1708

reason to love and to regret the dead Field-Marshal. From the very outset of the war, and in the teeth of Dutch generals and Dutch field-deputies, Overkirk had loyally and steadfastly supported the Englishman on whom the mantle of William had descended. One of his last acts, on the last day of his life, was to sign an order, at the Duke's special request, for the final abolition of the pike in the Dutch service.[1] Half an hour afterwards he passed away. He was called by Goslinga, and by the angry Tories,[2] obsequious This impertinence completes his title to the veneration of posterity.

The body was conveyed to Holland, to be buried at Overkirk. Preceded by a numerous detachment of horse and foot, and followed by Marlborough and his principal officers, the coffin was borne from Rousselaere in mournful silence along the road to Ghent. Three-quarters of a mile beyond the town, the troops halted, while the dead Field-Marshal rode for the last time between the sorrowing ranks, and the last salutes were fired. Then his aide-de-camp and an escort of 150 cavalry took charge of the corpse. They were furnished with a special passport from Vendôme; and as they passed by the city of Ghent on their way to Sas, the French commander of that fortress sent them his tribute to an old and gallant foe.

Having satisfied himself that Eugène had now sufficient powder to finish the siege,[3] Marlborough turned his attention to the grave problem of provisioning the two armies. Supplies were running low; and to procure and to economise such food as the country still produced, it was necessary to adopt the most energetic methods. The troops were compelled to subsist for a period of six days on the rations ordinarily allowed for four, the value of the difference being handed them in cash Strict precautions were taken against misappropriation and waste. Marlborough paid, and paid well, for all that his officers seized, but the peasantry, with a prudent eye to their own requirements

---

[1] Murray, vol iv., p 282 Letter of October 29 to the States, as to calling in 190 pikes from the Dutch Guards, and rearming them with muskets or firelocks.

[2] Portland MSS · E Lewis to Robert Harley, October 15, 1708 (Hist MSS Comm, 15th Report, Appendix, part iv, p 509)

[3] Murray, vol v, p. 267 Marlborough to Wratislaw, October 17, 1708.

in the approaching winter, persisted in withholding large stocks from this obligatory market. Far and wide, villages, castles, and even churches, were ransacked by the allied troopers for concealed grain. And the local authorities of Courtrai and the surrounding district were admonished by the Duke in a minatory note that, unless they exhibited more zeal for the service, he would be constrained to avail himself of " other measures "[1]

Indignant at the remarkable degree of success which had attended Cadogan's efforts to maintain the lines of communication with Ostend, Vendôme determined that the post of Leffinghe must at all costs be wrested from the allies. On the 18th, therefore, assisted by his galleys and sloops, he advanced by way of the dyke, and opening trenches, and erecting batteries, laid siege to this insignificant village in proper form. But on the night of the 20th, 300 of the Dutch and English infantry which garrisoned the place, crossed the canal, completely surprised the French, killed or wounded 100 of them, dismounted their cannon, and carried off forty prisoners. Vendôme resorted now to sapping; but he lost heavily from the fire of the defenders. On the 24th, Erle threw into Leffinghe a mixed force of English, Dutch, and Spaniards, 1,250 in all, and withdrew the old garrison, which was very exhausted. That same night, the French assaulted the village in five columns. Marching waist-deep in water, they surprised the new-comers, who were either negligent or drunk, and with trifling loss to themselves, captured the position and everybody in it, besides a large magazine of powder and £80,000 in gold. Vendôme reported his exploit to Versailles in pompous language. His sense of proportion or his sense of humour was to seek on this occasion. For while he was taking Leffinghe, he had already lost Lille

From the 4th to the 20th, Eugène had been busily extending his lodgments on the counterscarp, draining the moat, and erecting new batteries against the body of the place. On the evening of the 20th, Boufflers, fearing an assault, lighted an enormous conflagration in the breach. At

[1] Murray, vol iv., p 266: Marlborough to local authorities of Courtrai, October 17, 1708.

8 a.m. on the morning of Sunday, the 21st, Eugène opened fire with fifty-six cannon and thirty-five mortars and howitzers. The effect was crushing. Within twenty-four hours it became evident that Lille might be exposed, at any moment, to the horrors of a storm Boufflers had been instructed by the King that such a calamity was not to be allowed. Accordingly, on the afternoon of the 22nd, with the concurrence of his principal officers he decided to surrender The melancholy duty of hoisting the colour of its Colonel's company above the breach devolved by the rule of seniority upon the old and glorious regiment of Touraine. The order was received with natural emotion. Nobody volunteered for the service, and the soldier who was eventually commanded by the officer of the guard to undertake it, smashed his musket in two upon the ground

Hostages were immediately exchanged, and an armistice for thirty hours was accepted by both sides. With mutual congratulations besiegers and besieged now fraternised together. " The enemy and we were good friends," wrote a British officer. " They brought out good Burgundy, and we drank, caroused, and gasconaded each other by turns."[1] Eugène, who had been that day to Menin, learned the news on his return. He wrote at once to Boufflers, complimenting him on his heroic defence, and according him the extraordinary privilege of drawing up the terms of his own capitulation " I will make no alterations," he said, "unless there be something contrary to my honour or my duty, but that I do not apprehend from so gallant a man as yourself "[2]

The conditions were quickly settled. The city of Lille, with such ammunition and stores as it still contained, was to be delivered to the allies. The wives and families of the French officers and soldiers, and all the cavalry which had entered with Luxembourg, were to retire to Douai. The sick and wounded were to be transported to the same place, or, if they preferred, they were to remain in Lille at their own expense. Prisoners, taken during the siege, were to

[1] MSS of the Earl of Mar and Kellie, p 468 Lieutenant William Nodding to the Earl of Mar, October 14 1708 (Hist MSS Comm)
[2] *Histoire du Prince Eugène de Savoye*, t. iv., p. 39. Letter from Eugène to Boufflers.

be exchanged. The garrison were to evacuate the town, and to retire into the citadel on the 25th; and the allies were not to assume possession before that date. Boufflers and his men had well deserved this honourable treatment. They had yielded only after sixty-two days of open trenches. They had lost no fewer than 4,500 of their number, or exactly half of their original strength. And they had inflicted 12,000 casualties on the besiegers.

The fall of Lille, " the first and fairest "[1] of the French King's conquests, resounded over Europe like the crack of doom. At a time when her financial resources were intolerably strained, France could ill afford to lose this populous centre of wealth and commerce. At a time when her military prestige had already been profoundly humbled, she could ill afford to see this masterpiece of Vauban's skill wrested from her by an enemy, who, according to every maxim of the game, should have paid a terrible penalty for his imbecility or his presumption. For though, in a sense, the honour of the nation had been saved by Boufflers, not even the sublime figure of Boufflers could divert the attention of the whole world from the outstanding and amazing fact that a French army of more than 100,000 men, outnumbering the total forces of the allies, and interposing between them and their base, had for sixty-two days remained little more than idle spectators of the Marshal's magnificent resistance. This army was commanded by Vendôme, and accompanied by Berwick, both generals of high repute; many of its officers were men of proved capacity and valour; it included in its ranks the most distinguished corps in Europe, the *Maison du Roi ;* its cavalry was numerous, and as Luxembourg's exploit had demonstrated, of admirable quality; it was well fed, well equipped, and furnished with a powerful artillery. But the spirit of its infantry had been effectually broken on the day of Oudenarde—how effectually was demonstrated once for all at Wynendael. Virtual paralysis of the entire organism had resulted. In the words of Clausewitz, already quoted, " if we speak of the destruction of the enemy's armed force, we must expressly point out

1 Lediard, vol. ii., p. 303.

that nothing obliges us to confine this idea to the mere physical force, on the contrary, the moral is necessarily implied as well."

Having vainly endeavoured to persuade Boufflers to surrender the citadel in addition to the town, Eugène attacked that formidable work on the 29th. Luckily, the fine weather, which had broken during the interval, returned when it was again wanted   Eugène proceeded by the tedious, but inexpensive method of the sap.   "We go on very slowly, being very careful of losing as few men as possible,"[1] wrote Marlborough to Godolphin on November 6. And ten days later he observed. "We have great management both of our men and ammunition "[2]   It was a prudent policy. " For we cannot yet guess," said the Duke, " when the campaign may end, but as soon as we have the citadel, we shall then be more at liberty to act against the enemy, and I do assure you that our intentions are to do all that lies in our power to bring them to action."[3]   Meantime, it was necessary to feed the allied troops; and to the solution of this increasingly difficult problem Marlborough addressed himself with his accustomed energy.   The stringent measures already adopted were ruthlessly enforced.   " I admit," said the Duke, referring to the compulsory purchase of corn, " that it is a little hard upon the peasants, but of two evils it is necessary to choose the lesser.   Better that they should suffer than that the army should perish for want of bread "[4]   On the luckless French across the frontier his hand again fell heavily.   On October 25, he dispatched thirty squadrons and ten battalions into the country of Artois, where they seized and fortified La Bassée.   Advancing as far as Lens, they possessed themselves of all the corn they could discover, and forwarded it to Lille.   Owing to the flight of the peasantry, the troopers were compelled to do the threshing themselves. Marlborough paid them for this work at the rate of a crown a sack.   On November 3, the Duke's army made a general forage to the very walls of Ypres.   On the 5th, Cadogan

---

[1] Coxe, vol ii., p 328, Marlborough to Godolphin, November 6, 1708.
[2] *Ibid* , p. 329, November 16, 1708.
[3] *Ibid* , p 328, November 6, 1708
[4] Murray, vol iv , p 295 Marlborough to Fagel, November 8, 1708.

reinforced the detachment at La Bassée with ten squadrons. But these measures proved insufficient. " We are more apprehensive of wanting bread than of anything the enemy can do,"[1] wrote Marlborough to Godolphin on November 6. Accordingly, on the 7th, he dispatched Lord Stair with ten squadrons and ten battalions to Dixmude. On the 9th, Stair attacked a French post in the neighbourhood of that town, and captured the garrison of 200 men. The people of the country and of the country of Furnes had been ordered by the French to carry their corn to Ypres Stair required them to carry it to him, on pain of military execution. Proper payment was made, plundering was suppressed, by Marlborough's orders, with the utmost severity; and very soon a good supply of corn, cattle, and sheep began to arrive at Lille. But even so, the stock of corn was inadequate for the requirements of the army. " Not everyone knows, or takes into consideration," said Marlborough, " that we have need of nearly a thousand sacks a day."[2] Reinforced with five battalions and six squadrons, Stair advanced to Loo, and under constant pressure from the Duke redoubled his exertions. He lost a Prussian detachment of two battalions and two squadrons, which the French cut off at Hondschoote; but he succeeded in extorting 6,000 sacks of grain from the country of Furnes. Marlborough wrote to him almost every day, and sometimes twice in one day. The text was always the same: " All our happiness depends upon your getting a good quantity of corn."[3] Stair had some idea of surprising Furnes or Gravelines; but the Duke, though he would have valued the capture of Gravelines, now that Ostend was isolated, would consent to nothing that might interfere with the vital business of feeding the army. Meantime, the troops at La Bassée were by no means idle; and on the 13th, they extended their field of operations by the seizure of St. Venant. Marlborough's work was well seconded by Eugène, who rigidly economised the provisions thus hardly obtained. As the result of these activities,

[1] Coxe, vol ii , p 328. Marlborough to Godolphin, November 6, 1708.
[2] Murray, vol iv , p 300. Marlborough to Fagel, November 11, 1708.
[3] Ibid , p 299 Marlborough to Stair, November 10, 1708.

" both armies," says a contemporary writer, " lived in parsimonious plenty."[1]

On the morrow of the surrender of Lille, it naturally devolved upon the belligerents to take stock of the situation, strategic and political. Marlborough had formed the opinion that the time was ripe for the conclusion of a general peace He considered that France, shamefully humiliated in the field, ravaged and insulted in her border provinces, and robbed of one of the wealthiest of her cities and proudest of her fortresses, was probably now in a proper mood to submit to terms which would be acceptable to the coalition. If only she were convinced that, in the event of her continued resistance, the allies intended to press their advantages with the utmost means at their disposal, he judged that she would infallibly seize the present opportunity lest a worse thing should befall her When therefore he dispatched to the British government the news of the capture of Lille, he pressed them, at the same time, to obtain from Parliament an augmentation of the forces in the field. This suggestion he repeatedly urged upon Godolphin. Writing on November 6, he said that, in the absence of another victory, " the only way of having a speedy and good peace, is to augment the troops, so as that we may enter France the next campaign with a good superiority, and that the fleet may be assisting to us."[2] And on the 16th, he said· " I must again press you to take what I believe to be the only way of bringing France to a speedy and good peace, which is, that you should not only resolve in England upon an augmentation of troops, but lose no time in prevailing with the States-General to do the same, for their declaration would have a greater effect in France "[3] He added that he was exerting his own influence in Holland to this end, and that the field-deputies agreed with him entirely Identical opinions were expressed by Lord Stair, in a letter of October 24 to the Earl of Mar. Stair suggested that the States-General should " propose to the Queen to make an augmentation in this country next year of 20,000 men " " The very

[1] T Brodrick, 1713, *A Compleat History of the Late War,* p 265
[2] Coxe, vol. ii., p 329: Marlborough to Godolphin, November 6, 17c8
[3] *Ibid* , pp 329, 330, November 16, 1708.

proposal," he said, " would break the heart of the French. They know the troops are ready, and they are persuaded we can find the money when we have a mind to it."[1]

So convinced was Marlborough that the moment was favourable to a peace, that, on October 30, he took a very unusual step. He wrote to Berwick, suggesting that Louis should instruct Burgundy to make written propositions to the Dutch field-deputies, to Prince Eugène, and to himself. He also hinted at the possibility of a six months' armistice, an idea which had emanated apparently from M. de Surville at the time of the surrender of Lille. He admitted that Eugène was bitterly opposed to a suspension of arms; but for himself he undertook that, if his suggestion were followed by the French government, he would labour to the utmost of his power to promote an accommodation. As an evidence of sincerity, he added that, in the event of his success, he trusted that the offer, made to him by d'Alègre in 1706, would still hold good. In choosing Berwick as his intermediary, the Duke was actuated by a variety of motives In August and September some correspondence, in which he had announced his weariness of the war and his anxiety for a peace, " stable, permanent, and consonant with the interests of my country,"[2] had already passed between them. He had intimated then that the Dutch government should be first approached, but Berwick had replied that, in view of previous rebuffs, it would be " contrary to the dignity of the King " to make further overtures to Holland. The letter of October 30 had therefore the appearance of an alternative proposal. Moreover, the Duke was naturally desirous of increasing the credit and importance of his sister's son at the French Court And in embarking upon a secret negotiation, which, if it became public property, could easily be misrepresented by his numerous enemies, he very prudently selected as agent a man on whose personal affection and stainless honour he could implicitly rely.

Berwick immediately forwarded a copy of this important

---

[1] MSS of the Earl of Mar and Kellie, p 468: The Earl of Stair to the Earl of Mar, October 24, 1708 (Hist MSS Comm)
[2] Legrelle, *Une négociation inconnue entre Berwick et Marlborough 1708-1709*, p. 17.

communication to Torcy, the Minister for Foreign Affairs, at Versailles. In a covering letter, he observed that, although as a general rule he mistrusted everything that Marlborough wrote, on this occasion he believed the Duke to be in earnest. In his memoirs he remarks: " Nothing could be more advantageous than this advice of the Duke of Marlborough; it opened to us an honourable way of putting an end to a burthensome war. . . . There was not the least appearance of duplicity in what he wrote."[1]

Marlborough's letter was judiciously timed. The French commanders were seriously considering the new situation created by the loss of Lille, and grave differences of opinion had already manifested themselves. On November 1, Chamillart arrived to take part in the deliberations. He was accompanied by Chamlay, whose knowledge of the topography of the Spanish Netherlands was unrivalled among the soldiers of France. On the 3rd, a council of war was held at Saulchoi near Tournai. Burgundy, Berry, Vendôme, Berwick, and Bergueick were also present. Vendôme insisted that they " ought to march to the Duke of Marlborough and give him battle ",[2] but after Wynendael, even Vendôme, incurable optimist as he was, could hardly have expected such a proposition to be taken seriously. He next suggested that they should continue to hold the canals from Nieuport to Bruges, and from Bruges to Ghent, and the Schelde from Ghent to Tournai and Condé, thus blockading " every road by which the enemy could return, in order to reduce them to the alternative of being starved to death or suing for peace."[3] This strategy had already been examined by Berwick, and by him pronounced impossible, but it found great favour at Versailles, and Chamillart had virtually been instructed to authorise its adoption Nevertheless, Berwick assailed it without mercy. He insisted that the army, large as it was, was quite unequal to the task of securing this immense line of waterways, and that Marlborough could force a passage whenever he chose He recognised that the allies might prefer to remain where they were, but he pointed out that, in that event, the French cavalry would be utterly ruined

[1] *Berwick's Memoirs*, vol ii , p 48   [2] *Ibid.*, p. 49.   [3] *Ibid*

if it attempted to winter in a country already stripped of
forage, and that the enemy, in the meantime, could live
at the expense of Picardy and Artois, not a single soldier
being available for the defence of those provinces   His own
plan was to abandon the ambitious and perilous design
of cutting off the allies from their base, to station a sufficient
force behind the canal for the preservation of Ghent and
Bruges, and to march with the remainder of the army to
the protection of the frontier provinces.   To the civilian
mind of Chamillart this safer and sounder strategy seemed
vastly less attractive than Vendôme's.   The idea of enclosing a hostile army in a semi-circle of rivers and canals
was exactly the idea to fascinate a person of the class
which makes war on maps and nowhere else.   So Chamillart
decided that, as long, at any rate, as the citadel of Lille
held out, the army should continue in their present situation, strengthening their works with the spade, and covering their front with inundations, which were to be produced
by the destruction of the dykes.   Both Berwick and
Chamlay declared that this last device was impracticable,
as it eventually proved to be; and Chamlay subsequently
wrote to Louis to warn him against the hazardous extension
of the army in the face of an enemy " so vigilant and so
rashly enterprising."[1]   Nevertheless, the strategy of Vendôme prevailed.   His flatterers at Versailles lamented
" the unhappy destiny of those conquerors who were about
to be imprisoned without any resource ",[2] and French
ministers and agents at foreign courts confidently gave out
" that the confederate army was so cooped up, they would
soon either be famished or obliged to abandon Lille."[3]

Possessed as he was with this fantastic notion that the
victors of Oudenarde, Wynendael, and Lille, were virtually
entrapped, Chamillart concluded that Marlborough's desire
for an armistice, as a preliminary to a general peace, was
directly begotten of fear.   Louis and Torcy, however,
ascribed it to anxiety for his own future.   They had per-

[1] Pelet, t. viii , p 510 Mémoire de Chamlay, 13 novembre, 1708
[2] Saint-Simon, t. vi , ch xxxi , p 405
[3] Lediard, vol ii , p 366 (see also Marlborough's letters of November 30
to Manchester, and December 10 to Moles and Stanhope, printed in
Murray vol iv)

suaded themselves that he was losing popularity in England,
that he had every reason to dread a change of ministry,
that the Queen would be unable to protect him for ever,
that he had quarrelled with the Elector of Hanover, that
he was jealous of Eugène's glory, and in short, that his
own position, as the virtual head of the coalition, was in
fact so uneasy and so insecure that he was eager to retire
from it on the best possible terms.   Under the influence
of these ideas, which they communicated to Burgundy,
Berwick, and Chamillart, they instructed Berwick to
decline his uncle's offer, but to express the willingness of
France to enter into secret conferences between a couple
of selected representatives.   Berwick's letter was drafted
by Chamillart, and dispatched on the 5th.   It emphasised
the desire of Louis for peace; but it altogether rejected the
notion that France should commit herself to definite proposals in the manner suggested   It declared that a "solid
peace" could never be secured except by the way of secret
conferences, at which the more delicate questions might
be discussed and adjusted.   It contended that, in the
existing position of the armies in the field, peace itself
would be easier to arrange than the conditions of an
armistice.   And it flatly accused Marlborough of initiating
the correspondence as a method of escape from a military
situation which "those experienced in war"[1] regarded as
likely to culminate in the destruction of the allied armies.

French diplomacy in that epoch would never have been
justly esteemed the most brilliant in Europe, had this
effusion been typical of it.[2]   "M. de Chamillart," says
Berwick, "dictated to me the answer I was to make, and
I thought it such an extraordinary one, that I sent it in
French to show the Duke of Marlborough that it did not

[1] Legrelle, p 35· Réponse de M le duc de Berwick au duc de Marlborough, composée par M de Chamillart, 5 novembre, 1708
[2] Many years later, writing in reference to the difficulties which beset
the negotiations of 1709 and 1710, Bolingbroke declared his opinion of
this incident as follows. "I know most certainly that France lost . . . by the
little skill and address of her principal minister, in answering overtures
made during the siege of Lille by a principal person among the allies,
such an opportunity and such a correspondence as would have removed
some of the obstacles that lay now in her way, have prevented others,
and have procured her peace" (*A Sketch of the History and State of Europe*,
letter viii).

come from me "[1]   The effect which it produced can readily
be imagined. Marlborough was astonished and disgusted
to discover that the French government was still dwelling
in a fool's paradise   In his reply, which was dispatched
on the 6th, he did not condescend to discuss the military
situation with ministers so blinded, or with " those experienced in war," who advised them so fatuously. He simply
observed that he was " very mortified " that any motive
other than " the desire for peace "[2] should be attributed
to the action he had taken. While he concurred in the
view that the terms of an armistice would not be very
easy to arrange, he adhered to his previous opinion that
proposals for a general peace should be advanced in the
manner he had suggested   He promised, however, that,
if secret conferences were opened at the Hague, he would
do his utmost to facilitate a settlement, when the armies
went into winter-quarters. In conclusion, he demanded
the return of his original letter, which had been deliberately
retained by Chamillart, an error both in tact and tactics,
that was subsequently condemned by Torcy

M. Legrelle has examined this incident in an elaborate
treatise, based upon the study of ministerial archives. He
arrives at the conclusion that from first to last Berwick's
judgment was at fault, and that Torcy and Chamillart,
on the other hand, exhibited all the qualities of discerning
and patriotic statesmen. M Legrelle is not the first historian who, amid the intricacies of original documents,
has lost a firm hold on facts. His whole argument is
vitiated by two entirely false assumptions   He supposes
that Marlborough's desire for peace was a new and sudden
development, so inconsistent with his character and record
that it could only be explained upon some subtle and
sinister hypothesis. And he supposes that the military
situation of the allied army was as desperate as Chamillart
imagined it to be. Both suppositions are grotesquely
erroneous. In accepting the vulgar slander that Marlborough's policy was always to prolong the war, because
he made money out of it, M Legrelle ignores that volu-

---

[1] *Berwick's Memoirs*, vol ii , p 49
[2] Legrelle p 37. Marlborough à Berwick, November 6, 1708.

minous private correspondence, in which over and over again the Duke gave utterance to his passionate longing for peace and for his own retirement   The sincerity of these letters, written for the most part to persons with whom it was unnecessary, and probably impossible, to practise the arts of simulation, cannot reasonably be challenged. They deserved more attention from an author so partial to the study of original documents as M. Legrelle.   As for the notion that Marlborough was so frightened by the alleged peril of the allied army that he endeavoured to gain time and to cheat the French of their strategical advantages by the manœuvres of a dishonest diplomacy, Berwick's comment is the best that can be made.   "This reasoning," he says, "I own, was beyond my penetration."[1] Berwick was the best soldier in the French army of Flanders. His greatest defect, in the military sense, was an excess of caution.   He therefore would have been the last man in Europe to underrate the immensity of the risks which the allies were supposed to be running   Yet he regarded Chamillart's theory as preposterous at the time. When, in the light of subsequent events, he wrote his memoirs, he did not, and he could not, qualify his opinion. For Chamillart and Torcy there was some excuse.   They were not soldiers.   They were simply clever people, who blundered after their kind, because they tried to be too clever.   But it is strange indeed that any modern historian should range himself with them.   "A glance at the map," says M. Legrelle, will show how far the invaders had advanced beyond "the sphere of action which prudence prescribed for them."[2]   But a glance across the centuries will show in true perspective what manner of fighting men were Marlborough and Eugène, and what measure of contempt has always been felt by soldiers of their class for such paper strategy as that which even the orthodox Berwick regarded from the first as a pretentious and ruinous futility.

On his return to France, Chamillart reported that the reconciliation between Berwick and Vendôme was purely superficial, and that Burgundy's vacillation was the direct

[1] *Berwick's Memoirs*, vol. ii , p 48   [2] Legrelle, p 96

result of their constant antagonism Louis decided to transfer Berwick to Alsace. So little was doing in that quarter that the Elector of Bavaria had already quitted his command, and taken up his abode at Mons. Nevertheless, Berwick departed gladly on the 16th for Strasbourg. He was so happy to escape from a false position that he forgot to pay his valedictory respects to Vendôme

All this time Eugène was slowly but surely progressing in his attack upon the citadel Although, as Godolphin complained in a letter of the 23rd, the allies had been " in the field a month longer than ever was known,"[1] it was Marlborough's intention to await the success of his colleague, and then, provided only that the weather did not become unendurable, to recover Ghent and Bruges. The weather was an important consideration; but the French theory that the allied army was itself besieged, and would infallibly be starved, does not appear to have entered into the Duke's calculations. The army was still living " in parsimonious plenty," notwithstanding the fact that the enemy had invented frivolous pretexts for plundering the numerous sutlers and purveyors who followed the drum, and had subsequently revoked all their passports. " Such a proceeding," said Marlborough, who was more concerned for the innocent victims of it than for any effect it may have had on his own position, "is quite contrary to our maxims, and we have always taken advantage of any opportunity to convince everybody that, when war is necessary, it can be carried on without the repudiation of all humanity and good faith."[2] For the rest, the Duke assumed that, whenever he chose, he could force the lines of the Schelde with ease (as Berwick and Chamlay had maintained), or if not with ease, at least after an action so decisive that it must terminate the war He would have preferred to demonstrate the truth of this assumption in his own good time; but the French insisted that he should do it sooner.

The indefatigable Bergueick had never entirely abandoned his insidious designs on Brussels, where the House of

[1] Coxe, vol ii., p 330· Godolphin to Marlborough, November 12/23, 1708
[2] Murray, vol. iv , p 388 Marlborough to the Elector of Cologne. January 2, 1709, and to Boufflers, February 8, 1709

Bourbon could count on numerous adherents. In the
middle of November, he put forward a plan for the capture
of the city He suggested that, if the Elector of Bavaria,
whose personal popularity in the Spanish Netherlands, and
particularly among the ladies, was always very considerable, were suddenly to appear before the place at the head
of a small army, the garrison might be easily overpowered
with the assistance of the disaffected party among the
citizens. His plan was sanctioned, and preparations for
its execution were immediately put in hand. A force of
8,000 men, to be drawn principally from the garrisons of
Mons, Charleroi, and Namur, was selected for the service.
It consisted of fourteen battalions of foot and eighteen
squadrons of horse, including the Elector's Life Guards,
and it was provided with engineers, field-guns, and a siege-
train It was to concentrate at Hal on the 21st, and to
summon the capital on the 22nd. Brussels was a place
incapable of a prolonged defence. But the garrison consisted of 5,000 foot and 1,000 horse, under the command
of Pascal, a resolute and experienced officer, who was not
the man to be intimidated by mere demonstrations. The
success of the enterprise depended largely on the secrecy
and rapidity of its execution But for several days prior
to the 21st, it was gossip of a sort among the French officers,
and it was certainly known to Marlborough on the 20th.
And although the Elector joined his army at Hal on the
21st, it was not until noon on the 23rd that he appeared
before Brussels and summoned Pascal to surrender. The
slowness of his march was caused by icy rains, which ruined
the highways and exhausted the troops. When Pascal
returned an ironically polite refusal, a long delay ensued.
The Elector was waiting for his cannon, which, owing to
the deplorable state of the roads and the insufficiency of
the cart-horse teams, did not arrive until the 25th Meantime, the partisans of France made no movement Pascal
and the Dutch deputies took the necessary steps to maintain order among the citizens, while to encourage the
garrison, they issued gratuitously to every man a daily
allowance of a pound of meat, two quarts of beer, and four
glasses of brandy.

Marlborough was kept well informed of the Elector's proceedings by the governors of Ath and Audenarde. But remembering the unfortunate precedent of Bruges and Ghent, he did not allow the apparent danger to Brussels to divert his attention from Antwerp. On the 22nd, he instructed Erle to reinforce that garrison with five of the best English battalions at Ostend and a detachment of dragoons. A Walloon regiment was also dispatched to the same point; and the Dutch government took similar steps from the side of Holland. At the same time, the Duke apprised Pascal by more than one express that he was not forgotten, and adjured him to maintain the capital until " the last extremity "[1]

The situation which had arisen did not find Marlborough and Eugène in any sense unprepared The contingency was one which they had frequently and carefully examined. It had always been their fixed resolve to preserve Brussels at all hazards. And they had long since settled in their own minds a plan of operations appropriate to the case.

Between the 22nd and the 24th, Marlborough recalled the various detachments which had been engaged in the business of provisioning the army, and sent away his heavy baggage to Menin. On the evening of the 24th, he ordered ten battalions and twenty squadrons to march forward upon Harlebeke on the Lys. A few hours later, the entire army quitted Rousselaere, and proceeded by a parallel road towards Courtrai on the same river. On the morning of the 25th, Eugène, having left thirty battalions and thirty squadrons before the citadel of Lille, moved with nineteen battalions and fifty squadrons upon Roubaix It had been Marlborough's original intention to essay the passage of the Schelde on the night of the 25th. But his troops, like those of the Elector, suffered so severely from the rain and the condition of the roads, that it was 8 o'clock on the morning of the 26th before the last of them were over the Lys. Eugène halted at Roubaix until his colleague was ready This unforeseen loss of a day did not embarrass the Duke, because he was well aware that " the wretched

---

[1] Murray vol iv , p 237· Marlborough to Pascal, September 24, 1708

weather must disconcert the enemy "[1] as much as the allies. He himself had been in very bad health for more than a week, a fact which he studiously concealed from the army, lest the news of it should reach England and distress his wife. But he was "resolved," as he wrote to Godolphin, "to venture everything rather than let them take Brussels."[2] It was typical of his famous serenity of mind that, in the midst of this fateful crisis, he could indite a graceful letter of thanks to M. Espagnol of Lille, who had sent him a present of some bulbs for the gardens of Woodstock.[3]

Reports of the movements of the allied troops came quickly to the French in their position behind the Schelde. On Berwick's departure, Vendôme had planned an attack upon the army of Eugène, but the necessity of covering the siege of Brussels had compelled him to postpone this project For his own security he was not at all afraid. As 65 battalions and 80 squadrons under La Motte were holding the canal from Bruges to Ghent, he had only 57 battalions and 125 squadrons to hold the Schelde from Ghent to Tournai.   But, on the 17th, he informed Louis that Marlborough's army was so widely dispersed that, before it could concentrate against the line of the Schelde, La Motte would have ample time to arrive upon the scene. "Consequently, sire," he affirmed, "we risk nothing " Burgundy wrote in a much less confident tone, pointing out that Marlborough, by reason of his central situation, enjoyed a dangerous advantage.   A personal inspection of the French position by no means reassured the Prince. From Pottes to Escanaffles the line seemed formidable enough; but from Escanaffles to Ghent it exhibited several points of weakness.   Audenarde, indeed, was blockaded by a triple line of works, running from outer defences of the place to the adjacent hills, but D'Artaignan reported that this fortification was absurdly large, and needed 20,000 men to garrison it properly In the direction of Gavre and Ghent, the possibilities of a successful attack were very apparent. Moreover, the strength of the current of the Schelde and

---

[1] *Ibid*, p 322 Marlborough to Chanclos, November 22, 1708
[2] Coxe, vol ii , p 331 Marlborough to Godolphin
[3] Murray, vol. iv , p 320. Marlborough to Espagnol, November 22, 1708

the skilful manipulation of the sluices of Audenarde frustrated every attempt to form fresh inundations. Burgundy
came to the conclusion that Vendôme's optimism was by
no means justified. D'Artaignan notified Chamillart that
the line was not impregnable; and other officers took a
similar view.

On the 24th came numerous reports that the allies had
called in all their detachments, and were moving towards
the Lys It was strongly rumoured that Brussels was
their objective; but the idea of an attack upon the canal
between Bruges and Ghent, an idea to which Marlborough
deliberately gave currency, was also mentioned. Throughout the two succeeding days, the French commanders were
almost hourly apprised of the doings of the enemy.
Grimaldi, the governor of Bruges, who obtained his information from a servant of one of the Dutch generals,
sent express after express to Burgundy with full accounts
both of what was being done and of what was intended.
Confirmatory intelligence arrived from other, and equally
reliable, sources. The opinion was formed by various
officers that Audenarde and Gavre were the threatened
points. Burgundy took the alarm. On the morning of
the 26th, he reinforced the more exposed positions, and
sent orders to La Motte to dispatch D'Estrades from Ghent
with eight battalions and six squadrons to Gavre. Vendôme
would have gone to Gavre in person, but he was suffering
from a complication of gout and colic. He told Burgundy,
however, that there was no need for excessive hurry, as
the enemy had not yet crossed the Lys. He is said to
have repeated the same statement when they were over the
Schelde.

From Tournai to Audenarde was twenty miles. This
immense front was defended by an army which numbered
not more than 35,000 men Burgundy was at Saulchoi,
near Tournai, with 13 battalions and 90 squadrons, Guébriant
at Pottes with 10 battalions, La Chastre at Escanaffles with
5 battalions, Souternon at Berchem with 3 battalions and
10 squadrons, Nangis at Melden with 9 battalions, and
Hautefort on the heights of Audenarde with 14 battalions,
25 squadrons, and 20 guns. All these detachments lay

well within supporting distance of one another. But the state of the roads was very unfavourable to rapidity of concentration. Moreover, if the allies attacked between Audenarde and Ghent before D'Estrades arrived at Gavre, they could turn the whole line without striking a blow

Nevertheless, such was the insane confidence of Vendôme, that on the evening of the 26th he wrote to Chamillart in these terms: " We are told that the enemy propose to force a passage over the Scheldt or over the canal. Which-ever they select, you can assure His Majesty that we are ready to give them a good reception. . . . I will only say that, judging by all that reaches me, the enemy are in a desperate situation, and I know not how they will extricate themselves . . You will be so kind as to read this letter to the King."[1] The last sentence was the fatal one. Even Louis' unbounded faith in Vendôme could not survive this missive, and its sequel.

Burgundy wrote at the same time, but in a much less complacent strain. He expressed the hope that all would go well, but he frankly told the King that a reverse was possible, and that he had warned the Elector of Bavaria to be prepared for the worst. Diffident and nervous as he evidently was, he unfortunately allowed himself to be infected by Vendôme's conviction that, in any event, there was still plenty of time. He had intended to march to Berchem that very day, but Vendôme dissuaded him, promising him to accompany him thither on the morrow instead So the young prince went to bed and to sleep at Saulchoi. When he awoke, it was too late

Marlborough at Courtrai, "tormented with a sore throat,"[2] and so ill and weak with fever that he was compelled to travel in a litter, exhibited now an unrelenting energy, which alone secured him an enormous advantage over his lethargic opponents. Though the rear of his drenched and foot-sore columns did not get up till 8 on the morning of the 26th, at 3 in the afternoon he ordered the march to be resumed. It was then and there that he upset the calculations of Vendôme, and made certain of the success

[1] Sautai, *Une opération militaire*, Appendice II , p 65. Vendôme à Chamillart, 26 novembre, 1708
[2] Coxe, vol ii , p 335 Marlborough to Godolphin, November 28, 1708.

of the plan which he had concerted with Eugène. This plan was in all respects characteristic of its authors. It would probably have been easier to force the canal between Bruges and Ghent than to force the Schelde between Ghent and Tournai. But such an operation would have entirely uncovered Lille, and if successful, would have carried the army to Brussels by the most circuitous of roads. Marlborough chose the direct path, which lay through Audenarde. To enter that town itself, and debouch from it in face of the triple works beyond it, was out of the question. The Duke had therefore selected three other points of attack. Eugène, on the right, was to march upon Escanaffles, Lottum, on the left, upon Gavre, and he himself, in the centre, upon Berchem He knew that Eugène's attempt was the least promising of the three. But if either of the other two were successful, the line would be forced; and if both of them were successful, Hautefort's detachment outside Audenarde might, with the assistance of the garrison, be enveloped and destroyed

At 2 o'clock, Lottum, who had the longest road to travel, set off for Gavre. His command consisted of 16 battalions and 40 squadrons, with 6 guns and 14 pontoons. Chanclos, the governor of Audenarde, who had specially studied the locality, accompanied the column. It was the same Chanclos who had guided the nocturnal march of the allies, when they forced the lines of Brabant in 1705 [1] Six battalions were dispatched to Audenarde, where the same number were already in garrison. The officer, commanding in Chanclos' absence, was instructed to hold himself in readiness to co-operate with Marlborough on the right and Lottum on the left in a combined attack upon Hautefort's works. Marlborough's army was preceded by a detachment of eight battalions, with the pontoons and field-guns, under Cadogan, who directed his march through Waermaerde on Kerkhove, which is over against Berchem. Cadogan had personally reconnoitred the river at this point Marlborough followed with 40 battalions and 100 squadrons He had timed himself to arrive at Kerkhove about midnight. In unison with these movements,

1 See Vol. I., Chapter XI , "The Lines of Brabant," p. 290.

Eugène was advancing from Roubaix upon Autryve, which is opposite to Escanaffles. All the columns were already in motion, when at 5 o'clock the bearer of Vendôme's complacent dispatch set off for Versailles.

The pitiless rain had now ceased, but the night, though fine, was cold with the coldness of late autumn just verging into winter. There was little likelihood of error or confusion, for the sky was illumined by a resplendent moon. The troops were in excellent spirits. Officers and men alike forgot their own weariness in their anxiety to burst the vaunted barrier, which stood between them and the beleaguered capital. They knew that Pascal was already attacked, but they were ignorant of the result. Only the sullen booming of a distant cannonade, borne through the silence of the night over forty miles of flat meadow-land and marsh, inspired them with the hope that they were still in time.[1]

Lottum's column, moving swiftly and in admirable order, traversed the northern side of the battlefield of Oudenarde, and crossed the great highroad to Ghent. Here a dispatch-rider from the army of the Schelde, with letters for La Motte, blundered right into the line of march, and was made prisoner. It was midnight[2] by the village steeples, when they reached the river-bank over against Gavre. No challenge greeted them across the water, no sound of hostile movements broke the stillness of the sleeping countryside. The business of laying the pontoons was instantly begun. Timber had been forgotten; but the nearest cottages were levelled to supply the deficiency By 2 o'clock the work was finished. The Dutch grenadiers of Fagel's regiment were the first to cross. Lifting their noses in the air, they sniffed comically, and observed that they could already smell the gin and cheese of their native Holland, and that at that moment every man of them was worth three Frenchmen.[3] It was a small thing, but it showed the joyous and unconquerable spirit which animated the soldiers of Marlborough. These grenadiers had been marching, with but little interval for repose, for two days, and half of the time

[1] *Mémoires de Goslinga*, p. 86
[2] *Ibid* Goslinga, who was present, gives the time " midnight," but Lediard and Boyer give the time as 4 a m   [3] Goslinga, p ¿6

in rain and mud; and now they were taking their lives in their hands at the hour when human courage is at its lowest ebb For troops that can be facetious under such conditions, nothing is impossible

The rest of Lottum's infantry followed, and the cavalry joined them at dawn. A thick fog obscured the country; but some peasants, whom the soldiers seized, declared that there was no enemy in the vicinity, though they understood that a detachment from Ghent was to be expected in the course of the morning.[1] Lottum, in obedience to the orders which he had received, drew up his men in a position covering the bridges, dispatched his report to Marlborough, and awaited further instructions Between 8 and 9, some of his cavalry, scouting on the left, distinctly heard the music of a French march Advancing towards the sound, they were challenged by a couple of dragoons, who fired on them with pistols, and dashed off into the fog. D'Estrades, with his eight battalions and his six squadrons, was close at hand. Lottum wheeled to the left to meet this unseen danger. Presently the fog lifted, and the sun shone brilliantly. The French were so skilfully posted in broken and wooded ground, a mile and a half away, that it was impossible to estimate their numbers. The two detachments remained facing one another till noon, when an officer arrived with orders from the Duke to move on Audenarde.

. The operation, as a whole, had been crowned with complete success. At midnight, Cadogan came down to the Schelde between the villages of Kerkhove and Elsegem. He had designedly selected a portion of the river, where the right bank, being dominated by the left, could be swept by the fire of his artillery. Having previously ascertained that the French patrols rode by the churchyard of Berchem at intervals of two hours, he watched by the light of the moon until he saw one pass. Immediately afterwards he ordered the pontoons to be laid, and a battery of thirty guns to be erected Souternon, who was at Berchem with three battalions and eight squadrons, had been continually

---

[1] Goslinga, p. 86, but other authorities say that there was actually a French force in garrison in a château

on the alert   The information which he received on the
afternoon and evening of the 26th was of the most alarming
kind   Convinced that the enemy were not only moving
but were already at hand, he had warned Vendôme of the
imminence of the peril, and had decided to spend the night
in the saddle. His attention, however, had been drawn
to his left, where he had actually heard the distant rumble
of Cadogan's march, and had assumed that it was caused
by a column of baggage-waggons   When the news arrived
from his right that the allies were passing the river between
Kerkhove and Elsegem, he galloped to Berchem, drew
out his small command, and hurried them away to the
threatened point   Daylight had not yet broken, and the
fog was rising from the river, but as he advanced at the
head of his cavalry, he plainly perceived that a hostile
force, which he estimated at ten battalions and ten squadrons, was already in position on the right bank. At the
same time, he was saluted by a volley from the battery across
the water.

Souternon halted, and took counsel with his officers.
The enemy had the advantage both of numbers and situation.   Moreover, it was impossible to come at them at all
without defiling between the river and an inundation under
a flanking fire from Cadogan's cannon.   Every officer save
one, who was a Spaniard, discountenanced the attempt.
This circumstance was characterised by Vendôme, in his
report to Chamillart, as " very shameful for the nation."[1]
And certainly it would seem that, if Souternon had rightly
appreciated the issues involved, he would have risked the
loss of his detachment in a vigorous attack.   The preservation of so small a force was a matter of no moment in
comparison with the importance of checking the progress
of the allies at this initial stage   But he accepted the
advice of his officers, and fell back on Berchem, where he
lined the hedges with his infantry, and stood his ground
under the fire of Cadogan's guns. He was hoping that
Nangis, who was at Melden with nine battalions, and whom
he had already summoned to his aid, would hasten at the

[1] Sautai, *Une opération militaire*, Appendice II, p 84 Vendôme à
Chamillart, 29 novembre, 1708

call But Nangis hesitated, and not unnaturally, to march through open country across the front of Cadogan's position Very little time was allowed to Souternon. The head of Marlborough's column was rapidly approaching; and the Duke himself was at hand. Satisfied that he would be supported, Cadogan ordered his men to carry Berchem. Souternon did not await the onset He quitted the village by its southern side, sent orders to Nangis to join Hautefort, and retreated towards Escanaffles, with a loss of twenty men and some baggage-waggons.

Meanwhile, Eugène had led his column to the Schelde at Autryve, had occupied the château, and had begun to erect a battery. Riding in person to Waermaerde, he met Marlborough, and learned that Cadogan's detachment had crossed the river. At the same time, he was informed that La Chastre was on the alert at Escanaffles, and that the French artillery had opened fire from the right bank by the light of the moon He instantly resolved to convert his attack into a demonstration, to send back six battalions and twenty-four squadrons to Lille, and to march on with the remainder to the support of Marlborough at Kerkhove.

But long before the Imperialists could arrive, the Duke's army had been pouring across the four bridges, which Cadogan had laid, and rapidly extending its front in the direction of Melden Marlborough, who had quitted his litter and mounted his charger, directed an immediate advance through Melden upon Audenarde. Nangis was now retiring upon Hautefort's corps. The leading squadrons of the allies engaged his rear-guard But the Irish brigade and the brigade of Bourbonnais, which together constituted the nine battalions under the command of Nangis, offered a very desperate resistance, setting fire to the houses and bridges on the stream of Etichove, and disputing every foot of ground with their pursuers. Hautefort, in the meantime, aware that the allies had crossed the river both above and below Audenarde, perceived the trap, and hastily prepared to elude it Having decided to retreat upon Grammont, he called in all his outposts, ordered his cannon and baggage to start at once, and anxiously awaited the coming of Nangis. Nangis arrived before noon. Thereupon Hautefort fired his camp, and with twenty-four battalions and twenty-five squadrons began his retirement. The allies, though Nangis had escaped them, did not abandon the chase. But they had now to deal with an entirely fresh rear-guard, consisting of two columns of cavalry, sustained by 400 grenadiers. A sharp action ensued. On the side of the French, a regiment of dragoons and a regiment of Irish horse particularly distinguished themselves; on the side of the allies, Albemarle, whose charger was shot under him, led on his carabineers with conspicuous courage. Marching briskly, but in excellent order, Hautefort succeeded in reaching Enghien with his artillery intact He was complimented by Chamillart for his fine retreat. At dusk, near Grammont, the allies abandoned the pursuit. They had sixty casualties,[1] but they had taken three standards and a pair of kettle-drums, with the bulk of the enemy's baggage and bread-waggons. The French losses, in killed and prisoners, were, according to Sautai, 45 officers and 700[2] men. Thus with a brutal and exasperating simplicity the English general had shattered into fragments the hypothesis upon which his pacific overtures had been repulsed by Chamillart, that hypothesis which was beyond the understanding of Berwick, but which, in modern times, has been valiantly resuscitated by M. Legrelle.

Vendôme and Burgundy did nothing. They were not even spectators of their own disgrace. The sleeping camp at Saulchoi had been awakened at daybreak by the booming of cannon from the direction of Audenarde. Vendôme had driven off in his chaise towards the scene of action. Burgundy had followed at 8 o'clock. But even Vendôme was constrained to recognise that the game was up He fell back on Tournai with 31 battalions and 100 squadrons, while Burgundy amused himself with a game of tennis.

The main body of the allies halted for the night on the hills beyond Audenarde. It was decided that Eugène and his men should return to Lille upon the morrow. But

---

[1] Boyer and Lediard but the *Military History* says that 100 privates were killed

[2] Murray, vol iv , p 332 Marlborough, writing to Eile on December 3, says, " nearly 1,000 prisoners," besides killed

before dawn, Marlborough's untiring army passed on towards Brussels. In the Duke's own words, " the cry came so loud "[1] from the beleaguered city that he was compelled to ask his soldiers for this final effort. At Oombergen, half-way on the road to Alost, they again encamped after an exhausting march. But the Duke, who, if he had studied his own health, would have been in bed,[2] dashed forward at the head of sixty squadrons and two battalions of the Guards   He entered Alost at 6 the same evening.   Good news met him there.   Brussels was saved.

The Elector of Bavaria, working with double teams of horses, had at last contrived to bring up his artillery.   At 9 o'clock on the morning of the 26th he opened fire from a battery of eight pieces   Pascal's guns, which were admirably served, responded, with damaging results   It soon became obvious that, unless the friends of France among the citizens took active measures, the project must collapse.   But the municipal authorities, observing an attitude of strict neutrality, kept perfect order in the town. The Elector determined now upon a gambler's throw. Towards evening he began to bombard the outworks with a couple of mortars.   At 7, he engaged the defenders of the counterscarp in a duel of musketry

It was the roar of this preliminary fire-combat which reached the ears of Lottum's soldiers as they stepped out towards the Schelde.   At 9, the French attacked in two places   " There ensued," says the chronicler, " the most furious, obstinate, and bloody engagement that ever was known."[3]   Animated by their officers, the Dutch and English vied with one another in a reckless heroism, which barely sufficed them against the gallant ardour of the foe. Nine times the French assaulted the works.   At two points they secured a foothold.   But at 6, on the morning of the 27th, the defenders, sword in hand, expelled them from both lodgments.   Fighting continued until 10, when urgent messages were dispatched to Marlborough, and every preparation was made to resist to the last.   But the Elector recognised that his little army was too exhausted by fatigue

[1] Murray, vol iv , p 326 Marlborough to Boyle November 20 1708
[2] Co   vol ii p ?15 Marlborough to Godolphin, November 28, 1708.
[3] Boyer vol vii , p 149

and exposure, and too crippled by its losses, to resume the
assault. Several of his best officers had fallen; and of his
seven engineers, five had been killed and two taken prisoners
Having thrown a few bombs into the city in the vain hope
of exciting disorders among the inhabitants, he determined
to withdraw quietly under cover of darkness. But this
movement was destined to assume the undignified character
of a rout. At 9 that evening, a cavalry officer, who had
seen with his own eyes the detachment of Lottum in position
at Gavre, galloped in with the news. Immediately afterwards came a second messenger with the alarming intelligence that the governor of Ath had surprised St Ghislain,
an important outpost of Mons. The Elector knew that
Mons was denuded of troops. He knew that, if the allies
were already across the Schelde, their cavalry would soon
be astride of his communications with that valuable fortress
At 10 o'clock, therefore, with one regiment of dragoons
and five squadrons of Life Guards, he fled. D'Arco followed, as best he could, with the main body, many of whom
disappeared on the march.[1] Twelve cannon, two mortars,
three waggons of gunpowder, and 800 wounded, including
nearly 100 officers, were abandoned to the victors. This
desertion of the wounded was described by Marlborough
as " most scandalous."[2]

On the morning of the 29th, the Duke, accompanied by
Augustus of Saxony, entered Brussels amid the acclamations
of the populace. He "received," in his own words, " great
compliments of thanks for so seasonable a relief from the
Council of State, the States of Brabant, and the whole
magistracy."[3] He found that the casualties of the garrison
amounted to 600[4] or thereabouts. The survivors he
rewarded with a month's pay Having dined with Pascal,
whom he warmly congratulated, he returned in the evening
to Alost.

Notwithstanding the fact that the enemy's strategy had
been generally condemned by the most respectable military

---

[1] The total losses of the French, including desertions, were estimated
by the allies at from 3,000 to 4,000
[2] Coxe, vol ii , p 336 Marlborough to Godolphin, November 29, 1708.
[3] Murray, vol iv , p. 326 Marlborough to Boyle, November 29 1708,
[4] Boyer says that they were between 500 and 600 The *Military Life*
says that they were nearly 700 But Millner puts them at 413.

opinion of the time, the news of Marlborough's triumph created no little sensation in the capitals of Europe. The French were hopelessly discredited The magnitude of their vapourings was everywhere contrasted with the futility of their performance. " The abandoning those lines, on which they had been working for many weeks," says Burnet, " was a surprise to all the world their councils seemed to be weak, and the execution of them was worse; so that they, who were so long the terror, were now become the scorn of nations."[1] For several days Louis was kept in ignorance of the truth. When he learned it, he was inexpressibly humiliated. He did not conceal the bitterness of his feelings from Vendôme That general, however, laid all the blame on Souternon; and he actually had the effrontery to declare that he had always been opposed to the system of defending the Schelde. But Louis' disillusionment was now complete. And the popular disgust in France was deep and universal.

Marlborough's operation, (for the part which his colleague played in it was comparatively slight,) excited the admiration of every soldier by reason of the swiftness, the facility, and the insignificant loss with which it was accomplished. In Burnet's words, " a very hot action " had been anticipated. " Some of the general-officers told me," says the Bishop, " that they reckoned it would have cost them at least 10,000 men "[2] The astounding result was due to the fact that Marlborough on this, as on so many other occasions, surprised his enemy. When it is remembered that the French were in receipt of daily, and almost hourly, intelligence of the advance of the allies, this explanation may appear paradoxical Certainly, the French commanders were well aware that an attack was imminent. In one sense, therefore, they were not surprised. But how imminent it was, they altogether failed to grasp. When Vendôme and Burgundy went to bed on the night of the 26th, they imagined that, if they moved from Saulchoi on the ensuing morning, they would arrive in ample time Considering the pitiable condition of the roads, and the fatigue which the allies had already undergone, they believed

---

[1] Burnet vol. iv., p 196.   [2] Ibid.

that no general, worthy of the name, would deny his soldiers
a reasonable amount of rest before he hurled them against
entrenched positions, protected by inundations and a
formidable river.   The memory of Oudenarde should have
taught them that they were not dealing with an ordinary
antagonist.   They reckoned without the singular spirit
which distinguished Marlborough's men in this campaign,
and above all, they reckoned without the tremendous
energy of Marlborough himself   At Courtrai, on the
morning of the 26th, the Duke lay ill in bed, he was taking
medicine; he was " tormented with a sore throat "; he was
compelled to travel in a litter.   But he knew that his men
would rise to the occasion, if only he could rise to it himself.
His was the triumph of mind and will over the weakness
of the flesh   For the rest, the details of his plan were
admirably contrived.   While the false rumour of a movement against the canal tied La Motte to one extremity of
the line, and the advance of Eugène to Roubaix tied
Burgundy and Vendôme to the other, the points actually
selected for attack were so judiciously chosen both upon
strategical and tactical grounds, that success was virtually
assured beforehand.   Yet Marlborough, in writing to his
wife, modestly ascribed the victory to divine providence
" Considering," he said, " the pains they had taken by
fortifying every place of the river, where they thought
we could pass, I think it next to a miracle our surprising
them as we did."[1]   And writing to Godolphin, he said
simply· " God favoured our passage of the Schelde "[2]

It was fortunate for France that, in opening thus easily
the direct road to Brussels, the allies did not, at the same
time, annihilate the corps of Hautefort.   Hautefort's
escape would seem to have been due, in part at any rate,
to some misunderstanding or misconduct in the execution
of the Duke's orders   The officer, who commanded the
garrison of Audenarde in Chanclos' absence, and who had
been reinforced on the 26th with six battalions of foot,
had been instructed to co-operate in the enveloping movement against Hautefort's corps.   If, at any time between

[1] Coxe, vol ii , p 337 Marlborough to the Duchess, December 6, 1708
[2] Ibid , p. 340 Marlborough to Godolphin, December 6, 1708.

dawn and midday on the 27th, the works outside Audenarde had been vigorously assailed by the occupants of that fortress, it is obvious that Hautefort might not have got off so lightly, if at all   But nothing of the kind occurred. The fact is certain   But the reason of it is obscure, notwithstanding the very remarkable account which is to be found in the memoirs of Goslinga.

Goslinga prefaces his narrative with a characteristic anecdote. He tells how, prior to the forcing of the Schelde, he one day found Eugène in contemplation of the strategical situation as it appeared upon a map. Goslinga remarked that, if only his advice had been taken on the morrow of the victory of Oudenarde, the French would have been blockaded instead of the allies.   The Prince replied emphatically that Goslinga was right, and that, in that event, not a man of the enemy would have escaped [1]   In view of the immediate sequel this story seems singularly inept.   For never was the essential inefficiency of such blockades more signally demonstrated. If Goslinga is speaking the truth, Eugène must have been a master of irony.

When Marlborough was making his final dispositions at Courtrai, Goslinga resolved to attach himself to Lottum's column   Aspiring to add fresh laurels to those which he had reaped at Oudenarde, he concealed his intention from his colleagues, who in the ordinary course would probably continue with the main body of the army.   At 4 on the morning of the 26th, he visited the Duke. Marlborough was in bed, pretending to be ill.   But his malady was mental rather than physical   Evidently he realised at last the full horror of the situation to which his criminal rejection of Goslinga's strategy had reduced the allies.   Presently Cadogan and Chanclos arrived. Chanclos remarked that, if Lottum's column were successful, it ought to advance against Hautefort's flank. Marlborough listened, but said nothing. Goslinga supported Chanclos, and Cadogan concurred, "at least in appearance."[2] Then Marlborough expressed the opinion that Lottum should be guided by circumstances and his own judgment.   But on the assumption that what was proposed might prove to be feasible,

[1] *Mémoires de Goslinga*, p 83   [2] *Ibid*, p 84.

the Duke sent six battalions into Audenarde. They were to attack the enemy in front, while Lottum attacked his right flank.

Goslinga remained with Marlborough's column until after Lottum had started At 4 in the afternoon, imagining that he had successfully hoodwinked his colleagues, he stole away to the left, and one hour later overtook Lottum. After some potations with the Dutch generals, he was congratulating himself on the success of his manœuvre, when to his amazement and disgust he perceived the deputies, Rechteren and Van Colleen. With childlike candour, he explains that he was " mortified " He adds that he regarded their presence as an evil omen, and that several of the generals took the same view He assumed that either Marlborough or Cadogan had told them of his whereabouts, as nobody else, save Gueldermalsen, whom he trusted, was aware of it. This portion of the narrative betrays a certain confusion of ideas. Rechteren and Van Colleen had as good a right as Goslinga to ride with Lottum's column; and the assumption that they joined it, solely because he had done so, is gratuitous. And why should their presence be regarded by Dutch officers, of all people, as an evil omen ? Goslinga's memoirs, as a whole, convey, and are intended to convey, the impression that it was not the idiocy of his civilian compatriots, but the natural depravity of the English commander, which ruined hopeful enterprises. The admission, however, as coming from him, is a very valuable one   That Goslinga was " mortified "[1] can well be believed. He was wounded in his immense vanity by the reflection that the glory which he had antici- pated for himself alone might be shared by others

After Lottum's detachment had crossed the Schelde, a council of war was held. Lottum declared that he had been directed to entrench himself upon the right bank, to inform Marlborough of his situation, and to await fuither instructions Goslinga and Chanclos were amazed. In reply to their enquiries, Lottum announced that his oiders did not empower him, in the absence of opposition from the enemy, to move on Audenarde As he was a man of

[1] *Mémoires de Goslinga*, p 85

honour, Goslinga considers that he was speaking the truth.
Goslinga told him that six battalions had been sent into
the town for the express purpose of combining with his
detachment in an attack upon the French works.   Chanclos
confirmed this fact, and argued that, after a march of only
two leagues over an excellent road, they would catch the
soldiers of Hautefort in their beds.   Lottum accepted these
statements, but steadily declined to exceed his own orders,
unless he received an authorisation from the field-deputies,
as representing the Dutch government.   Goslinga gave it
him at once; but Rechteren and Van Colleen, out of
" damnable jealousy,"[1] refused to assume their share of
the responsibility.   All the generals, including Lottum
himself, endeavoured to persuade them, but in vain.   They
were acting as the instruments of Marlborough, who had
resolved by the exercise of a base duplicity to ruin a
design, of which he personally " could not have the glory."[2]

It is to be observed that, for this occasion at any rate,
Goslinga drops his monotonous calumny that Marlborough
was unwilling to beat the French too much   He substitutes
for it the altogether preposterous suggestion that this
world-famous and consistently triumphant commander was
envious of such honour as his subordinate officers might
gain in the efficient execution of a plan, which he himself
had devised   Stupid malignity could go no farther.   By
the very immensity of his renown, Marlborough was lifted
above all ordinary temptation to an odious vice, from
which by nature he was singularly averse.   Envy of Eugène
was indeed ascribed to him by certain of his enemies.
Their testimony is false, but it is not, upon the face of it,
egregiously foolish   Lottum was a good and gallant
soldier, but envy of Lottum was an absurdity of which
Marlborough was incapable.   In justice to Goslinga, who
after all was not mentally deficient, it must be admitted
that his words are susceptible of another interpretation
His reference to the " damnable jealousy " of Rechteren
and Van Colleen supplies a clue   It may well be that, in
the depths of his inordinate conceit, the field-deputy honestly
believed that he, Sicco van Goslinga, the true and rightful

[1] *Mémoires de Goslinga*, p 83   [2] *Ibid*

victor of Oudenarde, the amateur of French kettle-drums, was the dangerous competitor, whom Marlborough condescended to baffle by a squalid trick which deprived the Grand Alliance of one of the fruits of victory

But Goslinga has more to tell. At noon he proposed an attack upon the French detachment from Ghent. Lottum approved the idea, but pleaded, as before, that he was bound by his orders. When Marlborough's messenger arrived, Goslinga repeated his suggestion. But beyond an idle reconnaissance nothing was done If his advice had been adopted, Goslinga considers that the detachment from Ghent could have been destroyed, and that Ghent itself might even have surrendered. When Lottum's column eventually arrived at Audenarde, the officer who commanded there expressed surprise at its failure to appear sooner, and told Goslinga that he had remained on the alert throughout the night with the six battalions. Yet Marlborough actually censured this man, who was an excellent soldier, and whose premature death was hastened by his undeserved disgrace. For the rest, Goslinga after mature consideration decided to conceal this long and melancholy story from everybody except Eugène, who was, of course, disgusted at such horrible disclosures.

Presumably, Chanclos decided to conceal it also, and Lottum, and Orkney, and Wurttemberg, and Athlone, and Bauditz, and the other officers, who took part in the discussions at Gavre Unless they all with wonderful unanimity decided to conceal it, there is a reasonable presumption that some traces of it would have survived in the documents and records of the time. But for this, as for most other portions of the fantastic fabric of romance which the Dutchman has erected to the condemnation of Marlborough, corroboration is lacking. It is known that the garrison of Audenarde, though reinforced for the occasion, did nothing. It is said that their commander alleged in his own defence that he had received a counter-order from the field-deputies. It is stated by Schulenburg that Marlborough accused the field-deputies of delaying Lottum's march, and of meddling and muddling in matters which they did not understand. It would be difficult, if not impossible, to reconcile these stories with one another, or with the narrative of Goslinga. But one proposition can be advanced with confidence Whatever may have passed in private between Marlborough and other persons, the final orders which he gave to Lottum were assuredly the right ones. The Duke's object was, before all else, to force the Schelde. He could not foresee that any of the three attacks would certainly succeed; but he knew that Lottum's chances were by far the best. If Lottum crossed, and entrenched himself at the head of his bridges, both the other columns, in the event of failure at Kerkhove and Autryve, might still have passed at Gavre. But if Lottum had moved off to Audenarde, and Marlborough and Eugène had been repulsed, Lottum would have been destroyed, and what was worse, the Schelde would not have been forced. Moreover, it is simply incredible that an ailing general, who was more than sufficiently absorbed in a multitude of anxious details, should have had time or energy to spare for the paltry intrigues of personal malice. And in flatly declining to believe that, for any reason whatsoever, Marlborough jeopardised the success of a most delicate and critical operation by deliberately issuing ambiguous or conflicting orders, that most competent French historian, M. de Sautai, is on the safest of safe ground.

"The forcing of the Scheldt," wrote Marlborough to Godolphin on the 29th, "was not only necessary for the saving of Brabant, but also for the sending more ammunition to Lille."[1] The magazines of that city, as well as those of Menin and Courtrai, required to be replenished; and the army of Eugène had need of an additional supply. At Brussels, the Duke arranged that two hundred waggons should be collected at Ath, and loaded there with one thousand barrels of powder and a stock of flour To protect his restored communications, he encamped the main body of his forces between Beirlegem and Audenarde, on December 1, while Dedem with twenty battalions recrossed the Schelde and occupied the left bank, and Hompesch with eight battalions and thirty-eight squadrons took post at Menin. On the preceding day, he had detached Dompré

---

[1] Coxe, vol. ii., p 336 Marlborough to Godolphin, November 29, 1708.

with forty squadrons to the assistance of the handful of troops, which had surprised St. Ghislain, and which was now surrounded there by a small army under Hautefort and Albergotti. But, St Ghislain having fallen before Dompré could arrive, the Duke instructed him to proceed to Ath, and furnish an escort for the convoy, which started on the 3rd It reached Menin on the 5th. Its arrival contributed directly to the surrender of the citadel of Lille. In the absence of Eugène, the besiegers had established themselves on the second counterscarp on November 26, and had been expelled by the garrison on the 28th On his return, the Prince apprised Boufflers of the successful passage of the Schelde and of the flight of the Elector of Bavaria, and offered him most honourable terms. But Boufflers, though his stock of ammunition had fallen very low, and though he and his men were eating horseflesh, still held out. For he knew that, at that advanced season of the year, every day gained by the garrison diminished the enemy's chances of recovering Ghent and Bruges On December 1, the besiegers again obtained possession of the second counterscarp On the 7th, their batteries being ready to breach the walls of the citadel itself, Eugène once more summoned the place He warned Boufflers that, if the garrison submitted to an assault, the survivors would all become prisoners of war. At the same time, he invited the Marshal to inspect the ample supplies of powder and provisions, with which the besiegers were now furnished. To preserve his troops, who numbered 4,000, Boufflers, acting on the King's instructions, consented to treat for a capitulation, which he obtained upon excellent terms. In their intercourse with this, the noblest of their foes, Eugène and his officers omitted nothing which would testify to their veneration for his self-sacrificing valour. The Marshal and his men departed on the 11th. Boufflers and Luxembourg travelled in Eugène's own carriage. They were escorted to Douai by 400 of the Prince's cavalry, whom the Marshal, chivalrous to the last, quartered in that town for the night, and handsomely entertained at his own charges. This " hero in spite of himself,"[1] as Saint-

---

[1] Saint-Simon, t vi, ch xxxii, p 424

Simon calls him for his unaffected modesty, was received
and rewarded by Louis as he deserved. And the same
authority records that not in all France, not even in the
envious Court of Versailles, was there a single tongue that
did not applaud the King's generosity.

The fall of the citadel of Lille finally released the armies
of Eugène and Marlborough from their prolonged entangle-
ment   The annual withdrawal into winter-quarters was
now many weeks overdue.   Continuance in the field had
been rendered tolerable solely by the abnormal mildness
of the autumn. But on December 3, it rained, and on the
night of the 4th, it began, says Hompesch, " to freeze so
very hard, that our soldiers long for fighting, were it only
to warm themselves."[1]   At Lille, the ice lay so thick upon
the moats, that, in Millner's phrase, " many bridges " were
provided, if an assault had proved necessary.[2] " Both
our horse and foot," wrote Marlborough, on the 6th,
" already suffer very much by the cold weather "[3] And
on the 10th, he wrote " I never in my life felt colder
weather than we have had for the last three days."[4]
The French retired into their frontier fortresses, and their
Princes returned to Paris, " fondly believing,"[5] to quote
Lediard, " that the confederates, tired out with the fatigues
and difficulties of a long and active campaign, would have
been satisfied with their last important conquest."   But
Marlborough did not intend to leave his work unfinished.
" We must have Ghent and Bruges, let it cost what it
will,"[6] he wrote to Godolphin. While Ghent and Bruges
remained in French hands, it was still possible for Louis to
argue that France, after all, had something substantial to
her credit in the balance-sheet of the campaign   Until
those cities were retaken, the winter-quarters of the allies
would be exposed to continual annoyance, while communications by road with Lille, Menin, and Courtrai would be
perpetually threatened, and communications by river

---

[1] Boyer, vol vii , p 155 Letter from Hompesch, December 5, 1708
[2] *Millner's Journal*, p 247, November 26, 1708
[3] Coxe, vol ii , p 340 Marlborough to Godolphin, December 6, 1708.
[4] *Ibid* , p 341: Marlborough to Godolphin, December 10, 1708
[5] Lediard, vol ii , p 402.
[6] Coxe, vol ii , p 340 Marlborough to Godolphin, December 6, 1708.

absolutely blocked. Marlborough desired to leave all
things in readiness for a vigorous, offensive campaign upon
the French frontier in the ensuing spring. He believed
that, if the strategical position of the allies were perfected
now by the recovery of Ghent and Bruges, and if the raising
of additional troops were sanctioned by the Dutch and
British governments, the French would sink from demoralisation to despair, and early in the ensuing year would
accept whatever terms were dictated to them by the Grand
Alliance. " I think," he wrote on December 3 to Godolphin, who had protested against the prolongation of the
campaign, " I think the taking of Ghent and Bruges,
with the augmentation which I hope will be made by
England and Holland, will procure an honourable and
safe peace."[1]

While the army lay at Beirlegem, the Duke wrote to
Walpole to impress upon him the " necessity of raising recruits by Act of Parliament on the parishes or hundreds."[2]
In the same strain, he declared to Boyle that " it would be
of the greatest service to the public . . . if an act could
be obtained for levying men upon the counties, as has
been formerly proposed "[3] He also broached the subject
of an additional levy to the King of Prussia As to the
question of financing the foreign contingents, " I know,"
he said, in writing to Godolphin on the 3rd, " I know the
difficulties of Holland to be so great, that I hope every
honest man in England will be contented with their furnishing only one-third in the augmentation; for it is most
certain that they now subsist only by credit, and that the
ill-affected in that country have no hopes left but that
England will insist upon their giving one-half "[4]

All this time, the Duke was busily preparing for the siege
of Ghent. He was principally concerned for the supply
of forage. " Forage being very scarce in these parts,"
wrote Hompesch on the 5th, " our horses will somewhat
suffer; but when men must be sacrificed to obtain a fair
and honourable peace, there is no reason to complain of

[1] *Ibid*, p 338· Marlborough to Godolphin, December 3, 1708
[2] Murray, vol iv., p 335. Marlborough to Walpole, December 3, 1708.
[3] *Ibid*, p. 341 Marlborough to Boyle, December 6, 1708
[4] Coxe, vol. ii , p. 339: Marlborough to Godolphin, December 3, 1708.

the share horses must have in these difficulties."[1]   But
it was impossible to allow the cavalry to be ruined.   On
December 3 the Duke wrote to Walpole as follows: " In
a few days we shall be obliged to furnish the horse with
hay and oats that we must bring from far, . . . which will
occasion a considerable extraordinary charge, so that you
must move that a latitude be allowed in the funds given
in Parliament for defraying it, though I hope about forty
or fifty thousand pounds may answer Her Majesty's quota "[2]
And in a letter of the same date to Godolphin, he said:
" If we continue the army together, we must subsist them
with dry forage, which is very difficult and expensive."[3]
The need was so urgent that it was dangerous to await the
consent of the Cabinet.   Having obtained the concurrence
of the Dutch government, Marlborough, on his own responsibility, sent Cadogan on the 6th to Brussels to enter into
contracts, in conjunction with the deputies, for a three
weeks' supply.   It was essential that, upon the fall of the
citadel of Lille, the allied forces should be in a position to
invest Ghent without a moment's avoidable delay.   For
the French in that city were working day and night to
strengthen their defences; and the frost continued with
undiminished rigour.

The spirit and resolution which the Duke displayed at
this juncture are deserving of the highest admiration.   The
weakness which had well-nigh prostrated him on the eve of
the passage of the Schelde had not yet disappeared.   " The
truth is," he confessed to Godolphin on November 29,
" that I am very ill in my health, so that if we should have
very ill weather, it may kill me.   But I must venture
everything, rather than quit, before we have perfected this
campaign.   My heart is in England, and nobody has greater
desire for the enjoying quietness there than myself; but
should I take ease at this time, I should hurt the Queen
and my country more than my whole life could repair."[4]
He was greatly encouraged by the admirable temper of

---

[1] Boyer, vol vii , p 155 · Letter from Hompesch, December 5, 1708.
[2] Murray, vol. iv., pp 335, 336: Marlborough to Walpole, December 3, 1708
[3] Coxe, vol ii , p 338 · Marlborough to Godolphin, December 3, 1708.
[4] *Ibid.*, p 336: Marlborough to Godolphin, November 29, 1708.

the troops. Even the German auxiliaries were persuaded
to remain. " Our men," he wrote to Godolphin on December 6, " are very hearty, and desirous of taking those two
towns, so that I hope they will suffer a great deal before
they grumble."[1] In truth, the betrayal of Ghent and Bruges
still rankled in the breasts of Marlborough's soldiers   The
English, in particular, resented their exclusion from places,
which they had used, since Ramillies, as their regular
winter-quarters.[2] Nevertheless, the Duke knew well how
much, in reality, depended on his own presence. " You
are so pressing in your letters for my return," he wrote
to Godolphin, " that I must tell you the truth, and beg
you will not think it vanity, that if I should leave the
army, it would not be in anybody's power to keep them
in the field."[3] It would have been easy and pleasant to
abandon the campaign when the citadel of Lille was taken.
Yet the very man who, by Goslinga's account, seized
every opportunity of prolonging the war, was now flouting
the established rules of the military profession, and sacrificing himself and demanding equal sacrifices from others,
solely because he was convinced that he saw his way at
last to terminate the struggle by one final and extraordinary
effort. The soldiers were worthy of the captain whom
they adored. For it was fated that the essential baseness
of his nature should be hidden from such babes, and revealed
to Sicco van Goslinga alone.

On the 11th, Marlborough decamped from Beirlegem,
and moving northwards, took post between Melle and
Meirelbeke. For the convenience of the investing forces,
he proceeded to lay bridges over the network of rivers
and canals, of which Ghent is the centre. Eugène's army
passed the Schelde on the 16th, and halted at Eename.
The Prince rode on to Melle, where a council of war was
held. On the 17th, the Imperialists, reinforced by twenty
of Marlborough's squadrons, crossed the Dendre at Grammont, and encamped at Cammerge to cover the siege.

The garrison of Ghent consisted of thirty-four battalions
and twenty squadrons, a small army. It was fully equipped

[1] *Ibid*, p 340 Marlborough to Godolphin, December 6, 1708
[2] *Milner's Journal*, p. 252, December 8, 1708
[3] Coxe, vol ii., p. 336. Marlborough to Godolphin, November 29, 1708.

with artillery of all sorts, and abundantly supplied with
ammunition. The city was victualled for two months,
although it contained a population of 80,000, over and
above the soldiery The fortifications, in comparison with
those of such places as Lille or Tournai, were obsolete;
but they included an excellent counterscarp, and owing
to the numerous water-ways and inundations, they were
difficult of access. The command was entrusted to the
unfortunate La Motte, whose influence at Versailles procured
him this fair opportunity of obliterating the disgrace of
Wynendael

That the citizens of Ghent were uneasy at the sight of
Marlborough's army, and more particularly of his ammunition boats, can well be imagined. So far as they dared,
they endeavoured now to atone for their recent treachery.
Marlborough was informed, on the 15th, that they had
angrily refused to participate in the defence or to surrender
to La Motte the keys of their magazines, that they were
grievously perturbed at the prospect of a bombardment,
and that they might even be expected to rise against the
garrison. He contrived to transmit to them a verbal
message, thanking them for their zeal for King Charles,
and expressing the hope that it might not be necessary
to proceed to extremities, as bombs were unable to distinguish between friends and foes. On the 17th, he received
" a deputation from the clergy, the magistrates, and the
commonalty of the town," who came, as he informed
Boyle, " to desire we would not destroy their buildings
with our bombs and fire-balls. But I told them, since
they had brought this misfortune upon themselves by their
own folly or negligence, they must either assist us against
the garrison or expect we should use all manner of extremity
to reduce them to their duty. I likewise charged them
to declare to the Spanish and Walloon troops . . . that
if they would immediately quit the French interest and
come over to us, they should be favourably received into
the King's service "[1] The Duke was aware that these
troops were on very bad terms with their French commanders. He therefore embodied his offer in a formal

[1] Murray, vol. iv , p 362: Marlborough to Boyle, December 17, 1708

proclamation, signed by himself and by the Dutch deputies. Several copies of this document were surreptitiously introduced into the city.

On the 18th Marlborough completed the investment of the place. But the circumference of Ghent was fifteen miles, and the communications between the posts of the besiegers were extremely bad. " The roads," said Marlborough, "are so deep and broken in this low country that it will take us some days to make them practicable for bringing the cannon from the water-side to the batteries "[1] Moreover, a thaw having set in, the enemy were enabled to increase the artificial inundations, which obstructed the approaches to the place. Marlborough laboured indefatigably to drain the waters, to create magazines of forage at Melle, and to organise the regular supply and distribution of provisions to the investing army. " At this time," he wrote to Godolphin on the 24th, " we have very fair weather, which we make use of for hutting and covering ourselves, so that we may resist ill weather, if we must have it, for the soldiers as well as officers are convinced of the necessity of having this town."[2] On the 24th and 25th, he opened the trenches at three separate points. On the 25th and 26th, there was a dense fog, under cover of which the besieged sallied out in force on the latter date. They captured a brigadier and a lieutenant-general; but after the first surprise, they were quickly driven in   On the 27th, Fort Rouge, which commanded the canal of Sas van Gent, surrendered with 200 men   On the 28th and 29th, Marlborough was confined to his room with a cold and a painful sore throat, the result of fog and the dampness of the trenches. But his train of 150 cannon and mortars had now arrived. The batteries having been erected, orders were issued to open fire at dawn on the 30th, and at 10 o'clock to employ red-hot shot and bombs. The orders were never executed. For at noon on the 29th La Motte sent out a trumpeter with an offer to treat.

Saint-Simon says that La Motte was absolutely incapable

---

[1] *Ibid*, p. 366. Marlborough to Walpole, December 20, 1708
[2] Coxe, vol II, p. 343 Marlborough to Godolphin, December 24, 1708.

of cowardice or treason, and that he simply lost his head.
Both on public and private grounds he might well have
been expected to hold out until the last.   When Chamillart
realised that the allies were certainly determined to besiege
Ghent, he wrote to La Motte on December 17 in a singularly
outspoken strain.   He dwelt upon the exceptional importance of the place and the necessity of using " all possible
means to protract the siege," that it might " cost the allies
very dear "; he urged La Motte " to dispute the ground
inch by inch," as Boufflers had disputed it at Lille; and
he declined to give any instructions as to " the preservation of the troops " in the last extremity, because, as he
explained, " a long time "[1] should elapse before such a
contingency could arise.   Speaking as a friend, and not
as the Minister for War, he frankly declared that, if, as the
reward of long and faithful service, La Motte was to secure
the coveted baton of a Marshal of France, he must ardently
embrace the present opportunity of recovering the good
opinion of the King, and of expunging the memories of a
too facile capitulation at Ostend and a too ridiculous fiasco
at Wynendael   This letter failed to reach its destination.
It was intercepted by Marlborough, who was not a little
edified by the perusal of it   But it did no more than
emphasise considerations, which must have been already
apparent to La Motte.   He surely required, as an old
historian remarks, " no extraordinary capacity to conceive
of what prodigious consequence it was to France that
Ghent was preserved, or at least that it was held out to the
last."[2]   Yet after four and a half days of open trenches,
and before the besiegers' batteries had begun to play, he
asked for terms   He was in want, according to Marlborough, " both of money and forage."[3]   But neither
money nor forage was indispensable in the circumstances.
It was also alleged that he had need of lead.   But Villars
observed that he had sufficient of that commodity to last
him till the end of the world, since all the churches were

[1] Lediard, vol ii , p 406· Chamillart's letter to La Motte, December 17,
1708
[2] Campbell, *The Military History of Prince Eugène and John, Duke of
Marlborough*, vol ii , p 87
[3] Murray, vol iv , p 389 Marlborough to Boyle, January 3 1709

covered with it. La Motte maintained, in his own defence, that the fortifications of Ghent were obsolete, and that he was anxious to save his army for the King's service. Both excuses were inadmissible. Saint-Simon alleges that he was stupid enough to be persuaded by the arguments of a pusillanimous officer of Swiss. Although Saint-Simon alleges also that the populace were quiescent, it is not improbable that the presence of 80,000 discontented and terrified civilians affected the general's nerves The people of Ghent had a turbulent record. Fear is a potent motive; and fear was rampant in the conscience-stricken city, where the sentiments of Marlborough's soldiery were not unknown. " If it should have come to a general storm," says Sergeant Millner, both garrison and inhabitants "could have expected but very little favour "[1] from an army, exasperated by what they regarded as the foul play of the citizens, as well as by their own sufferings and hardships.

Happily for the reputation of Marlborough's men, the horrors of Badajoz were not anticipated at Ghent. On condition that he were permitted to march out with the honours of war, La Motte proposed to surrender both town and castle within four days, if the allies were not compelled to abandon the siege in the meantime. Marlborough, though he knew that Boufflers had returned to Douai on the 28th, readily agreed. On the 31st, he wrote to the magistracy of Bruges and to Grimaldi, who commanded twenty battalions and nine squadrons in that town, offering them similar terms. But in the night of January 1, acting on instructions from Boufflers and the Elector, Grimaldi evacuated Bruges, and retired across the frontier. The garrisons of Plasschendaele and Leffinghe followed his example

La Motte marched out of Ghent on January 2. Marlborough and Eugène were in the saddle at the head of their men. " The garrison was so numerous," wrote the Duke to Boyle, " that they were from 10 in the morning till near 7 at night before all had passed through the gate."[2] " It is astonishing," he told Godolphin, " to see so great numbers of good men to look on, and suffer a place of this

[1] *Millner's Journal,* p 254 December 19, 1708
[2] Murray, vol iv., p. 389 Marlborough to Boyle, January 3, 1709

consequence to be taken, at this season, with so little a loss."[1] Small wonder that the officer, commanding the Spanish troops, refused to sign the capitulation, and that his was not the only case.

Marlborough visited the town incognito the same evening. On the 3rd he inspected the fortifications, "which," he reported, "I find in so good a condition that they might have given us much more trouble."[2] The populace received the victors with acclamation   The authorities entertained the Duke and his officers at the town hall with great magnificence, and that night the city was illuminated. " Some, however," says Lediard, " believed this joy to be fictitious."[3] Marlborough prudently acted on the assumption that it was genuine. " A general amnesty " was granted to the citizens, " and a new confirmation of all their privileges."[4] In Burnet's judgment they " did not deserve so good usage." But they had paid heavily for their treachery, and they had been thoroughly well frightened. Severity, in all the circumstances, would have been highly injudicious. For, as Marlborough had written only three weeks before to Godolphin, " not only the towns but the people of this country hate the Dutch."[5] It was thanks to England, and to England's general, that the whole of the Spanish Netherlands had not, long since, imitated the example of Ghent and Bruges.

In his rage and disappointment, Louis refused to see the messenger who brought La Motte's dispatch. He sent that general a *lettre de cachet*, banishing him to his country estate near Compiègne. He had expected the city to hold out for six weeks, assuming that the allies could keep the field so long. In Maffei's opinion, it could, with the co-operation of Grimaldi's small army at Bruges, have held out all the winter. As if to intensify the bitterness of the humiliation which the King and the people of France had now to suffer, no sooner had La Motte capitulated than the weather changed. On the 3rd and 4th, it rained and snowed incessantly; and on the morning of the 5th, a

[1] Coxe, vol ii , p 315. Marlborough to Godolphin, January 3, 1709
[2] Murray, vol iv , p 389. Marlborough to Boyle, January 3, 1709.
[3] Lediard, vol ii , p 419.   [4] Burnet, vol iv., p 198.
[5] Coxe, vol. ii , p 340. Marlborough to Godolphin, December 6, 1708.

severe frost set in, " a most violent frost "[1] (says Burnet),
" which continued the longest of any in the memory of
man." " It was scarcely possible," says the same historian, " to keep the soldiers alive, even in their quarters,
so that they must have perished, if they had not broke
up the campaign before this hard season "[2] Villars took the
same view " That horrible frost," he declared, " which was
so fatal to all the fruits of the earth . . . would have been no
less deadly to Prince Eugène and the Duke of Marlborough,
if the garrison had been able to defend itself two days
longer."[3] Such a coincidence, following immediately upon
the singular meteorological conditions, which had attended
the siege of Lille, enabled the pious, and even the impious,
to draw conclusions very gratifying to the Bishop of Salisbury " It made great impressions," he says, " on many
of the chief officers, which some owned to myself; though
they were the persons from whom I expected it least."[4]
Marlborough had been always a steadfast believer in divine
providence and the efficacy of prayer. " This campaign,"
he wrote to Godolphin on the 3rd, " is now ended to my
own heart's desire; and as the hand of the Almighty is
visible in this whole matter, I hope Her Majesty will think
it due to Him to return public thanks, and, at the same
time, to implore His blessing on the next campaign."[5]

Eugène set off on the 3rd for Brussels, and Marlborough
on the 4th. Having settled the disposition of the troops
in winter-quarters, they entrusted the command to Tilly,
and departed on the 9th for the Hague.

Thus ended a campaign, which was certainly one of the
most extraordinary, one of the most picturesque, and one
of the most instructive in the annals of war. In the military
history of that epoch it stands out conspicuous, if only
because it furnishes so many examples of rules successfully
violated and maxims defied with impunity. Marlborough,
and Eugène paid no deference to text-books, when they
marched an army fifty miles in sixty hours, and flung it

[1] Burnet, vol iv, p 198.
[2] Westerloo in his Memoirs alleges that men and horses were actually
frozen to death as they marched
[3] *Vie de Villars* t ii, p 29   [4] Burnet, vol iv, p 198.
[5] Coxe, vol ii, p 346· Marlborough to Godolphin, January 3, 1709.

across a considerable river in the teeth of a fresh and numerically superior opponent. They paid no deference to text-books, when they invested a fortress of the resisting capacity of Lille, although the water-ways were not in their possession, and a hostile force, greater than their own two armies combined, threatened the flanks of their long communications with Brussels They paid no deference to text-books, when to this same force they offered battle in an open plain, though the odds in numbers were two to one in favour of their antagonists. They paid no deference to text-books, when, in the late autumn, with hospitals full and magazines empty, with provisions running low and every road to the capital barred by an entrenched enemy, they resolved to open up fresh communications by way of Ostend, and at all hazards to continue the siege. And they paid no deference to text-books, when they remained before the citadel of Lille throughout November, or when, without relaxing their hold upon their prey, they suddenly turned upon Vendôme and burst his impregnable line of the Schelde as though it had been paste-board, or when, in the depth of winter, instead of dispersing their war-worn armies, they invested Ghent and terrified it into surrender on the eve of the hardest frost within the memory of living man. The unbroken success, which attended these daring and repeated breaches of the accepted axioms of war, proved conclusively that there was more in the art, as practised by Marlborough and Eugène, than Louis and Chamillart and Villeroi had once imagined, when they comforted themselves with the reflection that the Duke was nothing but a gambler, dangerous only because he was reckless to the point of desperation " I think," wrote Marlborough to his Duchess, " we may, without vanity, say that France will, with terror remember this campaign for a long time."[1] France was confronted with the mystery of genius; and she was appalled by it.

From first to last the French had possessed great advantages. They enjoyed the active sympathy of a majority of the people of the country, a circumstance, which, at the very outset, and without the expense of a battle or

[1] Coxe, vol ii , p 340· Marlborough to the Duchess, December 10, 1708

a siege, gave them the fortresses of Ghent and Bruges and the control of the water-ways, and which constantly afflicted the allies with an embarrassing anxiety for the safety of Antwerp, Brussels, and the other cities of the Spanish Netherlands. They enjoyed a superiority of numbers, which at Oudenarde was considerable, and which, at Mons-en-Pevèle and Wynendael was absurdly disproportionate. They enjoyed an altogether abnormal share of those opportunities, which the cautious generals of that epoch seldom offered to an opponent, but which resulted naturally from the audacious risks taken by the allies. And finally, they enjoyed those additional opportunities, which the unprecedented length of the siege of Lille conferred upon them, and which, upon any reasonable calculation of possibilities, they were not entitled to expect. Yet, notwithstanding these great advantages, they accomplished nothing, and worse than nothing   Two exploits, and only two, stood to the credit of the French soldier   One was Boufflers' defence of Lille, the other Luxembourg's dash across the allied lines.   The glory, in the one case, was shared among 8,000 men, in the other among 2,000   Yet more than 100,000 were in the field for France.   What is the explanation of these very inadequate results ?   It is, after all, a simple one.   In war, all advantages are eventually worthless, if they be not accompanied or ultimately followed by actual or potential superiority in combat.   The acquisition, by civilian connivance, of Ghent and Bruges, created an atmosphere of prosperity, which the military collapse at Oudenarde immediately afterwards showed to be artificial. The refusal to fight a battle for the salvation of Lille drove home the same lesson.   Neither situation, nor numbers, nor fortresses, nor field-works, nor positions, nor rivers, nor cities, nor conspiracies of them that dwell therein, can ever compensate an army for proved or conscious inferiority under the vital test of battle.

It is true that, in one respect, Marlborough and Eugène were remarkably fortunate.   The exceptional weather favoured them consistently.   But no weather, however exceptional, could have justified them in taking such hazards as they took, and in giving such chances as they gave.

At Oudenarde, by Marlborough's own confession, he pre-sented the enemy with "too much advantage." The project of besieging Lille was, in Feuquières' phrase, "chimerical." It depended upon a service of gigantic convoys, the uniformly safe arrival of which, posterity, according to the same author, would refuse to credit. It succeeded, in the words of Villars, "against all the rules of war" The victory of Wynendael was something of a miracle; and Feuquières, in all his vast experience, could find no precedent for it. But if Webb had been beaten, "the consequence," by Marlborough's own admission, "must have been the raising of the siege the next day." The passage of the Schelde was accomplished virtually without loss, though the enemy's works at Audenarde "had more the appearance of the ramparts of a fortress than ordinary lines," and though the general-officers of the allies had anticipated 10,000 casualties. The siege of Ghent, undertaken in the depth of winter, astounded the military opinion of the day by its shocking foolhardiness. What then was that virtue, in which Marlborough and Eugène trusted, and never trusted in vain ? They relied, without doubt, like Wellington in the Waterloo campaign, upon their own proved skill, and their own vast knowledge of the possible in war. They relied also upon the notorious dissensions among the French commanders. But from first to last, the one, permanent, preponderating, and decisive asset, upon which they relied to overbear all odds, and to extricate them from all entanglements, was the superb *moral* of their soldiers. To say thus much, is not to detract from the merits of Marlborough and Eugène, from the vigilance and daring of the one, or the magnificent tenacity of the other For this spiritual power on which they leaned was, in the main, a power which they themselves had created, and which they alone sustained. The splendid confidence which they displayed had nothing in common with the audacity of ignorance or the heroism of despair. On the contrary, it was, in the highest sense, scientific. For it was based entirely upon knowledge—knowledge of themselves, knowledge of their men, and knowledge of their foe.

In forming the opinion that, provided the members of the Grand Alliance prepared more strenuously than ever for war, a satisfactory peace was now within their grasp, Marlborough did not reason from the great results achieved in the Spanish Netherlands alone. In the other theatres of the struggle, the campaign of 1708, unlike its predecessor, had yielded no compensating triumphs to the French arms. On the Rhine, the Elector of Bavaria, disgusted at the trick which Marlborough and Eugène had played upon him, and jealous of the glory which they had reaped as the outcome of it, sulkily declined to take the offensive; but the French, on the other hand, though they were enabled by his inactivity to detach troops for Flanders, accomplished nothing of any moment. In Italy, the Duke of Savoy had been slow to take the field. A dispute with the Court of Vienna in regard to the investiture of a part of the Montferrat having been settled in his favour through the interposition of England and more particularly of Marlborough, he moved at last in July, and traversing Mont Cenis and the Little St. Bernard, appeared to threaten Dauphiné and even Lyons. Villars, who at the head of an inferior force, was entrusted with the defence of the frontier from Geneva to the sea, exhibited all his accustomed energy and skill. But when, at the end of October, the operations were suspended on account of heavy snows, the Duke of Savoy had captured the fortresses of Exilles, Perusa, and Fenestrelles, and was master of the passes of the Alps. He had also compelled the French government to detach troops from Roussillon to the assistance of Villars. Marlborough, while he recognised that the Duke had " opened the way into France,"[1] regarded his performance

---

[1] Murray, vol. iv , p 247: Marlborough to Lord Raby, October 1, 1708.

as a disappointing one on the whole. But the enemy, at any rate, could extract no encouragement from it.

In Spain, no second Almanza had darkened the prospects of the House of Hapsburg. Thanks to the prudent measures which, at the instigation of Marlborough and Godolphin, had been adopted in the Peninsula, the Bourbon armies, though not yet entirely checked, progressed but slowly. Early in February, on the landing of the first contingent of German and Italian troops at Barcelona, Galway and Das Minas sailed for Lisbon with 1,800 Portuguese. " The success of our friends in Catalonia," wrote Marlborough to the Earl on the 7th of June, " will very much depend upon the diversion you make."[1] But Galway, who was now the ambassador of England as well as her general, speedily discovered that no diversion of any importance was to be expected from the Portuguese government. The army was indeed dispatched to the frontier, but it was not permitted to undertake any serious operations. Galway's place at Barcelona, as general of the English, was filled, upon Marlborough's recommendation, by James Stanhope, who still retained his appointment as envoy to Charles. Starhemberg, the Austrian commander-in-chief, arrived at the end of April. Henceforward the fortunes of King Charles were no longer embarrassed by those scandalous jealousies and diversions which had long originated in the self-seeking personalities of Peterborough and Noyelles. " I learn with satisfaction," wrote Marlborough to the King on June 26, " the harmony which reigns among all the generals."[2]

Orléans at Zaragoza was preparing to besiege Tortosa. On June 12 he invested that fortress with 22,000 men. Noailles, marching to join him with 7,000 French regulars and 3,000 Spanish volunteers, found his progress barred by the Prince of Darmstadt, who occupied a strong position on the Ter with 4,000 men. In June, Noailles, having been weakened by a detachment for the army of Villars, retired to Roussillon. But the siege of Tortosa, notwithstanding the valour and activity of the garrison, was vigor-

[1] Murray, vol iv , p 54· Marlborough to Galway, June 7, 1708.
[2] Ibid , p 82 Marlborough to the King of Spain, June 26, 1708.

ously pressed. Starhemberg, who had taken the field with 10,200 Germans, Italians, English, Dutch, and Portuguese, was much too weak to relieve the place. Sir John Leake with the fleets of England and Holland had quitted Lisbon on May 8. Approaching Barcelona, he fell in with ninety French barques, laden with provisions for the army of Orléans, captured sixty-nine of them, and dispersed the rest. This booty was very welcome to the allied troops in Catalonia, which were none too well supplied Leake anchored at Barcelona on the 26th, detached a small squadron to cruise upon that coast, and sailed on the 30th for Italy, to procure reinforcements for Starhemberg.   On June 8 he reached Vade on the Gulf of Genoa, where he dispatched Norris to Milan, and the Dutch Vice-Admiral Wassenaer to Turin. Charles wanted money as well as men; and Marlborough instructed the British representative at Turin to raise a loan in Italy, if it could be got " upon reasonable terms "[1] Marlborough had faith in the policy of " showing the flag " " It is likely," he said, " the arrival of our fleet may retrieve our credit in these parts."[2]   Though Marlborough had never ceased to urge the vital importance of sending an early succour to Starhemberg, it was not until July 15 that Leake set sail for Catalonia. He carried with him 2,200 horse and 3,600 foot, as well as the young Princess of Wolfenbüttel who was betrothed to Charles. He reached Mataro on the 26th. He was fifteen days too late. Tortosa had fallen on the 11th.

Starhemberg immediately advanced to Cervera. Orléans retired to Agramont, and there entrenched himself. Most of his French troops having been recalled to Flanders he could do nothing For three months the two armies remained in their camps, and then retired into winter-quarters. But in November D'Asfeld captured Denia in Valencia, and in December he took the town of Alicante; but the castle, which was defended by the English and the Huguenots with romantic heroism, held out until the ensuing April

These French successes were altogether eclipsed by an

[1] *Ibid*, p. 59. Marlborough to Stanhope, June 11, 1708.
[2] *Ibid*, p 56: Marlborough to Mr. Chetwynd, June 11, 1708.

event which was the greatest triumph that had attended
the Mediterranean strategy of Marlborough since the
capture of Gibraltar. To secure the fullest benefit derivable
from that strategy, it was essential that an English squadron
should winter within the Straits. All the allied governments and all their generals and diplomatists realised this
truth. That none realised it more strongly than Marlborough
himself, is clearly shown by numerous and emphatic passages
in his correspondence. He pressed it continually upon the
British Cabinet. But objection was taken by the Admiralty,
who in the absence of a commodious harbour and assured
victualling, very properly declined to risk their ships.
Spezia had been suggested as a suitable place, but Marlborough, in a letter of June 26 to Stanhope, wrote as fol-
lows· " You know I am sufficiently convinced of the necessity of a squadron wintering in the Mediterranean, but it
is certain all our seamen are against it, alleging the men-
of-war cannot be secure and have all the necessaries to
enable them to keep the sea in the port of Spezia."[1] He
wrote in similar terms, on the same date, to the King of
Spain; but he also said that he was using his utmost endeavours to promote the desired end Marlborough was
a great strategist He fully understood that the essential
unity of war is unaffected by the element on which it
happens to be waged. But he was too good a soldier not
to know that he must not dictate to sailors upon questions
of seamanship. As an islander, he naturally perceived
more clearly than the statesmen of Central Europe the
proper distinction between the two professions. In answer,
it would seem, to protests from Vienna, he wrote to Wratislaw on July 18 as follows· " There is nobody who does not
concur as to the necessity of keeping a winter squadron
in the Mediterranean, but when all is said that can be said,
the opinion of the admirals and the officers of the navy as
to the harbour and the other requirements of the fleet must
prevail. It is certain that they are the best judges of such
things, and Sir John Leake is not without instructions in
the matter; but I must tell you plainly that so far as I
can discover, these gentlemen consider the only safe and

[1] Murray, vol. iv., p 84: Murray to Stanhope, June 26, 1708

suitable harbour is Port Mahon. I have written to Mr Stanhope, urging him to spare no efforts to obtain possession of it; once this is done, there will be no further difficulty, and you must allow me to say, as I have said before, that every word you may write upon this subject, and every order that may be given in England, must be absolutely subject to the judgment of the fleet; that is very easy to understand. Mr. Stanhope's project is always in our thoughts, and so are the measures whereby it may be executed, and I hope that everybody concerned will diligently contribute to its success."[1] On the same day, and in a similar strain, he addressed himself to Sinzendorf in the following terms· " It is quite certain, as I am informing Count Wratislaw, that Admiral Leake has the Queen's orders to station a winter squadron in the Mediterranean. But the use of the navy is limited by conditions which do not apply to the land forces. There are many more precautions to be taken, and you and I are not competent to be judges of them. In these matters we must refer to the admirals and the officers of the fleet, who are principally concerned in them, and who, I am sure, will do their utmost. If we could have Port Mahon, all difficulty would vanish, and I have already written to Mr. Stanhope, urging him to spare no efforts to obtain possession of it."[2] In the letter to Stanhope, which had been dispatched three days before, Marlborough had declared that it was " certain our seaofficers are the best judges what may be done with safety in this case." But he had added in his own handwriting this significant postscript· " I am so entirely convinced that nothing can be done effectually without the fleet, that I conjure you, if possible, to take Port Mahon, and to let me have your reasons for any other port, so that I may continue to press them in England "[3] This correspondence alone is positive proof of Marlborough's title to be regarded as a master of the use of sea-power, and as a war minister of England not unworthy to be ranked with Chatham himself.

" I conjure you, if possible, to take Port Mahon " With that exhortation for his supreme and indisputable warrant,

[1] *Ibid*, p 118 Marlborough to Wratislaw, July 18, 1708.
[2] *Ibid*, p 119· Marlborough to Sinzendorf, July 18, 1708
[3] *Ibid*, p 107 Marlborough to Stanhope, July 15, 1708

Stanhope, who had wintered in England, and who had almost certainly discussed the project with Marlborough in person, did not hesitate to act. In August, with Starhemberg's assistance he prepared an expeditionary force of 2,000 English, Spanish, and Portuguese, with ten guns and some mortars. But Leake was no longer at Barcelona. With 1,000 Spanish troops and 600 English marines on board, he had sailed for Sardinia. Arriving off Cagliari on the 11th, he summoned the place, threw in a few shells the same night, and on the morning of the 12th, disembarked his troops and marines together with 600 sailors. Thereupon the governor, who was detested by the people, surrendered. The entire island followed suit. In Cagliari the allies obtained " a good fortified harbour conveniently near Italy "[1] In Sardinia they obtained a magnificent granary invaluable to the army of Catalonia. The inhabitants presented them at once with 1,400 tons of corn, which were speedily shipped to Barcelona. Two thousand horses, destined to serve as remounts for the army of Orléans, became the booty of the conquerors, and the majority of the Spanish garrison enlisted under King Charles. While Leake lay off the island, he was apprised by Stanhope that everything was now in readiness for an attack upon Port Mahon, that the transports were about to sail from Barcelona, and that the fleet must proceed forthwith to Minorca to participate in the operation. Naval opinion was not at all favourable to this project, but naval opinion was overborne by the resolute Stanhope, who knew very well what he was about, and who carried Marlborough's letter in his pocket. Stanhope sailed from Barcelona with the transports on September 2. On the 13th he fell in with Leake, who was cruising off Port Mahon. On the 14th he landed in the vicinity of that town. The inhabitants surrendered immediately; but the powerful fortress of St. Philip and its dependent works refused to yield. Preparations were made to besiege it, but the rocky nature of the ground and the deficiency of horses caused considerable delay. The season being now so far advanced, Leake sailed for England on the 19th, leaving behind him a

---

[1] Parnell, *The War of the Succession in Spain*, ch. xxviii , p 253.

squadron of seventeen ships under Rear-Admiral Whitaker
On the 20th, the *Dunkirk* and the *Centurion* anchored
off Fornelles, an excellent harbour, situated at the north-
eastern corner of Minorca, and suited to the needs of Stanhope's transports They engaged the fort, and after a
severe action compelled it to surrender. On the 22nd,
400 of Stanhope's men appeared before Ciudadela on
the western side of the island. The place capitulated
without resistance. By the 28th everything was ready
for the attack upon St. Philip. This formidable work was
manned by a garrison of 1,000 French and Spaniards,
amply provided with provisions and artillery. But Stanhope, with the assistance of the navy, brought up no fewer
than forty-two guns and eighteen mortars. He breached
the defences on the 28th, and the same day, by the gallant
rashness of some English grenadiers, whom he promptly
supported, he secured a lodgment at the foot of the inner
glacis. On the 29th the governor surrendered Contrary
to the terms of the capitulation, Stanhope arrested the
French troops in retaliation for the barbarous and perfidious
conduct of D'Asfeld in Spain. The place contained 3,000
barrels of powder and 100 cannon. The price which the
allies paid for it was forty killed and wounded; amongst
the slain, however, was Captain Philip Stanhope, of the
Milford, the general's brother, " a young gentleman of
great hopes, who was extremely regretted "[1] " This conquest," wrote Stanhope to Marlborough, " has cost me
very dear; but since he died in doing service to Her Majesty
and his country, I shall think his life well bestowed, as I
should my own."[2]

Marlborough had the glorious news on October 30. It
is a highly significant circumstance that his letter to Berwick, suggesting that the time was ripe for peace, bears the
same date Port Mahon, in the Duke's judgment, was a
more important conquest than Lille. He could not believe
that the French resistance would outlast the loss of both
The opinion which he entertained of the strategical value of
this great acquisition was emphatically endorsed in France.

[1] Boyer, vol vii , p 190
[2] Letter to the Duke of Marlborough of September 30, 1708, printed in
Lord Mahon's *History of the War of the Succession in Spain,* p 257.

The governor was delivered to a court-martial at Toulon, expelled from the army, stripped of his pensions and his cross, and committed to prison with his principal officers, and finally banished to a remote province   "With this conquest and Gibraltar," said Saint-Simon, " the English found themselves in a position to dominate the Mediterranean, to pass the winter there with entire fleets, and to blockade all the ports of Spain on that sea."[1]   It was no wonder that Stanhope should have prophesied that Port Mahon would be " to France in the Mediterranean what Dunkirk has been to us in the Channel,"[2] and that he should have written to Sunderland that " England ought never to part with this island, which will give the law to the Mediterranean both in time of war and peace."[3]   Unfortunately, Minorca belonged of right to Charles. The resources of diplomacy, however, might yet secure it for England, and Stanhope, by way of a preliminary move, garrisoned Port Mahon with English troops alone.

Whitaker sailed from Minorca to Italy to convey a third detachment of Imperialist troops to Catalonia   He continued in those waters through the winter, and to excellent purpose   For the Pope, who had refused to recognise King Charles, and who had long exhibited his partiality for the House of Bourbon, was now at open war with the Emperor.   Encouraged by the Court of France, and taking advantage of the absence of the Imperialist forces, under Savoy, he hired troops at his own expense, endeavoured to raise an armed league of the princes and states of Italy, and threatened Joseph with the temporal as well as the spiritual power   Marlborough realised the danger to the coalition of this new complication.   He instructed Meadows, the ambassador at Vienna, to " insinuate to the ministers " there that " no time should be lost in acting against the Pope with the greatest vigour "[4]   The British government, which was highly incensed at the encouragement given by Clement to the Pretender, had been meditating revenge. Leake's instructions had contemplated the destruction of

---

[1] Saint-Simon, t xi , ch ccii., p 202
[2] Mahon, *History of the War of the Succession in Spain*, p 258.
[3] *Ibid* , Appendix, p. 75   Stanhope to Sunderland, September 30, 1708
[4] Murray, vol iv , p 278: Marlborough to Meadows, October 25, 1708.

Civita Vecchia, which Marlborough had described as "certainly very reasonable, if we can have any proof that the Pope contributed to the late intended invasion."[1] Clement pretended that he had not contributed in kind; but his blessings and his prayers he could not deny. When, therefore, in November the Imperialists advanced into the Papal territory, Whitaker made ready to support them from the sea. But Clement, who had already been alarmed by the capture of Port Mahon, decided now to treat. At the last moment, the Austrian ambassador desired the British admiral to suspend the bombardment of Civita Vecchia. In January, 1709, Clement yielded to the Emperor's demands, and agreed to recognise King Charles. Thus the coalition was relieved from what Marlborough designated as "a terrible embarrassment "[2] And thus the Duke's prophecy that the capture of Port Mahon would "greatly contribute to hold the Princes of Italy in check "[3] was fulfilled.

The year 1708 furnishes an instructive example of the manifold uses of the navy in amphibious war. The seizure of a permanent base in the Mediterranean was beyond all comparison the principal achievement of the fleet. But it had also frustrated the Pretender's raid on Scotland, it had co-operated with the army in Flanders by threatening a descent upon the French coast from Boulogne to Cherbourg, and by restoring communications through Ostend; it had co-operated with the army in Catalonia by transporting large reinforcements from Italy, by destroying the enemy's provision ships, by securing in the island of Sardinia an inexhaustible source of food-supply, in the winter, trusting to its naval base, it had threatened to bombard the port of Rome, terrified the Pope, and contributed to the collapse of his projected combination of Italian states against the House of Hapsburg. But busy as it was in Europe, it would still go hunting for pieces of eight in American waters. Notwithstanding the number and diversity of these services, the protection of commerce was nowise neglected. The convoys were so prudently timed, and the cruisers so judiciously stationed, that, as Burnet says, ' we

[1] Murray, vol iv , p 12 Marlborough to Boyle, May 14, 1708
[2] Ibid , p 460 M b gh to the Marquis de Prie, March 2, 1709.
[3] Ibid , p 286 Marlborough to Wratislaw, October 31, 1708

made no considerable losses."[1]   In short, the Admiralty
which at the beginning of the year had been so bitterly
and so unscrupulously assailed, was before the end of it,
entirely rehabilitated.   And the vindication of Marlborough's Mediterranean strategy was complete.

The extraordinary duration of the campaign in Flanders
had compelled Godolphin to face the new Parliament in
November without that sense of comfort and support
which he invariably derived from Marlborough's presence.
He had continually pressed the Duke to return to England
in the autumn, if only for forty-eight hours,[2] and in a letter
of November 9 he had gone so far as to declare that " unless
that can be compassed very, very soon, it will be next
to impossible to prevent ruin."   His disappointment was
shared by the Queen, who appeared " much concerned "[3]
at so long a separation from the only member of her
ministry whom she now regarded as a friend.   But even the
termination of the campaign did not release the general
from his duties on the continent   He was detained by the
double necessity of preparing for a more vigorous conduct
of the war, and of watching the anticipated negotiations
for peace.   Before the surrender of Ghent it had been
strongly represented by the States-General that both
Marlborough and Eugène should continue in the Netherlands throughout the winter.   But inasmuch as the one
commander was imperatively called to London and the
other to Vienna, a compromise was ultimately effected.
Marlborough was to reside at the Hague during January
and February, and Eugène during March and April.

That the Duke was secretly pleased to be constrained by
circumstances to absent himself from England at this point
there can be little doubt.   As early as May 6 he had warned
his wife that he would " try to arrange to stay abroad next
winter "[4]   In spite of his loyalty to his colleague and his
Queen, if not, indeed, because of that very loyalty, he
hated the notion of a contact with domestic politics
more intimate than that which he already obtained from

[1] Burnet, vol. iv., p 202.
[2] Coxe, vol ii., p 358: Godolphin to Marlborough, November 2, 1708
[3] Ibid , p 330· Godolphin to Marlborough, November 12/23, 1708
[4] Ibid , p 217. The Duke to the Duchess, May 6, 1708.

the bulky and unpleasant contents of his letter-bags. In the midst of the exacting labours and responsibilities of an abnormally prolonged and arduous campaign, he had been pestered by a correspondence with the Queen, the Duchess, and Godolphin, which would have ruined the temper and the nerves of any but the most patient man in Europe. Judging that their successes at the general election had made them the absolute masters of Parliament, the Junta had now adopted an even more haughty and menacing tone. Maynwaring had warned the Duchess in April that, in the event of Whig victories at the polls, it would be "impossible to keep them together"[1] without substantial concessions. Godolphin, who desired to appease them by the admission of Somers and Montagu to the ministry, found himself confronted by the sullen resistance of the Sovereign who, if she was angry at the sacrifice of Harley, was furious at the disgraceful interference of Sunderland in the Scottish elections.[2] Godolphin's offers to resign left her unmoved Sarah's tempestuous remonstrances did much more harm than good It was to Marlborough and to Marlborough alone, that his colleague looked for effective assistance in the miserable struggle with the Sovereign. All through the summer and autumn of 1708 the Duke was labouring to mitigate an evil which he despaired of curing. He despaired of curing it, because he knew that he had something much more serious to combat than the Queen's inveterate dislike of Whiggery and her personal detestation of the Whig leaders. He knew that Anne was not left altogether without resources. Under the pressure of their misfortunes the moderate Tories and "the Tackers" were tending now to coalesce. St. John was urging Harley to come to terms with Bromley and the champions of the Church. Marlborough was informed of this movement. "I do not take Mr. Bromley for a great negotiator," he wrote to the Duchess on August 23, " but a less able man than himself will reconcile Lord Rochester and Mr. Harley at this time. I believe you may depend upon it that they will be all of one mind, and that they think themselves

[1] *Private Correspondence of Sarah, Duchess of Marlborough,* vol. 1 , p 105: Mr Maynwaring to the Duchess of Marlborough, April 9, 1708
[2] See Chapter XIX "Dunkirk, Ghent, and Bruges"

assured of the hearts of the Prince and the Queen, which
is a very dismal prospect."[1]   Bromley was in fact in correspondence with Harley.   They reckoned on the support
of the gentry and the clergy, and they were deliberating
as to the best lines of attack in the ensuing Parliament [2]
The immediate danger, however, lay not in Parliament,
where the combined forces of Toryism could be steadily
voted down by the cohorts of the Junta.   It lay rather
in the secret counsel and encouragement which a reviving
opposition could extend to the Queen through the instrumentality of Mrs. Masham.   What Maynwaring called " the
senseless farce of Harlequin and Abigail "[3] was still running.
In a letter to the Duchess the Queen spoke of " Masham
and me."[4]   " I do not wonder," said Maynwaring, " that
the expression . . . made you sick, for it is very ridiculous."
" I am very sorry to see by yours," wrote Marlborough to
his wife on July 19, " that the Queen is fonder of Mrs.
Masham than ever; I am sure, as long as that is, there
can be no happiness, I mean quietness."[5]   " Sooner or
later," he wrote on August 2, " we must have her out of
the hands of Mrs. Masham, or everything will be labour
in vain "[6]   " The account you give me of the commerce
and kindness of the Queen to Mrs Masham," he wrote on
the 6th, " is that which will at last bring all things to ruin "
And on the 9th he wrote " The Tories have got the heart
and entire possession of the Queen, which they will be able
to maintain as long as Mrs Masham has credit."[7]   At
first he had deemed it possible to attack the new favourite.
" I can't but think," he wrote to the Duchess on August 6,
" some ways might be found to make Mrs Masham very
much afraid."[8]   But a fortnight later he had changed his
views.   " I am sure," he wrote on the 23rd, " that the
interest of Mrs. Masham is so settled with the Queen, that
we only trouble ourselves to no purpose, and by endeavour-

[1] Coxe, vol. ii , p 291· The Duke to the Duchess, August 23, 1708
[2] Portland MSS : W. Bromley to Robert Harley, September 18, 1708
(Hist MSS Comm , 15th Report, Appendix, part iv , p 504)
[3] *Private Correspondence of Sarah, Duchess of Marlborough,* vol 1 , p 113 .
Mr. Maynwaring to the Duchess of Marlborough, April, 1708   [4] *Ibid.*
[5] Coxe, vol ii , p 279· The Duke to the Duchess, July 19, 1708
[6] *Ibid* , p 282 The Duke to the Duchess, August 2, 1708
[7] *Ibid* , p 286 The Duke to the Duchess, August 9, 1708
[8] *Ibid* , p 283 The Duke to the Duchess, August 6, 1708

ing to hurt, we do good offices to her, so that in my opinion we ought to be careful of our own actions, and not lay everything to heart, but submit to whatever may happen."[1]

Nevertheless the Duke took infinite pains to soothe and to persuade the indignant Queen, and to stave off as long as possible the ultimate catastrophe. He succeeded in the end in preserving Sunderland from her just resentment, although her threats to dismiss his son-in-law from her service perturbed him greatly, and were the principal cause of the serious illness which prostrated him on the eve of his march from Assche to the field of Oudenarde.[2] Writing to Anne on August 2 he expressed his surprise that anybody should have been able, in his absence, to induce her to entertain the idea of giving " me so great a mortification in the face of all Europe, at a time when I was so zealously endeavouring to serve you, at the hazard both of my reputation and of my blood." In the same letter he reminded her that something more than his own personal feelings would be involved in the disgrace of a minister who was also a member of the Junta. " For God's sake, Madam," he wrote, "consider that, whatever may be said to amuse or delude you, it is utterly impossible for you to have ever more than a part of the Tories; and though you could have them all, their number is not capable of doing you good."[3] But although he was willing to advise her in general terms, he refused to be drawn into the particular controversies between the Junta and her Writing on July 23 he said: " As I have formerly told Your Majesty that I am desirous to serve you in the army, but not as a minister, I am every day more and more confirmed in that opinion " At the same time he declared to her that he considered her " obliged in conscience, and as a good Christian, to forgive and to have no more resentments to any particular person or party, but to make use of such as will carry on this just war with vigour."[4] Mrs. Morley, who still hoped to extract from Mr. Freeman some evidences of sympathy and support

[1] *Ibid*, p 291 The Duke to the Duchess, August 23, 1708.
[2] See Chapter XX , " Oudenarde," p 125
[3] Coxe, vol ii , p 283 Marlborough to the Queen, August 2, 1708
[4] *Ibid*, p 2'1 Marlborough to the Queen, July 23, 1708

which she might use to her own advantage in her constant troubles with Mr Montgomery, did not conceal her disappointment. An incautious phrase in the letter which Marlborough wrote to his wife on the morrow of Oudenarde gave the Queen an opportunity of insisting that he should be more explicit. " I do, and you must," he had written, " give thanks to God for His goodness in protecting and making me the instrument of so much happiness to the Queen and nation, if she will please to make use of it."[1] The Duchess showed this letter to the Queen, who immediately requested the Duke to explain the intention of the concluding words, which she professed to regard as highly mysterious. Marlborough parried the stroke. " What I then meant," he said, " as I must always think, is, that you can make no good use of this victory, nor of any other blessing, but by following the advice of my Lord Treasurer, who has been so long faithful to you."[2] Such amiable generalities were little to the Queen's liking. " I am very sorry," she said in her reply, " to find you persist in your resolution of not advising me concerning my home affairs."[3]

Marlborough's methods, though less exasperating, were quite as ineffective with the Queen as those of the Duchess and Godolphin. From the Junta, on the other hand, he got no gratitude for his pains. On the contrary, they accused him of lukewarmness, if not of insincerity. They pretended to believe that he had encouraged Somerset's attempt to divide their party.[4] They affected to regard him as secretly leagued with the Sovereign to compass their destruction. They threatened a revival of the attack upon the Admiralty, to strike at Anne through the Prince of Denmark and at Marlborough through his brother George. Their mutterings and their menaces were only too faithfully reported by the Duchess, whose comments showed that, in her judgment, they were not wholly undeserved. In her judgment her husband should have accepted the advice of Maynwaring and should have dis-

[1] Coxe, vol. ii., p 265 The Duke to the Duchess, July 12, 1708.
[2] *Ibid* , p 283 · Marlborough to the Queen, August 2, 1708
[3] *Ibid* , p 284. The Queen to Marlborough
[4] See Chapter XIX , " Dunkirk, Ghent, and Bruges," p. 115

played "something more of warmth and zeal"[1] towards
the leaders of the Whigs. Marlborough endured it all with
admirable patience. He submitted the digests of his proposed letters to the Queen to the Duchess and Godolphin
for their approval. He begged his wife to believe that he
would never be "so indiscreet as to employ the Duke of
Somerset in anything that is of consequence."[2] He repeatedly told her that he considered his brother George
"in as wrong measures as is possible."[3] He reiterated his
assurances that he should "always be ready to join with
the Whigs in opposition to the Tories,"[4] who would, he
predicted, attack him in the ensuing winter "with all the
malice imaginable."[5] "I am fully convinced," he said,
"that the Tories would ruin me."[6]

Lonely and difficult as was the path which Marlborough
deliberately chose to tread in this unhappy labyrinth, it
was assuredly the path of honour. While his loyalty to
Godolphin constrained him to acquiesce in his colleague's
policy of paying out driblets of blackmail to the Junta,
his loyalty to his Sovereign forbade him to bully her in
the interest of politicians whom she had always regarded
as the enemies of her religion and her authority Over
and over again he told his wife, with an emphasis which
he might have known would be very unpalatable to her,
and her associates, that he was, before all else, the Queen's
friend. On July 19 he wrote: "I own to you I have a
tenderness for the Queen, being persuaded that it is the
fault of those whom she loves, and not her own, when she does
what is wrong "[7] On August 6 he wrote. "You know my
resolutions by my former letters of being firm to the Whigs;
and if they support the Queen, they will make me more
capable of serving them and my country."[8] On August 9,
he earnestly requested that letters which had passed between
Anne and himself, and which he enclosed for the perusal

---

[1] *Private Correspondence of Sarah, Duchess of Marlborough*, vol 1, p. 103
Mr Maynwaring to the Duchess of Marlborough, April 6, 1708.
[2] Coxe, vol ii., p. 279. The Duke to the Duchess, July 19, 1708
[3] *Ibid*, p 284 The Duke to the Duchess, August 6, 1708
[4] *Ibid*, p 288 The Duke to the Duchess, July, 1708
[5] *Ibid*, p 290 The Duke to the Duchess, August 20, 1708.
[6] *Ibid*, p 286 The Duke to the Duchess, August 6, 1708.
[7] *Ibid*, p 280 The Duke to the Duchess July 19, 1708
[8] *Ibid*, p 286 The Duke to the Duchess, August 6, 1708

of Godolphin and the Duchess, " be torn to pieces, so that they may never hurt Mrs. Morley whom I can't but love and endeavour to serve, as long as I have life; for I know this is not her fault, otherwise than by being too fond of Mrs. Masham, who imposes upon her "[1] On August 16 he wrote. "I love the Queen with all my heart "[2] On August 20 he wrote· " I love her and my country."[3] And on September 27 he wrote: " I can't entirely agree with your opinion of the Queen; I must own I have a tenderness for her, and I would willingly believe that all which is amiss, proceeds from the ambition and ill-judgment of Mrs. Masham, and the knavery and artfulness of Mr Harley "[4] Unerring, therefore, was the woman's instinct which prompted Anne to cling so tenaciously to the friendship of Marlborough in spite of the very scanty consolation which she derived from his guarded epistles. She knew at any rate that if the Duke would not run counter to the advice of Godolphin, he would at least protect her against the menaces of the blackmailers. In July they were threatening to move an address in the ensuing session in favour of an invitation to the Electoral Prince of Hanover to take up his residence in England, an ancient project[5] which they very well knew that the Queen detested. Anne wrote immediately to Marlborough. She begged him to ascertain if anything was known of such a suggestion in the Prince's circle, and to " contrive some way to put any such thought out of his head." " I shall depend upon you," she said, " to do everything on the other side of the water to prevent this mortification from coming upon her that is, and ever will be, most sincerely,"[6] etc.

Though sentiment, and very admirable sentiment, dictated the attitude of Marlborough towards the Queen throughout this trying period, it cannot really be contended that his judgment was by any means at fault. Browbeating and intimidation were not the methods most likely to prevail with a woman and a Stuart, particularly at a

[1] Coxe, vol ii p 286 The Duke to the Duchess, August 9, 1708
[2] Ibid , p 289· The Duke to the Duchess, August 16, 1709
[3] Ibid , p 290· The Duke to the Duchess, August 20, 1709
[4] Ibid , p 297 The Duke to the Duchess, September 27, 1708
[5] See Vol I , Chapter XIII. " 1705–1706," p 35
[6] Co e, vol ii , p 267. The Queen to Marlborough, July 22, 1708

moment when political forces of a very formidable order were steadily organising themselves against her tormentors. With a full consciousness of the folly of such courses, Marlborough warned the Duchess that the Hanoverian project was "very dangerous,"[1] and expressed the opinion that the Whigs should think twice before they engaged in it. For himself he insisted steadily on a free hand in dealing with the Queen "I must be master of judging of my actions towards the Queen,"[2] he said on one occasion, and on another: "I must be master of my own actions, which may concern the Queen personally." Sarah's way led straight towards catastrophe. On August 31, the day of the Thanksgiving for Oudenarde, a public and scandalous scene between Mrs Morley and Mrs Freeman was narrowly avoided. The Duchess, as Mistress of the Robes, had selected and arranged the jewels which the Queen was to carry at the service in St Paul's. The result was not approved by Anne, who preferred to follow her own taste, or, as Sarah alleged, the taste of Mrs Masham. As the royal carriage proceeded on its way through the crowded streets its two occupants were all the while engaged in an embittered dispute over this paltry affair. The unseemly squabble was actually resumed in the Cathedral itself The sermon was preached by the Bishop of St Asaph, who referred to Marlborough "as crowned with fresh laurels every year, because it seems that they wither faster in our unkindly climate than elsewhere" Moved by this or some similar suggestion of the moment the Duchess introduced her husband's name into the whispered altercation "He has now no interest with you,"[3] she said. "It is untrue," retorted Anne The wrangle continued until Sarah, fearful lest their rising tones should be overheard, and forgetful, as she had too long been, of their relative positions, peremptorily told the Queen of England to hold her tongue. The thoughtless words sank deep The full indignity of her situation flashed upon the Sovereign. When Sarah subsequently sent her a written remonstrance, enclosing a letter from the Duke, complaining of

---

[1] *Ibid*, p 288 The Duke to the Duchess, July, 1708
[2] *Ibid*, p 282 Marlborough to the Duchess, August 2, 1708.
[3] *Memoirs of the Life and Conduct of the Duchess of Marlborough*, p. 180.

the incident of the jewels, and remarking that " Your Majesty chose a very wrong day to mortify me,"[1] she replied as follows " After the commands you gave me in the church, on the thanksgiving, of not answering you, I should not have troubled you with these lines but to return the Duke of Marlborough's letter safe into your hands."[2] Sarah endeavoured to justify herself in a second epistle, and subsequently in a tempestuous interview, at which she fiercely denounced the intrigues of Harley and bitterly reproached the Queen for preferring his creatures to the lords of the Junta. The angry voices of the disputants were heard in the ante-chamber, and when the Duchess, who was virtually ordered to quit the royal presence, passed out among the courtiers, the tears of rage were still shining in her eyes   The Queen was discovered in a condition of distress which she was unable to conceal   Gossip is never at a loss to draw the correct inference from circumstances such as these.   The world believed that Sarah's power was declining, and acted on its belief.   She who had formerly been worshipped was now not even feared   Homage was openly paid to the rising favourite   Even the Whigs looked coldly and neglectfully upon the woman who had ruined herself for them.   Smarting under the humiliations which she had never schooled herself to suffer, the Duchess confided to her husband that she too was sick of both political parties, and announced her intention of abandoning a hopeless struggle.   Marlborough concurred.   He had already written that " till the Queen changes her humour and resolutions, the less the conversations are the better."[3]   On learning that the Duchess had now determined neither to speak nor to write to her mistress, he assured her that she would " find a good effect of it in one month "[4]   For himself, he said that he did not propose to " mention her any more this campaign."   " For my own part," he declared, " I am quite weary of all business, and if amongst all these disagreeable bustles, I could be so happy as to have liberty of remaining quiet

[1] *Memoirs of the Life and Conduct of the Duchess of Marlborough*, p 180.
[2] Coxe, vol ii , p 295· The Queen to the Duchess
[3] *Ibid* , p 290 The Duke to the Duchess, August 23, 1708
[4] *Ibid* , p. 297 The Duke to the Duchess, October 1, 1708

with you, I should be at the height of my wishes." And
again on October 1 he told her. "If I am to be happy,
it must be with you."[1] Throughout this unpleasant
correspondence, as indeed throughout all his correspondence
with the Duchess, some place was invariably found for the
language of love.

Towards the end of August Marlborough and Godolphin
simultaneously offered to resign. Anne refused to release
them. "I hope," she wrote to the Duke, "you will both
consider better of it, and not do an action that will bring
me and your country into confusion "[2] In the same letter
she came with disconcerting directness to the vital point.
The Junta, she said, had misconducted themselves "in
the last Parliament, and . . ever since the rising of it; for
from that minute they have been disputing my authority,
and are certainly designing, when the new one meets, to
tear that little prerogative the crown has to pieces " She
asked "why a handful of men must awe their fellow-
subjects." " To be short," she exclaimed, " I think things
are come to, whether I shall submit to the five tyrannising
lords, or they to me." And she requested Marlborough
to advise her of " the best expedient " whereby she might
escape such thraldom. It was not in the Duke's power
to frame a satisfactory answer. The answer which he sent
was very long and very ineffective. The Queen had stated
the brutal facts with too much plainness.

It was perfectly true that, as he insisted, ministers from
whom she had withdrawn her " trust and confidence " in
favour of " insinuating busy flatterers," could not be
expected to continue indefinitely in office, only to be
" answerable for other people's follies, or worse." But
equally, when he declared that so long as she harkened to
his advice and Godolphin's, she would be " in no danger
of falling into any hands but "[3] theirs, he was enunciating
an obvious fallacy. For his advice was merely an endorse-
ment of Godolphin's; and Godolphin's was merely an echo
of the fulminations of the Junta It was totally irrelevant
to dwell upon the long and faithful service which they two

---

[1] *Ibid.*   [2] *Ibid*, p 291 The Queen to Marlborough, August, 1708.
[3] *Ibid*, p 293 · Marlborough to the Queen.

had rendered her in the past. For in the past they had always known and shared the Queen's views, which were intensely hostile to government by faction, particularly the faction controlled by " the five tyrannising lords." It was they who had now changed, not she. To quote her own words, " My thoughts are the same of the Whigs that ever they were from the time that ever I have been capable of having notions of things and people, and I must own I can see no reason to alter mine."[1]

As the time of the opening of Parliament approached the complaints of Somers and the threats of Sunderland warned Godolphin of the fate in store for the ministry upon the first important division in the House of Commons. In the second week of October he met the Lords of the Junta at Newmarket, and finally surrendered himself to those inexorable taskmasters According to Erasmus Lewis, his "submissive protestations" were received by Wharton " with all possible scorn and contempt."[2] Wharton declared that Godolphin knew very well " it was his last stake, and that he could subsist no longer without them."[3] But the Junta required something more from the Prime Minister than abject professions of his attachment to the principles of Whiggery. They required the Attorney-Generalship for Montagu, the dismissal of Admiral Churchill, and the resignation of the Prince of Denmark. The Prince, who had always pursued a moderate and judicious course in politics, and who had materially assisted Godolphin in procuring the removal of Harley, had latterly incurred the displeasure of the Junta, both because he had refused to abandon Churchill, and because his natural resentment at the partisan attacks upon the Admiralty was tending to drive him into the arms of the Tory party. But he was guilty of another and a far graver offence in the eyes of these artists in jobbery He was in the way Once he were out of it, his office could be given to Pembroke, who could then resign the Lord-Lieutenancy of Ireland in favour of Wharton, and the Presidency of the Council in favour of Somers. Godolphin did what he could to pay the price demanded.

---

[1] Coxe, vol ii , p. 284· The Queen to Marlborough
[2] Portland MSS : Erasmus Lewis to Robert Harley, October 15, 1708 (Hist MSS Comm , 15th Report, Appendix, part iv , p 509)
[3] *Ibid.*

In the matter of Admiral Churchill, he was compelled to invoke the assistance of Marlborough. To Marlborough the sacrifice of his brother was a peculiarly odious item in the blackmailer's bill, and one which hitherto he had steadily refused to consider. But loyal as always to Godolphin, he now consented to meet it. On October 19 he wrote to Churchill as follows. " If you do not take an unalterable resolution of laying down that employment before the Parliament sits, you will certainly do the greatest dis- service imaginable to the Queen and Prince, the greatest prejudice to me, and bring yourself into such inconveniences as may last as long as you live, and from which it is wholly impossible to protect you "[1] For the rest, Godolphin was now materially and unexpectedly aided by the domestic affliction of the Queen The Prince, who had suffered for years from asthma, was seriously ill. Anne, who nursed him always with the tenderest devotion, and who watched with apprehension the daily decay of his strength, was no longer in a condition to hold out against her enemies Mrs Masham had complained to Harley in the summer that the Queen's courage was failing. As the Prince grew worse it failed entirely.' She assented to Montagu's appointment to the Attorney-Generalship She promised to assent to Pembroke's appointment to the Admiralty, and to the transfer of his offices to Wharton and Somers. But for a week she could attend to no other duties save those of the wife who is about to become a widow. On November 8 the Prince died " He had his astma," wrote Mar, " a spitting of blood, a lethragie, an hidropsie, and something of a palsie. He was a very good man."[2] He was. But Erasmus Lewis has recorded (and the accuracy of the statement is virtually admitted by Burnet) that it was " not to be imagined how joyful some men "[3] were at his decease Anne was terribly dis- tressed. " My poor aunt," wrote Mrs. Masham to Harley

[1] Coxe, vol. ii , p 357 · Marlborough to Admiral Churchill, October 19, 1708.
[2] Earl of Mar and Kellie MSS The Earl of Mar to his brother, Lord Grange, October 28, 1708 (Hist MSS Comm , p 469) See also Saint-Simon, t. xii , p 158
[3] Portland MSS · Erasmus Lewis to Robert Harley, November 2, 1708 (Hist MSS Comm , 15th Report, Appendix, part iv., p 510)

on the 6th, "is in a very deplorable condition." All
resistance to the Junta was now at an end. Churchill
disappeared. Somers and Wharton obtained their desires.
Somers affected to believe that he owed something to
Marlborough and sent the Duke his "humble thanks."[1]
Wharton, having appointed Addison his chief secretary,
repaired to his new government where he so comported
himself that even Macaulay could say of him that "he was
not only licentious and corrupt, but was distinguished
from other libertines and jobbers by a callous impudence."[2]

The Duchess of Marlborough had neither spoken nor
written to the Queen for some weeks. But she went to
Kensington at the last moment, and was present when the
Prince died. She led her grief-stricken mistress from the
chamber, and subsequently accompanied her to St James's.
Mrs. Masham complained to Harley that the Duchess was
always with the Queen and would not leave her alone "so
long as to let her say her private prayers."[3] But no
permanent reconciliation resulted The circumstances, indeed, were very unfavourable to such an issue. For Sarah
was the agent and the friend of those who were gloating over
the corpse. Sarah was entirely identified with the cause
of Whiggery. Whiggery had won a famous victory over a
dying man and a broken-hearted woman. But the woman
was still the Queen of England; and as she recovered from
the first shock of her bereavement, she set herself, like
Mary, Queen of Scots, "to study revenge"

The "tenderness" for his Sovereign, to which Marlborough had boldly pleaded guilty months before this last
affliction came upon her, must have caused him many a pang
when he read the story of her loss and of the manner in which
her hour of natural weakness had been utilised against her
by remorseless politicians The news of the Prince's death
was, by his own admission, one of the causes of the illness

[1] Coxe, vol ii , p. 359 Somers to Marlborough, November 30, 1708
[2] Macaulay's *Essays*, vol ii *The Life and Writings of Addison* See also
Swift's, *A Short Character of Thomas, Earl of Wharton* One paragraph from
this brutal indictment may be quoted "He goes constantly to prayers in
the forms of his place, and will talk bawdy and blasphemy at the chapel
door He is a presbyterian in politics, and an atheist in religion; but he
chooses at present to whore with a papist "
[3] Portland MSS : Abigail Masham to Robert Harley, November 6, 1708
(Hist. MSS. Comm., 15th Report, Appendix, part iv , p. 511)

which prostrated him on the eve of the forcing of the Schelde.[1] It was no wonder that he welcomed the exigencies of war and of diplomacy which detained him for a time on the continent. For the rest, both Godolphin and he had now the momentary and bitter satisfaction of the black-mailed. They were delivered from the fulfilment of a threat which had served its purpose. In the Parliament, which met on November 27, the men who professed to regard the war as a sort of religious crusade magnanimously condescended in exchange for salaries and offices not to obstruct the strenuous prosecution of it. The Junta's original candidate for the speakership was one of the most virulent critics of the Admiralty, Peter King. But before the death of the Prince, Godolphin had persuaded them to substitute for a person, who was very obnoxious to the Sovereign, a moderate Whig, Sir Richard Onslow. As part of the bargain, King had been jobbed into the recorder-ship of London, and Anne had been induced to bestow upon him " the honour of knighthood as a particular mark of her royal favour and esteem."[2] The opposition, who had hoped that the Whig vote would be split between King and Onslow, were ready in the event to put up Sir Thomas Harmer But Onslow alone being nominated, the choice was made unanimously. Parliament was opened by commission. The Queen's speech dwelt upon the desirability of " a considerable augmentation "[3] of troops, and the certainty that the creation of a naval base at Port Mahon would necessitate " some extraordinary expenses."[4] In their address to the throne both Houses requested the Queen to " moderate her grief "[5] in the interest of her own health. The Lords told her that they were " more and more convinced, that no peace can be safe and honourable until the whole monarchy of Spain be restored to the House of Austria."[6] But they also requested her to use her " most pressing instances " with the allies " to shew a suitable vigour, and particularly with those, the interest of whose family is more nearly concern'd in this present war "[7] The Parliament proceeded to set a good example

[1] Murray, vol iv., p 324. Marlborough to Boyle, November 27, 1708
[2] Boyer, vol vii , p 233.   [3] Ibid , p 253   [4] Ibid , p 254.
[5] Ibid , p 256   [6] Ibid   [7] Ibid.

to the coalition. They consented to an augmentation of 10,000 men, and they voted seven millions for the army and navy. The difficulty of recruiting engaged their close attention. Several expedients had already been tried, and had been found inadequate. Under various statutes, enacted since the beginning of the war, insolvent debtors, willing to enlist, could claim their discharge from prison, able-bodied men, having no visible means of subsistence, could be forcibly pressed, and the bounty payable to volunteers had been raised from 40s. to £4. Marlborough in his letters[1] to Boyle and Walpole was advocating now some form of compulsory service. The traditional hostility of the Tories to military despotism,[2] and of the Whigs to despotism of any sort, rendered such proposals impracticable But the government succeeded in passing an Act which doubled the reward payable to parish constables, who produced new victims for the recruiting officers, and which granted a premium of £3 to the overseers of the poor in respect of every such case occurring in their parish. "Military service," as Mr Leadam observes, "was converted into an agency for ratepayers' relief." The Duke regarded these makeshift devices with qualified enthusiasm. "I wish with all my heart," he wrote to Walpole on January 16, "it may have the end purposed. But in all events I most earnestly recommend to you the hastening of the officers into the country as fast as they arrive, and to give them all possible assistance, for in this hard weather in all probability they may get more men in one day than in a week hereafter "[3]

The opposition attacked the ministry in both Houses, but with small result. On December 24 the Commons, having unanimously voted their thanks to Major-General Webb " for the great and eminent services performed by him at the battle of Wynendael," and Webb having responded "in a very handsome and modest speech," Bromley improved the occasion with malicious sneers at Marlborough. He observed that " he did not disapprove the method of returning thanks to such generals as performed their duty,

[1] Murray, vol iv , p 334 Marlborough to Walpole, December 3, 1708, p 341 . Marlborough to Boyle, December 6, 1708
[2] Vol I , Chapter II , "The Exorbitant Power of France," p 35
[3] Murray, vol. iv , p 397. Marlborough to Walpole, January 16, 1709.

which, however, had been more frequently done of late, than heretofore; but that he could not but take notice, that not only the thanks of both Houses, but also great rewards had been bestowed upon another commander."[1] The evident intention of the Tories to exploit the case of Webb for party purposes was more injurious to that gallant soldier than it was to the government. For notwithstanding his indubitable claims and the admitted injustice which he had suffered in the official news-sheet, the Whig majority of the Peers declined to entertain a motion for a vote of thanks. Moreover, within ten days of Bromley's effort, both Houses presented the Queen with a congratulatory address upon the achievements of a campaign which had "given many opportunities to Your Majesty's General, the Duke of Marlborough, to shew his consummate ability, and all the great qualities necessary for so high a trust."[2]

Finally, on February 2, 1709, the Commons passed a vote of thanks to the Duke for his "great and eminent services" and "indefatigable zeal." The Speaker transmitted it to Brussels. "Nothing," said Marlborough in his reply, "can give me more satisfaction."[3]

More elaborate, though not much more effectual, were the attempts made in both Houses to found an indictment of the ministry on the circumstances of the Pretender's recent raid. It was alleged, and apparently with some justice, that the present defences of Scotland had been dangerously neglected It was insinuated, and possibly with some truth, that the arrests of suspected persons in that country had been calculated as much with an eye to the gerrymandering of the Scottish elections as to the safety of the state It was erroneously contended that British strategy on this occasion had been defective both by land and sea. And it was darkly hinted that, if a proper search were to be instituted for the friends of James, it should begin in the Cabinet. "Even among the apostles themselves," said Haversham, the protagonist of the opposition in this connection, "he that bore the bag prov'd the traitor"[4] But it was impossible to make much capital

[1] Boyer, vol vii, pp 270, 271　　　[2] Ibid., p 273
[3] Coxe, vol ii, p 377, February 13, 1709　　　[4] Boyer, vol vii, p 281

out of an episode which had terminated so ingloriously for
the enemies of England; and ministers, steadily supported
by the Whigs, experienced no difficulty in retaining the
confidence of Parliament.

Certain of the government's legislative proposals deserve
attention here. A bill to encourage the naturalisation of
foreign Protestants was carried in the teeth of the opposition of the Tory party and of the City of London. The
measure was hotly attacked upon social, commercial,
economic, religious, and national grounds. It was particularly obnoxious to the High Churchmen, who endeavoured,
but without success, to insert a clause making conformity
a condition of naturalisation. Burnet of course "spoke
copiously"[1] against them. By this time the cup of Anglican
bitterness was filled to the brim. It was destined before
the year was out to overflow, and with startling consequences for the ministry.

Recent events in Scotland had proved the desirability
of assimilating the treason laws of that country with those
of England. A bill to effect this purpose, though resisted
by the Scots in both Houses, was eventually carried. But,
lest it should be thought that the government were contemplating a vindictive policy, they followed up this measure
with an Act of Grace, which granted a general pardon for
high treason. The historians, including even Coxe, seem
rather to go out of their way to suggest that this indemnity
must have been peculiarly comforting to Marlborough and
Godolphin. But others besides Marlborough and Godolphin, and others besides Tories and Jacobites, had corresponded with the exiles at St Germains. If Marlborough
and Godolphin were so specially concerned, it is somewhat
curious that, although they had been eight years in power,
they had not hitherto thought it worth while to protect
themselves in this fashion.

The government's prosperity was more superficial than real.
Writing to Marlborough on December 24, Godolphin described
its actual condition as "very uncertain and precarious,"
and "full of all manner of distractions and jealousies."[2]

[1] Burnet, vol iv., p. 213
[2] Coxe, vol ii., p 379. Godolphin to Marlborough, December 24, 1708.

The Queen could not forgive the Lord Treasurer for his last capitulation to the Junta. She treated him with studied coldness, while her intimacy with Mrs Masham and with the Tory friends of Mrs Masham increased daily It had therefore become an open question whether power was in fact lodged in the hands of the Prime Minister, as blackmailed by the Junta, or in those of the new favourite as inspired by Harley. The Junta themselves were so far in doubt upon the point that Godolphin and Sarah both suspected them of " making up to Mrs. Masham." Three out of the five members of the insatiable syndicate were now provided for; but Halifax and Orford were still unemployed. Halifax, in particular, was furious at his exclusion from power. On Sarah and Godolphin, and above all on Marlborough, he poured out the torrents of his insolence and rage Sunderland took up the cudgels on his behalf. Sunderland, too, had a special grievance of his own. To facilitate the management of Scottish affairs, Godolphin procured the creation of a third Secretaryship of State, which was bestowed in February upon the Duke of Queensberry. The justice and policy of this arrangement did not appeal to Sunderland. Justice and policy were poor compensations for the loss of a considerable slice of the patronage hitherto wielded by the stern republican. His temper had never been of the best; but in this sad affliction he even quarrelled with his devoted mother-in-law. Sarah's Whiggery was not proof against the arrogant airs of the Whig chiefs. At this time she denounced them all, and none more than Sunderland But Godolphin still clung, with simple and pathetic tenacity, to his old idea that, if only Marlborough would return, all these troubles might be cured. On January 4, he wrote that he knew of no remedy equal to the Duke's presence, because his authority " when it appeared plainly, would be of so much weight as to extinguish much of this uneasiness." And on January 10 he wrote· " So much advantage is taken of your absence, and I suffer so much, that . . . the life of a slave in the galleys is paradise in comparison of mine."[1] Marlborough appears to have formed a more modest estimate

---

[1] *Ibid* Godolphin to Marlborough, January 10, 1709

of his own ability to calm the ruffled waters of domestic politics. It was now his settled resolution to withdraw himself entirely, if possible, from all affairs save those of diplomacy and war. His object was, as he told his wife on January 7, " to serve my Queen and country to the best of my understanding, without being either minister or favourite."[1] He considered that the behaviour of Sunderland looked " like madness."[2] He resented the personal attacks which were made upon him by Halifax; but he regarded their present antics without apprehension because he knew that, with three of their number in the ministry the Junta had given hostages to fortune, and that the crude device of threatening to destroy the government was no longer applicable. He was sorry for Godolphin. He rejoiced at his wife's new attitude to the strife of parties. For the rest, he wrote to her continually of his country's safety and his own retirement. " When England is safe, I had rather anybody should govern than I,"[3] he said   And again, " I shall esteem myself happy, if England be safe, and that I may have leave of living quiet with you "[4]   And again · " I swear to you solemnly that your love and quiet I prefer to all the greatness of this world, and had rather live a private life than be the greatest man England ever had."[5]

The months of January and February were spent by Marlborough partly at Brussels and partly at the Hague, and were devoted largely to the tedious and difficult business of organising the military resources of the coalition. No sooner had the numerous forces, with which the French had conducted the recent campaign in the Netherlands, gone into winter-quarters beyond the frontier, than the Duke was apprised by his admirable intelligence department that, notwithstanding the severity of the weather, sixty battalions and about as many squadrons were marching from the Rhine, from Dauphiné, and even from Spain towards Picardy and Artois. Writing to Godolphin on February 13, he spoke of the alarming reports of " the vast

[1] Coxe, vol ii , p 383: The Duke to the Duchess, January 7, 1709.
[2] Ibid., p. 384. The Duke to the Duchess, February 7, 1709
[3] Ibid , p 383: The Duke to the Duchess, November 28, 1708
[4] Ibid   The Duke to the Duchess, January 16, 1709.
[5] Ibid. : The Duke to the Duchess, November 28, 1708.

numbers of troops they have in all their towns, and that all
their villages and farm-houses between the Sambre and the
Meuse are full of their horse."[1] On the 14th he informed
Sinzendorf that regiments from Roussillon and Spain
had actually arrived at Valenciennes,[2] that all the garrisons
were swarming with soldiers, and that the châteaux and
the hamlets were packed with them. Boufflers had returned
to the frontier, and the rumour ran that the French would
open the next campaign in the early spring with the siege
of Lille In reality, Louis had approved a project of
Chamillart for the recovery of Lille in the middle of winter.
Of this design, which was ultimately abandoned, Marlborough knew nothing. He imagined that the object of these
imposing preparations was to intimidate the Dutch into
an unfavourable peace, or possibly to begin the campaign
with a desperate battle In any event it was necessary to
make some adequate response. The Dutch were sadly
crippled by their enormous expenditure upon the siege of
Lille, but they were so far impressed by the proceedings
on the frontier that the Duke had little difficulty in persuading them to vote an augmentation of 6,000 men. The
10,000 men voted by the British Parliament, he hoped to
procure from Saxony and Prussia The negotiations with
the Elector of Saxony were simple ; but those with the King
of Prussia were more than usually difficult. Frederick had
grievances against Holland, and grievances against the
Emperor, and grievances against Marlborough himself.
The Grand Chamberlain, the Grand Chamberlain's wife,
and Lord Raby, the British ambassador, were all discontented. At first, it seemed as if instead of increasing his
contingent the King would withdraw it altogether. Then
he offered cavalry instead of infantry. Marlborough's
letters to the Court of Berlin were characterised by all his
accustomed suavity and tact; but it was only by the exercise of extreme patience, and with the skilful assistance of
General Grumbkow, whom he specially dispatched to
Berlin, that he at last obtained an augmentation of six
battalions and nine squadrons, or 5,000 men in all. Soldiers

---

[1] Ibid , p 389 Marlborough to Godolphin, February 13, 1709.
[2] Murray, vol iv , p 448: Marlborough to Sinzendorf, February 14, 1709

could have been got elsewhere with less trouble. But while the French relied upon numbers, Marlborough relied upon quality, and he never made any secret of his opinion that, for quality, he preferred the subjects of the King of Prussia to any troops save the British

The Emperor had readily consented to allow the army of Eugène to winter in the Low Countries. He also agreed that 2,500 recruits should be dispatched to Starhemberg from Italy under the protection of the English fleet. But he refused to permit the intervention of the maritime powers in his chronic feud with the Hungarian Protestants, and he engaged once more in dangerous bickerings with the Duke of Savoy. That prince was proposing to march upon Lyons with 50,000 men. Marlborough, though he had little faith in the project, did not oppose it. He did what he could to promote a good understanding between the Courts of Turin and Vienna. He insisted that the Austrian contingent of 20,000 men at present serving under the Duke of Savoy must on no account be weakened by detachments whether for Spain or elsewhere. And he repeatedly urged that the withdrawal of French forces from Spain, Dauphiné, and the Rhine provided an opportunity for vigorous action in those quarters

Even his own government made trouble for Marlborough at this anxious time. Seven British regiments, quartered for the winter at Antwerp, had been assigned by Parliament to the army in Spain Marlborough protested vigorously. On February 7, he warned Godolphin that, if England persisted in this folly, " at length my Lord Haversham will be gratified by our being beaten, for a great superiority at last must undo us "[1] On February 11 he wrote again. " Is it possible that men of good sense, and that mean sincerely well to the common cause, can be in the least doubt that if the enemy make their greatest, and, indeed, their only effort in this country, but that we must do the same, or expect to be beaten ? which I pray God Almighty to prevent, for that would be a fatal blow. If any orders have been sent me for the march of these seven regiments, I do most earnestly beg you will once more lay

[1] Cox , vol 11 , p. 388. Marlborough to Godolphin, February 7, 1709

before Her Majesty and the lords of the Cabinet Council my apprehensions."[1] These representations were happily successful.

Finally, in the Spanish Netherlands, the obstructive tactics pursued by certain members of the Council of State had resulted in the starving of the military forces maintained by the recovered provinces. Marlborough and the Dutch deputies were at length compelled to remove the offenders. In reporting the matter to King Charles, the Duke declared that, but for this drastic action, " the troops would surely be dead of hunger."[2]

Before quitting the continent, Marlborough performed one of those characteristically gracious acts which won for him an exalted place in the hearts of Frenchmen. Having learned that Boufflers was seriously ill at Ypres, and that he would welcome the services of a Brussels doctor, who had formerly attended him, the Duke directed the man to ·proceed at once to the bedside of the Marshal. At the same time he wrote that he was no less interested now in the restoration of the Marshal's health than he was in the old days of their friendship, " when we served together under M. de Turenne."[3]

On March 8, the Duke embarked at Ostend, and after a long and perilous crossing, reached London on the 12th On the 13th he took his seat in the House of Lords In presenting him with the " hearty and unanimous thanks " of that chamber for his " great and eminent services," the Lord Chancellor observed: " I cannot but conclude, without acknowledging, with all gratitude, the Providence of God, in raising you up to be an instrument of so much good, in so critical a juncture."[4] Marlborough replied that there were " very few things "[5] which could give him more satisfaction than the approbation of the Peers

His visit to England lasted less than a month. During that time he was an eyewitness of the new situation at Court which had hitherto been only portrayed to him in

[1] Ibid., p. 389: Marlborough to Godolphin, February 11, 1709.
[2] Murray, vol. iv., p. 468 Marlborough to the King of Spain, March 7. 1709.
[3] Ibid , p 440 Marlborough to Boufflers, February 12, 1709
[4] Boyer, vol. vii , p. 316   [5] Ibid

the letters of Sarah and Godolphin. He noticed, moreover, that, even to himself, the Queen's manner had changed. And he was more than ever conscious that both he and Godolphin were tolerated rather than trusted by the haughty Junta In these circumstances it must have been with a sense of relief that he sailed from Deal on April 7. After a slow passage, rendered dangerous by fog, he reached the Hague on the 9th.

XXIV.—THE MISERY OF FRANCE

WHEN Lille and Port Mahon fell, Marlborough formed the opinion that if, upon the conclusion of the campaign, the allies prepared with increasing vigour for another, France would consent to an acceptable peace without further bloodshed. Proceeding upon this hypothesis, he wrote his letter of October 30 to Berwick The foolish reply, which Berwick was directed to send, showed conclusively that the military situation in the Netherlands was not in the least understood by the French government. Marlborough corrected their misconceptions, when he burst the lines of the Schelde with consummate ease. He completed their disillusionment, when he recovered Ghent and Bruges in the depth of winter. At the beginning of 1709, therefore, he had still good reason to hope that the opinion which he had formed in the preceding autumn would prove to have been justified.

But the vast concentration of troops, which the French effected on their north-eastern frontier during January and February, went far to shake his confidence in their pacific aspirations. It is probable that, with the object of stimulating the exertions of the various powers, Marlborough made the most of the facts But the facts remained; and though he recognised that they might be perfectly compatible with a politic desire to influence negotiations for peace, he inclined, until the end of April, to the view that Louis was at heart resolved upon a final throw in the spring or early summer.

Before the end of 1708 he had been aware that clandestine agents, clothed with varying degrees of responsibility, had begun to canvass both the French and Dutch governments as to the possible basis of a peace. The most active of these intermediaries was Petkum, the minister of Schleswig-Holstein at the Hague, who, keeping in close touch with Heinsius, maintained at the same time a permanent correspondence with Torcy. Petkum informed Heinsius in December that France was willing to treat on the assumption that all Italy, except the Milanese, should be bestowed on Philip. When Marlborough reached the Hague in January, he agreed with the Grand Pensionary that this proposal need not be rejected forthwith, and that Petkum might be instructed to follow it up. But others besides Petkum were fishing in the same waters. Bergueick, who was employed by the Court of Madrid, was assuring the Dutch statesman, Vanderdussen, that Philip was prepared to offer the Republic a favourable treaty of commerce. On January 15 Vanderdussen replied that, unless Spain, the Indies, the Milanese, and the Netherlands, as well as, a favourable treaty of commerce, were secured beforehand, no business could be done in Holland. From these subterranean currents of diplomacy Marlborough could derive no positive conclusion. But considering them in conjunction with the previous record of the French Foreign Office, with the notorious eagerness of the Dutch to end the war, and with the military movements beyond the frontier, he was justified in at least suspecting that Louis intended no more than to sow dissensions among the allied powers, and to diminish the ardour of their preparations for the next campaign.

In the opinion of the British government, there was a real danger that the temptation to effect a separate bargain with France might be greater than Holland could resist. To obviate that danger, Godolphin and Somers, who were acting now in the closest union, reverted to the precedent of 1706. Before he quitted Ghent, Marlborough was instructed as to the essential conditions upon which England would consent to treat. They were three. Firstly, the entire monarchy of Spain must be restored to Charles. Secondly, the just pretensions of the Emperor, the King of Prussia, the Duke of Savoy, and the other allies, must be duly satisfied. And thirdly, Holland must be granted a favourable treaty of commerce and a sufficient barrier for her national security. Marlborough knew well that, as soon as he mentioned the word " barrier " at the Hague, he would be asked to explain why England still refused to assent to the Barrier Treaty Accordingly, on January 3, he wrote home, requesting that Godolphin and Somers would elaborate their views on that delicate topic.

The question of the Barrier Treaty, which had remained dormant for nearly two years, had recently been revived. In December the Dutch were alarmed by a story that Marlborough had again been promised the government of the Spanish Netherlands, and this time for life The story was true. The offer had been made after Oudenarde, and by the King of Spain himself. In his letter (which is dated August 5, and is now preserved in the Brussels archives), Charles had expressed his approval of the " prudent dissimulation," which had characterised the Duke's attitude towards the claims of Holland. " I do not doubt," he wrote, " but that you will never allow the Netherlands, under the pretext of that pretended barrier, to suffer any diminution either in their area or as regards my royal authority in them, which authority I wish to place in your hands."[1] Mindful of what had happened in 1706, he recommended that the renewed offer be kept a secret from the Dutch. Marlborough had replied that he would make every sacrifice to prove himself worthy of so distinguished a favour. To Godolphin he had written· " This must be known to nobody but the Queen; for should it be known before the peace, it would create inconveniences in Holland."[2] He had added that, if, when that day came, Anne should not " think it for her honour and interest that I accept of this great offer, I will decline it with all the submission imaginable." Godolphin had concurred with the Duke and with King Charles as to the importance of secrecy. But the Dutch had now got wind of the facts, and were exhibiting their former nervousness. They assumed, and not incorrectly, that Charles thought to purchase Marlborough's influence for the House of Hapsburg. In an interview with the Duke, the field-deputy, Pesters, hinted broadly at this aspect of the matter. According to Pesters' report of December 17, 1708, addressed to Heinsius, a

[1] *Brussels Archives,* quoted by Gachard, *Histoire de la Belgique,* p 337. Charles to Marlborough, August 5, 1708
[2] Coxe, vol ii , p 316. Marlborough to Godolphin.

curious scene occurred. "In God's name," exclaimed
Marlborough, "what have I to expect from King Charles ?
He has more than once bestowed on me the government
of the Low Countries. I have the patent." (Here the Duke
pointed to his strong-box, and then corrected himself,
saying, "No, I have left it in England.") "But when I
learned that it was displeasing to your Republic, I renounced
the idea, and I renounce it for ever No, in truth, Pesters
(he always calls me 'Pesters,' when he wishes to speak
with sincerity), if they offered me in Holland the office of
Stadtholder, I swear by God and by my own damnation,
I would not accept it. I am greatly misjudged. I know
of what I am suspected, but my sole thought, after I shall
have done my utmost to secure a good and durable peace,
is to retire into private life. Nevertheless, if a governor
were required for the Low Countries, I do not know why
I should be less agreeable to the Republic than another,
but I assure you that I have no thoughts of it."[1] It is
certain that the Duke was lying He did desire the government of the Netherlands; and he did intend to accept it
when the war was over, if the Queen assented, and if his
wife's pronounced dislike of the idea could be removed.
The desire and the intention were both so natural and so
proper in themselves that the Dutch, as sensible men,
could attach no credence to his denials. They knew in
their hearts that he was lying, and they knew, or they
ought to have known, that, thanks to the enormous clamour
which they had raised over the question of the patent in
1706, he could not, upon public grounds, take any other
course.

But the situation had altered since 1706, and altered
greatly in their favour Although they were still as nervous
as ever lest Marlborough's influence should be wholly used
for Charles, they had begun to realise that Marlborough's
influence was no longer what it had been. On the death
of the Prince of Denmark, the control of British policy
virtually passed to the Whig Junta. The voice of Somers
was stronger now in the counsels of the Cabinet than the
voice of Marlborough Holland gained immensely by the

---

[1] *Heinsius Archives* H Pesters to Heinsius, December 17, 1708 (Rijks-
Archief [State Archives] at the Hague).

change. For it was a Whig tradition, or rather a Whig principle (everything which that party advocated was always elevated to the rank of a principle), to cultivate the closest friendship with the Calvinist Republic. Another Whig principle was the security of the Hanoverian Succession. But Holland would not guarantee the Hanoverian Succession except in return for a Barrier Treaty. Consequently, the Junta were desirous of concluding a Barrier Treaty as speedily as possible. Vryberg, the Dutch minister in London, reported to Heinsius, on December 21, that Somers and the Whigs were eager to settle. Vryberg's information was correct. On January 8, Godolphin wrote, in reply to Marlborough's request for further information, that, while England could on no account consent to the inclusion of Ostend in the proposed barrier, she was ready to agree to all else which the Dutch themselves " could reasonably desire."[1] The mail, containing this letter, and six other mails as well, were ice-bound for weeks. They did not reach Marlborough until February 2. When, therefore, the Duke arrived at the Hague on January 15, he could only say that he was not instructed on the question of the barrier. Heinsius was disappointed. He wrote to Portland, threatening that, if Marlborough, on his return from Brussels to the Hague in February, did not prove more accommodating, the States would send Buys to England. The Whigs were vastly perturbed at this suggestion, for Buys was the leader of the peace party in Holland, and he was known to have had relations in the past with Harley. To show that such a measure was unnecessary, they renewed their protestations of good faith, and even expressed their willingness to send a special envoy to the Hague to conclude a Barrier Treaty.

Still following the precedent of 1706, Godolphin, on February 7, forwarded to Marlborough a set of preliminaries, which, in the opinion of the British Cabinet, should be jointly accepted by England and Holland before they entered into any negotiations for peace with France. The preliminaries, which Marlborough and the deputies had

[1] Coxe Papers, vol. xxvii.. Godolphin to Marlborough, January 8, 1709 (Brit. Mus. Add. MSS., 9104)

II.   20

agreed upon in 1706,[1] had never been communicated to the States, who probably would have refused to ratify them. Those which Godolphin now put forward were three in number—the restitution of the whole Spanish monarchy, the erection of barriers for Holland and Savoy, and the recognition by Louis of the Protestant Succession, coupled with the expulsion of the Pretender from French territory. Nevertheless, when Marlborough returned from Brussels to the Hague on February 19, he took the line that both the question of the preliminaries and the question of the barrier could very well stand over until after he had paid his approaching visit to England   And to this line he adhered, though Godolphin wrote to him on the 15th, apprising him of the threat to dispatch Buys to London, and urging him to expedite the business of the Barrier Treaty   The Duke's policy was procrastination, pure and simple.   It was directly opposed to the policy of the Junta, who were genuinely anxious to come to a settlement with the Dutch as soon as possible.   When Vryberg told Sunderland, on February 26, that Marlborough pretended that he had no powers, Sunderland said, " I cannot imagine what reasons my Lord Duke can have for doing so."   He added that a treaty between England and Holland, covering the three questions of the barrier, the Protestant Succession, and the preliminaries of peace, would be better than " if our generals lay encamped upon the plains of Paris." Vryberg was delighted, and expatiated to Heinsius on the virtues of the Secretary of State, " who does not hesitate even to gainsay his father-in-law's opinions, when he thinks they are not right."[2]

If a peace were long delayed, Marlborough's tactics were almost certain to fail, because it was not with him, but with the Junta, that the last word would rest   But they were the only tactics whereby he might possibly achieve his object, which was the postponement of the barrier question until hostilities were terminated, and France was willing to concede the demands of the Grand Alliance. The Dutch believed, or affected to believe, that, in pursuing

[1] See Vol I , Chapter XV , pp 429, 430
[2] *Heinsius Archives*. Vryberg to Heinsius, February 26, 1709.

this object in opposition to the wishes of his own government, he allowed his judgment to be seduced by the promise of the patent. But there is no reason to suppose that, if the promise of the patent had never been made, his attitude would have been other than what it was That attitude was perfectly consistent with his whole record from the commencement of the war. Though Marlborough was before all else a patriotic Englishman, and though he invariably set the interest of England above that of every other country, he had laid firm hold of the fact that, in the struggle with " the exorbitant power of France," the interest of England was identified with the common interest of the Grand Alliance As the organiser and the soldier of the coalition, he made it his business to oppose all sectional movements, which tended to diminish the energy, by impairing the harmony, of the machine as a whole. It was in this lofty and far-seeing spirit that he looked on every issue of strategy, diplomacy, and domestic politics which came before him. It was in this same spirit that, at the very outset of the contest, he had insisted, in the teeth of Rochester's opposition, that England should set the allies a signal example of self-sacrifice by exerting her naval power in the Mediterranean instead of in the acquisition of Spanish colonies and Spanish gold It was in this same spirit that, amid the execrations of " the Tackers " and the pathetic moanings of the Dutch, he had carried the soldiers of England and Holland to the banks of the Danube. It was in this same spirit that he had continually imperilled his own position at the Court of Vienna by his remonstrances upon the bitter subject of the Hungarian rebellion, by his fearless rebukes to the Austrian ministers for their unworthy suspicions of England, and for their refusal to send Eugène to Barcelona. So too, in 1706, and again in 1709, it was in this same spirit that he regarded the question of the Barrier Treaty He fully recognised that the interests of the coalition as a whole, and the interests of every member of it, imperatively demanded that, as one result of the war, Holland should secure an effective barrier against French aggression. For if Holland and Belgium, or either of them, were to fall into the hands of Louis, the independence of the British Isles, and consequently of all Europe, would be vitally menaced. But he did not understand by an effective barrier the annexation of the Spanish Netherlands to the United Provinces, or such an assumption of sovereign rights by the Dutch as would be tantamount in practice to annexation For in either eventuality the Spanish monarchy would be unjustly despoiled, and the strategical and commercial position of England would be weakened in favour of that maritime power, which was her chief competitor, and which, even in Marlborough's lifetime, had terrified the citizens of London with the thunder of its guns On the other hand, he was aware that the ideas of an effective barrier, which found favour at Barcelona and Vienna, were impossible and absurd. Sinzendorf's instructions in 1706 had made that plain. It followed, therefore, that, whenever the question came up for settlement, grave dissensions would arise between the members of the Grand Alliance. Marlborough desired to postpone that evil day until after the common enemy had been reduced to submission. The Junta, on the contrary, desired to close with the Dutch immediately. Their arguments made no impression on the Duke. He attached but little weight to Holland's guarantee of the Protestant Succession, because Holland, for her own sake, would be obliged, in any event, to oppose the restoration of the Pretender Moreover, the value of the guarantee, if it ever had any, had been considerably depreciated since 1706 by the Union with Scotland He attached no weight at all to the sentimental connection between the Whigs and the Dutch To Marlborough, as a loyal subject of the British Crown and a loyal member of the Church of England, the political and religious dogmas of the Dutch made no appeal But for him the question was not one of personal predilections at all. Calvinism and Republicanism were not British interests. Still less were they interests of the Grand Alliance. Where his country's safety and well-being were concerned, these doctrines could exercise no more fascination over the mind of Marlborough than they had exercised over the mind of Cromwell, who might have been more naturally expected to appreciate their charms. One contention of the Junta, and only one, the Duke regarded as relevant and even serious. The Junta were honestly afraid (and Godolphin fully shared their fears), that, unless a Barrier Treaty were promptly arranged, Holland would withdraw from the Grand Alliance Marlborough, who knew the Dutch far better than Godolphin or any other member of the Cabinet could know them, did not believe that they would proceed to that extremity. He considered that the ideas of a secession and a separate peace with France were being cleverly manipulated from the Hague to frighten the Whigs into the immediate conclusion of a Barrier Treaty. He was afraid that the same ideas would be used, with equal effect, to frighten them into the conclusion of a Barrier Treaty, not only unseasonable in time, but improper and indefensible in substance. He foresaw that, if such manoeuvres were successful, the Grand Alliance, in face of a still unconquered foe, might be shaken to its very foundations. And he greatly feared lest, once they had obtained what they wanted, the Dutch themselves would cease to exhibit any genuine concern in the vigorous prosecution of the war.

Marlborough sailed from Ostend on March 8. On the following day, Rouillé, a special envoy from Louis to the Dutch, passed through Brussels on the road to Antwerp. Bergueick had visited Versailles, and had reported to the King the result of his correspondence with Vanderdussen. Observing that Vanderdussen made no explicit reference to Naples and Sicily, Louis had instructed Rouillé to open a negotiation on the hypothesis that Naples and Sicily might be granted to Philip. The States appointed Buys and Vanderdussen to meet Rouillé at Moerdyke. Subsequently the envoy was allowed to proceed to Woerden near Utrecht, where he could more easily confer with Dutch statesmen. This important affair was unknown to Marlborough when he sailed from Ostend. He heard of it for the first time in London, when the whole story became the common property of the coffee-houses and the streets. He was both surprised and indignant, and he did not hesitate to complain that he had been duped by Heinsius. But it was the publicity of the negotiation that annoyed him most. The French took every opportunity of trumpeting it abroad. One of Rouillé's secretaries declared that " his master had the peace in his pocket, and was sure of Holland "[1] The Spanish Netherlands were infested with the agents of Torcy and Chamillart " Peace-gentlemen are trotting about this neighbourhood in fine style,"[2] wrote Albemarle, the military governor of Brussels, in a letter to the Grand Pensionary. But when he proposed to lay them all by the heels, he was warned by Pesters that they were provided with passports. Heinsius affected to be astonished at the indiscretion of the French. But he did not deceive Marlborough. The Duke had no difficulty in penetrating the diplomacy of both France and Holland. France deliberately courted publicity, because it was calculated to disturb and alarm the Grand Alliance. Holland as deliberately connived at it, because it was calculated to terrify the British government into a premature and improper Barrier Treaty

His immediate concern, however, was to mitigate the unpleasant impression, which would certainly be created at Vienna by what he himself described in a letter to Raby, as " the unaccountable proceedings of Holland."[3] He wrote to Sinzendorf and Wratislaw, expressing his conviction that Rouillé had no other object than to sow dissension and mistrust among the allies, that the Dutch had already repented of their error, and that the intrigue would end in nothing But to guard against the possibility of danger, he promised to return at an early date to the Hague. He told Hoffmann, the Austrian resident in London, that he hoped to delay negotiations until the opening of the next campaign, when he would endeavour to extort better terms. He warned Heinsius " to lose no time in acquainting Prince Eugène " (who was now on his way to Holland) " with what you think proper, to prevent his being jealous."[4] He himself wrote to the Prince, referring to the alarm, which Rouillé's mission had excited in England, and urging

<hr>

[1] *Heinsius Archives* . Cadogan to Heinsius, March 12, 1709.
[2] *Ibid :* Albemarle to Heinsius, March 11, 1709
[3] Murray, vol iv , p 472 Marlborough to Lord Raby, March 15, 1709.
[4] *Heinsius Archives:* Marlborough to Heinsius, March 8/19, 1709.

him to hasten to the Hague. But if Marlborough could
allay, he could not dissipate the anger and suspicion of the
Emperor. Even his own good faith was questioned at
Vienna " It is almost incredible," wrote Wratislaw, on
April 15, " that you should have had no previous knowledge of the arrival of M. Rouillé."[1] The terms of an address,
presented to the Queen, on March 14, by both Houses of
Parliament, augmented the anxiety of the Austrian ministry.
This document insisted that no peace would be acceptable,
unless the King of France acknowledged the title of Anne
to the throne, recognised the Protestant Succession, expelled
the Pretender from French territory, and demolished the
fortifications and harbour of Dunkirk. Obviously, it had
no other intention than to place upon record those points
which were of immediate and vital concern to England
alone. Yet Wratislaw chose to assume that, because
nothing was said as to the restoration of the Spanish
monarchy, England was weakening upon that important
principle, which had been several times affirmed by Parliament. The assumption was entirely gratuitous. When
Marlborough returned to the Hague, he was provided with
instructions, which, if Wratislaw could have seen them,
would have completely reassured him. In view of " the
alarm and jealousies," which had resulted from Rouillé's
mission, the Duke was to impress upon the Dutch " the
opinion of the Queen that no negotiation for peace should
be concluded with France, until the preliminaries are
adjusted between England and the States." He was " to
announce her hope that the States will concur in her sentiments and those of her people, so often expressed in the
address of Parliament, that no peace can be safe or honourable unless the whole Spanish monarchy be restored to the
House of Austria." Then followed, on behalf of England,
the heads enumerated in the address of March 14. And
finally, he was " to announce Her Majesty's desire, that other
preliminaries should be required for the security and interest
of the States, particularly a barrier, for which a treaty
had been so long depending."[2]

Marlborough arrived at the Hague on April 9. Of all

[1] Blerheim *Archives* Wratislaw to Marlborough, April 15, 1709
[2] Coxe, vol ii., p. 394.

the diplomatic tasks which he had ever undertaken, none
was so difficult and delicate as that upon which he had
now embarked. Eugène, who was awaiting him, had been
furnished with instructions which conflicted sharply with
the views and aspirations of the Dutch. As regards the
barrier, the Prince was to maintain, as Sinzendorf had
maintained in 1706, that the towns composing it were to
be extorted from France, and that the upkeep of the garrisons
was to be found by Holland. As regards the preliminaries
in general, he was to insist that whatever compensation
might be granted to Philip, Sicily and Naples could never
be surrendered by the House of Hapsburg. To confound
the Dutch, he was to explain that, upon strategic grounds,
Sicily and Naples were as vital to the safety of Austria as
the Spanish Netherlands to the safety of Holland, and that,
if Philip were to have either, the Emperor would prefer
that he should have the Spanish Netherlands In both
these matters, each of the disputants expected to prevail
over the other with the assistance of the British Cabinet.
But the British Cabinet, though it regarded the Austrian
conception of a Dutch barrier as ridiculous, was proposing
preliminaries of peace, which would almost certainly encounter a great opposition from the Dutch. To increase
the uneasiness of the Duke's position, he himself was
suspected in Holland of being the creature of the Hapsburgs,
while he, who had formerly moulded the policy of England
before he declared it, was now become little more than the
mouthpiece of the Whig Junta

From his first interviews with Heinsius, as also with Buys
and Vanderdussen, who were conducting the negotiation
with Rouillé, Marlborough was confirmed in the opinion
that the French were " only seeking to amuse " the Dutch,
and " to gain time."[1] Buys and Vanderdussen were
haggling with Rouillé over the towns, which Holland
required from Louis for the purposes of her barrier; and
Rouillé, who was in constant communication with Versailles, was slowly and painfully conceding them one by
one. Marlborough reported that the Dutch were more
than ever desirous of terminating the war, but that even

[1] Murray, vol. iv., p 476 Marlborough to Boyle, April 12, 1709.

the warmest partisans of peace regarded the present propositions of France as inadequate. He also inferred with
satisfaction that no decisive step would be taken " without
the participation of the High Allies "[1] But, on the whole,
the diplomatic situation was obscure The Duke, however,
was firmly resolved that the French should reap no military
advantages from Rouillé's mission. He proceeded without
delay to complete his preparations for the forthcoming
campaign, and although the extreme backwardness of the
season pointed to a late beginning, he ordered the army
to be ready to take the field at twenty hours' notice. He
was commonly reported to have declared that, if France
had no further offers to make, the allies must treat in the
summer upon French soil with 150,000 plenipotentiaries.

Shortly after his arrival, Marlborough revealed to Heinsius, in a private and unofficial manner, the instructions
of the British Cabinet in regard to the preliminaries of
peace Heinsius was "a little surprised" He said that
he was "very apprehensive France would never be
brought to those terms" Marlborough replied that he
could "not depart from any one article," and that considering the notorious exhaustion of France, it was to be
expected that she would eventually give way. Heinsius
was not convinced. He told the Duke, "in confidence,"
that Holland was "under worse circumstances" than
France, and that, if the negotiations were broken off, " the
great towns and the commonalty would lay it entirely "[2]
at the door of England. He promised, however, that no
proceeding, disagreeable to England or the other allies,
should be sanctioned by the Dutch government, if he could
possibly prevent it For the present, he recommended
that Marlborough should not disclose his instructions,
except in so far as they related to the barrier and the
Protestant Succession In this suggestion both Marlborough
and Eugène acquiesced. In subsequent interviews, the
Duke was repeatedly warned by Buys of "the ill consequences that might attend the breaking off this negotiation
by our insisting on the entire monarchy of Spain."[3] But

[1] *Ibid*, p 477· Marlborough to the King of Spain, April 16, 1709
[2] *Ibid*, p 476· Marlborough to Boyle, April 12, 1709
[3] *Ibid*, p 479 Marlborough to Boyle April 16 1709.

Godolphin objected strongly to a policy of reticence. " The longer you defer proposing the matter of your instructions," he wrote on the 15th, " the greater difficulty you will find in having them complied with."[1]

But it soon appeared that there was an excellent reason for delay During Marlborough's absence in England, Heinsius had declined to discuss the question of the barrier with Cadogan. But he raised it immediately upon the Duke's return. He was met at once with a request for a written statement of the Dutch demands He was unable to refuse, though Holland was as reluctant now as she had been in 1706 to commit herself in a formal document to the acceptance of terms, which, however high she fixed them, were bound to fall short of annexation. The States proceeded to discuss their claims. On the 16th, Marlborough warned Boyle that he was afraid their decision might be characterised by extravagance. His fear was justified. On the 18th, they sent him a deputation The interview lasted " above two hours."[2] At the outset, he assured them of the Queen of England's sympathy, and of her sincere desire for the erection of a reasonable barrier. He also endeavoured " to cure them of any jealousy " arising out of his own supposed partiality to the Hapsburg interest. On their side, the Dutchmen opened the ball with the announcement that the number of towns, which they required for their barrier, had increased since 1706 Marlborough replied that it was his business to aid them as far as possible; but he expressed the hope that they would insist only upon places " absolutely necessary for their own security."[3] Otherwise, he said, it would be impracticable to justify their position to Charles, or to the world at large. He then requested them to submit a complete list of barrier fortresses, with a statement for their reasons for the inclusion of each. This they undertook to do. Referring subsequently to the question of cost, they hinted that the Spanish Netherlands would be expected to furnish not less than £300,000 for the upkeep of the garrisons. Marlborough

[1] Coxe Papers. Godolphin to Marlborough, April 15, 1709 (Brit, Mus. Add MSS., 9104)
[2] Coxe, vol ii , p 398
[3] Murray, vol iv , p 481. Marlborough to Boyle, April 19, 1709

replied that, until the places were known, and the number of troops was determined, it would be premature to discuss the cost. But he told them plainly that, in fixing the amount of the burden to be borne by King Charles' subjects, regard must be had to the necessities of the civil administration of the country, and in his report to Boyle, he observed that, so far as his own information went, the revenues of the Spanish Netherlands could not endure such a charge. On the 19th, he was presented with the list of fortresses. It was something of a shock. Eugène, who visited him that day, discovered him " in great distress."[1] The document was certainly a remarkable one. Simulating a moderation to which they were altogether strangers, the Dutch omitted no fewer than seven names from the original list of 1706. They omitted Luxembourg, Thionville, Charleroi, Mons, Ypres, Furnes, and Maubeuge. Luxembourg and Thionville, however, had little value for Holland, though much for the Empire. Ypres, Furnes, and Maubeuge had already been promised them by Rouillé, and were intended to be reinserted at the conclusion of peace. Mons was dropped in deference to English criticism; and both Mons and Charleroi were rendered less important now by reason of the new demands. On the other hand, the places mentioned for the first time were Hal, Lierre, the Castle of Ghent, Fort Perle, St. Donas, Damme, and Knocke Theoretically, therefore, Holland was but substituting seven new ones for the seven she had dropped. But actually she was increasing the total by three. Actually, also, the proposed barrier was not a barrier at all. It was a fortress system, which would dominate the entire Spanish Netherlands. The coast was to be commanded by Knocke and Fort Perle, Bruges and the canal by Damme and Fort Donas, the Schelde by Fort Perle, Dendermonde, and the Castle of Ghent, the plain of Brabant by Lierre and Hal, the Meuse by Namur, and the frontier of France by Menin, Lille, Condé, Tournai, and Valenciennes. " It encloses what might be thought a great kingdom," wrote Marlborough to Godolphin on the 19th. " I hope

[1] *Feldzüge des Prinzen Eugen*, Supplement-Heft zum 11. Bande, ii. Serie, p 60 Bericht an den Kaiser, April 19, 1709.

to persuade them from some of it," he said, "so that I beg very few may see it."[1] Meanwhile, he did not communicate it officially to Boyle and the Cabinet. Godolphin was furious. He denounced the Dutch proposals as showing "very little consideration for King Charles, any more than for the Queen." He expressed his admiration for "the great modesty of the States,"[2] who demanded so much for themselves, while they objected to England's request for the demolition of Dunkirk. And he gave it as his opinion that the Dutch were more concerned to gratify themselves and the French than to promote the common interest of the Grand Alliance.

It was probably because he foresaw that Holland's demands in respect of her barrier would be very unreasonable, that Marlborough had agreed to postpone the formal declaration of England's views as to the preliminaries of peace. For, obviously, it would be difficult for the Dutch to talk to him of moderation, now that he was in possession of their own outrageous statement of claim. Accordingly, on the 23rd, he acquainted the Pensionary with his instructions "in form," and with "what Her Majesty insisted on positively as part of the preliminaries." Heinsius told him that the negotiation with Rouillé was progressing so badly that a rupture seemed imminent, and warned him to be ready to take the field forthwith. But in his report to Boyle, while he expressed "an entire confidence" in the Pensionary's sincerity, Marlborough declared that there was "a thorough inclination for peace "[3] among the Dutch, and that a rupture was, in his judgment, improbable. In a letter of the 24th, to Moles, he took the same view, basing it mainly on the prevalent disorder and embarrassment of the finances of the Republic.

The Duke informed Boyle, on the 24th, that he was strongly disposed to pay a flying visit to England, that he might explain the diplomatic situation in full to the British government The necessity of such a course became evident, when the Dutch delivered to him, in draft, the "project" of their Barrier Treaty. In this document, the

---

[1] Coxe, vol ii , p 398: Marlborough to Godolphin, April 19, 1709
[2] Ibid · Godolphin to Marlborough, April 12/23, 1709
[3] Murray, vol iv , p. 486 Marlborough to Boyle, April 23, 1709.

list of fortresses, originally demanded in 1706, was incorporated, subject of course to the additions and omissions, of which Marlborough had already been notified It contained, moreover, some new and startling features. For example, it empowered the Dutch government, in time of war, to throw their troops into any and every town of the Spanish Netherlands without exception. It imposed upon that country an annual charge of 3,250,000 louis towards the maintenance of Dutch garrisons in the barrier fortresses It annexed the territory of Upper Guelderland to Holland without compensation to Charles, who was not even to take possession of the Spanish Netherlands until peace had been concluded, though the Dutch garrisons were to enter into occupation immediately In return for these extraordinary advantages, Holland was to endeavour to induce Louis to acknowledge Anne and the Protestant Succession, and she was not to make peace except in conjunction with England. The "project," as a whole, was so outrageous, that Marlborough was naturally eager to escape for a time from the importunities of those who had had the effrontery to present it. He dared not tell them what he thought of it. He dared not tell the Kings of Spain and Prussia that he had even seen it But he warned Frederick, who was holding Upper Guelderland as a security for moneys owing to him, that the Prussian minister should be fully instructed on the subject; and he urged Charles to dispatch a special envoy to the Spanish Netherlands. Heinsius attempted to dissuade him from visiting England, and argued that his departure at this juncture would create a bad impression in Holland. Marlborough pretended that he was constrained by private reasons On April 29, he quitted the Hague, taking the "project" with him He reached London on May 2. His arrival set all tongues wagging; and rumours of the imminence of peace were rife

Even the Junta, notoriously tender as they were towards the interests of Holland, refused to stomach the "project." For not only were the Dutch demands unjust and unreasonable in themselves, but they were put forward under circumstances, which suggested, and which were deliberately

intended to suggest, that a refusal would be followed by
the secession of Holland from the Grand Alliance The
thinly veiled threat was odious enough to Marlborough,
who believed that Holland was only ' bluffing.' To the
Junta, who believed that she was in deadly earnest, it was
peculiarly bitter, thus to be wounded in the household of
their friends. When artists in blackmail are themselves
blackmailed, the spectacle is at once instructive and agreeable. But the situation was too serious for Marlborough
and Godolphin to do full justice to its delicious irony.
Without delay the Cabinet fell to work upon the grotesque
" project " When they had finished with it, it was un-
recognisable. From the list of towns they deleted Ostend,
which dominated the whole coast, and Dendermonde, which
dominated all Brabant. The right of Holland to flood the
Spanish Netherlands with troops, they restricted to the
single case in which France should be the attacking power,
and in which war was openly declared. For the support
of the Dutch garrisons, they proposed the formation of a
special fund out of the revenues of such places as had not
belonged to the Spanish monarchy at the death of Charles II.
The clause, forbidding Charles III to take possession until
a general peace had been arranged, they eliminated altogether. The problem of Upper Guelderland they reserved
for the arbitrament of the Queen On the other hand,
instead of an empty engagement on the part of the Dutch
to use their good offices on behalf of Her Majesty's title
and the Protestant Succession, the British Cabinet demanded
from Holland a pledge to continue the struggle until these
two points had been conceded, until the entire Spanish
monarchy was surrendered, and until the fortifications of
Dunkirk had been dismantled and its harbour destroyed.
The result of their labours, the " counter-project," as it
was called, was to be communicated to the Dutch, when
Marlborough returned to the Hague.

The Duke knew well that it would be one man's work
for months to chaffer with the government of the Republic
over the question of the barrier. It would be physically
impossible for him to undertake the task, and at one and
the same time participate in the negotiations for peace

and supervise the preparations for war Nor could he, if the negotiations came to nothing, combine the discharge of his absorbing duties in the field with the tedious and uneasy business of haggling with Holland. Before he quitted the Hague, therefore, he had written to London, advising the appointment of a second plenipotentiary. The difficulty now was to select the man Sunderland and Halifax were both suggested Sunderland was rightly deemed unsuitable by reason of his violence and want of tact Halifax possessed the diplomatic experience, which he had gained at the Hague in 1706, but he was not well liked by the Dutch, and he cherished a grudge against Marlborough and Godolphin, who since that time had given him no employment Nevertheless, Godolphin and Somers offered him the post. Halifax refused it, alleging that a Barrier Treaty would assuredly be unpopular in England, and that, if Marlborough had thought otherwise, he would never have proposed to divide the honour with a colleague. Mr. Geikie[1] considered that the Duke's conduct was justly deserving of Halifax' sneer. But even assuming that a genuine necessity for the appointment of a coadjutor had not existed, Marlborough would have been perfectly entitled to cast upon another the execution of a policy, for which he was not responsible, and of which he entirely disapproved. He was not the master of the Cabinet, but he was not its maid-of-all-work. No man is under a moral obligation to appear before his contemporaries or before posterity in a character, which he himself considers as either odious or absurd. It may be, as Mr Geikie holds, that the conclusion of a Barrier Treaty was now become unavoidable, and that the British government could not, if they would, have discovered any alternative. But even so, there was no reason why Marlborough should be compelled to negotiate it. On the contrary, there was a very cogent reason why he should have nothing to do with it The question could be regarded from another standpoint besides the low and personal one which Halifax adopted The most valuable asset of the Grand Alliance was Marlborough's

[1] Roderick Geikie, The Dutch Barrier MS in the library of King's College, Cambridge

unique influence over the princes and the states, which composed that heterogeneous and fissiparous body. The less he was identified with a transaction, which would almost certainly be displeasing to every one of the allies excepting Holland, the more likely he was to preserve intact that reputation for justice and impartiality, which more than anything else had held together the ill-assorted atoms of the coalition. None was more conscious of this truth than Marlborough himself. If, therefore, he had not, in fact, required the services of a colleague, he would have been well advised, in the interest of the common cause, to pretend that he required them.

Eventually, the Cabinet selected Lord Townshend A comparatively young man, possessed of considerable learning, an amiable disposition, an ingratiating address, and a clean record, Townshend is said to have been beloved by everybody that knew him [1] Burnet has certified to the soundness of his Whiggery. It was therefore an appointment to which the Dutch could take no serious exception.

Having drafted their " counter-project," and nominated their second plenipotentiary, the Cabinet reconsidered the question of the preliminaries of peace Those which had been already supplied to Marlborough, were reaffirmed. But he was further instructed to propose a renewal of the Grand Alliance, all the signatories becoming also guarantors for the fulfilment of all the conditions of peace. If the French remained obdurate until the campaign opened, it was to be competent to the allies to increase their demands. On May 15, Marlborough and Townshend sailed from Margate. After a bad passage, they reached the Hague on the 18th.

During his stay in Engand, the Duke had modified his opinion of Louis' attitude towards a general peace. He saw good reason now to believe in the sincerity of overtures which he had previously regarded with grave suspicion. For Louis had taken a remarkable step On May 6, four days after the Duke's arrival in England, Rouillé had been joined by a colleague, whose position in the French government was in itself a powerful evidence of good faith. On

[1] Macky, *Characters of the Court of Great Britain,* p. 89 (" Charles, Lord Townshend ")

that day, no less a personage than the Secretary of State
for Foreign Affairs, the Marquis de Torcy, arrived at the
Hague, and immediately visited the Grand Pensionary
The astonished Heinsius told him that they must not confer
without the consent of the States.   This condition having
been duly fulfilled, Torcy was admitted, on the 7th, to an
interview, at which Buys and Vanderdussen were also
present.   He was subsequently informed that the States
could bind themselves to nothing " till they knew the sentiments of the Queen of Great Britain, by the return of the
Duke of Marlborough "[1]   There were Englishmen who
regarded it as a suspicious coincidence that first Rouillé,
and then Torcy, should seek, as it were, to take advantage
of Marlborough's visits to England to tamper with the
Dutch.   But the correct behaviour of Holland destroyed
the edge of all such criticism.   The coming of Torcy was
an impressive fact, which could not easily be explained
upon some sinister hypothesis.   When Villars first heard
of it, he concluded that peace was assured, and that the
basis of the treaty had already been settled by informal
agreement.   On no other supposition could he imagine
that " the minister would . . . thus expose himself to the
risk of receiving an affront."[2]   If Louis desired but to
delude and to cajole the allies, he could have effected his
purpose as well through Rouillé or another as through
Torcy.   It was not essential that he should go out of his
way to humble himself before the Europe which he had
aspired to subjugate.   It was not essential that he should
instruct his Secretary of State for Foreign Affairs to knock
like a suppliant at the door of that very Heinsius, whom,
thirty years before, Louvois at Paris had insolently
threatened with the Bastille.   In international politics
such luxury of self-abasement is not cultivated for its own
sake.   It was only to be understood on the assumption
that, this time, Louis was in earnest, and was resolved to
make almost any sacrifice to demonstrate the fact.

And such an assumption was abundantly justified by the
known circumstances of France in the spring of 1709.
Overmatched by the arms and resources of the allies on

[1] Boyer, vol viii , p 3.   [2] *Vie de Villars*, t. ii., p 42.

land and sea, disorganised in her finances and ruined as to her maritime commerce, expelled from Italy and the Spanish Netherlands, and reeling under the terrible wounds she had newly received at Lille and at Port Mahon, she seemed to be fighting at last for little more than her own existence. Even her extraordinary powers of recuperation were paralysed now. For, in the short breathing-space, which ensued upon the termination of the prolonged campaign of 1708, the hand of God fell heavily upon her. The bitter frost, which set in on January 5, before the troops of the allies had retired into their winter-quarters, continued, without intermission, excepting for a partial thaw of ten days, until March 3. It was general throughout Europe and the British Isles. But in France, which was least able to endure it, it was characterised by exceptional severity. So intense was the cold that every river in the land was frozen to its mouth, champagne congealed in the cellars, and at certain places on the coast ice formed upon the sea. The ten days' thaw, between January 24 and February 4, which was followed by violent snowstorms and a return of the frost in its most extreme form, wrought incalculable mischief. The olives, and the vines, and most of the fruit trees were destroyed. Even the warmest south was not exempt. The grain perished in the earth. The season of spring was a season of desolation and despair The loaf rose to famine prices; and it was difficult to import corn from Africa and the Levant, when, summer and winter, the English cruisers were sweeping the Mediterranean Sea. The mortality among the cattle, and particularly the sheep, presaged as great a scarcity of meat as of bread. Game dropped dead in the forests and the fields; and even the rabbits expired in their burrows. In the capital, where the government made every effort to maintain an artificial appearance of plenty, business was interrupted, the courts of law were closed, the opera was suspended, public amusements and private entertainments ceased, popular disorders broke out, the death-rate doubled, and the births and marriages decreased by one-fourth. The rich died fast, but not so fast as the poor In the provinces, the highways were littered with the carcasses of men and beasts.

In Burgundy, the people lived on herbs and roots. Far and wide, the emaciated peasantry abandoned their villages and flocked into the towns, where the inhabitants were already unable to support themselves, and the hospitals were crowded with scurvy-stricken multitudes. A horde of two thousand descended upon Clermont-Ferrand from the mountains of Auvergne. Hundreds of men, women, and children, wandered over Touraine in troops, intent upon arson and pillage The forest of Orléans-swarmed with savage vagabonds. Brigandage became almost universal. At Amiens the principal market was plundered in broad daylight. Châteaux and convents were attacked and rifled upon every side. In the prevailing scarcity of money, the half-starved troops upon the frontiers remained penniless. No army suffered so much as the army of Flanders, which was quartered in a country already ruined by the war. Credit collapsed; and at Lyons the great house of Samuel Bernard stopped payment. Neither private charity nor the efforts of the administration could cope with the frightful welter of misery, destitution, and disease. Louis and his advisers recognised the critical condition of the country. They contrasted it with the state of England, where the merchants were actually exporting wheat to Portugal in exchange for gold, and where, on March 4, more than two million pounds were raised for the government by public subscription in the City of London, in the space of four hours, and "near one million more would have been subscribed that very day, if there had been room."[1] It was no wonder, therefore, that the King of France was surrounded by advocates of peace, and even of peace at any price. It was no wonder that Chamillart, writing to Villars on March 29, should sorrowfully confess that "the long duration of a war, out of all proportion to the King's finances, has placed us under the hard necessity of receiving law from our enemy."[2] It was no wonder that, at a council held at Versailles on April 28, after bitter tears of grief and humiliation had been shed, the offer of the Secretary of State for Foreign Affairs to

[1] Boyer, vol vii , p 295.
[2] *Vie de Villars*, t ii., p. 39 Lettre de M. de Chamillard, 29 mars, 1709

proceed in person to the Hague should have been accepted. And it was no wonder that Marlborough, who was well informed from a variety of sources as to the appalling situation of the French people, should have been convinced by the coming of Torcy that Louis was in earnest at last.

The Dutch had so conducted their negotiations, first with Rouillé, and subsequently with Torcy, as to lend no colour to the theory that they were prepared to desert the Grand Alliance   The firmness, not to say the arrogance, of their demeanour destroyed this last hope of French diplomacy.   When Marlborough arrived on the 18th, they had already extorted the consent of Torcy to their own demands, and were insisting upon those of England. Immediately upon his arrival, the Duke had a conference with Eugène, and another with Heinsius and the President of the States.   That same evening he was visited by Torcy, who remained for a couple of hours.   On the morning of the 19th Torcy attended the Duke's levée, and afterwards accompanied him to Prince Eugène.   At night, Marlborough and Eugène together had an interview with Heinsius.   The Duke was more than satisfied with these discussions   They entirely convinced him of the loyalty of Holland and the sincerity of France.   " By the joy that seemed to be in His Grace's countenance yesterday," wrote Hare on the 21st, " all seemed to go well, at least as to these two points, that the French were resolved to have peace on any terms, and the Dutch determined to do nothing without us "[1] " M. de Torcy has offered so much," wrote Marlborough to Godolphin on the 19th, " that I have no doubt it will end in a good peace."[2]   On the same date, he wrote in similar terms to his wife, and even instructed her to prepare " the side-board of plate,"[3] and to send in a claim to the Lord Treasurer for a canopy, to be used in the ceremonial appropriate to the solemn functions which he expected to ensue.

Marlborough's belief in the sincerity of the French government was founded partly upon certain facts, of which he alone among the representatives of the allied powers had any cognisance.   At his first interview with Torcy, after

---

[1] Hare MSS · Letter of May 10/21, 1709 (Hist. MSS Comm , 14th Report, Appendix, part ix , p 222).
[2] Coxe, vol ii , p 402   [3] Ibid.

a graceful reference to the high regard, which, in his private capacity, he had always entertained for the King of France, he alluded to the secret correspondence with d'Alègre and with Berwick. Torcy, who imagined that the Duke was only waiting for a price to be named, replied that the attitude of Louis was unchanged, and that his pecuniary proposals still held good. He then explained that Louis was willing to resign the Spanish monarchy as a whole, but that he ardently desired compensation for his grandson, or an equivalent for himself. If Marlborough could procure Naples and Sicily for Philip, or even Naples alone, or if he could preserve either Dunkirk or Strasbourg for France, Louis was prepared to pay him two million livres. For Naples and Dunkirk together, for Strasbourg and Dunkirk together, or for Naples and Strasbourg together, the figure was three million livres. For Naples, Sicily, Dunkirk, and Strasbourg, all four, it was four million livres. This delicately graduated offer was based upon elaborate instructions, forwarded to Torcy by the King himself. The effect of it was altogether disappointing According to Torcy's own narrative (and Torcy's credibility in this connection is beyond suspicion), Marlborough listened, blushed, and passed on to other topics. He spoke of the Pretender, whom he called the Prince of Wales, declaring that it would be to that young man's advantage to quit France, and emphasising his own desire to serve the son of his old master He spoke of his Whig colleague, Townshend, describing him as "a very honest man," but "a kind of inspector," in whose presence he was bound always to use the language of " an obstinate Englishman "[1] in regard to the House of Stuart. He spoke of the folly of the British people, who desired the destruction of France, and who failed to realise that peace was now become their highest interest. He referred to his own longing for tranquillity in his old age; he piously ascribed the successes of the allies to the Almighty, who had welded the soldiers of eight nations into one harmonious whole, and he warned the Frenchman, though always in a modest tone, that, if it became necessary to resume the struggle, the army would

---

[1] *Mémoires de Torcy*, t. ii., p. 109

not be deterred from invasion by lack of supplies since corn
could always be transported by the fleet to Abbeville.   But
though he talked thus freely of a variety of matters, he
never reverted to the proffered bribe.   And when, at a
subsequent interview, Torcy once more approached the
subject, "he blushed, and seemed desirous of changing the
conversation."[1]   He had gained his end, the only end for
the sake of which he ever alluded to the correspondence
with d'Alègre and Berwick.   He had finally satisfied himself
that Louis was at last determined to secure peace.

Various reflections are suggested by this episode.   But
only two aspects of it need be noted here.

In the first place, it sheds a curious light upon the gravest
of the standing charges against Marlborough's reputation.
His enemies have depicted him as a monster of avarice
and treachery.   To those odious vices, France, according
to the unimpeachable testimony of her Foreign Minister,
now made deliberate and forcible appeal.   According to
the same unimpeachable testimony, the Duke did not
condescend even to notice the temptation.   When it was
repeated, he steadily ignored it.   One swallow does not
make a summer.   A man may still be a drunkard, though
credible witnesses depose that on a particular occasion he
refused the finest champagne.   But Torcy's story does not
stand alone.   Marlborough's repeated refusal of the patent
for the government of the Spanish Netherlands is another,
and a signal, example of his loyal and disinterested conduct.
General accusations, advanced by prejudiced persons, and
circulated by paid liars, ought always to be received with
some caution.   When they conflict directly with reliable
evidence as to matters of fact, they become worse than
suspect.

Secondly, it must be remembered that, even if Marlborough had accepted the gold of Louis XIV, he could
hardly have been convicted under the moral code of that
epoch.   For a bribe was regarded then as one of the legitimate resources and lawful perquisites of diplomacy.
Between those engaged in international negotiations, pay-
ments of money frequently passed as a matter of course,

[1] *Mémoires de Torcy*, t ii , p 127.

and almost as a matter of etiquette. The ministers of
Charles XII of Sweden, for example, were the regular
pensioners of England; and when Marlborough himself went
to Leipzig, he went prepared to outbid the French ambassador in the Swedish market. It may be that his waning
influence at London and the Hague would have been insufficient to procure for France what Torcy asked. But he
did not make the attempt. He had long been weary of the
war; he had long been desirous of a private life; and he
was certainly fond of riches. Yet when this fair opportunity
came to him, he, who is so often represented as an unscrupulous money-grubber, went out of his way to be
honest above the standard of his age and generation.

Marlborough's optimism was tempered by one misgiving
In accordance with the plan, upon which the allies had
wisely determined to proceed, Louis was to be presented
with certain preliminaries, on his acceptance of which an
armistice was to be declared   If, at the expiration of a
stipulated period, these preliminaries had been fully executed,
the armistice was to continue, while the numerous details
of a general peace were finally adjusted; but if, on the
other hand, the preliminaries, or any of them, remained
unfulfilled, the war was to be resumed. Now, one of the
preliminaries was the restitution to Charles of the entire
monarchy of Spain   Portions of that monarchy, such as
Brabant and the Milanese, had already been recovered by
force of arms. Portions of the residue, such as the Walloon
fortresses, it was obviously competent for Louis to restore.
But it was not within the power of a King of France to
assign the country and the people of Spain, by a stroke of
the pen, to a Hapsburg prince   Louis could formally
acknowledge Charles; he could recall his troops from the
Peninsula; he could order his grandson to return to Versailles. But if Philip chose to ignore the order, and if,
notwithstanding the withdrawal of their French auxiliaries,
the Spaniards chose to support him, what then ?   Either
the allies must consent to abate their terms of peace, or they
must be prepared to continue the war in one of its theatres,
and that, from some points of view, the most difficult.
This dilemma had always been foreseen. Torcy himself

had long since prophesied it to Petkum, in a letter of
October 30, 1707.[1] Stanhope was fully alive to it, for he
had frequently confided to Marlborough his "apprehensions
that a treaty of peace will not immediately put an end to
the war in Spain." It was evidently troubling the Duke
five weeks before he met the French minister. For, on
April 16, he had written to Moles, recommending that
Charles should leave nothing undone to win himself a following among the Spaniards, and above all, among the
ruling class, "that when it comes to a question of peace,
and France is obliged to give her orders for the recall of
the Duke of Anjou, we may encounter no reverse on that
side." "I am sure," he added, "that you are already
thinking of it, but it is a matter which to us is so essential,
that I cannot forgo this slight reference to it "[2]

It is probable, however, that Marlborough as yet entirely
failed to realise how firm was the resolution of the great
majority of the Spanish people never to accept King Charles,
and how formidable was that power, which, even if they
were abandoned to their own resources, they could still
oppose to the efforts of the Grand Alliance. They were,
in fact, determined to stand by Philip to the last; and
Philip was no less determined to stand by them   Louis
had already hinted that the growing pressure on the northern
frontier of France might compel him to withdraw every
French soldier from Spanish soil at no distant date. He
had even referred to the expediency of accepting peace
upon any terms. Unshaken by this prospect, his grandson
had replied, on April 17, as follows "My own resolution
has long been taken, and nothing in the world can make
me change it. God has set the crown of Spain upon my
head, I shall keep it there as long as I have a drop of blood
in my veins. This much I owe to my conscience, my honour,
and my subjects' love. I am sure that they will not
abandon me, whatever happens, and that if I expend my
life at their head, as I am determined to do, even to the
very last extremity, to remain with them, they will shed

---

[1] Round MSS Torcy to Petkum, October 30, 1707 (Hist. MSS Comm ,
14th Report, Appendix. part ix , p 322)
[2] Murray. vol iv , p 478, April 16, 1709. Marlborough to Moles,
April 16, 1709).

their blood, with equal cheerfulness, to keep me   Were I
capable of such cowardice as to resign my kingdom, you,
I am certain, would disown me as your grandson . . . I
will never sign a treaty unworthy of me. I will never quit
Spain save with my life, and I should infinitely prefer to
perish, disputing the ground foot by foot at the head of
my troops, rather than do anything which would sully, if
I may say so, the honour of our House."[1] The temper of
this epistle was the temper of the subjects of him who
wrote it. It was rumoured throughout the Peninsula
that the negotiations in Holland were deliberately intended
by Louis to culminate in the desertion of his grandson.
At once the popular fury exploded against France, while
the popular enthusiasm for Philip rose to heights which
it had never before attained. Two military events assisted
to inflame and to confirm the national spirit.   On April 18,
after a five months' defence, illustrated by circumstances
of the most romantic gallantry, the garrison of Alicante
marched out with the honours of war   Byng and Stanhope
had vainly endeavoured to relieve them. Their capitulation
left Charles without a foot of Spanish soil beyond the borders
of Catalonia. On the side of Portugal, Fronteira and
Galway had taken the field, in April, near Campo Mayor,
with 15,000 men, only 2,800 of whom were English. Contrary to Galway's advice, Fronteira passed the Caya, on
May 7, and engaged a Spanish army equal in number to
his own. As at Almanza, the Portuguese cavalry behaved
disgracefully. Both wings galloped off the field without
striking a blow, and though the Portuguese infantry showed
great steadiness, and the English came stoutly to their aid,
retreat was inevitable   Five guns were lost, and a British
brigade of 80 officers and 900 men laid down their arms
The fact that the victorious army was entirely Spanish in
its composition struck the imagination of the Spanish
people. As Stanhope pointed out to Marlborough, on
June 15, it increased the probability that "a treaty of
peace will not immediately put an end to the war in Spain."[2]

---

[1] Noailles, *Mémoires politiques et militaires*, t. iv., p. 45. Philippe V à Louis
XIV, 17 avril, 1709.
[2] Coxe Papers Stanhope to Marlborough, June 15, 1709, vol xl. (Brit.
Mus Add. MSS, 9117)

For it was proof positive that Philip's position was not, of necessity, dependent on the support of France. Torcy had realised that truth as long before as October, 1707, when he wrote the letter to Petkum which has already been cited.

The attitude, which the people of Spain adopted at this juncture, must have astonished many, who recollected the furious resentment, which the treaties of partition had formerly aroused in that country. By expelling Philip now, the Spaniards would have secured the integrity of their empire; by retaining him, they ensured its dismemberment. For one thing was certain. So long as the Hapsburg claimant was excluded from the throne, the Spanish possessions in Italy and the Netherlands, which the allies had recovered on the field of battle, would never again form part of the Spanish monarchy. Yet the mass of the nation adhered to Philip with an enthusiasm, which seemed to stultify all they had said and done when they were confronted with the treaties of partition. Their conduct, however, was neither so paradoxical nor so perverse as it appeared. Their inconsistency, in fact, was more superficial than real. A partition, which results from the fortune of war, differs essentially from a partition, which foreign powers presume to impose in time of peace A people, which has accepted trial by battle, can accept an adverse verdict without loss of honour; but no people can tamely submit to external dictation, and retain its self-respect. In 1702, the allies proposed a division of the Spanish monarchy; in 1709, on the contrary, they insisted that the Spanish monarchy should be preserved intact On both occasions, they incurred the hostility of the great majority of Spaniards, and for the same reason. That haughty race declined to recognise the right of foreign powers either to distribute its dominions or to dominate its kings. It repudiated, with disdain, " the chimerical and insolent pretensions of the English and the Dutch "[1] It would take no orders of any description from the potentates and parliaments of alien and heretic states. It stood, in short, upon that noble principle which was the very genesis and life-blood of the Grand Alliance, the principle of national inde-

[1] Noailles, t iv , p 13. Phillippe V à Louis XIV, 12 novembre, 1708

pendence. In engaging in a conflict with the Spanish people upon this issue, the coalised peoples of Europe were virtually engaging in a conflict with their own ideal of nationality. Morally, they were assuming a false position; practically, as the event proved, they were assuming an impossible one.

But Europe, as yet, was blind to the intensity and the profundity of Spanish patriotism The diplomatists, assembled at the Hague, recognised indeed that it would be easier for them to agree about the ultimate destiny of Philip than to give effect to their agreement. Marlborough, writing to Cadogan on May 24, particularly noted the evil influence of " the ill news from Portugal "[1] upon the course of the negotiations. Hare, in a letter of the 21st, commented with unjust severity on Galway's misfortune, and expressed anxiety as to the effect it might produce on both Dutch and French.[2] For the rest, however, the prospects of an early peace grew steadily brighter. On the 20th, Marlborough, Eugène, and Townshend returned the visits of Torcy, who presented them for the first time to Rouillé. It is unnecessary to recite in detail the numerous conferences and discussions which ensued, and which continued for an entire week The proceedings were characterised by remarkable firmness and unanimity on the part of the allies. Only once was their harmony disturbed. On the 23rd, Sinzendorf arrived. Eugène, like Marlborough, required assistance; but it does not appear that Eugène, like Marlborough, was vilified on that account. Sinzendorf took exception to the list of towns which the Dutch proposed to require from France for the purposes of their barrier. Eugène supported his colleague; and, for the moment, Marlborough was afraid that " all had been undone."[3] But the Dutch stood fast, and the Austrians were compelled to yield. As to Torcy and Rouillé, their attitude from day to day was one of gradual, and not ungraceful, concession. On the 20th, they granted the demands of

[1] Murray. vol iv , p 499: Marlborough to Cadogan, May 24, 1709.
[2] Hare MSS , May 10/21, 1709 (Hist MSS. Comm., 14th Report, Appendix, part ix , p 222)
[3] Coxe Papers. Letter to Godolphin, May 29, vol xxviii (Brit. Mus. Add. MSS , 9105)

England and Holland; but when it was insisted that Alsace should be restored to the Empire, they broke up the conference, and sent for their passports. On the morning of the 21st, however, they were easily persuaded by Petkum to resume the negotiation. They now consented to surrender Strasbourg, but this offer having been declined as inadequate, they again sent for their passports, and actually took formal leave of Marlborough and Eugène. These demonstrations made no impression on the allies. The passports were issued; but Torcy and Rouillé were warned by the States that, if they departed now, they would not be permitted to return. Perceiving the futility of their manœuvres, the Frenchmen affected to be convinced a second time by the arguments of Petkum and other representatives of neutral states. On the 23rd, they dispatched an express to Versailles, and once more reopened the discussions.

To cut short these interminable and wearisome conversations, which Marlborough compared to the proceedings in committees of the British Parliament, the allies decided to formulate their demands in writing On May 28, Torcy was presented with the complete set of the preliminaries of peace, embodied in forty-four articles, and signed by all the plenipotentiaries of the coalition Briefly, this document declared that an armistice would be granted for two months, during which time the entire Spanish monarchy must be surrendered to Charles, the fortresses of Furnes, Knocke, Menin, Ypres, Lille, Condé, and Maubeuge formally made over to Holland, the fortifications and harbour of Dunkirk destroyed, the Pretender expelled from France, Newfoundland ceded to England, and Strasbourg, Kehl, and Breisach evacuated in favour of the Emperor. If these conditions were fulfilled, the armistice was then to be renewed, and the details of a general peace to be finally adjusted. "In case," said Article XXXVII, "the King of France executes all that is above mentioned, *and that the whole monarchy of Spain is delivered up and yielded to King Charles III as is stipulated by these articles, within the limited time,* 'tis agreed, that the cessation of arms between the parties in war shall continue till the conclusion

and ratification of the treaties which are to be made."[1]
This article crystallised the issue, which was, in effect,
the only vital issue. In ordaining that the renewal of the
armistice should be dependent on the absolute surrender
of "the whole monarchy of Spain," it raised the delicate
question of Louis' ability, and willingness, to persuade or
to coerce his grandson. The allies foresaw that, even after
Louis had faithfully executed those of the preliminaries
which it was obviously competent for him to execute, the
greater part of the Spanish monarchy might still remain
in the actual possession of Philip. For this contingency,
they provided in Article IV, which contained the following
paragraph: " But if it should happen that the said Duke
of Anjou does not consent and agree to the execution of
the present convention, before the expiration of the term
aforesaid, *the Most Christian King, and the Princes and
States concerned in the present treaty, shall, in concert, take
convenient measures to secure the full execution thereof*"[2]

Torcy and Rouillé refused to sign They represented
that they could not commit themselves to all the preliminaries without exceeding their powers But Torcy
undertook to start immediately for Versailles, that he
might explain the position to Louis, and procure a ratification under the King's own hand. That very day he
departed, leaving Rouillé behind him, and promising that
a definite decision should be received not later than June 4
Although, in certain quarters, the refusal to sign excited
both surprise and misgiving, the opinion was widely held
that peace was at hand.

Marlborough shared in the prevalent belief. " I flatter
myself," he wrote to Wratislaw on the 31st, " that the
situation, in which they find themselves, will oblige them
to accept "[3] " I do verily believe," he wrote to his wife,
on the same date, " the condition of France is such that
they must submit to the conditions we have given them."[4]
In a similar strain, he wrote to Stanhope on the 27th.

[1] Lamberty, t v,. p 289. " Préliminaires pour la paix avec la France,"
28 mai, 1709   [2] *Ibid.*
[3] Murray, vol iv., p. 500. Marlborough to Wratislaw, May 31, 1709.
[4] Coxe Papers The Duke to the Duchess, May 31, 1709 (Brit Mus Add.
MSS , 9105).

On June 4, when he was still in ignorance of the event, he expressed the same view in a letter to Eugène, who had gone to Brussels. On June 4, also, he was actually in communication with Godolphin in regard to the return of the British troops and the payment of all arrears to the foreign auxiliaries. That very day, a French courier left a note from Torcy for the Prince of Savoy at Brussels, and proceeding to the Hague on the 5th, delivered Louis' answer to Rouillé. The King declined to ratify the preliminaries.

Rouillé announced his master's decision in a tone surprisingly haughty. Louis entered specific objections to several articles, including the XXXVII. But the plenipotentiaries of the allies unanimously refused to recede from any one of them. They were supported in this attitude by the States-General Rouillé was warned that, if France persisted in rejecting the terms now proffered, the allies would consider themselves free to enlarge their demands upon a future occasion. " Pressed to declare if he had any secret orders tending to peace," the Frenchman virtually admitted, on the 8th, that Louis would sign, if Article XXXVII were dropped. For answer he received his passport the same evening At the last moment, Petkum proposed that France should surrender two or three towns as an equivalent for Article XXXVII. But this device was regarded merely as an attempt to bribe the Dutch with an enlargement of their barrier. On the morning of the 9th, Rouillé took his departure.

Surprised and disappointed as he was at the turn of events, Marlborough resolutely refused to abandon hope. " I am apt to think," he wrote to Somers, on the 7th, " the French Court will soon be convinced of their error and accept of the terms that are offered them."[1] And Hare, in a letter of the same date, observed · " I dare say, if Rouillé carries the jest so far as to leave this place, he will return before he goes to Paris, and that one way or other we shall have peace without fighting for it."[2] On the afternoon of the 9th, the Duke set out to join the army. Passing by

---

[1] Murray, vol iv , p 504· Marlborough to Somers, June 7, 1709
[2] Hare MSS.. Letter of June 7, 1709 (Hist MSS Comm , 14th Report, Appendix, part ix , p 224).

Rotterdam and Antwerp, he reached Brussels on the 11th, some hours in advance of Rouillé, who had started before him. In company with Eugène, he determined to try his fortune at a final interview with the French envoy. Orders were issued to detain Rouillé when he stopped to change horses, but through some misunderstanding they were not obeyed, and the opportunity was lost

The failure of the negotiations astonished Europe. The suffering people of France received the unexpected tidings with the stupefaction of despair. But not for long did they succumb to this unmanly weakness. In a circular letter, addressed to the governors of provinces, the King appealed to the nation in language of superb dignity and pathos. Having shown how, in return for a bare armistice of two months, France had been required to strip herself naked before her implacable foes, he touched with indignant scorn on the suggestion that he himself should expel his grandson from Spain, and protested that it was " against humanity " to believe that the allies had ever imagined him to be capable of such an action   " Although the tenderness I have for my people," he said, " be as hearty as for my own children, although I bear a part in all the ills which the war makes such faithful subjects undergo, and I have shown to all Europe that I sincerely desire to make them enjoy peace, I am persuaded they would themselves oppose the acceptance of it on conditions equally opposite to justice and to the honour of the French nation." In conclusion, he declared that he had set his trust in God, " hoping that the purity of my intentions will draw the divine blessing on my arms "[1] And simultaneously he addressed a second letter to the archbishops and bishops of the realm, exhorting them " to excite again the fervency of prayers in their respective dioceses " These moving documents achieved their full purpose The proud and warlike nation was profoundly touched. The rich sent in their plate to the Treasury The poor flocked to the frontiers, where at least they could find bread for their bellies, and powder and steel wherewith to chastise the

[1] Lamberty, t v , p. 300: Lettre du Roi de France aux Gouverneurs des Provinces

authors of their misery. The people applauded the action
of their monarch. They appreciated the confidence which
he reposed in them, and they determined to show him that
it was not misplaced These "odious pretensions,"[1] as
Noailles called them, these "revolting propositions,"[2] as
Villars termed them, must be resisted to the death.

The net result of the abortive negotiation was therefore
a clear advantage to France. This advantage did not
consist in a waste of the coalition's time, for owing to the
cold and wet, and the general backwardness of the season,
the campaign must, in any event, have opened late [3] It
did not consist in a neglect of the coalition's preparations,
for Marlborough and Eugène, "trusting little to the shews
of peace,"[4] had left nothing undone to ensure the readiness
of the army for the field. The gain to France was essentially a moral one. Inspired by a new and unanimous spirit
of loyalty to the throne and devotion to the fatherland,
the nation rose superior to its calamities, and confronted
its triumphant foes with an assured and resolute air, which
nothing in its material circumstances appeared to justify.

This very unpleasant, and wholly unforeseen, consequence
of their diplomacy did not escape the observation of the
allies They now considered, or affected to consider, that
Louis, from the outset, had been working solely for this
end, and that he had all along intended that the protracted
and laborious negotiation should be shipwrecked on the
XXXVII article of the preliminaries They represented
his proceedings as "a masterpiece of French artifice."[5]
"A chicane," Godolphin called them, and "a deliberate
insincerity."[6] Louis had only himself and his own record
to thank for it, if the statesmen of Europe regarded him as a
monster of sagacious perfidy. But, on this occasion, the
statesmen of Europe were wrong. Posterity has declined
to swallow a theory, which was only advanced at the time

---

[1] Noailles, t. iv., p 57
[2] *Memoires de Villars*, Appendice 250 Villars au Roi, 6 juin, 1709.
[3] Hare MSS Letter of May 21, 1709 (Hist MSS Comm., 14th Report,
Appendix, part ix , p 223).
[4] Lediard, vol. ii., p 455
[5] *The History of the Treaty of Utrecht* (1712), p 46
[6] Coxe Papers: Godolphin to Marlborough, May 31, 1709 (Brit. Mus.
Add MSS , 9105).

in the teeth of an overwhelming presumption to the contrary.[1] Posterity has accepted the judgment of Lecky, who declares that "Louis, resolving on peace at any price, submitted to the allies the most humiliating offers ever made by a French King," only to be met with an additional demand "as impolitic as it was barbarous." And the same authority observes that "there are few instances in modern history of a more scandalous abuse of the rights of conquest than this transaction."[2]

In truth, the allies had badly overreached themselves. They were right to be severe, for Louis had conspired against the liberties of Europe. They were right to be cautious, for Louis had kept bad faith both in peace and war. But they were guilty of a stupendous folly in insisting that a King of France should turn his arms against his own grandson. For thus they compelled a proud and sensitive race, every man of which has ever been a potential warrior, to find new resources in itself at a moment when all resources seemed to be exhausted. "Louis XIV," says Bolingbroke, "had treated mankind with too much inhumanity in his prosperous days to have any reason to complain even of this proposition. His people indeed . . might pity his distress. This happened, and he found his account in it."[3] The responsibility for so criminal a blunder rests upon the British, Dutch, and Austrian governments. For the House of Hapsburg, which was demanding the restitution of what it claimed as its lawful inheritance, some excuses may be found. For Holland, too, it may at least be urged that, eager though she was to humble the tyrant who for years had menaced her existence, she acted in this matter as the obedient servant of those Whig ministers, from whom she hoped to obtain in return her Barrier Treaty. England, in fact, controlled the issue. The Junta could have saved the situation, had they wished. But the Junta regarded the preliminaries as erring, if at all, on the side of leniency. They regarded it as no more

---

[1] Even Hallam, who is very reluctant to allow that Godolphin and the Junta might have erred, admits that there is "no decisive evidence" of Louis' insincerity *Constitutional History of England*, vol iii, p 210 (see note at the bottom of the page).

[2] Lecky. *England in the Eighteenth Century*, vol i, pp 57, 58.

[3] *Letters on the Study and Use of History*, letter viii

than reasonable to demand that Philip should be removed
from the Spanish throne by the hand which placed him
there.[1] It was always one of the vices of their party to
subordinate the common instincts and the common sense
of mankind to the dictates of an arid logic.

In the summer of 1709, it was perfectly futile to approach
the Spanish problem as it might have been approached
in 1702, or even in 1706   Owing entirely to the inordinate
duration of the war, Philip was now so firmly established
in the hearts of his subjects, as to be practically independent
of the support of France.   Consequently, he could only
be expelled in one of two ways.   A French army might
march to the assistance of Starhemberg and Galway, as
was contemplated by the preliminaries, which Louis had
refused to sign; or the coalition might make its peace with
France, and might subsequently concentrate its entire
forces upon the peninsula.   Godolphin regarded this second
alternative as extremely objectionable.   He believed, and
not without reason, that, if peace were concluded between
the Grand Alliance and France, the burden of recovering
Spain would devolve upon England alone.   For he believed
that Holland would contribute nothing, and Austria, next
to nothing, to the common task.   He believed, moreover,
that France could not be trusted to remain quiescent while
Philip was being driven from the Spanish throne.   In his
view, therefore, as in the view of the Junta, it was preferable
to continue the war under the old conditions, and he openly
rejoiced at the collapse of the negotiations.   " I am very
glad," he wrote to the Duke, on May 31, " that by your
great precaution and the firmness of Holland their artifice
is pretty well discovered and so far eluded that I hope
nobody will be the worse but themselves for this shameful
proceeding "[2]   Marlborough, however, did not concur.
Moderation was not, in his judgment, a conspicuous feature
of the preliminaries as a whole.   On the contrary, in a
letter written to Stanhope a week before Louis' refusal
was received, he described them as " the utmost that we
could dare to expect "[3]   Stanhope emphatically agreed,

[1] See, for example, Burnet, vol vi., p 22
[2] Coxe Papers: Godolphin to Marlborough, May 31, 1709 (Brit. Mus.
Add. MSS., 9105).
[3] Coxe, vol ii , p 409. Marlborough to Stanhope, May 27, 1709.

and characterised them as "beyond what we ever could imagine or hope."[1] Evidently, therefore, Marlborough considered that the coalition's claim had been drawn upon the amplest scale, and that something less might reasonably have been accepted. As to the stipulation that Philip, if he refused to go, should be ejected by French bayonets, the Duke made no secret of his own opinion. "If I were in the place of the King of France," he said, "I should venture the loss of my country much sooner than be obliged to join my troops for the forcing of my grandson."[2] Why, then, did he not resist the inclusion of this article in the list of preliminaries? There were several reasons. In the first place, he no longer controlled the policy of England; in the second, he was daily losing his influence over the statesmen of Holland; and in the third, he honestly believed at the time that the condition of France was so depressed that no humiliation was too gross for her to endure.

Europe had been so long habituated to regard the Duke as the dominating personality of the Grand Alliance, that the full effect of the recent changes in the domestic politics of England was not yet understood even by his own country-men. In many quarters, therefore, the failure of the negotiations was ascribed to him The Tories openly alleged that he preferred war to peace, because he found war more remunerative. The charge was as unjust as it was untrue, but he could make no effective reply to it without disclosing to the world the divergence between his own views and those of the ministry which he served. Torcy, however, is a faithful witness as to the Duke's real attitude on this question. Marlborough told him privately that, if Louis abandoned Philip, the allies could easily recover Spain for Charles afterwards. When Torcy quoted these words in the presence of the plenipotentiaries, Marl-borough did not disown them. He simply said, in accord-ance with the views of his employers, that the settlement must be final, and that the coalition must not be left with a second war on its hands. On a subsequent occasion, both Marlborough and Eugène declared, in Torcy's presence, that, as a military problem, the conquest of Spain alone

[1] Coxe Papers : Stanhope to Marlborough, June 22, 1709 (Brit Mus. Add MSS., 9117)
[2] *Heinsius Archives:* Marlborough to Heinsius, July 10, 1709.

would not be difficult. But Heinsius and Townshend
dissented from this opinion, and declined to be influenced
by it Moreover, the Duke's private correspondence
reveals his true sentiments. To Stanhope he wrote, on
May 27, that he considered the obnoxious provision as to
the employment of French troops against Philip to be
quite unnecessary, because " when the French have delivered
us all the cautionary towns, and complied with everything
else on this side, we shall have the better end of the staff."[1]
And to Godolphin he wrote, on June 16: " I have as much
mistrust for the sincerity of France as anybody living can
have, but I will own to you that, in my opinion, if France
had delivered the towns promised by the preliminaries, and
demolished Dunkirk and the other towns mentioned, they
must have been at our discretion, so that if they had played
tricks, so much the worse for themselves "[2] Godolphin,
who totally disagreed with him, replied, on the 27th, as
follows: " I shall keep your opinion in that matter to
myself, because, if it were known, I am afraid it might
discourage people both here and in Holland."[3]

Goslinga would not have been Goslinga, had he neglected
so admirable an opportunity of enlarging on his favourite
theme He was very indignant at the rupture of the negotiations. He considered that, if Louis could not be otherwise
induced to ratify the preliminaries, Article XXXVII ought
to have been omitted by the Grand Alliance. In support
of this opinion, he privately delivered an oration to Marlborough with all his accustomed vigour and freedom. He
was in ignorance, of course, that he was preaching to the
converted, and in ignorance he was permitted to remain.
For Marlborough, who was only too painfully aware of the
field-deputy's magnificent talent for indiscretion, ignored
his argument altogether, and simply requested him not to
create dissensions among the allies, who had acted throughout with complete unanimity. This treatment did not
astonish Goslinga, because, as he explains, previous experiences had convinced him that Marlborough " passionately
desired the continuance of the war, through resentment at
the refusal of the governorship of the Low Countries, and

[1] Coxe, vol ii , p 409 Marlborough to Stanhope, May 27, 1709.
[2] I id , Marlborough to Godolphin, June 16, 1709
[3] Ibid., p 410: Godolphin to Marlborough, June 27, 1709.

through ambition and covetousness of money."[1] He subsequently discoursed upon the same topic to Eugène, who showed himself more than sympathetic. " I am very glad," said the Prince, " to find that these are your sentiments; they are mine too In four campaigns we should not obtain what we might have now by a stroke of the pen and without spilling a drop of blood."[2] Eugène, moreover, gave him permission to repeat the substance of this interview to his friends at the Hague. Trouble resulted, and it became necessary to make representations to the Prince upon the subject But Goslinga appears to exult over the fact that the mischief was already done. As his patriotism cannot be questioned, his judgment must be inexorably condemned For it was playing the game of France with a vengeance, deliberately to use the failure of the negotiations as an apple of discord among the allies. Marlborough, who was fully conscious that Goslinga's was not the only tongue that would accuse him of wickedly prolonging the struggle, acted in this matter like a high-minded statesman. His wise and self-denying reticence was requited, both at home and abroad, with the basest calumny He, whose renown had long been the most illustrious in Europe, was accused of ambition, he, who had just refused a bribe of four million livres, was accused of avarice.

For the rest, it is highly significant that Eugène, who, like Marlborough, served a government, which regarded the preliminaries as erring on the side of leniency, and who, unlike Marlborough, was personally interested in the humiliation of Louis XIV, should nevertheless have shared his colleague's views as to Article XXXVII The fact itself does not rest upon Goslinga's testimony alone. " The Prince of Savoy," wrote Marlborough to Lord Townshend, on June 13, " is of opinion that we should have explained the 37th Article and have made it easy, thinking the French were sufficiently in our power when they had put us in possession of the towns this is only for your own information "[3] Upon a question of the higher strategy (for such, in effect, this question really was), the combined judgment of the two greatest soldiers of that age was preferable to the most mature decision of the Cabinets of London and Vienna.

---

[1] *Mémoires de Goslinga*, p 101   [2] *Ibid*, p. 102.
[3] Murray, vol iv, p. 505 · Marlborough to Lord Townshend, June 13, 1709.

XXV.—TOURNAI

Louis had sincerely desired peace, and honestly ensued it; but he too, like Marlborough and Eugène, had not neglected to prepare for war As early as March he had chosen the generals who were to command upon the threatened borders, Berwick in Dauphiné, Harcourt on the Rhine, and Villars in Flanders. The last appointment he would have assigned to Boufflers, had Boufflers' health been equal to the task. But Villars was the better choice. By common consent the cloud in the north-east was the blackest of all the black clouds impending over France. Villars, the fortunate, Villars, the unbeaten, Villars, who in 1703 had menaced Vienna itself, who in 1705 had barred the path across Lorraine to Paris, and who as late as 1707 had overrun Wurttemberg and Brabant, was before all others the best fitted to confront the storm

The Marshal arrived on the Belgian frontier in the middle of March. "I was unable," he says, " before starting, to formulate a plan of campaign, because I did not know whether I should find an army there. The enemy were reporting and stoutly asseverating, in all their journals, that it would be impossible to create one, or at any rate to maintain one. As a matter of fact I found the troops in a deplorable condition, without clothes, without arms, without bread."[1] The famished soldiery were selling their uniforms, and even their weapons. The officers suffered no less than the men. As the terrible results of the ruinous winter became more and more apparent, Villars realised that he would be compelled to face the forthcoming campaign without magazines. Such corn as could be discovered, was only to be purchased at an outrageous price. And Villars had no money in his treasury. It was as much

---

[1] *Vie de Villars*, t. ii., p. 30.

as he could do to procure for the army a bare subsistence from day to day.

In one respect, however, Villars was more than satisfied with the condition of his command   He noticed from the outset the recruits, of whom there was no deficiency, were men, possessed of unusually good physique, and accustomed to fatigue. " The misery of the countryside "[1] was driving the tough peasantry of France to exchange the starvation of the villages for the semi-starvation of the frontiers. He was struck, moreover, by the resolute bearing of his lean and leggy soldiery, and by their air of patient fortitude. When, as was his wont in the most depressing circumstances, he moved amongst them, with words of comfort and exhortation, he would often hear them say, " M. le Maréchal is right, there are times when it is necessary to suffer."[2]

But Villars was too good a general to believe that this army, with all its resignation and pathetic courage, could face the victorious and confident veterans of Marlborough and Eugène in the open field. Without money, and without bread, it is still possible to win battles, but without *moral*, it is impossible.   The problem of restoring that *moral*, which from the day of the Schellenberg to the day of Wynen-dael had steadily dwindled towards vanishing-point, was the grand problem which Villars had now to solve.   He did not deceive himself in regard to it.   He did not imagine that in one campaign he could raise the spirit of the French soldier to the level at which Condé, Turenne, and Luxembourg had left it.   For the present, his object was to create a force which, if it were attacked in an entrenched position, could be trusted to stand its ground with a reasonable expectation of repelling its assailants.   To this end he exerted to the utmost his exceptional powers of invention and rhodomontade   He gave currency to a tale that, before quitting Paris, he had demanded nine million livres in cash for the uses of the army, and that he had refused to start for the frontier until the money was paid over.   This promising legend was reproduced in the Dutch newspapers, where he himself perused it with the parental pride which only authors know   Although he experienced no little

[1] *Ibid* , p. 34.   [2] *Ibid*,

difficulty in providing the troops from day to day with an inadequate quantity of rye and oats, he brazenly pretended that he possessed a superfluity of flour, and that a sufficient subsistence for the summer was assured. " Villars," says Saint-Simon, "set to work to boast like a bully, and to advocate insane proposals in his usual style. He breathed of nothing but battles, he gave out that nothing but a battle could save the state, and that he would fight one in the plains of Lens at the outset of the campaign."[1] The same authority records that the swaggering demeanour of the Marshal excited the disgust of men of sense. But Villars had never been popular among the courtiers, whose censure he derided and whose approbation he despised. He considered it his business to revive confidence not only in the army, but in the government itself. Referring to the anxiety which the proximity of Marlborough and Eugène excited at Versailles, he wrote to Chamillart as follows· " I highly esteem these two great generals; but just as our countrymen exalt them to the skies, so too there are perhaps some Germans who honour me with a little attention."[2] To Torcy he wrote in April that " a successful battle at an early date " was the " sole resource " of France, and that he should fight one " in good heart."[3] In May, when Torcy was at the Hague and the allies were representing that the French army was in no condition to take the field, Villars encouraged the ambassador in a long dispatch, in which he insisted that his command was at its full strength, that subsistence for June and July was assured, and that the men were as eager as himself to encounter the enemy.

But talking and writing were not the only weapons which the Marshal used. He occupied some advanced posts, which threatened the enemy's communications with Menin and Lille, carried off the labourers repairing the roads, and rendered the passage of convoys impossible otherwise than by an exiguous service of boats upon the Schelde. Had he been able to accumulate a sufficiency of flour, he would have laid siege to Courtrai. By these activities he improved the condition and raised the spirit of his army. " It

[1] *Mémoires de Saint-Simon*, vol. xiii., p 93
[2] *Vie de Villars*, t ii , p 35 Lettre à M de Chamillart.
[3] *Ibid* p 42 Lettre à M de Torcy, 21 avril.

seemed," he says, " that the very extremity to which we
were reduced, inflamed the courage of the troops; and I
have never seen them in such good heart."[1] He succeeded,
moreover, in partially dispelling the gloom which enveloped
Versailles. " It is from you alone, Monsieur," wrote
Madame de Maintenon on April 8, " that we derive any
consolation."[2] On May 26 she informed him that the
ladies of St. Cyr were so impressed by the miracles he
was performing on the frontier that they regarded him
as a saint.[3] The King, to whom Villars had reported the
melancholy situation of Max Emanuel at Mons, replied
that the Elector had only himself to blame for the loss of
Bavaria. " If you," he said, " had remained there, I have
reason to think that things would not have turned out as
they have."[4] Early in May the Marshal was summoned
to a council of war at Marly, where he speedily discovered
that he could obtain neither instructions nor assistance.
" I put my confidence in God and in you,"[5] was the King's
last word at parting.

Notwithstanding his extravagances of language, Villars
fully realised the responsibility of his position. Even
Saint-Simon admits that. He admits also that there was
a method in the Marshal's madness. Undoubtedly this
bragging and valiant Gascon, who, because he had done
much, had a right to talk much if he thought it expedient,
exercised a beneficial influence on the government and the
army at a moment of definite crisis. Torcy, returning from
the Hague with the preliminaries in his pocket, read them to
Villars at Douai. The Marshal, as he wrote to Louis, could
not disguise his indignation. He declared at once that it
was impossible for the King to accept such terms. He
learned with delight of " the noble, wise, and just resolution " to continue the struggle. " I was at the head of
your infantry," he said, " when the courier brought me
Your Majesty's despatch. At the opening lines, which
indicated your decision, I showed my satisfaction to the
troops, who all responded with a shout of joy and eagerness
for battle."[6]

[1] *Ibid*, p 51.
[2] *Ibid*, p 38 Lettre de Mme de Maintenon, 8 avril
[3] *Ibid*, 26 mai.   [4] *Ibid*.. Lettre du Roi, 29 mars.
[5] *Ibid*, p 45   [6] *Ibid* p 54 Lettre au Roi, 6 juin.

Marlborough and Eugène quitted Brussels on June 12, and took the way to Audenarde. Having successfully circumvented a French party, which was lurking in the neighbourhood, they arrived at Alost, where they learned that the roads across the country " were almost impracticable "[1] through the continual rains. They therefore proceeded by the causeway to Ghent. At a council of war, on the 13th, it was unanimously decided to defer the concentration of the army until the weather became more settled and the roads had been repaired. On the 15th the two commanders visited Nivelles and reviewed the Prussian troops. On the 17th they set off for Lille. Orders were issued to the several detachments to move upon Courtrai and Menin " as fast as the unseasonable weather and continual rains would permit "[2] At Courtrai, on the 17th, Marlborough and Eugène were disagreeably surprised to learn from Dopf that very little flour had been accumulated there or at Menin, and none at all at Lille. Marlborough wrote strongly on the subject to the States Deputies at Brussels, urging them to bring pressure to bear upon the contractors [3] He wrote also to the magistrates of Bruges[4] and Ghent,[5] and to the Council of State at Brussels, insisting that such provisions as had arrived from England and Holland, or elsewhere, should be forwarded without delay. Prompt measures were essential, if the army, as it advanced into the plains of Lille, was to get sustenance for man and beast. That city itself had suffered frightfully from the severe winter; and Marlborough had received " a dismal account of the scarcity of forage on the ground, besides that the French ravage and destroy the little there is before them to distress us the more when we approach them."[6]

The two commanders arrived at Lille on the evening of the 18th Here they were informed that Villars had been entrenching himself between Lens and La Bassée since the 14th. " It were to be wished," wrote Marlborough to Heinsius, " we had better weather that we might join

[1] Murray, vol iv , p 504. Marlborough to Lord Townshend, June 13, 1709.
[2] Ibid., p. 510: Marlborough to Boyle, June 20, 1709
[3] Ibid , p 508· Marlborough to the States Deputies, June 18, 1709.
[4] Ibid., p 512 Marlborough to the Magistrates of Bruges, June 22, 1709.
[5] Ibid , p. 512 Marlborough to the Magistrates of Ghent, June 22, 1709
[6] Ibid , p 507· Marlborough to Mr. Secretary Boyle, June 16, 1709.

him before he has finished."[1] But the army was not
assembled in the neighbourhood of Menin until the 21st.
On the 22nd it advanced to Roubaix, and on the 23rd to
the plains upon the southern side of Lille. Marlborough
took up his quarters at the Abbey of Loos, and Eugène at
the château of Lompret. The forces under their command
amounted to at least 110,000 men, a total which was never
reached on any other occasion during the whole war.

Even the indomitable Villars could hardly contemplate
so immense an accumulation of confident and war-hardened
troops under the greatest commanders of the age without
a tremor. Many of his general-officers were quite unnerved
by the spectacle. They urged him to fall back to a less
exposed position behind the Scarpe; and when he refused,
they publicly complained of his temerity in an unrestrained
fashion well calculated to destroy that *moral* which he had
been painfully building up among the soldiery Chamillart,
who, though an honest and able man, was unequal to the
exceptional emergency which had now arisen, had been
removed from the War Office in June. To his successor,
Voisin, Villars wrote in reference to the suggestion of a
retirement to the Scarpe, " I ask whether the army is to
defend the kingdom, or the kingdom to cover the army."
In the same letter he appealed to a maxim of Turenne to
the effect that " he who would absolutely avoid a battle
makes a present of his country to him who seeks one."[2]
He added that the criticisms of his officers " render the
burden which I bear very heavy. You will never hear that
my countenance gives anybody reason to suspect that I
find it so; but one has one's bad nights."[3] He also suggested that the presence of some of the princes of the blood
might silence the ' croakers.' But only the English
Pretender, the Chevalier de St. George, was permitted to
serve.

The line which Villars was proposing to defend was the
most advanced line which it was in his power to occupy.
It extended from Aire and St. Venant on the left through
Béthune and Douai to Valenciennes on the right. The

[1] *Ibid* , p 509· Marlborough to the Pensioner, June 19, 1709.
[2] *Vie de Villars*, t ii p 56 Lettre au Ministre, des 14 et 16 juin
[3] *Ibid.*

French were still in possession of Ypres, Tournai, and Mons; but the capture of Lille had largely neutralised the strategical value of those fortresses. From Lille the allies would safely enter France. But Villars was determined to abandon not an inch of French territory which it was possible to hold with any reasonable prospect of success. In selecting the line from Aire to Valenciennes, he selected the foremost position capable of defence against the allied army. On the 14th he concentrated the bulk of his forces at the point of his extensive front which lay within the shortest march of Lille. He fixed his camp between Hulluch and Cuinchy, a little to the south of La Bassée. Here his extreme right was protected by the canal of Douai, and his extreme left by the fortress of Béthune, while both flanks were completely covered by streams and marshes which the heavy rains had rendered impassable. His centre was partially defended by inundations, and by villages which he occupied and fortified with redoubts, but he strengthened it from end to end with a rampart fifteen feet thick and a ditch eighteen feet wide When the allies advanced to Lille, he ordered a second ditch to be dug at a distance of thirty paces in advance of the first. "Nothing," he says, "is more dangerous to an enemy"[1] That he was right, the allies had formerly proved to their cost, when they expended their fascines on the hollow road which lay before the Bavarian entrenchments at the Schellenberg Moreover, the Marshal cleared the ground of every tree and bush that would afford cover to assailants, or impede the fire of the defence. His batteries were posted with excellent judgment. But they were manned most strongly on the heights of Cambrai, which dominated the highroad for Lille. Finally, he constructed redoubts between Béthune and St. Venant to cover a march in that direction.

Villars had 80,000 men under his command, including a numerous and admirable cavalry, and he continued to feed and pay them somehow. The King and the nobility were melting down their plate for the service, and by threats of military execution, the Marshal compelled the nearest towns to disgorge their reserves of grain. Though the

[1] *Vie de Villars*, t. ii., p. 61.

soldiers were reduced at times to half and even quarter rations, and though they sometimes saluted the Marshal with the cry of " give us this day our daily bread,"[1] their spirit continued to be excellent If only the enemy could be induced to deliver a frontal attack upon them, they might be expected to render an excellent account of themselves.

There was at least a possibility that the Marshal's wish might be gratified. It is not to be supposed that Marlborough had forgotten that project of an advance on Abbeville, which he had reluctantly abandoned in the preceding campaign in favour of the siege of Lille. Lille being now in his possession, as well as Ghent and Bruges, certain of the risks attending such a movement were greatly diminished. But the situation at the end of June, 1709, differed from the situation at the end of July, 1708, in one essential respect. When Marlborough desired, after Oudenarde, to march towards Abbeville, the French army which he was proposing to ignore was a beaten army under generals notoriously divided. But the grim and desperate forces, assembled in the lines of La Bassée, by no means answered to the same description. Uncorrupted by luxury, and infuriated by suffering, they were commanded by an enterprising and energetic soldier, whose faith in his own star they fully shared. Marlborough knew well that, in the face of such an antagonist, there was a limit to the number of points which he could safely throw away.

The army of Villars must be destroyed, or at least put out of action, before the allies could venture to begin their march upon Montrocul and Abbeville.

Upon the receipt of reliable information from Arras to the effect that Villars was determined to stand his ground, Dopf and Cadogan rode out on the 24th with an escort of 1,200 horse to view his position and examine the approaches to it They obtained the impression that it was impregnable. Cadogan is said to have disguised himself as a peasant, and to have narrowly escaped capture in his anxiety to ascertain the truth. Their report was so unfavourable that Marlborough and Eugène decided to abandon the idea of a direct attack upon the French army.

[1] *Ibid.*, p 60

According to information supplied to Villars, this resolution was only taken after a heated discussion, at which Marlborough and Eugène insisted upon a battle and the Dutch field-deputies refused to allow it. Neither the narrative of Goslinga nor the correspondence of Marlborough lends any colour to this story. " If it had been reasonable," wrote the Duke to his wife on the 27th, " this letter would have brought you the news of a battle, but Prince Eugène, myself, and all the generals, did not think it advisable to run so great a hazard."[1] It is at least conceivable that, at another time, Marlborough might have been eager to make the venture. But on the collapse of the negotiations with Torcy, the war had entered, in Marlborough's opinion, on a novel and peculiar phase. Although both sides had professed the utmost indignation at that collapse, and although the French had formally revoked the whole of the offers which they had made, while the allies had announced their intention of increasing their demands, the Duke remained firmly convinced that peace might be expected at any moment. The parties had approached so near to an agreement, and the economic distress of France was so extreme that he could not induce himself to believe that the rupture was final. If he were correct in his judgment, there was no necessity, for the present, at any rate, to accept great risks. For the present it would suffice to maintain the existing pressure on the French nation.

His strategy was probably modified by these ideas Recognising that starvation was now become a powerful ally, he had already instigated both the Dutch and English Admiralties to concentrate their attention both in the Baltic and the Mediterranean, upon the cornships bound for French and Spanish ports. By an Order in Council the right of seizure had been extended to neutral bottoms. " They sent," says Burnet, " to all places for corn to preserve their people," and notably to the coasts of Barbary. But " many of the ships that brought it to them," says the same authority, " were taken by our men-of-war." Marlborough believed that France could not much longer endure

[1] Coxe, vol. n , p 420: The Duke to the Duchess, June 27, 1709.

the strain. Proceeding upon that hypothesis, he readily agreed that it was unnecessary to sacrifice thousands of lives in an assault upon the lines of La Bassée.

The council of war decided that the position which Villars had adopted must be turned. But if it was to be turned by the left, the fortress of Ypres must first be taken, and if by the right, the fortresses of Tournai and Mons According-ing to Goslinga, Marlborough was in favour of the former plan, and everybody else of the latter. There was some-thing to be said on both sides. Ypres, though well pro-tected by inundations, was, on the whole, a less powerful place than Tournai, but it was strongly garrisoned. Tournai was a place of exceptional strength, and its citadel, a masterpiece of Vauban's genius, was regarded by the great Condé as the first in Europe, but its garrison had been dangerously reduced by Villars, who was persuaded that if the enemy did not attack him in his lines, they would invest Ypres. Goslinga pretends that, in advocating the siege, Marlborough had his eye upon Dunkirk. The state-ment is without foundation. Unlike the Dutch, whose paramount motive was the acquisition of more and more towns for their barrier, Marlborough was swayed by con-siderations of pure strategy. It was not upon Dunkirk that his eye was fixed, but upon the French sea-board from Calais to Abbeville. But believing, as he did, that peace was at hand, he was not disposed to insist upon this aspect of the question. If, however, it were to be regarded as a matter of no ulterior importance by which flank the lines of La Bassée were turned, so long as they were turned, he recognised that the evident fact that Villars was alarmed for the safety of Ypres would greatly facilitate the in-vestment of Tournai. Moreover, in establishing itself before Tournai, the allied army would cover Brussels and Brabant.

Had Villars known, or even suspected, that Tournai was in danger, he would have endeavoured to reinforce the garrison, and possibly to interfere with the preliminary motions of the allied army. But the secret was well kept. On both sides it was believed that the lines were to be attacked. The reconnaissance of the 24th, the appearance of Marlborough's pioneers, on the same day, on the roads leading to La Bassée, and a second reconnaissance of the 25th, which only confirmed the results of the first, all pointed to one and the same conclusion. On the 25th, "dispositions were made," says Hare, "for a march, which everybody moreover took for granted was towards the enemy, though nobody could tell how it was possible to come at them."[1] All the information which reached the French camp was to the same effect. It was duly confirmed by the reports of deserters. On the morning of the 26th, a council of war was held "to take, as 'twas industriously given out, proper measures to attack the French"[2] Thereupon the heavy baggage was sent off to Lille. At 9 in the evening the army marched. Eugène and the Imperialists advanced at first towards La Bassée, and then struck away towards the north-west, as though they intended to turn the lines on the side of St. Venant. Marlborough moved southward with his centre and right, as if to effect a similar manœuvre on the side of Douai; but behind this screen, his left defiled in silence and without beating a drum by way of Pont-à-Trenin upon Tournai. At 7 on the morning of the 27th, the astonished soldiery beheld in the distance the grey and massive towers of the most majestic cathedral in the Spanish Netherlands "Hardly anybody suspected whither we were going," wrote Hare, "and this morning, to the surprise of ourselves as well as the enemy, we find ourselves before Tournai."[3] Marlborough came up with the main body in the course of the day and encamped between Antoing and the Douai road. On the march he had detached a force under the Prince of Orange to drive the French from the fortified posts of St. Amand and Mortagne. Orange executed his orders without losing a man. Meantime, Dompré, who had been left at Alost with nine squadrons and five battalions, appeared upon the eastern side of the Schelde, where he was joined by Lumley, with thirty squadrons and ten battalions At nightfall the army of Eugène arrived, and set up its tents to the north of

[1] Hare MSS., p. 224, June 27, 1709 (Hist. MSS Comm, 14th Report, Appendix, part ix). [2] Boyer, vol. viii., p. 22. [3] Hare MSS., p. 224, June 27, 1709 (Hist. MSS. Comm., 14th Report, Appendix, part ix.)

Marlborough's, thereby completing the investment of the place.

Villars had been entirely deceived. He had remained under arms all night, expecting to be attacked More nervous for his left than for his right, he had reinforced the garrison of St. Venant, and had proceeded in person to the neighbourhood of the fortress He had ordered 500 horse to advance towards Eugène's line of march, lighting many fires upon the skyline, as though the entire French army were at hand [1] Throughout the 27th, he imagined that Marlborough and Eugène were waiting only to take advantage of some false motion on his part. When their armies disappeared into the east, and he eventually discovered that Tournai was invested, he pretended to be highly delighted. " It was a great solace,"[2] he says. He was fully entitled to claim that he had foiled for the time being the project of invasion. But he was by no means satisfied with that honour alone. He affected to believe that the manœuvres of Marlborough and Eugène had been solely designed to entice him to a combat in the open field, and that the investment of Tournai was a mere afterthought, and was only undertaken at the last moment, when, thanks to his great perspicuity and restraint, these manœuvres had entirely failed. He even asserted that he had purposely left the city insufficiently garrisoned that it might serve as a bait to the allied generals; and without any regard for the reputation of the unfortunate governor, he calmly predicted that the siege " would of course occupy them for the entire campaign."[3] In short, he showed, as usual, that his talent for ' saving face ' amounted to genius. Unfortunately he has succeeded, to a certain extent, in hoodwinking posterity. Mr. Belloc, who has examined the matter at some length, recognises that Villars' version is exaggerated; but for Marlborough and Eugène he can say no more than that " the determination to besiege Tournai . . . had been reached at least as early as the 26th." He adds that " there is no positive evidence . . . one way or the other."[4] But he is wrong. The language employed by the

[1] Vie de Villars, t. ii , p 63.   [2] Ibid
[3] Ibid , p 64   [4] Hilaire Belloc, Malplaquit, p 33.

old historians[1] implies that the decision to besiege Tournai was taken as early as the 24th, that is to say, immediately after the first reconnaissance. That it was in fact taken on that very day, is proved beyond dispute by Marlborough's dispatch to Dompré, directing him to march from Audenarde at dawn on the 27th, and to approach as near as possible to Tournai without crossing the river, where he would be joined by another corps with final instructions.[2] This document bears date the 24th.

Surville, who had done so well at Lille, commanded in Tournai. The numbers of the garrison fell short of 7,000. So complete was the surprise, that many of the officers were absent on leave, and when Marlborough's vanguard appeared, three battalions of foot and a regiment of dragoons were actually under orders to join the army of Villars, and to start within a couple of hours. The majority of the men were young troops They were well supplied with ammunition and bread, but very deficient both in meat and money. As soon as Surville perceived that the allied forces were closing in upon the place, he sent out a party to secure the cattle in the neighbouring fields. But they were all made prisoners, with the exception of nine or ten dragoons, who escaped to Condé; and the cattle were duly restored to the peasantry. Though Villars pretended to believe that the defence could be maintained for "at least four or five months," he knew very well that the garrison had been dangerously depleted, and he showed his uneasiness by his conduct. On the 29th, he endeavoured to throw in a detachment of seven or eight hundred horse from Mons and Condé; but the allies were thoroughly prepared, and the design miscarried. A second attempt, undertaken on the night of the 30th, with 1,000 horse and dragoons, each carrying a foot-soldier, met with a similar fate The redoubtable Luxembourg was ordered to the neighbourhood of Valenciennes with twelve squadrons of dragoons; but he found no opportunity of doing at Tournai what he had done at Lille These demonstrations. no less than the efforts of individual officers to join

[1] Boyer, vol viii , p 22, and *The History of John Duke of Marlborough*, p. 272.
[2] Murray, vol. iv., p. 516: Marlborough to Dompré, June 24, 1709.

the beleaguered garrison, served only to encourage the allies by convincing them that the place was undermanned, and that Villars knew it

The governors of Condé and Valenciennes having opened their sluices, the besiegers were at first embarrassed by the flood of water which came down the Schelde. But they constructed bridges at Chercq above the town and at Constantin below it, and working diligently, they completed the lines of circumvallation on the eastern side of the river by July 4, and on the western, two days later. All this time, the heavy artillery, protected by the garrisons of Menin and Warneton, was descending the Lys to Ghent, and thence ascending the Schelde towards Tournai. Villars in his lines of La Bassée was a helpless spectator of these proceedings He could do no more than threaten the posts upon the Lys. A detachment under D'Artaignan, assisted by another from the garrison of Ypres, carried Warneton on July 4 They then attacked Fort Rouge, which was held by no more than fifty men; but they were twice beaten off, and on the approach of a force which Marlborough had dispatched to the scene, they hastily retired with 700 prisoners. This small success (and even Villars admitted that it was " not very important "[1]) they owed, according to Goslinga, entirely to the Duke's negli gence. Thereafter, ten squadrons and six battalions were stationed at Deulemont to observe the movements of the French in the valley of the Lys.

Marlborough in person directed the siege. He organised three separate attacks, one under the Prussian general Lottum, against the citadel, one under the Saxon general Schulenburg, against the gate of the Saint-Fontaine, on the left bank of the Schelde, and one under the Dutch general Fagel, against the gate of Manville on the right bank. Sixty battalions, seven of which were British, were selected for the operation. They broke ground on the night of the 7th. " The trenches," wrote Marlborough in his report to Boyle, " were considerably advanced, and our men covered before the enemy perceived they were at work, so that we sustained very little loss, which I take

---

[1] *Vie de Villars*, t ii, p 63.

to be a good omen."[1] The besiegers, however, suffered no little inconvenience from " the excessive continued rains."[2] Marlborough complained that the downpour had continued " this month past,"[3] and that hitherto they had had " nothing like summer weather ",[4] and Hare lamented the hard condition of " the poor creatures "[5] in the trenches, who were " up to the knees in dirt."[6] But even this depressing deluge had its uses. The closing of the sluices at Condé, Valenciennes, and Bouchain, had materially lowered the waters of the Schelde; and owing to the obstruction of some boats which the French had sunk above Audenarde in the preceding campaign, it was necessary at one point to cut a new channel. But thanks to the abundant rains these difficulties were surmounted, and the artillery and stores came up from Ghent without " the tediousness, expense, and toil of land-carriage."[7]

*   *   *   *   *

The MS of this chapter is incomplete. The citadel of Tournai surrendered September 3, 1709 —G. W T.

---

[1] Murray, vol iv , p 536· Marlborough to Mr Secretary Boyle, July 8, 1709.

[2] Ibid., p 540: Marlborough to Mr Secretary Boyle, July 11, 1709

[3] Ibid. [4] Ibid

[5] Hare MSS . Letter of July 8, 1708 (Hist. MSS. Comm., 14th Report, Appendix, part ix).

[6] Murray, vol iv., p. 540 : Extract of a letter from Mr Cardonnel to Mr Walpole, July 11, 1709.

[7] Boyer, vol. viii., p 31

XXVI.—MALPLAQUET

MARLBOROUGH and Eugène decided that the fall of Tournai should be followed by the siege of Mons. After the campaign was finished, and Mons had shared the fate of Tournai, the French pretended that it was a place of no particular importance. They thought differently in 1691, when the capture of that one town by Louis and Luxembourg was deemed an adequate counterblast to the conference of the powers at the Hague. And Villars himself thought differently, if his efforts to save the fortress are any criterion of the value which he attached to it.

The investment of Mons was by no means an easy operation. To prevent it, Villars had only to occupy in force the old lines which ran behind the Trouille from Mons to Maubeuge. And situated as the armies then were, the French were much nearer to those lines than the allies. Goslinga, that most self-satisfied amateur of war, considered the enterprise hopeless, and prophesied its complete failure. But Marlborough and Eugène had a better knowledge than Goslinga of the capabilities of the officers and men whom they commanded. On August 31 they dispatched Lord Orkney, with twenty squadrons and all the grenadiers of the army, to attempt the surprise of St. Ghislain, which guarded the passage of the Haine. On September 3 they ordered the Prince of Hesse-Cassel, with 60 squadrons and 4,000 foot, to take the same road. The Prince's instructions were to invest Mons on the southwest. If he found Lord Orkney in possession of St. Ghislain, he was to cross the Haine, on the western side of Mons. In the alternative, he was to cross it on the eastern side, and pass the lines of the Trouille. In either event the allied army would follow and support him

Setting out from Orchies at 4 in the afternoon, the Prince of Hesse pushed forward with extreme diligence. Arrived

in the neighbourhood of St. Ghislain, he learned that
Orkney had been unable to surprise that post. He therefore continued his march on the northern bank of the
Haine till he arrived at Obourg, where he crossed at 2 o'clock
on 'the morning of September 6. Though hampered by
perpetual rain and the badness of the roads, he had accomplished fifty-six miles in fifty-three hours, a remarkable
feat At 7 he advanced from the east towards the lines
of the Trouille, which he entered at noon.

Villars meantime had not been idle. Uncertain as to
the intentions of his enemy, he dared not concentrate in
either direction. But as soon as he ascertained that the
allies had a design upon Mons he instructed the garrison
to send out a detachment to the assistance of the three
regiments of dragoons which held the lines of the Trouille;
he ordered the troops at St. Ghislain to support his
movement, and he dispatched the Chevalier de Luxembourg
with thirty squadrons and the regiment of Picardy to the
defence of the threatened point. But Luxembourg came
too late. Hesse-Cassel was already within the lines. The
dragoons and the detachment from Mons were too feeble
to resist him. And the officer who commanded at St.
Ghislain, observing that the entire army of the allies was
marching towards the Haine, very properly declined to
quit his post. Luxembourg at first was minded to give
battle But it speedily appeared that Hesse-Cassel was
supported by the main body under Marlborough and
Eugène. Luxembourg therefore called in the dragoons,
ordered the detachment of the garrison to return to Mons,
and himself rejoined Villars, who had pushed forward as
far as Quievrain. It was useless to attempt the recovery
of the lines, for though the Marshal had excellent cavalry
at Quievrain, the infantry of his army was not yet concentrated. Hesse-Cassel was thus enabled to advance un-
opposed to the south-west of Mons, where he occupied a
position from Jemappes to Flameries. The same day
Marlborough and Eugène arrived at Obourg, passed the
Haine, and invested the place upon the east. Hesse-Cassel
modestly received the congratulations of his generals, and
Goslinga allowed that he had been mistaken.

Meantime the French army was gathering at Quievrain. On the evening of September 7, they passed the Honeau and encamped between Athis and Montroeul. Villars was determined to save Mons. If a battle were necessary, he would not shirk it. But two miles from his front his path was barred by a broad belt of forest, stretching almost from St. Ghislain on the Haine to Maubeuge on the Sambre. This obstacle could be skirted at its northern extremity, where a passage existed between the woodland and the Haine; it could be traversed only at the gap of Boussu, and farther south at the gap of Malplaquet. The first of these three approaches was blocked by Eugène's army, and the second by Marlborough's. But the gap of Malplaquet was still open

On the 8th Villars rested his men, and fed them as well as he was able. That night he ordered the Chevalier de Luxembourg to set forward with a detachment of cavalry and seize the gap of Malplaquet. At 6 on the next morning the whole army followed. Screened from observation by the forest, they marched swiftly and without beat of drum. At 8 o'clock Marlborough and Eugène, with an escort of 30 squadrons and 400 grenadiers, rode out to the mill of Sart to reconnoitre. Patrolling towards the gap of Malplaquet the cavalry discovered Luxembourg's troopers. Auveigne rode forward, and found that the gap was already held by a powerful force. And in the far distance he caught a glimpse of the French army, moving in four columns towards the plateau of Malplaquet.

The allies were taken at a disadvantage. If Villars chose to pass the gap, the left of Marlborough's army was the only force immediately available to dispute his progress. The right could not be brought forward for some hours. Eugène's army was six miles farther to the rear. Many of the cavalry were foraging, and not a few of all arms were plundering the countryside. The situation was critical. But Marlborough and Eugène retained their nerve and judgment. They reflected that the forest was a friend to both sides, and that Villars was probably as ignorant of their dispositions as they had been of his. While, therefore, they dispatched urgent orders for every horse and man to join them forthwith, they drew out the infantry of Marlborough's left in two lines, and pushing up as many guns as possible to the eastern extremity of the gap, began at once to cannonade the enemy. The broken nature of the ground permitted the French general no very clear view of the numbers of the enemy. By 3 o'clock Marlborough's right was also in position. Heavy rain retarded the arrival of Eugène's army till the ensuing day. But enough had been done to impress Villars. He halted at the western end of the gap. His artillery replied to Marlborough's, and his troops began to entrench. Instead of attacking he would wait to be attacked.

Had Villars flung himself upon the enemy that afternoon, he might perhaps have destroyed them in detail, and won a momentous victory. Had he known at how great a disadvantage he would have taken them, he might perhaps have made the venture. Wellington declared that the best general was he who could best divine what was passing on the other side of the hill. It would seem that Villars ought to have been better informed of what was passing on the other side of the forest. He was, however, uncertain of the truth. And it is a question whether in any event he ever intended to do more than accept a battle in a position of his own choosing.

After his bombastic orations to his soldiers and his grandiloquent epistles to the King, the conclusion was a somewhat tame one. Certainly Villars was a braggart. But he knew that rhodomontade alone could never restore the spirit of the French army. Nothing less than an indubitable victory in the field could do that. And how was he to obtain such a victory ? Here again the problem was largely one of *moral*. The forces were numerically equal. Assuming that the generalship was equal (and Villars was not the man to assume less), *moral* would be the deciding factor. To secure the fullest possible benefit from that factor, there was only one course to take. Villars must not wait to be attacked. He must himself attack.

For in war the moral advantage is not upon the side of the defence. As a general rule the assailants, merely because they are the assailants, assume that the enemy recognises

and dreads their superiority in discipline and valour. This
is especially and very naturally the case when the enemy
has not the excuse of inferior numbers. And in the particular instance of the French nation, it must be remembered
that their instinct is always to attack. The most aggressive
form of war is the form most congenial to their temperament. They are sincerely happy in no other.

But Villars, who knew his countrymen well, hesitated to
apply his knowledge. At the thought of dashing his
ragged and ill-fed soldiery, many of whom were ignorant
of war, and almost all of victory, upon the confident and
well-fed battalions of Marlborough and Eugène, his heart
misgave him. He knew the truth of Marshal Saxe's dictum
that "the first onset of the French is hardly to be resisted."[1]
But if, in this instance, it were resisted (and the veterans
of Marlborough and Eugène were not the men to be easily
appalled), if it were resisted, how many times could an
army composed of recruits and of survivors of Blenheim,
Ramillies, and Oudenarde be induced to return to the
charge ? A decided repulse would be followed by a tremendous counter-stroke, which would annihilate the only
force that stood between Paris and the invader. Villars
recoiled from the responsibility. He decided to assume
a strong position and wait to be attacked. By this decision
he practically forfeited his chance of a great victory. But
he also minimised the probability of a severe defeat. He
virtually played for a drawn battle. It is difficult to say
that he was wrong. In the existing position of French
affairs to fight without being beaten would have been an
immense advantage.

It cannot, however, be maintained that the position which
he chose was the best that offered Feuquières[2] has shown
that he should have entrenched himself on the plateau to
the west of the gap of Malplaquet, and received the allies
as they debouched into the open with a converging fire
from his broader front. The position which he actually
occupied was very different. Across the western extremity
of the gap, which was a mile and a half in width, and which

---

[1] Marshal Saxe, *Reveries*, ch. vi., p. 136.
[2] *Mémoires de Feuquières*, t iv , p 53

sloped gently down towards the enemy, he placed his centre. His wings he thrust forward on the edges of the woods to right and left. The centre he covered with trenches and earthworks, and the wings with ditches and palisades. From end to end of this concave line he distributed his infantry and cannon, his cavalry he ranged in the rear, on the plateau of Malplaquet. He thus created an infernal semi-circle of fire with 80 guns and 90,000 men to feed it. No army could enter such a hell, and live. None but maniacs would attempt it. If Villars imagined that Marlborough and Eugène were so intoxicated by success as to rush head foremost into so obvious a death-trap, he little understood the men with whom he had to deal. Their practised eyes perceived at once the defects of the French position. They saw that the dense, but not impenetrable forest, which covered his projecting wings, might also cover movements that would turn his flank   They saw that in the middle of the gap, and not far in advance of the French lines, was a small wood, the wood of Tiry, which Villars had neglected to occupy, and which could be utilised to mask an advance against his centre. And they saw that his fine cavalry, though exposed to the fire of their cannon, would be impotent until his centre had been forced, and his army virtually defeated. They perceived at once that the strength of such a position was more apparent than real. It was in fact too apparent. All that Villars had done the allies could see; but much of what they might do would be hidden from his view.

Marlborough and Eugène decided that if Villars stood his ground, they would attack him. Goslinga, the only Dutch deputy present on the 9th, consented. Though it was impossible to overbear the united opinion of the foremost captains of the age, there were officers in the allied army who considered that opinion bad. And other critics, wise after the event, have asserted that in the actual circumstances a battle was unnecessary and unjustifiable. It is of course conceivable that Mons might have been invested and taken, as Lille had been invested and taken, without a battle. But Vendôme's army had been fresh from the humiliation of Oudenarde; Villars and his men on the other hand were full of fight. Marlborough and Eugène appreciated the distinction. They had also learned from a captured officer that Villars had obtained the King's permission to hazard a battle. They may therefore have considered that the investment of Mons in the presence of a spirited and unbeaten foe was impracticable. The question, however, is not really material. For Marlborough and Eugène were thinking not of Mons, but of Paris. The fact which oppressed Villars, the fact that these 90,000 Frenchmen in the gap of Malplaquet were all that stood between the allies and Paris, was for Marlborough and Eugène the governing consideration. The instinct which told them to destroy the army of Villars, before he could change his mind, and before the permission to fight could be withdrawn, was a true instinct. They were afterwards accused of inhumanity by that foolish class of persons who in all ages have imagined that battles can be won without fighting. In this instance the accusation is more than usually irrelevant. The stroke which they designed to deal at Malplaquet was a final, and therefore a merciful one. Though they could not hope to win so bloodless a triumph as Ramillies, they might nevertheless achieve a second Blenheim. And a second Blenheim must have ended the war.

But the time and the method of attack had still to be determined.[1] It has been asserted that Marlborough advocated an immediate advance on the afternoon of the 9th. The assertion could only have been made in error. Before the arrival of Eugène's army the numerical odds were two to one in Villars' favour. That Marlborough should have thought of giving battle under such conditions is incredible. But on the ensuing day, the 10th, after the Imperialists had joined, a real difference of opinion appears to have arisen. Observing that the French had never ceased, from the moment that they occupied the gap, to fortify it with every kind of field-work known to the art of the military engineer, Marlborough suggested the expediency of attacking before these artificial defences had attained perfection. Eugène, on the other hand, considered that

[1] Alison, *The Life of the Duke of Marlborough*, vol ii, p. 45, and Boyer, vol viii p. 51

it would be safer to await the coming of the eighteen battalions which had been left at Tournai, and which would
raise the number of the allied forces to an equality with
those of Villars. The idea of assuming the offensive with
an army appreciably smaller than that of the strongly
posted army was bold almost to rashness   But over and
over again Marlborough had found that judicious audacity
had served him well   On this occasion his opinion was not
adopted. The allies won the battle, and the detachment
from Tournai had a notable share in the victory.   But a
day and a night were gained by the French engineers, who
exacted in exchange for their labours a frightful toll of
blood.   Which of the two generals was right, is a point
too nice to be decided even by expert critics.   For where
Marlborough and Eugène differed, the most competent of
judges are unlikely to agree.

Throughout the 10th the guns plied steadily on both
sides.   The French continued to elaborate their works with
diligent ingenuity.   In the middle of the gap they erected
a chain of nine redans with intervals sufficiently wide to
permit the passage of cavalry.   The trenches joining these
redans to the wood upon the left, the wood of Taisnières,
were covered by the marshy source of a small stream.   The
trenches, joining them to the wood upon the right, the wood
of Laignières, were triple in formation; and in that quarter
the approaches on the side of the enemy were traversed
by stiff hedges.   In the afternoon the allies set to work
to construct a battery between the wood of Tiry and
the French left.   The two armies were so close to one
another that friendly conversations, inspired by mutual
curiosity, sprang up between the soldiers.   Some subaltern
officers began a kind of informal colloquy, which was joined
by others of higher rank and ultimately by Albergotti,
who commanded on the French left, and by Cadogan and
Hesse-Cassel on behalf of the allies.   The rumour spread
that peace had been declared.   Villars peremptorily cut
short the interview, but not until certain features of the
French position had been studied at close quarters by the
enemy's engineers, who, it is alleged, were openly sketch-
ing and making notes while their comrades talked.   The

French have always asserted that the whole comedy was a reconnaissance prearranged by Cadogan, if not by Marlborough and Eugène.

The plan of attack which the allied generals had devised was simple in the extreme. They proposed to begin with vigorous assaults upon the French wings. As soon as both or either of these assaults had so far succeeded as to weaken or outflank the centre, a third was to be delivered against the very heart of the position. But before nightfall on the 10th, they modified their plan in one important respect. Realising the enormous strength of the triple lines in front of Malplaquet, they decided to convert the assault upon the French right into a feint, and to devote their principal efforts to the opposite wing. On this understanding they made their final dispositions.

In front of the village of Aulnois the allied left, consisting of thirty-one Dutch battalions, commanded by General Tilly and the Prince of Orange, was to advance between the woods of Laignières and Tiry and deliver the feint attack upon the French right and right centre. Hesse-Cassel with twenty-one Dutch squadrons was to support this movement. In front of the village of Blaregnies, the headquarters of the allies, fifteen English battalions under Lord Orkney, supported by Auvergne with thirty Dutch squadrons, comprised the centre. On the right, the preparations for the true attack were of a very elaborate kind. The French left, following the contour of the forest of Taisnières, projected in the form of an angle. Against the southern face of this angle, Lottum was to operate with twenty-two battalions of Imperialists and British, while Schulenburg with forty more was to assail its northern face. A detachment of 1,900 men from the investing force before Mons was to penetrate the woodland opposite Sart, and endeavour to outflank the enemy's left. Farther north, Withers with nineteen battalions and six squadrons from Tournai, was to traverse the forest and turn the whole French position. The residue of the cavalry, nearly 200 squadrons, supported Lottum and Schulenburg. By this arrangement two-thirds of the allied army were concentrated against Villars' left wing alone. At the point selected for the real attack the numerical odds were four to one against the French.

The formation of the allies possessed the additional advantage of increased security. The bulk of their army being massed at the head of the line of communication, retirement, if retirement should become necessary, would be safe and easy. Marlborough and Eugène did not anticipate failure At the worst they discovered that, if after a series of sanguinary repulses they failed to carry the French position, the defenders would be too exhausted and too impeded by the nature of the ground to pursue them with vigour. But good generals never despise an enemy Every precaution was therefore taken to ensure an uninterrupted retreat. An adequate force was detached to cover the gap of Boussu. And lest the garrison of St. Ghislain should be tempted to dispute the passage of the Haine against a beaten army, 9,000 men were ordered to carry the place by storm that very night. They succeeded perfectly. The capture of this post not only prevented the possibility of a disaster, but also completed the investment of Mons.

Marlborough and Eugène passed the night in the full consciousness that they had left nothing undone to compass a crushing victory upon the morrow. Their soldiers, habituated to triumph and contemptuous of opponents who could never be induced to fight except behind artificial defences of the most formidable kind, looked forward with confidence and even pleasure to another combat under the leadership of generals whom they loved and trusted. Nor was the spirit of the French unworthy of that proud and warlike nation. Villars himself, who had done more than any man to revive the soul of the army, was astonished at the cheerful obedience and the proud demeanour of his ragged, ill-nourished troops. At the prospect of battle all that they had suffered, and all that their families were suffering at that moment, was forgotten. They remembered only that they had at last an opportunity of punishing those enemies who had humiliated the great King and had brought their country to the brink of ruin. Villars, as he moved among them, received the most flattering evidences

of his own personal popularity. So encouraged was he by
the bearing of the army that he wrote that day to Versailles
a letter full of hope. In it he said that the " vivacity "
and " ardour " of the troops " redouble my own desire
for a chance of meeting the enemy on equal ground, and
give me an entire confidence, with God's aid, of beating
him well."[1]   The words are characteristic in their calculated
falsity. Anything less like " equal ground " than the
ditches, ramparts, redans, palisades, and dense forests of
Malplaquet it would be difficult to imagine   Nor was he
himself devoid of deep misgivings. At the last moment he
marked out a fresh line of trenches on the plateau in the
very position which, according to Feuquières, he ought to
have occupied from the beginning.[2] He kept his soldiers
busy on this new work throughout the night. But he
failed to complete it, nor did he utilise it during the battle.
His conduct in this matter, like his conduct on the previous
morning when he first arrived at Malplaquet, was marked
by a note of hesitation, which was in strong contrast with the
masterly and masterful tactics of Marlborough and Eugène.

In this situation the French horse, and particularly the
Household regiments, set a splendid example of stoical
endurance. They did but reflect the spirit of the whole
army. With joyful alacrity the soldiers stood to their
arms   Resounding shouts of " Vive Villars ! Vive le
Roi !" greeted the Marshal wherever he rode. Realising
that his left was his weakest point, he took up his own
position at the junction of the centre with the wood of
Taisnières, while he delegated to Boufflers the command of
the right.

At 3 o'clock on the morning of the 11th the army of the
allied powers paraded in order of battle. When the sun
rose, a thick mist, depending like a curtain over the face
of the woods and flooding all the gap of Malplaquet, effectually obscured the French lines. The chaplains recited
prayers, and the soldiers listened in reverent and awful
silence. The regular allowance of spirit was distributed
to the troops in accordance with a custom which excited

[1] *Vie de Villars*, t. ii , 10 septembre, 1709: Villars au Roi.
[2] *Mémoires de Feuquières*, t. iv., p. 56.

the derision of the French, who have never been able to comprehend the physical needs of Teutonic and Scandinavian peoples. Under cover of the mist forty pieces of cannon were posted in the grand battery between the woods of Tiry and Taisnières. As the regiments filed off to their appointed stations, rude jests upon the subject of the enemy's field-works passed along the lines, the men affecting to complain that once more they were required to wage war on moles. Eugène regaled them with the music of the massed bands. He was in high spirits, for September 11 was his day, the day of Zenta   As he and Marlborough rode along the ranks, the mist began to disperse, the guns opened, and here and there a man was stricken down. The French artillery, though somewhat less numerous than that of the allies, was skilfully posted and splendidly served under the direction of that Saint-Hilaire, who as a child had seen Turenne drop dying from the saddle   But the guns of the allies made the better practice. For though Villars' infantry was shielded by the trenches, his cavalry, in full view upon the plateau, presented a large and vivid target, difficult to miss.

A little before 9 the signal was given, when the grand battery of the allies delivered a crashing volley against the French left wing. Thereupon Lottum's twenty-two battalions marched up to the guns, deployed to the right in three lines, and advanced to the attack of the southern face of the projecting angle of the wood of Taisnières   As their left flank was thus exposed not only to an enfilading fire from the guns of the enemy's left centre but also to an assault from the infantry posted there, Orkney brought forward his fifteen battalions and covered the movement. Marlborough in person superintended these hazardous tactics   At the same time Schulenburg was leading his forty battalions, also in three lines, against the northern face of the same angle. Eugène himself, exulting in peril, rode on with Schulenburg's men   Simultaneously with these two main attacks upon Villars' left, the 1,900 foot from Mons penetrated unseen into the woodland, and Withers' little army pushed boldly across the forest belt towards the left rear of the enemy's position.

The ground which Lottum and Schulenburg had to cross was traversed by a rivulet, which, taking its rise opposite the French left centre, encircled the fortified edge of the wood of Taisnières with a natural moat of water and marshland. As Lottum's men floundered forward through the swamp, they were smitten with a terrific fire, which disordered their line but did not check their charge. The French, who at this point fought under the eye of Villars himself, stood firm behind their works. There was a sharp grapple, and the assailants were hurled back across the stream. No better fortune attended Schulenburg and Eugène. On this side the French with the utmost coolness reserved their fire till the enemy was over the stream and marching fast upon the woods At pistol-shot range the allies got a volley which stopped them then and there. The left of the line recoiled, and engaged in a duel of musketry with the French, while the right, which had extended to avoid an impracticable swamp, joined hands instead with the detachment from Mons. These combined forces did indeed make some headway. They succeeded in clearing a skirt of the forest and in penetrating the interior, but only to be brought to a standstill by steady shooting from a stockade of felled timber, which had been so disposed as to bar the only passage open to any considerable body of assailants upon that flank. The first attacks had failed.

Nothing daunted, Lottum and Schulenburg dressed their ranks, brought up their second lines, and after a short breathing-space again went forward. This time Lottum had extended his left, which suffered in consequence more severely than before from the enfilading fire of the enemy's left centre. This post of perilous honour had fallen to the Buffs, who proved themselves well worthy of it. The spectacle of the redcoats reeling and staggering across the marsh was too tempting for the French Twelve battalions of their left centre passed the trenches and prepared to charge with the bayonet. Villars saw the movement, which was in itself correct and opportune. But he also saw that Marlborough had anticipated it. Auvergne's thirty squadrons had ridden to the front. The Duke lum-

self was with them, vigilant and calm Villars' quick
fancy showed him in an instant the twelve battalions swept
out of existence by that impending torrent of hoofs and
sabres. Before it was too late he recalled his impetuous
infantry to the shelter of the trenches. The dauntless
Buffs went on, and dashing over the breastwork turned
the right of the position. At once the whole line opposed
to Lottum began to weaken. After a furious struggle the
allies became masters of the southern face of the forest of
Taismères.

Meantime Eugène and Schulenburg had not been idle.
With undiminished courage they had returned to the charge,
only to encounter a resistance as determined as that which
had frustrated their previous effort. It was not until
Lottum's success began to threaten the flank and rear of
the defenders on the northern side, that any real progress
was made. Then slowly and reluctantly the French fell
back, and the whole of the projecting angle of the wood
was in the grasp of the allies But the wood itself was still
swarming with the enemy. The timber grew so close that
all possibility of ordered tactics was at an end. Every
man stumbled forward through the suffocating smoke as
best he could. Quarter was seldom given. Every tree
concealed a marksman, and combats of unexampled savagery
filled every glade with shrieks and blood. No precise
narrative of that hideous struggle has ever been compiled.
The materials do not exist, for no man saw how his neighbour died or fared. Certain French battalions were subsequently accused by their countrymen of misconduct. The
charges were never proved, nor could they be. They were
probably unjustified. Though individual cowardice was
of course exhibited on both sides, the mass of the French
displayed conspicuous courage, and only surrendered the
forest foot by foot, and tree by tree before the pressure of
overwhelming numbers. But always the allies gained
ground. And now the column under Withers, beginning to
emerge at La Folie on the left rear of the French position,
accelerated the retirement of the defenders of the wood.
Villars realised that he was outnumbered, and sent to
Boufflers for assistance.

Meantime the regiments in the Dutch service, which composed the left wing of the allies, had also engaged the enemy Marlborough and Eugène had ordered that this attack should be a feint, and that it should not begin until half an hour after the other had been launched. Only the second part of their instructions was observed. The Prince of Orange, who thirsted for distinction and who resented the change of plan which, in his opinion, assigned to his countrymen a less active part than their known valour deserved, seems to have resolved to convert the false attack into a true one. Impatiently he listened to the roar of the conflict round the wood of Taisnières. Drawn up in five columns before the village of Aulnois his thirty-one battalions awaited the signal. No sooner was the appointed moment come than he gave the word, and riding to the front led on the charge with reckless gallantry. At once the fringes of the wood of Laignières and the trenches and batteries across the road to Malplaquet were ablaze with deathly flame. Saint-Hilaire had disposed his guns with terrible ingenuity. In that zone of fire it seemed impossible to live. The Prince's staff went down almost to a man. His own horse was killed, but on foot and alone he still went forward The men were worthy of their leader For to the left the Scottish regiments in the pay of Holland swept the French grenadiers from the skirt of the forest; and all five columns from Laignières to Tiry, swaying and reeling in the tempest of musketry and grape-shot, rolled onward to the foremost trench and over it, and on again towards the second. But ere they could attain it, with a long glitter of lowered steel and a mighty roar of cheering, the French charged out upon the sorely smitten ranks and chased them from the lines.

The Prince of Orange had committed a cruel blunder. In defiance of his instructions, he had endeavoured in the teeth of a flanking fire to carry a triple row of entrenchments, manned by a force which outnumbered his own by two to one. Nothing but a miraculous success could condone such conduct. Nothing on earth could justify a repetition of it. But the Prince was no longer capable of considered action. Mad with the fighter's lust, he rallied his shattered troops, and mounting a second horse, renewed the charge. He was nobly followed; but the resistance of the French was fierce and more confident than ever. Orange was again dismounted, and again he strode forward on foot, and almost alone. He snatched a standard of a wavering battalion, and planting it with his own hands upon the trench, called to the men " to take care of their colours if they had no regard to him." All strove to emulate a leader so heroic. The Dutch Guards fell in heaps. Tullibardine perished at the head of the Highlanders of Athol. Of 200 Huguenot gentlemen, 194 were killed or wounded. But not an inch would the Frenchmen yield. Their officers indeed had no easy task to hold them back. At length the glorious regiment of Navarre, defying all restraint, burst like a flood over the trenches, and swept down upon the foe. At the sight of those lean and sunburned men, ragged as mendicants but terrible as doom, the much enduring infantry of Holland gave way at last. Banners which they had taken were wrested from their clutches, banners of their own, and a whole battery of cannon, became the booty of Navarre. Hesse-Cassel, leaping forward with his twenty squadrons, stayed the rout. Reassured by this timely support, the fugitives halted, and doggedly reformed, while the French returned in exultation to their lines.

And now an immense responsibility devolved on Boufflers. Thus far he had more than held his own. His assailants had been twice repulsed and terribly punished. His soldiers, following the immemorial instinct of their race, were panting to go forward. Should he, or should he not, command a counter-stroke ? Officers of high rank and proved ability came flocking to his side, and urged him to seize what appeared in their judgment a matchless opportunity. Let him launch the whole of the infantry of the right wing upon the demoralised enemy, and let the Household Cavalry support the movement. The allied left would be annihilated, their centre outflanked, and their whole army hurled back in ruin upon the Haine. Military imagination is more highly developed in the French soldier than in any other. The most uninstructed of the valiant

peasants who manned those blood-stained trenches pictured
to himself the splendid prospect which, as it seemed, a
word from Boufflers would unroll.   But the word was never
given.   Boufflers refused to move.   Contrary to the prevailing opinion of the moment, an opinion which the lapse
of years and fuller knowledge did but confirm in all who
formed it on the field of battle, he declined to quit his post.
So high an authority as Saxe, who was present in the army
of the allies, long afterwards declared that he was wrong.
The vanity of his countrymen, whose nervous anxiety to
explain away their defeats is unworthy of a people which
possesses an unparalleled record of victories, has tended to
emphasise the verdict of condemnation   That verdict may
be justified.   But nobody should venture to adopt it without a careful examination of the arguments upon the other
side.   The two armies were equal in numbers.   They were
so arranged that in the centre of each this equality was
preserved.   But each had massed a preponderating force
upon its right wing   So long as these dispositions remained
unaltered, the French, if they would strike, must strike
with their right or not at all.   But what is obvious now,
was not of necessity obvious to Boufflers.   He had no
means of knowing that he could dispose of twice as many
men as the Prince of Orange.   It was one of the defects
of the position selected by Villars that the enemy's arrangements were largely masked from the observation of the
French.   Boufflers possessed no certain information as to
his opponent's strength.   He only knew that he had been
attacked with a vigour and determination which seemed to
suggest that the assailants were unconscious of any dangerous
inferiority in numbers.   Numbers of course were not the
sole consideration.   It was represented to Boufflers that
the spirit of his men was such that the half-beaten enemy
could never endure their onset.   Assuming this forecast to
be correct, Boufflers had still to consider the possible effects
of a forward movement of the right wing on the battle as
a whole.   Villars had already sent to him for aid, and he
had been compelled to refuse it.   The left was therefore in
difficulties.   It might be crushed, and the centre also,
before an advance of the right wing could make itself

sufficiently felt to afford any relief to the rest of the army. Balancing the chances, he decided that he could not take the risk. It may be demonstrable now that, had he done so, he would have won the battle. But he was not to know that He was an old man, and he made, as old men are apt to do, the choice of caution. He was also a lieutenant, and like a good lieutenant he acted in the spirit of his chief. This is his true defence. Villars from the beginning had played for safety. In refusing to deliver a counter-stroke, Boufflers did exactly as Villars had done, when he marched to attack the enemy's army and halted at the first sight of it, when he found it in inferior numbers and left it alone to concentrate, and when he laboriously prepared to receive behind his field-works the blow which he himself had set out to deliver. The highest duty of a subordinate officer is so to grasp the conception and so to absorb the spirit of his chief, that in every emergency he will act as the chief himself would have acted in his stead. To all appearance Boufflers fulfilled this duty to perfection when he resolutely declined to be persuaded into a more daring movement than any that Villars had hitherto essayed. To censure him is also to censure the very ideas upon which Villars himself had proceeded throughout.

No sooner was Marlborough satisfied that the forces of Lottum and Schulenburg had taken a firm hold of the forest of Taisnières, than he hastened to see for himself how the situation was developing on the left wing. As he rode along, a wild-eyed horseman came galloping to meet him. It was Goslinga, whose native courage had carried him into the thickest of the battle Distracted by the awful carnage of his countrymen, he was now careering wildly over the field in search of the man whose skill in war he esteemed even more than he mistrusted his motives in politics. As they rode on together and Marlborough beheld the pitiable wreckage of the Dutch army, he realised profoundly how much the allies had lost by the death of Overkirk. Coming at length to the Prince of Orange, he expostulated with him on his inconsiderate ardour. Presently Eugène himself arrived. The two generals succeeded in explaining to the Prince that not thus were false attacks delivered. They instructed him to menace the enemy continually and to maintain a perpetual fire, but not to renew the assault with the bayonet until Boufflers' flank had been turned by the advance of the centre and the right. Then they galloped away to their original stations. Their return was opportune. Disappointed in his hope of obtaining assistance from Boufflers, Villars had withdrawn the Irish and the Champagne regiments from the centre, and flung them into the wood of Taisnières, where they had more than checked the advance of Lottum and Schulenburg The allies were at a standstill or even recoiling, when Eugène reappeared amongst them. Order and courage were restored at once. Led by the Prince himself, the troops returned with vigour to the attack. The French resisted desperately. Eugène, who manifested not the slightest regard for his own safety, was wounded by a bullet in the head. But he flatly refused to seek a surgeon. "If," said he, "I am fated to die here, to what purpose can it be to dress the wound ? If I survive, it will be time enough in the evening."[1]

Slowly but certainly the allies pressed on. The French, driven piecemeal from the shelter of the trees, drew up, as fast as they emerged, on the plateau beyond The allies did not pursue them, but, weary and disordered, formed as best they could along the western fringe of the forest. Meantime on the extreme right, Withers was engaged with the infantry that manned the hedges of La Folie His cavalry had been ridden down by the Carabineers, but his movement was still full of menace to the French army.

It was now noon. Villars had marshalled no fewer than fifty battalions on the edge of the plateau. He was meditating a charge which should smash the straggling line of infantry before him, and hurl the shattered fragments back into the recesses of the forest. His tactics at this crisis of the battle were such as the French soldier understands and loves Gaily the bayonets came down to the charge The Marshal, as careless of himself as was Eugène, rode out before his men. But fortune was against him. A musket-ball struck him below the knee. He reeled from the saddle.

[1] Coxe, vol ii , p 453

But he refused to quit the ground. A chair was brought; but no sooner was he seated in it than he swooned away. They carried him from the field, and with him the last hope of a victory for France. The grand movement which he had conceived, he alone was competent to conduct. Disheartened by his fall, the fifty battalions continued irresolute upon the plateau. The opportunity passed. Eugène was busily dressing his ranks, and making ready to advance. But fear of the French cavalry restrained him. At length, however, seven twelve-pounders were got across the wood. With these he opened fire upon the flank of the enemy's horse, and forced them to recede.

And now the decisive moment had come. But Marlborough's was the eye that saw, and Marlborough's the hand that struck. Returning from his interview with the Prince of Orange, he had perceived at a glance that the withdrawal of the Irish and the Champagne regiments had perilously weakened the French centre. No sooner was he satisfied that Eugène had established himself on the farther side of the wood of Taisnières than he gave the word to Orkney to advance. With a proud and joyous confidence, begotten of accumulated years of victory, the British infantry swung forward. The French Guards, whose bravery on this occasion, according to the testimony of their own countrymen, consisted solely in their uniforms, discharged one volley and fled. The Bavarians fought well, but they were overmatched. In an instant the long wave of scarlet and steel had topped the trenches and redans. But Orkney checked it there. For Marlborough's purpose was to utilise the enemy's defences as cover for his own advance. The infantry occupied the captured works. The grand battery, dividing into two sections, went forward to right and left, and opened a converging fire upon the crowded plateau. All was ready for the stroke which Marlborough loved the best. Close behind Orkney rode Auvergne with his thirty squadrons, and Hesse with his twenty-one. Then came the British, Prussian, Hanoverian, and Imperialist cavalry. All the horsemen of the allied army stood like a suspended flood, impatient to burst through the channel which Orkney's redcoats had laid bare. The first to pass

it was Auvergne. The movement was a critical one. For
five hours the French cavalry had endured the fire of the
allied guns with stoical fortitude. At last their opportunity
had come. Boufflers himself was there to see that they
took it. Greedily they watched Auvergne's troopers trotting
out from the redans. When twenty squadrons were
through, they delayed no longer. In a furious charge they
swept the half-formed line of Dutchmen back in confusion
upon Orkney's foot But Orkney's foot, secure behind the
works, with steady volleys checked their onset. The
twenty squadrons rallied, and strengthened by others, again
rode forth into the open. Again the French dashed down
and drove them, desperately struggling, back to the shelter
of the flaming parapets; and again the pursuit was stayed.
Time after time, led on by Boufflers himself, the Frenchmen
charged, and charged effectively; but every time they
staggered and recoiled before the rolling fire of the British
infantry, while more and more of the allied horse pushed
through into the fight. Auvergne was in at last, and Hesse,
and, squadron after squadron, the British, the Prussian,
and the Hanoverian horse came on. Hesse, wheeling to
the left, threatened the flank and rear of the trenches which
Orange had striven in vain to carry from the front. At
once the defenders began to waver; and Orange, attacking
now for the fourth time, swept all before him. The great
body of the French cavalry, unable to make head against
the combination of musketry and cannon, rolled farther
and farther back on the plateau. But here the combat
was renewed with undiminished fury. The wide heath of
Malplaquet was smothered in a swirl of galloping steeds
and glinting steel. A tradition long survived among the
French soldiers that in this encounter certain of their
regiments bore themselves ignobly If such were indeed
the case, the allies have left no record of the fact. By
common consent the Household troops and the Gendarmerie
exhibited the superb valour that was always expected
of them. Old Boufflers, heading no fewer than six charges,
fought like a trooper in the thickest of the swords. But
the allies had ever the upper hand. The climax came when
Eugène himself passed the redans at the head of all the

horsemen of the Imperialist army, and threw this last
reserve into the fray   Then Boufflers ordered the right
wing to retreat.   The left had already begun a retirement
in the direction of Quievrain.   The centre now fell back
upon Bavai, and the right upon Maubeuge.   All three
columns marched in compact order.   The cavalry protected
the rear.   Discipline was easily maintained   For the
soldiers, indignant and dejected at the issue of the day,
were in spirit not defeated.   Some squadrons of the allies
watched them as they went.   But the retreat was practically unmolested.   The victors were too weakened by their
losses and too exhausted by their efforts to pursue an enemy
whose demeanour to the very last was wonderfully firm.

So ended one of the bloodiest battles ever fought   The
French had 11,000 casualties at the very least, and the
allies twice that number, or about 20 per cent. of the
total forces engaged.   The allies captured fifteen guns.
Colours were taken by both sides.   Much was said at the
time, and much has been said since, in disparagement of
the victory.   But the magnitude of the achievement cannot
be denied.   The French had selected a position of some
natural strength.   They had spent the greater part of two
days and nights in fortifying it to their taste with the aid
of every device known to the artillerist and the engineer.
In less than six hours they had been forced out of it and
driven from the field by an army which in numbers was
no more than their equal.   This was a splendid feat of
war.   It presupposes in the allies a marked superiority not
only of tactics, but also of disciplined courage.   Malplaquet
was a great battle and a great victory.

The French soldiers, bewildered and resentful, declined to
recognise defeat.   Those of the right wing considered that
they had won, and those of the left that they had by no
means lost.   All alike pointed to the captured colours, to
the orderly and uncontested retreat, and above all to the
hideous carnage of the enemy, as proofs of the unreality
of the alleged victory   Always hypercritical of their
commanders, they maintained that, had the right wing
been permitted to deliver a vigorous counter-stroke, an
amazing triumph would have been the sure result.   Villars

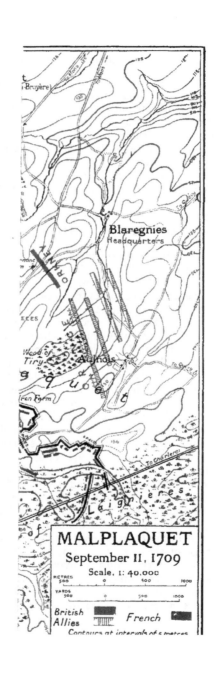

Blaregnies
Headquarters

Wood of
Tiry

Malhois

MALPLAQUET
September 11, 1709
Scale, 1: 40.000

METRES
500   0   500   1000

YARDS
500   0   500   1000

British
Allies   French

Contours at intervals of 5 metres

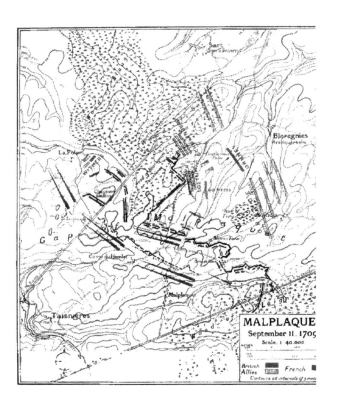

MALPLAQUE
September 11. 1709
Scale. 1 40.000

British
Allies   French

Contours at intervals of 5 metres

himself, in pursuance of his system, adopted a similar tone. But for his untimely wound he would have made short work of Marlborough and Eugène. The loyal Boufflers struck the same note. He even overdid it. His dispatches to Versailles excited the ridicule of the courtiers, and of the enemies of France. A satirical echo of this sentiment is to be found in the *Tatler* :[1]

> " Sir,
>
> " This is to let Your Majesty understand, that to your immortal honour and the destruction of the confederates, your troops have lost another battle. Artagnan did wonders, Rohan performed miracles, Guiche did wonders, Gattion performed miracles, the whole army distinguished themselves, and everybody did wonders. And to conclude the wonders of the day, I can assure Your Majesty, that tho' you have lost the field of battle, you have not lost an inch of ground. The enemy marched behind us with respect, and we ran away from 'em as bold as lions."

But despite the weakness of his epistolary style, Boufflers saw more deeply into the heart of things than did his critics. For Villars, though beaten, had achieved his ultimate end, while Marlborough and Eugène had failed in theirs. Villars had planned a battle which should restore the *moral* of the French army. Marlborough and Eugène had planned a battle which should annihilate the French army. The battle had been fought. The French army had not been annihilated. But from that time onward it began to recover its *moral*. The evidence of this fact is overwhelming. The knowledge of it was soon the common property of Europe. " The Dutch," wrote Harley, " murmur that their troops are ruined; and what is worst, the French have recovered their reputation, not only amongst themselves, but also with the allies, and it is a dangerous thing to have a good opinion of the courage of an enemy."

France was saved at Malplaquet as surely as at Valmy. Valmy was little more than a skirmish and much less than a battle; Malplaquet was one of the greatest actions in

---

[1] *The Tatler*, No. 77, October 6, 1709.

history. And yet, while Dumouriez' triumph is a household word in France, and long processions make pilgrimage to the monument of Kellermann, Malplaquet is only a name, and barely that, to the countrymen of Villars and of Boufflers. They have raised no stone to mark this sacred ground, they never wander in these haunted woods. These gallant gentlemen and peasants are forgotten, because, like their fathers before them, they served the King, and held the common faith of Christendom.

APPENDIX I

A.—THE BRITISH INFANTRY AT THE SCHELLENBERG

No British regiment inscribes the name of Schellenberg upon its banners. What principle, if any, governs the distribution of battle honours in this country, it passes the wit of man to discover, when a victory so gallantly purchased and so valuable in its results is officially ignored.

If Blenheim had never been fought, the Schellenberg would have been famous, as famous at least as Oudenarde, where the British losses were trivial in comparison. But the greater triumph entirely eclipsed the lesser.

The case of the Schellenberg is not the only one (though it is certainly the worst) in which Marlborough's men have received hard measure from the authorities. Captain C. B. Norman, in his admirable book, *Battle Honours of the British Army*, presents the following table, " as showing the scanty recognition accorded to the regiments which fought under Marlborough, the generous recognition of those which fought under Wellington."

Marlborough's Battles for which no Battle Honours have been Granted.					Wellington's Battles for which Battle Honours have been Granted.				
	Officers.		Men.			Officers.		Men.	
Engagements.	K.	W.	K.	W.	Engagements.	K.	W.	K.	W.
Schellenberg	32	85	638	1,419	Sahagun ..	—	—	2	18
Liège ..	11	20	142	365	The Douro	—	10	23	86
Menin ..	34	80	551	1,994	Almaraz ..	2	12	32	101
Lille ..	17	43	447	1,093	Arroyos dos				
					Molinos ..	—	7	7	51
Douai ..	13	61	638	1,093	Tarifa ..	2	3	7	24

Inadequate appreciation of the work of Marlborough's men is not confined to official quarters. It seems to have become a kind of convention, to which even writers of authority submit, to disparage the part played by the British Army in the War of the Spanish Succession. Great emphasis is continually laid upon the fact that, when Marlborough took the field, the English were by no means the only soldiers comprised in his command. And the argument is supported by comparative statistics of the casual-

ties incurred by the several contingents of the allied forces
An example of this standpoint may be found in an article by
General Sir E. Barrow, K.C.B., entitled, " The English Genius in
War," and published in the *National Review*, April, 1910.   The
writer admits that under Marlborough, " that incomparable
general," as he calls him, " the British infantry learnt the meaning of fire-discipline as applied to the musketry of that day, and
was trained to fight in line relying on platoon-fire."   He admits
that, in the reign of George II, the inheritance from " the great
days of Marlborough " of the tradition of " rigid training in what
was then called the platoon-exercise " produced " a personal
proficiency in handling arms and a methodical fire-discipline,
which rendered the British infantry of that day far superior to
any of its opponents."   But he argues from an examination of
the casualty-lists of Blenheim, Ramillies, Oudenarde, and
Malplaquet, that " however glorious the campaigns of Marlborough may have been, they do not necessarily imply or illustrate any marked superiority of the British soldier over those of
either our allies or our enemies of that period."

It is true, of course, that Marlborough's armies were composed
of men of more than one nation.   So were Wellington's, and
particularly the army which he led in the Waterloo campaign.
Figures alone are very unsafe guides in a matter of this kind.
It is absolutely certain that, before the war was half finished,
Marlborough's men had acquired among the enemy a reputation
out of all proportion to their numerical strength.   That fact is
proved conclusively by Louis' letter of May 6, 1706, to Villeroi
If by that date there was no evidence of " any marked superiority
of the British soldier over those of either our allies or our enemies
of that period," why should the King instruct the Marshal that
it would be " very important to have particular attention to that
part of the line which will endure the first shock of the English
troops " (see Vol I , Chapter XIV., p 377) ?   And why should the
Marshal obey the order with a slavish fidelity which was one of
the main causes of his ultimate defeat ?   To estimate the share
of the British soldiers in the victory of Ramillies by their losses
alone is not only to do them a grave injustice, but totally to mis-
understand the nature of that battle.

The historians who delight in reminding the public that
Blenheim, Ramillies, Oudenarde, and Malplaquet were, only in a
very qualified sense, British victories, invariably ring the changes
on those four battles alone   Yet presumably they have read
the story of the Schellenberg, and of the four sieges, Liège, Menin,
Lille, and Douai, cited in Captain Norman's table.   One hesi-
tates to think that they purposely suppress whatever fails to
coincide with a conventional theory.

The British losses at the Schellenberg were not only heavy in
themselves, but they exceeded those of any other contingent
engaged.   The following table is printed in Millner:

Contingents.				K.	W.	Total.
Imperialists	..	..	..	284	1,182	1,466
Dutch	..	..	..	378	933	1,311
Hanoverians	..	..	..	204	451	655
Hessians	..	..	..	97	223	320
British	..	..	..	452	1,084	1,536

The opinion which Louis and Villeroi had formed of the superiority of the British troops was based upon experience, upon the experience of the Schellenberg, Blenheim, and the lines of Brabant. But wherein did that superiority consist ? So far as the cavalry at any rate were concerned, it was to some extent tactical (see Appendix B). But so far as all arms were concerned it was indubitably moral. The psychology of the British soldier in action is difficult to analyse. But three attributes of immense value obviously emerge, a passionate desire for close fighting, an unintelligent inability to recognise defeat, and an assumption of the enemy's inferiority, originating not in vanity but in absence of imagination. These ideas were not inelegantly conveyed in the compressed Latinity of the Emperor's phrase (" miro ardori et constantiæ ").

B.—MARLBOROUGH'S CAVALRY AT RAMILLIES

The defeat of the French and Bavarian cavalry, and particularly of the Maison du Roi, by a body of allied horsemen consisting largely of the despised Dutch, was a thing which no Frenchman could understand. Three explanations were suggested, and were generally accepted—in France.

(1) It was alleged that Marlborough concentrated an overwhelming number (if not all) of his cavalry on his left wing, and that Villeroi made no reply to this movement.

This is a half-truth. It is a fact that, for reasons already stated in Chapter XIV., Villeroi declined to weaken his left. But at the opening of the battle Marlborough's left wing consisted of 48 Dutch squadrons, supported by 21 Danish ones, or 69 squadrons in all. Opposed to them were 78 squadrons of French and Bavarians. At this point, therefore, Villeroi at the outset enjoyed a preponderance of strength.

The 21 Danish squadrons engaged and destroyed 14 squadrons of French dragoons. Meantime the remaining 64 squadrons of French and Bavarians, including the Maison du Roi, were charged by the 48 Dutch squadrons. In this encounter the Dutch, though outnumbered by 4 to 3, held their own. This was the first phase of the combat.

In the second phase, Marlborough threw in 18 squadrons which he had summoned from his right, and the Danes attacked the enemy's wing on its right flank.   The allied squadrons (assuming that none of them had been put wholly out of action) now numbered 87 to the enemy's 64.   The balance was now in their favour to the precise extent to which it had formerly been against them.   It was now that they obtained the mastery.

In the third phase, Marlborough brought up 21 additional squadrons from his right.   The odds, in squadrons, were now 108 to 64, or nearly 7 to 4.   But the issue had already been decided.

(2) It was alleged that the 4 regiments of Bavarian cuirassiers, who together with the Maison du Roi composed the first line of the French, behaved very ill, and that the whole of the second line abandoned the field without striking a blow.

The imaginary spectacle of the 13 squadrons of the Maison du Roi, contending unaided against more than 100 squadrons of the allies, seems to have afforded no little consolation to public opinion in France.   And certainly there were elements of truth in this account.   The Household did display their accustomed valour.   The greater part of the second line did fail in the performance of their duty.   But the 4 regiments of Bavarian cuirassiers appear to have been well handled, and they, at any rate, did not by any means disgrace themselves.

In any event, it is somewhat difficult to see how the admission that the vast majority of the French cavalry of the right wing was not only defeated, but was actually too frightened to fight, assists the French case.

(3) It was alleged that the allies made use of novel tactics

Saint-Simon says that, when they charged, they opened to engulf the French, and then surrounded them   Feuquières and La Colome assert that the allies charged in four lines, but Feuquières adds that, just before the shock, the second and fourth lines closed up with the first and third.   It is very unlikely that the formation in four lines was adopted in the first phase of the combat.   But at some period in the third phase, when Marlborough had brought up two separate reinforcements of 18 and 21 squadrons, eye-witnesses may have actually seen four lines. French authorities also assert that the allies charged without any intervals between their squadrons, and that passing between the intervals in the French line, they took their opponents in flank and rear.   Saint-Simon's story that the allies opened to engulf the French is probably explained by this manœuvre.

The fact (for it seems to be a fact) that no intervals divided Overkirk's squadrons at Ramillies is highly interesting   Colonel Maude (in *Cavalry : Its Past and Future*, p. 98) quotes an observation of Frederick the Great to the following effect .

" Je ne laisse aucune intervalle entre mes escadrons, parceque les escadrons séparés les uns des autres prêtent autant de flancs à l'ennemi .   . je veux que l'impetuosité de leur charge force l'ennemi à plier avant qu'ils puissent se mêler avec lui "   Colonel

Maude goes on to say "The difficulty of working without intervals is sufficiently familiar to all cavalrymen, indeed, it is so great that I have repeatedly heard it said that it is impossible Yet here we have the practice of one of the most experienced employers of the cavalry arm in battle, to show that with a sound elementary training of the horse and rider the impossible was attainable . . . An Englishman who had served many years in the Austrian cavalry . informed me that in 1848-50, when he was quartered at Milan, they used often to charge 12 squadrons in line without interval, and that as far as his experience went, if the men were well grounded in individual horsemanship to begin with, no special difficulty was felt."

Frederick's cavalry achieved perfection. Their efficiency resulted from a combination of attributes, of which the ability to charge without intervals was one That this ability should have been possessed by Marlborough's continental horsemen forty years before Frederick used the language cited by Colonel Maude, is to say the least, remarkable The French appear to have regarded it as an extraordinary innovation They almost suggest that it was unfair. In reality it was one more proof of the superiority of Marlborough and his men to those who had previously been esteemed the foremost soldiers in Europe.

The true explanation of the result of the cavalry combat at Ramillies is simple. The allies owed their success to three causes

(1) The enormously improved *moral* of the Dutch This alteration was wholly effected by Marlborough, of whose military genius it is a conspicuous illustration

(2) The excellent training and horsemanship of the allied troopers, who could charge without intervals and could rally promptly.

(3) The admirable tactics of Marlborough and his officers (e g , the swift attack which crushed the 14 squadrons of dragoons, the timely use of the 18 squadrons from the right, Wurttemberg's flank charge, and the demoralising effect of the 21 squadrons of reserve)

On p. 68 of the work already quoted, Colonel Maude makes the following observation· " The evidence I have been able to collect is quite inadequate for the formation of any opinion as to the degree of excellence attained by Marlborough's cavalry." He is here referring to the English. I cannot avoid the conclusion that this brilliant and instructed writer has fallen at this point into an excess of caution.

The English did not participate in the great charges at Ramillies. But if the successful execution of difficult movements under fire and in the face of the enemy is any criterion of discipline and horsemanship, the advance of Lumley's squadrons over the marshes on the extreme right, when Orkney was attacking Offus, must not be forgotten. Discipline and horsemanship had already been exhibited by the British cavalry on a larger scale at Blenheim, when they traversed the swampy meadows of the Nebel, and again at the passage of the lines of Brabant, when they crossed the hollow road to Tirlemont   That they could rally promptly is proved by the repeated charges which they made on both these occasions.   No runaway gallops, such as neutralised the initial successes of Rupert's horsemen, are recorded to their discredit

It is certain that, from the outset, their *moral* left nothing to be desired   Eugène recognised that fact at a glance when he reviewed them at Gross Heppach. Moreover, they were penetrated through and through with the proper cavalry spirit.   At Blenheim the French Gendarmerie (a corps d'élite) fired from the saddle, no such folly was ever reported of Marlborough's men   What the Duke understood to be the true rôle of cavalry, and what he required of his English regiments at any rate, is clearly stated by General Kane, himself a combatant at Ramillies   After insisting on the importance of horsemanship, Kane goes on to say that a good cavalry must "handle their swords well, which is the only weapon our British horse make use of when they charge the enemy, more than this is superfluous.   The Duke of Marlborough would allow the horse but three charges of powder and ball to each man for a campaign, and that only for guarding their horses when at grass, and not to be made use of in action." (Kane's *Campaigns*)

Marlborough used the mounted arm for his decisive strokes. It was therefore only natural that he should have devoted special attention to its development   It was natural also that he should aim at the lofty standard of training and tactics, set by his own countryman, Oliver Cromwell, whose cavalry has never been excelled, except by Frederick's   That under his command the English regiments, and most of the continental ones as well, were educated to a point at which they exhibited almost all the essential characteristics of perfect cavalry seems to me to be historically established

In one respect alone they probably fell short of the ideal   "Seeing that it is quite certain," says Colonel Maude, "that up to the beginning of the Seven Years' War no continental heavy cavalry ever attempted to charge with closed files at a gallop, it is highly improbable that the British cavalry ever achieved this feat either."   Marlborough thoroughly understood the principles upon which cavalry should act   He relied upon shock   Shock is produced by a combination of cohesion and pace. The pace, at the moment of impact, should be the highest of which the horses are capable, but it should never be attained at the sacrifice of cohesion.   It is better to charge knee to knee at the trot than in a loose and disorderly manner at the gallop   Only the most perfectly trained cavalry can ride home at the gallop and still preserve their line unbroken and compact   Doubtless Marlborough worked continually towards the highest standard.   Each successive campaign must have added something to the efficiency of his squadrons. But in default of direct evidence to the contrary, the great charges at Blenheim and Ramillies must be assumed to have been delivered at the conventional pace of the period, the trot At the same time, it must be remembered that the trot is a somewhat elastic term, and is not incompatible with a high degree of speed

In charges on a smaller scale the highest standard was perhaps sometimes attained as early as 1706 It is distinctly asserted (see Boyer, and Cranstoun) that in the pursuit after Ramillies cavalry were charged by the 4 squadrons of the third and sixth Dragoon Guards, and infantry by the 3 squadrons of the Scots Greys, at the gallop. There is no reason to assume that in either instance the files were not kept closed.

APPENDIX II

SLANDER

IT has often been said by vacuous gossips and interested slanderers that two royal concubines, Arabella Churchill and Barbara Villiers, founded the greatness of the house of Marlborough. " Everybody agreed," wrote Grammont, " that a man who was favourite of the King's mistress and brother of the Duke's, was starting well and could not fail to make his fortune."[1] In this sentence, however, logic is partially sacrificed to epigram The facts, moreover, so far as they are known, offer but a fragile support to the suggestion of the cynical Frenchman.

Arabella joined the Duke of York's household some years before her brother But the date of the commencement of her intrigue with James has never been determined The assumption that it began before John Churchill came to Court, or even before he obtained his commission in the Guards, is only an assumption. Nor is it, of possible conjectures, by any means the best Arabella's four children by the Duke were born between the years 1670 and 1674 That circumstance, taken in conjunction with an entry in *Pepys' Diary* of January 12, 1669, causes the balance of probability to incline towards a date subsequent to the opening of her brother's military career It is, however, unnecessary to labour a point, which only malice could have raised There was never any need to discover a sexual origin for such simple events as Churchill's entry into the Duke of York's household and the Guards Both brother and sister owed their situations to the same cause, the self-sacrificing loyalty of their father to the House of Stuart. Once established at Court, Churchill's personal charm and exceptional talents sufficiently explain the rapidity of his success But though it be granted that her brother cannot be shown to have profited by her dishonour, modern opinion is still dissatisfied. The Churchills, father and son, were gentlemen and Churchmen both. Yet, apparently without compunction, they permitted a woman of their family to live in open and acknowledged shame. They took no steps to remove her from Court. The father continued to hold a position under the Crown. The son was the servant and the friend of his sister's seducer. Modern opinion upon this subject, as upon most of the men and the events of the past, is saturated and vitiated with an insidious anachronism, most

---

[1] *Mémoires de la vie du Comte de Grammont* (1731), ch. xi., p. 393

difficult to purge away. The common kind of lie, if not easily overtaken, is easily exposed. But that state of completed ignorance, that passive mendacity which Plato has called " the lie in the soul," is hard to combat. In history it perverts whatever it touches. The men and women of history are constantly condemned by judges, who are never masters of their case, who know next to nothing of the environment and atmosphere in which their victims lived In the present instance, if a man would understand the position of the Churchills, he must understand two things which have long ceased to have any counterpart in modern life. In the first place, society at the Court of Charles II, as at every other Court in Europe, took its tone from Fontainebleau and Versailles. Now Louis XIV honoured his mistresses before all the world, and he expected, and indeed required, that all the world should honour them likewise. Consequently, a woman who became mistress to a king, or as in Arabella's case, to a king's heir, suffered no loss of caste or self-respect. She might even gain in both Even to-day, when royal mistresses are no longer publicly acknowledged, little, if any, stigma attaches to their names And secondly, it must be considered how deeply the idea of the divinity of royalty had sunk into the mind of the English nation The clergy taught it as a theory, and almost as a theology. The people saw, in the miraculous efficacy of the royal touch, a practical proof of the verity of the doctrine. The language which was commonly used about Charles I would have seemed blasphemous in the ears of any who did not firmly believe that kings were beings of a superhuman order Persons in this condition of mind would easily, and even logically, extend the constitutional maxim, "The King can do no wrong," to the ethical sphere They might even come to regard it as a woman's plain duty to minister to the pleasures of these godlike beings. Josephus tells a story of a very virtuous and pious matron, whose virtue and piety were her undoing Her unsuccessful lover having assumed the character of the deity Osiris, she yielded cheerfully upon religious grounds what no arts of the seducer could ever have extorted from her. Boccaccio has a similar tale of the personation of the Angel Gabriel. Some such reasoning undoubtedly influenced the majority of minds in the seventeenth century To talk of the Churchills as trading on Arabella's shame is to pervert history. Where there is no offence against the opinion of society there is no shame.

Almost everybody has heard of John Churchill's intrigue with his beautiful kinswoman, who is variously known as Barbara Villiers, Mrs. Palmer, Lady Castlemaine, and the Duchess of Cleveland. The episode appears to have been public property from the beginning Adorned and illustrated, as only the malignant diligence of political rancour can adorn and illustrate, it has been public property ever since. To the mercenary pen of

the crapulous Mrs. Manley it was a godsend. Macaulay loved
to dwell upon it with that insufferable loftiness which is the
privilege of Whigs and prigs. And in more recent times it proved
mightily pleasing to the vulgarity of a Bradlaugh

The story never rested upon any better foundation than
common talk. Aristotle said that general belief in a thing is no
bad criterion of its truth   But a history of the seventeenth
century, which relied implicitly upon popular rumour, would
be obliged to record that the majority of notable persons lived
in promiscuous adultery and died by the hand of the poisoner.
There are, however, two tests whereby this kind of evidence may
be judged. If a report can be shown to have originated from
persons who were in a position to know the facts, or to have been
commonly retailed by such persons, and if those facts were not in
themselves impossible or absurd, it may be accepted as in all
probability true, at any rate in its essential features.   Now the
scandal about Churchill and the King's mistress was not merely
the prurient gossip of hackney-coachmen or citizens' wives   It
passed current in the society in which they both lived, and was
actually exported to France by the French ambassador   The
first of the two tests is therefore satisfied   As to the second, the
possibility of such an intrigue can hardly be questioned   For
it is nowise incompatible with the known character and situation
of the persons involved

Lady Castlemaine was to Charles II what Madame de Montespan was to Louis XIV, the most beautiful creature in the royal
seraglio and the most imperious. Like Madame de Montespan
also, she bore more children to her lord than any other of his
favourites   But here the parallel ends   Madame de Montespan
lived circumspectly under Louis' protection, and when it was
withdrawn, she adopted the fashionable pose of the Frenchwomen
of her day and became a most edifying recluse. Lady Castlemaine, on the contrary, while simulating a ferocious jealousy
of Charles' infidelities, scandalised even the licentious world in
which she moved by the almost Homeric catalogue of her para-
mours. Years afterwards, at the age of sixty-four, when her
children by the King were approaching middle life, and she
herself was a grandmother, she permitted her passion for a handsome vagabond to render her publicly ridiculous. In the days
when Churchill first appeared at Court her ripe beauty and her
unabashed laxity were the talk of the town. She was bitterly
satirised in broadsheets which were hawked about the streets
of London   In a licentious novel written in French and published at Cologne, both she and Charles were lampooned for
the edification of the continent. The virtuous Evelyn, coupling
her with Nell Gwynn, describes her as a " curse of our nation "[1]
The susceptible Pepys, who went everywhere and saw everybody,
and whose taste in women was sufficiently catholic, over and over

[1] *Evelyn's Diary*, March 1, 1671.

again awards her the palm of transcendent loveliness. Having feasted his eyes, in the Privy Garden at Whitehall, upon her " smocks and linen petticoats, laced with rich lace at the bottom," he observes that they were the finest " that ever I saw."[1] and that it did him good to look at them. One of her portraits by Lely he calls " the so much desired by me picture of my Lady Castlemaine, which is a most blessed picture, and one that I must have a copy of "[2] She had dark blue eyes and auburn hair, and a very majestic manner The fact of her physical fascination is not open to dispute. But nobody has placed on record the secret of that charm which, despite her notorious irregularities, enabled her so long to retain her sovereignty over the fickle and satiated Charles. It may be that her tragical airs and tempestuous outbursts, whereof it is written in Pepys that she " hath nearly hectored him out of his wits,"[3] stimulated an appetite that had been cloyed by universal acquiescence. Burnet says that the King's " passion for her, and her strange behaviour towards him, did so disorder him, that often he was not master of himself, nor capable of minding business "[4] But whatever may have been the key wherewith she could unlock the heart of Charles, it is easy enough to understand how Churchill, who was just emerging from boyhood, fell beneath the sway of what Macaulay has described as " that superb and voluptuous loveliness which . . . overcame the hearts of all men."[5] Their kinship (she was his second cousin once removed), the very difference in their ages (she was twenty-eight and he twenty), would help to smooth the way, if indeed it needed any smoothing For Barbara Villiers never waited to be wooed. Obedient solely to the whims of a capricious temper, which spurned the brilliant Rochester and capitulated to a rope-dancer, she selected such persons as pleased her and summoned them authoritatively to her side. Once her choice was made, she carried all by storm A coarse word, flung from her carriage-window as she drove round Hyde Park, indicated to Wycherly that he found favour in the eyes of her who could easily make the fortune of a dramatist It is improbable that Churchill offered any resistance to her passion. Possibly he paid her his court from the first with all the cool audacity which invariably distinguished him That mature beauty which appeals peculiarly to youth, that dangerous charm of the woman of the world which fascinates the inexperienced, enormous riches, infinite power, the universal admiration of mankind, everything in short which could excite the vanity and gratify the senses of a boy of twenty, Churchill beheld in Lady Castlemaine, and beholding, doubtless desired.

That he was for a considerable period one of her favoured lovers, may be taken as an established fact. But history is

1 *Pepys' Diary*, May 21, 1662 2 *Ibid*, October 20, 1662
3 *Ibid*, August 7, 1667 4 Burnet, vol 1, p 101.
5 Macaulay, vol 1, ch iv, p. 210.

under no obligation to accept the alleged particularities of the affair. Grammont's assertion, for example, that Churchill himself publicly and habitually bragged of his conquest, is improbable Conceited young men, especially of Grammont's nationality, are prone to " kiss and tell." But Churchill was possessed of three qualities, modesty, caution, and good taste, any one of which would have sufficed to restrain him from such vulgar folly Nor is it obligatory to credit the facetious anecdote of the sudden irruption of the King into the lady's chamber, and the ignominious descent of the lover from the window. This kind of tattle possesses but little value It may be believed or not, according to taste That her child, Barbara, born in 1672 and disowned by Charles, was in fact Churchill's, may well be true. But Pope's allegation that Churchill, after accepting largely of her money,

> " Lived to refuse his mistress half a crown,"

is palpably false The Duchess of Cleveland was a wealthy woman to the end of her days It has been suggested that the reference is to an incident at the gaming table, where the Duchess, an inveterate gambler, was temporarily in need of a loan. This explanation hardly mends matters. It is not the plain meaning of the verse Nor did the Duke play for half-crowns Even Macaulay resists the temptation to incorporate this gorgeous specimen of the lie epigrammatic in his unrivalled collection. Pepys declares that she was " so great a gamester as to have won £15,000 in one night, and lost £25,000 in another night at play, and hath played £1,000 and £1,500 at a cast."[1]

The story of Barbara's generosity, which Pope, for the sake of an antithesis, declares to have been so evilly requited, deserves more serious consideration, not indeed by reason of its own importance, but solely in consequence of the base uses to which it has been put by Churchill's slanderers In the year 1674 he purchased from Lord Halifax an annuity of £500. The investment proved an excellent one for him, for he was twenty-four, and the price which he paid was only £4,500. But Halifax's speculation was not so rash as at first sight it seems to modern eyes Human existence in those days was shorter, in the average, than it is to-day, and more exposed to abrupt termination by pestilence, assassination, or the duel Moreover, a young and ambitious soldier, bent upon distinguishing himself by personal prowess in the field, could hardly be regarded as ' a good life ' But whence did he procure so large a capital sum ? Play ran high at the Court of Charles II, and Churchill possessed the qualities essential to success at cards. It is, however, unlikely that his natural prudence would have permitted him to gamble on so dangerous a scale Tradition declares that the money came from the Duchess. This story, which rests on nothing worthy of the name of evidence, is not inherently improbable.

[1] *Pepys' Diary*, February 14, 1668.

The lady was rich, and though Burnet calls her "ravenous," like most women of her kind she gave as easily as she got. Where she got this particular sum, is of no consequence. It may have been the price of an office or an intercession. Those who love to trace all action to obscene causes, will find an indecent anecdote on the subject in Pope or Lediard.

Now many estimable persons, who find it in their hearts to excuse a young man's intrigue with a beautiful woman older and more experienced than himself, regard it as unpardonable that he should accept her money   Had Churchill presented £4,500 to Lady Castlemaine, they would not be offended   Yet logically and ethically the two cases are indistinguishable. The world, however, has no respect for logic or ethics. Its judgments are those of that moral eccentricity, 'the man of honour'   This standard is a variable one. In the twentieth century, as it happens, 'the man of honour' is presumed never to take a woman's money. And therefore Churchill is condemned. But common fairness, to say nothing of the historic or the scientific sense, requires that if Churchill is to be tried by the code of 'the man of honour,' the code selected must be that of his own day, and not that of ours. If he be so tried, he is certainly acquitted. The standpoint of society in the seventeenth century differed widely from its standpoint in the twentieth. In that age the fortunate lover frequently made his fortune. The world would merely watch and whisper. Often it was amused, generally it was envious, but always it was complacent

But the edge of calumny is not to be turned aside thus easily. Churchill's traducers insinuate, and even assert, that, so far as he was concerned, the intrigue with Lady Castlemaine was neither refined by affection nor palliated by desire   They represent it as a shameless barter between the lust of a mature and sensual woman and the avarice of a greedy and calculating boy. But this conception of Churchill's motive is a wholly gratuitous assumption. There is no reason to suppose that the affair originated in anything but the mutual inclinations of two singularly attractive personalities   And if Lady Castlemaine, being rich, desired to help a kinsman and a lover, who was poor, the impulse did her credit. And if Churchill accepted her help, the ethical argument whereby he is to be condemned has still to be elaborated.

The judicious investment of the money seems also to have been regarded as an aggravation of Churchill's infamy. The moralists do not explain what better disposition he could have made of it   He might easily have put it to more questionable uses. Many young soldiers would have squandered it on play. Some would not have hesitated to transfer the guineas of one mistress to another or to the women of the town. Churchill preferred to adopt a course, which must have relieved his parents of the burden of his maintenance, and which must assuredly have accorded with the wishes of his benefactress.

The change in public sentiment on matters of this kind is well illustrated by two of Marlborough's historians, Coxe and Lediard. Coxe, who wrote a century after Marlborough's death, glided swiftly and easily over the story of his connection with Lady Castlemaine. Lediard, a contemporary of the Duke's, who less than a dozen years after his death published a Life of him, which is dedicated to his success, and which is nothing less than a sustained panegyric, sets down the worst that his worst enemies have suggested on this unsavoury topic with a satisfaction and a complacency that can barely be distinguished from approval

That interested calumniators should have sought to vilify the name of one of the greatest Englishmen that ever lived, is natural enough. But that they should have met with so much success in their despicable business, is entirely discreditable to the English nation Where else in Europe would it have been possible to depress the reputation of a man, who had served his country well, merely by citing the more or less legendary details of a youthful amour ? The attempt, if made, would cover the makers of it with derision in any land save that in which the national sense of proportion has been vitiated by the national malady of Puritanism. Churchill deliberately broke the Seventh Commandment. In itself the offence admits of no justification. And he, who lived and died a loyal member of the Church of Andrewes and Herbert, of Ken and Collier, had not even the same excuse as many men of fashion of his day, who were real or professing agnostics. But one swallow does not make a summer, nor one intrigue a Rochester. So far as is known this was Churchill's solitary lapse Despite the temptations to which his physical beauty, personal charm, and extraordinarily successful career exposed him, he maintained throughout a long life a purity in his relations with women, which was almost unique at that period, and which would have been remarkable at any. Yet to this day his good name suffers A cloud is popularly supposed to rest upon his early manhood. It rests in reality upon his malignant traducers and incompetent critics. Neither common sense nor elementary justice should have permitted his countrymen to accept their historical facts and their moral judgments from the hired pen of such a filthy libeller as Mrs. Manley, herself a lewd liver, or from such unscrupulous partisans as the Tory, Swift, who broke the hearts of two faithful and affectionate women; and the Whig, Macaulay, whose idol, William III, the champion of Protestantism, for years flaunted an ugly mistress in the face of a beautiful and devoted wife.

APPENDIX III

TANGIER, SOUTHWOLD, AND MAESTRICHT

THE regular army, which Churchill had entered, and which he was destined to render so illustrious, differed sadly from the renowned and formidable force of the present day Its origin was as recent as the King's restoration. Its numbers were contemptible. Its organisation was defective. Its discipline was an evil compound of barbarism and laxity. Outside the British Isles it had no reputation and almost no record. At home it enjoyed neither respect nor popularity. " Methought," wrote Pepys, after a review of the Household Troops in Hyde Park, " all these gay men are not the soldiers that must do the King's business, it being such as these that lost the old King all he had, and were beat by the most ordinary fellows that could be "[1]

Yet a time had been when England stood high above all the nations of the continent in military prestige At Falkirk, Crecy, Poitiers, Najara, Agincourt, and Verneuil, her soldiers had earned the admiration of Europe. And the lustre of her national exploits had been, if possible, enhanced by the achievements of her private adventurers Princes and peoples had competed to purchase the wisdom of her captains and the terrible skill of her archers To the tactics of English officers and the long-bows of English yeomen Portugal owed the astonishing victory at Jubaroth And the inscription on the tomb of Sir John Hawkwood in the cathedral of Florence still testifies to all the world that this English soldier of fortune was the most accomplished commander of his time

But more than two centuries had passed since those gallant days The decline of feudalism and the rise of great monarchies had reduced England to the rank of a second-rate power. Her insular position and her small population had deprived her of the motive and the means for effective intervention in the politics of Europe Her sanguinary civil wars and her domestic distractions, both secular and religious, had absorbed, to a large extent, the combative energies of her people. On the sea, indeed, she had fiercely battled with Holland for her trade, and with Spain for her very existence. On that element her arms were known and feared But of the land-forces of the British Crown Europe in 1667 knew practically nothing. Even as soldiers of

[1] *Pepys' Diary*, July 4, 1663.

fortune the English had long yielded their pre-eminence to the mercenaries of Switzerland, Germany, and Spain.

Yet the stock was not exhausted; the ancient strain had suffered no deterioration. From time to time such stout adventurers as Captain John Smith, or such adventurous gentlemen as Sir Philip Sidney, " the good Lord Willoughby," Lord Herbert of Cherbury, and " the fighting Veres," reminded the nations of the continent that the island of the Black Prince and Henry V, of Chandos, and Hawkwood, and Talbot, still nurtured a race redoubtable in war. It could not even be said that the mastiffs slumbered. For more than once they had sharpened their teeth on one another's throats, with such results as were signally manifested when Cromwell's red regiments went into action at the battle of the Dunes. But better far than these isolated and spasmodic exhibitions of British pugnacity was the nation's unshaken confidence in itself. What Kinglake wrote of the nineteenth century was equally applicable to the seventeenth— " in truth the English knew that they were a great and a free people, because their fathers, and their fathers' fathers, and all the great ancestry of which they come, had been men of warlike quality " However foreign statesmen might affect to ignore her political influence and foreign soldiers to deride her military worth, the English in the days of Charles II had never ceased to believe in England and to cling tenaciously to those proud traditions of the past, which were enshrined in the popular literature of ballad and chronicle. Never once had the common people abandoned their old conviction that, man for man, they could always give odds to foreigners And that conviction, which nowadays is often cheaply and ignorantly derided, was based upon indubitable exploits of the Hundred Years' War. Its survival in England should occasion no surprise. For, more than a century after Talbot's death, it still survived in France Writing of the year 1546, Montluc, no friendly witness, has recorded that his countrymen at that epoch persisted in believing that " one Englishman always beat two Frenchmen, and that your Englishman never ran away, and never surrendered "[1]

Churchill did not join the army for the sake of swaggering along the Mall in a gold and scarlet coat, which doubtless set off his fine figure to the admiration of the ladies of the City and the Court. He chose it as a profession and a career. And he therefore desired, what every true soldier desires, a speedy opportunity of acquiring experience and achieving distinction in other fields than the parade-ground and the Park.

There were in Europe at that time two recognised academies of warfare, in both of which the military art could be learned to the best advantage On the eastern boundary of the Empire smouldered perpetually that tremendous struggle with the Turk, wherein no less a soldier than Eugène of Savoy received his early

[1] *Commentaires de Montluc* (Collection par M Petitot, t. xxi , p 72).

training, and whither he returned in old age to win his latest laurels. In Flanders, the Rhenish provinces, and Franche-Comté, the periodic efforts of the French monarchy to extend the frontiers of France at the points where France was weakest, provided a school of arms, in which the Duke of York himself, and many noblemen and gentlemen of England, had studied war under its most renowned masters And here, no doubt, if he had been at liberty to choose, John Churchill would have preferred to make his first campaign But an ensign in the King's Foot Guards was restricted to such opportunities of learning his trade as the King's service might afford. And for Churchill, as for many thousands of his successors, the first call was to the continent of Africa.

The seaport of Tangier, which passed to England when a Portuguese princess became queen to Charles II, was a troublesome possession. On the land side it was closely and continually beset by savage tribesmen under one of those fanatical pretenders, of whom Northern Africa produces a seemingly inexhaustible supply. Its seaward batteries had exchanged shots with the battleships of Holland. Its occupation by the English was a cause of extreme irritation to the Spaniards, who were not ashamed to intrigue with the Moors against the garrison The Portuguese had left it in a dilapidated condition The rebuilding of its fortifications and the construction of a harbour-mole involved a large capital outlay The annual expense of its maintenance was considerable. An entire regiment had been raised for its defence. Its climate was unhealthy Nor were the benefits to be derived from it immediately apparent to the ordinary Englishman The House of Commons and the nation regarded it with a jealous eye. They saw in it nothing but a costly inutility and a dangerous pretext for the existence of a standing army. The retention of Tangier was in fact as unpopular as the surrender of Dunkirk When Clarendon fell, the mob of London insulted him with this doggerel,

> "Three sights to be seen,
> Dunkirk, Tangier, and a barren Queen "

Charles II is not popularly regarded as one of the founders of the British Empire. English hypocrisy and English Whiggery between them have blasted his reputation for all time He was, however, one of the few, who in the seventeenth century perceived the proper line of imperial policy, and strove to follow it in the teeth of prejudice, ignorance, and cant. Pepys, whose opinion on the point is final, has testified to his extraordinary knowledge of naval matters. And Pepys' judgment is certainly confirmed by the wisdom which the King displayed in the abandonment of Dunkirk and the occupation of Tangier The national finances could not support the upkeep of both places. For naval purposes Dunkirk was useless to England. But

Tangier provided her with that which she had never yet possessed, a base from which her maritime power could operate in the Mediterranean. It gave her also the command of the Straits, and enabled her to frustrate the concentration of the Atlantic and Mediterranean squadrons of both France and Spain It was a refuge for English merchantmen and a station for English privateers. It was convenient for the suppression of that African piracy, which preyed upon the commerce of the civilised world As a trading port, it offered immense possibilities And the permanent presence of the English flag at a point, where it must be daily sighted by the seamen of all nations, added materially to the prestige of the English name. All these advantages were apparent to the King. Expert opinion, both at home and abroad, was unanimous. The soldiers and sailors agreed with the merchants and the diplomatists that Tangier was an " incomparable jewel," and " the most important place in Christendom for His Majesty and the good of our nation." But the English people remained unconvinced One consideration alone should have lightened their blindness The astonishing anxiety of France, Spain, and the United Provinces, to compel the evacuation of Tangier, was conclusive evidence of its strategic value. Louis XIV gave the most significant proofs of his uneasiness. After an unsuccessful attempt to establish a footing of his own on the African coast, he fell back upon the heroic expedient of constructing a canal from the Mediterranean to the Bay of Biscay.

It was not in the course of his ordinary, regimental duty that Churchill went to Africa At that time it would have been considered hardly politic to send the Foot Guards so far afield. Libellers of the more indecent sort allege that the Duke of York desired to remove him from the Duchess, who had manifested an excessive preference for his society. Others of the same school substitute the King for the Duke, and Lady Castlemaine for the Duchess. To these professional liars such discrepancies mattered not at all. Nothing mattered, in comparison with the insinuation of a sexual motive Posterity, however, may safely assume that, with the laudable zeal of the ambitious subaltern, Churchill volunteered for active service and was accepted He seems to have passed some portion of the years 1669 and 1670 at Tangier. Though many contemporary documents, relating to the occupation, are extant, no record of his adventures has as yet been brought to light. Tradition says that he took part in several engagements with the Moors, and that he acquitted himself with credit. Enough is known of the history of the garrison to show that this service was no child's play. As many as 20,000 Moors hovered around Tangier, and lay in ambush for parties from the town. Twice already they had caught the British in their toils. On the first occasion they destroyed a detachment of 400 men. On the second, the governor, the Earl of Teviot, a Scottish soldier,

who had risen high in the service of France, was one of many
officers who perished His name stands first upon the roll of
those illustrious warriors of his race, who like Abercrombie,
Gordon, and Wauchope, have died for Britain in Africa   The
character of the enemy has changed but little in two centuries
and a half.   Cruel, fanatical, and elusive, the Moor of Churchill's
day was very like the Moor, who in more recent times has defied
the military enterprise of France. But the musket of the
seventeenth century was far from conferring on its possessor the
overwhelming superiority of the modern rifle. The handful of
regular troops and gentlemen-volunteers, who held Tangier for
England, had not that advantage of weapons, which could compensate them for their inferiority of numbers. They depended
rather upon discipline, and upon that contemptuous valour,
which has always distinguished British soldiers in the face of
savage foes   Churchill was perhaps fortunate to bring off his
experience unscathed. He had begun well. No better education
in military resourcefulness could be imagined than campaigning
at Tangier with that valiant regiment, which is to-day " The
Queen's " (West Surrey). But more precious by far was the
insight, which he then and there acquired, into the strategical
importance to England of the Mediterranean Sea and of the
Straits of Gibraltar. In daily and direct contact with the
soldiers and sailors, the merchants and diplomatists, who had
come to understand what as yet was hidden from the English
people, he learned a lesson which he never forgot. In 1682
Whiggery forced Charles II to abandon the place, which had
been so expensively fortified and improved and so tenaciously
defended for twenty years. But twenty years later, when
Churchill found himself in responsible control of the strategy of
England in European war, he remembered the lesson of his
youth and signally applied it.

Two years after Churchill's return from Tangier he obtained
the opportunity for which he longed. In the spring of 1672
England and France declared war against the United Provinces
By land, the principal burden of the struggle naturally devolved
upon the French   But Charles II had agreed to furnish a contingent of 6,000 British troops, who should serve in the armies of
Louis XIV. For an English officer, who seriously desired to
learn his business, the occasion was unique. The campaign gave
promise of furnishing the finest models in every department of
warlike science   The Dutch, though inferior in numbers and
military quality, were obstinate fighters   To crush them, " very
near 177,000 "[1] men were about to take the field   This, the
largest regular army that had hitherto been seen in Europe, was
commanded by Turenne and Condé, the one unrivalled in strategic
combination, the other in fighting battles   With them were
associated two officers, whose names have become household
words—Martinet, the instructor and disciplinarian, and Vauban,

[1] Lediard, vol. 1., p. 23.

the maker and taker of tremendous fortresses   And behind them
stood the tireless administrator, Louvois, whose genius created
and maintained this vast machine of war in the highest condition
of efficiency and vigour

Early in May Louis began his march   He carried all before
him.   "The King of France," says Burnet, "came down to
Utrecht like a land-flood "[1]   In two months he was almost at the
gates of Amsterdam   The resistance encountered was of the
most trivial kind   Considered as an operation of war, the passage
of the Rhine, so much extolled by the poets, historians, and
painters of that age, possessed but little importance.   But considered as an example of preparation and organisation, the whole
campaign was a masterpiece   Most of his biographers have
asserted that Churchill enjoyed the advantage of participating
in it.   An English detachment, commanded by the Duke of
Monmouth, was indeed present   But Churchill was detained at
home by sterner work   With five companies of his regiment he
was serving in the fleet.

If the Dutch were weak on land, they were strong upon the
water   In a contest with France and England for the mastery
of the sea they had no reason to despair   Had they been ready
in time, they might have destroyed their enemies in detail.
But De Ruyter appeared in the Channel too late to prevent a
junction between the English fleet under the Duke of York and
the squadron from Brest under the Comte d'Estrées   On board
the English ships 3,000 regular troops were acting as marines.
And many gentlemen-volunteers, in accordance with the gallant
custom of the time, shared with them in this hard and perilous
service.   Churchill was near his master, for the " King's Company "
had been assigned to the admiral's flag-ship, *The Prince*   The
combined navies (" a goodly yet terrible sight,"[2] says Evelyn, who
saw them from Dover) sailed proudly through the Straits   De
Ruyter fell back to the shelter of his own coasts, while the allied
squadrons, which were anxious to victual and water, dropped
anchor in Solebay.   Here, on the morning of June 7, De Ruyter
surprised them   Many of the sailors were still ashore, when a
French frigate signalled the approach of the enemy, who were
standing down in two lines before a north-east wind.   At once
the drums beat, and the constables hurried the laggards from
the ale-houses to the boats.   Though the allies had 101 ships of
the line to De Ruyter's 91, the odds were heavily against them.
The wind blew hard upon a dangerous coast.   They had neither
space nor time to manœuvre.   Confusion and separation resulted, the English tacking to the north and the French to the
south.   De Ruyter, who was indubitably the most accomplished naval commander of the time, detached a small division
to amuse the French, and fell with the whole of his remaining
force upon the English.   The battle which ensued was one of

[1] Burnet, vol. i., p 359   [2] *Evelyn's Diary*, May 14, 1672

the most desperate in the annals of the British navy. Like the classic combat of Syracuse, it was fought in full view of an excited multitude, whose emotions are described in the ancient ballad.

> " I cannot stay to name the names
> Of all the ships that fought with James,
> Their number or their tonnage,
> But this I say the noble host
> Right gallantly did take its post,
> And covered all the hollow coast
> From Walderswyck to Dunwich "[1]

Two hundred miles to the north, the fishermen in Bridlington Bay listened awestruck to the cannonade. The citizens of Calais heard it plainly, and dispatched swift horsemen to Paris with the news. Ensign Churchill found himself in the hottest of the fighting From the outset *The Prince* was specially selected for attack. Two fire-ships, the torpedoes of that age, were loosed against her. She sank one and disabled the other. But she was cruelly punished by the Dutchmen's broadsides Her captain was killed, and 200 of her crew were put out of action Before 11 o'clock she was a partial wreck. James shifted his flag to the *St Michael*, and subsequently to the *London* All day long the conflict raged. Lord Sandwich, the second-in-command, a cautious seaman, who imagined that his courage lay under suspicion, stood by his burning ship to the last, and perished in the waves It is said that d'Estrées meditated tacking to the relief of his hard-pressed allies. Had he attempted it, he would certainly have been annihilated. At sunset the Dutch withdrew. Both sides had suffered terribly, and both claimed the victory in what De Ruyter called the severest of the thirty-two actions in which he had been engaged The battle was in fact indecisive. But the strategical advantages remained with the Dutch. For the allied navies were far too crippled to co-operate with Louis in the invasion of Holland.

The Guards did well and had many casualties. Churchill was selected for promotion over the heads of his seniors. The Lord High Admiral's regiment, a body of musketeers, who acted as marines, had lost four captains in the battle The Duke of York was colonel. It was probably upon his recommendation that one of these vacancies was allotted to Ensign Churchill.

On land the rapid progress of the French arms reduced the Dutch to the extremity of exasperation and despair In the last resort they opened the dykes They met invasion with inundation. Meantime, Europe, alarmed by the aggrandisement of France, hurried to their assistance. In August, the Elector of Brandenburg and Montecuculi, the Emperor's general, who had served with distinction in the Thirty Years' War and had won imperishable glory against the Turks, appeared upon the Rhine

---

[1] " A song on the Duke's late glorious success over the Dutch " *Naval songs and Ballads*, C H. Firth.

with 40,000 men. Condé and Turenne hastened to oppose them. The position was now reversed. The French, who had begun the campaign by an irresistible attack, were compelled before its close to stand strictly on their defence

In January, 1673, Monmouth's regiment of infantry, which had served under Condé in Lorraine, went into winter-quarters at Arras and Douai   Meantime orders had been issued to raise a second contingent of eight companies, drawn from other battalions   Captain Churchill's company of the Lord High Admiral's regiment was one of those selected   The King displayed a particular interest in the undertaking   Many gentlemen of name, hoping to secure commissions, enlisted in the ranks   In December this new corps, which was commanded by Lieutenant Colonel Bevil Skelton, a former captain of the Guards, embarked at Dover. Landing at Calais, they proceeded at once to join the battalion of Monmouth at Arras and Douai   A party of officers, of whom Churchill was one, obtained permission to visit Paris, where they were presented to the King by Grammont.   Little did Louis, now at the zenith of his glory, imagine that the handsome boy in a scarlet coat was destined to humble his power in the dust.

From the outset the question of precedence created friction between Monmouth's regiment and the newcomers, who were not a draft of recruits but a picked body of seasoned soldiers, chosen from regiments senior to Monmouth's. The tension existing between these two bands of high-spirited foreigners caused some anxiety to the French authorities at Arras.   Eventually the point at issue was referred to Charles himself   His decision was adverse to the claims of Monmouth's men.   But Monmouth got his revenge.   When the campaign of 1673 began, his regiment joined Turenne, while Skelton's, much to its disgust, was left without active employment

Turenne, by brilliant operations, conducted in the depth of a severe winter, had compelled the Prussians and Imperialists to retire with ignominy   The Elector indeed was so disheartened that he withdrew for a time from the coalition   Despite this great success, Louis decided that the campaign of 1673 should proceed upon less ambitious lines than its predecessor. The principal object which he proposed to himself was the capture of Maestricht   Maestricht was a place of immense strength, invaluable as a base for the reduction of the United Provinces and the Spanish Netherlands. In the preceding year Condé had urged him to besiege it. But, following Turenne's advice, he had merely masked it. He now prepared to invest it in person. The operation was to be covered by two armies   In the north, Condé, acting if possible in combination with the allied fleets, was to keep the Dutch forces fully occupied. In the east, Turenne was to hold the Imperialists at bay.

In June the investment began   Ten days later the trenches

were opened. Monmouth was present, and, though Skelton's regiment was still unemployed, Churchill accompanied him. Presumably he had obtained permission to go upon this special service as a volunteer The privilege was not to be despised. Vauban himself was directing the operations, which astonished both besiegers and besieged Never before had science conferred upon the assailants of a fortified place so much immunity combined with so much power Churchill had now an opportunity of studying the highest development to which the art of the military engineer had at that time attained. He had also a chance of personal distinction, which he did not fail to seize The attack upon the counterscarp was ordered for the evening of the day on which Monmouth was the Lieutenant-General on duty in the trenches. At 10 o'clock the cannon gave the signal Simultaneously the attack was delivered in three separate places. The assault upon the counterscarp and demi-lune before the Tongres Gate succeeded A hundred of that superb force, the King's Musketeers, led on the column. One among an ardent band of volunteers was Churchill Another, a cornet of horse, whose presence there was contrary to orders, but whose reckless daring atoned in Louis' eyes for his disobedience, was Louis Hector de Villars, whom thirty-seven years later all the world knew as the hero of Malplaquet and the victor of Denain The fire from the palisades and ramparts was said by men experienced in war to have been the hottest they had ever faced But the assailants never flinched They discharged one volley; and then, over bursting mines, and through tempests of shattering grenades, surged up the counterscarp sword in hand. The Dutch were driven from both counterscarp and demi-lune. Three times they returned, and three times they were repulsed Then sullenly they withdrew, leaving the French to fortify the position which had been so gallantly won.

The garrison, who numbered 6,000, under the command of Fariaux, a valiant Frenchman in the service of the enemy, did not acquiesce in their defeat. At noon on the ensuing day, which was Sunday, they sprang a mine beneath the demi-lune with murderous effect, and fell furiously upon the working-party and their guards. Surprised and outnumbered, the French gave way. Monmouth was at dinner when the news came. Alarmed for the safety of his prize, he instantly dispatched a body of the King's Musketeers to the scene. But they came too late. Fariaux was already in partial possession of the demi-lune Thereupon the Duke and Churchill made for the trenches. They were followed by twelve private gentlemen of the English Life Guards Other Englishmen of quality, nine in all, with half a dozen of the Duke's pages and servants, joined them as they went along. The situation admitted of no delay. To advance by the trenches was to sacrifice time to safety. The English did not hesitate. Monmouth, a famous runner, sprang

over the parapet, and raced across the open under a heavy fire
Close at his heels came Churchill and the rest. The gentlemen
of the Life Guards flung away their carbines and drew their
broad-swords. Arrived at the demi-lune, the little party fought
their way in through a sally-port. Their appearance rallied the
Musketeers, who were retiring. The combat was renewed and
vigorously sustained till reinforcements arrived   Once more,
and finally, the Dutch were driven from demi-lune and counterscarp. The Italian regiment, the best in the town, was ruined.
But the handful of English suffered severely   Churchill was
among the wounded   And France that day lost one who is
counted for ever among the paladins   D'Artagnan, Dumas'
D'Artagnan, was killed
The importance of this success became speedily manifest.
After twenty-three days of investment, and thirteen of open
trenches, Maestricht fell
The conduct of the English was the admiration of both armies.
Churchill's behaviour in particular acquired him a great reputation   Where all were brave, his bravery had been prominent.
Louis XIV publicly thanked him in the presence of the troops,
and promised to recommend him to the King of England.   It
was not upon the money-bags of Barbara Villiers, but upon the
blood-stained counterscarp of Maestricht that the foundations
of the house of Marlborough were truly laid
In England the glory gained at Maestricht was grateful to the
national pride. A model of that fortress was constructed in the
ensuing year in a meadow at Windsor, and was duly attacked
and defended by the Guards " to the greate satisfaction of a thousand spectators,"[1] including Mr. Evelyn and Mr. Pepys. Monmouth himself directed the assault. He was now embarked upon
that fatal tide of popularity, which ultimately tempted him to
his doom   He told the King that he owed his life to Churchill.
Whether he spoke the precise truth or merely the language of
generous compliment, the words have now a tragic irony. For
to Churchill more than to any man he was destined to owe his
death

[1] *Evelyn's Diary*, August 21, 1674

APPENDIX IV

SEDGEMOOR

On Thursday, June 21, 1685, Monmouth's three ships cast anchor at Lyme, famous for its heroic defence against Prince Maurice in the Great Rebellion. Landing at the head of some eighty followers, he at once dispatched his emissaries into the surrounding country, where the ground had already been well prepared. In the market-place at Lyme he caused to be read a manifesto, composed by Ferguson, and described by Burnet as " full of much black and dull malice "[1] In it he proclaimed " war against James, Duke of York, as a murderer and an assassin of innocent men " and as guilty of the " barbarous and horrid parricide " of the late King. Recruits flocked to his standard in droves As many as 1,500 joined him in the first twenty-four hours. The business of arming and drilling went on apace. The King had no regular troops within striking distance. But the militia of the adjacent counties began to assemble. It was James' intention that they should blockade the invader in Lyme On Saturday those of Dorsetshire were mustering at Bridport, only eight miles away. Monmouth determined to attack them at once. Their weapons and equipment offered a tempting bait to an army that was miserably deficient in both. Success at the outset, moreover, would engender confidence. It might even induce the militia, who for the most part sympathised with the pretender's cause, to desert to him in a body.

On Sunday the attempt was made. At dawn Lord Grey, with some 400 of the rebels, aided by a thick mist, and by the enemy's entire neglect of the most elementary precautions, succeeded in surprising Bridport. In hurry and confusion the militia rushed to arms. The odds were all in favour of the assailants, but at the very moment when victory seemed surely in their grasp, Grey and his untrained cavalry, smitten with a sudden panic, wheeled to the rear, and galloped madly back upon the road to Lyme. Thereupon the infantry also retreated, but in good order, and with a dozen prisoners and thirty horses. The royalists had ten killed, including a couple of gentlemen-volunteers Seven of the rebels were slain, and twenty-three taken Monmouth's first essay had miscarried ignominiously

The need of capable leadership was depressingly apparent. But before he had been many hours in England, evil fortune robbed the Duke of the best of his officers. Fletcher of Saltburn,

[1] Burnet, vol ii., p. 262.

having shot and killed Dare in a stupid squabble about a horse, was obliged to fly the country Fletcher was a man of birth and a man of parts, and in both capacities he was sorely missed.

On Monday the Duke set out for Taunton with 3,000 men and 4 guns. The Devon militia under Albemarle, and the Somerset militia under Luttrell, were converging from Exeter and Chard respectively upon the town of Axminster. Monmouth, however, arrived in Axminster before them, and immediately took up a strong position. Some skirmishing ensued But though they were not inferior to the rebels in military value, and were very superior in numbers, neither of the militia regiments showed any stomach for the work. They retreated in disorder, and of the Somerset men, "half, if not the greatest part," went over to the Duke. Monmouth made no attempt to press his advantage. He continued on his way to Taunton, which he entered on Thursday, June 28

His enterprise was assuredly a desperate one. But judged, as it generally is, by the result, it is apt to appear more desperate than it actually was. Subsequent events proved that Monmouth was both ill-informed and badly advised. But at the outset he had specious and not unreasonable grounds for hope. In the first place, he relied upon the western counties, where Puritanism predominated among the middle and lower classes, to furnish him with a secure base and with the raw material of a numerous and fanatical infantry. Secondly, he believed that noblemen and gentlemen would join him in sufficient numbers to lend prestige to his cause and to supply him with a cavalry not wholly contempt-ible Thirdly, he expected that some at least of the King's troops would desert to the banner of one, whom they had formerly known as a daring and popular officer Fourthly, he counted upon an organised rising in Cheshire and another in the capital itself And fifthly, he trusted to Argyle to create a powerful diversion in Scotland. Of these anticipations only the first was realised. Had all or most of them been fulfilled, or even partially fulfilled, the rebellion could not have been suppressed without a bloody and protracted struggle. It might even have succeeded in the end.

Meantime, the government had not been idle. On the day of Monmouth's landing the Mayor of Lyme dispatched his servants with the news to the loyal gentry of Somerset and Devon, and himself rode off to Exeter to inform Albemarle From Honiton he sent an express to London, which was reached at 4 a m on Saturday morning. The Privy Council was instantly convened Confirmatory evidence soon came to hand. Riding night and day, two burgesses of Lyme alighted at the door of Sir Winston Churchill, the member for the borough. Lord Churchill and he conducted them immediately to Whitehall. The most energetic measures were taken Parliament displayed the utmost loyalty. A sum of £400,000 was voted for the King's use. Monmouth

was attainted, and a reward of £5,000 was offered for his apprehen‑
sion. All the militia of the western counties was enrolled.
Professional soldiers were deputed to advise the lords‑lieutenant.
James requested the Prince of Orange to lend him the British
regiments in the Dutch service. Such regular troops as were
instantly available were ordered to proceed forthwith to Salisbury.
The command, with the rank of Brigadier, was bestowed upon
" our trusty and well‑beloved John, Lord Churchill, Colonel of
our Royal Regiment of Dragoons "[1] The choice was a good one.
Churchill was an officer of experience, as experience went in
England at that time; he possessed an intimate knowledge of the
country in which he was to operate and of the people inhabiting
it, and from personal contact he understood thoroughly the
character and capacity of the man to whom he was opposed.

On Saturday, the very day on which the news arrived, Churchill
set off. With him went two troops of his own dragoons, and four
troops of the Earl of Oxford's Horse (The Blues). Five com‑
panies of the Queen Dowager's Regiment of Foot (The West
Surrey), under Colonel Kirke, were to follow as quickly as
possible; and a train of artillery was to join him from Portsmouth.
On Wednesday, the 27th, he reached Bridport. On Thursday,
the 28th, he was at Axminster, in the heart of his own country.
On Friday, the 29th, he arrived at Chard, midway between Taun‑
ton and Lyme There he was in a position to join hands with the
militia of Dorset and Devon. He was also established upon
Monmouth's line of retreat, if retreat were in any circumstances
contemplated. On the following day, however, this door was
finally closed The King's ships appeared off Lyme One of
Monmouth's had already left. But the other two surrendered.
Forty barrels of powder, and helmets and cuirasses for some
four or five thousand men, formed part of the capture.

When Churchill arrived at Chard, Monmouth was at Taunton,
" a very factious toun,"[2] where he had been welcomed with
extraordinary enthusiasm by a community which cherished
always the traditions of the Great Rebellion Soon he had more
recruits than he could arm. But the nobility and gentry still
held aloof. Consequently he still lacked the material of a
cavalry that could be relied on not to run away. At Taunton he
proclaimed himself king, declared that his father had been
poisoned by " James, Duke of York," and offered a reward for
the head of that " usurper." But despite these impudent follies,
he now began to realise the extreme difficulty of his enterprise
His strategical plan was a daring one He proposed to seize
the important city of Bristol, where he would find many adherents
and abundance of arms and supplies From Bristol he intended
to advance through Gloucestershire, effect a junction with his

[1] *The History of the Second Queen's Royal Regiment, now The Queen's
(Royal West Surrey) Regiment,* Colonel John Davis, vol ii , p 22
[2] Dalrymple, vol ii p 23 James II to the Prince of Orange, June 17,
1685

friends from Cheshire, and move in overwhelming force upon the capital   A scheme, so bold and so ambitious, obviously depended for success upon the rapidity of its execution.   It was absolutely essential that the Duke should be in Bristol before the regular army arrived from London   But Monmouth, trained among the professional soldiers of the continent, and deeply impressed by his own easy triumph over the Covenanters at Bothwell Bridge, attached undue importance to the instruction of his undisciplined troops.   He was drilling when he ought to have been marching.   He was squandering golden hours   In military value his men were not greatly inferior to the militia, in which the majority of them were accustomed to serve   And the militia could not be trusted to oppose him either at Bristol or elsewhere.   Not tactical precision but time was the predominant factor in the situation.   And the wasting of the time, which he devoted to a futile attempt to place his soldiery upon an equality with the regular forces, destroyed him

On the day of his arrival at Chard, Churchill began at once to get touch of the enemy   Some twenty of his cavalry, patrolling in the direction of Taunton, encountered an equal number of the rebel horse   After a brisk engagement, in which twelve of Monmouth's men were killed, the rebels retired upon their supports, and the King's troopers drew off to Chard with a loss of only one killed and two wounded.   Monmouth could derive no sort of encouragement from this affair   It by no means dissipated the unfavourable impression created by the misconduct of his cavalry at Bridport   At least two years are requisite for the training of a horse-soldier; and Monmouth's men had not been embodied two weeks.   They knew how to ride, and there is no reason to suppose that they were inferior in constitutional courage to their comrades of the infantry   But the fault lay less with the men than with the horses, many of which had not even been broken to ordinary purposes, and were now required to face the exacting test of war

Churchill, who had been joined at Chard by Kirke, had undoubtedly considered the feasibility of destroying Monmouth's army before the main body of the King's troops arrived from London.   On July 1 he wrote to the Duke of Somerset: " I have forces enough not to apprehend the Duke of Monmouth, but quite contrary, should be glad to meet with him, and my men are in so good heart "   He seems to have hoped that the militia, stiffened by the excellent regiments which he commanded, would be sufficient for the task.   Moreover, he was instructed by Sunderland that James desired him to occupy Bridgwater and bar the road to Bristol   But the information which he collected at Chard compelled him to abandon all such ideas.   The militia of those counties which formed the immediate theatre of operations were wholly untrustworthy.   Hardly a man of them would fight, and not a few were prepared to follow the example of those

who had already deserted   Indeed, two days after Churchill's
arrival at Chard, a couple of Somerset companies went over to
the rebels   In these circumstances he had no option but to
await the coming of his reinforcements   In the meantime, if he
was too weak to attack, he was also too strong to be attacked.
But there was one risk.   At any moment Monmouth might awake
to the importance of celerity, and might carry Bristol with a
rush   He was deterred solely by his nervous dread of attempting
anything serious until such time as his followers should have
acquired some semblance of discipline.   Churchill, who had
served with him in the field, and knew him thoroughly, realised
the necessity of playing on his fears.   He realised that the more
active and enterprising the royal troopers showed themselves,
·the greater would become the anxiety and hesitation of the rebel
commander.   By efficient scouting and the assiduous collection
of intelligence, he could maintain perpetual touch with the rebels
without any danger to himself; by clinging to their flanks, cutting
off their stragglers, and routing their cavalry in vigorous skirmishes, he could harass and depress them to the last degree, and
by the diligence of his patrols, and the terror which the mere
presence of the royal troops inspired, he could prevent, or at any
rate impede, the increase of their numerical strength.   His own
intimate knowledge of the country and its inhabitants fitted him
well for the execution of such duties.   And in his superb cavalry,
supported by his dragoons, he possessed a force pre-eminently
adapted to carry out his plans.   The more Monmouth saw of
Churchill's men, the more diffident he would grow of his own, and
the more likely would he be to fritter away invaluable time in the
vain hope that he could drill his army into shape, or that recruits
of better quality would come to his assistance.

On July 1, after discussing and rejecting a proposal to turn and
attack Churchill, Monmouth marched to Bridgwater with 7,000
men, while Churchill's column, moving on parallel lines, came
to Langport.   Bridgwater showed itself, if possible, more enthusiastic for the Duke than Taunton   To meet the difficulty of
arming his recruits, he issued an order under the style of " James
R." for the constables and tything-men to search the country
round for scythes.   On the 2nd, in pouring rain, the rebels set
out for Glastonbury.   Churchill's tireless troopers soon made
their appearance on the right   Hour after hour they hovered
upon the flank and rear of the army, as it toiled onward through
the mud.   Some of those who took part in the retreat from
Quatre Bras to Waterloo, when the rain descended in torrents
and Napoleon's cavalry rode menacingly behind and beside the
line of march, have recorded with what joy the British infantry
beheld their mounted comrades executing the Duke of Wellington's orders to " drive those fellows off."   No such spectacle
cheered the hearts of Monmouth's men.   Grey's unhappy horsemen proved quite unequal to their work.   Eighty of them

collapsed before a charge of forty of the Horse Guards, who chased them almost to the shelter of the rebel pikes and scythes. Attended always by these tenacious companions of the road, the drenched and dispirited column tramped into Glastonbury, and kindled its fires among the ruins of the abbey

Meantime the main body of the royal army was rapidly advancing from the capital. But Churchill was no longer in supreme command. Some days after his departure from London he had been superseded by the Earl of Feversham. The military reason for this new appointment was not very obvious. Feversham's record was not superior to Churchill's, and his reputation in the army was by no means high Certainly he was the older man by ten years, and by far the better born, but whatever accession of authority he derived from those circumstances, was more than counterbalanced by the unpopularity attaching to his foreign origin Of the two, Churchill would have been by far the better choice. But James has been very unduly censured for his action in this matter. It is ridiculous to expect him to have seen in Churchill the future victor of Blenheim and Ramillies. He liked and trusted both men Feversham, however, was the nephew of Turenne, who had been a generous friend to James, Duke of York, in the days of his exile James, King of England, was not unmindful of his debt of honour to the dead. Nor was Feversham merely the elegant imbecile depicted by Macaulay. Even Burnet admits that he was " an honest, brave, and good-natured man "[1] And he certainly understood as much about the art of war as did the frivolous Monmouth, or indeed the great majority of British officers of that time.

It goes without saying that Churchill was bitterly disappointed at his supersession. He seems to have regarded it as a reflection on his loyalty as much as on his capacity The war being a civil war, this aspect of the question could not be overlooked When Monmouth at Taunton assumed the royal title, he sent a letter to Churchill at Chard, claiming the allegiance of his old companion-in-arms. Churchill administered a dignified rebuff by way of reply; and at the same time, he forwarded the Duke's letter to the King. But far away in London the government, overwhelmed with anxiety, may conceivably have repented of its hasty selection of a general. Some among the King's advisers may well have recollected that Churchill and Monmouth had once been famous friends, and had hazarded their lives together on the counterscarp of Maestricht They were now within a few miles of one another in the heart of a country where Monmouth had many supporters, and where Churchill's family had large interests and connections. It might be said that common prudence demanded the appointment of a commander-in-chief who would be exempt from any special temptations to play the traitor That James himself had doubts of the fidelity of his

[1] Burnet, vol. ii., p 264

favourite, is altogether improbable. But he may have been willing to appear to show deference to the judgment of those who had Churchill, of course, could hardly be expected to appreciate these considerations. He only knew that he was deprived of a great opportunity, and that possibly his loyalty was suspect. His private correspondence shows that he was both disappointed and hurt "I see plainly," he wrote to Clarendon, "that the troble is mine, and that the honor will be another's "[1] But he wisely determined to manifest no resentment. Throughout the campaign he continued to display such zeal and ability as won him the commendation of Feversham and the gratitude of the King

Feversham quitted London on June 30 Having ordered his troops to concentrate at Bath, he himself, with 200 horse, made rapidly for Bristol On the road, he detached Oglethorpe with a party in the direction of Andover and Warminster to ascertain the situation of the rebel army. He also sent instructions to the Duke of Somerset to destroy the bridge over the Avon at Keynsham. On the 2nd, he reached Chippenham, where he found Pembroke with the militia of Wiltshire and Hampshire. At noon on the 3rd he entered Bristol. Beaufort and Somerset were there with the militia of Gloucestershire, Monmouthshire, and Herefordshire. That same day Monmouth marched from Glastonbury to Shepton Mallet Churchill, still moving on parallel lines, came to Somerton, where he was joined by his brother, Colonel Churchill, who, with a strong detachment of horse and foot, including five companies of the Queen's Regiment, had escorted the train of eight guns from Portsmouth. Skirmishing between the mounted men of both armies still continued. The royal troopers were very active, and brought in many prisoners, among others " Jarvice, a felt-maker—a notorious fellow."[2]

It was Monmouth's design to cross the Avon at Keynsham and attack Bristol on the Gloucestershire side, where the defences were weakest. Turning to his left on the 4th, he struck away towards Pensford Churchill replied by moving upon Wells The lines of march continued to be parallel, but Churchill was now upon Monmouth's left, instead of, as hitherto, upon his right, and the rebels ran a risk of being caught between the royal armies. Early that morning Feversham returned from Bristol to Bath, where he found Oglethorpe, who reported the advance of the rebels to Shepton Mallet. Feversham ordered him to ascertain their subsequent movements At midnight the commander-in-chief received the information that Monmouth was encamped at Pensford, only four miles from Keynsham

[1] General Viscount Wolseley, *The Life of John Churchill, Duke of Marlborough*, vol 1 , p 306.
[2] Dummer's Journal, June 23, 1685; Pepysian Library, No 2490, Magdalene College, Cambridge. Quoted in *The History of the Second Queen's Royal Regiment*, vol ii , p 47

Instantly he dispatched the whole of his cavalry to Bristol. He himself followed with the foot.

Monmouth knew nothing of these movements. Having detached a party to repair the bridge at Keynsham, he passed the night at Pensford A little before daybreak on the 5th, when Feversham's cavalry were entering Bristol, the rebels advanced to Keynsham and passed the Avon Monmouth decided to assault the city under cover of darkness Meanwhile, to refresh his wearied troops and to suggest to the enemy that he had abandoned his design on Bristol, he recrossed the river and encamped at Keynsham. By this time his army is said to have numbered no fewer than 1,000 horse and 8,000 foot; but many of his men were very indifferently provided with weapons. They spent the day in repose and in preparation for the attack on Bristol. The city was the second in the kingdom It contained an abundance of arms and money. Its political, commercial, and strategical value was enormous If Monmouth took it, his cause would not be easily put down. He knew that the ramparts were dilapidated He knew that the militia, who composed the garrison, were disaffected He knew that he had friends among the citizens who had promised to open the gates. But he did not know that the royal cavalry was already there, and that the royal infantry was following fast

But he learned the truth before nightfall Oglethorpe, with one troop of the Blues, and one of militia horse, was still scouring the country to the west of Bath The rebels kept no proper watch Oglethorpe was equally careless. The consequence was that this handful of royal cavalry rode unconcernedly into Keynsham before they discovered the presence of the enemy, whom they at first mistook for the militia Then Oglethorpe's conduct went far to redeem his previous error. In modern manœuvres an umpire might have declared him to be out of action. But he instantly charged the astonished rebels with such vigour that he routed their horse, broke through their foot, and finally galloped out of the town with but scanty loss to himself Some of his troopers were taken, but fourteen of the enemy were killed upon the spot. This incident, so characteristic of the English soldier at his best and worst, did not tend to encourage either the insurgents or their leader. A prisoner told the Duke that Feversham was at hand with 4,000 men Monmouth imagined that Oglethorpe's party was the advance-guard of Churchill's column, and that Churchill and Feversham were converging upon Keynsham to crush him between them. Later in the day, his scouts reported that the royal army was actually at Bristol. Thereupon he abandoned the project which had brought him to the banks of the Avon. This decision was fatal. In the words of Wolseley, " the capture of Bristol was the last chance upon which Monmouth had any right to calculate."[1]

[1] Wolseley, vol. 1 , p. 299.

At first he proposed to make for Gloucester, pass the Severn, destroy the bridge behind him, and push on to Cheshire. But in deference to the opinion of his officers, who were afraid lest Churchill's cavalry should succeed in holding him until Feversham's infantry came up, he decided to try Wiltshire, where he was advised that 500 horse were ready to join him He likewise resolved to attempt the capture of Bath, which in Feversham's absence invited an attack. This last, says Wolseley, " was a foolish plan, and could lead to little even if successful "[1]

Starting at nightfall on the 5th, he struck away to the right along the south bank of the Avon. Churchill was now at Pens-ford, close upon the heels of the rebels, and well informed of all their movements While his horsemen watched them on the road to Bath, he himself prepared to join forces with Feversham Marching out of Pensford on the morning of Friday, the 6th, he took the way towards Bristol A mile beyond the town he halted, and hanged " Jarvice the felt-maker," who died " obstinately and impenitently."[2] Leaving behind him this deterrent example for the benefit of the disaffected of those parts, he resumed his march Presently he was met by an order from Feversham to rejoin at Bath, whither the commander-in-chief was now returning by the north bank of the Avon. Monmouth, in the meantime, halted on the hill to the southward of that city and in mere bravado summoned it to surrender The citizens killed his messenger and treated his message with disdain. Without attempting to avenge the insult, the rebel army wheeled off to the right and headed for Wiltshire A march of seven miles through a mountainous country brought them to the village of Philip's Norton, where they halted for the night. That same evening Feversham and Churchill joined hands at Bath. Exclusive of militia, their combined forces were not far short of 3,000 men The cavalry numbered 700, the infantry nearly 2,000; and there was Churchill's train of 8 guns. The artillery from London had not yet arrived

Early on the morning of Saturday, the 7th, Feversham paraded his army on the outskirts of Bath He very properly intended to attack the rebels at once For more than a fortnight the insolent pretender and his deluded adherents had been at large in the Western counties It was high time to assert the King's authority On political, even more than on military, grounds Monmouth should be forced to a decisive engagement. Feversham had dispatched a party to ascertain the movements of the enemy. The officer in command reported that, according to the statements of the peasantry, the rebels were still at Philip's Norton. Feversham dispatched a second party of household cavalry with orders to bring back no hearsay evidence but to reconnoitre the enemy until they drew his fire. Monmouth was about to take the road, when the royal troopers alarmed his rear-

[1] Wolseley, vol. 1., p. 299.   [2] Dummer's Journal.

guard After a few shots had been exchanged, the Duke of
Grafton, who had been detached with 500 foot and Churchill's
dragoons, arrived upon the ground It was now raining heavily.
Grafton's instructions were to pursue the rebels and to hold
them in play until the main body could get up. Despite the
villainous weather and the steepness of the ways, he had marched
with great rapidity; he now attacked with equal vigour The
approach to Philip's Norton from the north lay through a narrow
lane, a quarter of a mile long Monmouth lined the hedges with
his infantry and set 50 musketeers behind a stiff barricade, which
had been erected at the entrance of the village Grafton himself
led in a body of 45 grenadiers to the support of the household
cavalry, and essayed to force a passage. The rebels resisted
stoutly. The fighting in the lane and at the barricade was very
fierce As soon as Feversham arrived, he ordered Churchill with
a company of grenadiers to advance to the assistance of the Duke.
Monmouth threw forward both horse and foot upon Grafton's
flank, and almost succeeded in enveloping the handful of troops
already engaged But Feversham called up the horse-grenadiers
and easily intimidated the rebel cavalry. Nevertheless Grafton,
whose behaviour that day bore witness to the fact that not all
the bastards of Charles II were disloyal, was virtually surrounded.
He found himself alone with twenty troopers. He refused to
accept a horse which was offered him by a non-commissioned
officer of the Blues; but he caught another, which was already
wounded, and eventually cut his way out with the survivors
of his party The cavalry and dragoons were so closely packed
in the narrow lane that, in Feversham's opinion, they would have
been badly mauled if Monmouth had delivered a vigorous
counter-stroke. As it was, however, they retired steadily, the
movement being covered by Churchill with Grafton's 500 foot
and dragoons. Churchill in turn was warmly assailed by the
rebels. Feversham drew up his horse on a gentle rise at the
mouth of the fatal lane; here he was rejoined by Churchill, who
was not pursued, and the main body of the royal infantry having
now arrived, the line of battle was speedily completed. The
artillery was delayed by the badness of the roads, but as soon as
it appeared it was ordered to the front. It played upon the
rebels with good effect. Monmouth posted two small pieces in
the lane, and two on an adjacent elevation, and replied to the
best of his ability. For a couple of hours the cannonade continued, while the rain beat pitilessly down. Feversham desired
to pass the night in that situation; but his tents had not arrived,
and he could procure no shelter for his troops. Accordingly, at
4 o'clock he retired north-eastward upon Bradford. Oglethorpe with a party of horse remained behind to watch the
enemy's movements. Monmouth resumed his march the same
evening in the direction of Frome. Both armies were soaked and
considerably maltreated. In Feversham's no fewer than fifty

had been killed. The rebel dead are said to have numbered eighteen.

In this sharp skirmish Monmouth's foot had fought well and had inflicted a distinct check upon the enemy, whose subsequent withdrawal to Bradford could be construed as an admission of defeat Yet the rebels were in no mood of exultation. The abandonment of the design on Bristol, the failure at Bath, the retrograde nature of the movement on Frome, the knowledge that the royal army was concentrated, the sight and sound of its formidable artillery, and the physical exhaustion induced by fighting and marching in the heavy rain, had depressed and demoralised these untrained soldiers As many as 2,000 are said to have deserted between Philip's Norton and Frome Such discipline as had hitherto existed was entirely relaxed, and plunder and licence became the order of the day.

Monmouth himself was horribly cast down. At Frome he found that a convoy of arms and stores, which he was expecting there, had been captured by the loyal militia of Wiltshire under Lord Pembroke. He realised that the promises made by his friends in that county could not be fulfilled He learned, for the first time, of the complete failure of Argyle. He learned also that the troops from Holland had landed at Gravesend. He had no information of the projected rising in London, although the absence of the royal army had provided the ringleaders with a favourable opportunity. He had seen with his own eyes at Philip's Norton the splendid regiments which were now within striking distance of his half-armed and despondent followers. He knew only too well that a price of £5,000 was set upon his head, for he had already been "shot at thrice by his own men." Gloomy and unnerved, he summoned a council of war on the afternoon of Sunday, the 8th It was actually proposed— whether by Monmouth or by some of his advisers, is uncertain— that those who had landed at Lyme should slip away that night to Poole and escape to Holland. This infamous suggestion was eventually rejected in favour of a retirement to Bridgwater, where numerous recruits were said to be assembling But the same evening three of the Duke's principal officers deserted.

Meanwhile, Feversham's men spent Sunday in repose at Bradford. They had need of rest. From the time when the main body quitted London on June 30, to the time when the rear-guard tramped into Bradford a little before midnight on Saturday, July 7, they had marched incessantly for eight days on end. Churchill's column had worked longer and harder still; and the Dorset militia, which had accompanied it, were so exhausted that Feversham dismissed them to the easier duty of maintaining order in their own county

Feversham experienced a certain difficulty in divining the enemy's intentions. He was considering the expediency of detaching Churchill to hold the road to Bristol, while he himself

barred the way to London, when he learned from Oglethorpe
that Monmouth designed to move upon Warminster. On
Monday, the 9th, therefore, he marched southward to Westbury,
with the object of attacking the rebels. But instead of moving
upon Warminster, they continued still at Frome. The same day
Feversham was joined by the artillery from London, with its
escort of five companies of Dumbarton's regiment He also
received a supply of tents, which, according to Shere, the officer
in command of the guns, " came very seasonably."[1] The
billeting of the soldiers in towns and villages was attended by
grave abuses. " Unless we encamp," said Shere, " the country
will be ruined, for we have been hitherto much their greater
enemies than the rebels." Moreover, dependence upon towns and
villages hampered the mobility of the royal army. The retreat
to Bradford, for example, was due entirely to the want of tents.

Feversham was now instructed by Sunderland that, in the
King's opinion, Churchill should not again be detached from
the main body. Lord Wolseley infers that James " evidently
doubted Feversham's military skill and wished him to have
Churchill at his side as an adviser."[2] This inference is needlessly
unjust to the commander-in-chief. Seeing that the royal army
was supposed to be outnumbered by the rebels in the proportion
of three to one, any division of forces was to be deprecated unless
absolute necessity compelled And now that their camp
equipment had arrived, the King's soldiers had nothing to do
but to stick together and to stick to the enemy.

On the 10th, Monmouth retired from Frome to Shepton
Mallet Feversham occupied Frome the same day. The advance
of the royal army created a wholesome consternation in the
disaffected area. The effect produced by the appearance of
Churchill's cavalry has been well described by one who witnessed
it " Terror marched before them," he said, " for we could hear
their horses grind the ground under their feet almost a mile before
they came." But Churchill himself was by no means satisfied
Writing to his wife from Frome, he said, " We have had abundance of rain, which has very much tired our soldiers, which I
think is ill, because it makes us not press the Duke of Monmouth
so much as I think he should be, and that it will make me the
longer from you, for I suppose until he be routed I shall not have
the happiness of being with you."[3] He consoled himself, however,
with " her picture," which she had sent him by Lord Colchester.
" I do assure you," he wrote, " that it was very welcome to me,
and will be, when I am alone, a great satisfaction to me, for the
whole world put together I do not love so well as I do you, for I
swear to you I had much rather lose my own life than lose you."[4]

Continuing his retreat, and losing always by desertion on the

[1] MSS of the Earl of Dartmouth Henry Shere to Lord Dartmouth,
July 1, 1685 (Hist MSS Comm , 11th Report, Appendix, part v., p 126).
[2] Wolseley, vol. 1 , p 303.
[3] *Ibid* , p. 304.			[4] *Ibid.*

way, Monmouth halted at the cathedral town of Wells, where his demoralised adherents indulged in one of those iconoclastic orgies, which are a perpetual reproach to the name of Puritanism Early on Friday the 13th, he entered Bridgwater for the second time. It was only eleven days since he had quitted that town, in some depression, it is true, but not without daring hopes, he returned to it now in a condition of mind indistinguishable from despair.

Meanwhile, the royal army was ploughing laboriously through the mud in pursuit of the rebels. Having rested on the 11th at Frome, they marched on the 12th to Shepton Mallet, and on the 13th by Glastonbury to Somerton They rested again on Saturday, the 14th; but two[1] parties of horse, which they dispatched towards Bridgwater, boldly approached the town, skirmished successfully with Monmouth's men, and returned with the intelligence that he had broken down the bridges, and was fortifying the place as if he would endure a siege. His intentions were difficult to fathom, for he changed them almost from hour to hour. But Churchill suspected the truth, or something very like it. " I find," he wrote, on the 14th, to Lord Clarendon, " by the enemy's warrant to the constables, that they have more mind to get horses and saddles than anything else, which looks as if he had a mind to break away with his horse to some other place, and leave his foot entrenched at Bridgewater."[2] It is justly observed by Wolseley that " a peculiar gift, one of the instincts that mark the born general," was an essential characteristic of Churchill's genius "From apparently small indications he possessed the power of divining his enemies' plans." In the present instance he was not far wrong Monmouth had reverted to his original design He had resolved to march a second time for Keynsham, effect a junction at Gloucester with his friends from Cheshire, and execute a dash upon London, where, according to his latest information, 3,000 men were waiting only for a leader

Feversham in person reconnoitred the country in the direction of Bridgwater and chose the village of Middlezoy for his next encampment. But a better situation was subsequently discovered at Weston Zoyland, and thither, on Sunday, the 15th, the royal army marched. Less than four miles now separated the combatants. From the tower of the parish church of Bridgwater, Monmouth could descry the tents of his pursuers.

Generals, trained like Feversham in the rigid school of continental warfare, excelled in nothing so much as in the selection of a strong camp The position of the royal army at Weston Zoyland was a fair example of this art Sedgemoor, the flat, low-lying region to the east of Bridgwater, bounded on the north by the Polden Hills and on the south by the River Parret, had been, in the days of the Saxons, an extensive swamp. But in

[1] One of these was a troop of Churchill's dragoons.
[2] Wolseley, vol. 1 , p 306

1685, though it was still liable to inundation, it had been partially
drained by huge ditches, locally known as " rhines." These
ditches were at all times dangerously deep in mud; but heavy
rains, such as those which had recently fallen, filled them with
water to the brink. One of them, the " Bussex Rhine," traversing
the moor from the north-east towards the south-west, intersected the Bridgwater road at a point about half a mile to the
west of the village of Weston Zoyland, and then swung sharply
round towards the south-east. It provided Feversham with a
ready-made entrenchment, which, being in the shape of a loop,
enabled him to form a convex line of battle, a thing highly recommended by the text-books. In this position he posted his
infantry and guns, the infantry to the north of the Bridgwater
road and the guns to the south of it. In the village behind them
he quartered his cavalry and dragoons. The militia he left at
Othery and Middlezoy, some miles to the rear. Thus strongly
encamped, he proposed to rest his soldiers till the morrow. He
believed with Churchill that Monmouth was about to march a
second time towards Keynsham. In that event, it was very
desirable that the royal army should be fresh for the pursuit.

Though Monmouth had made a pretence of fortifying Bridgwater, and also of retiring upon Taunton, it was still his real
intention to double back towards the Avon. But late in the
day he abandoned this plan, which promised little, for a more
audacious one which promised all. A certain Godfrey, a farmer
who lived near Weston Zoyland, and who had observed the disposition of Feversham's troops, informed him that so much
laxity and confidence prevailed among them that a surprise
under cover of darkness was perfectly feasible. Having listened
to Godfrey's tale, Monmouth ascended the tower of Bridgwater
parish church and carefully examined the enemy's lines through
a spy-glass. Even at that distance he could distinguish the
uniforms of Dumbarton's regiment and the Foot Guards. He
gazed upon them with mingled apprehension and regret, for
he had seen them in the field, and he knew their fighting quality.
But he particularly remarked the separation of the infantry from
the artillery, and the distance of the cavalry from both. Convinced of the possibility of success, he consulted his officers.
Godfrey was sent back to Weston Zoyland to ascertain whether
any entrenchments had been thrown up. He returned with the
intelligence that there were none. But, curiously enough, he
appears to have made no reference to the Bussex Rhine. The
military value of this familiar object entirely escaped him.
Yet Monmouth, at any rate, should have known of its existence.
For twice in the last fortnight he had marched across Sedgemoor,
and no fewer than eight Weston Zoyland men were serving
in the ranks of the insurgents.

Monmouth decided to attempt a surprise. It was a bold
determination, but a proper one. Presented with a great and

unexpected opportunity he had the sense to prefer it to a more
considered, but less promising, plan. But to what extent was
he entitled to count upon the feasibility of a surprise ? Macaulay
alleges that Feversham " even at this momentous crisis .   .
thought only of eating and sleeping "[1] It is impossible to substantiate the charge   Feversham's dispositions for the safety of his
camp were entirely adequate. At Borough Bridge on the Parret
he posted a troop of Churchill's dragoons   In Penzoy Pound,
an enclosure 350 yards to the westward of his guns, he placed a
picket of 50 musketeers   On his left front, on the main road
to Bridgwater, he had patrols and sentries and a guard of
40 horse. On his right front, at Chedzoy village, he had 100
horse and 50 dragoons under Sir Francis Compton, with an advanced party before them, as well as sentries and patrols   He
ordered Dumbarton's regiment to keep 100 men under arms
throughout the night   And finally he instructed Oglethorpe
with a troop of Life Guards to watch the Bristol and Keynsham
roads to the north-east of Bridgwater, and ascertain which route
the rebels selected for their anticipated march towards Gloucestershire   With these arrangements Lord Wolseley has no fault
to find. Feversham himself rode out to see them properly
executed. If, therefore, Monmouth was so credulous as to believe
that Feversham had neglected the ordinary duties of a general,
he was counting upon the chances which did not exist. Probably,
however, he believed nothing of the kind. He trusted rather,
and with very good reason, to Godfrey's assertion that Feversham
was badly served   Penetrated with professional contempt for
their amateur opponents, and convinced that Monmouth's ideas
of strategy were restricted to the art of running away, the officers
and men of the royal army had ceased to cultivate the virtues of
vigilance and sobriety. They ridiculed the suggestion that the
enemy could be capable, under any circumstances, of an offensive
movement. In short, the very weakness of Monmouth's position
had now become his strength   It is to the credit of his military
instinct that he realised that fact

The tactics which he adopted were probably the best that
could be devised. The column was to proceed along the Bristol
road for a distance of two miles, when it was to wheel to its right
into the open moor. Fetching a wide compass to the north-east
of Chedzoy, it was to move circuitously upon the right front
of the royal infantry without attracting the attention of Compton's men. The horse were to push rapidly forward on the left,
and passing unseen in the darkness round the enemy's right flank,
to burst into Weston Zoyland, capture or kill the royal troopers
in their beds, fire the village, and charge the royal infantry in
the rear   If all went well, Feversham's army would be destroyed
long before his powerful artillery, which was stationed on his
extreme left, could come into action   It was an admirable plan;

[1] Macaulay, vol 1 , ch v., p. 295.

but it had one obvious weakness If the Bristol and Keynsham roads were watched, it must collapse at the very beginning. Monmouth did not know that this duty had been assigned to Oglethorpe and a troop of Life Guards There was a bare chance that Feversham might have neglected the precaution There was a much better chance that, whoever was chosen to do the work, would do it badly. Monmouth took the risk.

But he made one serious error of judgment He entrusted his cavalry to Grey When he was reminded that Grey had failed conspicuously at Bridport, he answered: " I will not affront my Lord, what I have given him in charge is easy to be executed "[1] But nocturnal operations are never easy to be executed, and with such troopers as Grey commanded, even a Cromwell or a Zeydlitz could not have answered for the event. Monmouth paid dearly for his complacency.

The distance to be traversed was nearly six miles. Two-thirds of the route lay across the open moor, and it would be necessary to pass a couple of drains, the Black Ditch and the Langmore Rhine But Godfrey undertook to act as guide. Orders were issued that the strictest silence should be maintained, that anyone who made a noise should be instantly stabbed, and that, until they were in the midst of the enemy's camp, there should be no firing.

At 11 o'clock on Sunday night the rebel army set out from Bridgwater. Before 5 on Monday morning its panic-stricken remnants were re-entering the town. The story of what happened in the interval falls naturally into three parts, each part representing a period of approximately two hours.

From 11 to 1, the rebels were marching, undiscovered and unsuspected, towards the royal camp They moved at first in a single column, the infantry leading At Peasy Farm, on the edge of the moor, they left their baggage-waggons and one of their guns. Then Godfrey brought them to the Black Ditch, which they crossed in safety at the ford Re-forming in two columns, the infantry on the right and the cavalry on the left, they proceeded towards the Langmore Rhine. Though the moon shone brightly, a thick mist, which rendered all objects invisible at fifty paces, enveloped the landscape and greatly favoured their chances of concealment Unfortunately, it also perplexed their guide, who brought them indeed to the Langmore Rhine, but not to the crossing. Delay and confusion ensued. Some of the horses stuck fast in the mud, and some of the men lost themselves on the moor; but eventually a passage was effected. The foot re-formed on the opposite bank, while the cavalry continued their advance. One o'clock sounded from the tower of Chedzoy church. The rebels were almost within striking distance of the enemy, who had as yet no inkling of their presence On the whole, fortune had so far favoured their

<hr>

[1] Dalrymple, *Memoirs*, vol 1, p 183

enterprise. Monmouth's calculations had been justified by success. But the fault was not Feversham's. At 11 that night, at the very time when the rebel column was defiling out of Bridgwater, the general who, according to Macaulay, " thought only of eating and sleeping," made the round of his camp, inspected the guards and sentries, and finally rode out to Chedzoy, where he waited for news from Oglethorpe   Judged by his performances in this campaign, Oglethorpe was a courageous but incompetent officer.   " Although," says Wolseley, " he crossed both the roads he was ordered to examine, he could not have pushed the smallest patrol along either in the direction of Bridgwater "[1]   Otherwise he must have seen or heard something of 3,500 men, 42 waggons, and 4 guns, which were actually on the move   A little before midnight, however, he dispatched a trooper to Chedzoy with the report that all was quiet.   At that very moment Monmouth's column had completed the first two miles of its march, and was wheeling off the road on to the moor. Feversham, having received this report, returned to Weston Zoyland   At 12 45 he reached his quarters, undressed, and went to bed.   Shortly after his departure, Oglethorpe and his men rode into Chedzoy   They must have crossed the track by which Monmouth was approaching, and they must have crossed it not many minutes in advance of the head of his column.   But no collision occurred.   Though nothing can be said for the failure of Oglethorpe to discover the enemy on the Bristol road, in justice both to his men and to Compton's it must be remembered that out on the moor the rebels were shrouded in the mist, while the sound of their trampling was partially muffled by the softness of the peat   Determined to unravel the mystery, Oglethorpe continued on his course until he struck the main road from Weston Zoyland to Bridgwater.   Following it westward to within half a mile of the town, he halted and dispatched four of his troopers to the bridge with instructions to pose as rebels and ascertain from the sentries what Monmouth was about

The second period, from 1 o'clock to 3, was the critical and decisive one   As Grey pushed forward with the rebel horse, a shot was fired, whether by accident, or by one of Compton's vedettes, or, as was subsequently alleged, by a traitor in the ranks, it is impossible to determine   But the alarm was given. The drums beat, the trumpets pealed, and the royal army rushed precipitately to arms.   For a few brief minutes, confusion and dismay reigned supreme   Grey had still time to execute his purpose.   Pressing on towards Weston Zoyland, he was suddenly confronted by the unexpected obstacle of the Bussex Rhine. Having just dismissed Godfrey, whose services were supposed to be no longer required, he was unable to find the crossing At this moment Compton came galloping in from Chedzoy, charged through a portion of the rebel horse, and got safely back

[1] Wolseley, vol 1, p 324.

to camp. Even now, with a little insight and dash, Grey might have won the battle   But he was deficient both in nerve and coolness   Had he borne to the left, he would have turned the flank of the royal foot, and he would have discovered the ford. Unfortunately for him, he wheeled to the right and carried the bulk of his horsemen across the front of the enemy's line Beyond the trench the matches of Dumbarton's regiment were gleaming through the fog   The officers, knowing that three large parties of royal cavalry were out that night, and uncertain whether the dark mass before them represented friends or foes, permitted it to pass.   But Captain Berkeley of the Foot Guards, which regiment stood next to Dumbarton's in the line, cried out, "For whom are you ?"   "For the King," came the answer "Which King?" replied Berkeley.   "King Monmouth, and God with us," shouted the rebels.   "Take this with you," said Berkeley, and gave the word to his company, who instantly discharged a well-aimed volley. The next company followed their example, and their next. Untrained marsh mares and colts could not endure such treatment   The rebel cavalry fled back into the night.   At Peasy Farm, two and a half miles to the rear, the drivers of the baggage and munition waggons were infected with the panic of the runaways and immediately abandoned the field.

But now Monmouth himself brought up his infantry at the double. The men had orders to charge home with the steel. If those orders had been punctually obeyed, even at this stage a victory might have been won   But demoralised by the spectacle of their panic-stricken horse, and by the startling apparition of the Bussex Rhine, the rebels came to a standstill, and opened at once a disorderly and erratic fire. The King's infantry, with the exception of Dumbarton's regiment, made no response. One who served in the royal army, and who censures its "supineness," "preposterous confidence," and "undervaluing of the rebels," testifies to the cheerful and disciplined alacrity with which, after the first moments of alarm, the six battalions of foot made ready to receive the enemy The behaviour of the soldiers gives scanty support to the local tradition that many of them were drunk. Churchill, who had never been to bed that night, was present on the right of the line almost from the beginning of the action, and was directing the defence, in so far as any direction was possible. But in the earlier stages of such a confused, nocturnal engagement, the safety of the royal army depended rather upon the steadiness of the men and the decision of their subordinate officers than upon the control of any in supreme command   It was only after the breathless excitement of the first encounter that leadership began more and more to assert itself   And whose leadership ? Almost every movement of tactical importance was ascribed by the public opinion of the time to the initiative of Churchill. But considered as evidence, the public opinion of the time is worse than worthless. At the first sound of the trumpet Feversham hastened to the point of danger. It is true that Churchill was on the ground before him. But the Whig legend, which depicts the commander in-chief as carefully adjusting his cravat in front of a looking-glass in Weston Zoyland, while the battle was being won by his lieutenant, is an appropriate decoration of the pages of Lord Macaulay. It ought not to have disfigured those of Lord Wolseley.

When Feversham arrived, Monmouth's three field-pieces had come into action on the left of his foot, and under the management of a Dutch gunner were making good practice on Dumbarton's regiment and the Guards. Churchill had already ordered up the royal artillery, but it was slow in coming, for it had 500 paces of soft ground to travel, and horses and drivers could not be discovered in the darkness. Fearful lest his infantry should be provoked by punishment into a premature offensive, Feversham forbade them to cross the Rhine. Then he hastened off to superintend the disposition of his horse, who were rapidly arriving from Weston Zoyland. These he divided between his two wings. And now Oglethorpe, who had at last learned the truth at Bridgwater, came galloping in, collecting on the way the guard stationed on the main road. Feversham carried this reinforcement behind the line of his infantry and added it to the cavalry of his right. Then he himself conducted the whole of that wing across the ditch. Oglethorpe, who was on the extreme right, perceived before him some remnants of the rebel horse endeavouring to form. He instantly charged them and drove them finally from the field. But Feversham kept his men well in hand. He ordered Oglethorpe to wheel to the left and in conjunction with the rest of the wing to assail the rebel infantry in flank.

Returning now to the centre, Feversham found that, under Churchill's direction, everything was going well. With the assistance of the carriage-horses of the Bishop of Winchester, himself an old cavalier, who was present in the royal army by the King's command, six cannon had been hauled to the right of the line. Three of them were posted on the right of Dumbarton's regiment and three in front of the Foot Guards; and they responded with deadly effect to Monmouth's artillery. The remainder of the guns, as fast as they arrived, were placed in the intervals of the line. Recognising that the brunt of the battle was upon his right, Feversham intended to transfer the Coldstreams from his left centre to the decisive point. But he found that Churchill had anticipated him and was already moving the Queen's and Queen Dowager's regiments from the extreme left, where they were practically out of action, to the support of Dumbarton's and the Guards. Thereupon the commander-in-chief rode off to rejoin Oglethorpe. Having completed his manœuvre, Churchill ordered a troop of his own dragoons, which had hitherto acted as a guard for the artillery, and another which had been billeted in Weston Zoyland, to form on the left of the Royal Foot. As the day was beginning to break, he himself led them across the Rhine and chased the rebels from their guns

The third and last phase endured from 3 o'clock to 5 In the pallid light of dawn the cavalry of Feversham's left passed the Rhine and attacked the rebels in flank They were boldly met and vigorously repulsed A similar check had already befallen Oglethorpe on the opposite wing But the situation of the rebels was now desperate They were surrounded upon three sides. Their artillery was silenced All their horse and many of their foot had fled Their stock of ammunition was exhausted and could not be replenished, for the waggons had been left behind at Peasy Farm and had long since disappeared Monmouth, who had fought bravely enough at first, was riding for his life towards the north In Burnet's words, " he left the field too soon for a man of courage, who had such high pretensions "[1] Yet two battalions still stood firm and hurled back the household cavalry with pike and scythe. " The slain," says Evelyn, " were most of them Mendip miners, who did greate execution with their tooles, and sold their lives very dearly."[2] Not until the King's infantry came pouring across the ditch and charged straight upon their front, did these valiant peasants abandon the unequal contest A horrible butchery ensued On the open moor and in the full light of day the work of pursuit was easy. It was mercilessly done The King's cavalry, infuriated by the obstinate resistance of an enemy whom they despised, gave little quarter to the fugitives. Some, who retreated to the enclosed ground about Chedzoy, eventually escaped to Bridgwater, but many were hunted to their death among the ditches and cornfields. Five hundred prisoners, 79 of whom were wounded and 5 dying, were packed into the church of Weston Zoyland. Monmouth's army was annihilated. In killed alone it lost more than 1,500 men, or nearly half its numbers The total of Feversham's casualties did not exceed 400.

No attempt was made to rally at Bridgwater Within a few hours Churchill entered the place at the head of a thousand men. Feversham followed more slowly He was laden with prisoners and busy with hanging them. Oglethorpe carried the news of victory to James, who rewarded him with a knighthood, though " he ought," says Lord Wolseley, " to have been dismissed the army for incompetence and carelessness "[3] As there was no longer any enemy to fight, Feversham's forces were dispersed as rapidly as possible A detachment remained at Bridgwater under the command of Colonel Percy Kirke, an officer of good birth and exceptional ability, who differed from

[1] Burnet, vol ii , p 264   [2] *Evelyn's Diary*, July 8, 1685
[3] Wolseley vol i , p 29

the Kirke of ancient legend and modern, sentimental fiction almost as markedly as his contemporary, Dundee, from the " bloody Clavers " of Puritan mythology But, because he continued the process of hanging the prisoners under martial law, the Whig historians have pilloried him for ever. Churchill and Feversham returned to London. Churchill was eager to rejoin his wife " I shall be at no ease," he wrote from Wells on July 19, " till I am in your arms, whom I love above my own life "[1] The King rewarded him with the colonelcy of the 3rd troop of Life Guards, a lucrative and honourable appointment. The 1st troop, and the Garter, were bestowed on Feversham

So terminated this brief, and not particularly glorious, campaign Public opinion, which then, as ever, displayed but little understanding of military matters, concentrated itself entirely on the victory of Sedgemoor. But the issue was not decided at Sedgemoor. It was decided on the day when Monmouth came to Keynsham Bridge, too late by a few hours to carry Bristol by assault The time, which he consumed in his march from Lyme to the Avon, he imagined to be well spent on trying to train his followers to encounter a disciplined army Divining his nervous anxiety to secure this impossible result, Churchill played upon it to the uttermost. Throughout his career, no soldier ever realised more fully than Churchill the preponderating importance of the moral over the material in war. The moral effect of his activity, prior to the concentration of the royal forces at Bath, was the determining factor in the campaign. He not only destroyed the self-confidence of the rebels, and intimidated many who would otherwise have joined their ranks, but he succeeded to perfection in confirming the low opinion which Monmouth himself had formed of his men's ability to face the King's soldiers in the field. Every hour that Monmouth was frightened into frittering away on drill and exercise, brought Feversham nearer to Bristol. On the preservation of that city everything turned When Churchill ensured its safety, as he, and not Feversham, undoubtedly did, he wrecked the strategy of Monmouth and rendered his ultimate destruction a question of time alone

The subsequent course of the campaign, though richer in dramatic interest, is inferior in military importance. Civil opinion, at any rate, has failed to grasp this point. It has also treated the responsible commander with evident injustice. As regards the interval of nine days, which elapsed between the concentration of the royal forces at Bath and the battle of Sedgemoor, Churchill himself appears to suggest that the operations of the army during that period were deficient in vigour and celerity But Churchill was highly aggrieved at his supersession by a foreigner, and he was smarting under the conviction that in matters of strategy Feversham deliberately ignored him

[1] *Ibid*, p 341

Yet he admits that the weather and the state of the roads were distinctly adverse to rapidity of movement   Lord Wolseley agrees with Churchill that Feversham was slow.   He also complains that Feversham was perpetually ignorant of his enemy's doings and intentions, and that he did not harass the rebels as Churchill had harassed them   It would be very presumptuous to challenge the verdict of so high an authority, but it is permissible to observe that that verdict would seem to have been based upon an imperfect apprehension of the historical facts. From the report which Feversham transmitted to James after the action at Philip's Norton,[1] it is abundantly clear that he was very much alive to the necessity of destroying the rebel army as quickly as possible   But his men and horses were extremely fatigued; his troops, though regulars, were in many cases neither trained in the actual business of war nor inured to its hardships; and he was gravely embarrassed by the badness of the roads and the heavy rains.   On the other hand, the enclosed nature of the country was all in favour of an enemy who desired to avoid a decisive engagement   Regarding his antagonists as " a company of vagabonds,"[2] and the whole campaign as little better than an affair of police, Feversham reasoned, as a Frenchman of his class and profession would naturally reason, that no honour was to be got by taking risks   Indecisive encounters, like that at Philip's Norton, were to be avoided   The essential thing was to make a clean sweep of the enemy at a single stroke.   He therefore rested his troops, both horse and foot, and husbanded their strength as much as possible.   He had only 700 horse in all, and if he did not use this arm as Churchill had used it, the reason may have been that he was afraid of using it up.   The imperative considerations which governed the action of Churchill had ceased to operate   The crisis was past   Bristol was no longer in peril.   It was infinitely more important now that the royal troopers should be fresh for the decisive shock than that they should worry Monmouth's column on the march.   The rebels were sufficiently dejected already, and from Philip's Norton to Bridgwater they deserted wholesale   As to the allegation that Feversham never knew what Monmouth was about, the facts do not support it   It is certain that he was not well served; but, despite the inefficiency of his subordinates, he seems to have learned as much as it was possible to learn of the plans and intentions of an opponent who never had any, or changed them almost from hour to hour   Whether it be true or not that, throughout these nine days, he was dilatory in his movements and perfunctory in the acquisition of intelligence, the fact remains that, at the end of that period, he successfully accomplished, on his own lines, the task which he set himself to do.   He annihilated the rebel army at a blow   And this, in reality, was his unpardonable

[1] MSS of Mrs Stopford Sackville, vol 1, p 9: Earl of Feversham to James II, June 28, 1685 (Hist MSS Comm)   [2] *Ibid*

offence. To punish him for such a crime against Whiggery, his performance was decried, and his personality was ridiculed. It is to be regretted that Lord Wolseley should have allowed his judgment to be affected by contact with these vindictive distortions of the truth.

Such glory as the royal arms achieved in the battle itself was ascribed by public opinion at the time to Churchill rather than to Feversham   Indeed, it was openly suggested that, but for the vigilance and coolness of Churchill, the royal army would have been cut to pieces.   James II, a practical soldier, who understood war vastly better than ninety-nine out of a hundred of his subjects,[1] was fully satisfied with the conduct of both his favourites   Of Churchill it was said in the official report that he " performed his part with all the courage and gallantry imaginable "[2]   If the King was unduly prejudiced in favour of Feversham, it must be remembered that the nation was far more unduly prejudiced against him   The army and the Tories disliked him because he was a foreigner ; the Dissenters and the Whigs detested him, because he beat them utterly, and because he hanged them without mercy   Between the two parties his reputation enjoyed but little chance   The stories of his incapacity, negligence, and sloth, are crude exaggerations when they are not transparent lies.   Yet Burnet, who after all was a serious historian, permits himself to say that Feversham " had no parties abroad," " got no intelligence," and " was abed without any care or order "[3]   The facts show, and Lord Wolseley agrees, that at Weston Zoyland Feversham encamped in a " well-chosen " and " strong " situation.   The facts also show, and Lord Wolseley also agrees, that his dispositions for the night were adequate, and such as " would have protected him against surprise, had Compton and Oglethorpe known their work and done it properly "[4]   He himself made the round of the guards, and he continued in the saddle and on the moor until nearly 1 o'clock   But he committed two mistakes   Proceeding, as he was, on the hypothesis that Monmouth would break away towards Gloucestershire on Sunday night, he ought to have been dissatisfied with Oglethorpe's report that nothing of the kind was in progress, and he ought certainly to have remained on the alert until he learned what the enemy was actually doing or meditating   But whether he went to bed, or whether he sat up, he would still have been surprised   Doubtless he was very tired, and properly anxious to prepare himself for what he anticipated would be a fatiguing day.   Doubtless also he trusted to the arrangements, which he had made, to protect him against sudden attack.   Such confidence was misplaced and constituted his second error.   Accus-

---

[1] The King's own description of the battle is by far the clearest and the best of all the contemporary accounts · Hardwicke State Papers, vol 11, p 305   [2] Lediard, vol 1 , p 57   [3] Burnet, vol. 11., p. 264   [4] Wolseley, vol. 1 , p 323

tomed as he was to serve in the war-hardened armies of France, he failed to realise how deficient in most of the military qualities, except valour, were the regular forces of the British Crown. Officers like Oglethorpe were almost hopelessly incompetent. Men like those who furnished the vedettes around Chedzoy, and who discovered nothing of the rebel column, until after they had passed the Langmore Rhine, must have been either very ignorant of their elementary duties, or very undisciplined in the performance of them. It is not necessary to accept the tradition of the countryside that the King's soldiers were drunk, but they certainly despised the enemy, albeit upon totally insufficient grounds In any event, they were not material upon which Feversham could rely to save him from a surprise. Had he been an Englishman, he would probably have realised that fact, as Churchill realised it He already knew by experience that his cavalry was none too efficient in some of the primary functions of the mounted arm. But he neglected to profit by his knowledge At the same time, from the extreme severity of the censure passed upon him, one might almost imagine that never before or since was a general surprised by a nocturnal march. Better soldiers than Feversham have been not only surprised, but well beaten in addition, which Feversham was not Lord Wolseley insists that he, and he alone, must be held responsible for the narrowness of the margin by which the royal army escaped disaster By the same strict rule, he, and he alone, is entitled to the credit of the victory If Feversham must be blamed for the faults of Oglethorpe and Compton, Feversham must be applauded for the merits of Churchill It is a pity that Churchill's admirers should have imagined that they were doing him a service by belittling Feversham The process can add no lustre to the name of Marlborough.

Over the subsequent fate of the beaten rebels many easy tears have been expended For the most part, they got what they deserved, or what, at any rate, all who go about to destroy governments by force of arms, know well beforehand that they must be prepared to expect Rulers, who are too timid or too soft-hearted to defend themselves, find none to defend them; and any established authority, which does not strike hard when it is struck, will speedily learn that its right to exist at all can be challenged with success For the rigorous measures which James adopted against Monmouth and his adherents, plenty of precedents could be adduced. Henry VIII, for example, laid a very heavy hand upon those Catholics of the north, who participated in the " Pilgrimage of Grace " Yet Henry VIII was a popular monarch in his own time and is by no means execrated in ours In this same West Country, and within the memory of many who fought at Sedgemoor, Oliver Cromwell meted out sharp justice to the Royalists who had engaged in Penruddocke's rising, which was a trifle in comparison with Monmouth's.

Yet Oliver Cromwell is still regarded as an enlightened statesman   The law of high treason was plain.   In respect of all
persons who had appeared in arms against the government,
the juries could find but one verdict, the judges (of whom there
were others besides Jeffreys) could pass but one sentence   The
elementary fact that the sufferers, unlike the innocent victims of
Shaftesbury and Titus Oates, were after all guilty, is too often
overlooked   Why James, of all men, should have been expected
to show them leniency, it is impossible to say   They belonged to
a faction, which, having failed in its attempt to deprive him of
his birthright by constitutional methods, claimed now to deprive
him of it by force.   They had publicly denounced him to his
subjects as a usurper and a fratricide   They had menaced all
who continued to serve him with the penalties of high treason.
And they were not men who could safely be despised   They
were not men whose language was necessarily more powerful
than their performance.   Their opinions and aims were identical
with those of the party which had murdered Charles I.   They
spoke the same cant; they listened to the same harangues from
the same breed of fanatics, and they were led by officers, some
of whom had served in the very army which stood between the
people and the scaffold in Whitehall   Monmouth's insurrection
was in fact the death-convulsion of that militant Puritanism,
which in the preceding generation had destroyed the Parliament,
the Church, and the Monarchy itself   If James considered that
the kind of justice which their fathers thought good enough
for his father was the kind of justice which they merited, the sentiment was natural enough.   Whether, in acting on it, he was well
advised, is another question.   But it is a question of expediency
simply   Governments must determine for themselves to what
extremities they should proceed in dealing with their mortal
foes   If they determine wrongly, they will pay dearly for their
error   Confronted by an armed uprising of that arrogant and
persecuting faction which had assassinated his parent and driven
him and his kindred beyond the seas, James II crushed it without
mercy.   It may be that his policy convicts him of unwisdom; but
in all the circumstances, it does not convict him of abnormal vindictiveness or lust of blood

Of the King's justice few of the rebels and their abettors
had any right to complain.   But they had every right to complain of the gross brutalities and the indecent buffooneries which
accompanied the administration of it, and which constituted a
wanton aggravation of their sufferings.   Much of the sympathy,
to which they would not otherwise have been entitled, they
owed to the atrocious behaviour of Jeffreys on the Bench

Churchill was no foe to severity, when severity was obviously
both politic and humane.   And therefore it is written that, in
the very crisis of the rebellion, when the safety of the second city
in the kingdom was trembling in the balance, he hanged " Jarvice

the felt-maker " on the outskirts of Pensford [1] But from the cool and systematic carnage of political proscriptions his amiable nature turned with disgust. Only twice during the judicial reign of terror, which followed the battle of Sedgemoor, does the name of Churchill appear with any prominence; and on each occasion the circumstances were such as did it honour. When the sister of a condemned rebel, Benjamin Hewling, whose brother, William, had already suffered the extreme penalty, came to London to intercede with James it was Churchill who procured her an audience As they waited together in the ante-chamber, he told the unhappy creature how sincerely he longed for her success; but at the same time he warned her that the marble chimney-piece, on which he laid his hand, was not harder than the King's heart His kindness availed her nothing, for his forebodings were verified. When Lord Delamere, one of Monmouth's accomplices, was tried for his life before thirty of his peers, whom Jeffreys had carefully selected, it fell to Churchill, as the youngest of the thirty, to give the first vote. Delamere was certainly guilty, but the only witness against him was shown to have committed perjury. Though the King himself was present, Churchill unflinchingly voted for acquittal, and every one of the twenty-nine others followed his fearless example. James' comment to the Prince of Orange was, that Delamere " had good luck, as well as just judges."[2] He might have added that Churchill and his fellows had cheerfully embraced the opportunity of reminding Jeffreys that the peers of England did not take their orders from such sordid ruffians as he In neither of these cases did Churchill act in accordance with his own apparent self-interest His intervention on behalf of Benjamin Hewling could win him no favour with a master, whose will was firmly fixed upon merciless repression. He must have known that his action at the trial of Delamere might be construed as a direct affront to the royal authority, not only by Jeffreys but by James himself. Yet, acting in the one instance as an English gentleman, and in the other as a worthy member of the proud order to which he had been newly raised, he proved that he possessed both a generous heart and the courage to obey its dictates

These are hard cases for Churchill's professional detractors to resolve. But they are not the hardest. Everybody knows that, while Jeffreys was conducting his " campaign " in the West, there existed in the capital a scandalous traffic in pardons This abomination was open, flagrant, and unashamed Yet no particular odium appears to have attached to it. Feversham, the Maids of Honour, even the Queen herself, took part in it. One would naturally expect that Churchill, whose whole life is alleged by respectable writers to have been dominated by the most de-

---

[1] It is curious that Lord Wolseley, whose book is very minute in detail, should omit all reference to this incident

[2] Dalrymple, vol ii , p 54

grading avarice, would have coined fortunes at this shameful
mint. As the King's favourite, and as the son of the Parliamentary representative for Lyme Regis, he had large and peculiar
opportunities Yet nowhere is it recorded that he took any
advantage of them Just as the name of Churchill does not
appear beside that of Algernon Sidney in Louis' pension list,
so it is not to be found with that of Mary of Modena in the ignoble
catalogue of the retailers of the royal clemency.

Churchill had done his duty as a soldier, and done it with
distinction. For himself, he had nothing to regret But for
Monmouth, for the tragical ending of that life which he himself
had preserved on the counterscarp of Maestricht, he must have
experienced a profound pity. Nor could he, on the field of
Sedgemoor, have beheld unmoved the slaughter of those stout
West Country folk, the raw material of what he believed to be the
finest infantry in the world For the rest, though he was no
politician, he probably rejoiced, in common with the majority
of contemporary Englishmen, at the collapse of a movement which
menaced both the civil and the religious institutions of the realm.
" Had it not pleased God," wrote Evelyn, who had lived through
the Great Rebellion. " to dissipate this attempt in the beginning,
there would in all appearance have gather'd an irresistible force
which would have desperately proceeded to the ruine of the
Church and Government, so general was the discontent and expectation of the opportunity. For my owne part, I look'd upon
this deliverance as most signal. Such an inundation of phanatics
and men of impious principles must needs have caus'd universal
disorder, cruelty, injustice, rapine, sacrilege, and confusion, an
unavoidable civil war and misery without end."[1]

[1] *Evelyn's Diary*, July 15, 1685

APPENDIX V

SALISBURY

THROUGHOUT his life Churchill hated domestic politics, and, to the utmost of his power, avoided them. But there were times when domestic politics refused to be ignored. And such a time was now at hand The history of England in the seventeenth century is largely the history of a quarrel between the House of Commons and the Monarchy It is fashionable to assume that in this quarrel the House of Commons was fighting to secure the liberties of Englishmen and the Monarchy to subvert them. This assumption was, and still is, wholly gratuitous It was strenuously repudiated by Charles I, who, upon the scaffold, with his dying breath, denied it It was rendered ridiculous by the mere existence of that Cavalier party, which, though beaten in the appeal to force, always represented the larger half of national opinion. And it was never for a moment conceded by their descendants, Tories, who regarded with complacency the overthrow of Parliamentary government during the latter years of the reign of Charles II The group of country gentlemen, merchants, and lawyers, who composed the Whig and Puritan party in the House of Commons, may have been perfectly within their rights in refusing to vote the expenditure necessary to the efficient maintenance of the public service, unless in return for every vote the head of the executive resigned to them some portion of the prerogative, which had been bequeathed him by his predecessors But that the cause of this oligarchy was entirely and essentially the cause of the nation is what nobody can prove The majority of the nation refused to identify its interests or its liberties with the triumph of Puritanism and Whiggery. To this majority Churchill by birth, by inclination, and by deliberate choice, had always belonged.

But the secular controversy was complicated and embittered by the religious one. " Church and King " had been the war-cry to which the Cavaliers had charged on many hard-fought fields Laud had followed Strafford to the block They, who had driven the squire from his hall, had also hunted the parson from his vicarage. They, who had breached the walls of Basing and of Raglan, had also polluted and defaced the sanctuaries of Winchester and York Charles I, who might have saved himself by sacrificing the Church of England, preferred to perish as her

432

veritable martyr. While Charles II wandered in beggary over
the face of Europe, the Church's children received her sacraments
in secrecy and fear After the Restoration the doctrines of
passive obedience and of divine right were diligently inculcated
from the Anglican pulpits in almost every parish The cause
of the Church and the cause of the Monarchy seemed to be one
and indivisible. But it was reserved for James II to show that
they were not so James was a sincere and determined zealot.
He was resolved that England should return to her old allegiance
to Rome What Henry VIII could do, James II conceived that
he could undo. The one great obstacle in his path was not the
Puritan who raved against the " Scarlet Woman," but the
Anglican, who was alleged to be her secret lover. Rome knew
well, and had always known, which of these two was her more
dangerous antagonist. James II shared her knowledge But
he was not the first, as he has not been the last, to misjudge the
strength of the hold which the Church of England has always
possessed upon large and influential masses of the nation He
struck at her openly and boldly He fondly imagined that the
clergy and laity, who had so cheerfully supported him against
that rabble of republicans and fanatics which had followed his
brother's bastard to Sedgemoor, would submit with holy resignation to his chastening blows Many Englishmen, and almost all
foreigners, have failed to understand the Church of England
But nobody has ever paid more dearly for this mistake than did
James II.

The Tory party, confiding fully in his honour, had opposed the
efforts of the Whigs and Puritans to exclude him from the
throne of his ancestors In return he set before them a cruel
choice. Between their loyalty as subjects and their faith as
Churchmen, they must now decide It was a strange and
barbarous dilemma for the simple folk who composed the bulk
of the Tory party In their minds the two ideas of the altar
and the throne had by long association and by splendid and
pathetic tradition been welded into one It seemed to them
incredible that the King should assail the religion for which his
own father had perished But as the development of his policy
left little room for doubt, incredulity gave way to amazement,
and amazement to indignation The answer to the question,
if an answer must be given, was plain Both the Monarchy and
the Church were divine institutions Conflict between them
was hideous and unnatural But if there was to be war in heaven,
the English Churchman knew under which banner he must be
found He would fear God before he would honour the King.

The Whigs had long been ready for rebellion. But the Whigs
by themselves were impotent When under compulsion of the
King's religious policy the Tories joined them, successful rebellion
began to be possible The Revolution is always regarded as the
triumph of Whiggery Certainly it was a great triumph for

Whiggish principles   It was the vindication of a theory, the apotheosis of a philosophy. But, considered as a piece of practical politics, it was essentially the work of the Church of England and the Tory party

Churchill's opinion of the painful situation, which the King had deliberately created, was in no way peculiar to himself. Though not a politician, his principles were Tory, and he thought as other Tories thought   Like them he had detested the Exclusion Bill, but like them he was not prepared to stand quietly by while the Church of England was destroyed   And despite the delicacy of his position as the King's friend, he made no secret of his views   When in 1685 he went as ambassador to Paris, he told the Earl of Galway (who repeated his words to Burnet) that "if the King was ever prevailed on to alter our religion, he would serve him no longer, but withdraw from him "[1] Writing to the Princess of Orange in December, 1687, Anne declared of him that " though he is a very faithful servant to the King, and that the King is very kind to him, and I believe he will always obey the King in all things that are consistent with religion, yet, rather than change that, I dare say he will lose all his places and all that he has."[2]   It is evident that he spoke his mind freely to various persons   Nor did he at the same time endeavour to deceive his master   By his studious avoidance of political topics, he clearly showed his disapproval of the King's proceedings   But Burnet says that when he did speak, he spoke always in favour of "moderate counsels."[3]   It is alleged by one who professes to have been present, that at Winchester in the autumn of 1687 he ventured respectfully to remonstrate with James upon his religious policy, and was severely snubbed for his pains.   It is clear that upon the broad issue in dispute, his mind was fully made up, and that he never attempted to disguise what his sentiments were, and what, if the King proceeded to extremities, his conduct would assuredly be.

When that bold, but not very exemplary young person, the Duke of Grafton, represented to his uncle the danger of the course which he was pursuing, James was indignant. " You yourself have no conscience," he exclaimed. " True," replied Grafton, " but I belong to a party which has a great deal."[4] Grafton's case was that of many who played a prominent part in the overthrow of James. The Jacobites always adduced the lives and characters of these men as evidence of the insincerity of the contention that the Revolution was undertaken in defence of the Protestant religion   The Jacobites were wrong   Their conclusion did not follow from their premises   But the premises were true enough.   And the taunt was a bitter one for those to whom it applied.   Churchill, however, is not among this number.

[1] Burnet, vol 11 , p. 399
[2] Dalrymple, vol. 11 , appendix to book v , No vii   The Princess Anne's letters to her sister   [3] Burnet, vol 11 , p. 399.
[4] This story is told in Burnet, vol. 11., p 420

Even Macaulay admits that Churchill " believed implicitly in the religion which he had learned as a boy " And Hallam, who in vituperation of Churchill more than holds his own with Macaulay, recognises that he preferred rebellion to " open apostasy "[1] Some have denied that a man of his character could be actuated by any but material motives This judgment largely begs the question. A man's character is known only by his actions And the action by which, more than by any other, the character of Churchill is popularly judged, is his desertion of James. But no estimate, however low, of the character of Churchill can seriously affect the question. Many immoral persons have possessed sincere religious convictions. He is either a very shallow thinker, or very ignorant of the world, who supposes that every sinner who goes to church is a hypocrite. It is written that David, the adulterer and assassin, was " a man after God's own heart." James II, whose private life was notoriously vicious, risked all and lost all for the faith of Rome Moreover, modern opinion is at a loss to understand how great was the part which religion played in the public and private life of the seventeenth century The present age, which is distinguished by its arrogant self-sufficiency and its unscientific disregard of the recorded experience of the human race, hopes all things from political and economic change In Churchill's day men had grasped the truth that all solid amelioration is from within They realised that for time, as for eternity, it is the spiritual and not the material which counts. Therefore it was that so many were willing to dare and suffer for what they conceived to be the right religion And therefore it was that they inflicted, and endured, the sternest persecutions In setting the cause of God's Church as he conceived it, above all other causes, Churchill was at one with the best opinion of his age, and perhaps with the best opinion of all time.

He could easily have escaped from the dilemma created for him by the King's policy. He could have turned Papist. The example of Turenne furnished an illustrious precedent. Instances of remarkable conversion were perpetually before his eyes. The Secretary of State, Sunderland, and the Poet Laureate, Dryden, were the most conspicuous. Had Churchill joined this fashionable company, James would have been delighted His system of appointing none but Roman Catholics to places of importance was rendered difficult by the dearth of talent among the exiguous band of the nobility and gentry of that persuasion. Churchill as a convert would have been more than certain of some exalted office in the State Unfortunately for the theory of those who would depict him as a melodramatic villain, there is no sign that he ever contemplated this profitable baseness. From first to last he pursued an undeviating course He would serve the King against all the Whigs and Puritans in England, but he would

[1] Hallam, *Constitutional History*, vol. ii , p 656

never follow him to the destruction of the Church. Since the King decreed that he must be a traitor either to the throne or to the altar, he knew how to choose He joined the conspiracy of which William of Orange was the head

Few figures in English history are better known than William's, the hero of Macaulay's prose epic But no eloquence could ever win for him from posterity that affection which was denied him in his lifetime To Englishmen he was and will remain, " Dutch William " Yet he came, in fact, of the English blood royal He was the son of James' own sister, and, prior to the birth of the " Old Pretender," he was, after Mary and Anne, the next in the line of succession to the English throne. His real position has been frequently misunderstood He has been represented, and with truth, as the champion of Whiggery, as the liberator of England, and as the defender of the Protestant faith Yet it cannot be gainsaid that the champion of Whiggery was also an autocrat, the liberator of England was also a persistent favourer of Holland and the Dutch, and that the defender of the Protestant faith was an ally of Papist princes and even of the Papacy Such inconsistencies are only superficial Whig and Tory, England and Holland, Protestant and Papist—in comparison with his life's ambition William cared for none of these things They were but means to his ultimate end, which was in reality nothing less than the overthrow of the gigantic menace of the French monarchy William was playing a tremendous game in which England was a valuable piece. In him another maritime republic had produced another Hannibal, who was marshalling the nations against another Rome. In the contest between Louis and the rest of Europe, the power of England could turn the balance. William knew that the domestic policy pursued by James meant one of two things At the worst it meant that, as in 1673, England would be actively allied with France, at the best that, torn with discord and corrupted with foreign gold, she would remain an idle spectator of the struggle Neither eventuality suited William He wanted the wealth and the valour and the navy of England to be cast into the scale He believed that they could turn it against Louis. To accomplish this end he was prepared to pose as the champion of any and every principle which might recommend him to the great majority of the English people.

He had long been familiar with the intricacies of English politics Many of the foremost men in England were personally known to him He well understood that an invasion, which was not supported by the bulk of the two great parties in the State, could achieve no success that would be of permanent value to his large plans The England, of which he had need in the European conflict, was an England united and at peace within herself. He therefore proceeded with the utmost caution Early in 1687 he sent, as ambassador to James II, the diplomatist Dykvelt, with secret instructions to sound the men who spoke with most authority for English parties or exercised most control over English affairs Dykvelt succeeded beyond expectation Nottingham and Danby for the Tories, Devonshire and Russell for the Whigs, Halifax for the "Trimmers," and Compton, Bishop of London, for the Anglican clergy, gave him to understand that his master could rely upon their sympathy and co-operation It was evident, therefore, that William would receive national, and not merely partisan, support. But even so the enterprise might fail if the armed forces of the Crown remained faithful to James Admiral Herbert undertook to answer for the fleet. For the army, which contained many Roman Catholics, nobody could answer. But the officer, whose influence was greatest in military circles, was undoubtedly Churchill He was already known to William, who recognised his ability and was anxious to secure his services The British Army was numerous and brave; but, if Churchill refused to fight, William was convinced that many of all ranks would follow his example

Churchill, moreover, could be useful in another quarter. Through the instrumentality of his wife he could manage the Princess of Denmark. Anne's proximity to the throne, her well-known zeal for the Church, and her personal popularity, rendered her necessary to William's plans. Devoted though she was to her religion, it was possible that, in the struggle between public and private duty, a woman of her simple and affectionate disposition might need the direction of a sterner will William believed that in Mrs. Freeman's hands Mrs Morley would make no mistakes It was not indeed for the safety of the Church of England that Sarah was concerned For Sarah was incapable of religious enthusiasm She regarded all beliefs with equal indifference, but not all believers. From personal and political motives she heartily abhorred the Roman Catholics. And she considered that her own material prosperity was jeopardised by the policy of James "It was evident to all the World," she says, "that as Things were carried on by King James, every Body must be ruined, who would not become a Roman Catholic."[1] Though Anne was not the woman to waver in the Church's cause. her situation was a delicate one She might frequently have need of encouragement and counsel Lady Churchill could be trusted to supply her with both. It must therefore have given no little satisfaction to William to learn that Dykvelt was in touch with the one man who, better than anybody in England, would answer for King James' soldiers and King James' daughter. Nor did Churchill, cautious though he was, confine himself to verbal answers When the ambassador returned to Holland in June, 1687, he carried with him a batch of letters from eminent Englishmen to his master. One of them was in Churchill's hand. In it he asserted that the Princess of Denmark

[1] *Conduct of the Duchess of Marlborough*, p 82

" was resolved, by the assistance of God, to suffer all extremities even to death itself, rather than be brought to change her religion " For himself, he added, " My places and the King's favour I set at naught, in comparison of the being true to my religion." And he concluded with a declaration that, though he could not " live the life of a saint," he was determined, " if there be ever occasion for it, to shew the resolution of a martyr "[1]

From this time onwards William maintained the closest relations with his friends in England, while James, completely unaware of the extent of the disaffection which he was exciting, steadily pursued his plan for the destruction of the English Church. With bitter resentment the Tory party watched the development of a policy which was forcing them to reconsider the very foundations of their political faith But the King drove blindly on. Neither the tyranny of the Court of High Commission, nor the toleration of Dissenters, nor the boldness of the Jesuits, nor the advancement of Roman Catholics to situations of trust excited so much alarm as the direct attack upon the Universities and the prosecution of the Bishops The mass of the people were profoundly moved. Though the Whigs might talk of constitutional liberty, and expatiate upon their theory of the sovereign power, the nation as a whole understood that this was the Church's battle. London has witnessed many wild enthusiasms but seldom any comparable to that which blazed around the seven Bishops The Puritanism of the capital was notorious. Yet the most popular preacher of the time was the saintly Ken, the highest of High Anglicans The churches of London could not contain the throngs that pressed to hear him. Prominent among the vast congregations was the Princess of Denmark Meantime, the number of the conspirators grew continually But angry and fearful as the Tories were, they might still have been inclined to postpone overt action, had not the birth of a son to James reduced them to despair. The persecutions which must have ended at the death of the King seemed destined by this event to continue in perpetuity. William perceived that his hour was come But he very properly demanded a formal invitation bearing the signatures of men representative of great interests. Such an invitation was dispatched to him on June 30, 1688 (O S), the very day of the acquittal of the Bishops. On July 8, " One of the King's Chaplains," says Evelyn, " preached before the Princess on Exodus xiv. 13, ' Stand still and behold the salvation of the Lord,' which he applied so boldly to the present conjuncture of the Church of England, that more could scarce be said to encourage desponders "[2] In the same diary, under date August 10, stands this entry· " Dr. Tenison now told me there would suddenly be

[1] Dalrymple's *Memoirs*, vol 11 , appendix to book v , p. 62 Lord Churchill to the Prince of Orange, May 17, 1687
[2] *Evelyn's Diary*, July 8, 1688.

some greate thing discover'd. This was the Prince of Orange intending to come over." It is evident that the secret was a tolerably open one So open was it that the conspirators must have trembled greatly for the success of their project and the safety of their own heads. So open was it that it could no longer be concealed from the King of France. The man who was the last to see the peril was the man whom it most concerned. Neither the loud and repeated warnings of Louis, who was thoroughly alarmed, nor the military and naval preparations of William, which went on unceasingly, made any impression upon James. James was entirely guided by his Secretary of State, the Earl of Sunderland, a recent convert to the Church of Rome And Sunderland, at this critical moment, had joined the great conspiracy. Of his motives, so far as they can be estimated, the less said the better, but of the service which he rendered to England and to Europe it is impossible to speak too highly. When Louis represented that the forces which William was collecting were destined for the invasion of England, it was Sunderland who persuaded James that Louis was an idle alarmist. When Louis proffered the assistance of 30,000 soldiers and a fleet, it was Sunderland who easily convinced James that to accept would be equally humiliating and impolitic. When Louis warned the States that he had taken the King of England under his protection, it was Sunderland who incited James publicly and formally to resent this action as a piece of insulting patronage. Except for Sunderland, Louis might have saved James But thanks to Sunderland, more than to any other Englishman, the King seemed paralysed and blind. Not until the last days of September did he begin to see and to act. But then it was too late.

He had at his disposal a regular army of 40,000 men, more than sufficient to repel the force which William had collected. He had also a navy which, owing largely to his own personal supervision, had attained to a degree of high efficiency But he little dreamed that both services were honeycombed with treason. He never imagined that William, for all his military and naval preparations, expected to achieve his object without a battle. He knew indeed that several of his subjects were at the Hague in person, but he did not know that three-fourths of the remainder were there in spirit William, however, was better informed. Only one fear disturbed his quiet confidence All other measures having failed, it was still in Louis' power to save James in his own despite. A French invasion of the Spanish Netherlands might have ruined William's plans But Louis either indignant at the treatment which his overtures had received, or miscalculating the issues which depended on the event of the conspiracy, left the King of England to his fate. To William's immense relief, he sent his armies to the Rhine, where they carried all before them He never made a worse mistake. For this local and temporary triumph he paid heavily throughout the ensuing quarter of a century When France permitted England to be annexed by the coalition, she sounded the doom of her own ascendency in Europe.

On October 29 (O S.) William put to sea. A severe storm scattered his ships and drove them back to harbour. Though the damage done was insignificant, he published an exaggerated account of his losses, which was intended to deceive King James. But the rejoicings at Whitehall were short-lived On November 1 the Dutch fleet put out a second time. At first they shaped a course towards the Yorkshire coast, but, the wind blowing very strongly from the east, they abandoned the attempt and headed for the Straits of Dover. A powerful squadron, under the Earl of Dartmouth, was lying in the mouth of the Thames, where it was forced to remain by the very same gale that sped the Dutch armada down the Channel On November 5, a date, which, by reason of the nature of the quarrel between James and the Church of England, was regarded by the conspirators as most auspicious, William cast anchor in Torbay and began to disembark his forces When Dartmouth eventually got to sea and started in pursuit, he encountered such heavy weather that he was compelled to take refuge at Spithead

The news from Dover that the Dutch had passed the Straits was highly disconcerting to King James, who had already disposed his forces on the supposition that the blow would fall upon the northern coast. It now became necessary to revise his plans and to arrange for a concentration of the entire army at Salisbury The distances to be traversed, the lateness of the season, and the poor condition of the roads, rendered delay inevitable William wished for nothing else. To secure a base at Exeter, to refresh and organise his troops, to attend the arrival of those who had promised to declare for him, and to await the expected disintegration of King James' forces, he had need of time. And time he had certainly obtained by a judicious manipulation of the advantage which the use of the sea confers upon an assailant, whose enemy is compelled to move overland by means of communication vastly inferior to his own

Of all the conspirators who were implicated in William's project, only a few, like Herbert, Burnet, and Russell, had the good fortune to be actively and openly engaged The great majority had been doomed, from the very nature of the case, to long hours of torturing anxiety. All through October they went in extreme peril of arrest The King's Jesuit advisers, who had good reason to suspect certain of the ringleaders, urged him to secure them. But the last and greatest service which, before his own dismissal, Sunderland rendered to the cause of the Revolution, was to dissuade his master from a course which would have seriously hampered William's plans Nevertheless, the King was greatly perturbed. Late in October William circulated in

England a declaration in which he alleged that he had been
" earnestly solicited by a great many Lords, both spiritual and
temporal."[1] It does not appear that Churchill had as yet fallen
under suspicion Yet, knowing the tremendous importance of
the part which he intended to play, he must have watched every
move in the great game with painful fascination His mind was
fully made up He followed the line which he had taken at the
commencement of the crisis without faltering to the end He
had no part nor lot in the King's policy. He did not even
pretend to regard it with approval. Unless it were utterly and
finally abandoned, he was determined to use his best endeavours
to frustrate it. On August 4, he had written to William in these
terms·

" SIR,
" Mr Sidney will lett you know how I intend to behave
myselfe I think itt is what I owe to God and my contry. my
honour I take leave to put into your Royalle Hinesses hands,
in which I think itt safe if you think there is annything else
that I ought to doe, you have but to command me, and I shall
pay an intiere obedience to itt, being resolved to dye in that
relidgion that itt has pleased God to give you both the will and
power to protect
" I am, etc , etc ,
" CHURCHILL."[2]

The time for the fulfilment of this momentous pledge was now
at hand. And the conspirators had carefully matured their plans
They did not propose to assist the Prince of Orange by inciting
the regular army to mutiny and seize the capital, or indeed by
anything in the nature of a military *coup d'état*. Proceedings
of this kind, even if successful, would have been highly unpopular,
and might conceivably have resulted in a national reaction in
favour of James The idea of government by prætorian bands
had been detestable to Englishmen since Cromwell's time. The
policy adopted was less violent, but infinitely more effective.
Whether he won or lost it was James' interest to fight as soon
as possible. A victory would strike terror into the hearts of the
disaffected, and a defeat would not of necessity promote the
Prince's cause among a proud and insular people, who would
scarcely relish the spectacle of continental mercenaries advancing
in triumph over the corpses of Englishmen The conspirators
understood that a pitched battle must in nowise be permitted.
All armed collision on a great scale must be postponed until such
time as the Prince's strength and the King's weakness rendered
it impossible. To this end they decided that every device of
official procrastination must be utilised to delay the concentration
of the troops at Salisbury. Such forces as succeeded in arriving

[1] *The Life of King William III*, p. 124
[2] Wolseley, vol ii , p 12

early at the front were to be paralysed by the desertion of officers who, like Kirke and Trelawny, the colonels of the two Tangier regiments, Grafton, the colonel of the Guards, and Churchill himself, were deeply committed to the plot   By these methods they hoped to impose upon the King a bloodless settlement of his controversy with the Church and nation. Their sagacity was proved by the event

Immediately upon the news of William s landing, James pushed forward all his available cavalry and dragoons into the west. Their function was to check the advance of the invading army, while the slowly moving infantry and ponderous artillery were mustering behind them   James' strategy was correct enough, and would probably have served its purpose had William contemplated a dash upon Bristol or upon the capital itself But William was in no hurry On November 9 he entered Exeter, where he continued for ten days He was, in fact, disappointed by the very meagre support which he at first received from the nobility and gentry He even began to imagine that he had been betrayed. His unexpected appearance in the west at a time when his partisans had prepared to receive him in the north accounted in reality for this delay   But before he had been a week at Exeter there occurred an event which augured well for the success of his undertaking On November 11. thanks to the machinations of the conspirators, it happened that the officer in command of the troops already assembled at Salisbury, was himself a conspirator This was Edward, Viscount Cornbury, of the loyal house of Clarendon. Falsely alleging that he had received orders from London to attack an advanced detachment of the Dutch at Honiton, he marched three regiments of horse to Axminster, a distance of fifty miles, and at sunset, on the 13th, moved out against the enemy The singularity of the operation excited suspicion among the loyal officers. It was evident that the three regiments were about to be entrapped Two of them refused to follow their commander, and turned back in the nick of time But Cornbury and such other officers as were entrusted with his secret succeeded in joining William and in carrying an entire regiment with them.

To James, who was on his way to Salisbury and had already reached Winchester, the blow was a severe one Though Cornbury, apart from his birth, was a person of small ability or importance, that fact itself was ominous. The King suspected that only the most powerful prompting could have driven so ordinary a young man to so extraordinary an action. And he saw his army, his solitary bulwark, already weakened by desertion and demoralised by mutual suspicion. At first he was disposed to abandon his journey But Feversham, his commander-in-chief, urged him to push on to Salisbury, where his presence would inspire the troops On November 17 he set out Churchill, whom he had made a lieutenant-general, accompanied

him, as did two other prominent conspirators, the Duke of
Grafton, and the Prince of Denmark   On the 19th he arrived.
On the 20th he reviewed his troops, rewarded the men who had
refused to follow Cornbury, and declared that all who desired
to leave him were at liberty to do so.   On the 21st he proposed
to visit an advanced post at Warminster, where Kirke commanded.   But he was pestered by a violent attack of bleeding at
the nose from executing this design   It was afterwards said that
Churchill and Kirke had contrived a plan for seizing him in his
carriage and delivering him to William   James himself believed
this story, and considered that Providence had intervened to
save him.   It is most improbable that any such plan existed.
William would not have been grateful to those who presented
him with so embarrassing a prisoner.   Another and a darker
tale, which accuses Churchill of meditating the assassination of
his master, rests upon no testimony worthy of the name, and,
if it ever reached the King's ears, was regarded by him as unworthy of credence   It is, however, certain that by this time the
treason of Churchill and his associates was strongly suspected by
Feversham and others.   They urged the King to make several
arrests   James refused.   With a pathetic confidence, which to
some at least of the conspirators must have rendered their
treason unspeakably painful, he trusted them to the last.   But
they had taken the alarm   At a council of war, which was held
immediately after the abortive attempt to visit Warminster, it
had been decided, in opposition to the arguments of Churchill
in favour of a forward movement, to fall back behind the Thames.
From this and other circumstances, Churchill divined that he
was no longer safe   That same night, accompanied by Grafton,
Berkeley, and some other officers, and followed by twenty of the
Royal Dragoons, he quitted Salisbury.   On November 23 he
joined the Prince of Orange at Axminster.

It is said that the veteran Schomberg said to Churchill when
he arrived, " that he was the first lieutenant-general he had ever
heard that had deserted from his colours "[1]

If William's own general really permitted himself to reproach
a British officer for doing that which William's own manifesto
had urged the entire British Army to do, Churchill was not the
man to be vastly perturbed by such maladroit effrontery.   Nor
was he the man to recognise the verdict of a court of honour in
the native insolence of a German mercenary.

Before his departure, Churchill wrote the King a letter[2] which
deserves to be quoted in full.   It was as follows:

" SIR,
        " Since men are seldom suspected of sincerity, when they
act contrary to their interests, and though my dutiful behaviour

[1] Macpherson, *Original Papers*, vol 1 , p 162
[2] State Papers Domestic. First Bundle for 1689   Quoted in Wolseley,
vol ii , p 41

to your Majesty in the worst of times (for which I acknowledge my poor services much overpaid) may not be sufficient to incline you to a charitable interpretation of my actions, yet I hope the great advantage I enjoy under your Majesty, which I can never expect in any other change of government, may reasonably convince your Majesty and the world that I am actuated by a higher principle, when I offer that violence to my inclination and interest as to desert your Majesty at a time when your affairs seem to challenge the strictest obedience from all your subjects, much more from one who lies under the greatest obligations to your Majesty. This, Sir, could proceed from nothing but the inviolable dictates of my conscience and a necessary concern for my religion (which no good man can oppose), and with which I am instructed nothing can come in competition. Heaven knows with what partiality my dutiful opinion of your Majesty has hitherto represented those unhappy designs which inconsiderate and self-interested men have framed against your Majesty's true interest and the Protestant religion; but as I can no longer join with such to give a pretence by conquest to bring them to effect, so I will always, with the hazard of my life and fortune (so much your Majesty's due) endeavour to preserve your royal person and lawful rights, with all the tender concerns and dutiful respect that become, Sir, your Majesty's most dutiful and most obliged subject and servant,

" CHURCHILL "

If Cornbury's desertion had dismayed the King, Churchill's overwhelmed him. He saw plainly that effective resistance to the Prince's progress was now impracticable. The army was probably disloyal and palpably demoralised. The strategic retirement which had already been arranged, degenerated into a precipitate retreat. The first day's march was to Andover. One who was present at that town has left a vivid picture of what he saw. " I can never forget," he wrote, " the confusion the Court was in, . . . the King knew not whom to trust, and the fright was so great that they were apt to believe an impossible report just then brought in that the Prince of Orange was come with 12,000 horse between Warminster and Salisbury. Upon hearing it the Lord Feversham, the General, never questioned the truth, but cried out. ' Zounds, then Kirke be asleep.' This I was an ear-witness of. Everybody in this hurly-burly was thinking of himself, and nobody minded the King, who came up to Dr. Radcliffe and asked him what was good for the bleeding of his nose." On the ensuing day Prince George of Denmark and the Duke of Ormond followed Churchill's example. " Poor man," said Lord Lichfield, " they will leave him so fast they will not give him time to make terms."

And now the northern counties were all ablaze. Delamere had risen in Cheshire and had entered Manchester at the head of

fifty of his tenantry Danby with 100 horse had seized York
Devonshire had ridden in arms from Derby to Nottingham, where
he had published a manifesto of revolt And day by day noblemen and gentlemen from all parts of the country brought in
their dependents, mounted and armed, to William's camp. As
symptoms of the utter alienation of loyal sentiment, such movements were alarming. But from a standpoint purely military
they had less importance Once victorious over William's
disciplined bands, the regular army would have made short work
of these high-spirited amateurs in war. But from the hour of
Churchill's desertion the idea of victory, or even of resistance,
had ceased to enter into James' calculations

On Monday, November 26, he arrived in London, only to be
greeted with the bitter tidings that the Princess Anne had disappeared from Whitehall When Anne was apprised that the
military conspirators had put their designs into execution, and
that her father was returning to his capital, she knew that it was
time to depart. Herself a conspirator, she dreaded to face the
relative whom she and her husband had so deeply injured. She
declared to Lady Churchill, "That rather than see her Father,
she would jump out at the Window "[1] But, in truth, her principal terror was for her adored Mrs. Freeman "Indeed," says
Sarah, " I had Reason enough on my own Account, to get out
of the Way."[2] James had already issued orders for her arrest.
But Sarah's assertion that the flight of the Princess was wholly
unpremeditated is incredible Reason and the weight of evidence are equally opposed to it The contingency had been foreseen, and provision had been made. Sarah had received her
instructions, and when the crisis came she followed them to the
letter She sought out Compton, Bishop of London, who was
the man appointed to manage the escape On the evening of
Sunday, November 25, Anne retired as usual to her apartments,
but not to bed At midnight she descended by the back stairs.
She was accompanied by Lady Churchill and Mrs Berkeley
Compton and the Earl of Dorset were waiting near the "Cock-
pit " with a carriage. They drove forthwith to the Bishop's
house in the City, and next day to Copt Hall, a place of Dorset's,
in Epping Forest Thence they proceeded to Nottingham,
Compton, who as a young man had served in the Life Guards,
riding in advance with pistols in his holsters and a broadsword
on his thigh. Anne received an enthusiastic ovation from the
northern rebels. Sarah also had her triumphs. Her radiant
beauty made an inevitable impression on the heart of young
Colley Cibber, who waited at table when Devonshire entertained
these welcome guests.

The story of the Revolution has been often told This is not
the place in which to rewrite it Churchill's part in the drama
was virtually concluded on the night of November 21 when he

---

[1] *Conduct of the Duchess of Marlborough*, p 81.   [2] *Ibid*

rode from Salisbury into the west. But he could still be of
service to William and to the nation. On December 10, James
fled from Whitehall. Pursuant to his orders Feversham thereupon proceeded to disband the army. Panic and rioting ensued
in London. To embarrass William the forces of anarchy had
been deliberately let loose William, who had now arrived at
Henley, at once dispatched Churchill and Grafton to the scene.
By exerting all their authority over their old regiments, and
over the Household troops and the army generally, they succeeded in mustering a sufficient array of disciplined men to protect
the capital from further outrage. In this important duty
Churchill's personal influence and consummate tact were invaluable Grafton, who displayed his usual reckless courage,
narrowly escaped assassination

It remains to consider the ethical aspect of Churchill's behaviour at this crisis in his own and the nation's history The
dominant motive of his conduct was sincere attachment to the
religious faith in which he had been born. It was certainly not
his material interest to abandon a master who had raised him
so high, that he might attach himself to an adventurer whose
own fortunes, to say nothing of his favours, were problematical.
The point, however, does not require to be laboured. What
Macaulay has conceded to Churchill's credit may be taken as
beyond the region of dispute

But many have thought that, however pure and lofty may
have been Churchill's motive, gratitude to the King should have
rendered him incapable of active treason James himself held
this opinion strongly. It is, however, fundamentally unsound.
In point of fact, Churchill's private obligations to James were
far less overwhelming than is commonly supposed. Before the
Restoration his family had done and suffered much for the
House of Stuart. He himself was born under his grandmother's
roof, because his father's own home had been confiscated by
rebels. He started life with nothing but his sword and his talents,
because the paternal fortune had never recovered from the
penalties of loyalty Charles and James, recognising their
indebtedness to this family, provided John and Arabella Churchill
with places at Court. At this stage, the Stuarts and the
Churchills could perhaps cry quits. Subsequent events did
nothing to modify the position For if Churchill rose high in
the royal service, he rose as much by conspicuous merit as by
any favour He was worth what he received. Arabella certainly
was not in James' debt Whatever she may have got, she had
given all. But even assuming that Churchill was under strong
personal obligations to James, those who reason that he was
thereby stopped from military action antagonistic to the King's,
set the argument not merely upon a low plane, but upon an
entirely false one. It was not for a man so highly placed as
Churchill to regulate his public conduct by private considerations.

Blind devotion to a master, which in a valet or a groom may be a virtue and a duty, would not have been a proper motive for a peer of England whose action could not fail to exercise a powerful influence in current affairs Apart, moreover, from his mere rank, Churchill in 1688 was one of the most prominent personages in the State His authority in the army was unrivalled The duties of a situation such as that to which he had attained took precedence of any which he might owe to the patron who had helped him to attain it This also is a point which should need no labouring It is almost a truism The story of Thomas à Becket, who resisted to the death the master who had made him, is the classical example.

Having once determined that he was constrained by duty to defend the Church of his fathers against the monarch who was contriving her destruction, Churchill had next to consider the question of ways and means. In joining the conspiracy of which the Prince of Orange was the head, he joined the only movement which possessed a reasonable chance of achieving the object which he had at heart So far his conduct is above reproach But was he justified in continuing to serve a King whom he intended to desert in the hour of trial ? There are those who hold that the treason of Salisbury was infinitely less odious than the long course of dissimulation which preceded it But the issue is by no means so simple as it appears to the eye of popular morality. William was playing a game which could not be played successfully with all the cards upon the table A plot, in which the principal plotters make a public confession of their intentions, will speedily develop into a futile and perhaps a bloody burlesque When Churchill took a hand he was bound to abide by the maxims of the game Suppose, for example, that at any time during the two years which preceded the Revolution he had resigned his offices, had managed to avoid arrest, and had repaired to the Hague Such a course, while it would certainly have been straightforward and would have effectually silenced those critics who accuse him of the blackest treachery, would have placed the Church's cause in extreme peril For it would have opened even James' eyes to the real nature of his nephew's designs The King would have appealed to the patriotism of the nation, who had little love for the Dutch. A war with Holland would probably have ensued, a war in which the army and navy of England would assuredly have rendered no bad account of themselves. From such a struggle James would have emerged with redoubled strength to prosecute his religious policy to its appointed end

For the leader of a rebellion and the maker of a revolution morality means, or should mean, something more than a righteous quarrel. He is bound by the strongest sanctions to be satisfied, before he acts, of the prospects of success. Upon his prudence and practical wisdom will depend not only the safety of the cause which he upholds, but the happiness and even the lives of numbers whom he exposes to the vengeance of the authority which he assails. For him, therefore, to divorce morality from expediency is in the highest degree immoral. Whoever can appreciate the truth that, in certain circumstances, the treason which fails is ethically worse than the treason which prospers, will be slow to denounce the dissimulation of Churchill in that unmeasured language which is the distinctive mark of superficial or malicious criticism.

But whatever standard is applied to Churchill must, of course, be applied to the other conspirators If Churchill is to be condemned because he did not openly declare himself, William of Orange must be equally condemned. Nor can Mary and Anne, and Sunderland and Danby and Compton, and innumerable other leaders in Church and State escape the like censure Indeed, Churchill's dissimulation was infinitely less repulsive in its details than William's Much has been made of an alleged assembly of officers (at London or Salisbury), where James is said to have received assurances of loyalty from Churchill and others who, within a few days, abandoned him. At such a moment such a profession could hardly be avoided. But it seems a trivial thing in comparison with the policy of William, James' own son-in-law and nephew, be it remembered, who had made a practice of sending ambassadors to the English Court with instructions to intrigue against his uncle, who had publicly prayed for the Prince of Wales at a time when he was arming to rob him of his birthright, and who had formally and repeatedly denied that his military and naval preparations had any connection with the politics of England. These methods were essential to the success of the conspiracy Had William and his English associates, or any of them, openly avowed their intentions, the Revolution could not have happened To condemn Churchill, therefore, is to condemn the conspiracy which issued in the Revolution, and is in reality to condemn the Revolution itself. Such a conclusion is not of necessity absurd But many of Churchill's critics appear to be ignorant that their reasoning involves them in this result.

There are some precisians who consider that, even if duplicity can be excused, the military crime of desertion is unpardonable But Churchill's duty as an officer of the King's army stands upon the same footing as his other duties to the King, whose friend and trusted servant he was All these obligations were cancelled by the supreme claim of his religion. What William thought, or professed to think, of this particular problem, can best be studied in the manifesto which he addressed to the British Army, before starting for England, and in which the following passage occurs.

" We hope, likewise, that you will not suffer your selves to be abused by a false Notion of Honour, but that you will in the first place consider what you owe to Almighty God and your Religion, to your Country, to your selves, and to your Posterity, which you, as Men of Honour, ought to prefer to all private Considerations and Engagements whatsoever "[1]

If this was anything better than the most odious cant, one would suppose that the mouths of William's admirers would have been for ever stopped from abuse of Churchill's desertion of King James Yet of all the pack which have been snarling at his heels for two hundred years, the Whig Macaulay is the foremost and the shrillest Macaulay's motives will appear hereafter. It is perhaps unnecessary to say that they had no relation whatever to the actual issue.

Churchill's Jacobite judges stand on firmer and cleaner ground. Yet they, too, are influenced by a consideration not strictly pertinent to the moral issue They cannot forget that, after William himself, and possibly Sunderland, no man contributed so much as Churchill to the great catastrophe. When James went to Salisbury, the odds were already heavy against him If at that moment anything on earth could have saved the Crown of the Stuarts, it was the sword of Marlborough Half a generation was to elapse before that surpassing genius flashed out upon the battlefield of Blenheim Yet already his talent for war was highly esteemed. The belief that Churchill, and Churchill alone, might have turned the tide, and did not, made James implacable to his old servant long after he had pardoned others whose treason was at least as dark. This same belief, which was wonderfully confirmed by his achievements in the War of the Spanish Succession, explains not a little of the vindictive malice wherewith Churchill was pursued by Jacobites and High Tories, both in his life and in his death They loathed him less for what he had gained by his action at the Revolution than for what they had lost, or believed that they had lost. It was not the mere fact of his defection, it was not the preference, which he was stupidly alleged to have given to his private interest, it was not even those circumstances which are commonly, and most unfairly, supposed to have aggravated his conduct and placed it in some rare and peculiar category of infamy, it was none of these things that caused him to be singled out for special obloquy by the partisans of the House of Stuart. It was not, in short, for his treason but for his talents that he stood condemned.

In Stuart partisans this attitude is natural, but in the mass of Churchill's contemporaries and of posterity, it is neither just nor decent They who, for whatever cause, set store by the Revolution, should not be forward to revile the one man who might have stayed it and did not. Nor should they who call it " glorious," because it was accomplished without the effusion of blood, hasten to denounce the great soldier who could, if he would, have exacted a terrible price for it, but who deliberately preferred what he regarded as the highest of public causes to " all private Considerations and Engagements whatsoever."

[1] *The Life of King William III*, p. 131

APPENDIX VI

FLANDERS AND IRELAND

SOCIAL disorder and constitutional anarchy ensued upon the flight of James. Though the energy of William and Churchill speedily suppressed the one, the other still remained   Nor was the problem easy of solution   William's ideas of an appropriate settlement did not coincide with those of the Tory party.   The Tories, desirous of bridging, as far as possible, the indubitable breach which they had made in their famous principles, proposed a regency.   William would not hear of it.   They then suggested that Mary alone should assume the Crown.   But Mary, like the dutiful wife that she ever was, refused the offer.   Such a contest could have only one issue.   The Tories represented a majority of the nation, but William was the man in possession   England at that moment could forgo these devices for saving the face of an embarrassed party, but she could not afford to quarrel with her deliverer.   In the end, the Crown was conferred upon both the Prince and Princess of Orange, and in the event of both their deaths without issue, upon the Princess of Denmark.   "The lawyers disputed," says Evelyn, " but necessity prevailed."[1] Churchill, like the rest of the Tories, appears to have entered upon the destructive work of the Revolution without any constructive plans   His wife declares that she " imagined that the Prince of Orange's sole Design was to provide for the Safety of his own Country, by obliging King James to keep the Laws of ours, and that he would go back as soon as he had made us all happy "[2] Churchill himself may conceivably have entertained similar views. But in common with the bulk of his countrymen, he accepted a settlement which was dictated by expediency if not by necessity. Sarah did more   She exerted herself to reconcile the Princess Anne to the new constitutional arrangement.   Anne was distinctly aggrieved by the action of the Convention Parliament in preferring the claims of William to her own   At first she was disposed to exhibit her resentment and to become the centre of an opposition   Such conduct would have been both undignified and futile.   Fearful lest the King and Queen should ascribe it to her influence, Sarah summoned Tillotson to her aid.   Together they persuaded the Princess to submit with a good grace to what,

[1] *Evelyn's Diary*, February 21, 1689
[2] *Conduct of the Duchess of Marlborough*, p 83.

450

" as Things were then situated,"[1] was the best, and indeed, the only possible solution.

William showed himself well satisfied with Churchill's services. He gave him the rank of lieutenant-general, made him Gentleman of the Bedchamber, and raised him to an Earldom. Churchill selected the title of Marlborough, which had previously existed in the family of Ley, with whom he was distantly connected on his mother's side It was a name of good omen to the Englishmen of that period. In 1665 an Earl of Marlborough, a good and valiant man, had perished gloriously in a sea-battle with the Dutch

For a Prince of Orange the Crown of England was a splendid prize. But William valued it, as he valued all things, only in so far as it contributed to the fulfilment of his life's purpose, the humiliation of the might of France While he talked to his new subjects of their religion and their rights, he was mentally estimating the contingents and the subsidies which they could furnish to the coalised powers If the English were unable as yet to appreciate his point of view, their bellicose temper was entirely to his satisfaction With them, war with France was more than inevitable; it was already popular. Louis had welcomed James as a friend and an ally, and in the spring of 1689, had assisted him to land in Ireland, where Tyrconnel and the Catholics were practically supreme The Commons addressed the King in favour of a resort to arms In May hostilities were proclaimed.

Louis was assailed on every side. Turn where he would, to the Pyrenees, to the Rhine, to the Flemish frontier, he saw his enemies in array. But he had two allies, the Turks in the east, the Irish in the west, whose activity relieved him not a little from the pressure of attack England, at any rate, until she had relieved her flank from the Irish peril, could not intervene effectively upon the continent. Sound strategy demanded that, before any operation was undertaken in the Low Countries, the Jacobite forces in Ireland should be annihilated. But William, who was none too well advised as to the possibilities of Irish resistance, and who was, moreover, impatient to bring home to Louis the strength of the coalition's new ally, committed the error of attempting too much. In May he dispatched Marlborough to Holland, where a contingent of 8,000 strong, the flower of the British Army, had already arrived. In the same month he sent Kirke with an inadequate detachment to the relief of Londonderry. In August, Schomberg landed in Ulster with 10,000 men, mostly raw troops, who were unequal to the work before them, and who perished in crowds from privation and disease. The consequence was that, when the year ended, Ireland remained in the possession of James and his French auxiliaries. The success which in the meantime had attended Marlborough was no compensation for this strategical disaster.

It is possible that in shipping so many of the finest English

[1] *Ibid.*

regiments to the continent while he relied upon foreigners and newly raised levies for the conduct of the war in Ireland, William was influenced by political rather than military considerations. In truth, the old soldiers of King James were not altogether safe material to employ against their former master   The Revolution had sorely wounded the professional pride of the British Army. Both officers and men considered, illogically perhaps, but none the less sincerely, that in surrendering the kingdom without a battle, they had humiliated themselves in the eyes of Europe Their jealousy was excited by the presence of the Dutch troops, whose discipline and good conduct gave rise to unfavourable comparisons   In March, 1639, these sentiments took a practical and dangerous shape.   The Royal Scots, a regiment which even at that time was ancient and renowned, was one of those under orders for Flanders   On the road to Harwich they mutinied at Ipswich and started by forced marches for Scotland   Pursued by mounted and superior forces they were overtaken in Lincolnshire and compelled to surrender   William treated them with as much clemency as firmness   They returned to their duty and their illustrious career   But William may well have thought that the sullen and difficult temper of such regiments was better suited to foreign warfare than to civil strife beyond St. George's Channel   But foreign warfare itself was unpopular among the men, who suspected that they were to be transferred to the service of Holland.   William found it necessary to correct this impression by the issue of a proclamation.

The continental campaign of 1689 is not difficult to understand   The allies had four armies in the field.   In Flanders the Spaniards and Dutch under Vaudemont threatened the northeastern frontier of France   Farther south the Dutch, English, and Swedes, commanded by the Prince of Waldeck, were proposing to operate in the country between the Sambre and the Meuse.   On the Rhine the Elector of Brandenburg, with an army of Prussians and North Germans, was meditating the capture of Bonn, while the Duke of Lorraine, with the Emperor's forces, had formed a design upon Mainz.   The French, on the other hand, outnumbered by their enemies, stood strictly on the defensive.   But at every point they fared badly   On the Rhine, where their cavalry was largely untrained, they went in terror of the Emperor's horsemen   Lorraine, an excellent general, passed the river, took Mainz, and marching down the left bank, assisted Brandenburg to complete the reduction of Bonn.   Thus easily this natural barrier of the Rhine was lost to France.   In Flanders, Vaudemont advanced to Courtrai   The French retired before him, and took refuge in their fortified lines between the Lys and the Schelde.   Meantime the fourth army under Waldeck, though too weak to take a decided offensive, had manœuvred successfully against the enemy and had been victorious in the one notable engagement of the whole campaign

To this army Marlborough and the English contingent were attached. On their first arrival in Holland the English had created an unfavourable impression. In numbers they were far below their proper strength. They were discontented, suspicious, and insubordinate. Their officers were half paid   Their arms and equipment were bad.   Their physical condition seemed little suited for the fatigues of the field   The one military quality, which nobody denied them, was courage.   But the talents of Marlborough effected a sudden change.   Landing at Rotterdam on May 17, he proceeded at once to Maestricht, where he conferred with Waldeck.   Waldeck was one of William's men, a commonplace, unimaginative soldier, well schooled in the pedantry of European war   Though no officer possessed a more complete knowledge of all that part of the military profession which can be taught in battle, he was always unfortunate   Like all foreigners, he had a poor opinion of the English army. But, adorned with more intelligence and refinement than most of his class, he was captivated by the charm and the good sense of Marlborough, and delighted with his energy.   Reinforced by detachments drafted from other regiments, and reduced by judicious rigour to a proper discipline, the English contingent gradually began to excite the admiration of the very general who had at first regarded its inefficiency with despair   Marlborough was assisted by excellent officers, such as Tollemache, whose reputation in the army was second to his own, and Charles Churchill, his brother, the colonel of the Buffs, whom he made a brigadier.   By the middle of June the whole army was encamped between Tirlemont and Judoigne   On the 20th they marched for Fleurus   The French, under Marshal d'Humières, were at Haine, near Mons.   Weakened by desertions and by a flood which destroyed 1,000 horses and many tents and stores, they were by no means anxious to fight.   But Waldeck continued his advance.   On July 1 he was between Charleroi and Namur with 35,000 men   On the 3rd he wrote to William that thus far he could not sufficiently praise the English, and on the 6th he reported that, not counting the sick, the English numbered 6,000 foot and 500 horse, "the whole so well ordered that I have admired it, and I can say that Monsieur Milord Marlbrouck and the Colonels have shown that their application has had a good effect "[1]   On the 30th Waldeck retired to Nivelles, where he suddenly descended upon Fontaine l'Évêque.   D'Humières fell back   Reinforced by 4,000 Luxembourg horse, Waldeck passed the Sambre at Marchienne on August 6, and encamped at Ham-sur-Heure.   On the 14th he moved south and took up a position one mile to the north of Walcourt, a small fortified town, which

[1] S P Dom K Wm's Chest, No 5, f 62, quoted by Captain H R Knight in *Historical Records of the Buffs, East Kent Regiment, 3rd Foot, formerly designated the Holland Regiment and Prince George of Denmark's Regiment*, vol 1, p 290

he occupied with a regiment of Luneburgers, 600 strong. Meantime, d'Humières had also passed the Sambre and was moving towards Walcourt from the south-west. During these manœuvres contact had been established between the outposts of the armies, and skirmishing had already occurred. But neither general was eager for a battle, except at an obvious advantage.

The ancient town of Walcourt, famous throughout Catholic Europe for its miraculous Virgin, stands upon a considerable eminence in the midst of a picturesque country of woods and hills. The locality is totally unsuited for the formal tactics of a pitched battle. On ground so difficult and broken, caution was the highest part of generalship. But caution was precisely the quality in which the Marshal d'Humières did not excel. A brilliant courtier, splendid and profuse in his mode of living, and endowed with the most amiable and fascinating of manners, he had risen to the summit of his profession at an early age. But gossip whispered that his good fortune was attributable less to his military talents than to the beauty of his wife, which was supposed to have enslaved the heart of Louvois. At the battle of Cassel in 1677 his impatience committed the right wing to a hazardous movement that threatened to involve the entire army in disaster. He was now to demonstrate even more conspicuously his unfitness for the highest command

On the morning of the 25th a numerous detachment of Waldeck's army went out into the country to forage   Marlborough was one of the officers who superintended this important work To guard against a sudden descent of the French, Colonel Hodges with 600 Englishmen of the Sixteenth Foot (now the Bedfordshire Regiment) and some 300 Dutch horse and dragoons, was stationed at the hamlet of Batte Fer or Forges, about two miles south of Walcourt. Hodges was a brave and skilful officer, who had proved his quality in the hard fighting round Tangier   About 9 o'clock the outposts gave warning of the approach of a large body of cavalry   It was the vanguard of the French army   Cannon were immediately fired as a signal to the foragers to return to camp. In the meantime Hodges made ready to hold the enemy in play. The approach to Walcourt from the south runs through the valley of the Heure, a narrow gorge not easy to be forced by mounted men. In and about the hamlet of Batte Fer or Forges, the English infantry awaited the attack. The Dutch horse rode out to skirmish with the enemy. But d'Humières' cavalry, an arm in which he was particularly strong, came on in overwhelming numbers, till they were checked by the fire of English foot. For nearly two hours this one battalion stood its ground. By 11 o'clock almost all the foragers were safe in camp   Marlborough and other officers rode out to Batte Fer or Forges. Cavalry was pushed forward in support of Hodges. But now the main body of d'Humières' army had arrived. Infantry and dragoons advanced to carry the village. Thereupon Hodges evacuated the position, and retiring for a short distance, occupied a mill, which he held stubbornly till he received express orders to abandon it. Wheeling and firing as the French pressed forward, the English infantry retreated slowly and in good order, till they reached the summit of the high ground adjacent to the hill of Walcourt on its eastern side. Then they returned to the camp They had done well. Their losses amounted to no more than two officers and thirty men Tangier, as a school of war, was certainly justified in their valiant colonel It was now high noon. D'Humières had accomplished nothing, and he ought to have realised that there was nothing left to accomplish. But, irritated by the obstinate resistance of the handful of English, he conceived the mad idea of carrying the post of Walcourt by assault. Walcourt was not a fortress of the latest type. But it stood on a steep hill, it was partly covered by a river, and its ancient ramparts furnished an adequate protection against musketry and field-guns Though the garrison numbered not more than 600, they had confidence in their defences and still more in the proximity of the whole of Waldeck's army, which was itself inaccessible to attack unless the town were first carried These considerations were lost on d'Humières Encouraged by a gentleman of the Court, who told him that there were several breaches in the walls, he ordered his artillery to cannonade the place and drew out nine battalions to deliver the assault. Three separate points were selected for attack. Over river and stream and marsh, and up the precipitous heights, went the French infantry, only to recoil again and again before the accurate fire of the Luneburgers. Waldeck threw forward both horse and foot to the eminence east of the town There also he planted a battery which replied to d'Humières' guns But, the French refusing to relinquish their audacious project, it became necessary to reinforce the garrison. This operation was difficult by reason of the nature of the ground. At 2 o'clock, however, it was effected by Tollemache under a heavy fire. D'Humières' enterprise was now hopeless But still the assaults continued At one time two hundred men of the French Guards marched up to the grey walls of the town, and, with a courage equal to that of the assailants of Hougomont, coolly prepared to make a bonfire of the gates. They were almost all shot down A little before 6 the moment arrived for a counter-attack Meantime Waldeck's army was waiting impatiently for the word On the western side of the town, Schlangenberg advanced with the Dutch infantry On the east, Marlborough fell upon d'Humières' flank with the English Life Guards, supported by two English battalions The French gave way in disorder. Fortunately for d'Humières his cavalry was commanded by one of the most brilliant officers in the French service. If Marlborough was there, so also was Villars. By his masterly tactics the wreckage of Louis' superb infantry was saved In the light of subsequent events the encounter of these two in the valley of the Heure was strange and almost prophetic Not for twenty years were they to meet again on the field of battle And it was destined that then, as at Walcourt, Villars should be summoned to save his country from the incompetence of generals who knew more of the courtier's than the soldier's art.

The ground was unfavourable to close pursuit. D'Humières escaped annihilation. But he was badly beaten He left six guns in the hands of Waldeck. His eight battalions of the Guards were completely ruined The loss in officers was especially heavy. The killed and wounded could hardly have been less than 2,000 Six hundred dead were counted around Walcourt alone. The losses of the allies were comparatively trifling The casualties among the defenders of Walcourt did not exceed forty, and among the army in general, 300

The conduct of the English gave great satisfaction to Waldeck. In his report to William he declared that " Colonel Hodges and the English . . did marvels," and that " Marlborough is one of the most gallant men I know."[1] William was delighted And the people of England were delighted. Walcourt was not a great battle, but for them it had a great and splendid significance. Like Stuart's victory at Maida in 1806, it demonstrated to all the world that for the English army, unknown and unhonoured though it was upon the continent of Europe, the military prestige of France had no terrors

The French Court was " much concerned "[2] As for d'Humières, his reputation was ruined In the ensuing year he was superseded by Luxembourg. The severest judgment passed upon his conduct was that of Feuquières   " I have no instructive reflections to make upon this subject," wrote that able but remorseless critic, " except to say that this combat should never be cited, save as an example to avoid."[3] Waldeck was so pleased with his success that in the next campaign he set a similar trap for Luxembourg at Fleurus But he had mistaken his man. And Fleurus ended in a crushing disaster for the allies.

The battle of Walcourt was the virtual end of the campaign. Waldeck recrossed the Sambre and retired to Genappe and then to Hal The French followed, but at a respectful distance. Sickness raged among the allied troops. The English, who were deficient in shoes and clothing, suffered severely. So bad was their condition that Waldeck was obliged to send four regiments back to Breda. In the middle of September both armies were reinforced. At Waldeck's approach the French, who were at Lessines, fell back to a strong position at Leuze.

[1] Prince of Waldeck to the King, S P Dom K Wm's Chest, No. 5, f 96, quoted by Captain H R. Knight in *Historical Records of the Buffs,* p 293

[2] *London Gazette,* August 29, 1689.

[3] *Mémoires de Feuquières,* t. iii., p. 262.

Waldeck was now obliged to part with the remainder of the English contingent, who were quite unfit for further service. A few days later both armies withdrew into winter-quarters. Marlborough returned to England.

It was evident to William that the summer of 1690 must be devoted to the reduction of Ireland, where James and his French allies were still in possession of all save Protestant Ulster. Ulster, too, might have been theirs, had Louis realised the strategical importance of Ireland at this moment. Though no great naval battle was fought in 1689 or the beginning of 1690, the French navy was stronger than the combined fleets of England and Holland. It was used successfully to cover the dispatch of troops and supplies to James. But it was not used to prevent either Kirke or Schomberg, or eventually William himself, from crossing St George's Channel. The French forces in Ireland were sufficient to create a troublesome diversion, but they were not sufficient to conquer the entire country in 1689, or even to hold their own in 1690. Properly supported both on land and sea, James and Lauzun might have maintained their ground for years, they might even have invaded England and driven William from the throne. But Louis, whose eyes were ever fixed upon the Rhine, neglected the opportunity. Even so William could not afford to permit his enemies to continue upon British soil. Early in June, 1690, he crossed to Ulster and took the field at the head of 36,000 men.

Marlborough did not accompany him. It has been suggested, and perhaps truly, that Marlborough was unwilling to appear in arms against his old master. This delicacy happened to harmonise with William's plans. In quitting England at a time when the command of the sea was at the best an open question, he was naturally anxious to leave behind him at least one soldier in whose ability he had the highest confidence. During his absence the government remained in the hands of Mary, assisted by nine Privy Councillors whom William had selected from both Whigs and Tories. The Whigs were Devonshire, Dorset, Monmouth, and Russell, the Tories, Caermarthen, Pembroke, Nottingham, Lowther, and Marlborough. Marlborough also received his commission as commander-in-chief of all the forces in England during William's absence.

It was not long before the courage and capacity of Mary and her advisers were put to the severest proof. No sooner had William departed than Tourville, the most accomplished seaman that France at that time possessed, appeared off the Devonshire coast with a fleet superior in numbers to the combined navies of England and Holland. Herbert, whom William had created Earl of Torrington, took command of the allied squadrons at St. Helen's. But whether from prudence or treachery, he showed no disposition to engage the enemy. As Tourville sailed eastward, Torrington retired towards the Straits of Dover. The

government became alarmed   They had reason to suspect that
Tourville's movements had been preconcerted with the English
Jacobites.   Several of the more prominent of that faction, including the Queen's uncle, Clarendon, were promptly committed
to the Tower   And Torrington received peremptory orders to
bring the French to battle.   He obeyed, but not in the true
spirit of the British sailor.   On June 30, off Beachy Head, he
permitted the Dutch to become closely involved, while he himself, with the bulk of the English ships, maintained the action
at the longest possible range   The Dutch were honourably
beaten, the English were disgraced.   The shattered squadrons
took refuge in the mouth of the Thames   Had Tourville followed
up his victory, he might have annihilated his enemies   But
even as it was, he had secured for a time the mastery of the sea.

England's danger was extreme.   There were not 6,000 regular
troops in the island   William's crushing victory upon the
Boyne, while it raised the spirits of the people, did not immediately affect the situation   Tourville controlled the seas   On
the one hand, he could bar the return of William from Ireland;
on the other, he could easily transport an army of French veterans
across the Channel.   And these veterans were available.   Luxembourg had relieved the pressure on the north-eastern frontier of
France by routing Waldeck at Fleurus.   D'Humières, with 20,000
men, was encamped within easy distance of Dunkirk.   England
lay open to invasion by the foremost military power in Europe
To James, who thoroughly understood the art of naval warfare,
the magnitude of the opportunity was apparent   Returning to
France from the Boyne, he implored Louis to seize it

In this dark hour the bearing of the English people was beyond
all praise.   The animosities of party were forgotten; the voices
of faction were hushed   The Jacobites went in silence and in
terror of their lives   An immense majority of the nation, without
distinction of class or creed, rallied in arms to the support of the
lonely and beautiful Queen, who showed herself in nowise unworthy to wear the crown of Elizabeth Tudor   From sea to
sea the country swarmed with fighting men   The peasantry,
the yeomanry, and the shopkeepers looked to the nobility and
gentry of the realm as to their natural leaders, and then, as
ever in such moments of national peril, they did not look in vain.
The story of that summer in England is a proud story to read.
Unfortunately it is too often read without discernment.   Dema-
gogues, desirous of blinding the people to the necessity of national
preparation for war, grandiloquently proclaimed that what-
happened in 1690 would happen now.   Doubtless the courage of
the nation is still high   Doubtless the spirit, which was exhibited
then, would in like circumstances be exhibited again   But
something more than spirit and courage are required to encounter
victoriously the valour that submits to discipline and the enthusiasm that is organised by scientific skill.   And in any case

the events of 1690 prove nothing. England's gallant levies were never launched against the battalions which Condé and Turenne had trained.

Had the issue been tried, the event can hardly now be estimated. It must, however, be admitted that in that age the odds were not so overwhelmingly in the invaders' favour as they would be to-day. If Marlborough had no army in the continental sense of the term, he had, nevertheless, an abundance of soldiers. Both in temper and physique his recruits were perhaps the finest in the world And already they had a useful knowledge of the rudiments of war The nation, which sprang to arms on the morrow of Torrington's defeat, was a nation which almost without exception could manage a horse and handle a weapon. Many among the peasantry had learned in the militia the elements of drill Not a few of the gentry had served under the generals of France and Holland. From such material, and with a nucleus of 6,000 regular troops, a formidable army could certainly be formed Fighting on their own ground, and animated by the intense hatred of the French, which was at that period innate in the English character, they might well have delayed the invaders until such time as the fleet could put to sea once more, and William could return from Ireland. They might even have achieved a great victory. For we know now, what nobody knew then (though there were some who dimly suspected it), that he who would have led them in the field was a greater than Luxembourg. Had Marlborough lost a battle in defence of London, it would have been the only battle that he ever lost

But Louis missed his opportunity. The rout upon the Boyne had disgusted him with adventures overseas And he very properly placed little confidence in James' assertion that the English were eager to welcome home their rightful king But if James was wrong in his politics, he was right in his strategy. His opinion, however, was politely ignored. July was fast running out, the Dutch and English fleets were rapidly refitting, the improvised army of England was learning its business day by day under the eye of Marlborough, and still the French did nothing. At length they did move. On July 22, Tourville anchored in Torbay and landed troops The promised rising of the Jacobites did not come, but the whole of Devonshire and Cornwall precipitated themselves upon the invaders. The French burned a hundred houses in the innocent fishing-town of Teignmouth, and promptly took to their boats Such an achievement had better been left undone. Among a people, whose love of hard fighting has always been as conspicuous as their humanity in war, it excited nothing but derision and disgust.

Within a month from the battle of Beachy Head, Louis' opportunity had passed. Tourville had returned to Brest. The allied fleets were again at sea. Marlborough perceived that all danger of invasion was at an end, and that the time had arrived to deliver an effective counter-stroke. The point, which his infallible judgment selected for attack, was the south-west coast of Ireland. The precise operation which he proposed was the capture of the harbour towns of Cork and Kinsale. He realised that if once an English army were firmly established in that region, the principal communication between France and Ireland would be destroyed. It would become impossible for Louis to reinforce the Jacobite army, which was still defying William from behind the walls of Limerick and Galway. Even the retreat of the French contingent which had fought at the Boyne might be cut off. The plan was a sound one. As early as January Sir Robert Southwell, the Secretary for Ireland and himself a native of Kinsale, had advised the King to attack the rebels simultaneously from north and south. William had not accepted the suggestion, possibly because it would have necessitated the employment of troops whom he dared not move from England so long as there existed a genuine risk of a French invasion. But now the moment had arrived. Marlborough laid his completed plans before the Queen. A majority of her nine advisers, partly from dislike of Marlborough and partly from inability to comprehend the strategical position, urged her to reject them. This was the first occasion, but it was by no means the last, on which ignorance and prejudice endeavoured to frustrate the designs of the foremost soldier of that age. Fortunately, Marlborough was endowed with a serene and patient temper. Nobody was better able to conceal the justest feelings of resentment and contempt. He quietly reiterated his proposition and exposed the fallacies in the arguments of his opponents. Mary referred the whole matter to the King. The critics had no chance with one who understood the principles of war. Greatly to the vexation of the majority of the council of nine, William at once accepted Marlborough's plans and ordered him to execute them himself with the least possible delay. The season was already far advanced. It was known that the health of English soldiers suffered severely upon Irish soil, particularly in autumn. Fearful lest the prospects of his campaign should be jeopardised by climatic conditions, Marlborough urged forward the preparations with the utmost vigour. Nor did he, in the meantime, neglect two necessary precautions. While he kept himself well informed of the military situation at Cork and Kinsale he deliberately created at home " the fog of war." The gossips of the London coffee-houses were regaled with the story that, in revenge for the burning of Teignmouth, the government meditated a descent upon the coast of Normandy. Even to the Admiralty the truth was not officially divulged. The secret, however, was suspected by many. Lauzun and Tyrconnel speedily got wind of it. Already they were heartily sick of Ireland. There was nothing which they so much dreaded as to be permanently cut off from France Without delay and without regret they abandoned a country where they had achieved nothing but disaster. They left the Duke of Berwick, Marlborough's nephew, in nominal command They took with them the remnants of that French contingent which had constituted the most dangerous element in the Irish problem. A strategical advantage of the first magnitude was thus obtained by the mere rumour of Marlborough's project.

On August 26 the Earl set out for Portsmouth On the 30th he embarked his troops. Adverse winds detained the flotilla for more than a fortnight. Not until September 17 did it put to sea Meantime, William, beaten by Irish valour and the Irish climate, had abandoned the siege of Limerick and returned to London He had left behind him instructions that 5,000 men from the forces already in Ireland should co-operate with Marlborough upon his arrival in Cork

The flotilla, including the convoy, numbered eighty sail. Marlborough, who suffered as usual from violent sea-sickness, made the passage on the *Grafton*, a vessel of 70 guns, which was commanded by the Duke of Grafton This young prince was the son of Marlborough's old love and kinswoman, the Duchess of Cleveland They had fought together at Philip's Norton and Sedgemoor, and together they had deserted James at Salisbury. William had suspected Grafton of Jacobite propensities, and had deprived him of the colonelcy of the 1st Foot Guards But regarding him as too dissipated a person to be really dangerous he had subsequently given him a man-of-war Grafton exhibited a strong taste for a naval life,[1] and much was expected of his career upon the sea. Gallant and energetic, the Duke was resolved to show in Ireland that one at any rate of King Charles' bastards could perform some signal service for the State On the evening of Saturday, September 20, the flotilla reached the entrance to Cork harbour. On Sunday morning they stood in, and having silenced a battery which guarded the mouth, dropped anchor for the night On Monday, after demolishing a second battery, they came with the tide to West Passage, which is seven miles inland from Cork. Here, on Tuesday, Marlborough disembarked his army The enemy appeared in some force, but attempted nothing serious Marlborough formed a camp and dispatched a formal summons to McGillicuddy the Governor, who treated it with disdain On Wednesday 600 sailors and marines were landed Headed by Grafton, who was not too proud to work with his hands among his men, they speedily brought ashore the artillery, ammunition, and supplies. That same afternoon, after a march of nearly six miles, Marlborough approached the southern suburb of Cork The resistance which he encountered was of the feeblest. After some ineffectual skirmishing the Irish set fire to the houses and retired.

[1] *Evelyn's Diary*, November 6, 1679.

But Marlborough's army was not the first of the besieging forces to appear before the town. On the preceding evening the advance-guard of the detachment of 5,000 men from the army of Ireland, which William had ordered to co-operate with the Earl, had arrived upon the heights to the north of Cork. Ever since he sailed from Portsmouth, Marlborough had been in communication with Ginkel, the Dutchman who now commanded in Ireland. Marlborough had specially asked that British soldiers and British officers should be sent him. Ginkel, having carefully arranged that no British forces should be available, apologised for his inability to oblige him, and assigned him 5,000 Danes, Dutch, and Huguenots under the Duke of Württemberg. This trick was played in accordance with a deliberate policy. The foreign generals who surrounded William, deemed it essential to their interest to establish the proposition that the British army in general, and British officers in particular, were good for nothing. Ginkel hoped that Marlborough would fail. He probably expected that friction between Württemberg and the Englishman would tend to paralyse operations. And he was determined that, in the event of a success, the British should be compelled to share the glory with the foreigners.

Tettau and Schravemor, who commanded the advance-guard, were prepared on Wednesday afternoon to storm the northern suburb. But the Irish did not await the onset. Imitating their comrades on the southern side they fired the houses, and withdrew into the city. The dominating position of Shandon Castle was thus abandoned to the besiegers.

Although in the age of Vauban and Coehoorn the fortifications of Cork were obsolete, the natural defences of the place were not to be despised. Situated on an island in the River Lee, it was bounded upon the north and south by channels of running water, and upon the east and west by treacherous marshes. It was entirely surrounded by a wet ditch and by limestone walls, which were strengthened by twelve towers. Beyond the river it was protected on the north by Shandon Castle, and on the south by two important works known respectively as "Fort Elizabeth" and "The Cat." These three positions overlooked the city. But the garrison, which numbered 5,000, was not strong enough to hold them all. The Danes were already in possession of Shandon Castle and were erecting batteries there. On Thursday morning Marlborough discovered that in abandoning the southern suburb the Irish had also evacuated "The Cat." He occupied it immediately and constructed batteries, which began at once to play upon Fort Elizabeth and upon the town itself.

It was unnecessary to open trenches. The suburbs afforded sufficient cover to the besiegers. Nothing indeed could save the city but the destruction of Württemberg's army by the Duke of Berwick, who was only fifty miles away with 8,000 men, or the decimation of the British forces by exposure and disease. But

Wurttemberg was too quick for Berwick, and marched safely into the northern suburb on Friday evening Berwick ordered McGilli-cuddy to fire the town and cut his way out before he was entirely surrounded McGillicuddy ignored the order. He hoped for a protracted siege, whereby Kinsale would assuredly be saved and the British army probably ruined But he was counting without the energy of Marlborough, whose batteries were already hard at work

Wurttemberg's arrival at once created a difficulty. Taking his stand upon his royal birth, he claimed the command of the entire army. As a prince of a royal house, he objected to serve under one who had been born a mere gentleman His contention was irrelevant and thoroughly bad. The question was not a social but a military one. Marlborough was Wurttemberg's senior in military rank Marlborough had been appointed by Queen Mary to the command of the British expedition against Cork and Kinsale. Wurttemberg was merely the officer commanding a contingent which had been instructed to co-operate with Marl-borough's army. With his habitual sauvity of manner the Earl endeavoured to convince the Duke that his claim was unreason-able But the Duke refused to be convinced He even lost his temper Marlborough retained his, despite the provocation The situation was ridiculous. But it was necessary to find a way out. Arbitration would have involved delay. Besides, there were no arbitrators whom the English general could trust. He therefore suggested the antique device of exercising command upon alternate days. Wurttemberg was induced by a Huguenot officer to accept this compromise. Such an arrangement had nothing to recommend it save necessity. But on the present occasion it was rendered innocuous by the tact of Marlborough. The first day being his, he chose, as the watchword, "Wurttem-berg." The Duke was charmed, and responded on the second day with "Marlborough." Thereafter, though the dual com-mand continued, the German co-operated amicably with the Englishman, whose infinite superiority he soon perceived.

Marlborough had decided to breach the eastern wall of the city. The point selected was some sixty yards north of the river. By 4 o'clock on Saturday afternoon the fire of the heavy guns had created a practicable breach The tide was rising, but there was still time for the column of assault to pass the stream. Marlborough was preparing to deliver his attack, when McGilli-cuddy, whose men were somewhat shaken by the bombardment to which they had been subjected, opened negotiations for surrender These negotiations he succeeded in prolonging until the river had become impassable Then he rejected the terms proposed. That night some of the garrison made an ineffectual attempt to escape. At dawn on Sunday the batteries reopened fire. The *Salamander* came up the river at high tide, and turned her guns upon the breach and town. By noon all was

ready for the assault   A Danish column, 1,000 strong, forded
the northern arm of the river, and, driving the Irish from their
trenches in the marshes, advanced steadily towards the breach.
    It was now 1 o'clock. In the southern suburb, Marlborough's
brother, Brigadier Charles Churchill, with 1,500 British infantry,
stood waiting for the falling of the waters. At length the word
was given   As the column moved off, many volunteers, noblemen and gentlemen all, following the good and gallant fashion
of the time, sprang forward to its head. Conspicuous among
the brilliant group was the handsome Grafton, who bore himself
that day not unworthily of the house of Villiers and the house
of Stuart   Undeterred by the close and heavy fire which opened
on them from the ramparts, the stormers plunged into the river.
The water was up to their armpits, and the tide ran strongly.
But English soldiers, led as these were led, are not easily stayed.
Certainly the garrison of Cork were not the men to stay them.
With little loss they struggled through, formed again upon the
bank, and chased the Irish from their trenches in the marsh.
The Earl of Grafton, careful of the soldiers' lives, wished to bring
artillery to bear upon the breach at this close range. He was
calmly examining the ground, when a bullet fired at 140 yards
struck him in the shoulder   He fell, mortally wounded. Cast-
ing a cloak over the body, the column dashed on and seized the
counterscarp   Here they halted, and again re-formed for the
final charge. It was never made. At 3 o'clock, McGillicuddy
hoisted the white flag and sent out to treat for terms.
    Marlborough, who had lost a day through McGillicuddy's
pretended negotiations, was in no mood to grant the garrison
the honours of war. He insisted on immediate surrender
Rather than endure the last assault, they yielded   That night,
some of the besiegers passed the breach and began to loot the
city. But on the following morning Marlborough entered in
person and speedily restored order. He found himself with
4,000 prisoners on his hands, including the Earl of Tyrone and
Lord Clancarty.
    Grafton lingered for eleven days. Before the end, he ex-
pressed himself as happy in his death, but less happy than he
would have been had he left his country in better case. His body
was carried to England, and buried at his wife's home of Euston.
He was only twenty-six. Whatever of evil he had done in his
short life lies hidden in the grave. Be it remembered only that
he died for England in the forefront of her battle-line
    Marlborough knew that he had little time to lose if he would
capture Kinsale before the advance of autumn rendered operations
impossible for English troops   Kinsale, situated at the mouth
of Bandon River and upon the left bank of it, was a poor town
in itself, but by reason of its fine, natural harbour, which formed
the principal means of communication between Ireland and
France, it enjoyed a strategic importance superior to that of

Cork. The harbour was defended by two works, the "Old Fort" and the "New." The "Old Fort" stood upon the right bank of Bandon River, and the "New" upon the left. The "Old Fort" was an obsolete work, but the "New" had been constructed as recently as 1678, and carried 100 guns.

Cork surrendered on the afternoon of Sunday, September 28. Early on Monday 300 of Marlborough's cavalry and 100 of his dragoons set off for Kinsale. The distance was less than eighteen miles, but the roads were bad and had been damaged by heavy rain. It was two hours after noon when the horsemen reached the vicinity of Kinsale, and dispatched a trumpeter to the Governor, Sir Edward Scott, who was in the "New Fort." Very favourable conditions were offered him, in the event of immediate surrender. But he was warned that, if he awaited a regular siege, he would assuredly be hanged. He retorted by dismissing the trumpeter with the menace of a similar fate. Thereupon the cavalry and dragoons galloped straight for Kinsale They were none too soon. Every preparation had been made by the garrison to burn the place, and the flames were actually kindled, when the horsemen dashed in and trampled them out. Marlborough was fortunate in this success For if the two forts were to be regularly invested, the shelter of the town would be necessary to protect his troops from the injurious effects of the advancing season. Lord Wolseley indeed finds fault with him for delaying the departure of his horse till Monday morning. And certainly, had they started Sunday afternoon, the prospect of surprising Kinsale before it could be burned would have been more assured.

The "Old Fort" was immediately summoned. But the commander defiantly refused to yield. On Wednesday, three regiments of foot marched in from Cork. Marlborough himself arrived on Thursday morning. He was surprised to find that the works were far stronger than his information had led him to anticipate. He subsequently told Burnet that, had he known the truth, he would never have undertaken the operation so late in the year. He perceived at once that the "New Fort" could not be reduced without heavy artillery His siege-train was at Cork, and in the existing state of the roads, some days must elapse before it could reach Kinsale. Meanwhile he determined to waste no time upon the "Old Fort," which, according to deserters, contained not more than 150 men. He ordered Tettau to carry it by assault

That same night Tettau embarked 800 infantry in boats and passed the river a mile above the town. They landed at a point three-quarters of a mile from the fort. At dawn they surprised the garrison. The attack was skilfully delivered. It was assisted by the explosion of a magazine. Two hundred of the Irish were taken prisoners, and more than two hundred killed. A few escaped in boats to the "New Fort." It was a brilliant exploit   Only in the hour of victory did the assailants realise that the garrison was more than three times as numerous as they had supposed.

Hoping that Scott's resolution might be shaken by this disaster, Marlborough again summoned the "New Fort." But Scott replied that it would be time enough to capitulate when another month had elapsed.   Trenches were at once opened. The English made their approaches from the north, the Danes from the east   By October 7, the besiegers were within pistol-shot of the counterscarp.   And now Sarsfield moved towards Kinsale.   His cavalry were reported at a distance of only twelve miles.   But he contented himself with ravaging the country and made no serious effort to relieve the place.   On the 11th the great guns arrived   The bombardment was now maintained both day and night.   Mining proceeded with considerable success.   By the 15th all was ready for the assault, when Scott demanded terms   Marlborough, whose army was already suffering badly from service in trenches that were knee-deep in rain-water, willingly granted the garrison permission to march out with all the honours of war, and to betake themselves with arms and baggage to Limerick   He himself wanted no more prisoners, and he knew that at Limerick they wanted no more mouths to feed.   Accordingly on the following day Scott departed with 1,200 men   Marlborough's booty was by no means contemptible   Besides the hundred pieces of cannon, he found immense supplies in the "New Fort"   But 250 of his men had been killed and wounded during the siege.   Many more had died from disease, and many were in hospital.   He was therefore well pleased that, despite all obstacles and risks, his enterprise had been crowned with complete success, and that he had kept his promise to the Queen.

Having appointed his brother, Brigadier Charles Churchill, as governor of Kinsale, and having distributed his army in winter-quarters, Marlborough took ship for England, and landed at Deal on October 28.   He was graciously received by William, who declared, " No officer living, who has seen so little service as my Lord Marlborough, is so fit for great commands "[1]   Among the nation at large he was enthusiastically acclaimed   His popularity was well deserved.   For as Lord Wolseley says, " in twenty-three days Marlborough had achieved more than all William's Dutch commanders had done both in Ireland and abroad during the whole of the previous year "[2]   And the historian of the British Army has placed it upon record that, " in the matter of skill, the quiet and unostentatious captures of Cork and Kinsale in 1690, were far the most brilliant achievements of the war; and these were the work of John, Earl of Marlborough."[3]

[1] Macaulay, vol ii., p 216.
[2] Wolseley, vol ii , p. 216.
[3] The Hon. J. W. Fortescue, *A History of the British Army*, vol.i., p. 350.

For the year 1691 William formed two resolutions. In Ireland the work, which he and Marlborough had so well begun, must be carried to a prosperous conclusion, on the continent the allies must be stimulated to greater activity, and the disaster of Fleurus, if possible, avenged. A conference of the coalised princes assembled in January at the Hague. William himself presided The total of the armed forces of the alliance for the forthcoming campaign was fixed at 220,000. The numbers of the various contingents were determined, and every arrangement made for a gigantic effort The proceedings of the congress created an impression in Europe which Louis decided to correct In March, when armies are still supposed to be in winter-quarters, Luxembourg and Vauban suddenly appeared before the important frontier fortress of Mons with 100,000 men William, by extraordinary exertions, succeeded in raising a force of less than half that number But he could accomplish nothing Mons fell. The soldiers returned to their garrisons And William himself came back to England in vexation and wrath.

The allies were placing five armies in the field In the Pyrenees, in Piedmont, upon the Rhine, in Flanders, and in Ireland, they made ready to challenge the power of France. For the command in Ireland nobody had stronger claims than Marlborough. It was therefore with bitter disappointment that his admirers, who were the great majority of the English nation, learned that the King had passed him by in favour of the Dutchman Ginkel. But if he was deprived of the opportunity which an independent command would have given him, he was able to participate in war upon the grand scale. William, in person, was to lead the army of Flanders. As in 1689, the English contingent in that army was assigned to Marlborough.

Early in May William and Marlborough arrived in Holland. William lingered for a time at his favourite residence of Loo, but he dispatched Marlborough and Solmes to Anderlecht, on the outskirts of Biussels, where a camp was forming under the supervision of Waldeck. The work of concentration proceeded none too smoothly; and Waldeck welcomed the assistance and advice of the Englishman, who had impressed him so favourably in the campaign of 1689. Many of the difficulties of the moment were created by that obvious stupidity of the Dutch government, which in later years hampered the genius of Marlborough on innumerable occasions Louis had entrusted the army of Flanders to Luxembourg, a personal enemy of Louvois, but a general who possessed and deserved the entire confidence of his countrymen Luxembourg's instructions were to cover Mons, and to protect the frontiers. The obvious interest of France was not to fight battles against superior numbers, but to gain time. For time, as Louis knew, was a powerful solvent of confederacies It was, however, expedient to remind the nations that, though William could summon congresses at the Hague, he could not shield the guilty from the vengeance of France. Accordingly Luxembourg, advancing from Courtrai to Lessines, began to threaten Brussels, while Boufflers, moving with a smaller army, planted his batteries against Liège, a city which had broken its neutrality For five days and nights this rich industrial centre endured a merciless bombardment On the approach of a relieving force, Boufflers withdrew. He was warmly congratulated by Louis on his signal chastisement of the insolent burghers. Luxembourg, in the meantime, had swooped down on Hal, which is almost at the gate of Brussels At the rumour of his coming the garrison fled by night to the camp at Anderlecht. Though urged by Louvois to level Hal to the ground, Luxembourg contented himself with destroying its fortifications He reconnoitred the camp at Anderlecht, but he found it too strong to be attacked In fact his own situation at Hal began to be none too safe William himself had arrived, and the allied army, which outnumbered Luxembourg's, was ready to move Accordingly the French fell back to Braine-le-Comte, where they menaced Brussels while they protected Mons

Though the English contingent was but a small fraction of the allied army, Marlborough and his officers did not want for good society Never since Henry VIII went to the siege of Boulogne had a King of England appeared in arms upon the continent. The English aristocracy was not minded that he should appear alone. The descendants of the men, whose banners had been borne at Poitiers and Agincourt, flocked into the field as volunteers. The courtier and the man of fashion followed William of Orange to Flanders as they had followed James, Duke of York, to his seafights with the Dutch The luxury and foppery of many of these gallants exposed them to much ridicule. Nor did the campaign afford them many opportunities of displaying a courage which even the satirists could not dispute.

William's object was the recovery of Mons But before he could invest it, he must slip past Luxembourg And Luxembourg, who, if he was less than Condé and Turenne, was only a little less, stood ever on the watch To deceive him, and if possible draw him into a position where he might be outmanœuvred, William, after moving to Louvain, turned south towards the Sambre. Marching through a country, where the extraordinary height of the rye astonished English eyes, as it astonished them more than a century later in the Waterloo campaign, he encamped at Gembloux. Luxembourg, though urged by Louvois to bombard Brussels as Boufflers had bombarded Liège, evaded a task which he regarded as both impolitic and inhuman, and moving upon parallel lines to William, came down towards the Sambre and encamped at Estinnes. And now the allies, having been joined at Gembloux by the Landgrave of Hesse, whose train of artillery, drawn entirely by white oxen, "made a very fine show upon the march,"[1] crossed the Sambre and halted at Gerpinnes, six miles south of Charleroi. Luxembourg also passed the river and came to Boussu. William appeared to be meditating an attack upon the French frontier. To frustrate an advance in the direction of Dinant, Boufflers ravaged the country upon that side, while Luxembourg, posting himself at Florennes, covered Philippeville and barred the road to the south.

Only a few miles of wooded country separated the armies But Luxembourg would not attack, and he could not be attacked with any prospect of success So close were the two encampments that twice the French were startled by the sound of firing in the north To William at Gerpinnes had come glorious tidings, which possessed a special interest for Marlborough The news of the storming of Athlone, followed in a few days by that of the victory of Aughrim, caused great rejoicing in the camp of the allies On each occasion the whole army drew out upon parade and discharged three volleys with all its musketry and cannon. Whatever were the issue of the campaign in Flanders, the Irish peril was at an end, and England's flank was cleared at last. The French government had thrown away its greatest opportunity In Lord Wolseley's words, "had Lewis employed in Ireland half the army which Luxembourg had been moving uselessly from camp to camp in Flanders, he could easily have destroyed Ginkel and re-established James in Dublin Castle"[2]

The situation of the two armies was now such that William had a fair chance of realising his true objective, the investment of Mons. On July 28 he struck his camp, and wheeling to the right through the territory of Walcourt, already so familiar to Marlborough's eyes, crossed the River Heure and encamped at Cour. Thence he sent forward 2,000 men to seize the town of Beaumont, a fortified place of the same type as Walcourt. Luxembourg in person observed the earlier stages of the march. Perceiving that an attack upon the allied columns was impossible on ground so difficult, he returned to Florennes It was evident that, unless he could gain a march on William, Mons would be invested But the country to be crossed was almost impracticable to large bodies of men and horses, and had in fact never before been traversed by an army. But Luxembourg, like Turenne, had confidence in the marching abilities of the French soldier. With the utmost diligence he led his forces to Cerfontaine, where he halted and dispatched his heavy baggage to Chimay At 10 in the evening, after a brief rest, he set on once more, without beat of drum or sound of trumpet In five columns he plunged into the woods, where often there was no path save that which was cut by his indefatigable sappers. All night the French

[1] Edward D'Auvergne, *The History of the Campaign in Flanders for the Year 1691* (1735), p 87
[2] Wolseley, vol ii., p. 239.

pushed forward. Soon after dawn they began to debouch upon the line of heights to the westward of Beaumont. By 7 o'clock they were encamped in a situation of great natural strength, which William himself had intended to occupy. When a few hours later the main body of the allies arrived at Beaumont, from their camp at Cour, they were astounded to see the French already in position and covering the way to Mons   The King exclaimed that Luxembourg's army must have wings   Assuming that the country which the French had traversed was impenetrable, he had rested at Cour instead of pushing on to Beaumont   This delay lost him the advantage.

William was furious and eager for battle   The French, very weary but very delighted at the success of the trick they had played upon the Dutchman, contemplated the preparations for attack with amused interest.   The scene was picturesque in the extreme   Down in a green and smiling valley ran a tiny river. Beyond, on its steep hill, rose the pretty town of Beaumont, its ancient ramparts now bristling with pike and musket   North and south, as far as the eye could reach, gleamed the gay and varied uniforms of the allied forces.   The son of James II and Arabella Churchill, who was a volunteer in Luxembourg's army, may have recognised the scarlet coat and the handsome face of his mother's brother.   For it was possible to distinguish both persons and regiments.   Here were infantry and engineers making ready to bridge the stream   There on the height above moved a battery which would cover the operation.   Yonder, surrounded by a brilliant staff, rode the King of England himself.   As a spectacle, it was superb.   But Luxembourg, at any rate, regarded it as nothing more.   Confident in the superiority of his position, he never troubled his tired battalions to stand to their arms   The allies, on the contrary, remained in order of battle for twenty-four hours.   William drew up minute instructions for the guidance of his officers, and distributed his artillery in advantageous posts   But nothing came of it   A few rounds from Luxembourg's batteries quickly dispersed the builders of bridges, and sent the allied cavalry scampering from the heights.   Enthusiastic volunteers cantered down into the valley and discharged their pistols and their challenges across the stream   And nobody was killed. Waldeck and the timid generals of his school protested against fighting.   And William, though he had the support of as fine a soldier as Vaudemont, yielded to the majority.   History has preserved a charming picture of Marlborough at this moment   A Prussian officer, the Comte de Dohna, has recorded in his memoirs a conversation which he had with the commander of the English contingent, when the army was drawn up in expectation of battle at Beaumont.   Marlborough, who in the course of the campaign had formed an intimacy with the Prussian, led him with pride along the English regiments, and asked him if he did not think that such troops were invincible.   De Dohna, who observes that they were " fine troops and brisk,"[1] replied with Teutonic stolidity that there were those on the other side who held similar views as to French prowess, and that therefore it was unsafe to prophesy success. The story is characteristic of Marlborough No English general ever had a better understanding of the nature and capabilities of the English soldier. Having worked and fought among the men of all nations, he had formed an opinion which was not based upon insular ignorance and pride. At a time when the British army was derided on the continent, his confidence in the military superiority of his countrymen was already boundless And his trust was well requited. For if Marlborough believed in the English soldier, the English soldier came presently to have in Marlborough a faith devout almost to fanaticism.

And here, for William, the campaign virtually ended. Foiled in his grand attempt on Mons, he blew up the fortifications of Beaumont and marched to Charleroi, and thence by Genappe to Tubize. The road lay over the field of Fleurus, where the soldiers gazed with horror on the unburied bones and skulls that still littered the scene of Waldeck's overthrow in 1690. They felt as Napoleon's armies felt in the retreat across the Borodino and the flight through Quatre Bras.

Luxembourg encamped once more at Soignies. Eating up the supplies of the country as he went, he moved by easy stages to the neighbourhood of Tournai. The allies advanced to Leuze. But William was weary of the fruitless game. Leaving the command to Waldeck, he departed with an escort of 3,000 horse for the Hague.

Louis was well pleased. His great antagonist emerged from the campaign with diminished prestige The magnificent congress at the Hague had not prevented the fall of Mons or the destruction of Hal or the bombardment of Liège. It had not prevented Luxembourg from protecting the frontiers of France while he victualled his forces in Hainault and Brabant. It had not enabled William to win a battle or to recover the fortress which he had lost. But the humiliation of the allies was not yet complete The resourceful soldier at Tournai was preparing to give them another and a sterner lesson in the art of war. He had obtained his master's permission to strike a blow with the cavalry, his favourite arm. But secrecy was of the essence of success. Pretending that all serious work was over, he went on September 18 to the theatre at Tournai, where he witnessed a performance of Molière's " Le Médecin Malgré Lui." At the conclusion " Le Bourgeois Gentilhomme " was announced for the morrow. "To-morrow," whispered Luxembourg in the ear of the Duc de Maine, " we shall have another comedy, but perhaps the dénouement will be tragic."[2] Then he galloped to the camp, and

---

[1] *Mémoires du Comte de Dohna* (1833), p 152
[2] Ségur, *Le Tapissier de Notre-Dame*, p 258

threw himself down upon a bed of straw.   At dawn came a horseman from M de Marsilly, who was watching the enemy at Leuze,
with intelligence that Waldeck was moving.   At once the trumpets sounded and sixty squadrons sprang into the saddle
Villars was the first to take the road.   Luxembourg followed,
riding fast and in joyful mood.   Before daylight on September 19,
Waldeck struck his camp at Leuze and began to retire.   The
army defiled across the Catoise, a narrow stream with marshy
banks   The rearmost proceeded in a leisurely and careless
fashion   It was assumed that the French, like the allies, were
thinking only of their winter-quarters, and that in any event they
were not within striking distance.   Consequently no precautions
were taken to ensure the safety of the rear-guard   No parties
were scouting in the direction of Tournai, and no infantry were
posted at the bridges   When the sun rose, the landscape remained
shrouded in a clinging fog.   By 10 o'clock the right wing and
the centre of the army had passed the Catoise   The rear-guard,
which was composed of the Dutch cavalry of the left wing,
began to follow   All had passed save fourteen squadrons, when
a body of 400 horse trotted out of the mist and halting on the
rising ground in the direction of Leuze, coolly regarded the scene
at a distance of only 500 paces   The Dutch paused in their
march and prepared to chastise such insolence   But the numbers
of the enemy appeared to grow.   Thereupon the squadrons
which had already crossed the Catoise wheeled about and began
to return to the assistance of their comrades.   But still the Dutch
hesitated to attack   For the 400 seemed always to increase
They were cleverly manipulated   Villars was there

And a greater than Villars was at hand   The Dutch, who
had assumed that these mysterious cavaliers formed part of a
detachment from Mons or St. Ghislain, were presently astonished
to behold the haughty standards and resplendent uniforms of the
Household Cavalry of France.   But even then they refused to
believe that any considerable number of Luxembourg's men
could be at Leuze   Still less did they imagine that Luxembourg
himself was come.   They therefore continued to return across
the Catoise.   Their right was covered by the River Ligne and
their left by the village of Blicquy, where some infantry had lined
in the hedges   But there was insufficient space for so large a
body of cavalry to deploy.   As fast as they arrived, they drew
up in a deep formation of several lines.   But before their preparations were complete, the French threw out a body of dismounted dragoons who engaged the infantry in Blicquy   And
now the Dutch, realising at last that it was they, and not the
enemy who were in peril, began to retire   But it was too late.
Led by Villars the first line of the French horse, sword in hand,
charged down at full gallop.   The Dutch troopers received them
at ten paces with a shattering volley from the saddle.   It availed
nothing.   Villars' squadrons, though a mere handful in comparison, struck like a thunderbolt upon the crowded masses and split

them to the heart   Never was the superiority of shock, the true
tactics of cavalry, more signally displayed   Close upon the
heels of Villars came Luxembourg himself with the Gendarmerie.
The French, though still outnumbered, carried all before them.
Despite the heroic leading of their officers, and notably of Overkirk, the Dutch cavalry was shivered into fragments, and
driven helter-skelter over the plain.   The French delivered no
fewer than five consecutive charges.   Luxembourg, who carried
nothing in his hand but a cane, had a narrow escape   He was
attacked by a Dutch trooper,[1] whom he dexterously slashed across
the face   The man reeled, and before he could recover, he was
cut down by the French   Towards the end of the action the
victors began to lose their heads.   Men and horses alike got
out of hand.   But in the hour of glorious intoxication, Luxembourg retained his judgment unimpaired   As he looked beyond
the Catoise, he saw long lines of scarlet-coated foot coming up
towards the bridges at the double.   Marlborough was returning
with the English infantry, those " fine troops and brisk," whose
invincibility he yearned to demonstrate   Luxembourg had no
desire to test their quality   With infinite difficulty he succeeded
in checking the pursuit, and in withdrawing his weary men and
panting steeds from the range of the English musketry.   And so,
with trumpets sounding and standards tossing in the wind, the
victorious squadrons wheeled proudly off the field   They had
lost some colours, but they had captured many more than they
had lost.   In all the bitterness of impotence Marlborough
watched them go   There was not a horseman of them all whose
sword was not dripping with the blood of the enemies of France.
    It was a fine exploit   The broken horse fled fast and far
Some of the fugitives drew rein at Ath, but the governor, when he
saw that every man had a sword-cut behind, refused to admit
them.   Ever since the battle of Fleurus the Dutch had gone in
wholesome fear of the French cavalry.   Leuze completed a
demoralisation, which afterwards bore evil fruit at Steinkirk.
The casualties were very numerous   So, too, were the casualties
of the French, especially in officers   It is impossible to ascertain
the exact numbers lost, or even the exact numbers engaged.
All the figures were deliberately misrepresented by both sides.
But there can be no doubt that the French were in a minority,
and that by superior dash and tactics they gained a brilliant
triumph   If it cost them dear, its moral effect both upon the
allied army and upon European opinion was well worth the price
But Louis was not quite satisfied   He regretted his losses, but
he regretted still more that the humiliation which he had designed
for William had descended only upon Waldeck   William, however, received his share.   It was truly said of him, that the fall of
Mons and the combat of Leuze showed that in this campaign he
took the field too late and quitted it too early

[1] Sir George Arthur says " a gentleman of the Life Guards "   See *The
Story of the Household Cavalry*, vol 1 , p 258.

APPENDIX VII

DISGRACE

WITH the possible exception of Sunderland, no single Englishman contributed so much to the success of the Revolution as Marlborough Nobody appreciated that fact more clearly than William But William was never so infatuated as to imagine that · the Churchills had done what they had done from attachment to the House of Orange. While, therefore, he possessed the most signal and convincing proofs of Marlborough's power, he had no guarantee of his personal fidelity. Such a situation was in itself unfavourable to mutual confidence. It was greatly aggravated by a variety of special circumstances

From William's standpoint the position of the Princess of Denmark seemed similar to that of Marlborough. Anne was extremely popular Her action at the Revolution had carried a distinct political value Her proximity to the throne secured her the devotion of that large majority, who still in their hearts regarded the Monarchy as hereditary and not elective Her known love of the Church of England ensured her the support of that most influential class, the country clergy Like Marlborough, therefore, she had power. Like Marlborough, also, she could hardly be supposed to have deserted her indulgent father for the love of her ungracious cousin She might even be regarded as a person aggrieved. For William had assumed the crown in violation of her better right. These considerations alone sufficed to render the Princess an object of suspicion to a monarch whose authority rested upon a very precarious basis Even her husband, the most innocuous of men, was made to suffer for the King's jealousy During the Irish campaign of 1690 he was treated by William with insulting neglect, and in the summer of 1691, when he had volunteered for service at sea and had actually prepared his equipment, he was forbidden at the last moment to join the fleet.

But neither Anne nor Marlborough was so suspect in William's eyes as the bond which existed between them. Individually they inspired him with mistrust, in combination they alarmed him He had relied upon Churchill, or rather upon Churchill's wife, to control the conduct of the Princess at the Revolution, and he had not been disappointed He had, therefore, the best of reasons for believing that the Marlboroughs could do as they would with a nature which was as pliant before " Mrs Freeman " as it was obstinate before all others. And he knew of no device for breaking this dangerous alliance. It might have been supposed that in the Queen he possessed an auxiliary who could counteract the influence of Lady Marlborough. But in reality Mary was worse than useless for any such purpose. Her very adoration of her husband was its own stumbling-block. She had little patience with anybody who refused to see that William was the best and greatest man on earth And what she regarded as unreasonable in others she considered to be positively undutiful in her own sister Anne, for her part, found it difficult to remain on affectionate terms with one who could barely conceal her dislike for dear " Mrs Freeman " Nor were " Mrs Freeman's " bitter tongue and haughty, uncompromising spirit forces on the side of peace. They rendered her particularly obnoxious to the King's mistress, Elizabeth Villiers, who collected from her sister, Lady Fitzhardinge, minute reports of all that was said and done in the Princess' Court In fact, these four women between them, with that petty vindictiveness which is characteristic of feminine strife, so aggravated the situation as to render a good understanding well-nigh impossible.

William and Mary had not been many weeks upon the throne before they came into collision with Anne and the Marlboroughs. After a preliminary skirmish over the accommodation provided for the Princess at Whitehall, battle was joined on the question of her income. William desired that it should be paid her in the form of an allowance from the Crown, while Anne preferred that it should take the shape of a Parliamentary settlement. William's method was founded upon ancient precedent. But ancient precedent, in the England of the Revolution, was not the best of securities If the public events of that period meant anything, they meant that henceforward the supremacy of Parliament was assured. An arrangement, which might have been satisfactory when the royal prerogative remained intact, and when the succession was still regarded as inviolable, assumed a different complexion, when the Monarchy began to be treated as elective, and when no limit was set to the encroachments of the House of Commons. If, in the future, Parliament was to be the source of all power, it was natural and reasonable that Anne should wish to derive her maintenance from the fountain-head Her attitude excited the King's displeasure As despotic in temper as any Stuart, he regarded it, or affected to regard it, as an affront to his dignity and an insult to his personal honour. His resentment increased when he ascertained that Lady Marlborough, during her husband's absence in Flanders, was diligently canvassing in the Princess' interest, and that the Tory party was practically unanimous for a Parliamentary settlement. Mary mentioned the matter to her sister, and enquired the meaning of it. When Anne replied that she understood that " her friends had a mind to make her some settlement," the Queen made answer, " Pray, what friends have you but the King and me ?"[1] Anne was indignant, and hastened to confide her grievance to Lady Marlborough, who doubtless fortified her in her resolution never to be dependent upon William's favour. It was speedily recognised that the Princess would never yield, except to the solicitations of her favourite Efforts were therefore made to win Sarah to the King's wishes Both Lady Fitzhardinge and the charming Earl of Shrewsbury, " the King of Hearts," essayed the task, but without success. Eventually Anne triumphed. She obtained a Parliamentary settlement of £50,000 a year Her friends having originally suggested £70,000, this decision was represented as a compromise. It was in reality nothing of the sort. The true issue was not as to the amount of her income but as to the source whence it should be derived A year later Anne begged the Countess to accept a present of £1,000 a year. Sarah hesitated, but after consultation with Godolphin, accepted. "It was his opinion," she says, "that there was no Reason in the World for me to refuse it; as he believed that the Settling of the Princess's Revenue had been chiefly owing to my Lord Marlborough's indefatigable Industry and mine."[2] Undoubtedly the Marlboroughs served the Princess well and faithfully in this affair Macaulay is of course satisfied that their conduct was dictated by the vilest avarice He does not condescend to produce his evidence The facts do not assist him They merely show that in a quarrel, in which Anne was in the right and William in the wrong, Sarah served her mistress with conspicuous success

Despite his great qualities, William was deficient in sympathy and imagination As a foreigner, not only by birth but by temperament and instinct, he stood at a painful disadvantage among a people which, more than any in Europe, abhorred foreigners Only by the most engaging tact and the most gracious charm could he ever have achieved popularity. But he displayed neither To his English courtiers he appeared frigid and even boorish; in the intimate circle of his Dutch favourites he was genial and at times hilarious Such manners disgusted the British aristocracy. "Mrs. Morley" and "Mrs. Freeman" dubbed him in their private correspondence, "Caliban" and "The Monster." Marlborough, though he naturally shared in the sentiments of his friends and of his class, was not much concerned with trivialities of this sort But he was concerned with William's preference for foreign generals. This preference was not a mere prejudice It was founded on two solid considerations, the inexperience of British officers and the insecurity of public affairs. But Marlborough knew something more of war than was to be learned at Hounslow and Blackheath. He was not only conscious of his own powers; he had demonstrated them more than once, and notably in Ireland. He justly expected that in the campaign of 1691 his services at

---

[1] *Conduct of the Duchess of Marlborough*, p 87.   [2] *Ibid*, p 91

Cork and Kinsale would be rewarded by an independent command
He was disappointed. Excessively prone as William was to over-
rate the importance of prolonged training in continental methods,
he did not underestimate the military genius of Marlborough.
On the contrary, he feared it And because he feared it, he
denied it opportunity. He suspected that the man, who had
carried an army from James to William, might one day carry
an army from William to James But such caution overreached itself When Marlborough saw that the career upon
which he had naturally and legitimately set his heart was blocked,
he began to reconsider his relations with the government which
blocked it. A motive for disloyalty was generated where none
had previously existed He made no secret of his grievance
Regardless of the hostility of Portland and the other foreign
favourites, he openly complained in society, and above all in
military society, that the British Army was systematically
slighted by a government that was British only in name. It is
even said that he did not conceal his indignation from the King.
And he spoke not merely for himself, in this matter he was the
mouthpiece of the nation at large.

Yet another cause of estrangement between Marlborough and
William grew up in the early months of the year 1691, when
Marlborough first joined that numerous company of prominent
Englishmen who were in correspondence with St. Germains.
The relations which he then reopened with the exiled family
continued under various forms to the accession of George I. It
must not, however, be supposed that he was at this, or at any
subsequent moment of his life, a Jacobite But like the majority
of men of rank, he had friends and kindred who still owned
allegiance to King James He had never ceased to communicate
with his sister's son, the Duke of Berwick, and his wife's sister,
the Duchess of Tyrconnel As a Tory, the son of an old cavalier
who had suffered for the cause, he sympathised in his heart with
the hereditary king. As an Englishman he resented the presence
of the Dutch. As a soldier, disappointed of the highest prizes
of his profession, he no longer identified his private interest with
the interest of William. But however strongly such influences
predisposed him to regret his old master, they never converted
him to the creed of the Jacobite. His real object was to ensure
himself against the contingency of a restoration There were
times in the early years of William's reign, as there were times at
the end of Anne's, when that contingency seemed perilously
near. Nobody had so much to dread from the return of James
as the deserter of Salisbury When Marlborough discovered
that others were secretly securing themselves against the possible
consequences of a second revolution, he deemed it only politic
that he, whose guilt in James' eyes was blacker than anybody's,
should follow their example His immediate purpose was to
obtain a written pardon under James' own hand. To this end

he implored forgiveness in the most abject terms But James was not satisfied with contrite language, he demanded practical proofs of repentance. Marlborough supplied them, after a fashion He revealed to the Jacobite agents in England official secrets which proved of real utility to these desperate conspirators, who carried their lives in their hands He furnished information as to the numbers and disposition of the British forces and as to the probable plan of the forthcoming campaign He induced the Princess of Denmark to address a penitent letter to the father whom she had abandoned in his hour of need. He even promised that, when opportunity arose, he would bring over a large contingent of the army to the service of their former sovereign. In Flanders, in the summer of 1691, James called on him for the fulfilment of this pledge. But without destroying the effect which he had already produced on the mind of his old master, Marlborough found means to evade an undertaking which was never intended to be kept. It was only in small things that he brought forth the fruits of repentance. But his shameful and humiliating system was rewarded with entire success. He obtained the pardon which he craved, and with it that sense of personal security, which he, in common with so many of his contemporaries in public life, most ardently desired.

William possessed an efficient secret service. He was well aware that he was surrounded by men, both Whigs and Tories, who corresponded with the exiled monarch. He knew that James was maintaining a regular intercourse with many of those most highly placed in the administration and the fighting services. But he was not perturbed. He understood the motive of this widespread anxiety for political insurance, and he took a most lenient view of it. Never a hypocrite, he realised that the methods by which he had deposed his uncle were themselves open to criticism He never expected from Englishmen that devout loyalty, which they had been accustomed to offer to their hereditary princes. It was not his wish that those who were willing to serve him as long as he was in fact king, should, in the event of a change of dynasty, be banished or beheaded. He was familiar with that appalling series of judicial murders and savage proscriptions, which, from the days of the Long Parliament, had disgraced the public life of England. There is a limit to the endurance of human nature, and that limit had been reached in English politics The time had arrived when men could no longer be induced to serve the State, if every turn of the party wheel was to bring them to the block and their wives and children to beggary. " No one," says a modern historian, " ever knew who would be on the throne in five years' time—whether Mary or William, Anne or some Hanoverian Prince, or the Pretender turned Protestant. This uncertainty made it hard for English statesmen to cease to be knaves. Ministers and ex-ministers, Tories and Whigs, admirals and generals, regardless of the fidelity they had sworn to the reigning monarch, corresponded with St Germains as well as Hanover, so that their fortunes should in all events be secure " William appreciated the true position He neither asked nor expected too much of that generation of Englishmen. So long as they diligently executed their official duties and did not engage in conspiracies for his assassination, they were at liberty, so far as he was concerned, to make what arrangements they liked for the protection of themselves and their families against the risks of revolution. This attitude was essentially broad-minded and magnanimous. It was also the only practicable one Had William removed from office all who in Church and State maintained a clandestine intercourse with their former master, the government of the country could no longer have been carried on He therefore deliberately closed his eyes to a practice which it would have been imprudent to attempt to punish There is evidence that he even turned it to his own uses, and that in certain instances letters were written to St Germains at his suggestion or with his concurrence

Posterity has been much concerned at the treachery of Marlborough to William It has been infinitely more concerned than was William himself Posterity in this matter is more royalist than the King. William was a great man, playing one of the greatest games that have been played on earth, and he saw things in their true perspective It would have been well if the historians had imported into their judgments something of the dignified restraint of him who had the biggest right to complain.

But though the knowledge that Marlborough was doing what Halifax, Shrewsbury, Godolphin, Russell, and many others were doing, could not induce William to dispense with his services, it could hardly fail to increase the tension which already existed between the two men Of the various causes of friction and suspicion which have been enumerated, no one by itself was sufficient to create a rupture But their cumulative effect was considerable William formed the opinion that Marlborough was the most dangerous man in the three kingdoms If ever it became expedient to make an example, there could be little doubt as to where the blow would fall. Portland, and Elizabeth Villiers, and even the gentle Mary might be trusted to see to it that " Mrs Freeman's " husband was the selected victim But Marlborough himself precipitated the catastrophe. Towards the end of 1691 he set on foot a project, which could not fail to render him extremely obnoxious to William. By all the devices of the astute canvasser he endeavoured to induce a majority of members of the House of Commons to address the King in the ensuing session on the subject of the foreigners William was to be asked, in the name of the people of England, to dismiss his Dutch friends from all offices of State and to send his 5,000 Dutch troops back to Holland. Such an address, if carried, would have placed him in a serious dilemma. To grant it, would have been politically dangerous and personally distasteful. To refuse it, would have been to revive that antagonism between the Commons and the Crown, which was supposed to have been abolished for ever by the " Glorious Revolution."

In Marlborough's design there was nothing essentially dishonourable or base. On this question of the foreigners he was in perfect agreement with the great majority of his countrymen. It may be that the English view was a narrow one; but it was one which the nation had a right to take, and a right to impress upon the King by all the methods known to experienced Parliamentarians. But the business had another aspect. In pursuance of his system Marlborough represented to the Jacobite agents that he was, in fact, preparing the restoration of King James. If William yielded and dismissed his faithful foreigners, invasion would be comparatively easy. If he refused, popular discontent would overthrow him. In either event Marlborough would answer for the army. James thought highly of the design, and hoped everything from its success. But it was never permitted to attain maturity. Certain of the Jacobite agents in England suspected the sincerity of Marlborough's aims. They judged, though upon what evidence has never been divulged, that he was playing for his own hand, and that if he struck the crown from William's head, he would set it on the head of Anne. Accordingly they took upon themselves to inform Portland of the plot.

Macaulay assumes that the suspicions of the Jacobites were justified, and that William believed them to be justified. Obviously it would have been to Marlborough's interest that Anne should ascend the throne. But the existence of a possible motive is not in itself a proof of guilt. Whatever William did or did not believe upon the information supplied to him by the Jacobites, it is certain that James, who was in a better position to know and sift the evidence than either William or Macaulay, considered it to be totally inadequate. His language is explicit and severe. "Some loyal subjects, who were indiscreet," he says, "*believing* that they served me, and *imagining* that what my lord Churchill did was not on my account, but on account of the Princess of Denmark, had the *imprudence* to discover the whole to Bentinck."[1]

It is quite unnecessary to assume that William believed what James refused to believe. For the rest, the Jacobite revelations were not entirely fresh. William was already aware of Marlborough's correspondence with St. Germains. He tolerated it largely because he had no belief in its sincerity. But the well-laid plan to compel him to dismiss the Dutch was another matter. He resented it deeply. He considered that it touched both his honour and his safety in a vital point. It seemed, in his

[1] J. Macpherson, Original Papers, p. 440: " A Memorial, November, 1692—After the affair of La Hogue."

eyes, to threaten the whole fabric of his European policy Of all the causes of his discontent with Marlborough this was the last and greatest

In the latter part of 1691 signs were not wanting of the gathering storm William had promised that Marlborough's services should be rewarded with the Garter A vacancy having arisen, both the Prince and Princess of Denmark wrote in August to the King and begged him to fulfil his pledge. The Prince besought this favour " for my sake, it being the only thing I have ever pressed you for "[1] But William ignored their wishes. Later in the year, when Marlborough solicited the appointment of Master-General of the Ordnance, he was refused That winter William was meditating a dash upon the port and shipping of Dunkirk But the French got wind of the secret William spoke to Marlborough on the subject "Upon my honour, Sir," said Marlborough, " I told nobody but my wife " The King remembered the Duchess of Tyrconnel "I did not tell mine," he retorted sharply.

A spark produced the explosion. One evening in January, 1692, Mary and Anne had a violent altercation in the Queen's drawing-room. Lady Marlborough was of course the principal topic in dispute Anne, who was shortly to become a mother, confronted the indignant beauty with her usual, passive courage. The sisters parted in wrath On the ensuing day, Marlborough, after discharging his functions as Gentleman of the Bedchamber, was suddenly dismissed from all his employments.

Great indeed was the scandal, and various were the rumours. Everybody put forward his own explanation of an event which had taken the country entirely by surprise. One traced it backward to the affair of Anne's Parliamentary allowance. Another ascribed it to the machinations of Portland. Some declared that Marlborough had been detected in a treacherous correspondence with St Germains, others that he was paying the penalty for the fiasco of Dunkirk The version, which found most favour with the mass of the people, attributed his disgrace to his fearless hostility to foreign soldiers and favourites In a sense, everybody was wrong, because all were right The fall of Marlborough was the result of many and various forces, each of which contributed a share not easy to estimate exactly. But in concentrating itself upon the question of the aliens, popular opinion was not greatly at fault That question outweighed all others in William's mind. Marlborough's plan of attack by Parliamentary address had seriously perturbed him Macaulay wrote with truth, " William was not prone to fear; but, if there was anything on earth that he feared, it was Marlborough."[2] That sentence explains everything. It also explains why the

---

[1] Dalrymple, vol iii , p 255, app to pt ii , bk vii . Prince George of Denmark to King William, August 2, 1691
[2] Macaulay, vol ii , p 320

Whig historian should have declared a relentless vendetta against one of the foremost makers of the Revolution.

Mary had hoped that the dismissal of Marlborough would involve as a corollary the dismissal of his Countess. She was speedily undeceived. The Marlboroughs continued to reside with the Princess of Denmark at Whitehall. At the end of three weeks, Anne, imagining that the tempest had subsided, carried Sarah to the Court at Kensington. Among the company assembled in the Queen's drawing-room the appearance of the Countess created silent consternation. If William was irritated, Mary was furious. Even Anne herself was abashed. The least disconcerted of them all was the haughty woman, whose presence at that time and place was an obvious indecency. Stung by the insult, Mary wrote, on the following day, a letter, in which she commanded Anne to dismiss the Countess. Anne refused. But knowing that she would not be permitted to reside with her favourite in any royal palace, she begged the Duchess of Somerset to lend her Sion House. William urged the Duke to veto the suggestion. But the Duke, who was reputed the proudest man in England, was not amenable to pressure. So "Mrs. Morley" and "Mrs. Freeman" retired in triumph to Brentford. Here, in April, Anne gave birth to a child, which died within a few hours. Mary visited her, and again requested her to dismiss the Countess. Anne again refused. They parted in anger, and for the last time. The responsibility for this unhappy estrangement cannot in justice be fastened upon Lady Marlborough. Bitterly as she resented the Queen's attitude, the position in which she found herself was so unenviable that more than once she begged to be permitted to retire from the Princess' service. But Anne was always overwhelmed at the very thought of separation, and passionately implored her "for God's sake," and "for Christ Jesus's sake," never to mention it again.[1]

The wrath of William and Mary pursued the Princess into her retreat. It even descended to paltry and ludicrous persecution. All who went to Brentford were made to feel that they were unwelcome at Kensington and Whitehall. When Anne visited Bath and was ceremoniously entertained by the municipal authorities, the Secretary of State, Nottingham, notified the tallow-chandler, who was Mayor of the borough, that no honours must be paid to the Princess under pain of Her Majesty's displeasure. At church the preacher was forbidden to follow the ancient custom of laying the text upon the Princess' cushion. She was even deprived of her guards, and was consequently plundered on the road by highwaymen. These petty insults served no useful purpose. They perpetuated the public scandal, and increased the King's unpopularity. The nation sympathised with Anne, who, in the words of a contemporary satire, was "neither to be regarded by day nor guarded by night."

[1] *Conduct of the Duchess of Marlborough*, pp. 100, 113.

Marlborough, likewise, was supposed by the mass of the people to have been badly used. They saw in him a successful, English soldier, ruined by the intrigues of jealous, foreign rivals A few weeks after his disgrace a wretch named Fuller, a disciple of Titus Oates, gave information of a Jacobite plot, which was speedily proved to be his own concoction Though Marlborough was not one of those whom he had named, public opinion rushed to the conclusion that all who were suspected by government were unjustly suspected, and that Marlborough had been sacrificed upon evidence no better than Fuller's.

Anne had been warned in January by an anonymous correspondent that it was intended to proceed against her favourite's husband for high treason Although at that time the writer may have been misinformed, the event did ultimately come to pass In the spring of 1692 the military situation gave rise to grave anxiety. Louis had decided to secure the command of the Channel and to land an army, under James, on English soil At Toulon and Brest the French squadrons were rapidly making ready for sea The ports of Normandy were swarming with 20,000 troops, half of them Irish The Jacobites of London and Lancashire were actively preparing to co-operate with the invaders. Admiral Russell, on whose vigilance and skill the safety of the nation depended, was in actual correspondence with James. William, who had gone to Holland in March to arrange the forthcoming campaign in Flanders, saw the necessity of vigorous measures Something more was needed than busy dockyards and well-filled camps. A blow must be struck against domestic traitors The persons of several notorious Jacobites were therefore seized. But William was not content with Jacobites. Early in May warrants were issued by the Privy Council for the arrest of Marlborough, Huntingdon, and Scarsdale, on a charge of high treason Marlborough was examined by the Council and committed to the Tower. The evidence against him was explicit One, Robert Young, had produced a written scheme for the restoration of James. This document purported to be signed by Marlborough, Cornbury, the Bishop of Rochester, and others. Treasonable letters, apparently in Marlborough's handwriting, were also forthcoming. The appearance of Cornbury's name seemed ominous. He it was who had begun the military desertions at Salisbury; and he was not unnaturally regarded as Marlborough's instrument But Young's character was bad Like Fuller before him, he belonged in fact to the school of Titus Oates Certain of the Privy Council suspected him so strongly that they refused to sign the warrant for Marlborough's arrest. Marlborough himself flatly denied the authenticity of the writings imputed to him. The Bishop of Rochester had no difficulty in proving that every one of the documents was forged Within three weeks all the prisoners were released, with the solitary exception of Marlborough.

It is doubtful whether the government at any time believed in the evidence of Young   But they used it as a pretext for a stroke of policy, which was designed to intimidate both the secret and notorious friends of the House of Stuart   During the imprisonment of the accused, the battle of La Hogue was fought. Under the very eyes of James and the impotent soldiery of France and Ireland, Louis' navy was annihilated.   The peril of invasion passed, and with it the principal justification for a policy of terror.

But Marlborough continued in the Tower.   The most dangerous man in England was not to be liberated too lightly   In these unhappy days the Countess bore herself with that haughty courage which never failed her.   She frequently visited her husband in his confinement, while in political and social circles she laboured unceasingly for his release.   She was supported throughout by the sympathy of Anne, and of all those friends who set the obligations of friendship above the smiles of royalty. There were some, however, who in the hour of adversity exhibited only their cowardice and ingratitude.   Sarah was not the woman to forget either class   At this sad time an additional misfortune befell both her and her husband in the death of their youngest boy, Charles.   Grief and anxiety were beginning to tell upon her health, when at last, after an imprisonment of six weeks, Marlborough was brought before the Court of King's Bench on a writ of Habeas Corpus and released on bail of £6,000.   Two of his sureties, Shrewsbury and Halifax, were made to suffer for their generosity.   Their names, as well as his, were struck off the roll of Privy Councillors.

But the affair by no means ended here   In October Marlborough petitioned the Court to discharge his recognisances, and was refused.   In November Parliament met.   " I hope," said Anne, in a letter written to the Countess, while her husband was still in the Tower, " I hope, when the Parliament sits, care will be taken that People may not be clapt up for nothing, or else there will be no living in Quiet for any Body, but insolent Dutch, and sneaking mercenary Englishmen "[1]   Care was taken   The House of Lords, instead of voting the usual address of thanks for the King's speech, proceeded forthwith to the discussion of certain questions of privilege arising out of the arbitrary action of the government   Marlborough, Huntingdon, and Scarsdale had been imprisoned upon testimony which law and common sense alike pronounced to be inadequate   But that was not all. The retention of bail and the refusal to discharge recognisances were alleged to be breaches of the privilege of the House   Always jealous for the dignity of their order, the peers summoned the Constable of the Tower, the solicitor for the Treasury, and even the judges, to appear before them.   All these important personages were rigorously examined   The debates were marked by

[1] *Conduct of the Duchess of Marlborough*, p 104.

extraordinary bitterness and heat. To terminate a controversy which was highly injurious to himself, William exercised the royal prerogative in favour of the aggrieved Lords The sympathy of Englishmen was with them, and particularly with Marlborough. But it was scarcely deserved. Though the action of the government had been arbitrary, it had been amply justified by the circumstances in which it was taken, and in the main it was beneficial and right In Marlborough's case, however, it was carried to an impolitic extreme. What was at the outset no more than a seasonable measure of precaution, ultimately took on the appearance of persecution, and augmented William's difficulties by increasing his unpopularity.

The debates on privilege were followed by others, no less acrimonious, on the appointment of foreigners to high commands in the British Army The nation was smarting under the losses which its splendid infantry had suffered in the battle of Steinkirk where the English believed that they had been sacrificed by the malice or stupidity of Count Solmes. The question was warmly argued in both Houses The peers, after a discussion in which Marlborough took an active part, presented an address to the King in favour of the claims of British officers William received it coldly, and ignored it.

Marlborough now withdrew into private life But he did not hesitate to incite his friends in both parties and in both Houses of Parliament to assail the King and all his works. And in common with many others, who, like himself, were no Jacobites, and who, unlike him, still occupied high positions in the public service, he continued his correspondence with St. Germains and his personal interviews with the agents of the exiled monarch. Now that he had forfeited the favour of William, it was more than ever his interest to ensure against the restoration of James For several years he pursued this system with considerable ability and success Though the selfish nature of his motive did not escape the observation of James, the sincerity of his intentions was at times accepted by the credulous exile. But generous as he was in promises, protestations, and pretended benefits, there is no evidence that he ever rendered a single substantial service to the Jacobite cause.

Of all the accusations that have been brought against him, the gravest arises out of events which occurred at this period. In the spring of 1694 the English government was planning a descent on Brest Transports were collected at Portsmouth, and 7,000 troops assembled on the Portsdown Hills When all was ready, considerable delay was caused by adverse winds Not until the beginning of June did the flotilla appear in Camaret Bay It was received with a bombardment from the batteries A close reconnaissance showed that the garrison were well prepared. Contrary to the general opinion, both naval and military, Tollemache, who commanded the land-forces, cast doubt upon the reality of the enemy's preparations, and insisted upon delivering an attack. With no little gallantry the attempt was made. But it ended in a disastrous repulse. Tollemache himself paid the penalty with his life.

Out of this melancholy affair Macaulay has constructed a terrible indictment of Marlborough. The expedition, which was intended to surprise the enemy, was itself surprised by the elaborate arrangements made for its reception. Why? Because, says Macaulay, at the last moment Marlborough betrayed the secret to James, who transmitted it to Louis, who at once instructed Vauban to do whatever was necessary to ensure the security of Brest. Vauban obeyed only too well. The English rushed into a trap And the blood of Tollemache, and of the soldiers and sailors who perished in the hopeless grapple on the beach, cries out for ever, from the pages of Macaulay, against the traitor Marlborough.

In the foundations of this indictment two elements of truth can be detected. It is a fact, an ignoble and humiliating fact, that on May 4, 1694, Marlborough learned the destination of the flotilla and communicated it to James. The original of his letter does not exist, but the authenticity of the copy need not be challenged. It is also a fact that, in anticipation of the projected attack, the garrison of Brest was strengthened with both horse and foot, and the defences were repaired and the artillery disposed under the eye of Vauban himself But it is quite impossible to show that between these two facts there existed any connection whatsoever. Indeed, it is easily demonstrable that there was none

The date of Marlborough's communication is May 4. Now if it can be proved that, when Marlborough's news arrived at Versailles, it was no news to Louis, that he had already been in possession of the truth for more than a month, and that he had already taken measures to frustrate the design of the English government. Macaulay's accusation is seen at once to be ridiculous. At Paris there exists a letter, in which the French King informs Vauban that the English are meditating a descent on Brest with 7,000 men and instructs him to take the necessary steps to give them a suitable reception. This letter bears date, April 4, thirty days before that of Marlborough's note, and five weeks before the contents of Marlborough's note could have been known at Versailles. Macaulay says that, on the receipt of the traitor's tale, the French government acted with " characteristic promptitude "[1] They did indeed. Small wonder is it that France was dreaded in Europe. A government, which knew how to act upon information five weeks before receiving it, would be a formidable foe even in the age of wireless telegraphy

By these two dates alone, April 4 and May 4, Macaulay's charge is completely refuted. Even if there were no corroborative evidence, the calumny is slain at one stroke. But there is corro-

[1] Macaulay, vol ii, p. 488.

borative evidence   Some, at any rate, of the sources, from which Louis learned the secret, are well known   In the first place, the preparations at Portsmouth spoke for themselves   It was obvious to all who had eyes to see that a maritime fortress of the first importance had been selected for attack.   The expedition was the talk of London for weeks, and despite all efforts at concealment, its real destination was guessed by many.   What London could divine, was not hidden from Paris   To the menace of the preparations at Portsmouth, the French government had replied by dispatching Vauban on a tour of inspection of the northern and western harbours, including Brest   Vauban was actually engaged in this task, when he received the King's letter of April 4, directing him to proceed at once to the place, which had by then been ascertained to be the threatened point   Secondly, it is known that Godolphin, the First Lord of the Treasury, who was Marlborough's friend and the probable source of Marlborough's information, himself communicated the secret of the project against Brest to an agent of James in England, not later than the third week of April   And thirdly, James has left it upon record that he was warned in good time of the true destination of the flotilla at Portsmouth by Sunderland's son-in-law, Lord Arran.   These are circumstances which by themselves virtually disprove Macaulay's story   Yet he wilfully ignored them, or deliberately suppressed them.   Had he known of the existence of Louis' letter to Vauban, what course would he have taken ?

Indeed, Macaulay's malice against the man, who had the audacity to make William tremble, knew no limits of decency or common sense.   Not content with charging the blood of Tollemache and the rest to Marlborough's account, he went out of his way to invent an ulterior motive, which could never have existed save in the heart of one, who was not only the basest but also the silliest of mankind.   Tollemache was at that time the only soldier of British race whose reputation could be mentioned in comparison with Marlborough's   Macaulay has, therefore, suggested that Marlborough arranged the catastrophe of Brest with the express purpose of removing a competitor from his path   But only a seer or an idiot would pretend to know that an action, whether successful or unsuccessful, would involve the death of the commander.   Possibly the risk of death might be greater in defeat than in victory   But if Marlborough wished to expose the life of Tollemache in battle, he adopted the worst method imaginable of achieving his end   To warn the French, was quite the most likely way of averting an encounter altogether. An officer of Tollemache's experience and skill would not be easily tempted to rush into a death-trap   That he was so tempted, does not affect the argument   Military men, from William downwards, were astonished when they learned the imprudence of his conduct   Their surprise must have been fully shared by Marlborough, who had served with Tollemache in

Flanders, and was well aware of his capacity for war. These considerations sufficiently reveal the ineptitude of a suggestion which is wholly gratuitous In dealing with Marlborough Macaulay is always malicious, and almost always dishonest, but in this instance he is also stupid.

Whoever, then, was responsible for the failure of the expedition against Brest, the guilt rests not on Marlborough He pretended, of course, that he was communicating to James an invaluable secret. But he very well knew that his intelligence was already stale, though precisely how stale, he was perhaps ignorant. He acted in strict accordance with the system which, in common with so many Englishmen, both Whig and Tory, he had long been pursuing. This system consisted merely in deluding James into a belief in their penitence and loyalty by a parade of services, which had no substance, and of promises, which never attained fulfilment It was a pusillanimous and unclean policy. But its moral turpitude need not be appraised more harshly than William himself appraised it These men were not genuine traitors, but for the greater security of their lives, their families, and their property, they played at being traitors The game was a dirty one, and never more dirty than when it was played in the uniform of the British Army Although the failure to surprise Brest is not attributable to Marlborough, it is a bitter and humiliating memory that one of the greatest of English soldiers should ever have condescended to pretend to such dishonour

The traffic with St Germains was not only discreditable, it was extremely dangerous From William himself these sham Jacobites had nothing to fear William knew the truth, and they knew that he knew it They knew also that he had adopted the course, at once magnanimous and politic, of ignoring their system of insurance against revolution But if, by some unlucky chance, the facts were to become public property, Parliament and the nation might take a less complacent view. At length, in 1696, the risk which they ran was forcibly brought home to them. In the summer of that year Sir John Fenwick, a Jacobite agent, deeply involved in conspiracies against the throne and life of William, was arrested and imprisoned To save his neck, he offered, if a pardon were assured him, to turn King's evidence. But William would promise nothing Fenwick's revelations must first be made, that the government might judge of their value before it paid the price. Fenwick agreed, and presently evolved a document setting forth with a fair degree of accuracy the story of James' dealings with certain persons, who were generally supposed to be loyal subjects of King William. The persons designated were Shrewsbury, Godolphin, Marlborough, Bath, and Russell William was annoyed Fenwick had told him nothing that he wished to know, and very little that he did not know already. The net had been spread for real Jacobites;

but these were only the masqueraders. Fenwick was left to his fate   His wife's devotion procured him a delay   By law two witnesses were necessary to his conviction, and she had contrived the disappearance of one   But in November Parliament met   Russell boldly raised the question of the confession   The Commons voted it a scandalous paper, and decided to proceed against the prisoner by Bill of Attainder   When the Bill came before the House, Fenwick was introduced and examined   Colonel Godfrey, the husband of Arabella Churchill, challenged him to give particulars of his intercourse with Marlborough, and of Marlborough's services to James.   But Fenwick was not to be drawn   The Bill, in spite of strenuous opposition, passed the Commons   In the Lords, where it was also resisted, Marlborough spoke in his own defence   He emphatically denied that he had ever seen or conversed with Fenwick since before the Revolution   This was true enough.   Fenwick had no first-hand knowledge of the intrigues of any of the persons whom he had named   He had merely repeated what was common talk among the real Jacobites   Bath and Godolphin also spoke.   Here, as in the Commons, nothing could be extracted from Fenwick himself.   The Bill passed the Lords, and received the royal assent.   Fenwick died, as he well deserved to die   His guilt was not in doubt   But the method of his conviction procured him a measure of sympathy.   Trial by Parliamentary majority was a crude and vicious parody of justice.   It should never have been employed by those who talked as largely about the liberties of Englishmen as did the politicians of the Revolution.

But Marlborough, and all who were equally guilty with Marlborough, were thoroughly alarmed.   They had adequate cause   While the Bill of Attainder was still before the Lords, it was discovered that the Earl of Monmouth (afterwards the renowned Peterborough) had been secretly instigating the prisoner to adopt a course which was calculated to produce the gravest consequences   Monmouth experienced a sort of vicious pleasure in giving a fall to anybody who had power or reputation to lose   He had at first suspected that his own name might figure in the confession   Reassured on this point, he found means to instruct Fenwick how best to establish the guilt of the persons accused   The advice which he gave was distinguished by its ingenuity no less than by its malice.   In Marlborough's case he suggested that the King be prayed to lay before Parliament the reasons which had induced him to dismiss the Earl from his employments   Failing to perceive how he could benefit himself by pandering to the peculiar spite of Monmouth, Fenwick disregarded his advice.   Monmouth, in a rage, both spoke and voted for the Bill of Attainder.   Fenwick's wife retaliated by revealing the intrigue   The Lords indignantly took up the matter and committed Monmouth to the Tower   The King removed him from the Privy Council and deprived him of his offices   But he had the satisfaction of knowing that he had frightened better men than himself. Godolphin, whose nerves were badly shaken, had resigned before Parliament met. He, and Marlborough, and the others whom Fenwick had denounced, abruptly terminated their correspondence with St. Germains. They never renewed it during William's life. Though they continued to communicate verbally with Jacobite agents, they refused henceforward to commit themselves in writing. And they were not the only prominent Englishmen who learned a lesson in caution from the case of Sir John Fenwick.

The system adopted by the fictitious Jacobites has been considered in relation to the person of King William. But it has also another aspect. In so far as it assisted and encouraged France, it touched the safety of the nation. It raises the question of patriotism as well as of private honour. Certainly the standard of public conduct, which prevailed among the governing classes at that period, was low. Marlborough failed to rise above it. He did as others did. But eminent historians would have been more usefully employed in examining and explaining a social phenomenon of exceptional interest than in heaping disproportionate abuse upon an individual manifestation of it.

How came it that gentlemen and officers were willing even to pretend to betray the interests of their country to a foreign and a hostile power? Undoubtedly they were influenced here, as they were influenced in regard to their private duty to William, by an overwhelming desire for personal security in any event. They were false to England, not because it helped Louis, but because it gratified James. But this explanation alone is hardly a sufficient one. There is another, which is often overlooked. In that generation patriotism itself was weak. Forces had long been at work, which had dulled and blunted it. Marlborough had not escaped them.

The Reformation, and the long and devastating wars which followed it, checked the growth of that national spirit, which throughout Europe had begun to flourish as feudalism decayed. Divisions of race were crossed and obliterated by divisions of creed. During the sixteenth and seventeenth centuries the Papists of all nations fought side by side against the Protestants of all nations. An English Calvinist, who regarded an Irish Kelt as a barbarous idolater, regarded a French Huguenot as a Christian and a brother. Theological animosity produced the same effect in Europe as political faction in the old Greek states, where aristocrats were leagued with foreign aristocrats, and democrats with foreign democrats. The English Revolution was one of the last and one of the most remarkable illustrations of this truth. The English had always been notorious for their hatred of foreigners. Yet they expelled an English-born monarch because he was a propagator of popery; and because he posed as a champion of Protestantism, they gave the crown to a Dutchman, who brought with him such an assortment of Dutchmen, Danes, Swedes, Swiss, Brandenburghers and blackamoors, as had never before been seen in these islands even in a raree-show This tendency towards religious ' solidarity ' had existed in Europe for a hundred and fifty years It showed how deep and how sincere were the convictions which inspired the combatants. But, of necessity, it loosened the obligations of patriotism and lowered the ideal of nationality Marlborough himself was subject to it. For he was pre-eminently the man of the Revolution.

A second cause lay deep in the foreign policy of Louis XIV. That he might execute his designs upon the continent without fear of English intervention, Louis conceived the idea of securing the neutrality of England by alternately bribing Charles II and the leaders of the Parliamentary opposition. These investments were attended with a remarkable measure of success But the effect upon the tone of public life was disastrous When the hereditary monarch and the elected representatives of a country are willing, for a price, that a foreign government shall dictate that country's foreign policy, the generation which grows up in so corrupted an atmosphere is little likely to have imbibed a clean and exalted spirit of patriotism It is often said that Charles II sold England to France, and it is as often forgotten that certain immaculate gentlemen of the House of Commons were not backward in the same commerce. Ignorant as is modern England of her own history, the name of Algernon Sidney is still familiar. It is a name which carries always a vague suggestion of high and honourable associations. Yet who remembers, how many indeed have ever heard, that it figured in the pension-list of Louis XIV ? On the contrary, it is still almost a synonym for civic virtue of the loftiest and sternest type. " When," says Dalrymple, " I found in the French dispatches Lord Russell intriguing with the court of Versailles, and Algernon Sidney taking money from it, I felt very near the same shock as if I had seen a son turn his back in the day of battle "[1] Marlborough, whom public opinion from his own time onwards has always regarded as a monument of avarice, was never, like Sidney, the hireling of France. Yet the same public opinion, passing lightly over Sidney's baseness, pauses to select Marlborough from a great multitude of offenders and to pillory him for all time. Why ? Sidney may have done much for the philosophy of republicanism, but for England he did nothing in particular. Marlborough saved Europe, and raised England to such a pinnacle of glory as she had never before attained. No Thackerays and Macaulays have found their account in abusing Sidney It is the way of England's moralists to punish most the men who have served her best Also, it was necessary to Whiggery to blast the reputation of the one man who made William

[1] Dalrymple, Preface, vol 1

of Orange tremble.   But though Marlborough was never himself
a pensioner of France, he knew intimately the inner history of
the reign of Charles II   Probably he knew all that Dalrymple
only discovered a century later.   As a young man he moved in
the centre of that vitiated world where France was bidding
alternately for the support of an English King and an English
House of Commons.   Assuredly it was not a school of patriotism
undefiled.

A third, and a more subtle, cause of degeneracy sprang also
from French soil.   It is easy to understand that men were
debauched by Louis' gold, and that their demoralising example
corrupted the principles of others   But somewhat more difficult
to trace is the malign influence of French sentiment upon the
patriotic instincts of certain classes of the English people

France, in the latter half of the seventeenth century, was beyond
dispute the foremost power in Europe   For that reason alone
the peoples and princes of the lesser states were continually
tempted to imitate things French   England, despite her intense
and notorious insularity, formed no exception to the rule   In
England, moreover, this general tendency was assisted by a
special circumstance   Both Charles and James, themselves the
offspring of a French mother, had passed a considerable portion
of their time of exile on French soil   Many noblemen and gentlemen had followed their example.   At the Restoration these
wanderers brought home with them a variety of French fashions
and French modes of thought.   Many historians have traced
the consequences upon the England of the later Stuarts   Because
Louis was an absolute ruler, Charles and James must be absolute
rulers also.   Because Louis maintained a professional army,
they must maintain one.   Because Louis had mistresses and
bastards, they must have them   Because in France women
played female parts upon the stage, Desdemona must no longer
be represented by a giant.   Because Corneille and Racine wrote
tragedies in rimed couplets, Dryden must do the same   All
these instances are well known   But there is another which
seems to have escaped attention. This France, a nation united
under a strong and centralised government, was a new portent
in European politics   She was the creation of three men,
Henry IV, Richelieu, and Mazarin, whose work was not completed until 1660.   The first sixty years of the century had been
one long struggle between the French monarchy and the slowly
declining forces of French feudalism.   This struggle had culminated in the wars of the Fronde, which were coeval with the
exile of the English cavaliers.   The political examples, offered
by the Fronde to the aristocracy of England, were of the very
worst description.   In that episode, as in all the similar episodes
which preceded it, and indeed, in the so-called wars of religion
which preceded them, French feudalism exhibited the most
brutal indifference to the sentiments of loyalty and nationality.

The nobles of France, in their contest with the King of France, never hesitated to ally themselves with foreign powers. Those world-famous commanders, Condé and Turenne, fought side by side with Spanish troops against their own countrymen When, subsequently, they returned to their allegiance, little, if any, odium attached to their treason They had but acted as many others of their class had acted, and as their fathers and grand-fathers before them It is not unnatural to conclude that these examples exercised a pernicious influence upon the minds of Englishmen, at any rate of those Englishmen who had passed much time in France. England, where the worst features of feudalism had never been developed, had long been superior to her neighbour in point of patriotism. But in the reign of Charles II a curious deadness to this sentiment began for the first time to manifest itself. It is not unreasonable to ascribe some part, at any rate, of the degradation of the English standard to the contaminating effect of French opinion One of the many Englishmen of good family, who were directly exposed to this infection at an early age, was Marlborough himself Some of the most impressionable years of his life were spent among gallant comrades of the French nobility by the camp-fires of Alsace and on the battlefields of the Rhine From Turenne and Condé he learned the art of war. From the countrymen of Turenne and Condé he may well have learned to extenuate the crime of those, who are guilty, in the admirable English phrase, of " comforting the King's enemies "

APPENDIX VIII

FAVOUR

In the last days of December, 1694, Queen Mary was attacked by the smallpox in its most malignant form. William, guilty as he was of years of neglect and unashamed adultery, nursed her with the desperate devotion of a lover. But not all the energy of his remorse could avail to save her. She died in the plenitude of her strength and of her majestic beauty. She had deserved more happiness. Endowed with all the courage and spirit of her race, she was ever distinguished by the truly feminine virtues of patience, gentleness, and piety. But throughout her married life she was sick with love of the man who, from her honeymoon to her grave, dishonoured and betrayed her. Brought up in a Court where impurity was the mode, and formed by nature not only to love, but to excite love in others, she never so much as dreamed of taking vulgar vengeance on her unworthy husband. Interest apart from his interest she had none. For him she did violence to her feelings as a child. For him she endured the insults of the Jacobites and the more intolerable cynicism of those who were not Jacobites. For him she bore with resignation his very infidelity.

And now she was dead; and William realised too late that he had perversely thrown away something the like of which could never again be his.

The political consequences of Mary's death were important. William's own position was seriously shaken by it. Many, who had cheerfully acquiesced in the joint sovereignty of husband and wife, offered but a grudging allegiance to the survivor. Some politicians, indeed, demanded whether in point of law allegiance could be still required, or whether the Revolution settlement was not, in fact, at an end. Moreover, in the gracious charm of the dead princess her countrymen of all classes had found a compensation for the morose and taciturn manners of an alien monarch. Now the King was alone with his unpopularity and his dubious title. One remedy was obvious. The breach with the presumptive heir should be healed without delay. A reconciliation with Anne, who was well liked by the nation at large, and who wielded no little influence in Tory and High Church quarters, would go far to silence criticism and to restore to the government those elements of strength which it had hitherto owed to the personality of Mary. If blood alone were considered (and the people had not yet abandoned their belief in hereditary

494

right), Anne, like Mary, had a better claim to the crown than her cousin. The King perceived that her support was necessary to the stability of his throne   Certain obstacles which had hitherto stood in the way of a settlement had now been removed.   Mary herself was no more   In the widower's existing mood of penitence Elizabeth Villiers counted for nothing   Even the powerful influence of " Mrs. Freeman " was labouring for peace   Though Anne had not seen her sister on her death-bed, messages had passed   By the management of Sunderland, she was now induced to write to the King in sympathetic and duteous terms; and by the same dexterous management, coupled with the arguments of Somers, the King was persuaded to grant her an interview.   Thereafter amicable relations were resumed   The Princess' guards were restored to her, and St   James' Palace was assigned to her as a residence, and everybody flocked once more to her drawing-room   Marlborough and his wife had done their best to promote this happy result   It was certainly not their interest to perpetuate the feud   William's expectation of life was bad.   In all probability in a very few years Anne would be summoned to assume the crown   When that day came Marlborough would assuredly be the greatest man in England.   He could therefore afford to wait.   But he did not desire to wait   He was now forty-four, and conscious of abilities which had never yet received their opportunity.   When Tollemache fell he had offered his services to the King, who had refused them   Now that Mary was dead and the King and the Princess were reconciled, his hopes of employment revived.   But for a time they were disappointed.   To all representations made on his behalf, William, who fully recognised his talents, had one reply, " I do not think it for the good of my service to entrust him with the command of my troops."[1]   So profound was the King's distrust of the man to whom he owed so much

In Shrewsbury and Sunderland, Marlborough possessed two friends, who neglected no opportunity of pleading his cause   But William was not easily moved.   In politics he attached no value to professions, unless they were grounded upon palpable self-interest.   Two years after Mary's death Fenwick's case so frightened all the pretended Jacobites that he judged it safe to begin to modify his attitude to Marlborough   As the months went on the decay of his own health became so terribly apparent, that he knew it to be no longer worth Marlborough's while to gamble in a revolution when the desired certainty was seen by all to be at hand   According to William's philosophy the time had now arrived when Marlborough might be trusted.   Early in 1698 they were " frequently " together.   In June of the same year the Earl's restoration to favour was publicly recognised   William had decided that the Duke of Gloucester, who had now attained

[1] Charles Talbot, Duke of Shrewsbury, *Private and Original Correspondence.* p 53 . The King to the Duke of Shrewsbury July 15, 1694

the age of nine, should have a household of his own   The question
of appointing a governor to the young prince gave rise to some
heart-burnings.   Anne herself was anxious that the post should be
conferred on Marlborough   The extreme Tories urged the claims
of Rochester.   William selected Shrewsbury   But Shrewsbury
declined the honour on the ground of infirm health, and took
the opportunity of recommending Marlborough in his stead.
The King hesitated.   Portland sought to prejudice the Earl's
chances, but Portland's opposition was more than neutralised by
the support of Keppel, the rising favourite.   The advice of
Sunderland turned the scale.   Marlborough was made governor
with a salary of £2,000 a year.   Anne was delighted.   And
doubtless, if Gloucester himself had been consulted nothing more
agreeable to his own inclinations could ever have been devised
To an English prince, whose nursery was a childish arsenal,
whose dearest toys were puppet soldiers, and whose only games
were the mimicry of war, the greatest of English generals would
appear the most delightful of governors.   " My Lord, teach him
to be like yourself," said William, when Marlborough kissed
hands on his appointment.   The Dutchman could be gracious
when he tried   Marlborough's critics find such language ironical
But in all the circumstances irony was out of place.   And the
sequel shows that the critics are wrong.

Having chosen a Tory for the Prince's governor, William
selected Burnet, the most Whiggish of bishops, for his preceptor.
Anne was too good a Churchwoman to be gratified; but she was
also too discreet to exhibit her displeasure   The bishop alleges
that he shrank from the honour.   Lady Marlborough, whose
political and religious sympathies did not coincide with those of
her mistress, probably smoothed his path   Marlborough himself,
though he had little enough in common with the pompous pro-
phet of Whiggery, respected his learning and his parts, and liked
him as a man   Burnet was easily taken by the charming tact
of one whose diplomatic gifts were destined to be the admiration
of all the Courts of Europe.   Governor and preceptor worked together in complete harmony   And when in the ensuing year,
the more vindictive Tories in the House of Commons endeavoured
to effect the removal of the bishop from his new office, Marlborough exerted himself to the utmost to defeat their plans.
He even induced his brother George, the biggest Tory of them all,
to absent himself from the House when the division was taken
The attack on Burnet failed   Had it succeeded, it would probably have been followed by an attempt to supplant Marlborough
himself in the interest of Rochester.

When Marlborough became governor to the Duke of Gloucester,
his name was once more added to the roll of Privy Councillors.
He was also restored to his rank and position in the army.   In the
following month he was placed among the nine " Lords Justices,"
who administered the regal functions during William's absence in

Holland   Nor were the outward marks of favour the only ones which he received   More gratifying still, and more significant was the fact that William consulted him in all affairs of State. William pursued the policy of trusting " all in all or not at all." And Marlborough was in many respects a man after his own heart.   In the England of 1698, an English peer, who, to real talents for war and for diplomacy, united a genuine contempt for faction and the strife of parties, was a counsellor not to be despised.   Before the year was out the King gave him a most signal and pathetic proof of personal confidence   At last the ignorant folly of the House of Commons, which after the peace of Ryswick was clamouring, as it has always clamoured on the slightest pretext, for the reduction of the armed forces of the Crown almost to vanishing-point, had driven William to a desperate resolve.   He would abdicate.   He would abandon to their doom a people which was too stupid or too complacent to make ordinary provision against its own extermination.   In December he communicated his intention to the Cabinet   He also communicated it to Marlborough, who was not even a member of the government.   He was subsequently persuaded to relinquish his plan.   But if Marlborough was not entirely his by this time, so flattering a mark of consideration must have won him finally.

Marlborough's position was now, to all appearances, assured In 1699 it was rendered even more secure by the retirement from Court of his inveterate enemy, Portland.   But though the King had need of him, and was no longer afraid to make use of him, the political circumstances of the time were such that Marlborough was more than once required to exert the utmost of his tact and judgment to preserve what he had won.   Much as he detested the strife of faction and would have wished to stand outside it, as a peer of the realm he could not divest himself of the obligations attaching to his rank.   A vote in the House of Lords, at a time when the numbers of that assembly did not exceed 200, meant more to the government, for or against whom it was given, than it means to-day.   And the vote of one, who stood so high in the favour of the presumptive heir to the throne, necessarily carried more than ordinary weight   It was natural, therefore, that Marlborough's Parliamentary conduct should be scrutinised by William with a jealous eye.   And it would have been indeed remarkable if Marlborough had invariably succeeded in reconciling his duty with his interest   On two occasions at least he is known to have given some offence to William.   By the support which he gave to the Prince of Denmark, in the matter of the repayment of a mortgage on some lands which the Prince had resigned, at William's request, to the Duke of Holstein, and again by his unconcealed sympathy with the Resumption Bill, whereby the Irish estates, which William had distributed among foreign favourites, were sold to pay the nation's debts, he incurred the displeasure of the King.   But these clouds were only temporary.

If Marlborough did what he considered right, he did it without unnecessary violence. William, moreover, was far too magnanimous to punish a man for standing by his friends and his principles in the teeth of his own advantage Indeed, when the first irritation was passed, he probably thought the better of him for it. At any rate, he selected him again in 1699, and yet again in 1700, to be one of the "Lords Justices." He also appointed George Churchill to a post on the Board of Admiralty.

In these last years of William's reign, when Marlborough knew that the curtain was soon to rise upon a scene in which he alone would play the dominating part, he neglected no opportunities of strengthening his position in the political world. As his daughters grew towards a marriageable age, he had naturally begun to consider in what quarters he should look for advantageous alliances It was unlikely that there would be any dearth of candidates The girls themselves had inherited beauty and graces of no common order. Marlborough could easily have selected husbands whose friendship was worth acquiring. But he loved his children too well to attempt to force their inclinations in a matter vital to their future happiness Neither he nor his wife had forgotten the circumstances of their own marriage. He was therefore overjoyed when he discovered that a genuine affection had grown up between his eldest daughter, Henrietta, and Godolphin's only son, Francis Godolphin was not merely his personal friend and the platonic admirer of the Countess; he was also a trusted courtier of the Princess of Denmark, and a certain participator in the favours of the coming reign. A cautious and sober politician, he possessed, moreover, no little influence among the more moderate of the Tory party. Neither he nor his son was rich. But just as Marlborough, who is popularly supposed to have been a monster of avarice, had himself married a penniless girl, in defiance of his parents' wishes, so now he regarded the comparative poverty of Francis Godolphin as no obstacle to an alliance which was in all other respects desirable The Princess was delighted at the union of two families devoted to her service She offered to present the bride with £10,000; but Lady Marlborough would not accept more than half the sum. Marlborough himself gave the same amount. In the spring of 1698 Francis and Henrietta were married.

The second daughter, Anne, was her father's favourite child Her intellectual powers and the sweetness of her disposition, even more than her physical beauty, won all hearts. In the year 1699, Charles, Lord Spencer, the eldest son of Lord Sunderland, came under the influence of her exceptional charm. This young man had early acquired a reputation for superior virtue and learning His mother, who was also Anne's godmother, ardently desired to arrange the match for her son, who, at the age of twenty-five, was already a widower, with a melancholy temperament and a harsh, unpleasing manner. Sunderland stood high in William's favour. He and Marlborough were friends. Each had rendered the other good service on more than one occasion. Lady Sunderland had a romantic affection for Lady Marlborough, so intense that it even excited the jealousy of " Mrs. Morley." Yet in spite of these obvious advantages, in spite also of the fact that Spencer would be a far wealthier bridegroom than was Francis Godolphin, Marlborough hesitated He did not like the man. Still less did he like his political principles, which were violently Whig, even to the verge of republicanism He " would often," says Swift, " among his familiar friends, refuse the title of Lord, swear he would never be called otherwise than Charles Spencer, and hoped to see the day when there should not be a peer in England." But Lady Sunderland was not to be baulked With the assistance of Godolphin she at length obtained the approval of the Countess, who, while she would have preferred a more amiable son-in-law, felt no repugnance to Spencer's political predilections

Marlborough gradually yielded to his wife's persuasion Doubtless he considered that a powerful friend in the Whig camp was not to be despised. But what he disliked in Spencer was not so much his Whiggery as the extreme violence of it. Sunderland, however, promised that his son would " be governed in everything public and private by Lord Marlborough." Sarah probably advanced the feminine argument that this ungentle creature would be speedily tamed by the winning devices of the irresistible Anne. It was certain that the two were sincere lovers. Being fully satisfied on that important point, Marlborough at length consented. The marriage was celebrated soon after Christmas, the bride receiving the same dowry as her sister and the same present from the Princess of Denmark

In July, 1700, the Marlboroughs were staying with the Sunderlands at Althorpe, when the news arrived that the Duke of Gloucester was seriously ill at Windsor. Always a delicate child, and the last survivor of seventeen, he had reached the age of eleven, thanks only to the most assiduous care and to the healthy breezes and dry soil of Campden House, where he had spent the greater part of his short life. And now the fate of the Denmark family was upon him. The festivity of his eleventh birthday had been followed by a malignant fever Marlborough reached Windsor in time only to see him die. Four days later he brought the corpse by torchlight to London, where it was buried in Henry VII's chapel at Westminster. The Jacobites exulted; but the nation as a whole was plunged in gloom As the law then stood the life of the Princess Anne was now the solitary barrier between James II and the succession. " I do not think," wrote William to Marlborough, " that I need use many words to tell you with what surprise and grief I have learned of the death of the Duke of Gloucester. It is so great a loss for me and for all England, that my heart is pierced with sorrow. I assure you that on this occasion and on all others I shall be very pleased to give you proofs of my friendship "

Death had deprived Marlborough of his honourable employment, but death was about to give him a generous compensation Five months elapsed; and the King of Spain was no more. He bequeathed his dominions by testament to Philip, Duke of Anjou, grandson of Louis XIV Louis accepted the will, and dispatched Philip to Madrid with this observation, " Henceforth there are no more Pyrenees."

To Louis it seemed that at last that old dream of Henry of Navarre, a French hegemony in Europe, was about to be realised. Combination of his own power with the power of Spain seemed irresistible. The one man that might venture to resist it was rapidly sinking into the grave. With a little diplomacy and possibly a little war, the ambition of his life would be secured. But he reckoned without the son of Elizabeth Drake

APPENDIX IX

CHAPTER XXVII —1710–1711

(The author never finished the story, but he had made notes for the last chapter, which are here printed, because, however briefly, they bring the tale of Marlborough's campaigns to an end.)

FROM 1707, Robert Harley, the proposer of disbandment in William's time, had been working to undermine the government England was at the mercy of three women Only Sarah had ability, but it was discounted by her meddling and arrogance " So long as she retained her ascendancy over Anne, things went unpleasantly for the Queen, but on the whole well for the country; when her ungovernable temper drove Anne into the arms of Mrs. Masham, the Queen led a quieter life, but the country suffered " Marlborough, who knew Sarah's influence to be waning, tried to secure permanence by asking, on his return after the 1709 campaign, to be made commander-in-chief for life. The request was tactless and unprecedented. Anne refused point blank. Marlborough for once showed ill temper Anne was right, but she was wrong when she gave a colonelcy to Colonel Hill, Mrs Masham's brother, not on the recommendation of the commander-in-chief. but on Mrs Masham's Marlborough resolved to resign. Somers remonstrated with Anne Marlborough should have insisted that either he or Mrs. Masham must go. But he accepted a compromise, which Anne regarded as a victory.

To get Marlborough out of England, Harley had him sent to Flanders to negotiate as to peace This came to naught In April, 1710, he rapidly passed the Lines of La Bassée, and besieged Douai It fell on June 26 Marlborough proposed to besiege Arras or to pass the Somme. Villars, who had failed to relieve Douai, was behind a new series of lines, his *ne plus ultra* Marlborough took Béthune, Aire, and St. Venant, all strong places, well defended They cost him 15,000 men. This closed a campaign less brilliant than some. But it completed communications with Lille, opened the whole line of the Lys, and made easy a joint action with a sea expedition from Calais or Abbeville Another Ramillies would have brought the allies near to Paris But Marlborough was extremely cautious now, and sacrificed his grander plans for fear of his enemies at home.

Anne promoted all the colonels of the year to be generals, so as to include Hill, regardless of expense, propriety, justice, or discipline In August, Godolphin was dismissed, and Harley appointed Lord Keeper in his stead. This was the fall of the government Marlborough's Secretary-at-War, Adam Cardonnel, was replaced by Granville. On Marlborough's return, the Duchess was dismissed, despite Marlborough's entreaties. And Marlborough was ordered to forbid the moving of any vote of thanks to himself in Parliament

Some of Marlborough's own officers, notably Argyll, turned against him Swift and St. John vied with each other in blackening Marlborough's character. They accused him of prolonging the war, and loving bloodshed for its own sake They even denied him courage and talent. He would have resigned, but for Eugène and Godolphin, who begged him to keep the Alliance together. But Harley was secretly negotiating with Louis.

1711.—The French, aware of the state of English politics, spent the winter in preparing a gigantic barrier on the northern frontier, solely to prolong the campaign. The lines ran from the coast of Picardy, along the Canche, thence to the Gy or Upper Scarpe (from Oppy to Montenescourt) Then the Gy and Scarpe were dammed to form inundations to Biache. Hence a canal covered the lines to the Sensée. Hence there were more inundations to Bouchain Then came the Schelde to Valenciennes. Then the line reached the Sambre, and so to Namur.

Just before the campaign the Emperor died. This meant the probable withdrawal of the Archduke Charles' candidature It meant the detention of Eugène at Vienna, and possible breaches in the Grand Alliance. Also Marlborough was weakened by five battalions, sent under Mrs Masham's General Hill to Newfoundland, an expedition which failed hopelessly.

Marlborough assembled the allied armies at Orchies, south of Lille. Villars lay behind the Sensée from Oisy to Bouchain. May 1, Marlborough moved to a parallel position Both armies did nothing for six weeks. Eugène came, and was recalled with his army. June 14, Marlborough moved a march west to the plain of Lens, to conceal his diminution. Villars did not attack, but moved down to a parallel position. Five weeks elapsed Villars detached a portion of his army to the Rhine. But he still kept the numerical superiority. He would not fight. He could not be driven out by a smaller force. Only strategy remained. The inundation of the Sensée between Arras and Bouchain was traversed by causeways defended by a fort at Aileux Marlborough knew that, if he took it, Villars would take it again, and rebuild it. So he decided to make Villars demolish it. So he sent Rantzau with a strong force, who easily took it Then he ordered the work to be strengthened, and stationed Hompesch on the glacis of Douai three miles off, with a large force to watch it

Hompesch was careless Villars surprised him, and was

repulsed only with difficulty. Villars was delighted Marlborough appeared indignant, but reinforced Hompesch and pushed on the work at Arleux When it was done, he left a weak garrison, and moved off two marches, and camped opposite the lines between Canche and Scarpe. Villars followed parallel, after detaching a force to attach Arleux The commander sent for aid. Marlborough sent Cadogan, who did not hurry himself Arleux fell Villars demolished the whole work. Marlborough pretended to be furious, and threatened a direct attack on Villars' lines Villars was elated Villars detached a force into Brabant Marlborough sent Albemarle to Béthune with 10,000, and all his baggage and big guns to Douai Now he was weaker than ever Yet he moved one march nearer to Villars, and repaired the roads towards the enemy. His men thought he was mad

Villars was delighted. He summoned every man from the lines and adjacent garrisons. He wrote to Versailles that he had brought Marlborough to his *ne plus ultra* August 2, Marlborough advanced to within a league, and that day and the 3rd set his horse to collect fascines. That night (3rd), he sent away all his light guns and vehicles under escort On the 4th he rode forward to reconnoitre His generals were amazed at his calm instructions. Just before the end, Cadogan galloped back to camp Marlborough rode in, and ordered preparations for a general attack in the morning.

Despair settled on the army The thing was hopeless Misfortune had rendered the "Corporal" reckless But meantime Cadogan with forty hussars was galloping five leagues to Douai. He found Hompesch with 12,000 foot and 2,000 horse Hompesch prepared to march that night.

At dusk a column of horse trotted out on the allied right The French wondered. Then orders were given to strike tents. The horse, having distracted the French, returned at 9, unseen, and the whole army faced left, and headed by Marlborough marched off into the east without a sound.

It was a fine, moonlit night At dawn they reached the Scarpe, fifteen miles in eight hours There they found pontoons, and on the other side the field artillery under Brigadier Sutton. They crossed Then came news that Cadogan and Hompesch had crossed at Arleux, at 3 o'clock. Marlborough pushed on with fifty squadrons The foot stepped out Villars heard of Marlborough's march two hours after he started Not for three more did he understand Then he galloped off with the "Maison." All but 100 were worn down by his furious riding He was too late At 8, Marlborough was over at Aubencheul-au-Bac, and setting his cavalry over the Scarpe, barred the way by Oisy. Villars blundered into the outposts His escort was taken. He escaped by miracle His cavalry came on, but Marlborough's infantry, dropping by hundreds, and dying on the road, raced

them. Between 4 and 5 p.m the whole army was over and in
position between Oisy and the Schelde   They had done forty
miles in eighteen hours.   So vanished the *ne plus ultra.*

Next day Marlborough rested.   Half his foot had fallen out
and straggled in slowly   Villars offered battle under Cambrai
Marlborough refused it, though the Dutch deputies urged it.
He meant to take Bouchain.   This they opposed, as dangerous
On the 7th he marched down to menace Villars, while he passed
his army over the Schelde   Fools have blamed him.   He was
not so mad as to attack a strong position with a smaller and
exhausted force.

Marlborough covered himself skilfully with trenches.   Perhaps
Villars was ordered from Versailles to let him pass the Schelde,
but not to take Bouchain.   But September 13, the garrison
surrendered, under Villars' nose   Marlborough wished to take
Quesnoy, but the Cabinet, having agreed with Louis, forbade it.

This brilliant campaign was decried in England   When
Marlborough reached the Hague, in November, he found he was
accused of fraud, extortion, and embezzlement.   £63,000 had
been paid him by bread-contractors.   Marlborough proved that
this was a regular perquisite for secret service, and (as he added)
2½ per cent of the pay of the foreign troops   The defence was
sound   But on December 31, he was dismissed from all public
employments.

Three weeks later the House of Commons ordered his prosecution.   Ormond was appointed commander-in-chief, and
confirmed in these very perquisites, a fine piece of effrontery
and folly

Marlborough left England, really a banished man.   He had
been insulted in the House of Lords, even by Argyll   The
Lieutenancy of the Tower was taken from Cadogan and given
to Hill   Stair resigned the colonelcy of the Greys in disgust.   At
Ostend (November, 1712), at Antwerp, all the way to Maestricht,
Marlborough was met with popular applause, with cannon,
with escorts of horse, etc.   Eugène stood fast by him.   Yet the
main responsibility rests, not with the Tories, but with the
Dutch deputies, who ruined the early campaigns.

MEMOIR OF FRANK TAYLOR

WHEN I think of my brother Frank, I see him always, as it were, in a series of pictures, and, if I am to try to write about him, all I can do is to show one by one to his friends those portraits which are painted in the picture gallery of my recollection.

The first picture is that of a schoolboy of thirteen or fourteen years, and because it was hung on its rail when I was a very little girl the outline now is dim and the colours dull. In this picture there are really two boys, for Frank and my elder brother were nearly of an age, and although opposites in temperament the boys counted almost as one entity in a family of seven This, perhaps, was as well, for Frank, once described by a prim but discerning maiden aunt as a rough diamond, was a dreamy, untidy, and forgetful person, in constant need of a buffer between him and the disgrace which at home followed his shortcomings. The two were inseparable, and indeed their only difference, and that a passing one, would be caused by arguments of the Cavalier and Roundhead variety, arguments in which the elder would be supported by my father, who took the side of the Parliament, while the younger with fervour and dialectic skill defended the lost cause of Church and King. Frank was no mean antagonist, for at an age when most schoolboys know little or nothing of the history of their own country and its place in Europe he had read voraciously and was ready to fight for his opinions He owed something, too, of his historical knowledge to the old London Grammar School which the boys attended and which, founded originally for the sons of those who had fought in the Napoleonic wars, faithfully instructed their descendants not only in Latin, Greek, Science, and Mathematics, but in the history and literature of their own country Indeed, the faithfulness of the school authorities in this respect allowed little time for games or play of any kind. My brothers left home at 8 in the morning, returning after 5 at night with several hours of homework yet before them This homework somehow must have stimulated Frank's gift of drawing. From the time he could hold a pencil he had begun to draw, and I can remember the dining-room table, strewn with lesson books, on closer scrutiny revealing all sorts of treasures of art Torn pieces of paper, old envelopes, backs of exercise books, the printed page itself, were covered with representations of two branches of art caricature, or studies of horse and foot soldiers of all periods and nationalities. Sometimes a book cover would be the canvas for a half-finished battle-piece

Frank had a passion for soldiers. If he was not drawing, then he was manœuvring mimic regiments of cavalry and infantry, all laboriously collected over a period of years from Christmas or birthday presents, and by the expenditure of exiguous pocket-money   The disposition of troops was not enough.   Topography also had to be considered, and I recollect what was to me a fascinating cardboard model, on which was painted a vivid blue lake and a vivid green plain, and to which was gummed an unhealthy-looking range of blotting-paper mountains. Later, by demonstration I understood that this was the background for Hannibal's great victory at Lake Trasimene.

At the seaside also, when I myself was beginning to yearn for greater creations than the making of sand pies, I used to watch with rapture the erection of a mediæval castle, with draw-bridge, bastions, and moat, and share all the feelings of the be-sieged at the approach of the invincible enemy, the incoming tide

Vaguely I began to realise that the brother, who, when he was not teasing or making a noise, had it in his power to open a world of romance by means of sand or pen, possessed a capacity above the ordinary for winning scholarships and prizes innumerable. This was especially brought home to me on the occasion of a prize-giving when a royal personage visited the Grammar School. A striped tent, red carpet, flowers, and palms, made the ugly playground an enchanted place, and of all the boys it was my brother Frank who mounted the red dais oftenest, who received the largest number of leather-bound volumes and the largest number of royal smiles from the disappointing princess, who, instead of ermine and a coronet, wore a homely bonnet and silk dress, a far less awe-inspiring garb than the academic gowns which crowded round.

It must have been about this time that my parents were in-vited to visit the headmaster to discuss possibilities for my brother's future. The school examination papers, as usual, had been set and corrected by a University examiner, who was so impressed by Frank's papers that he had taken the trouble to write to the school to enquire into the circumstances of this boy, whom he had never seen, with a view to urging his being sent to a University, preferably to Oxford

An attempt forthwith was made to get Frank into Merchant Taylors' School, in the hope of his obtaining later on an Oxford scholarship, but he was found to be just over the entrance age. As there was no other possible alternative within my parents' means, it was decided finally that he should remain at the Grammar School until he had passed the London Matriculation Examination. This he did when captain of the school at sixteen, and, in 1890, with the help of money saved from earlier school scholarships, he entered University College and began to work for the London Intermediate.

Again the occasion of a prize-giving was to impress, yet more vividly, my imagination   A great round building like the picture of a Roman amphitheatre, with tier upon tier of students and parents and friends, was better than a striped tent in a playground, and the beauty of the Slade school, seated in the front row with a red rose at her breast, was more like a princess than that kind, middle-aged lady who had been a real princess.   Besides, that evening, when Frank brought home his prizes, he brought with them a red rose.

At this time his verse-making, which began much earlier, took definite form, and short poems began to find their way into the Press.   The *Pall Mall Gazette*, the *St James' Gazette*, and the *Globe* constantly accepted his verses.   The theme of this early work was usually romantic.   Certainly the daughters of romance were many and various, and sometimes the passing shadow of Delia's or of Lesbia's beauty was sufficient to inspire him.

In the summer of 1891 he passed the London Intermediate, but meanwhile he had been further encouraged at University College to try for an open scholarship at Oxford, it being obvious that he was a more suitable candidate for Oxford Honours than for the London degree   A prize for French, won at this time, enabled him to obtain the private coaching which he needed, if he were to hope to compete for an open scholarship

At first, however, it looked as if his excellent general education had been at the expense of classical training, and he had no success.   But in April, 1892, he was offered an exhibition at St. John's College.   This award being hardly sufficient in amount, the authorities kindly arranged to hold over the exhibition until he should have competed, once more, in a scholarship examination about to be held at another college.   This time he won a scholarship at Lincoln College, where in the autumn of that year he began residence.

The next picture stands out clear and distinct   It is that of a young man in evening dress and a scholar's gown, standing in the rostrum of the Sheldonian theatre at Oxford.   He is tall, six feet three, and broad in proportion, with grey eyes, dark hair, and a pale, clear complexion.   Like this I saw him on the day of the Encænia, with the magic of the magic city round him, and the glamour of high success upon him, and I admired him (perhaps for the first time) with all a schoolgirl's admiration, an admiration which, in the language of a schoolgirl, I would have died rather than admit

This was in 1895 when he recited the Stanhope prize essay, "The Regent Moray"   He had already, in 1894, won the Newdigate prize for a poem on "The Age of Leo X. in Italy."

In 1896 his first volume of verse, *Ad Sodales*, was published by Mr. Blackwell. It was a good title. He was himself essentially a companion, and Oxford had been to him a place of companionship

It was this feeling, no doubt, which inspired his poem "Oxford," written nine years later, but which may perhaps be most aptly quoted here.

OXFORD

Here, where I know the face of every sky,
  The breath of every breeze,
Here, where a thousand grey stones smile and sigh,
  A thousand rustling trees,

From laughing homelands, from far wastes and fell,
  From lone, foe-circled posts,
Sere battlefields, and fields of asphodel,
  Hither they flock, loved ghosts

I see them cluster in the watermeads,
  Yellow with daffodils,
I hear their brazen horns, I hear their steeds
  Among the changeless hills;

And all along the willow-tufted shore,
  I watch the white foam fly
Fast from their flashing oar-blades, and the roar
  Buffets the blue May sky,

And sharply from the level marsh again
  I hear their skilled bats click,
And when late autumn dapples the brown plain
  With dank white mists and thick,

Again they move with Doric discipline
  About the springing ball,
And calm and clear above the popular din
  Their steady captains call

In every room there dwells some voice for me,
  Laughter and song and jest,
Of every haunted garden I am free,
  Of every hall a guest;

And still thy hallowed pinnacles and spires
  Of everlasting bells
Startle the long sleep of divine desires,
  Still chant the ancient spells,

And Time himself, forgetful of his flight,
  Loiters within thy coasts,
And sits and sings, dear land of old delight,
  City of darling ghosts

In 1896 my father died and there was much sadness and worry at home. Frank's work suffered at a critical time, with the result that he came out with a second class in Greats This was a severe disappointment. It put an end to any hope he may have entertained of a classical fellowship in his own college and probably helped to turn his mind from the thought of obtaining any fellowship It was clear to him now that he wanted to write, but it was also clear that literature could not be pursued without an income.

Finally he decided to enter for the Civil Service examination the following year. The next twelve months he spent at home in preparation, and in September, 1897, passed twenty-second in the Civil Service list. The following October he went with several of his Oxford friends to the Local Government Board.

As a civil servant he passed through the usual stages. He was private secretary to Mr Gerald Balfour and to Mr. Runciman. But although his work brought him promotion, it was a means to an end, not an end in itself   His literary record shows clearly where his real interests lay

In 1898 he won the Chancellor's essay prize, " The Newspaper Press as a Power both in the Expression and Formation of Public Opinion," and in 1905 the sacred prize poem, " Esther "

Frank was thus the winner of four University prizes, and in 1906 it seemed as if a belated offer of a fellowship might be made to him. That which would have been invaluable to him when he left Oxford had not the same attraction now that he had an established position. As a matter of fact, it came to nothing, owing to some carelessness on his part in not sending his application by a particular date, but all the same the incident, revealing as it did some recognition by his University, was a pleasant thing to him.

Over this period my brother contributed poems constantly to the Press, especially to the *Pall Mall Gazette* and the *Spectator*. These were romantic, political and topical, historical and military. A selection of military and patriotic verse was published in 1913, by Mr. John Murray, under the title *The Gallant Way*. He also wrote several plays, but it was like him after one or two rebuffs to make no further effort with his manuscript. One play, *The Carthaginian*, was published, in 1914, after his death, by Mr. John Murray

About 1905 he began to write the Life of the Duke of Marlborough. His reasons for so doing, the intention and scope of the work have been indicated in his preface

The consideration of this period of Frank's life brings me to the next picture in my gallery, of which there are probably other copies   Many of his friends must have in their own minds a picture of him in that most characteristic attitude with knees crossed, sitting either in a chair that rocked by nature, or in one that with ill effects to itself was made to rock, writing on some scrap of paper against a book held up rather close to his sight. He used to sit thus without desk or writing-table, but perhaps a chair or a small folding stand for any special books of reference beside him, in the library, which was in reality a common room and the centre of the family life in our house in St. John's Wood   There, conversations were held, questions discussed, problems solved, while the writer remained unmoved, apparently able to emerge from and to return to his own world at will and without permanent disturbance of his concentration. Circumstances which would have made literary work not only difficult but impossible for most people hardly seemed to affect him. He was imperturbable, never out of temper. Indeed his nearest approach to annoyance would be a rare remark to the effect that when certain persons had gone to bed there might be a little peace.

It was not surprising that the family, and that the friends of the family, drifted to this room. It was a comfortable and pleasant place The walls were lined with shelves filled for the most part with old dusty books picked up second-hand in Charing Cross Road and thereabouts—French memoirs, histories, a whole library of Marlborough authorities—while above was hung a medley of prints, prints of the Duke and the Duchess, of battlefields and sieges, of kings, princes and princesses, and of famous captains and fair women of England, France and Flanders

In these ways the history of the great Duke entered the life of those Frank lived with. It was an entrance often unnoticed and unrealised but none the less real. For although he never read his manuscript to anyone, his life was so permeated by his work that in a sense he lived what he wrote No one ever kept his special knowledge more to himself and no one shared it more with other people.

He read extensively at the British Museum, and any incident that struck him he would relate with the same simplicity and zest with which he would have told a story of present-day occurrence.

More directly, at a time when I happened to be teaching the reign of Queen Anne, he used to tell me what to read and would himself supply all the details of military history, which until they were presented by his peculiarly human method seemed to me indeed dry bones. For this reason when I came to read the manuscript after his death, the chapters dealing specially with Marlborough's great victories were far from being new to me. His power to make military history of interest to the ordinary person was increased no doubt by his intimate knowledge of the country in which the War of the Spanish Succession was fought in the Netherlands For many years my brother's holiday had been a walking tour in France or Belgium, and every step of the Duke's great march to the Danube, which culminated in the battle of Blenheim, he had himself followed

Surely we shall never forget the preparations for these holidays, the consulting of maps, the buying of small necessaries, the packing, and the final departure with all the enthusiasm of a schoolboy. He went sometimes with my elder brother and one particular friend, sometimes alone. The last days of the holiday were usually spent at the house of some French friends who were particularly attached to him, and where it had become a habit for certain members of the family to pay a yearly visit. But

if the departure is a vivid remembrance, how much more the
return, when he came back brown and well and even more full
of life and spirits than usual   Then, in the first five minutes, the
presents he had brought home for my mother and for me had
to be displayed, and the pictures and postcards, which mean so
much to those who have seen the places and so little to those
who have not, had to be admired, while for days and weeks we
listened to the descriptions of forest and valley, of hill and
meadow, of bathing in rivers, of walking long roads, of delicious
déjeuners, of wonderful wines, of madame's management, of
madame's charm—in short, of all the delights that fall to those
who spend their leisure in the "pleasant land of France."

Indeed, any who dared to prefer Norway or Switzerland
were considered to be victims of their own perverse folly, when
the hospitable and historic country of the Entente lay so much
nearer.   But if he had little sympathy with the mountain-
climber he had a supreme contempt for those who sought the aid
of machinery in their enjoyment.   An electric launch, a motor-
car, an aeroplane, all were alike abhorrent

At home he was an enthusiastic tennis-player. He was a
well-known member of the Marlborough Lawn Tennis Club.
(It was a curious coincidence that several of the roads in St.
John's Wood, where we lived, should have been called after the
great Duke and his famous victory of Blenheim.)   Any summer
evening I seem to see him now, in his white flannels, with his
long, swinging stride, returning from the club, pursued by some
small girl or boy out of Blenheim Terrace, for the sake of the old
tennis ball which they knew they would get from him. Himself,
one of the best players, he succeeded in making the club a
happy place for the indifferent player, who too often has a poor
time in such societies. His pleasure, when he found himself
elected on the committee, is an example both of his almost
boyish simplicity, and also of the interest he took in meeting
what might be termed, without offence, quite everyday people.
Indeed, his pleasure had never been taken in the society of the
so-called cultured and literary   He was too human and in a
sense too unworldly   In the same way that as a boy and as a
young man a certain independence caused him to stand indifferently with authorities, so later in life, when he might have
made friends with those who quite legitimately could have
helped him in his career, he seemed always to remain outside.
A total absence of anything like vanity, which did not
however exclude open delight at a favourable press notice, was
surely not the least of those characteristics which made him
welcome in any society in which he found himself. His sense of
humour, at once boyish, keen, and mocking, was so much a part
of him that I had almost forgotten to speak of it. He mocked
mercilessly at false sentiment, and at high sentiment also he
might sometimes have appeared to mock, for, with him, as with

certain natures, sincerity, strong feeling, intense reverence, took to themselves a cloak of mirth to hide their nakedness

The French have said that conversation is a lost art in England. Frank was a great conversationist. Perhaps for that reason he numbered among his closest friends both men and women of that nation.

As a canvasser at elections no one was more at ease with rich or poor, educated or uneducated; no one knew better how to present such causes as Protection and Preference, which he supported long before Mr Chamberlain became their public advocate   Too good a patriot to love party government, he identified himself wholeheartedly with the Conservatives as most likely to defend the principles he had at heart.   He worked for them at every election since 1892

He was essentially pitiful to any kind of suffering   Without any personal experience of illness, he seemed to understand by instinct its weariness   Daily visits, if they were permitted, daily letters, ridiculous postcards, were never forgotten by him should one of his friends be ill.

For all animals, too, his sympathy was keen.   Until of late years there was a bob-tailed sheep-dog in our neighbourhood, who as a puppy strayed from home on a wet winter's evening, and, having the sense to follow my brother, spent the night at our house instead of in the street   I remember, too, that when a curious crowd watched with the sympathy of words the agony of a cat that had been run over, it was my brother who fetched a chemist to put it out of its misery.

Perhaps his humanity and his scholarship can be best appreciated from reading the titles of the small row of books which he chose to have over his bed, in the large and rather bleak bedroom, with the window opening on to the tops of trees and its view stretching beyond the roofs to the heights of Hampstead   In these books—the Bible, the *Odyssey*, the *Iliad*, Rabelais, *Westward Ho! John Inglesant*—he certainly would have said that he found those particular principles which coloured his thought, moulded his convictions, and are to be clearly traced in his interpretation of the character of Marlborough   Frank had a quite simple religious faith.   Perhaps his intellect was great enough to know its own limitations.   Certainly he never knew what it was to doubt.   His loyalty to the Church of England, and at least his intellectual adhesion to the Catholic tradition of the Church of England, never faltered.   That he was inspired with an intense and burning patriotism, and that with Lord Roberts he feared for England's unpreparedness in the great European struggle which he believed to be inevitable, not only his books but his poems show.   His admiration for France, her history, her literature, her people, was only second to his love for England, and that he should have died six months before the cementing in blood and tears of that friendship he so much desired between the two nations can never cease to be a poignant regret.

And this brings me to the last picture in my gallery   These seven years it has been veiled, and only a very few saw it in the painting   It is the picture of a man in the prime of life, losing strength and grip day by day, going down before a mysterious illness which the doctors failed to diagnose, brought in a few weeks from robust health to pain, sickness, and death.   It is the picture of courage and patience, of Christian fortitude strengthened by the last rites of the Catholic Church, the picture of life broken but complete, of death triumphant but transformed

> Requiem eternam dona ei, Domine,
> Et lux perpetua illuceat ei

He died on December 5, 1913.   At that time no one knew how far the history of the Duke of Marlborough had advanced or whether there would be a complete section fit for publication.   When the scattered manuscript had been collected from a host of other papers, certain chapters were found copied in Frank's superficially clear, upright handwriting, ready for typing, and also other chapters, apparently finished, but presenting considerable difficulties before they could be deciphered   The writing was minute and indistinct, with sentences scored through or written above, and many words only to be distinguished by good eyesight and guessing.

After six months' close work I succeeded in piecing together a complete section of the Duke of Marlborough's life, from 1702 to 1709, and in addition certain other earlier chapters.   It then appeared that if the book was to be of use for reference it must be thoroughly documented   In some cases my brother had given the source of his quotations but hardly ever the volume or page, while in the majority of instances he left no indication of the authority consulted.   So I began my search with some packets of his British Museum slips and many odd notes, written often on scraps of paper, alone to help me. Then the war came, and all idea of immediate publication had to be abandoned.   At intervals during other work I returned to the Marlborough manuscript and to tracing the quotations to the sources from which my brother had taken them. Even now that the time has come for publication, I regret that, after years of research, there must still remain a few omissions in the references and therefore in the Bibliography. The chapter " Tournai " is incomplete, and I have left it incomplete because I wish to present my brother's work—and his work only—to the readers of that brave attempt which after all was so near completion, the Life of the Duke of Marlborough.

G. WINIFRED TAYLOR.

BIBLIOGRAPHY

CONTEMPORARY OR ALMOST CONTEMPORARY AUTHORITIES —I.

A —Histories, Documents, Letters, and Memoirs.

Archives at Blenheim Palace

Archives at Brussels

Archives of Heinsius (Rijks-Archief [State Archives] at the Hague).

Accomplished Officer, The. Written originally in French by A. R. London, 1708

Austrian Netherlands, A Journey through the [By John Macky.] London, 1732

Berwick, Maréchal de: Mémoires écrits par lui-même. 2 vols. Paris, 1778

Memoirs, written by himself 2 vols London, 1779

Blenheim Roll, 1704. Edited and annotated by Charles Dalton. London, 1899

Bolingbroke, Henry St John, Viscount Letters on the Study and Use of History London, 1779

Boyer, A The History of King William III London, 1702
The History of the Reign of Queen Anne digested into Annals 11 vols. London, 1703-13
The History of Queen Anne London, 1735

Brandenburg, Memoirs of the House of. London, 1757

Brodrick, T A Compleat History of the Late War 2 vols London, 1713

Burnet, Bishop. History of his Own Time 4 vols. London, 1818

Campbell, J · The Military History of Prince Eugène and of John, Duke of Marlborough. 2 vols. London, 1736-7

Cholmondeley, Sir Hugh, Bart, the Younger An account of Tangier, with some account of himself and his journey through France and Spain to that place, where he was engaged in building the Mole and a journal of the work carrying on. London, 1787

Coxe Papers. Add MSS British Museum

Cuypert, Gisbert Journal inédit d'un savant hollandais *Revue historique*, t 2, 1876

Dalrymple, Sir John, Bart.. Memoirs of Great Britain and Ireland. 3 vols London, 1790

Dangeau, Philippe de Courcillon, Marquis de. Mémoirs Ed. Mme. de Genlis. 3 vols Paris, 1817.

D'Auvergne, Edward (Chaplain to the 3rd Regiment of Guards), The History of the Campagne in Flanders for the Year 1691. 2 vols. London, 1735

Dohna, Christophe, Comte de: Mémoires originaux sur la règne et la Cour de Frédéric roi de Prusse Berlin, 1833.

Dummer Journal Pepysian Library. Magdalene College, Cambridge

EUGÈNE, FRANCIS, Prince of Savoy, the History of   By an English officer.
    London, 1741
    Mémoires ecrits par lui-même [or rather by Charles Joseph, prince
    de Ligne]   Paris, 1810.
EVELYN, JOHN   Memoirs (Chandos Library).   Ed by W. Bray.   London,
    1879
FELDZÜGE des Prinzen Eugen von Savoyen   Vienna, 1876.
FEUQUIÈRES, MARQUIS DE   Mémoires   4 vols   Paris, 1740.
GOSLINGA, SICCO VAN   Mémoires relatifs a la guerre de Succession de
    1706-1709 et 1711, etc   Leeuwarden, 1857
GRAMMONT, COMTE DE   Mémoires de la vie.   Par M le comte Antoine
    Hamilton   The Hague, 1731
HARDWICKE PAPERS   Miscellaneous State Papers, 1501-1726.   London,
    1778.
HISTORICAL MSS   COMMISSION.
    Ailesbury MSS , 15th Report, Appendix, part VII
    Athol MSS , 12th Report, Appendix, part VIII
    Bath MSS , vol 1
    Buccleuch MSS , vol II , part II.
    Coke MSS (belonging to Earl Cowper), vol III., 12th Report, Appendix,
        part III
    Dartmouth MSS , 11th Report, Appendix, part V
    Foljambe, F. J Savile, MSS , 15th Report, Appendix, part V
    Hare MSS , 14th Report, Appendix, part IX
    Hodgkin, J Eliot MSS , 15th Report, Appendix, part II.
    Leyborne-Popham MSS , 1899
    Mar and Kellie MSS , 1904.
    Portland MSS , vol. IV , 15th Report, Appendix, part IV
    Portland MSS , vol V , 15th Report, Appendix
    Round MSS , 14th Report, Appendix, part IX
    Rutland MSS , vol II , 12th Report, Appendix, part V
    Stopford Sackville MSS , vols. I , II , 1904-10.
HISTORY of the Campaign in Flanders in the Year 1708.   London, 1709.
HOWELL, J B   State Trials, vol. XIV
KANL, RICHARD (Brigadier-General)   Campaigns of King William and
    the Duke of Marlborough   London, 1747
LAMBERTY·   Mémoires pour servir à l'histoire du XVIIIe siècle.   14 vols.
    Amsterdam, 1735.
LA COLONIE   Mémoires de Monsieur de, Maréchal de camp des armées
    d'Electeur de Bavière.   2 vols.   Brussels, 1748
LA FARE, MARQUIS DE.   Mémoires   Collection des memoires relatifs à
    l'histoire de France par M Petitot, t lxv   Paris, 1819-1829.
LIVES of the two Illustrious Generals, John, Duke of Marlborough, and
    Francis Eugène, Prince of Savoy   London, 1713.
LORDS, Journals of the House of   Vol XVIII
LUTTRELL, NARCISSUS   State Affairs from 1678-1714   6 vols.   Oxford,
    1857
LUXEMBOURG, MARÉCHAL, DUC DE   Mémoires   The Hague, 1758.
MACKY, JOHN   Memoirs   Characters of the Court of Great Britain.
    London, 1733
MACPHERSON, J · Original papers   2 vols   London, 1776 (2nd Edit).
MAFFEI, MARQUIS DE· Mémoires   3 vols   Venice, 1741
MARLBOROUGH, Correspondance diplomatique et militaire du Duc de,
    du Grand-Pensionnaire Heinsius et du Trésorier-Général des Pro-
    vinces-Unies J Hop .   . Publiée d'après les manuscrits originaux
    par G G Vreede. Amsterdam, 1850.

MARLBOROUGH DISPATCHES. Edited by Sir George Murray. 5 vols. London, 1845.

MARLBOROUGH, JOHN, DUKE OF, the History of, by the Author of the History of Prince Eugène London, 1742

MARLBOROUGH'S, THE DUKE OF, new Exercise of Firelocks and Bayonets, appointed by his Grace to be used by all the British forces and the Militia By an Officer in her Majesties Foot Guard London

MARLBOROUGH, SARAH, DUCHESS OF, Memoirs of the Life and Conduct of. London, 1744

MARLBOROUGH, SARAH, DUCHESS OF, Private Correspondence of, illustrative of the Court and Times of Queen Anne; with her sketches and opinions of her contemporaries, and the select correspondence of her husband . . . John, Duke of Marlborough 2 vols London, 1838

MAUVILLON, E DE Histoire du Prince François Eugène de Savoye 5 vols. Vienna, 1741
    Lettres françaises et germaniques 1740

MÉRODE-WESTERLOO, FELD-MARÉCHAL, COMTE DE Mémoires Brussels, 1840.

MILLNER, JOHN (Serjeant in the Hon Royal Regiment of Foot of Ireland): Journal London, 1733.

MONTLUC, Commentaires de Messire Blaise de Collection des Mémoires relatifs à l'histoire de France par M Petitot, ser 1, t 20–22 Paris, 1819–1829.

NOAILLES, ADRIEN-MAURICE, DUC DE· Mémoires politiques et militaires pour servir à l'histoire de Louis XIV et de Louis XV par M l'abbé Millot 6 vols Paris, 1777

ORKNEY, Letters of the first Lord, during Marlborough's Campaigns, English Historical Review. April, 1904

PARKER, CAPTAIN ROBERT(Late of the Royal Regiment of Foot in Ireland): Memoirs of the Most Remarkable Military Transactions from the Year 1683 to 1718 Dublin, 1746.

PELET, J J G, and VAULT, F E. DE Mémoires Militaires relatifs à la Succession d'Espagne 11 vols Paris, 1835–1862

QUINCEY, MARQUIS DE. Histoire militaire du règne de Louis le Grand 7 vols. 1726

SAINT-HILAIRE, Mémoires de, publies pour la société de l'histoire de France par Léon Lecestre. 6 vols. Paris, 1903–1916.

SAINT-SIMON, DUC DE Mémoires   40 vols Paris, 1842

SAXE, MARSHAL Reveries or Memoirs upon the Art of War London, 1757.

SHREWSBURY, CHARLES TALBOT, DUKE OF, Private and Original Correspondence of. By W Coxe London, 1821.

STATE PAPERS, DOMESTIC Public Record Office (These are printed in the Calendar of State Papers, Domestic 1670–72)

STATE PAPERS, HOLLAND Public Record Office

STATE PAPERS, HANOVER Stowe MSS, British Museum

STATE PAPERS, IRELAND. Public Record Office (These are printed in the Calendar of State Papers, Ireland 1666–70)

STEPNEY PAPERS Add MSS, British Museum

TALLARD, MARÉCHAL DE: Campagne 2 vols Amsterdam, 1763.

TORCY, MÉMOIRES DE 3 vols. The Hague, 1757

UTRECHT, the History of the Treaty of London, 1712

VILLARS, Vie du Maréchal duc de. 4 vols Paris, 1784.

WILLIAM III, Life of 3rd edition London, 1705

B PAMPHLETS AND POEMS.

DEFOE, DANIEL An Enquiry into the Occasional Conformity Bill, by the
    Author of the "True Born Englishman" London, 1704.
    Legions Memorial London, 1701
    Tom Double 1704
    The Two Great Questions considered 1700

SWIFT, JONATHAN The Conduct of the Allies and of the Late Ministry
    London, 1712
    Some Remarks upon a Pamphlet entitled, A Letter to the Seven Lords,
    of the Committee appointed to examine Gregg By the Author
    of the "Examiner" Printed in the year 1711
    A Short Character of H[is] E[xcellency] T[homas], E[arl] of W[harton],
    L[ord] L[ieutenant] of I[reland] Published anonymously
    Poems, vol iii Aldine Edition, 1866

C NEWSPAPERS.

The London Gazette
The Tatler

LATER AUTHORITIES —II

A BIOGRAPHICAL

ALISON, ARCHIBALD· The Military Life of John, Duke of Marlborough
    Edinburgh and London, 1848

ARNETH, A RITTER VON Prinz Eugen von Savoyen 3 vols Vienna, 1858

CARTE, THOMAS The Life of James, Duke of Ormond with an
    appendix and a collection of letters 6 vols Oxford, 1851

CHURCHILL, JEAN, Duc de Marlborough, Histoire de 3 vols Paris, 1806.

COLVILLE, MRS Duchess Sarah New York, 1904

COXE, W Memoirs of the Duke of Marlborough 3 vols London, 1905

FEA, ALLAN King Monmouth London and New York, 1902

KAUSLER, F VON Das Leben des Prinzen Eugen von Savoyen 2 vols
    Freiburg im Breisgau, 1838

MALLESON, COLONEL G. B . Prince Eugène of Savoy. London, 1888

SCHONING, KURD W W G VON. Des General Feldmarschalls D G von
    Natzmer auf Gannewitz Leben und Kriegesthaten, mit den Haupt-
    begebenheiten des Garde-Reuter-Regiments Gensdarmes. Berlin,
    1838

SCHREIBER, FR ANT WILHELM. Max Emanuel, Kurfürst von Bayern
    Munich, 1861

SCHULENBURG, J M, REICHSGRAFEN VON DER· Leben und Denkwundig-
    keiten 2 vols Leipzig, 1834

SÉGUR, PIERRE DE Le Tapissier de Notre-Dame, les dernières années
    du Maréchal de Luxembourg, 1678–1695 Paris

SHIELD, A , and LANG, ANDREW The King over the Water. London, 1907

SICHEL, W S · Bolingbroke and his Times 2 vols London, 1901–2

STEBBING, WILLIAM Peterborough London, 1890.

SYBEL, HEINRICH VON Prinz Eugen von Savoyen Pitt Press Series
    Cambridge University Press, 1902

VOGÜÉ, C J M , MARQUIS DE Villars d'après sa correspondance 2 vols
    Paris, 1888.
    Le duc de Bourgogne et le duc de Beauvillier. Lettres inédites,
    1700–1708 Paris, 1900
    Mémoires du Maréchal de Villars 6 vols Paris, 1884–1904

WOLSELEY, GENERAL VISCOUNT The Life of John Churchill, Duke of
    Marlborough, to the Accession of Queen Anne 2 vols London, 1894

B MILITARY.

ALMACK, EDWARD The History of the Second Dragoons (" Royal Scots Greys ") London.

ARTHUR, CAPTAIN, SIR GEORGE, BART , Late Second Life Guards The Story of the Household Cavalry 2 vols London, 1909

BARROW, GENERAL SIR E The English Genius in War *National Review*, 1910.

BELLOC, HILAIRE. British Battles. Blenheim London, 1911.
British Battles: Malplaquet London, 1911.

CANNON, RICHARD The First or Royal Regiment of Foot London, 1847
The Sixteenth or the Bedfordshire Regiment of Foot London, 1847.

CARMICHAEL-SMYTH, COLONEL SIR JAMES: Chronological Epitome of the Wars in the Low Countries from the Peace of the Pyrenees in 1659 to that of Paris in 1815 London, 1825

CLAUSEWITZ, GENERAL CARL VON. On War Introduction and Notes by Colonel F N Maude, C B (late R E) 3 vols London, 1908

CREASY, EDWARD, SIR. The Fifteen Decisive Battles of the World London, 1894

DALTON, CHARLES. English Army Lists 6 vols London, 1892–1904.
Irish Army Lists, 1661–1685. London, 1909.
The Scots Army, 1661–1688 Edinburgh, 1909.

DAVIS, JOHN, LIEUT -COLONEL, F S A The History of the Second Queen's Royal Regiment now The Queen's (Royal West Surrey) Regiment 6 vols London, 1887

FERGUSON, JAMES: Papers illustrating the History of the Scots Brigade in the Service of the United Netherlands, 1572–1782 (Publications of the Scottish History Society) 3 vols Edinburgh, 1899

FORTESCUE, THE HON J W A History of the British Army London, 1899, etc
The Foot Guards London, 1915

GRETTON, G LE M , LIEUT -COLONEL. The Campaigns and History of the Royal Irish Regiment from 1684 to 1902.

HAMILTON, LIEUT -GENERAL SIR F. W. The Origin and History of the First or Grenadier Guards 3 vols. London, 1874

KNIGHT, H R , CAPT.. Historical Records of the Buffs, East Kent Regiment, 3rd Foot, formerly designated the Holland Regiment, and Prince George of Denmark's Regiment. Vol 1 London, 1905.

LAGRANGE ÉLISE, MME Guerre de la Succession d'Espagne. Le duc de Marlborough en Belgique Brussels, 1892

MAHON, LORD History of the War of the Succession in Spain London, 1832.

MAUDE, F N , LIEUT -COLONEL Cavalry. Its Past and Future. London, 1903
The Evolution of Modern Strategy from the Eighteenth Century to the Present Time. London, 1905.

MILLAN, J The Succession of Colonels to all His Majesty's Land Forces from their rise to 1742 London, 1742

MORRIS, WILLIAM O'CONNOR. Marlborough *The United Service Magazine*, 1899, 1900

NORMAN, C. B.: Battle Honours of the British Army from Tangier, 1662, to the commencement of the reign of King Edward VII. London, 1916

PARNELL, ARTHUR, COLONEL THE HON The War of the Succession in Spain. London, 1888.

REYNALD, H Succession d'Espagne. 2 vols Paris, 1883

SAUTAI, M T Une opération militaire d'Eugène et de Marlborough;
Le forcement du passage de l'Escaut en 1708. Paris, 1905.
Le Siège de la Ville et de la Citadelle de Lille en 1708 Lille, 1899.
La Bataille de Malplaquet Paris, 1904

TRIMEN, R.. The Regiments of the British Army. London, 1878.

WALTON, CLIFFORD, COLONEL, C B · History of the British Standing Army,
1660 to 1700. London, 1894.

WILKINSON, HENRY SPENSER. Britain at Bay London, 1909.
Edited by From Cromwell to Wellington. Twelve Soldiers.
London, 1899

C NAVAL

CLOWES, W C : All about the Royal Navy. London, 1891

CORBETT, SIR JULIAN S · Some Principles of Maritime Strategy London,
1911

FIRTH, C H Naval Songs and Ballads Publications of the Navy
Records Society, vol xxxiii , 1907

MAHAN, A T , CAPTAIN The Influence of Sea Power Upon History,
1660–83 London

D DIPLOMATIC

GEIKIE, RODERICK The Dutch Barrier MS at King's College Library,
Cambridge

LEGRFLLE, ARSÈNE· La Diplomatie Française et la Succession d'Espagne,
1659–1725 4 vols. 1888–1892
Négociation inconnue entre Berwick et Marlborough, 1708–1709.
Paris, 1893

SYVETON, GABRIEL· Louis XIV et Charles XII, etc. Paris, 1900.

E GENERAL.

CUNNINGHAM, A : The History of Great Britain from the Revolution in
1688 to the Accession of George I. 2 vols London, 1787

GACHARD, M Histoire de la Belgique au commencement du xviiie siècle
Brussels, 1880

GUIZOT, F P G General History of Civilization in Europe Edinburgh,
1839

HALLAM, HENRY. The Constitutional History of England 2 vols
London, 1872.

LANG, ANDREW A History of Scotland 2 vols Edinburgh and London,
1900

LEADAM, I S · The Political History of England, vol ix (1702–1760).
Edited by W Hunt and R L Poole 12 vols New York, Bombay,
and Calcutta, 1909

LECKY, W E H A History of England in the Eighteenth Century
7 vols 1892

MACAULAY, THOMAS BABINGTON Critical and Historical Essays 2 vols
London 1854
The History of England Popular Edition 2 vols London, 1895

NOORDEN, CARL VON Europaische Geschichte im achtzehnten Jahr-
hundert Bde. 1–3 Dusseldorf, 1870–1882

RANKE, LEOPOLD VON A History of England 6 vols Oxford, 1875

SOMERVILLE, THOMAS The History of Great Britain during the Reign of
Queen Anne London, 1798

WAKEMAN, H O The Ascendancy of France, 1598–1715 Period v
of European History. London, 1907

GENERAL INDEX

devastation of Bavaria discussed, 191 *ff*, joins forces with Eugène, 198, and the battle of Blenheim, Ch IX ; his consideration for prisoners, 239 *f*, his inaction after the battle discussed, 241 *ff*, the Margrave's jealousy of, 243, forced by German fears to besiege Landau instead of immediately securing the Moselle with a view to Paris offensive, 244 *f*. 247 *f*, 251, 259, takes Trèves, 250, and the problems of the higher strategy of the war in Hungary, Italy and Savoy, Portugal, and the Mediterranean, 251 *ff*, 256, visits the Courts of Prussia and Hanover, 257 *ff*, urges the invasion of France by the Moselle upon Holland, Vienna, and German States, 259 *f*, his use of surprise in strategy and tactics, 261, his tribute in the House of Lords to the British soldier, 262, the Queen's gift of the Manor of Woodstock and the palace of Blenheim to, 263, his invasion of France by the Moselle, "the real road," frustrated by Austrian lethargy, 271 *f*, Dutch timidity, 272 *f*, the jealousy of the Margrave, 273 *f*, 277, and the inertia of German princes on the Rhine, 275; confronted by Villars at Sierck, 275 *ff*, his disappointment and intention to resign, 280, returns to the Meuse, 279 *f*, 282 *ff*, his plan to surprise the French lines, 285 *ff*, and the taking of the Lines of Brabant, 294 *ff*, takes Tirlemont, 304, his desire to march instantly on Louvain opposed by Dutch generals, 305 *ff*, the miscarriage on the Dyle due to Schlangenberg's and the Dutch generals' spite against, 313 *ff*, his patriotic silence, 307, 315; appeals to the Hague for fuller powers, 311, 316, his design to attack the French at Overyssche frustrated by Schlangenberg and the Dutch generals, 326 *ff*, sympathy of people of England and Holland in his disappointment, 334 *f*, diplomatic success of his visit to Vienna, 346 *ff*., created a Prince of the Empire, 348; exigencies of the coalition necessitate visits to

Berlin and Hanover, 350, 352, Eugène's appeal for men and money for Italy to, 353, having experienced Dutch parsimony he negotiates quarter of a million loan in England for army of Italy, 353 *f*, 356, agrees to Godolphin's change of domestic policy in looking for support to the Whigs, 358, his Italian project, a plan for victory hampered by selfish policy of Kings of Prussia and Denmark and German princes, 366, 368 *f*, and finally abandoned after the disaster to the Margrave on the Rhine, 369 *f*, his pessimism at the continual frustration of his plans, 370 *f*, and battle of Ramillies, Ch XV ; personal risks taken by, at Ramillies, 382 *f*, his characteristic letter to the Duchess, 389 *f* ; the submission of Brabant and most of Spanish Flanders to, 392 *ff*, his hopes of peace, 398, governorship of the Spanish Netherlands offered by the Emperor to, 399, 402; his suitability for the post as strategist of the coalition, 402 *f*; jealous anger of the States at the offer, 404, the Queen's approval of the honour, 405, his irreproachable behaviour in declining the patent, 405; draws up an "acte" for administration of recovered provinces, 407, takes Menin, Dendermonde, Ath, 408 *ff*; his pleasure at Eugène's relief of Turin, 414; his disappointment at the anticlimax in Spain and failure of expedition to Guienne, 417 *f* ; magnificent welcome at Brussels to, 420; his uneasiness at Dutch indifference to common cause now that their own safety had been secured at Ramillies, 420 *ff*, 424 *f* ; goes to the Hague to settle preliminaries of peace, and to discover the Dutch definition of a barrier, 425, his reply to French peace proposals, 427; his instructions to discover essential conditions required by maritime powers before concluding any treaty of peace, 429 *ff*; Dutch and Austrian ideas of a suitable barrier irreconcilable in his opinion, 430 *ff*.; urges Sunderland's appointment to Secretary-

INDEX OF PLACE NAMES

PRINTED IN GREAT BRITAIN BY
BILLING AND SONS, LTD , GUILDFORD AND ISUR

②

66 → ·/ΛΛ3

Lightning Source UK Ltd.
Milton Keynes UK
UKHW011825020123
414736UK00005B/86